THE MAYA ROUTE
THE ULTIMATE GUIDEBOOK

THE MAYA ROUTE
THE ULTIMATE GUIDEBOOK

Richard Harris   *Stacy Ritz*

RAY RIEGERT   LESLIE HENRIQUES

Executive Editors

JOANNA PEARLMAN

Editor

GLENN KIM

Illustrator

ULYSSES PRESS

Published by: Ulysses Press
            3286 Adeline Street, Suite 1
            Berkeley, CA 94703

Library of Congress Catalog Card Number 92-62606
ISBN 0-915233-78-9

Printed in the U.S.A. by the George Banta Company

10 9 8 7 6 5 4 3 2 1

Managing Editor: Claire Chun
Editorial Associates: Lee Micheaux, Per Casey, William Kiester, Cynthia Price
Maps: Lee Micheaux, Phil Gardner, Per Casey
Cover Designer: Bonnie Smetts
Paste up: Karen Marquardt, William Kiester
Indexer: Sayre Van Young
Cover Photography: Front cover by Nik Wheeler;
   back cover by Allan Seiden (top), Nik Wheeler (bottom)

Distributed in the United States by Publishers Group West, in Canada by Raincoast Books, and in Great Britain and Europe by World Leisure Marketing

Printed on recycled paper

Note from the Publishers

An alert, adventurous reader is as important as a travel writer in keeping a guidebook up-to-date and accurate. So if you happen upon a great restaurant, discover an intriguing locale or (heaven forbid) find an error in the text, we'd appreciate hearing from you. Just write to:

Ulysses Press
3286 Adeline Street, Suite 1
Berkeley, CA 94703

It is our desire as publishers to create guidebooks that are responsible as well as informative. We hope that our guidebooks treat the people, country and land we visit with respect. We ask that our readers do the same.

Contents

Maps

The Best of the Maya Route

ADVENTURES
Jungle river trip to Yaxchilán *(Chiapas, pages 224–25)*
Volcano climbing *(Guatemala, pages 340–41)*
Jungle hiking *(Belize, page 396)*
Live-Aboard dive boats *(Belize, page 396)*

BEACHES
Playa Tortugas *(Cancún, pages 96–97)*
Playa Lancheros *(Isla Mujeres, page 103)*
Punta Chiquero *(Cozumel, page 115)*
Playas Tulum *(Quintana Roo, page 126)*

HOTELS AND RESORTS
Fiesta Americana Coral Beach *(Cancún, page 87)*
Cancún Puerto al Sol *(Cancún, page 89)*
Casa del Balam *(Mérida, page 169)*
Mayan Inn *(Chichicastenango, page 282)*
Posada de Don Rodrigo *(Antigua Guatemala, pages 292–93)*
Rum Point Inn *(Belize, page 392)*

JUNGLE LODGES
Mayaland *(Chichén Itzá, page 159)*
Hacienda Uxmal *(Uxmal, page 192)*
Tikal Inn *(Tikal National Park, pages 337–38)*
Chan Chich Lodge *(Belize, page 377)*
Chaa Creek Cottages *(Belize, page 385)*

MAYA SITES
Chichén Itzá *(Yucatán, pages 151–57)*
Uxmal *(Yucatán, pages 184–88)*
Palenque *(Chiapas, pages 215–20)*
Copán *(Honduras, pages 314–18)*
Tikal *(Guatemala, pages 330–35)*
Lamanai *(Belize, pages 374–75)*

Epilogue...

Upon confronting the colossal city of Nineveh, Jonah returned
to the still point of the Planet Earth, and there
planted a cherry tree. Golden beetles came, devouring every
leaf. Despairing, Jonah lifted his voice, crying to Great Heart:
"I waste my bones, blood and breath on this stubborn people."

Once again, Jonah crossed the sea. Upon returning he approached
the infant tree. Unfurling from each tiny bough were leaves,
pale, tender and green. Jonah and his wife wept and danced.
Lying down beside the tree, they spent the afternoon, listening
to the Earth...to the laughter of their daughters, playing.

Begun mid-February, 1979
Finished September 26, 1988
The one hundredth birthday
of Thomas Stearns Eliot,
a man
"whom one cannot hope to emulate"

Through and to the Glory of God

And His beautiful bride the bio-planet, Earth

NATIONAL PARKS

PRESERVES AND SANCTUARIES

RESTAURANTS

UNIQUE PLACES

VILLAGES

The Maya Route—La Ruta Maya

The chill morning mists of Guatemala's highlands are surrendering gently to the awakening day. Maya Indians, bent under massive bundles, straggle out of the pine forests and up the cobblestone streets to claim a few square feet of the central plaza. The sun breaks from behind a nearby ridge, scanning a harsh light across the growing clutter of Chichicastenango's Sunday market. As if aroused by its warmth, the drab bundles are flowering into a pastiche of colorful stalls. Amidst the drab necessities of daily life is the finest weaving to be found in the Americas.

At the southeast corner of the plaza, the devout—mostly women—make their little pilgrimages up the stone stairway to the whitewashed church of Santo Tomas. Reportedly built atop the ruins of a Maya temple, it still hears prayers to a pantheon of gods and spirits worshipped long before the arrival of Europeans.

We foreign visitors seem like time travelers from a different century—out of place in the age-old ritual of a Guatemala market. Yet, in truth we are now as much a part of this scene as the handwoven *huipiles* warming the shoulders of the Maya women. Despite our intrusive cameras, we are welcomed as prime customers. More efficiently than any government aid program, we are delivering foreign exchange directly to the people—with no bureaucratic middlemen.

And happy to do so, if our growing numbers is any measure. For there at 7000 feet in the volcanic Guatemala highlands, we were at a favorite way station on one of the world's fastest growing tourist destinations—"The Maya Route" or "La Ruta Maya" in Spanish.

The original Maya routes of the greater Yucatán Peninsula—like the famed silk routes of Asia—began in the mists of antiquity. They started as a network of foot trails of a people who arrived some three thousand years ago in Central America. Like the silk routes, the trails grew into major conduits of culture, trade, cooperation and conquest as villages grew into city-states and city-states into kingdoms. These people we know as the Maya eventually created an empire that lasted six times that of the Romans. They discovered the concept of zero in mathematics and developed a calendar the equal of the one we use today. They engineered and built vast temple complexes, left a legacy of great art and developed the only written language in the Americas.

Long before the arrival of Columbus, the Maya civilization had faded. The once-great cities lay in ruins—abandoned and battered by earthquakes, erosion and neglect. The encompassing rainforests had revived and drawn a suffocating green shroud over them. Some scholars think environmental destruction was the cause of the collapse. Others argue it was peasants uprising against a bloated aristocracy. "Overrun by enemies" is a currently popular theory. Most likely—the answer is a mix of the above. After 1492, diseases from Europe to which the Maya had no immunity decimated the survivors. Today, the Maya have recovered and in many areas outnumber those of European descent.

Just as the many silk routes became thought of as "The Silk Route," we think of "La Ruta Maya" in the singular though there are many routes. The term is most often used to describe a 1500-mile all-weather route that encircles the region like the drawstring on a treasure pouch. It brings travelers through or alongside the five modern nations that share the ancient Maya homelands—Mexico, Belize, Guatemala, Honduras and El Salvador. On it you pass within reach of more ancient cities and temple complexes than can be found in Egypt. It parallels the longest coral reef in the Americas, passes through tropical forests little changed since the pleistocene, and past villages that stand as living relics of an earlier time. More species of birds live along it than in all of Canada and the United States combined.

I am credited with coining and popularizing the catchy term "La Ruta Maya" in my article on the subject in the October 1989, *National Geographic* magazine. In truth, I borrowed it from an earlier time and used it both to describe today's encircling route and to symbolize the concept of multinational cooperation that I was recommending. The five nations share more than the common Maya heritage. Population pressures leave all of them saddled with endemic poverty that threatens their once vast tropical forests and the still-buried treasures of the Maya culture.

For poor people, conservation ranks a distant second to survival. Only if these assets become more valuable to the local people intact than as loot will they survive. When Columbus arrived in the Americas, the earth's largest tropical forest stretched some 5000 miles from Mexico to the tip of Brazil. Only 18 percent remains and most of that could be lost in this generation as land is cleared for farms.

It seemed that the only way to preserve the environmental and cultural assets of the region and stem the increasing poverty was for the five nations to put aside differences that had grown over the 500 years of European rule and work together. Regional promotion of their shared cultural and environmental assets as eco- and cultural tourist attractions seemed the first step.

When I proposed the La Ruta Maya idea, no two of the five nations were on friendly terms. Guerilla wars, human rights violations, border disputes, and territorial claims made the region a cauldron of violence and instability. Thousands of Guatemala Maya had sought protection from persecution by fleeing to Mexico. Guatemala claimed Belize and threatened to annex it by force. British troops were posted along the border to protect their former colony. Mexican loggers were openly stealing thousands of acres of Guatemala's northern hardwood forests. Almost 500 years after Guatemala split from Honduras, there was still not one paved road connecting the two neighbors. Well-armed looters were mining ancient Maya sites throughout the region, delivering millions of dollars worth of irreplaceable national treasures to the international art market.

In 1987, when I met Vinicio Cerezo, the first civilian President of Guatemala in 30 years, he immediately embraced the "La Ruta Maya idea." He asked me to promote it with leaders in the other four nations. I did. But it was his enthusiasm and foresight that fueled its acceptance. In October 1988, he convened a meeting in Guatemala of representatives of the five nations to consider joint promotion of regional tourism. This was perhaps the first meeting ever of officials of Mexico, Belize, Guatemala, Honduras and El Salvador. In August 1989, Cerezo and Mexico's President Salinas embraced publicly on their shared border to symbolize the end of 150 years of tension. They retired to a Guatemala ranch where they signed 13 agreements to cooperate in solving mutual problems.

By 1990, the five nations had formed "Mundo Maya," an official commission to promote regional cooperation. Guatemala officially dropped its claim to Belize in September 1991. Thousands of tourists annually cross the peaceful border between Belize and Guatemala to visit Tikal. Border crossing throughout the area has been simplified. There is talk of a common "La Ruta Maya" tourist visa.

A network of new flights makes air travel among the five nations easy. Looting of Maya art across the borders is no longer the large-scale industry of the past. New hotels and ecotourist lodges find themselves booked before they even open. The leaders of the five nations hope that "La Ruta Maya" will figuratively be the road to riches—that it will be a powerful tool for economic growth and environmental and cultural conservation.

Despite the progress, there are problems. Like a runaway train, environmental destruction has been hard to stop. The loss of rainforest is still escalating. Poverty continues to breed political, economic, and environmental problems. But the leaders are collectively applying the brakes. Dozens of parks and preserves have been formed. Environmentalists, once equated with leftist revolutionaries, have founded well-funded organizations that have become a powerful forces for conservation. Guerilla wars have stopped and the hope for long-term peace has never been better.

Traveling the "La Ruta Maya" has never been easier or more rewarding. Travel it once and you will return often, as I have. But even with this most up-to-date guide in hand, you can never—in one lifetime—complete your exploration of the amazing Maya world. Yet in trying you will get to know some of your closest neighbors. Remote though it may seem, the most distant point on the Maya Route is closer to Miami, New Orleans, Houston and Los Angeles than any of these cities are to New York.

Writers Stacy Ritz and Richard Harris alternate—like dueling banjos—in presenting the Maya Route. They're always in tune with their subject, compelling and fast-paced. You'll want to read *The Maya Route* before, during and after your own explorations of the Maya Route.

Bill Garrett
February 1993

Traveling the Maya Route

Where to Go

Three thousand years ago, in the fertile, sun-drenched lands of Mexico and Central America, the Maya created a civilization that knew no equal. Appearing mysteriously like early morning fog, they built magnificent cities, developed extensive trade routes and fashioned ceremonial centers that arched toward the heavens. Then, just as mysteriously, the Maya disappeared. What they left for today's traveler are sights that have no equal.

Today, the 1500-mile-long "Maya Route" runs down the length of the Yucatán Peninsula, crosses the jungles and mountains of Guatemala and loops through verdant Belize. The often dreamlike terrain varies from searing white beaches to impenetrable rainforest. Chilling stone faces stare out of the jungle and rivers disappear into steamy, darkening wells. Monkeys scramble through treetops and toucans wing across a cobalt sky. Offshore, aqua seas wash palm-covered islands dusted with powdery sand.

Along the route, hulking temples and step pyramids rise above jungle canopies, their summits rewarding with thrilling views across a velvety, forest-clad landscape. Thousands of stone dwellings, vast plazas and *sacbes*, or Maya-carved roads, testify to the greatness of their cities. The intricacy of Maya sculptures and stelae testify to their artistic genius. Their very creation defies explanation, for how could the Maya sculpt stone when they had no metal tools?

It is the mysteries, the hazy line between known and unknown, that make the Maya experience so enchanting. No matter where you travel along the route, speculation abounds. Did Quintana Roo's Cobá, for instance, actually boast 40,000 residents? At Belize's Lubaantun, how did the Maya craft such perfect stone buildings without using mortar? And does a stone fragment found at Chiapa de Corzo really hold the earliest recorded date in the New World—December 9, 36 B.C.?

Those secrets may remain forever locked within that ancient world. Yet a new Maya world—4 million descendants of those early Maya—still thrives along the route. Separated from the modern world by both geographic isolation and poverty, they cling to ancient customs, sowing the unforgiving soil for food and worshipping the planets for spiritual nourishment. Only in recent years has it been possible for travelers to visit their remote villages and experience firsthand one of the world's most complex and fascinating cultures.

Generations of isolation have preserved much of the Maya Route. This area half the size of Texas boasts more birds and animals than the United States and Canada combined. Chunks of jungle are still impenetrable, no doubt harboring the ruins of some yet undiscovered Maya cities. And the hemisphere's longest coral reef remains largely unspoiled.

Yet development and tourism have begun to leave their imprints on the region. Vast tracts of rainforest are ravaged daily for lumber and farming, and endangered species are slaughtered for the price of a meal. Flashy resorts and themed attractions are rising along once-barren coasts, kindling a get-rich-quick fever across the land.

But the Maya Route can still be saved. Moves are under way to curb development and preserve what's left of the rainforest. Dozens of wildlife reserves, including the world's only jaguar sanctuary, have been established in recent years. Travel programs encourage visitors to explore these reserves without harming them, thereby promoting conservation. Ecotourism, many say, is the key to preservation.

The Maya Route will most likely survive because it is tough and resilient. Born of Maya ingenuity and Spanish conquest, the region has long attracted outlaws—Spanish pirates and black loggers, escaped East Indian slaves and refugees from Yucatán's Caste War—who fused it with a reckless frontier mentality. That mentality fuels today's numbers, the cattle rustlers and political refugees, the illicit loggers and the shady businessmen, who find safety in the jungle. Banana plantations abound, but so do pot farms and illegal *milpas*, or slash-and-burn fields.

It is this raffishness, this tropical spice, that assures travelers of true adventure. Not necessarily danger, but the chance to experience the unexperienced. Exploring a cave whose walls hold thousand-year-old paintings. Watching an anteater tear through a termite nest deep in the

The Maya Route
La Ruta Maya

UNITED STATES

GULF OF MEXICO

CUBA

MEXICO

CARIBBEAN SEA

BELIZE

HONDURAS

GUATEMALA

EL SALVADOR

NICARAGUA

PACIFIC OCEAN

COSTA RICA

COLOMBIA

PANAMA

N

0   100 kilometers

100 miles

Cancún

Mérida   180 Valladolid

YUCATÁN

Cozumel

MEXICO

307

Campeche

QUINTANA
ROO

GULF OF MEXICO

261

186   Chetumal

Ambergris
Caye

CAMPECHE

TABASCO
Villahermosa

Belize
City

Belmopan

199

BELIZE

Tuxtla
Gutiérrez

CARIBBEAN SEA

CA
13

CHIAPAS   190

GUATEMALA

CA
1

9

HONDURAS

Guatemala
City

PACIFIC OCEAN

EL SALVADOR

rainforest. Or having your "hotel" valet arrive, wearing a boa constrictor and no shoes, to take your luggage in a bulldozer—the only vehicle available that day.

Indeed, the promise of the Maya Route, its ability to provide an endless odyssey, is the theme of this book. *The Maya Route: The Ultimate Guidebook* offers the best of the Maya experience, from river rafting through Maya villages to midnight jaguar treks, from elegant jungle lodges to seaside *palapa* bungalows. Each locale and excursion is described individually, with a focus on quality and value, the exceptional and the unique. Short sidebars give you insider information, featuring local folklore and history and tips on traveling along the "adventure coast."

For those whose idea of adventure is lying prone on a beach, *The Maya Route* also guides you through the resort islands and towns, including the famed megaresort of Cancún. Whether it's world-class hotels, jet-set dining and nightlife, or high-thrill watersports, you can find it all along "La Ruta Maya."

ABOUT "LA RUTA MAYA"

All through this book, we refer to the Maya Route or, in Spanish, La Ruta Maya. Although the term was coined with a whole region in mind, there is a single route that connects all the major points of the Maya land in a grand loop, from which the adventurous traveler will want to take many side trips. This book presents places on and near this Maya Route in the order you would encounter them along the way.

It was in October 1989 that *National Geographic* published a feature article titled "La Ruta Maya." Written by Bill Garrett, the journal's editor at the time, the article shook up the tourism industries of five countries as it wrapped several established tourist destinations—along with many more visited by only the most intrepid travelers—into a new, alluring package that virtually defined the term "ecotourism."

"La Ruta Maya" was a blueprint for an ambitious 1500-mile loop that would meander through five nations, linking all the major restored Maya ruins, the indigenous villages of today's Maya people and the environmental reserves that protect the region's rainforests and endangered species habitats. It would span the Mexican states of Quintana Roo, Yucatán, Campeche and Chiapas, then cross the breadth and length of Guatemala and continue to the Caribbean reefs of Belize. Spurs from the main route would extend into the ancient Maya regions of northern Honduras and El Salvador.

The first and most basic aim of Garrett's plan was to encourage regional, multinational cooperation to protect environmental and cultural assets. If the whole area could be promoted as a single travel destination, it would provide a steady flow of tourist dollars (and

deutschemarks, pounds, francs and yen) into one of the most impoverished parts of the Western Hemisphere. It would give peasant farmers a
reason to save the rainforest and government officials a reason to respect the Indians' rights.

La Ruta Maya made such good sense that it won instant and widespread international support. One result was the formation of the La
Ruta Maya Conservation Foundation, a Virginia-based nonprofit
group incorporated in October 1990. The foundation is researching
the feasibility of establishing environmentally sound people-movers to
reach isolated sites as an alternative to the destructive effect of roads.
Conveyances such as cable cars or electric narrow-gauge railroads,
they say, could offer unique opportunities to see, hear and photograph
the forests, resident animals and bird life with minimum environmental damage.

THINK METRIC

Whether you're getting gas, checking the thermometer or ordering a cerveza *(beer),
you'll notice the difference: everything is metric. All Ruta Maya countries, except
English-influenced Belize, are on the metric system, which measures temperature in
degrees Celsius, distances in meters and most substances in liters, kilos and grams.*

*To convert from Celsius to Fahrenheit, multiply times 9, divide by 5 and add
32. For example, 23° Celsius—the average temperature in Cancún during the
winter—equals [(23 x 9) ÷ 5] + 32, or (207 ÷ 5) + 32, or 41.4 + 32, or about
73° Fahrenheit. If you don't have a pocket calculator along (and you probably
should), just remember that 0° C is 32° F and that each Celsius degree is roughly 2
Fahrenheit degrees. Here are some other conversion equations and a conversion table:*

1 mile = 1.6 kilometers. 1 kilometer = .6 mile.

1 foot = .3 meter. 1 meter = 3.3 feet.

1 pound (libra) = .45 kilo. 1 kilo = 2.2 pounds.

1 gallon = 3.8 liters. 1 liter = .26 gallon (about 1 quart).

kilometers	to	miles	meters	to	feet
1.0		.6	1		3.3
2.0		1.3	2		6.6
3.0		1.9	3		9.9
4.0		2.5	4		13.2
5.0		3.1	5		16.5
10.0		6.3	10		33.0
25.0		15.6	25		82.5
100.0		62.5	100		330.0

The foundation is also actively encouraging a Eurail-quality bus system around the route. A pass would allow passengers to get on and off at will. Each of the five countries involved—Mexico, Guatemala, El Salvador, Honduras and Belize—would issue a tourist visa valid for the whole region.

Another action spurred by the Ruta Maya plan has been the formation of Mundo Maya, an unprecedented cooperative effort between all five affected nations to coordinate tourism programs throughout the region. Guatemala initiated the Mundo Maya program and, as a show of good faith, dropped its long-standing claim of sovereignty over Belize, for the first time recognizing its neighbor as an independent nation. The headquarters building for Mundo Maya is under construction in Belize City.

Central to the efforts of the La Ruta Maya Conservation Foundation are several projects that would protect ecosystems under UNESCO's Man and Biosphere program. The UNESCO qualifications are designed to ensure that environmentally sensitive areas will be preserved permanently and protected from future development. Unlike national parks and wilderness areas in the United States, UNESCO biosphere reserves (*biotopos* in Spanish) can be inhabited, with sustainable development allowed on the outskirts of a preserve to buffer an undisturbed core area. The proposed Maya Peace Park is the most ambitious of the Man and Biosphere projects along the Maya Route. Seeking to protect what remains of the Petén rainforest, the park will join three contiguous reserves—the Calakmul Biosphere Reserve in the state of Campeche, Mexico; the Maya Biosphere Reserve, which fills the whole roadless frontier of Guatemala's northern border; and the small Río Bravo Conservation Area in Belize.

Much of the Ruta Maya concept is still in the visionary stage. It may be a long time before we see such refinements as luxury buses in Guatemala, monorails in the rainforest or hassle-free border crossings. At present, the procedure for entering El Salvador is so burdensome that we recommend skipping the country all together. Accordingly, we have not included Salvadoran destinations in this book. La Ruta Maya is already a reality, however, and travelers to the region today will find themselves in good company along this adventure-filled route to the heart of a land where protecting natural environments and native cultures is imperative.

An introductory tour of the entire Maya Route takes about six weeks. You'll want to experience all of this fascinating region, though not necessarily all at once. However, if you only have a week right now, that's enough. The tropics have a way of luring you back time after time. Visit Tulum and Chichén Itzá this year, and next year you'll want to go to Tikal.

The Yucatán Peninsula's limestone and coral terrain bears many cenotes, or sink-holes, but not a single above-ground river.

The Ruta Maya truly has something for everyone, from travelers seeking high adventure beyond the edge of the civilized world to those whose main travel concern is keeping in touch with their stockbroker. Where you go really depends on what you want to do. All of the Ruta Maya countries possess stunning natural beauty, fantastic villages and ancient Maya sites, remarkable history and enough exotica to last a traveler a lifetime. They also offer sand, sun and sea—key ingredients for that kick-back-and-relax part of your vacation.

You'll find that the farther along the Maya Route you travel, the more challenging (and rewarding) your trip becomes. For those who are reading this book while basking on the beach behind a highrise Cancún hotel, we will tempt you to sample the fascinating world of the Maya, ancient and modern, just a few hours away. For seasoned, adventurous travelers, we will share hints for venturing deep into the rainforest and finding hidden ruins and biotopes that tourists hardly ever see.

THE MAYA ROUTE TODAY

Thirty years ago, **Quintana Roo** was unforgiving bush country where the most common visitors were outlaws and snakes. Today, the jungles have been transformed into high-class resorts that see millions of visitors from around the world. Its most famous resort, Cancún, is Mexico's most popular tourist destination and one of the fastest-growing cities in Latin America. Spanning the eastern coast of the peninsula, with the Caribbean Sea lapping at its shores, Quintana Roo is blanketed with tropical forest and trimmed with glistening white sand and cobalt water. As for beach life, this region fulfills just about every dream of paradise, from the opulence of Cancún and the rustic beauty of Tulum to the cast-all-your-cares-away mood of Isla Mujeres. Snorkeling and scuba diving are unparalleled in Cozumel's see-through seas, where divers flock for some of the best underwater scenery on earth. For lovers of archaeology, Quintana Roo boasts Tulum—the only Maya city right on the Caribbean Sea—as well as the obscure but overwhelming ruins at Cobá and Kohunlich.

Traveling west from Cancún by rental car or bus, visitors cross the state line into **Yucatán** and soon reach Dzitnup, where you can swim in a stalactite-hung *cenote* (natural underground pool) sacred to the ancient Maya, and visit the famous Maya/Toltec ruins of Chichén Itzá, as well as several lesser ruins in the vicinity. A side trip north to the coast takes in one of the world's largest flamingo colonies at Río Lagartos. Mérida, the capital of the state of Yucatán and the largest city on the peninsula, has colonial architecture and attractive plazas. It makes a good home base for exploring numerous Maya ruins in the area, such as Dzibilchaltún, Uxmal, Kabah and Labná.

The route southwest from Yucatán state to Chiapas passes through the Gulf Coast state of **Campeche**, where the capital city of the same name boasts an untouristy atmosphere and a colorful history. The old city is surrounded by stone fortifications erected to defend against pirate attacks. South of town are miles of pure white beaches, and a short drive to the east lies Edzná, a large restored Maya ruin that most tourists miss. Travelers who wish to bypass Guatemala and Belize can take a shorter loop tour of Mexico's Yucatán Peninsula, returning to Quintana Roo and the Caribbean coast through the jungles of southern Campeche and the Calakmul Biosphere Reserve, part of the proposed multinational Maya Peace Park.

Chiapas is a land of vanishing rainforest and high, cool mountains. At Palenque National Park (Parque Nacional Palenque) you'll see what many people consider the finest of all Maya ruins, with its elegant architecture, exquisite stone and stucco sculpture and fantastic jungle setting. An intriguing side-trip possibility for the adventuresome is an expedition overland, by minivan, on foot and by river boat to the remote Maya ruins of Bonampak and Yaxchilán.

Farther along the Maya Route, San Cristóbal de las Casas, in the heart of the Chiapas highlands, is the commercial center for a number of villages in the surrounding area. The streets teem with Indians in colorful *traje* (traditional clothes). Among the Tzotzil Maya villages nearby are San Juan Chamula and Zinacantán, both very traditional highland communities.

A side trip west from San Cristóbal, the small town of Chiapa de Corzo has been inhabited continuously for 3500 years. Once the colonial capital of Chiapas, it is now best known as the departure point for boat trips through the spectacular Cañón del Sumidero. Another side trip en route to the Guatemalan border will take you to beaches along Chiapas's Pacific coast.

If you enter **Guatemala** by road from San Cristóbal, you'll first come to Huehuetenango, a small city with a colorful marketplace and the site of Zaculeu, a large Maya ruin clumsily restored by the United Fruit Company. Farther along the route, Xela (Quetzaltenango) is the main commercial center for southwestern Guatemala. The city is surrounded by points of interest including picturesque Maya villages, as well as spas and gardens. The next major stop on this route is Panajachel ("Gringotenango"), the main town for Guatemala's most popu-

lar resort area, Lake Atitlán. This large lake is surrounded by small
Indian villages. The Maya ruin of Iximché is a short distance away, and
a longer day trip will bring you to the famous, colorful village of
Chichicastenango. Guatemala City, the largest city on the Maya
Route, offers food and lodging in all price ranges, as well as such
services as car rentals, medical facilities and embassies. The main tourist destination in the area of the capital city is Antigua Guatemala,
which was practically destroyed by an earthquake in 1773. Now an
historic district, it is home to most of Guatemala's American and European expatriates.

From the highway that runs east from Guatemala City to the Caribbean coast, travelers can make a side trip across the Honduran border
to visit Copán, one of the great showpiece ceremonial centers of the
ancient Maya world. Other attractions of eastern Guatemala include
the giant Maya stelae at Quiriguá, the Caribbean fishing port of Livingston and Río Dulce, a beautiful jungle river that provides habitat
for endangered species including manatees, tapirs and jaguars.

Buried deep in the northern Guatemala rainforest and teeming with
wild animals, the Petén is one of Central America's most remote regions. It is also one of the most thrilling, for here the classic Maya
civilization achieved its cultural, architectural and intellectual height,
as attested by the area's 100-plus Maya sites, including five skyscraper
pyramids that rise like giants from the jungle. The Petén's centerpiece
is Tikal, a 210-square-mile reserve protecting the ancient city that in
its 500 A.D. heyday was as large as any European city of the time.

Belize may be the Ruta Maya's smallest country, yet it possesses
enough natural and historical treasures to fill an entire continent. A
little larger than Massachusetts, this delightfully unusual tapestry of
European, Creole, Maya, Garifuna (African-Indian) and Mestizo

---

NO MORE "NO HABLO ESPAÑOL"

*If you learned some Spanish in school but are not fluent for lack of practice, you
might want to plan for some extra time in Guatemala, where "language schools" are
a booming industry. These schools arrange for you to live with the family of one of
their teachers. The total cost for a week's lodging, meals and 20 hours of one-on-one
Spanish instruction is under $100—one of the best bargains to be found along the
Ruta Maya. Wait until you arrive in Guatemala to select a "school," as you'll
want to meet the instructors and look at the household before making your choice.
There are more than 100 "language schools" in Antigua Guatemala and others in
Panajachel, Xela (Quetzaltenango) and Huehuetenango.*

(Spanish–Indian) peoples is a Central American anomaly: it is primarily English-speaking. It is also leading an heroic crusade for ecotourism, inviting visitors to check out its largely unexplored corner of the earth. Here, in more than 25 wildlife preserves, you'll discover gin-clear rivers where iguanas sun along the banks and jungles where monkeys swing through the treetops. You'll also find heavenly flora, genuine, down-to-earth people, and what is thought to be the largest concentration of Maya ruins anywhere. These include the late great cities of Xunantunich, Caracol, Lubaantun and Lamanai, most buried deep in the jungle and rarely visited. Add to all this a strand of jewel-like islands and the world's second-longest barrier reef, and you have one very special place, indeed.

When to Go

CLIMATE

Like most of the tropics, regions along the Maya Route have just two seasons: rainy and dry. Generally, rain falls and temperatures rise during summer and autumn months, from June through October—the least expensive time to visit the region. Daily rains can soak inland jungle roads, creating sludge trails that are impassable without four-wheel-drive vehicles. Late summer and early fall can also mean hurricane season, particularly along the Caribbean coast. It's not likely that you'll encounter one—they blow in every decade or so—but if you should, take it seriously: hurricanes are monsters that take lives and leave a path of destruction.

The months of July and August are the busy season in the relatively cool mountain highlands of Chiapas and western Guatemala. In San Cristóbal de las Casas, for example, where winter weather is cold and summers are perfect, European visitors (who typically come in the summer months) outnumber tourists from the United States and Canada by four to one. In the highland Maya villages that surround the town, fair-skinned foreign visitors are called not "*gringos*" but "*Alemantecas*" (Germans).

November to mid-April is the high and dry season—literally. Prices shoot up as much as 40 percent or more in response to the crowds flocking here to enjoy the idyllic balmy weather. Be aware that Christmas, New Year's and Easter pack the hotels wall-to-wall and the beaches towel-to-towel, sometimes with sky-high price tags attached. We usually find the May and October "shoulder seasons" pleasantly uncrowded, wonderfully economical and seldom unbearably hot—requiring at the worst two swims a day instead of one.

Here's what to expect from the climates of each Ruta Maya region (temperatures are Fahrenheit):

The **Yucatán Peninsula** is warm year-round, with temperatures that average in the 80s. During the summer, inland jungles can be suffocatingly hot and humid, while the Gulf and Caribbean coasts often stay comfortably cooled by trade winds. If you visit between May and October, you will likely experience *nortes*, nature's quick but tempestuous outbursts of thunder, lightning, wind and rain. They seem to come from nowhere and then disappear into nowhere, leaving a wake of intense blue skies and misty warmth. Winter brings dry weather, but the temperature drops only slightly, staying close to a perfect 75 degrees.

LA MORDIDA

In Mexico and more commonly in Guatemala, the custom of the mordida *persists. Literally, the word means "little bite"; actually, it means bribery of public officials. Both countries have been making serious efforts to eradicate the practice, at least where tourists are involved, because it horrifies many gringos, who fail to understand that public officials in the Third World are woefully underpaid. If you would tip a waitress for giving you the best possible service, then why not reward a traffic cop or border guard for exercising the discretion of his office wisely?*

If you find yourself in the position of having to discuss a bribe, never use the word mordida *or in any way suggest that you are asking the officer to do anything illegal. The very suggestion is highly offensive and could even land you in jail. Sometimes a small bribe is referred to as a* propina *(tip) or as an unofficial* honorario *(fee). More often, if you ask the officer whether there is another way the matter can be worked out, you will hear the following line of reasoning:*

"For me to fail to enforce the law would be a serious dereliction of duty and honor. It is for the court, not me, to assess a fine in a case like this. . . . But since you are a visitor in my country, and I like you, if you tell no one, I might let the delinquencia pass just this once. Of course, you must understand that in Guatemala it is customary to exchange a favor for a favor. Now that I am doing this favor for you, it would be the right thing for you to give me a regalo, a gift. For my wife. The amount is whatever you think is right. . . . Well, a little more than that. . . ."

If the idea of bribery bothers you, pay up anyway and report it to the government tourism office later. Anybody who is in a position to solicit a bribe can also cause interminable delay and hassle if you don't hand over the cash.

Mexicans are fond of saying, "There's a fiesta going on somewhere in Mexico every moment."

Chiapas is a land of extreme variations in altitude and climate. In the rainforest lowlands around Palenque and Yaxchilán, it is hot and humid year-round. A few hours away, in the highlands around San Cristóbal, nights are always chilly, winter temperatures can drop below freezing and you'll be glad if you have a room with a fireplace. The same is true of **Guatemala**. Lowland destinations like Quiriguá, Copán, Río Dulce and especially Tikal have the climate you'd expect in a tropical rainforest, while highland towns like Antigua and Huehuetenango are quite cool most of the time. If you venture higher into the mountains to Maya villages like Todos Santos, you should buy a warm wool jacket first. Throughout both Chiapas and Guatemala, the rainy season starts in mid–May and continues until October.

Summer rains increase dramatically in **Belize** as you head from north to south. Northern Corozal, for instance, averages 50 inches of annual rain, while Punta Gorda, only 200 miles to the south, gets an incredible 170 inches a year. During the rainy season, dependable afternoon showers give life to the forests and a welcome drop in temperatures for those who reside there. Temperatures along the coast and inland rainforests often reach 95 degrees by midday. During the dry season, from November through May, the thermometer registers in the comfortable low 80s. In the mountains of mainland Belize, the mercury drops into the 50s at night during winter, with perfect daytime weather in the 70s. Springtime creates crystalline waters in the offshore cayes, with visibility reaching an amazing 100 feet in some dive spots.

CALENDAR OF EVENTS

You may plan your Ruta Maya visit around a certain holiday or festival and join in the local spirit. As you may already know, Mexicans and Central Americans need no reason to celebrate, though they certainly have many. Indeed, writers from Octavio Paz to Alan Riding have described the fiesta as a vital liberation from solitude, stoicism and the restraints of poverty, whether the occasion celebrates a religious or patriotic event, a birthday or a wedding. Remember that because of the festivities, everything else practically shuts down, including government agencies, businesses and professional offices. In other words, if there's a holiday, forget about business and join the party!

Here are some of the more important events along the Maya Route:

JANUARY

Everywhere: **New Year's Day** (Día del Año Nuevo) is celebrated on January 1 as a national holiday, complete with parades, prayers and fireworks.

Yucatán Peninsula: Throughout Mexico, Christmas presents are given on January 6, the **Day of Kings** (Día de los Reyes), which marks the end of the month-long holiday season.

Chiapas: The **Fiesta de Enero** in Chiapa de Corzo, which runs from January 9 to 22, is marked by some of the most spectacular celebrations in Mexico, with parades, processions and masked dancers in the streets. The **Fiesta de San Sebastián** (January 16 to 22), one of the most important religious feast days at San Juan Chamula and San Pedro Chenalho, is observed with dancing, processions, incense and music in both villages. The **Fiesta de San Ildefonso** honors Tenejapa's patron saint on January 23.

Guatemala: The **Fiesta de Cristo de Esquipulas** on January 15 commemorates an apparition of the Black Christ that was seen by an Indian in 1595. Tens of thousands of pilgrims walk to Esquipulas from all over the country to visit a statue of the Black Christ. Recognized as having miraculous powers since 1737, this is the main spiritual symbol throughout Guatemala.

FEBRUARY

Everywhere: **Candlemas** (Candelario), observed as a religious holiday throughout Latin America, marks the midpoint of winter on February 2. Later in the month, Latin Americans revel in a week-long **Carnival** leading up to the austerity of Lent.

Yucatán Peninsula: **Candelario** is celebrated on February 2 with dancing, processions, bullfights and the blessing of candles and seeds. **Constitution Day** (Día de Constitución), a Mexican national holiday on February 6, means bank and business closings but no big public celebrations in the Yucatán. Mérida explodes with music, dance and fireworks for **Carnival**, as do Isla Mujeres, Cozumel and Campeche.

Chiapas: **Carnival** is spectacular in San Juan Chamula.

Guatemala: **Candelario** is celebrated throughout the country, especially in Chiantla, Huehuetenango and San Juan Ostuncalco, on February 2.

MARCH-APRIL

Everywhere: Throughout Latin America, **Holy Week** (Semana Santa)—the week leading up to Easter—rivals the Christmas season as the biggest holiday of the year. Everybody travels then. Expect crowds and high prices.

Yucatán Peninsula: **Holy Week** is a time for all-out street parties featuring passion plays, music and dancing in the plazas in Cozumel, Isla Mujeres and Campeche. There is a general exodus of city folk for the sea or lakeshore, where they picnic and camp.

Chiapas: **Holy Week** is one of the biggest events of the year in San Cristóbal de las Casas. On Saturday, the day before Easter, the whole town gathers to burn Judas in effigy. The festivities are extended for a second week, after Easter, as the **Fería de la Primavera de la Paz** (Spring and Peace Fair).

Guatemala: **Holy Week** (Semana Santa) is the biggest festival of the year in Antigua Guatemala. Travelers come from all over the world to witness it. Holy Week is the most important holiday of the year all over Guatemala.

Belize: Belize businesses close for **Easter Sunday** and the following Monday so locals can celebrate at home. On March 9, **Baron Bliss Day** pays homage to the man who left his $2 million fortune to this tiny country. Belizeans remember him with a day of fishing and sailing, an apt remembrance since the baron was devoted to both pursuits.

MAY

Yucatán Peninsula: **Labor Day**, May 1, is a Mexican national holiday, as is **Cinco de Mayo** (May 5), which celebrates the defeat of the French by the Mexican army at Puebla in 1862. Neither is celebrated in a very big way in the Yucatán or Chiapas, but banks and many businesses are closed. Later in the month, the city of Mérida livens up as it hosts its annual **International Song Festival**, which features performances of nearly 400 original songs, mostly in Spanish, from a dozen countries. **Corpus Christi Day** (late May or early June) occasions blessings of children all over the country.

Chiapas: The **Day of the Cross**, May 3, is a major ceremonial day in Tzotzil Maya villages, especially in San Juan Chamula.

Guatemala: **Labor Day**, May 1, is a Guatemalan national holiday. The **Day of the Cross**, May 2, is observed in Chichicastenango, as well as in Amatitlán, where a fair is held from May 1 to 5. The **Feast of Corpus Christi** (late May or early June) is marked by celebrations in Guatemala City.

JUNE

Chiapas: The **Fiesta de San Juan**, an important feast day in San Juan Chamula, is celebrated on June 24 with ritual horse races through the village as well as religious processions. This is also one of the biggest fiestas of the year in Santo Domingo Palenque. Nearby, the village of San Pedro Chenalhó celebrates the **Fiesta de San Pedro** from June 27 to 30.

Guatemala: Several villages on Lake Atitlán mark their patron saints' feast days in June: the **Feast of San Antonio de Padua** is observed in San Antonio de Palopó on June 12 and 13; the **Feast of San Juan Bautista** takes place in San Juan La Laguna from June 22 to 24; and the **Feast of San Pedro** is celebrated in San Pedro La Laguna on June 29.

JULY

Yucatán Peninsula: Dancing, fireworks and sporting events are all part of **Ticul**, a week-long fiesta commemorating the establishment of Ticul, a town northeast of Uxmal. Ciudad del Carmen, south along the coast from the city of Campeche, honors its patroness, **Nuestra Señora del Carmen**, with a big citywide fiesta.

Chiapas: The celebration of **Fiesta de San Cristóbal**, the biggest fiesta of the year in San Cristóbal de las Casas, lasts from July 17 to July 25. It is a time of pilgrimages and candlelight processions, and it coincides with San Cristóbal's peak tourist season. July 25 is also the date of the **Fiesta de Santiago Apóstal** in Amatenango del Valle.

Guatemala: **Fiestas Julias**, the state fair, fills Huehuetenango with revelry from July 12 to 18. Local fairs take place in Santiago Atitlán from July 23 to 25 and in Momostenango from July 28 to 30.

AUGUST

Yucatán Peninsula: **Assumption Day** is celebrated throughout Mexico on August 15.

Chiapas: Palenque has a big celebration on the **Fiesta de Santo Domingo de Guzman**, August 4. In Zinacantán, the **Fiesta de San Lorenzo**, August 8 to 11, is a time of flowers and processions. On August 30, music, incense and fireworks usher in the **Fiesta de Santa Rosa**.

Guatemala: The **Festival of Guatemala**, which marks the founding of the present capital, is observed in Guatemala City on August 15. Everything is closed.

SEPTEMBER

Yucatán Peninsula: Here and throughout Mexico, there are parades and fireworks on **Independence Day**, September 16. From September 27 to October 14, the **Fiesta de Cristo de las Ampollas** (Christ of the Blisters) in Mérida honors a sacred cross seemingly immune to fire.

Chiapas: From September 1 to September 5, the people of Palenque observe the **Fiesta de Santo Domingo**, their patron saint, in grand style. Throughout the state, the anniversary of Chiapas joining Mexico is celebrated on September 14, spilling into **Independence Day** celebrations on the 15th and 16th. In San Cristóbal de las Casas, the **Fiesta del Barrio de la Merced** on September 24 is a big civil celebration.

Guatemala: September 15 is Guatemala's **Independence Day**. The grandest celebrations are in Guatemala City and in Quetzaltenango, where it is the climax of a state fair that runs from September 12 to 16.

Belize: September means virtual nonstop celebrating in Belize. One of the biggest, most joyous national holidays, the **Battle of St. George's Caye** remembers the September 10, 1798, victory of the British over the Spanish. Every town joins in with a week of parades, jumpup street dancing and community-wide feasting. The British eventually gave Belize its independence on September 21, 1981, and Belizeans celebrate with **National Independence Day**. The whole country is like a carnival, and streets are filled with artisans, musicians, dancers, actors and every type of Belizean food imaginable.

OCTOBER

Yucatán Peninsula: A week of parades and dancing heralds in the **Fiesta de San Francisco de Asisi** on October 4. **Columbus Day** (Día de la Raza), October 12, is observed throughout Mexico.

Chiapas: A large market takes place in conjunction with the **Fería de San Francisco**, an authentically Mexican country fair and fiesta held in Amatenango del Valle October 1 through October 5. In San Juan Chamula, the **Feast of Our Lady of the Rosary** (Fiesta de la Virgen del Rosario) features music, dancing, costumes and a fair October 6 through 8.

Guatemala: The **Feast of San Francisco** is celebrated with local fairs in San Francisco El Alto and Panajachel from October 1 through 4. Later in the month, from October 15 to 18, similar fairs take place in Aguacatán and San Lucas Tolimán to observe the **Feast of San Lucas**.

Belize: Back-to-back holidays mean twice as much celebrating. October 12 brings **Columbus Day**, while October 13 is **Pan American Day.**

NOVEMBER

Yucatán Peninsula: **The Day of the Dead** (Día de los Muertos or Todos Santos) blends remembrance of the departed with cheerfully morbid revelry in a unique Indian-Christian tribute to death on November 1. Sugar skulls, altars, papier-mâché skeletons and toy coffins fill the streets of Yucatán cities, where strong Indian traditions survive. **November 20**, the anniversary of the beginning of the Mexican Revolution of 1910, is a national holiday.

Chiapas: The **Fería de Santa Cecilia** on November 22, followed up by the **Fiesta de la Caridad** on the 23rd and 24th, is one of the year's biggest festivals in San Cristóbal de las Casas.

Guatemala: **All Saints' Day** (Todos Santos) on November 1 and **All Souls' Day** on November 2 are observed throughout Guatemala. The most spectacular celebrations are in Guatemala City, Chichicastenango and Todos Santos Cuchumatán. The **Feast of Santa Catalina** on November 25 is a major fiesta in Zunil and Santa Catarina Palopó.

Belize: Pulsing drums and punta rock music signal the start of **Garifuna Day** in southern Belize. The November 19 festivities, centered in the Toledo District, mark the 1823 arrival of the Garifunas (African-Indians).

DECEMBER

Everywhere: **Christmas** (Navidad) is the holiest of holidays throughout the Ruta Maya region.

Yucatán Peninsula and Chiapas: The **Feast of Our Lady of Guadalupe**, patroness of Mexico, inspires parades, dancing and music nationwide on December 12. The Christmas season begins on December 16, the first night of **Las Posadas**, the Mexican tradition of nightly processions recalling Mary and Joseph's search for lodging in Bethlehem. Nativity scenes are the main form of Christmas decoration. **Christmas Eve** (Nochebuena) is also a time of holy processions and singing. **Christmas Day** is a national holiday, and the streets are deserted. **All Fools' Day** on December 28 is similar to April Fools' Day.

Guatemala: The **Feast of Our Lady of Guadalupe** is widely celebrated throughout the country, especially in Guatemala City, Chichicastenango, Sololá and Santa Lucía Utatlán. The **Change of Mayors** in Chichicastenango on December 31 is one of the most impressive ceremonies in the Guatemalan highlands.

Belize: December 26 marks **Boxing Day**, a national Belizean holiday.

How to Go

GETTING THERE AND GETTING AROUND

BY CAR   Traveling from the United States to the Ruta Maya by car is a challenging and time-consuming adventure. Not that it's particularly dangerous—just demanding. Most Mexican highways are two-lane roads, not limited-access freeways, and driving takes longer than you would expect. The drive to Cancún from Brownsville, Texas, the closest border crossing, is almost 2500 kilometers (1500 miles). It can be done in roughly 40 hours of actual driving time. To make the journey comfortably, without arriving in the Yucatán exhausted, allow at least a week. From El Paso, Texas, it's a 3600-kilometer (2160-mile) trip requiring 60 hours of driving, and from San Diego, it's 4800 kilometers (2880 miles)—more than 80 hours of driving.

If you are driving to the Yucatán from the U.S. border, plan well ahead for refueling and evening stops. Gas stations in Mexico are a government monopoly, and in much of the country they are few and far between. Never pass up an opportunity to fill your vehicle's tank. Driving after dark can be dangerous (the most common hazards being vehicles stopped in the traffic lane without lights and vehicles traveling without lights well after dusk—sometimes considered a display of machismo). In northern Mexico, especially, it can be a long way between towns large enough to have hotels or restaurants. For those with trailers, RVs or motor homes, private campgrounds abound in most parts of Mexico, and even in the smallest villages there are always informal sites where self-contained RVs can be parked—inquire locally.

In Mexico, unleaded gasoline is available at all Pemex stations. Gas is sold by the liter and costs significantly more than in the United States. Fuel prices run about the same in Mexico and Guatemala.

Traveling into Guatemala in your own vehicle has posed a problem in the past because unleaded gasoline has been completely unavailable. The Guatemalan government has now enacted a law that requires new cars sold there beginning in the spring of 1993 to have catalytic converters, so presumably unleaded fuel should be available.

Unleaded gas is not available in Belize—but there are not many cars in Belize. Fuel is sold by the gallon at about two-and-a-half times the price of gas in the United States.

For the red-tape aspects of arriving by car, see "At the Border—Motor Vehicle Requirements" later in this chapter.

CAR RENTALS   Renting a car eliminates the need for your own insurance and car permits as it lets you leapfrog over the thousands of

Take the optional extra insurance that lowers your deductible for damage to the vehicle—rental cars in Central America lead hazardous existences.

miles between your garage and the land of the Maya. Car rentals are widely available in cities that have commercial airports—Cancún, Mérida, Campeche, Tuxtla Gutiérrez, Guatemala City and Belize City. In other tourist areas that do not have local rent-a-car companies, travel agencies can arrange a rental car for you. It may take several hours advance notice or several days, depending on the place and the season. In fact, advance reservations are always wise if you're traveling during the high season.

Anyone 25 years or older, with a passport or tourist card, a driver's license and a major credit card, can rent a car in Mexico, Guatemala or Belize. Many international rent-a-car companies will reserve a car in advance and have it waiting for you upon arrival. However, it's best to confirm the reservation with the company's local office where you intend to pick up the car. The easiest way to do this is by fax (local fax numbers are available from the international companies).

Wherever you are in Mexico or Guatemala, always park in a guarded lot at night. In Belize, park in a well-lit area (we can't think of more than three guarded parking lots in the whole country).

Rental rates have increased dramatically in recent years and are generally higher than in the United States. The cost of renting a car is much higher in Cancún than in Mérida, so if you're flying into Cancún, you'll save by taking the bus or plane to Mérida and renting a car there. In the Yucatán, you get a bonus blast of nostalgia since most rental cars are new Volkswagen Beetles identical to the old ones. In Chiapas and Guatemala, Japanese and Korean cars are preferred. In Belize, most rental vehicles are four-wheel-drives (necessary for the super-rough and rocky roads), and rental rates are astronomical. Still, it's worth it for the freedom of having your own ride. Plus, public buses are snail-slow.

It is not currently possible to drive a Mexican rental car into Guatemala or vice versa. Those who plan to explore the entire Maya Route by rental car may find it necessary to fly between Mérida, Guatemala City and Belize City, renting a different car at each airport.

BY AIR   We think the best way to get from the United States to your starting point on the Maya Route is to fly. Commercial airlines fly frequently between the United States or Canada and the international airport at Cancún. There are also daily international flights to Belize City and Guatemala City.

For air travel to Cancún and the Yucatán Peninsula, you can take American, United, Continental, Northwest or either of the two Mexican airlines, Aeroméxico and Mexicana.

For service from the United States to Belize and Guatemala, the Honduras-based Sahsa Airlines has daily nonstop flights. Sahsa also offers an excellent "Maya World Fare," which gives you unlimited stops in the Ruta Maya region for $399 round-trip from Miami, New Orleans or Houston. (Note, though, that while Sahsa goes to all major airports in Central America, it does not go to Mexican destinations.) Other airlines serving Guatemala and/or Belize include TACA, LACSA and Aviateca.

Baggage allowances on international flights are generally the same as on U.S. domestic flights—two carry-on items small enough to fit under the seat or in an overhead rack, plus two pieces of check-through luggage. In addition, some Latin American airlines have a weight limitation—typically 40 kilograms (88 pounds)—on check-through luggage. All airlines allow considerably more baggage than you would want to carry around on this trip.

During special events, holidays and the November-to-May high season, make flight reservations at least two weeks to a month in advance. Air delays are common. So are flight cancellations—be sure to confirm your flight 48 hours before departure. Canceled flights seem to be a particular problem at Flores (the airport for Guatemala's Tikal National Park), where the next flight out may not be for several days.

All commercial airports in Latin America have an airport departure tax equivalent to about US$10 to $12, which must be paid in local currency at the time you check in.

When booking your international airline tickets, if you will be taking a connecting flight on your return trip, be sure to allow plenty of time. At the hub airport where you first land in the United States—probably Los Angeles, Dallas, Houston, New Orleans or Miami—you will have to wait for and claim your baggage, clear U.S. Customs, and recheck your bags before boarding your next flight. Allow one-and-a-half to two hours.

BY BUS   Buses are one of the cheaper modes of transportation in Mexico. Because the majority of Mexicans don't own cars, the bus system is used much more than in the United States, so you can generally get most anywhere by bus. From the U.S. border, you just about always have to go to Mexico City first, then catch a bus to the Yucatán from there. Depending on where you start from, it usually takes about 24 hours to travel by bus from the U.S. border to Mexico City, and the journey to Mérida takes another 24 hours.

Bus tickets are sold at the stations for cash (local currency only) on a first-come, first-served basis. Avoid bus travel around big holidays

(Christmas and Easter) unless you are able to buy tickets well in advance, which can't be done from the United States unless you work through a Mexican travel agency.

Buses are categorized as *primera clase* (first class) or *segunda clase* (second class). Throughout most of Mexico, most first-class buses are more comfortable than those in the United States, with air-conditioning, roomy seats and sometimes televisions that show Mexican video movies while you travel. In the inland areas of the Yucatán, first-class buses tend to be more run-down than elsewhere, but adequate, while on the Caribbean coast, the opposite is true: We took a first-class bus from Chetumal to Cancún that was more luxurious than the international flights to Cancún, Belize or Guatemala City.

Second-class buses, the notorious Third World "pigs-and-chickens" kind, are much slower and less comfortable. Lack of onboard restrooms makes second-class buses a dubious choice for long-distance travel. Considering the low cost of first-class bus tickets, budget is seldom a reason to settle for a second-class bus. You will have plenty of opportunity to have funky second-class bus adventures on shorter trips around the Maya Route.

BY TRAIN   Mexico's national railroad system, Ferrocarriles Nacionales de Mexico, is the cheapest—and slowest—mode of public transportation. Tickets are available through some U.S. travel agents, as well as at the train station. It takes from 24 to 48 hours to reach Mexico City from the U.S. border and another 36 hours to get to Mérida. Besides first- and second-class coaches, trains running between the border and Mexico City have more luxurious *primera especial* coaches with larger seats and air-conditioning, as well as more costly private sleeping compartments that must be booked well in advance. Trains that go to the Yucatán have neither, and some of them use the most decrepit passenger cars in the national railroad system. Taking the train

---

WATCH YOUR BAGGAGE...

There are persistent reports of theft problems on the Mexico City-Palenque-Mérida train. You have no alternative to carrying all your luggage on with you, which makes it vulnerable to thieves any time you fall asleep or leave your seat. In half a dozen train trips along this route, we've never experienced any such problems, but several foreign travelers we've talked to have lost their gear on this trip. Unless you're ready to split all-night guard duty with a traveling companion, don't take this train trip carrying any possessions that you can't risk losing.

from Mexico City via Palenque to Mérida is beautiful and memorable—but not comfortable.

BY SHIP   For travel to the Yucatán Peninsula, cruise ships offer glamour and comfort, with stops at several points along the Quintana Roo coast. Each year, luxury liners deliver hundreds of thousands of people to Cancún, Cozumel and Playa del Carmen. See the "Transportation" section in Chapter Four for names and phone numbers of the various cruise lines.

TRAVEL AGENCIES   All cities and larger towns along the Ruta Maya have a number of travel agencies, most of them located in the lobbies of larger hotels and in downtown commercial zones. These agencies do a lot more than just sell airline tickets and make hotel reservations. They often serve as clearinghouses for small tour operators and can help you arrange a motorcycle rental, a plane or four-wheel-drive trip to remote ruins, a horseback expedition into the mountains, a jetboat or raft trip down one of the region's spectacular rivers or any number of other adventures. Stop in and see what they have to offer. If nothing else, you'll come away with plenty of friendly suggestions to enhance your visit.

AT THE BORDER

PASSPORTS, VISAS AND TOURIST CARDS   United States and most Canadian citizens can visit Mexico without a passport or visa. You must, however, carry proof of citizenship in the form of a certified birth certificate or valid passport. Mexico accepts proof of citizenship in some other forms as well, but these are the only two proofs currently accepted by the U.S. Immigration and Naturalization Service when returning to the United States. A voter registration card is no longer accepted as proof of citizenship.

Naturalized U.S. citizens who do not have a valid U.S. passport must have an original certificate of naturalization or certificate of citizenship. Naturalized Canadian citizens need a passport. All European visitors need passports.

Anyone under age 18 must have proof of citizenship and the following documents: if traveling unaccompanied or with anyone other than their parents, a notarized letter of permission signed by both parents, a legal guardian or an individual passport; or if traveling with only one parent, a notarized letter from the other parent or legal guardian or an individual passport. Foreign students in Mexico are required to have an acceptance letter from the school and a letter certifying that they are financially secure, in addition to a tourist card.

When you enter Mexico, you will receive a tourist card, which you need to keep on your person at all times and surrender when you leave. You can speed up border-crossing red tape by obtaining these cards from a travel agent or Mexican consulate in the United States and typing them up before you leave, so that the *Migración* official only needs to sign and stamp it. You get your tourist card upon arrival if you are flying in to a Mexican international airport, before departure if you are taking a plane or bus from the U.S. border, or when you leave the *frontera* zone if you are traveling by car. Tourist cards are free, and bribery is no longer common practice on the Mexican border. Tourist cards can be issued for up to 180 days. (Most American expatriates who live in Mexico, instead of applying for extensions or resident status, keep their paperwork up-to-date by simply returning to the United States for at least 72 hours every six months and getting a new tourist card.) Multiple-entry tourist cards are also available. They are convenient, but not necessary, if you are planning to go to Guatemala or Belize and then return to Mexico. To apply for a multiple-entry tourist card, you need two copies of a photo that meets passport standards, and the procedure takes longer at the *Migración* desk than simply applying for a new single-entry card when you reenter Mexico.

All visitors to Belize, Guatemala or Honduras must have valid passports. Besides clearing immigration, you will need to show your passport when renting a car, cashing traveler's checks, or, in many cases, checking into a hotel.

Belize does not require visas (except for visitors from Cuba, Hong Kong and parts of Africa and the Middle East). Visitors who plan to stay longer than 30 days, however, should obtain an extension from the Belize Immigration Office (115 Barrack Road, Belize City; 2-33505). Extensions cost US$12.50.

Visitors to Guatemala must have either a visa (free, obtained in advance from any Guatemalan consulate in the United States or Mexico) or a tourist card (US$5, issued upon entry into Guatemala). Visitors who drive motor vehicles into Guatemala need visas. So do citizens of

---

PASAPORTE, POR FAVOR

If you want to travel deeper into Honduras or El Salvador, where there are a few minor Maya ruins, entry requirements can range from a visa to a tourist card to just a passport, depending on who you ask. If you are flying there directly, check with the nearest consulate at least two weeks before your departure and obtain either a visa or an official letter waiving any visa requirement. Many airlines require one or the other.

Unless you want to invite trouble from customs officials, carry prescription drugs in their proper containers. Remember, they search you for drugs when you leave Central American countries.

certain foreign nations. For example, the last time we traveled into Guatemala by bus from San Cristóbal de las Casas in Chiapas, Mexico, we made the acquaintance of a group of backpack travelers from the British Isles. Those with United Kingdom passports strolled across the border in five minutes for a $5 fee, but the poor soul with the Irish passport had to take an all-day trip back to the nearest Guatemalan consulate in Mexico for a visa.

To cross over to the great Maya ruins at Copán in Honduras, you need only your passport. Visitors staying 12 hours or less can get a special tourist card that does not cancel their Guatemalan visa or tourist card. If you stay longer than 12 hours, you are supposed to wait 72 hours before reentering Guatemala and must pay a new US$5 tourist card fee.

MOTOR VEHICLE REQUIREMENTS   For driving on the Ruta Maya, your current driver's license is valid. If you're bringing your own car, you'll need a Mexican car permit and Mexican auto insurance. To obtain a car permit (a special stamp on the owner's tourist card, issued for up to 180 days), you need proof of ownership—a current registration certificate and title. If the title shows a lien against the vehicle or if it is registered in another person's name or a company name, you need a notarized letter from the lien holder or owner authorizing you to take the vehicle to Mexico for a specified time. The owner or driver who has the car permit stamp on his or her tourist card *must* be in the car whenever it is being driven.

At this writing, the Mexican government has announced new regulations designed to stanch the flow of stolen cars from the United States to Mexico. Anyone bringing a motor vehicle into Mexico must show either a major credit card or a collision/comprehensive insurance policy valid for the duration of the stay. Otherwise, the owner may be required to post a cash bond guaranteeing that he or she will return with the vehicle to the United States. At the same time, the Mexican government has promised to simplify procedures for temporarily importing vehicles. For current requirements, contact a Mexican consulate in the United States or the U.S. Embassy in Mexico City (Paseo de Reforma No. 305, 60500 Mexico, D.F.; 5-211-0042).

Auto insurance policies issued in the United States are not valid in Mexico. Purchase motor vehicle liability insurance (and, if you wish, collision/comprehensive) before crossing into Mexico. It is sold by agencies on the U.S. side at all border crossings. Causing an auto accident is a crime under Mexican law, which presumes defendants guilty until proven innocent. This means that if you are involved in an accident that causes property damage, your vehicle will be impounded until you pay the damage and a fine. If any person is injured in the accident, you will go to jail.

The documentation you need to take your vehicle into Mexico is more than sufficient to bring it into Guatemala or Belize. Car permits in both countries are normally valid for 30 days. Guatemala does not require liability insurance, but as in Mexico, you risk hassles, delay and expense—and possibly jail—if you are involved in an accident without insurance. Belize requires liability insurance. Insurance costs considerably less in Guatemala and Belize than in Mexico—as little as US$1 a day. It is sold in border town mom-and-pop shops *inside* the country where it is valid. In Belize, you cannot buy car insurance or get a car permit on Sunday.

CUSTOMS REGULATIONS   When entering **Mexico** from the United States, you will be required to sign a form certifying that you are not importing contraband. Many travelers are surprised to learn that Mexico has a problem with smuggling from the United States. Stiff protective tariffs as much as double the price of goods made in U.S. factories, creating a temptation to circumvent the *Aduana* (Mexican Customs).

While rules are more liberal for foreign tourists than for Mexican citizens, you will be required to certify, among other things, that you are not bringing in more than one still camera and one movie or video camera per person, with a maximum of twelve rolls of film each. If your luggage should be inspected by Mexican Customs (which is unlikely), items travelers would be unlikely to use, such as kitchen appliances, will raise official eyebrows. So will more than one of the same item, especially electronics.

Just about the most trouble you can get into in Mexico is to be caught with a firearm or bullets in your possession. Latin American countries take gun control very seriously. The volume of red tape involved in importing a weapon legally is simply not worth it. Smuggling a box of ammunition into Mexico can carry a stiffer prison sentence than smuggling cocaine into the United States!

Guatemala's customs regulations, as they apply to tourists, are minimal and somewhat vague. As a practical matter, instead of physically inspecting your luggage, Guatemalan *Aduana* officials prefer to charge a small fee per bag for a tag certifying that they have inspected it.

Belize customs regulations are also liberal to tourists. However, they are notoriously slow at the Belize City international airport. This is especially true on Monday mornings, when Belizeans returning from weekend shopping sprees in Miami must itemize their purchases and pay duties. Customs officials literally check every corner of every suitcase. Twice, we waited nearly two hours in the boiling heat to clear customs. If you find yourself in this waiting-forever situation, slow down and remember—this is the tropics!

If you want to bring a pet into Mexico, Guatemala or Belize, you must have an International Health Certificate for Dogs and Cats (Form 77-043) signed by a U.S. veterinarian verifying that the animal is in good health, as well as a separate certification that it has been immunized against distemper and rabies within the last six months. A visa for your pet (in the form of a stamp on the veterinarian's certificate) costs US$20 when entering Mexico. Belize also requires an import permit, available from the Veterinarian Office in Belize City (2-45230).

U.S. CUSTOMS REGULATIONS   Even if you live there, the United States can be harder to enter than any of the Ruta Maya countries. When returning home, United States residents may bring back $400 worth of purchases duty-free. Anything over this amount is subject to a 10 percent tax on the next $1000 worth of items. In case customs officials question the values you declare, save the purchase receipts for goods you buy in retail stores and record your marketplace and street vendor purchases neatly in a notebook.

Persons over 21 are allowed one liter (or quart) of liquor duty-free.

Sportfish, shrimp and any seafood that can be legally caught in the Ruta Maya countries can be brought across the border. Many other fresh foods, however, are not allowed into the United States and will be confiscated.

Pirata (pirated copies of copyrighted books, records, cassettes, videos and computer programs, as well as clones of trademarked goods like designer jeans) are produced in Mexico. Bringing these items into the United States is strictly prohibited.

All items made from any part of an endangered species—such as the sea turtle, crocodile, black coral or ocelot—are prohibited in the United States and will be confiscated. Vendors of such items usually will not warn you that you can't take them home.

Ancient artifacts, such as pre-Columbian statues or colonial art, cannot be taken from their country of origin and will be confiscated if found in your possession. All archaeological finds are considered national treasures and the property of the country in which they were discovered.

For more details, write U.S. Customs (1301 Constitution Avenue, Washington, DC 20229; 202-566-8195), the U.S. Fish and Wildlife Service (Department of the Interior, Mailstop 430, Arlington Square, 1849 C Street NW, Washington, DC 20240; 202-208-5634) and

If you're staying in remote areas, bring a biodegradable liquid detergent to wash your clothes. Laundry facilities are scarce in the jungle!

TRAFFIC, World Wildlife Fund and the Conservation Foundation (1250 24th Street NW, Washington, DC 20037; 202-293-4800).

To avoid confiscation of prescribed drugs, label them carefully and bring along a doctor's certificate of prescription. As for contraband drugs, there's a war on. Smart travelers remain neutral.

Customs checks at the U.S. border can be swift or painstakingly thorough, depending on how suspicious you look. To avoid problems, dress neatly and declare your purchases.

GETTING READY

WHAT TO WEAR AND PACK   Pack light! A camera plus whatever else you can fit in your daypack would be perfect. A couple of freedom-loving Californians we met at a deluxe hotel in San Cristóbal went even further and started their month-long Ruta Maya trip carrying nothing but belt packs. Remember that you are going where beautiful handmade clothing is "almost free," as the street vendors say. So are colorful woven bags to carry it in. The less stuff you bring with you, the more stuff you can buy and bring back. There is nothing like lugging 75 pounds of suitcases around in search of a hotel to make one feel absurdly overmaterialistic.

Bring along a minimum of sporty, summery clothing. Pack T-shirts, shorts, swimsuit, sunglasses and a good pair of hiking boots. A flash-light with extra batteries is a must for exploring caves and for those nights when hotel generators shut down early. Trust that by the time you reach the chillier climate of the Chiapas and Guatemala highlands, you'll find a good selection of sweaters and jackets for sale in the streets and markets.

If you plan to visit fishing villages or remote Maya towns, especially those in the highlands where much is dominated by rigid tradition, you will want to keep your clothing modest so as not to offend the locals. No short-shorts, string bikinis, tight tops or other suggestive outfits, though all of these are perfectly acceptable attire in Cancún. Nudity is against the law in all Latin American countries. If you want to sunbathe in the buff, find a very private place to do so. Never visit a church in shorts. Women should always wear a skirt in churches, and men should wear a shirt and long pants.

For a health update on areas you'll be visiting, call the Centers for Disease Control in Atlanta at 404-332-4559.

When it comes to toiletries, larger towns along the Maya Route carry almost everything you'll find in the United States, sometimes at lower prices: toothpaste, deodorant, shampoo, soap, insect repellent, skin creams, shaving cream and batteries (buy the expensive ones; the cheapest kind often don't work). Imported items like tampons and suntan lotions are also widely available in larger towns, though they cost a bit more than in the United States.

Because tourism is a key industry along the Ruta Maya, 35mm film is easy to find. As in U.S. tourist destinations, tourist-trap prices prevail in the places where you're most likely to use up all your film and need more. In cities, film and batteries cost only slightly more than in the United States. You will find especially well-stocked camera stores at Chichén Itzá and in Mérida and San Cristóbal de las Casas.

Depending on where you travel along the Maya Route, you may have trouble finding quality, inexpensive books in English. In Mexico and Guatemala, for instance, books published in the United States cost much more because of high import tariffs. Except for tourist-oriented books on the Maya ruins, the selection of books in English is pretty much limited to mass-market bodice rippers and spy thrillers at larger Mexican newsstands. However, in the parts of Guatemala where American expatriates congregate, such as Antigua and Panajachel, English-language novels are recycled endlessly. You will find used-book or trade-in racks full of paperback potboilers left over from decades past at bookstores, hotels and restaurants where foreign visitors gather. In English-speaking Belize, where the literacy rate is over 90 percent, you'll have no trouble finding good books on all subjects. Many innkeepers stock superb libraries on Belizean and Maya history and culture and are happy to loan books while you're a guest. In archaeological areas across the Maya Route, you will find English-language books about the ancient Maya civilization that are not available in the United States. No matter where you plan to travel, don't forget to bring your copy of *The Maya Route: The Ultimate Guidebook!*

HEALTH PRECAUTIONS   No inoculations are required to enter Mexico, Guatemala or Belize. Cases of hepatitis, malaria, typhoid, cholera and other tropical diseases do occur but seldom afflict travelers. However, if you are planning to visit remote areas, your doctor may recommend tetanus, typhoid and gamma globulin (for hepatitis) shots and/or malaria pills.

You should definitely pack a first-aid kit. Include a good insect repellent, aspirin, adhesive bandages, cold capsules, vitamins, motion sickness tablets, calamine lotion or a small bottle of white vinegar (for insect bites), iodine or alcohol for disinfecting wounds, antibiotic ointment, water purification tablets, sunscreen, lip balm, diarrhea medicine and any prescription drugs you use. Anyone with a medical condition should consider wearing a medic alert identification tag that identifies the problem and gives a phone number to call for more information. Contact Medic Alert Foundation International (P.O. Box 1009, Turlock, CA 95381; 800-344-3226).

The illness most people encounter is diarrhea, euphemized as *turista* or Montezuma's revenge, caused by food and drink carrying unfamiliar strains of bacteria. A bout can range from a 24-hour case of mild cramps to an all-out attack with several days of fever, chills and vomiting, followed by a lousy feeling that lingers for weeks. We have suffered both kinds, and they are no fun. But not everybody gets sick in Mexico, Guatemala or Belize. Those who stay healthy use the best defense: prevention.

Avoid drinking tap water or ice made from tap water (commonly used in restaurants—ask!), and don't brush your teeth with tap water. Ask if your hotel has *agua purificada* (purified water). Many hotels in Cancún and in the resort areas of Belize have their own water purification system. In Belize City, the British government recently installed a modern purification system that seems to work just fine. In remote areas, motels and lodges usually provide bottled water in the rooms or will direct you to a grocery store that sells it. Always drink bottled liquids—mineral water, sodas, fruit drinks, soft drinks or beer—whenever possible. Remember, one drop of bad water can make you sick for weeks.

Eat with discretion. Consume only thick-skinned fruits that you peel yourself, such as oranges and bananas, and vegetables that are cooked through. Nuts with shells, such as peanuts and coconuts, are pretty safe bets, too. Avoid milk products; unpasteurized milk is frequently served in Mexico and Guatemala. Steer clear of raw seafood—*ceviche* is renowned for causing *turista*—as well as garden salads. Even if the produce was rinsed in purified water, it may have been fertilized (in the fields) with human waste, a common practice in some parts of Mexico and Guatemala.

Take it easy the first few days, especially with the more piquant varieties of Mexican food. If you sock your system with spicy food and heavy liquor right away, your stomach may seek revenge. In other words, eating jalapeño chicken followed by quesadillas and enchiladas chased by tequila slammers is asking for mucho trouble.

Be careful about street food. Meat, seafood, peeled fruit used in drinks and candies on which flies have taken their siestas are risky.

However, a lot of the food from stalls is delicious and very well prepared. If the facilities look clean and the food is hot off the grill, it's probably okay. Be the judge and take your chances.

Many people believe in preventive medicine. Some take a slug of Pepto-Bismol before every meal; others, a shot of tequila, believing it will extinguish any threatening organisms. The antibiotic Doxycyclin is commonly prescribed as a preventive, although it causes sensitivity to the sun—not a good thing in the tropics. We met several people, including former residents of Mexico, who swear by garlic pills as the best prevention. Juice of the *lima* (Mexican lime) is also a traditional way to ward off stomach problems.

If you take all the necessary precautions and still get hit with *turista*, try these remedies: Lomotil, the stopper-upper. Use sparingly. Not a cure, it's a morphine derivative that induces a kind of intestinal paralysis. Stop the dosage as soon as symptoms disappear. Paragoric, Kaopectate, Kaomycin, Imodium AD and Pepto-Bismol help keep the cramps down. Diodoquin, Mexaform, Streptomagnum and Donamycin are stronger over-the-counter cures available in Mexican drug stores. For diarrhea with a fever, you can take Septra or Bactrium if you are not allergic to sulfa drugs. But remember that prolonged use of any antibiotic is not good for your immune system and can make you more susceptible to other tropical diseases.

Manzanilla (chamomile) tea, popular in Mexico, soothes the stomach and often works wonders. Yerba buena (peppermint) tea is also soothing. Papaya restores the digestive tract. Light, easy-to-digest foods like toast and soup keep your strength up. Lots of nonalcoholic liquids—

SEA THIMBLES, SEA LICE AND STINGRAYS

If you plan to swim in the Ruta Maya seas, you should become acquainted with sea thimbles, sea lice and stingrays. The first is a tiny brown, thimble-shaped jellyfish that scoots along the surface of the water. If you swim along the surface, it will scoot with you and inflict little bites that later turn into big red welts. Sea lice also lurk on the surface and bestow measles-looking bites that itch for a week. Unfortunately, sea lice are invisible.

You can avoid sea thimbles simply by not swimming where you see them. You can't avoid sea lice, but you can minimize the bites by rinsing your body in fresh water as soon as you leave the sea. Rinse extra carefully underneath your swimsuit—the little guys hang out where there's clothing.

Like sea lice, stingrays are tough to see. The flat slippery creatures camouflage themselves in the sand along shallow areas and can deliver a wicked puncture with their stingers. Avoid being stung by shuffling away. If you're stung, see a doctor at once.

any kind—are important to prevent dehydration. Carbonated water with juice of a *lima* is another popular stomach soother.

Rest and relaxation will help your body heal faster than if you run around sick and wear yourself down further. The symptoms should pass within 24 hours or so, and a case of *turista* seems to have an immunizing effect—any subsequent bouts you may have will be less severe, and eventually your body will adjust to the foreign water. If you spend a month or more in Mexico and Central America, you may find that you have similar problems with the water back home when you first return—just like Mexican tourists, who suffer from *turista* when they visit the United States.

In rare cases, diarrhea may be a symptom of a more serious illness like amoebic dysentery or cholera. See a doctor if the diarrhea persists beyond three days, if your stool is bloody or foamy, or if you have a high fever.

For medical care, there are hospitals, medical clinics, dental offices and other health care providers, as well as the Red Cross, in all Ruta Maya cities, and in a number of smaller Yucatán towns. Private facilities are generally better-funded, better-equipped and less crowded than public hospital emergency rooms. Visits to doctors are relatively inexpensive, and hotels can usually recommend English-speaking physicians. Contact your health insurance carrier before you leave to find out the extent of your coverage while abroad.

For serious medical emergencies, Central American health care does not measure up to U.S. standards. Mexico has about half as many doctors per capita as the United States, and Guatemala and Belize have about half as many as Mexico. Central Americans who can afford it go to Miami or Houston for major surgery. For true emergencies, a San Diego-based service called Critical Air Medicine (toll-free from Mexico, 95-800-010-0268; from Belize or Guatemala, call collect to 619-571-8944) provides air ambulance service to anywhere in Mexico or Central America—24 hours a day, every day of the year.

AIDS ("SIDA" in Spanish) is reported to be epidemic in cities and towns along the Caribbean coast, though still uncommon in inland cities on the Maya Route and unheard of in rural areas. Most cases here are said to be transmitted through drug use. Take whatever precautions are appropriate for you. Condoms are not readily available in Mexico or Central America. Blood plasma may not be screened for the HIV virus.

MOSQUITOES   Ask anyone who's spent a night in the jungle and they'll tell you: The most ferocious animal is not a jaguar but a mosquito. Mosquitoes protect their territory in the Ruta Maya lowlands, known aptly as "The Mosquito Coast." The little buzzers are thickest in rainforests, swamp areas, and along the coastal bush. The best defenses are long sleeves and pants, along with a good repellent.

Belizeans burn abandoned termite nests to chase away mosquitoes, a defense practiced by the Maya people a thousand years ago.

What works for you may not work for someone else. People who wish to avoid DEET, the active chemical in most commercial mosquito repellents, may want to investigate other methods. Herb shops and health food stores in the U.S. sell good-smelling and more or less effective insect protection lotions made from oils and herbal essences. Some people swear by daily doses of Vitamin B-6 or garlic, others by tobacco smoke. The new electronic mosquito repellent devices, which emit a sound pitched at the high edge of human hearing, are supposed to drive mosquitoes away. We tried them out on a recent trip into the Petén rainforest and emerged from the jungle unbitten. Purchase one before you leave home; they're not readily available along the Maya Route.

Campers will find that mosquito netting is more important than a tent or sleeping bag. Hang a mosquito net over a hammock under a *palapa* in a campground like the ones at Palenque and Tikal and sleep comfortably (if not exactly privately) in paradise. Whether you're camping or spending your nights indoors, mosquito coils will keep the bugs away while you sleep.

For mosquito and other bug bites, lime juice takes the itch out, disinfects your wounds and acts as a repellent, too. Limes (*limones*, not *limas*) are sold in every village. An ointment called andatol, sold in pharmacies, also helps reduce itching. Be sure to clean bug bites daily, using an antiseptic on bad bites to avoid infection.

WOMEN TRAVELING ALONE

Women alone can expect different experiences depending on where they travel on the Maya Route. British-influenced Belize, for instance, is quite liberated when it comes to women's issues. Women traveling there can expect at least the same freedom and respect they enjoy in the United States. Mexico and Guatemala are a different story. Torn between the rising tide of feminism in Latin America and the age-old code of *machismo*, ladino men often behave toward North American and European women in bizarre and unpredictable ways. On the first day of a recent visit to Mexico, we encountered a taxi driver who requested a kiss and a restaurant waiter who gave a "discount" for *muy bonita piernas* (very pretty legs)!

Of course, these incidents may be annoying but they're rarely threatening. The best way we've found to handle them is to politely say "*No entiendo*" and walk away. Most men get the message. Women should know that incidents of sexual assault against *gringa* women whose solo sightseeing takes them to isolated places are on the rise all over Mexico and Central America. However, nowhere along the Ruta Maya is it as prevalent as in most U.S. cities.

The best defense is to have one or more traveling companions. Two or more women traveling together or a woman traveling with children will almost never be harassed. Today, many North American and European (as well as many Mexican women) travel independently by temporarily joining up with other woman travelers.

TRAVELING WITH CHILDREN

Should you bring the kids on a Ruta Maya adventure? That depends. Lots of Latin American women travel and sightsee with infants in arms, and tourist mothers we've met experienced no problems doing the same. In fact, thanks to the ladino reverence for motherhood, a baby is likely to mean special treatment, attentive service and sometimes lower prices all along the route. Although, for some people, traveling by public transportation with an infant could be one too many stressors, it is also true that many travelers find it fairly easy to enjoy the best of both worlds—parenting and adventuring.

Older kids? Take them along, by all means. It's easy in resort areas such as Cancún, Cozumel or Belize's cayes. As you move deeper into the land of the Maya, it can become more challenging and more rewarding, as well. Ancient temples and pyramids are great for climbing and poking into secret passageways, and the mysteries of vanished civilizations the ruins present can tantalize young minds for weeks on end. The jungle holds limitless fascination. You will be amazed at how quickly children can become fluent in Spanish.

Mexicans, Guatemalans and Belizeans adore children and are used to dealing with them in restaurants and hotels, though many hotels do not have cribs or baby-sitting services. Disposable diapers, baby food and medicines are widely available in bigger towns.

Remember to get a tourist card for each child. Children traveling with only one parent must have notarized permission from the other parent (or, if applicable, divorce papers, guardianship document or death certificate, authenticated at a Mexican consulate). Minors traveling alone must have a notarized letter of permission signed by both parents or guardians.

Prepare a junior first-aid kit with baby aspirin, thermometer, vitamins, diarrhea medicine, sun block, bug repellent, tissues and cold medicine. Parents traveling with infants will want to pack cloth diapers, plastic bags for dirty diapers, and a wraparound or papoose-style baby carrier. (In the Chiapas and Guatemala highlands, notice how mothers make baby carriers by tying long, narrow handwoven shawls.)

If you plan to tour by car with an infant, bring a portable car seat. For children of any age, be sure to bring along toys, books and art supplies to drive away boredom during long trips.

Pace your trip so your child has time to adapt to changes. Don't plan exhausting whirlwind tours, and keep travel time to a minimum. Seek out zoos, parks, plazas, outdoor entertainment and short excursions to amuse your child. Latin America's marketplaces are more fascinating than museums to many children.

DISABLED TRAVELERS

Physically challenged travelers can enjoy the Ruta Maya with proper planning. Most Latin American establishments and transportation systems do not provide special amenities, such as wheelchair access, for people with disabilities. You may want to get help from a good travel agent to track down hotels and other facilities to suit your situation. You may also wish to consult the comprehensive guidebook *Access to the World: A Travel Guide for the Handicapped* by Louise Weiss (Holt, Rinehart & Winston).

For more information, contact the **Society for the Advancement of Travel for the Handicapped** (SATH) (26 Court Street, Brooklyn, NY 11242; 718-858-5483); **Travel Information Center** (Moss Rehabilitation Hospital, 1200 West Tabor Road, Philadelphia, PA 19141; 215-329-5715, ext. 9600); **Mobility International USA** (P.O. Box 3551, Eugene, OR 97403; 503-343-1284); or **Flying Wheels Travel** (143 West Bridge Street, P.O. Box 382, Owatonna, MN 55060; 800-535-6790). **Travelin' Talk** (P.O. Box 3534, Clarksville, TN 37043; 615-552-6670), a networking organization, also provides information.

Persons in wheelchairs will have few problems visiting Chichén Itzá and Tulum, where the terrain is level and most walkways are smooth. The main walkway through Palenque is also smooth and level. Other major sites such as Uxmal, Cobá, Copán and especially Tikal, as well as most of the minor ruins, have rough, rocky trails or other obstacles that limit wheelchair mobility.

OLDER TRAVELERS

The Yucatán Peninsula, and particularly Quintana Roo, is popular among seniors as a vacation and retirement haven. Palenque and San Cristóbal de las Casas also attract more than their share of retired norteamericanos. Guatemala and Belize have been slow to follow, mainly because modern tourism facilities, including transportation and roadways, are still developing. Many older travelers to the Maya Route join escorted tours, leaving the planning to others. The **Amer-**

ican Association of Retired Persons Travel Experience (AARP, 400 Pinnacle Way, Suite 450, Norcross, GA 30071; 800-927-0111 or 800-745-4567) offers escorted tours to the Yucatán and Guatemala. An agency called **Elderhostel** (75 Federal Street, Boston, MA 02110; 617-426-7788) provides excellent educational programs in the Yucatán Peninsula for seniors age 60 and up. Programs cover Maya history, folk art and archaeology, and include field trips and instruction from university professors.

Be extra careful about health matters. Bring any medications you use, along with the prescriptions. Consider carrying a medical record with you—including your current medical status, medical history, your doctor's name, phone number and address. If possible, include a summary of your medical status and history translated into Spanish. See that your health insurance covers you south of the border.

VISITOR INFORMATION

Each country along the Maya Route has its own tourist information offices:

Mexico: To order an information packet about travel in Mexico, call the **Mexican Government Tourist Office** at its nationwide toll-free number (800-262-8900). For additional information, tourist cards and maps, contact one of the following Mexican Government Tourist offices in the United States or Canada:

70 East Lake Street, Suite 1413, Chicago, IL 60601; 312-565-2778

2707 North Loop W, Suite 450, Houston, TX 77008; 713-880-5153

10100 Santa Monica Boulevard, Suite 224, Los Angeles, CA 90067; 310-203-8191

405 Park Avenue, Suite 1402, New York, NY 10022; 212-421-6655

1911 Pennsylvania Avenue NW, Washington, DC 20006; 202-728-1750

128 Aragon Avenue, Coral Gables, FL 33134; 305-443-9160

2 Bloor Street West, Suite 1801, Toronto, Ontario M4W 3E2 Canada; 416-925-0704

Many major cities in the United States, Canada and Europe also have Mexican consulates. They can provide general travel information as well as specifics about legal aid and lawyers in Mexico.

Guatemala: Guatemala's tourist information agency, the Instituto Guatemalteco de Turismo, better known as **INGUAT** (P.O. Box 144351, Coral Gables, FL 33114-4351; 305-854-1544), can provide maps and tourist information. For help with specific problems, contact the nearest **Guatemalan Consulate**:

> 9700 Richmond Avenue, Suite 218, Houston, TX 77042; 713-953-9531
>
> 1138 Wilshire Boulevard, 3rd floor, Los Angeles, CA 90016; 213-482-7676
>
> 300 Sevilla Avenue, Ofecina 210, Coral Gables, FL 33134; 305-443-4828
>
> 57 Park Avenue, New York, NY 10016; 212-686-3837
>
> 1045 San Diego Mission Road, Suite 205, San Diego, CA 92108; 619-282-8127
>
> 2220 R. Street Northwest, Washington DC 20008; 202-745-4952

Belize: Because mainstream tourism is still relatively new to Belize, its only stateside tourist board can't provide much assistance. However, it can send you a comprehensive list of Belizean hotels and tour operators. Contact the **Belize Tourist Board** (415 Seventh Avenue, New York, NY 10001; 800-624-0686 or 212-268-8798).

For information on ecotourism in Belize, contact the **Belize Audubon Society** (Box 282, Belize City, Belize; 2-77369); the **Programme for Belize** (1 King Street, Belize City, Belize; 2-75616); or the **Belize Zoo and Tropical Education Center** (Box 474, Belize City, Belize; no phone).

How to Deal With...

LODGING AND DINING

Lodging along the Maya Route comes in many forms. International resort hotels along the Caribbean coast tend to be ultraluxurious and extremely expensive. In this book, we'll help you evaluate them ahead of time, and we'll also share the alternatives we've discovered, such as bargain-priced beachfront cabanas and small fishing village getaways.

Several of the major Maya ruins—Chichén Itzá, Cobá, Uxmal, Tikal—have what are commonly called "archaeological hotels" within walking distance. These jungle lodges are expensive (though their rates are much lower than you would pay in Cancún), and in these remote locations the amenities can be a little rustic (for example, their electricity comes from small gasoline-powered generators and may be rationed to a few hours a day), but their location makes the experience of staying there special enough to justify the prices and any mild inconveniences you might encounter. Archaeological hotels let you hike into the rainforest around Tikal to hear it burst into noisy life at dawn. They allow you an opportunity to wander through the abandoned ruins of Chichén Itzá before the first tour bus of the day arrives.

In the Spanish-speaking regions of the Ruta Maya, away from the jet-set resort areas on the Caribbean, you'll find an amazingly wide range of accommodations, from luxurious *clase internacional* hotels in the capital cities and charming colonial *posadas* (inns) where elegance is affordable if slightly faded to *casas de huespedes* (guest houses) that offer very simple, cheap lodging similar to youth hostels in the United States and Europe, but oriented more toward families.

Mexicans and Guatemalans love to travel, and that includes a lot of people who live far below the poverty line by U.S. standards. There are many very cheap lodgings where you can spend the night for the price of a hamburger. In general, hotel rates in Mexico today are about the same as you would pay in the United States for comparable accommodations. It's just that in Mexico there are more travelers who look for $3 rooms. We have chosen not to mention unexceptional rock-bottom budget lodging much in this guide, but those who are willing to sacrifice comfort to save money will have no trouble finding it.

In Guatemala, the types of lodging available are about the same as in Mexico, but the U.S. dollar exchange rate is so favorable that virtually all hotel rooms cost a fraction of what they would in either the United States or Mexico.

If you've been traveling in Guatemala, Belize accommodations will give you sticker shock. Except for no-frills motels in very remote towns, lodging prices are comparable to those on an expensive Caribbean island. Air-conditioning is nonexistent at many hostelries. Those that do offer it charge a premium, often twice as much as a room without air-conditioning.

It's standard practice for hotels in popular resort areas such as Cancún and the Belize cayes to raise their rates on weekends. During the high season (November to April on the coast, summer in the mountains) and around major holidays like Christmas and Holy Week, many hotels hike their rates way up and offer the American Plan (where room rates include three meals a day) or a Modified American Plan (dinner and breakfast), ensuring a captive audience for their in-house restaurants. During the off-season, they may switch to the less expensive European Plan (no meals included). Be sure to check when booking hotels in advance.

Reservations are essential during the high season and holidays, when the scramble for rooms can be fierce. Hotels at the archaeological zones are often booked up by bus tour companies months in advance. Confirm your reservation, preferably in writing, before you go. If the hotel reneges (hotels typically overbook during holidays to make sure they are filled if any parties fail to show), make a complaint to the local tourist office and swift action is likely to be taken. Many hotels demand a two-day (but sometimes up to 30-day) cancellation notice before refunding your deposit. Check on cancellation policies at the outset, and remember that cancellation by mail can be fiendishly slow. You can avoid these problems and lingering communications complications by using a knowledgeable, Spanish-speaking travel agent.

During the April-May and October-November "shoulder seasons," our favorite times to travel in the region, finding a nice room without reservations should be no problem except during Holy Week (the week before Easter). The hotel information in this guide should be enough to help you find the kind of lodging you want. If you are arriving in the evening, you'll usually find a few local hotel owners or their representatives hanging around the airport or bus station trying to recruit guests to fill their vacancies. You can take one of these rooms (inspect it before parting with your pesos) to rest up and get oriented, then move to someplace more special at your leisure the next day.

Throughout the Ruta Maya region, tourist areas are sharply defined. If you stray very far off the beaten path, you'll find that rural towns offer only very simple, very cheap lodging, often noisy and none too clean, and you will have to ask around (in Spanish) to find it. Reservations are unheard-of in these places.

In Mexico and Guatemala, room rates at all hotels are regulated by the government. A notice is posted inside the room door stating the maximum authorized rate per night. Outside of peak season, you will often find that the rate you are paying is lower than the authorized rate. If it is higher, you can complain to the national tourism agency or at least threaten to do so when you discuss the rates with the hotel manager. Oddly enough, in Guatemala the maximum rates are often posted in U.S. dollars rather than the local currency, quetzales.

PRICE CATEGORIES   This book's hotel and restaurant listings range from budget to ultra-deluxe, with an emphasis on unique or special midrange to upper midrange establishments. Hotels are rated as follows (prices listed are in U.S. dollars): *budget* facilities have rooms for less than $35 a night for two people; *moderate* hotels are priced between $35 and $70; *deluxe* facilities offer rates from $70 to $105, and *ultra-deluxe* have accommodations at prices above $105. Federal sales tax (called IVA in Spanish-speaking countries) on lodging is 15 percent in Mexico and Guatemala and 5 percent in Belize. Most Belizean hotels charge an additional 5 percent if you pay for your room with a credit card. Some resorts add a 15-percent service charge to their rates.

Restaurants are rated as follows: *budget* restaurants usually cost $5 or less for dinner entrées; *moderate*-priced restaurants range between $5 and $12 at dinner and offer pleasant surroundings and a more varied menu; *deluxe* establishments tab their entrées between $12 and $20, featuring sophisticated cuisines, plus decor and more personalized service; and *ultra-deluxe* restaurants generally price above $20. Restaurants in Mexico and Guatemala add a 15-percent IVA, and some resorts add a 15-percent service charge on top of that.

These ratings are necessarily very approximate because of fluctuating currency exchange rates and differing demand for tourist accommodations in various parts of the Ruta Maya region. For example, you'll find that most resort hotels in Cancún fall into the ultra-deluxe category, while in Guatemala only a handful of hotels in the entire country have room rates above the budget category.

STREET ADDRESSES

Confused by street names and directions? Relax. In Latin America, few places are neatly laid out. Maps almost always disagree. Spellings often differ. Streets may have more than one name—or no name at all. Some buildings have street numbers while others on the same street do not, and addresses are not always consecutive.

In coastal towns, the *malecón* (waterfront promenade) is a common point of reference. In all ladino cities and towns, the *zócalo* (main plaza or town square) is the key landmark.

All cities and towns in the Yucatán use a street-numbering system that seems hopelessly confusing at first but becomes a great navigation aid when you get the hang of it. All north-south streets are even-numbered, while all east-west streets are odd-numbered. See "Mérida" in the Yucatán chapter for a more detailed explanation of this system.

In the Chiapas highlands and Guatemala, city streets often have both a number designation, with *avenidas* (avenues) running north-south and *calles* (streets) running east-west, and a street name, which changes upon passing the *zócalo*, dating back to Spanish colonial times. For example, in Antigua Guatemala, Avenida 4, one of the streets that runs past the main plaza, is also called Calle del Obispo Marroquín north of the plaza and Calle del Conquistador south of the plaza. Street signs may give the avenue number, the name, neither or both. To make it easier to find your way around, we use street and avenue numbers instead of the colonial street names whenever possible.

Of course, you can forget all that in Belize. Most towns here have only a handful of roads (many without names), and getting around is as easy as strolling around the block. When asking directions, don't be surprised if you get a reply like, "Head toward the ocean and take a right at the third palm tree." The only place you'll need a map is in Belize City, and even there the streets are laid out in easy-to-get-around fashion.

MONEY, EXCHANGE RATES AND BANKS

Mexico has something of a reputation as an inexpensive vacation destination. In the 1980s, Mexico suffered a depression and runaway inflation that drove the exchange rate from 20 pesos to one U.S. dollar up to 3000 pesos to a dollar. This meant foreign visitors paid incredibly cheap prices for everything. As part of an economic recovery plan, the Mexican government froze the exchange rate against the dollar. Now, foreign tourists bear the brunt of inflation just as the Mexican people do, and there are few astonishing travel bargains left. The sales tax (IVA), which now stands at 15 percent, affects tourists virtually everywhere. In January 1993, the Mexican government deflated the peso and introduced the "new peso" to make day-to-day life less complicated and simplify financial transactions (people needed to carry around pocketfuls of the old bills).

After watching their pesos plunge in value during the 1980s, most Mexicans are receptive to transactions in other, more trustworthy currencies. In Cancún, U.S. dollars are accepted as readily as pesos, and many prices are posted in dollars. Elsewhere in the Yucatán and Chiapas, everybody who deals with tourists, from hotels and restaurants to small shops and street vendors, will accept U.S. dollars at an exchange rate about ten percent lower than you would get at the bank.

Guatemala's currency, the quetzal, is quite weak against the U.S. dollar. Until recently, the exchange rate was one-to-one, but it has now slid to five-to-one and will probably continue to fall. For services and Guatemala-made goods, the price in quetzales tends to run about the same as it would be in dollars in the United States, making this a country of amazing bargain prices.

On the other hand, Belize currency, measured in Belize Dollars (BZE$), is extremely stable. For the last few years, the exchange rate has stayed steady at BZE$2 to US$1. You'll have no trouble using U.S. dollars throughout Belize, though sometimes the exchange rate won't be as favorable.

Be smart and protect your vacation by carrying traveler's checks. Even if you get a slightly lower exchange rate (as you will in Belize), it's worth safeguarding your money. Well-known brands, especially American Express, are easiest to cash. You will need your passport, or

Mexico has deflated its currency and replaced the peso with the "new peso." The currency looks the same, but with three fewer zeroes. What once cost 10,000 pesos now costs 10 new pesos.

in Mexico your tourist card and a picture ID, to cash them. Canadian and European traveler's checks and currency can pose problems; some banks will not cash them.

Keep in mind that Maya villages have no banks, and it is usually impossible to cash traveler's checks there. On market days, there are often moneychangers around. At other times, only small-denomination local currency will work.

Most banks are open at 9:00 a.m., close between 12:00 noon and 2:00 p.m., and reopen until 6:00 p.m., Monday through Friday. They often have specified hours, which vary from bank to bank and day to day, for exchanging foreign money. In lieu of banks, *casas de cambio* give quicker service and are open longer hours, and the exchange rates are only slightly lower than at the bank.

Credit cards are just about as widely accepted in Mexico and Central America just as they are in the United States. Mastercard and Visa are the most popular ones; American Express cards are sometimes frowned upon because of their stiff fees to merchants.

If you need a financial transfusion while on the road, money transfers can be made via Western Union (*usually* taking one day) or via any big bank at home through one of its Mexican affiliates (which can take as long as five working days). Check before you leave home to see whether your bank offers this service.

TIPPING

While *propinas* (tips) are completely personal, the 15 percent guideline applies in Maya Route restaurants as elsewhere. Tip bellboys, porters, chambermaids and anyone who renders extra service the equivalent of at least US75¢ to $1. Taxi drivers in Mexico and Guatemala do not expect a tip. In Belize, tip taxi drivers as you would drivers back home. Gas station attendants deserve one (US25¢ to 50¢) if they wash your windows, check your oil or put air in your tires. Children often assault your car at stoplights or outside restaurants, madly cleaning your windows or begging to watch your car for a tip. Musicians often perform for tips on the town plaza. Even a small coin is much appreciated.

SIESTAS AND BUSINESS HOURS

One of the more famous Latin traditions is the siesta, a midday break lasting two or three hours, when establishments close while workers go home to eat and rest—generally from 1:00 to 4:00 p.m. or 2:00 to 5:00 p.m. Later, stores reopen until 7:00 p.m. or so.

Siesta is a hot-climate custom. In the cool highlands of Chiapas and Guatemala, people do not take siestas. Instead, business hours in towns like San Cristóbal de las Casas and Huehuetenango are pretty much the same as in the United States. In Belize, banks and some government offices close an hour for lunch. Otherwise, businesses remain open all day.

BARGAINING

In Mexico and Guatemala, haggling over prices is a tradition that unites Old World and New World heritages. When the Spanish conquerors arrived in the Aztec city of Tenochtitlán (now Mexico City), they found huge marketplaces where food and handmade products were bought and sold in a manner very similar to that used in European cities and towns at the time.

Today, Mexico and Guatemala hold on to the custom of bargaining in public markets, though not in retail stores. Price negotiations are a kind of universal language. By writing numbers on a pad of paper, you can do it even if you don't speak Spanish.

Price bargaining can be a lot of fun as long as you maintain a cheerful attitude. Don't look at it as a war of wits—because you're bound to lose. From earliest infancy, children watch their mothers sell things. They learn about salesmanship before they can walk. By the age of seven, their skill at separating tourists from their money is honed to a fine edge, and they know how to use those big brown eyes to tug on your heartstrings. Foreign visitors who come from societies where prices are fixed and haggling is rare only stand a chance of "winning" a negotiation by viewing each transaction as one where everybody wins.

It's only natural for market vendors to double or triple their asking prices when they see you coming their way. Your plane ticket to get to Mexico cost about as much as most vendors earn in six months. If you lived in a country where the average per capita income is $852 a year, as it is in Guatemala, you'd charge "rich" foreign tourists more than you charge your neighbors, too.

It doesn't matter whether you paid 25 quetzales for a shirt someone else might have gotten for only 15 quetzales. It doesn't even matter whether you paid less than you would pay in a store back home (unless you're hoping to make your fortune in the import business). What matters is whether you'll actually wear it when you get back home.

Some people enjoy bargaining. It's an extrovert game that pays off in savings. Give it a try. What have you got to lose? Cut the quoted price in half and start bargaining from there. Drift away and watch the vendor call a lower bid. But if you reach a good ballpark figure, don't quibble over nickels and dimes. So the vendor makes an extra 50¢. You undoubtedly got a great deal, too. Everybody wins.

If you feel uncomfortable haggling over prices, you'll probably reach the same result if you simply look at an item with longing and ask, "*¿No me da una discuenta?*" (Won't you give me a discount?), then wait patiently. The vendor will do all the work, running through repeated calculations and hypothetical price reductions before naming the bottom-line price.

Bargaining is rare in resort shops and boutiques, and in any store that tags the merchandise with fixed prices. In Guatemala and in smaller Mexican towns, shopkeepers are more likely to negotiate reduced prices for a quick cash sale. In all small retail stores, it's okay to inquire about discounts when purchasing multiple items.

MEXICO'S DEATH IN THE AFTERNOON

*The bullfight (*corrida de toros*), sometimes interpreted by foreigners as an act of cruelty to animals, is not for everyone. Yet it is one of the great national spectacles of Mexico, and better than any sport it captures the bravado, passion, color and pomp of the country.*

Imported from Spain a few years after Cortés conquered Mexico, the bullfight today can be seen in every major Yucatán Peninsula town. Generally, each corrida *features six bulls and three matadors. The ceremony begins with a* desfile, *the parade of matadors,* bandarilleros *(lancers on foot),* picadors *(lancers on horseback), various assistants and a team of mules to drag the dead bull away. After these players enter the ring and take their places, the bullfight continues in three acts, called* tercios *(thirds).*

What does the bullfight mean? Some interpret it as a ritual sacrifice, not unlike Maya sacrificial ceremonies. Or could it be a symbolic battle between man and nature, even a flirtation between man and woman (in which the matador, with his decorative costume and silken cape, plays a female role)? Perhaps more than anything, as one authority described it, the bullfight is a rendezvous with death, for both man and beast, and an attempt to outwit it.

TAKING PHOTOS

As you visit villages anywhere along the Maya Route or stroll through the markets in larger towns and cities, you will most likely admire the colorful, elaborately handcrafted traditional clothing worn by many Maya people. It is almost irresistibly tempting to try to capture indigenous people in photographs. It can also be frustrating to try. Maya people often seem to have a preternatural sense that warns them of tourists with cameras. They will wag fingers at you in warning not to try to take their picture, and if you look through the viewfinder you're likely see everyone in the market turning their backs to you. Sooner or later, you're sure to get the message: Most traditional Maya people don't want their picture taken—a taboo that we, as visitors, ought to respect.

One's image is a vitally important thing to many village people. Note how, in highland Maya churches, mirrors are hung around the saints' necks. When one's image is reflected in the mirror, the people believe, it establishes a direct spiritual link with the saint. Little wonder, then, that the same people do not want their images "stolen" by the machines of pale, rich foreigners.

In Chichicastenango, Guatemala, women often cover the heads of their infant children with special cloth sacks when foreign tourists are in the village.

We overheard a bus tour guide explaining, with a faintly patronizing attitude toward Indian "superstitions," that the purpose of this custom was to ward off the "evil eye." When we asked a young mother why

---

DON'T SHOOT!

In San Cristóbal de las Casas, Chiapas, you're likely to hear the story of a tourist— some say American, others German—who was killed several years ago in the village of San Juan Chamula for taking a snapshot inside the church. Some say that he (or she) was hacked to pieces with machetes, others that he was locked away without food until he starved to death.

Various versions of the tale have been circulating for decades, and most likely it never actually happened, at least not any time recently. It is certainly true, however, that tourists who violate the Chamula law against photographing the church are imprisoned, sometimes beaten, and in all cases their camera equipment destroyed. Similar penalties apply in some villages for any photography whatsoever, and in nearly all villages for photographing any religious ceremony. The grim legend of a death penalty for photography emphasizes just how strongly many Maya people feel about having their pictures taken.

she hid her baby's head, though, she explained that it was simply to protect him from having his picture taken. Maybe, in traditional cultures, the camera is the modern, high-tech equivalent of the "evil eye."

Yet there is more involved than mere superstition. To aim a camera at a person without consent and shoot is an assaultive act. After so many centuries as victims of armed invasion by foreigners, it is not unreasonable for the Maya people to take offense at photo assaults by *Alemantecas* ("Germans," the word commonly used by villagers today to mean all foreign visitors). Then, too, stories abound of village people who, while visiting the city, have been understandably horrified to find their own pictures in magazines or tourist brochures, accompanied by strange, incomprehensible foreign writing.

If you want to photograph the Maya people, ask first. With the coming of television to many villages, attitudes toward cameras are changing. Some people are more willing than in the past to pose for photographs, usually for a small payment. In particular, the "expelled people" who sell or beg in the streets of San Cristóbal de las Casas, who wear the traditional dress of their former villages but as exiles are less bound by traditional taboos and are in dire need of money, are almost always willing to be photographed for a fee. And if you converse with them for a while and let them get to know you, many people who would deeply resent having their likeness captured by a stranger are more than willing to offer it as a gift to a new friend.

Photography is best done in town, and not in people's own villages. If you do wish to take pictures in any village, be sure to visit the administrative office to familiarize yourself with official photography restrictions and prohibitions before you even reveal that you have a camera in your possession. This is a matter not only of courtesy but also of personal safety. The best policy, however, is to leave your camera back at the hotel safe when you visit traditional Maya villages.

PUBLICATIONS IN ENGLISH

U.S. magazines, newspapers and paperback books can be found in large cities and resorts along the Ruta Maya, at newsstands, department stores and gift shops in big hotels and airports. The *Mexico City News*, a daily English-language tabloid distributed throughout Mexico, is the most widely available English-language publication in Mexico. In Cancún, you can usually find the *New York Times* and the *Los Angeles Times*. In Antigua Guatemala, where a lot of expatriates from the United States live, the *Miami Herald* is usually available, and several hotels, restaurants and bookstores have trade-in sections of old English-language paperbacks.

All major Belize publications are in English. The country's newspaper is the *Reporter*, a quirky, homestyle tabloid that reports on issues

English is the official language in Belize and the unofficial second language all up and down the Caribbean coast.

from screwworm eradication to the number of Guatemalan "aliens" who sneaked across the border that week. Pick up a copy—it's local color at its best. More glossy, but still offering gossipy tidbits, is the bimonthly *Belize Currents* magazine.

SPEAKING SPANISH

Of course, you'll get more out of a Latin American trip if you speak fluent Spanish. But what if, like most people who live in the United States, you don't? Many people who have never studied Spanish worry more than they ought to about traveling to Mexico and Guatemala. One of the fundamental lessons foreign travel teaches is that it's perfectly possible for people to communicate even though they don't know a word of each other's languages. Words help, but it's your tone of voice, the expression on your face, and gestures or sign language that often count for more when it comes to making yourself understood.

The trip blueprinted in this book begins in Cancún, where English is spoken at least as much as Spanish, and takes you deeper into Spanish-speaking America by slow degrees. In the Yucatán Peninsula, English is the key to a good job in the tourist industry, and it is widely taught in secondary schools and colleges, so many people that you will meet as a visitor will speak at least a little English. As you travel into Chiapas and Guatemala, few locals speak any English at all.

Even in bilingual areas like the Yucatán, people will relate to you better if you attempt to speak Spanish, no matter how poorly. It pays in smiles if you study for your trip by practicing a few useful phrases like "*¿Cuánto vale esto?*" (How much is this worth?), "*La cuenta, por favor*" (The check, please), "*¿Tiene usted una habitación para la noche?*" (Do you have a room for the night?) and "*¿No habría modo de resolver el problema de otra manera?*" (Isn't there some other way to resolve the problem?). You'll find many others to build your repertoire in any of dozens of Spanish phrasebooks sold in U.S. bookstores. We like Lonely Planet's pocket-sized *Latin American Spanish Phrasebook*, which contains regionalisms of Mexico, Guatemala and other countries. Spanish language instructional cassette tapes can help you learn Spanish pronunciation, which is much more straightforward than English. (For a short list of vocabulary words, see the glossary at the end of the book.)

The most useful questions to learn are those that can be answered yes-or-no or with a number. It can be very frustrating to ask for directions, for example, and receive a cheerful reply so long, fast and complicated that you can't make sense of it. Better to ask questions like, "Is this the right way to. . . ?" and "How many blocks?" and "On the right or left?"

TIME ZONES

The Yucatán Peninsula, Chiapas, Guatemala and Belize all stay on Central Standard Time year-round, so the time throughout the Ruta Maya region is the same as the Central Standard Time Zone in the winter or the Rocky Mountain Daylight Time Zone in the summer.

MAIL

Mail from Mexico and Belize to the United States is quite reliable and generally takes less than two weeks to reach its destination. From Guatemala, mail takes two to three weeks, and letters or packages that look as if they might contain something valuable are at some risk of vanishing in the mail system.

The postage rate for packages from Guatemala to the United States is expensive enough so that it doesn't make much sense to mail purchases home—a good reason to travel light and leave plenty of luggage room for purchases. If you do mail packages home from Guatemala, you'll find it much less frustrating to use one of the shipping agencies in Panajachel or Antigua instead of trying to deal with the post office and Guatemalan Customs on your own.

If you want to mail goods to the United States from the Ruta Maya, you may send items of less than $50 duty-free to a particular address (but not your own) as often as every 24 hours. Mark the parcel "Unsolicited Gift—Value Under $50" and enclose a sales receipt.

While on the road, you can receive mail in Mexico or Guatemala at the main post office in any city via Lista de Correos (similar to General Delivery in the United States). Use this address format: [Your Name], Lista de Correos, Name of City, State (or Department), Country. The post office holds Lista de Correos mail for only ten days in Mexico (one month in Guatemala), then returns it to the sender. The post office will charge you a small fee, and you will need identification to pick up your mail. For more security, American Express offices will hold mail for cardholders and persons carrying American Express traveler's checks.

TELEPHONES

Calling into Mexico can be a frustrating experience, and to Guatemala it may be all but hopeless. However, recent changes have made the process somewhat easier. To call into Mexico, dial 011 (international code), 52 (country code), then the two- or three-digit city code, followed by the local number. Contact the international operator for city codes. The country code for Guatemala is 502.

Belize has an excellent phone system. Calling into Belize is usually as easy as calling long-distance in the United States. The country code for Belize is 501, and local codes differ depending on where you're calling *from*. If you're calling from abroad, use the one-digit abbreviated local code (available from an international operator). If you're calling within Belize, use the full local code, which has a zero prefix. For instance, to call Belize City from the United States, you would dial 2. To call Belize City from elsewhere in Belize, you would dial 02. (If this system sounds confusing, that's because it is!)

Many establishments in Mexico, Guatemala and Belize have no phones because of the expense and, in many communities, because it literally takes years on a waiting list to get one installed. For local or long-distance calls, your best bet is usually to ask your hotel manager for assistance in placing the call. You will pay any long-distance charges plus a small fee for the service.

AT&T and some other U.S.-based long-distance companies have special numbers you can dial in Mexico, Guatemala and Belize that will connect you with an English-speaking operator and let you charge international calls to your calling card, often at a lower cost than you would pay through the local phone company. Ask your long-distance carrier for a directory of international numbers.

To phone home without a calling card, go to a long-distance shop. They are called *casetas de larga distancia* in Mexico. In Guatemala, go to any office of **Guatel**, the national phone company. In Belize, go to any office of **BTL** (Belize Telecommunications Limited). You give your calling information to the person behind the desk and wait until the call goes through, which can take a few minutes or several hours depending on how busy international phone lines are. Then you take the call in a private booth and talk as long as you want. At the end of the call, you pay cash for it at the desk. These calls can be *very* expensive; it's easy to spend US$50 or more on a phone call home.

For placing calls unassisted, here are some key numbers to remember: long-distance operator: 91; international operator (English-speaking): 98; prefixes for dialing direct to the United States, Canada and Europe: 95 (station to station) and 96 (person to person).

In Mexico and Guatemala, you answer the phone by saying, "*Bueno.*"

ELECTRICITY

Electric currents are the same in Mexico, Guatemala and Belize as in the United States—110 volts, 60 cycles, compatible with all American portable appliances. If you need to convert appliances from other countries, bring your own adapters.

LAUNDRY

Your wash can be taken care of overnight at your hotel (sometimes quite costly) or in a few hours at a laundromat (inexpensive; the attendant puts your laundry into the washer and dryer and folds it for you) in any city along your route. In small towns and villages, women will often wash your clothes by hand for extra cash. Dry cleaners are found in the major cities.

PERSONAL SAFETY

Travelers from the United States often have a mistaken notion of Mexico and Central America as dangerous places populated by bandits, leftist guerrillas, brutal or corrupt police, torturers and midnight death squads. (Latin Americans often have the same kind of anxiety about visiting the United States, believing it to be a land dominated by organized crime, filled with shootings, racial prejudice and promiscuity.) Evil forces may exist; as foreign tourists, we almost never get a chance to find out. You may be surprised to find yourself feeling more at ease along the Ruta Maya than you do at home. The reason is simple: the crime rate is lower here than north of the border.

The fact is, traveling in the Yucatán or Chiapas today is probably as safe as strolling the streets of your own home town, and traveling in Belize is probably much safer. Mexico has its social problems, but violence is not one of them. Thanks to tough laws, almost nobody owns a handgun in Mexico. Images of *bandidos* are left over from a century ago and have no more present-day substance than the idea of wild Indians on the warpath in the American West.

Guatemala is another story. This is the quintessential "banana republic," the land where the word *desaparacidos* ("disappeared" political prisoners) was coined. Here, within the past ten years, in remote corners of the country entire Maya village populations have been massacred by the army for their land. There have only been democratic elections since 1985, and it remains unclear whether the president controls the military or vice versa. The military aid the government has been receiving from the United States since 1954 to fight leftist guerrillas is a large part of Guatemala's gross national product. Local government officials in rural areas are arrested for drug dealing and sent to the United States for trial. The restroom of an American-owned fast-food restaurant in Guatemala City was recently bombed by "terrorists." The U.S. Department of State warns that guerrilla activity continues on a sporadic basis in the departments (similar to states) of El Quiche, Huehuetenango, San Marcos, Petén, Escuintla, Suchitepequez and Saca-tapequez. The Guatemala Human Rights Committee presents a different viewpoint. A recent bulletin reported 14 "extrajudicial executions," mostly of Council of Ethnic Communities members, by government-backed "civil patrols," as well as 24 unidentified bodies believed to be death squad victims, in a typical one-month period.

All that is true. The good news is that as a tourist you will probably never encounter any of these dangers. As the U.S. Department of State reports (Advisory No. 92-47, March 13, 1992), "More than 120,000 American citizens visited Guatemala in 1991 and less than one percent had any problem with crime. Eighteen incidents of violent crime involving American citizen visitors were reported to the embassy in the past year." In the Guatemalan economy, tourism ranks second in importance only to coffee beans, and the government knows from experience that any unpleasant incident can drive away foreign tourism for years. Nor does any side in Guatemala's persistent political unrest want to incur the wrath of the United States, which would doom their cause. You will enjoy a healthy, protective dose of "tourist immunity" in Guatemala, and your chances of getting involved with death squads, guerrillas or terrorists are about the same as your chances of getting kidnapped by the Mafia while traveling in the United States: none.

Unlike its big neighbor to the southwest, Belize is sparsely populated and has little big-city crime. Belizeans are extremely proud, family-oriented and peace-loving (the police carry no guns). Traveling there is like traveling through a jungle version of the American Midwest—lots of country roads and friendly people. The female half of our writing team spent five weeks crisscrossing Belize in a four-wheel-drive by herself and had not one problem. Even in Belize City, where everyone seems to have an "I-got-robbed" story, she felt quite at ease.

In any city, it only makes sense to watch out for theft. The crime rate in Guatemala runs high, especially in Guatemala City, where it is about the same as in major U.S. cities. The difference is that foreign tourists are natural targets for theft because they stand out in a crowd and seem wealthy in a country where the average income amounts to US$72 a month.

Be aware that whenever you are in public, any *ladrón* (thief) who happens to be around will be checking you out. Use common sense. Watch out for pickpockets, purse-snatchers, and pack-slashers, especially in public markets and other crowded places. Carry your trip funds, passport and other important documents in a money pouch or hidden pocket inside your clothing. Keep cash in your side pocket, never a back pocket. In cities, carry day-packs under one arm rather than on your back. Don't leave wallets or cameras lying on the beach while you go for a swim or sitting on a café table while you go to the restroom. Better hotels offer safe-deposit boxes at no extra charge. Always lock your hotel room and car. Park in a secured lot at night. Don't leave radios, gifts, cassettes or other temptations visible inside the car. Never flash a large amount of cash. Dress with humility; a thief will focus on the best-dressed, richest-looking tourist around, so make sure it's not you.

Just like in the United States, certain cities have a well-deserved reputation for crime, and travelers should use extra caution when visiting them. Guatemala City is known for its *ladrones*. In Belize, Orange Walk Town and Belize City are also famous for petty thieves. When choosing a hotel, make sure it's in a safe part of town, preferably one that's frequented by travelers. All hotels recommended in this book are located in safe neighborhoods. As a general rule, downtown areas where there is a lot of activity after dark are safer than outlying neighborhoods of the city. Don't tempt fate by wandering around dark back streets late at night. If you're camping out, avoid lonely roadside stops or isolated beaches unless you're with a group. Stay away from drug deals. In short, exercise the same caution you would use at home. Observe these common-sense precautions, and feel fortunate that you are not in New York City, where—unlike in Guatemala—the petty criminals carry guns.

DRUGS

Marijuana, cocaine, crack and other drugs are widely available and sometimes used publicly up and down the Caribbean coast from Cancún, Quintana Roo, to Livingston, Guatemala. Foreign visitors will rarely have access to drugs elsewhere along the Ruta Maya, except that in some areas such as Palenque and Panajachel, American expatriates deal marijuana or magic mushrooms to other Americans.

The United States government pays Mexico, Guatemala and Belize a lot of money to enforce drug laws, and these substances are highly illegal. Possessing, using or exporting any of them can land you in jail, and getting out can take a lot of time and money. The legal systems in Mexico and Guatemala operate under the Napoleonic Code, which presumes the accused guilty until proven innocent. Foreigners are not allowed bail or a trial by jury and can be kept in jail for up to 13 months before trial. Prison sentences for possession may run from 7 to 15 years, and there is no parole or other early release program.

All things considered, when traveling in Latin America, it's probably better to stay out of the war on drugs.

The Sporting Life

CAMPING

By no means the organized activity that it is up north, camping in Mexico, Guatemala and Belize takes place in a handful of national parks and trailer parks and along scores of peaceful beaches. All beaches in Mexico are public by law, though a good bit of beachfront land is connected to private property—hotels, homes, *ejidos* (community-owned Mexican land)—which the owners may consider off-limits for camping. When in doubt, check with the facility nearest the spot you're interested in. Campgrounds in national parks such as Palenque and Tikal are operated by concessionaires and charge small nightly fees. In Belize, parks such as the Cockscomb Basin and Blue Creek offer little-known shelters deep in the jungle. Overnight stays are arranged through park caretakers. Camping in public parks or on beaches is prohibited except in designated campgrounds.

For further camping information, pick up a copy of *The People's Guide to RV Camping in Mexico* by Carl Franz with Steve Rogers (Santa Fe: John Muir Publications, 1989), which has detailed coverage of Chiapas and the Yucatán Peninsula.

Insects are likely to share your campsite. Bug spray, mosquito nets and insect coils can help make camping more enjoyable. Locals burn coconut husks to smoke out bugs.

Many campers on the Maya Route eschew tents and sleeping bags in favor of hammocks and mosquito nets, and many campgrounds offer *palapas*, thatch-roofed open-air structures under which you can sling your hammock. This hot-weather mode of camping doesn't offer much privacy, but the necessary gear is lightweight and very compact.

SWIMMING

Washed by stunning seas, crisscrossed with smooth-flowing rivers and pocketed with glassy lakes and *cenotes*, the Maya Route offers many wonderful ways to get your body wet. Swimming in this blessed region is not only rejuvenating, it's a trip back in time. Where else can you plunge down bottomless sinkholes where Maya priests once sought sacred visions? Or float along rivers where thousand-year-old temples line the shore?

Along the east coast, the cobalt Caribbean Sea laps at the edges of Quintana Roo and Belize, its offshore waters tamed by 185 miles of coral reef. Most days, the water is so clear you can drop a quarter and tell if it lands heads or tails. North and west of the Yucatán Peninsula, the Gulf of Mexico creates a shallow shelf that's bathtub warm for year-round swimming. To the south along the coast of Chiapas and Guatemala, the Pacific Ocean stretches ink-blue to the horizon. Add to these the spectacular jungle waterfalls of Chiapas, the deep, dream-like *cenotes* of the Yucatán and the soothing warm rivers of Belize, and you have myriads of heavenly possibilities for taking a dip.

Wherever you swim, remember that nature is in charge. In the ocean, conditions can change from good to bad in a matter of minutes. Erratic currents and powerful waves contain hidden pitfalls that can be avoided with a little awareness. Keep in mind that waves can be deceptive. They come in varying sets: one set may consist of seven small waves, followed by seven big ones; or seven big waves followed by one calm swell; or a series of small waves overshadowed by a sudden, big, angry swell. If you get caught in a wave about to crash you onto the shore, try to roll up and tumble with it rather than thrash against it. Remember that waves grow bigger and more surly during the full moon. Stay alert and never turn your back to the sea.

Surfing and body-surfing are sports of skill practiced in often-treacherous waves. Familiarize yourself with the techniques and take a few lessons in beginners' waters before you try anything bigger.

Rip currents threaten open sections of the Caribbean. These currents can be spotted by their ragged-looking surface water and foamy edges. If you get caught in one, don't struggle against it; instead, swim parallel to the shore to free yourself from its inexorable pull toward the open sea.

DON'T TOUCH THAT REEF!

Five years ago, Mexico's most popular lagoon was alive with dazzling brain coral, flamboyant fans and schools of fish so thick you couldn't see a snorkeler ten feet away. Today, El Garrafón is dead, a victim of its greatest admirers—tourists. Day after day, party boats from Cancún have dumped hundreds of snorkelers on the Isla Mujeres reef. And day after day, they stepped on and stole the precious living coral, spreading disease that turned it into a skeleton reef. Somewhere along the line, the fish all swam away.

Preventing another El Garrafón is as easy as not touching a reef. Even a slight brush from a fin is enough to damage a coral forever. Always anchor in the sand or grass flats, far away from the reef. If you can't see where you're anchoring, send a snorkeler down to check the sea bottom. And no matter how tempted you may be, never take a piece of coral. That small souvenir will destroy in one second what it took nature thousands of years to build.

Be careful in waters full of coral reefs. Coral edges are jagged and can make nasty cuts. Consider wearing rubber thongs in the water to protect your feet. Treat any cuts with alcohol and an antiseptic.

Above all, when you go swimming, use common sense in judging safety conditions. Strong surf, steep dropoffs at the tide line, whirlpools and eddies around cliffs all signal danger. If in doubt, don't go. Avoid swimming alone.

Beware of sunburn, the trickiest ailment of the tropics. Tan slowly and use plenty of sunscreen on sensitive areas: lips, nose, shoulders, even the tops of your feet.

Nude sunbathing is against the law in Mexico, Guatemala and Belize. Travelers get away with it on deserted beaches, where no one can be offended, but remember that Catholic traditions reign in Latin America, and ladino and Indian families find flagrant nudity disrespectful. Be discreet and cautious.

SCUBA DIVING AND SNORKELING

When it comes to underwater sports, few places on earth can match Quintana Roo and Belize. The coral reefs that run down the Caribbean coast are bewitching worlds that lure millions of scuba divers and snorkelers each year. Belize's Blue Hole, a 480-foot underwater sinkhole etched with stalactites and stalagmites, is one of the dive world's true wonders. And there are hundreds of other wonders waiting to be explored.

Dive shops abound along the Quintana Roo coast and throughout the Belizean cayes. Renting snorkeling or diving equipment is easy in any resort area. Scuba divers must have proof of certification (advanced open water certificate required for the Blue Hole and other challenging areas). Those who aren't certified can take resort classes (mini-courses) at the larger hotels. For true scuba enthusiasts, numerous Belizean islands offer dive resorts where you can dive from sunup to well past sundown. For information about these resorts, check the "Cayes Lodging" section of the Belize chapter.

FISHING

Along the Ruta Maya, Belize is rapidly emerging as an anglers' paradise. In fact, fishing ranks second only to scuba diving as the reason people journey to this charming country. A *Time* magazine writer, after visiting for the first time in 1991, remarked that "it is probably impossible to go fishing in Belize and not catch something." Indeed, the offshore waters teem with everything from hard-fighting snapper, jacks and barracuda to wahoo, grouper, kingfish and cobia. For the light-tackle anglers, the flats between Belize City and Ambergris Caye are renowned for their glassy aquamarine waters swimming with bonefish, permit and small tarpon. Numerous fishing lodges on Ambergris and other cayes offer guides and trips to the best spots. For the ultimate Belizean fishing experience, join a floating fishing safari. Arranged by **Angler Adventures** (P.O. Box 872, Old Lyme, CT 06371; 203-434-9624), the multi-day boat trips meander through the Belizean cayes, including some very remote, breathtaking locales.

On the Mexican Caribbean, Quintana Roo also offers endless opportunities to wrangle a fish. Deep-sea fishing charters are available from all the major coastal resorts. Saltwater fishing licenses are required. They are available from charter companies, marinas and fishing lodges.

HORSEBACK RIDING

Horse trips are a popular activity in Chiapas, Guatemala and Belize, especially in mountain areas. You will find few resorts with riding stables in these areas, but a number of expedition outfitters and small stables are eager to guide visitors into the backcountry on horseback. To find out about them, inquire at the tourist information office or a local travel agency or check tourist-oriented bulletin boards.

TENNIS AND GOLF

Tennis and golf are practically unknown in the ladino and Indian cultures, so nearly all tennis courts and golf courses are found at luxury tourist resorts. Most of these places offer equipment rental as well.

TWO

Ecotourism

It is hard to imagine that in just two centuries, more than 80 percent of   **57**
Latin America's tropical forests have been erased from the planet. Population explosions, frenetic development, widespread logging and slash and
burn farming—where forests are burned to clear land to grow crops and
raise cattle—are mainly to blame. Much has been written about the destruction, but little has been done until recently, with the advent of a
concept called ecotourism. The basic idea behind ecotourism is that visitors to a place can contribute to the environment and support the people
who live in that environment. If villagers can make a living from tourism, it is reasoned, then there's no need to burn off the forest for food.

But ecotourism means much more than that. In fact, this catchword
of the '90s has come to mean setting aside vast forests as sanctuaries
and preserves and controlling tourism to those areas. It means fighting
destruction of virgin lands planned for resorts, and encouraging refor-
estation in decimated areas. It means giving someone tempted to loot
a Maya ruin a job as a tour guide to those ruins. It means convincing a
family who doesn't know where their next meal is coming from to
help preserve the forest that provides that meal. And for a traveler, it
means safeguarding the areas you visit as if they were your own backyard. If you must leave something behind, let it be footprints.

Every day, new ecotourism programs are being created. Numerous
environmental organizations, as well as the governments of Mexico,
Guatemala and Belize, are working together to promote joint ecotourism programs. Several ecotourism "congresses" have been held to
address each country's environmental problems and needs. At each
one, environmentalists, government officials, developers, tour opera-

tors, hoteliers and others in the tourist industry have met for intense discussions. The 1992 congress in Belize included field seminars where participants learned more about such subjects as recycling and eco-sensitive diving and sportfishing.

Of course, ecotourism can only work if it is supported by tourists. To better enjoy and contribute to the Maya Route, we encourage travelers to follow this environmental visitor's code of ethics:

1. **Do not disturb wildlife and natural habitats.** Stay on trails, avoid using machetes and collecting plants or wildlife. Coral reefs are especially sensitive, and should never be touched. Even a slight brush with your fin can cause disease in the reef. Bird nests should be viewed from a safe distance with binoculars, and nesting sea turtles should be observed only with a trained guide. Do not feed monkeys and other wild animals, because it alters their diets and behaviors. Raccoons, who normally live alone, become pack animals when fed and spread diseases that kill them.

2. **Do not litter.** If you'll be in remote areas, take along a sack to carry out your garbage.

3. **Be conscious of helping local communities.** Use native tour guides—they *are* the best—and patronize locally owned inns and restaurants. Buy souvenirs from native craftspeople; the Maya villagers make marvelous handicrafts.

4. **Be culturally sensitive.** Remember that you are a guest in a country. Make an effort to learn the people's basic customs and follow them. For example, in Mexican restaurants, it is considered rude for a waiter to bring a check until he's asked. And don't expect everyone to speak English—the Maya Route is rich with languages, many that are quite exotic.

Ecosystems

GEOGRAPHY

Few regions in the world are as physically diverse as the Maya lands. Where else, in a space smaller than the state of Texas, do you find snow-dusted volcanoes and sun-parched desert, rain-drenched jungle and luscious green islands? These scenes lie within two major geographical settings: highlands and lowlands. The highlands begin near Chiapas and stretch through Guatemala, almost to the end of Central America. Here, along a spine of hulking volcanoes, the earth swells to heights of 13,000 feet, though most of the ranges average 3000 to 5000

National Parks, Reserves and Wildlife Refuges

A Xel-Ha National Park
B Sian Ka'an Biosphere Reserve
C Dzibilchaltún National Park
D Parque Natural Del Flamenco Mexicana
    de Celestún
E Calakmul Biosphere Reserve
F Palenque National Park
G Parque Nacional Cañón del Sumidero
H Parque Nacional de Lagunas de
    Montebello
I Reserva Natural El Manchón
J Biotopo de Quetzal Mario Dary Rivera
K Parque Naciones Unidas
L Parque Nacional Río Dulce and Biotopo
    Chacón Machaca
M Biotopo Cerro Cahui
N Tikal National Park
O Maya Biosphere Reserve
P Hol Chan Marine Reserve
Q Half Moon Caye Natural Monument
R Community Baboon Sanctuary
S Crooked Tree Wildlife Sanctuary
T Shipstern Nature Reserve and Butterfly
    Breeding Center
U Guanacaste National Park
V Blue Hole and St. Herman's Caves
    National Park
W Mountain Pine Ridge National Forest
    Reserve
X Cockscomb Basin Wildlife Preserve

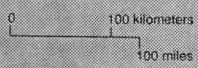

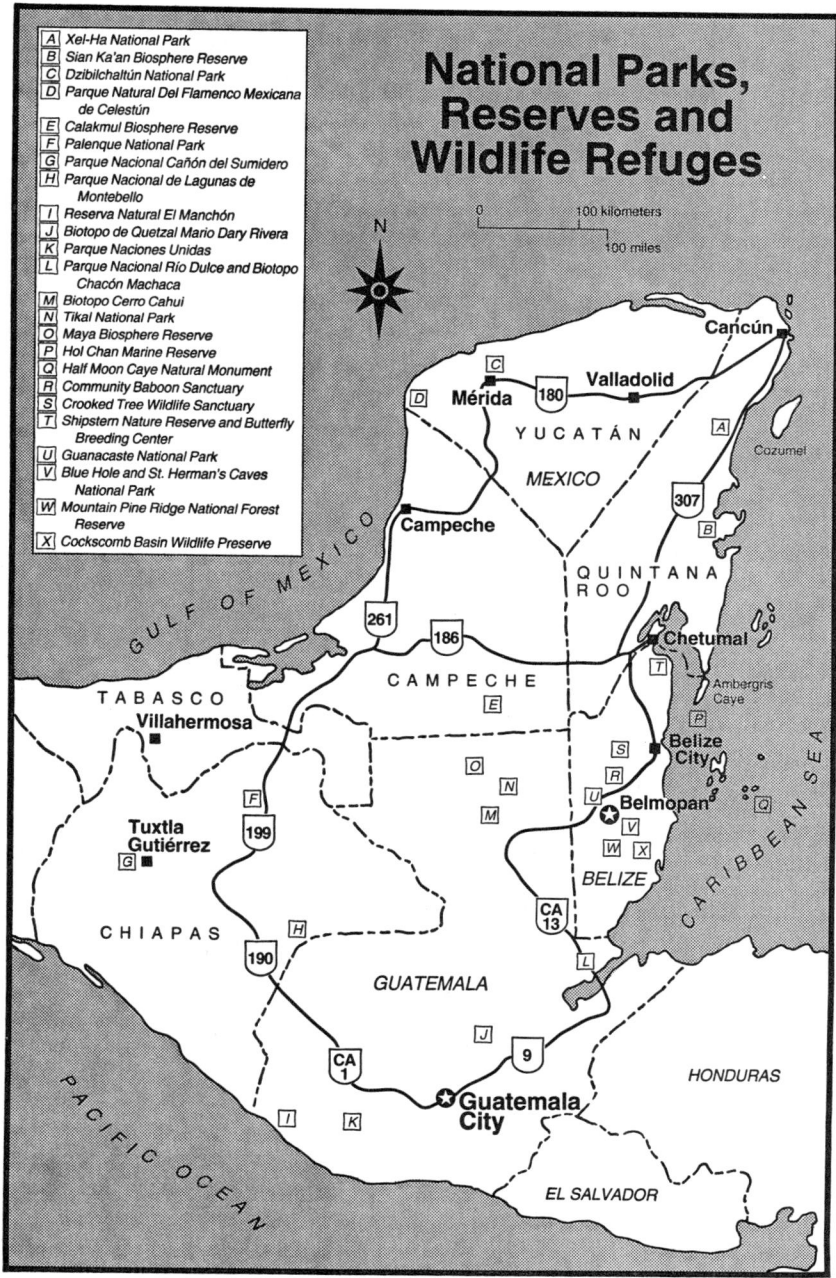

The word cenote was corrupted by the Spanish from the Mayan tzonot.

feet. Eons of rain and erosion have chiseled deep ravines, furrowed hills and smoothed out shallow valleys. On the northeast corner of the highlands, in the heart of Belize, the Maya Mountains stand alone, bordered by a wedge of limestone that defines the lowlands.

It is limestone that makes the lowlands so extraordinary. The Yucatán Peninsula is actually one great limestone shelf that extends down to Belize and Guatemala's Petén. The limestone around the Petén is the oldest and most rugged, carved with karstic hills and raised plateaus. From the air, you can see the vast flat shelf poking out into the frothy green Caribbean Sea on the east and the warm blue Gulf of Mexico on the north and west. A great barrier reef runs down the length of the shelf, providing a dazzling underwater edge.

Along the Yucatán's Caribbean coast, limestone erodes into silky, perfectly white sand that's forever cool (it's nicknamed "air-conditioned" sand). Islands pop up offshore, mountainous breaks in the sea's stream. Inland, most of the limestone is covered with hot, brambly, low-lying jungle that makes crop cultivation difficult. For centuries, the Maya slashed and burned areas to raise cattle and grow *maize* and other crops, though a patch of soil would only yield for two to three years. The 16th-century bishop Diego de Landa, who wrote much about the Maya, said that the Yucatán was "the country with the least earth that I have seen, since all of it is one living rock and has wonderfully little earth." It's no coincidence that today, thousands of beekeepers farm honey instead of crops.

The region's island strand continues off the coast of Belize, due south of the Yucatán. The terrain along Belize's coast is much like that of coastal Yucatán: low jungle with marshes interspersed with stunning beaches. Inland, Belize is a different story: flourishing, impenetrable jungle that ebbs and flows with the mountains. West of Belize is the Petén, swallowed in Eden-like jungle with double canopies of trees and cohune palms that reach four stories high.

There are few rivers or lakes in the lowlands; instead, the porous shelf is riddled with underground caverns and streams and pocked with millions of sinkholes, some dropping deep into the earth. These sinkholes, or *cenotes*, were crucial to Maya existence. The rains that collected here provided water not only for drinking and bathing but for irrigating crops. In fact, one theory about the mysterious demise of the Maya civilization is that a prolonged drought dried up their water supply. Some of the greatest ancient cities are set around fabulous networks of sinkholes.

Rivers begin again in Tabasco, an oil-rich region that lies northwest of the Petén and curves along the Gulf of Mexico. Known for its great, dependable summer rains, Tabasco is smothered with lush, humid rainforests that—thanks to their fruitful slash-and-burn potential—are disappearing at alarming speed. South of Tabasco, the state of Chiapas is wonderfully eclectic, with its gentle hills in the north, hot coastal plains in the south, and daunting volcanoes and cool, pine-clad mountains across its midsection.

Guatemala is the heart of the highlands, where rivers tumble down from soaring mountains and volcanoes—both inactive and active. Along the Pacific Ocean, volcanoes dump their silty ash onto the coast, creating black beaches that glisten like onyx. The searing hot Pacific region is also cloaked with fertile fields of sugarcane, coffee and cacao, and pasturelands for cattle. North of here lies the picture-perfect scenery Guatemala is famous for: glassy lakes cupped in pine forest, folded green hills, meandering streams and gushing rivers, and granite peaks that glisten in the subtropical sun.

FLORA

It would take volumes of books to do justice to the flora of the Maya Route—and that's just the beginning. Within this fabulously diverse region are desert cacti and water-gorged jungle plants, spiraling evergreens and island palms. There are strangler figs that can fell a 100-foot oak tree, and vines that will wound with their thorns and heal that wound with their leaves. And there are jungles so unimaginably dense they have buried whole cities for eons.

RAINFOREST MEDICINES

For thousands of years the rainforests have yielded plants, trees and shrubs prized for their medicinal value. These "healing" plants and their uses are carefully guarded secrets, passed down through generations of Maya bush doctors, though many Maya villagers also use the jungle as their backyard medicine cabinets. The leaves of the wild pineapple plant, for instance, can be heated and formed into a cast to set injured bones. The seeds from the custard apple are a sure cure for head lice, and the boiled vines of the bullhoof will stop internal bleeding.

But modern medicine, along with the destruction of many rainforests, has greatly reduced the practice of bush medicine. Ironically, it is modern medicine that's now focusing on those healing plants. Dozens of research projects, funded by major American health organizations, are underway throughout the Maya Route to find natural cures for cancers, AIDS and other diseases.

More than 4000 species of flowering plants decorate the Maya Route.

Along the Caribbean coasts of the Yucatán and Belize, the flora resembles many people's idea of tropical paradise: shade-giving papaya, mango and breadfruit trees; rambling bougainvillea and hibiscus bursting with brilliant color; and wind-blown palms, heavy with coconuts. Here, too, are the mangroves, propped along the shore, looking like bushes on stilts. Mangroves are crucial to the environment, as they provide nurseries for birds and animals and protect the shore from erosion. Inland, the Yucatán Peninsula does an about-face with its arid, scrubby forest that sprawls on a thin layer of soil atop the limestone. Where there is even less soil, thorny cacti take over.

Deeper into the Maya Route, across the heart of Belize and into Guatemala's Petén, are the rainforests and jungles that one associates with Central America. Here, in Eden-like settings, bromeliads and orchids grow as big as tree trunks and trees grow as tall as skyscrapers. Guanacaste trees, which can reach 400 feet high, are usually decorated with flowering air plants—making them nature's own Christmas trees. The bookut also grows tall and wide, with a canopy spanning about 40 feet. Howler monkeys love to eat its seed pods, though the pods' musky smell gives the tree its nickname of "stinking toe." The black oozing sap from the poisonwood tree inflicts angry blisters that last up to two weeks. The antidote, used since the time of the Maya, is to apply sap from the gumbo limbo. Near every poisonwood tree there's always a gumbo limbo.

But it is the cohune palm, with its thick trunk and elegant plumed fronds, that has come to symbolize Central American jungles. Preferring to grow on rich, deep, well-drained soil, cohunes were used by the Maya for building thatched homes and for cooking and making soap. In the foggy aftermath of a forest rain, they resemble wispy giants of the jungle.

Draping from the forest trees are vines that have long been used to heal sickness and provide food and water. The sinewy, water-gorged wild grapevine, for instance, supplies water so pure the Maya used it to cleanse newborn babies—a practice that continues today. The prickly "give and take" vine stabs with its spikes, then stops the blood flow with its leaves. And the gnarly bullhoof vine, when boiled and consumed as a liquid, will stop internal bleeding.

Riverbanks play host to the spiny bamboo, whose love of water makes it amenable to floods. The bamboo protects the banks from erosion, and protects itself with sharp barbs that can reach four inches in length. Few trees can protect themselves from the strangler fig, which slowly and methodically kills its prey. The strangler wraps its roots around a tree trunk until, after a few years, the roots grow and fuse and choke the tree to death. The trunk falls and becomes hollow, providing shelter for a variety of animals. Bats particularly love the damp, dark space where they can escape the light of day.

The jungles are also thick with tropical fungi that bloom with brilliant color and take on exotic shapes. Ferns cool the forest with their double ceiling canopies and provide food for many animals. In less dense areas, ferns also form soft green carpets that make openings in the forest. In the deep jungle, however, there is no space that does not escape the flora.

FAUNA

It is a feat of nature that a place so compact as the Maya Route should possess such a mind-boggling array of exotic animals. Here among the Maya mysteries live mysterious creatures like spiny anteaters and kinkajou bears, long-nosed bats and portly tapirs, scaly iguanas and gangly Jesus Christ lizards—who actually *can* walk on water.

These enchanting animals thrive in an amazing range of environments, from pine forests, dry savannahs, moist jungle and rainforest to offshore islands, low coastal plains and swamplands. However, as their homes quickly succumb to farming and development, many face extinction. During recent years, countries along the Maya Route have set aside dozens of protected sanctuaries where animals can flourish and people can view their worlds. With a little time and patience, one soon discovers how easy it is to witness this wonderful wildlife.

WHEN THE ANTS GO MARCHING

Even for the jungle, it's an uncanny sight: There you are, strolling through the forest, when you see leaves parading across the path. As you get closer, you notice the fluorescent green, thumbnail-size leaves actually have ants attached. In fact, each leaf is being lifted by a tiny ant who seems to have the strength of Hercules. Another ant pilots the leaf, sending codes to ants in the back of the parade to watch out for that stump, rock—or anteater.

Leaf cutter ants are some of the jungle's most ingenious residents. All day and all night they work chopping leaves and mounding them in piles that can reach six feet high. These compost piles turn into deep rich soil that trees love. What do the ants get out of it? They crave a fungus that grows on the cut leaves, kind of like ant caviar.

The giant jabiru stork is known in Spanish as el rey de ellos, *or "king of them all."*

The Maya Route, for instance, boasts the world's first jaguar preserve. The Cockscomb Basin Sanctuary in Belize has one of the world's densest populations of jaguars, whose hulking shoulders and huge paws make them appear quite menacing. Actually, the gorgeous spotted cat is rarely aggressive toward people, preferring to stalk smaller prey during the night. The Maya jungles are also home to smaller spotted cats—pumas, ocelots and margays—who, like the jaguar, are threatened because of widespread poaching.

A common but immensely fascinating jungle resident is the anteater, who constantly pokes its uninvited nose into termite nests. The anteater's long, slithery tongue is equipped with tiny prongs that keep the ants marching in the right direction—toward its stomach, where a special muscle crushes insect exoskeletons. Just as common and easy to spot are porcupines, armadillos, raccoon-like coatimundi and tapirs, nicknamed mountain cows.

Monkeys, too, abound in certain rainforests, though it takes a watchful eye to spy them scrambling through the treetops. Spider monkeys, with their lanky arms and legs and tails as long their bodies, are found only in the Yucatán Peninsula and Belize. Black howler monkeys have a slightly wider range that includes Guatemala. The howler's high-pitched scream—a common jungle morning sound—is often mistaken for a jaguar's call.

There's no mistaking the basilik, nicknamed the Jesus Christ lizard, as he sprints on two hind legs right across the surface of a river. He's a comical sight, really, a miniature dinosaur constantly on the run with nothing chasing him and nowhere in particular to go. The basilik's opposite is the iguana, who prefers to bask lethargically all day on a riverbank. Iguanas seem to be everywhere—including restaurant menus, where they're often listed as "bamboo chicken."

The Maya Route's offshore islands and coastal marshes teem with beautiful and bizarre birds such as the red-footed booby, which has golden white feathers and outlandish red webbed feet. Its name comes from its lack of fear—sailors to the New World used to walk right up and strike them on the head. Much less friendly is the frigate bird, whose gaunt, black silhouette gives it an ominous appearance. Despite its penchant for fish, the frigate refuses to get wet, and so is adept at swiping flying fish in mid-air. The cinnamon-colored jacana bird, which lives in marshes, ponds and rivers, is nicknamed the lily pad trotter: It gracefully hops across each pad on its pencil-thin legs. But the most famous of all Maya Route water birds is the jabiru stork. The largest flying bird in the Western Hemisphere, it reaches human proportions, growing as tall as five feet with an astounding wing span of up to ten feet. Unfortunately, it is greatly endangered, as fewer than 300 birds are thought to still be alive.

Inland, birds are flamboyantly colorful. The quetzal, Guatemala's national bird, is dazzling in its long-feathered turquoise coat. The tiny hummingbird shimmers in iridescent colors as it hovers motionless, sucking out flower nectar. Its incredibly high metabolism forces it to feed from dawn to dusk. The turkey-like curassow, who mates for life, boasts lacy crests and lustrous black or crimson feathers. Probably most associated with the jungle is the keel-billed toucan, who sports a crayola yellow bib and a fantastic, rainbow-hued beak shaped like a banana.

Tourism and the Environment

BIOSPHERE RESERVES

In the past, nature preserves were set aside for just that: nature. Local residents, let alone tourists, were not allowed within their bounds. But ecotourism started people thinking: Why not protect the environment *and* support local economies?

Biosphere reserves are designed with both these goals in mind. Within the bounds of a biosphere reserve, human activity is controlled but not prohibited. In recent years, Mexico, Guatemala and Belize have established biosphere reserves to help save some of the world's most com-

---

MAYA VILLAGE STAYS

*What better way to experience Maya culture than to stay in a Maya village? As part of a new, experimental ecotourism program, several Maya villages in Belize are welcoming visitors. In one of the best programs, called the **Maya Guest House Program**, travelers spend two days with the 225 residents of Laguna Village in southern Belize. During a stay, guests can help village women grind corn for tortillas, watch basket weaving and pottery making, help the men cut sugarcane and explore a local cave with 1000-year-old Maya paintings. At night, there's barefoot dancing around a bonfire.*

Profits from the program go to the village's education and sanitation fund, and to promote homestead farming instead of slash and burn. For information and reservations, contact the Toledo Ecotourism Association, P.O. Box 75, Punta Gorda, Belize, Central America; phone: 7-22119.

plex ecosystems. Restrictions vary within the reserves, but all prohibit large-scale development. Some, such as the 1.3-million-acre Sian Ka'an Reserve in Quintana Roo, allow limited fishing and hunting to support local villages. At the same time, residents are hired to do organic farming and to eradicate foreign plants that destroy native species.

Three of the most significant reserves lie at the crossroads of Mexico, Guatemala and Belize. The Yucatán Peninsula's Calakmul Biosphere Reserve, Guatemala's Maya Biosphere Reserve, and Belize's Río Bravo Conservation and Management Area join together to protect more than five million acres. But though physically connected, the reserves remain politically separate. Moves are now underway to combine them into a three-nation reserve called the Maya Peace Park—the Serengeti of rainforests.

Within these biospheres lie smaller biotopes—areas of uniform environment, plants and animals. The dense, Edenic jungle of Guatemala's Tikal National Park, with its large populations of howler monkeys and parrots, is a biotope. Outside the biospheres are dozens of national wildlife sanctuaries that welcome visitors. Most offer primitive facilities—you are, after all, a guest in the animal kingdom—but wonderful opportunities to witness exotic wildlife. Sanctuaries are best seen with an experienced guide, called a bush master. Many bush masters are descendants of the ancient Maya, and are remarkably well-versed in the flora, fauna and history of the region. Some do not wear shoes in the jungle—a sure sign they know their way around.

Many **tour companies** specialize in environment-oriented expeditions to countries along the Maya Route. A few of the best include:

ACROSS THE MAYA ROUTE:

> *Mayan Adventures*, P.O. Box 15204, Wedgewood Station, Seattle, WA 98115; (206) 523-5309.

YUCATÁN PENINSULA:

> *Amigos de Sian Ka'an*, Apartado Postal 770, Cancún, Quintana Roo, C.P. 77500 Mexico; 4-95-83.

GUATEMALA AND BELIZE:

> *International Expeditions*, No. 1 Environs Park, Helena, AL 35080; (205) 428-1700.

> *International Zoological Expeditions*, 210 Washington Street, Sherborn, MA 01770; (508) 655-1461.

BELIZE:

> *Great Trips*, 1616 West 139th Street, Burnsville, MN 55337; (612) 890-4405.

Sea and Explore, 1809 Carol Sue Avenue, Suite E, Gretna, LA 70056; (504) 366-9985.

Chaa Creek Inland And Jungle Expeditions, P.O. Box 53, San Ignacio, Cayo, Belize; 92-2037.

Float Belize, P.O. Box 48, San Ignacio, Cayo, Belize; 92-2188.

Mayaworld Safaris, P.O. Box 997, West Landivar, Belize City, Belize; 2-31063.

Native Guide System, P.O. Box 1045, 1 Water Lane, Belize City, Belize; 2-75819.

For information on environmental programs, contact one of these organizations:

La Ruta Maya Conservation Foundation, 209 Seneca Road, Great Falls, VA 22066; (703) 450-4160.

Mundo Maya Organization, 7A Avenida 14-44 Zona 9, Eddiferi La Galeria, Local 35, Guatemala; 2-340323.

Belize Audubon Society, 29 Regent Street, P.O. Box 1001, Belize City, Belize; 2-77369.

Belize Center for Environmental Studies, P.O. Box 666, Belize City, Belize; 2-45739.

Belize Zoo and Tropical Education Center, P.O. Box 474, Belize City, Belize (no phone).

Programme for Belize, 1 King Street, Belize City, Belize; 2-75616.

THREE

The World of the Maya

A journey along the Maya Route brings the traveler face-to-face with   **69**
the most tantalizing mysteries of ancient America. Anyone who walks
in the ruins of Chichén Itzá, Uxmal, Palenque, Tikal, Copán or other
Maya ceremonial centers is irresistibly drawn into speculations about
what that lost world must have been like. Ever since the great Maya
ruins were "discovered" in the 19th century, explorers, archaeologists
and tourists have sought clues about the ancient Maya people. Today,
academic theories abound and the fruits of painstaking inquiries fill
libraries and museums; yet scientific studies of the ancient Maya world
raise questions faster than they can be answered.

Many people view the Maya as an essentially warlike people in a
land ruled by the law of the jungle and swept by spasms of armed
conquest. Legends tell of human sacrifices in Chichén Itzá's sacred
well, and bas-relief sculptures on ball court walls depict life-or-death
athletic events. Faded murals at Bonampak show scenes of brutal conquest and slavery.

Others believe that the ancient Maya world was a peaceful kingdom
in which education and mystical wisdom reigned supreme. They point
out astonishing accomplishments in astronomy, architecture, mathematics, writing and the visual arts. According to legend, Uxmal served
as a university where arcane knowledge was shared, and none of the
lavish sculptures at Palenque show any hint of warriors or weapons.

Both views are likely true. When seeking to understand the ancient
Maya, we must keep in mind that the Maya people have lived for some
4000 years and that their culture has spanned a region unimaginably
vast to those whose sole mode of transportation was walking. Archae-

ologists divide the centuries of the Maya into four major eras: a primitive Preclassic Period, a magnificent Classic Period, a decadent Postclassic Period and an oppressive Hispanic Period.

The history of ancient Maya cities is a web of fact, fiction and guesswork. From hieroglyphs and sculptures, archaeologists know fairly complete historical backgrounds of some ceremonial centers, such as Palenque, right down to the exact dates when their leaders were born and died. Other places, such as Chichén Itzá, come to life mainly through doubtful and often contradictory legends, the truth of which experts have been debating for nearly a century. Of the early history of other sites, such as Uxmal, we know virtually nothing.

The raw material for understanding the past lives of these lost cities is a pastiche of accepted historical knowledge, local legends and superstitions, assorted crackpot theories and old manuscripts translated from even older Maya books. We offer a generous sampling of each throughout this guide—not because we're sure any of it is true but because the truth about the lost past is often found in the most unlikely places.

THE PRECLASSIC PERIOD (2000 B.C. to 250 A.D.)

About 4000 years ago, the Maya people began farming in the region bounded by the Caribbean Sea on the east, the Gulf of Mexico on the north and west and the Pacific Ocean on the south. They enjoyed a simple, comfortable, tropical way of life. They built thatched-roof huts, slept in hammocks and reaped the bounties of forests rich with fruit and game. They learned from neighboring Olmec people about the calendar and began to calculate time. They erected outdoor shrines and small temples to the god who brought the rain. They grew corn, runner beans and tomatoes, as well as cocoa beans, which were used as money throughout Mexico and Central America. The early Maya settlers spoke a single language from which all modern Maya languages derive.

The Preclassic Period ended around 250 A.D. as the Classic Maya civilization blossomed throughout the region. The conventional belief is that it happened suddenly, seemingly out of nowhere, around the time of the Roman Empire's decline. Yet it is equally possible that the scientific and cultural achievements of the Classic Period had been evolving for millennia before artists began recording them for posterity. Maya priests may have written glyphs in the dirt for a thousand years before carving them on stone monuments. Astronomers may have grounded their calculations in natural landmarks long before elaborate observatories were built in accordance with cosmic alignments. Because so few artifacts remain from that distant time, modern scholars will never know for sure.

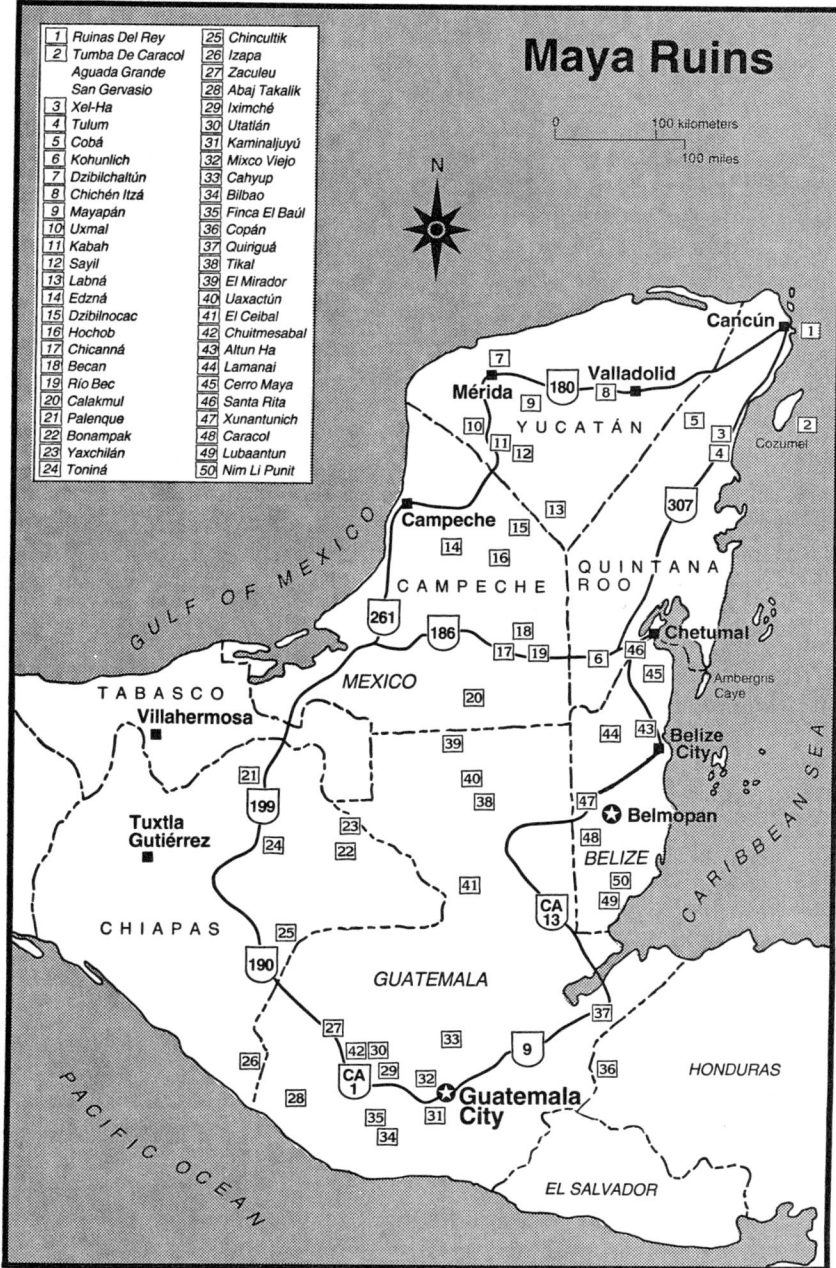

Maya Ruins

1	Ruinas Del Rey	25	Chincultik
2	Tumba De Caracol	26	Izapa
	Aguada Grande	27	Zaculeu
	San Gervasio	28	Abaj Takalik
3	Xel-Ha	29	Iximché
4	Tulum	30	Utatlán
5	Cobá	31	Kaminaljuyú
6	Kohunlich	32	Mixco Viejo
7	Dzibilchaltún	33	Cahyup
8	Chichén Itzá	34	Bilbao
9	Mayapán	35	Finca El Baúl
10	Uxmal	36	Copán
11	Kabah	37	Quiriguá
12	Sayil	38	Tikal
13	Labná	39	El Mirador
14	Edzná	40	Uaxactún
15	Dzibilnocac	41	El Ceibal
16	Hochob	42	Chuitmesabal
17	Chicanná	43	Altun Ha
18	Becan	44	Lamanai
19	Río Bec	45	Cerro Maya
20	Calakmul	46	Santa Rita
21	Palenque	47	Xunantunich
22	Bonampak	48	Caracol
23	Yaxchilán	49	Lubaantun
24	Toniná	50	Nim Li Punit

0   100 kilometers
100 miles

N

GULF OF MEXICO

PACIFIC OCEAN

CARIBBEAN SEA

Cancún
Valladolid
Mérida
180
307
YUCATÁN
Cozumel
Campeche
QUINTANA ROO
CAMPECHE
261
186
Chetumal
Ambergris Caye
TABASCO
Villahermosa
MEXICO
Belize City
Tuxtla Gutiérrez
199
Belmopan
BELIZE
CA 13
CHIAPAS
190
GUATEMALA
HONDURAS
Guatemala City
CA 1
EL SALVADOR

Scientists, using computer programs that decipher hieroglyphs and satellite photos that reveal unknown sites deep in the jungle, are uncovering something new each year.

The Maya civilization blossomed from an unremarkable farming culture into the glory and splendor of the Classic Period, and many theories have attempted to explain why. Early theorists speculated that Maya civilization sprang into existence as the result of contact with ancient Egyptians, Phoenicians, Cambodians or even the people of lost Atlantis. More recent theorists point to ancient Maya sculptures as proof that travelers from outer space visited earth long ago.

None of these theories have been proven false. All share a common, unspoken premise that "mere Indians" could only have achieved such feats of architecture, astronomy and art with outside help. The truth may be even more amazing: perhaps a single insight of genius on the part of an Indian whose identity remains unknown inspired a burst of creative energy that spread throughout a region larger than modern Italy to shape human accomplishment over a span of nearly seven centuries.

Exactly what revolutionized the Maya world, neither descendants of the ancient Maya nor archaeologists who study the question know for sure. The catalyst may have been a fundamentally new way of understanding time. It may have come from the invention of the Maya "long count" calendar, which enabled priests to conceive of enormously large time spans and make predictions thousands of years into the future. This new perspective may have made permanence more important, inspiring the creation of art and architecture designed to last into the distant future.

THE CLASSIC PERIOD (250 TO 900 A.D.)

The Classic Period lasted much longer than the time that elapsed between Columbus's first landfall in the New World and the end of the 20th century. Something mysterious ushered in this golden age of massive, ornate, brightly painted architecture, exquisite works of art, astounding advances in mathematics and astronomy, and the most sophisticated system of writing ever devised in the Western Hemisphere. The Classic Period dawned with the first hieroglyphic dates carved on Maya stelae, or carved stone monuments, and ended six-and-a-half centuries later with the last dates carved before stone sculpture halted so abruptly that some artists walked away leaving monuments unfinished. The greatest of the ceremonial centers—Cobá, Chichén Itzá, Uxmal, Palenque, Tikal, Copán and others—were built during the Classic Period, and all except Chichén Itzá were abandoned within a span of a few years around the end of the ninth century.

By the beginning of the Classic Period, dialects of the original Maya tongue had evolved into two separate languages, Yucatecan and Cholan, and communication became more difficult between the lowland people of the Yucatán and the highland people of Chiapas and Guatemala. Written language was the same in both areas. It consisted of about 1500 hieroglyph elements, some of them phonetic and others pictorial. Archaeologists do not know whether peasant farmers could understand the stelae inscriptions or whether reading and writing were the exclusive province of the ruling elite.

According to scholars who analyze pre-Columbian thought processes, the world view of the Maya was so different from that of traditional Western civilizations that any parallels drawn between their culture and that of ancient Egypt, Greece, Rome or medieval Europe are likely to be misleading. At the beginning of the 20th century, H. G. Wells wrote in his masterwork, *The Outline of History*: "It is as if the Maya mind had developed along a different line from that followed by the Old-World mind, had acquired a different twist to its ideas, was not, indeed, by Old-World standards a strictly rational mind at all. . . ."

Recent investigations into Maya thought, based on expanded understandings of Maya hieroglyphs, archaeoastronomy and symbolism, reveal that, far from suffering from the crippling mental aberration Wells imagined, Maya priests subscribed to a philosophy that people of European descent find hard to comprehend. The concept of duality— true vs. false, form vs. substance, mind vs. body—was foreign to Maya thought. Time and space formed a unified whole. Science and religion were one and the same. Earthly accomplishments mirrored cosmic purposes. The individual merged with the infinite.

It's no wonder that modern travelers experience a sense of awe upon visiting a ruin from the Classic Period, for the more we learn about the ancient Maya, the more we realize that theirs was a world of surpassing strangeness. We ponder lesser riddles—how they achieved such flawless and intricate stone carvings without metal tools; why some ball courts were much larger than others; how they derived astronomical formulas unknown to Western science until the 20th century; whether

---

LOST TRIBE OF ISRAEL?

The Church of Latter Day Saints, founded in 1830 at about the same time ancient Maya civilization was being "discovered," believed that the Maya were members of the lost tribe of Israel who had learned to build pyramids in the time of the Egyptian pharaohs; their life in the New World is the subject of the Book of Mormon.

By the end of the Postclassic Period, the two Maya languages had fragmented into 35 different languages. Most of these languages are still spoken today.

or not they practiced human sacrifice. Yet, what we feel while confronting artifacts left behind from a culture that evolved in directions alien to our own, poses the fundamental mystery.

The Maya of the Classic Period were ruled by lords who claimed authority through legendary god-king ancestors. The throne was passed down from father to son. Each region had its lord, and each lord lived in a palace flanked by temples at the center of the city. He employed priests, scientists, artists and warriors to govern the common people, most of whom lived in huts scattered across a broad agricultural zone on the outskirts of the city.

Many Maya leaders attained great wealth, and flaunted it. They ate meals smothered in chocolate sauces made from cocoa beans, which served as money. They wore headdresses graced with quetzal plumes, another form of money. Their jewelry and masks were fashioned from jade, the most precious commodity in the Maya world.

There were rigid class divisions. The nobility flattened the skulls of their children starting at birth to distinguish them from the masses. Some experts suggest that this practice may have altered not only their appearance, but the functioning of their brains, as well. Knowledge was probably passed along in teacher-student relationships, but whether peasants could gain admittance to the universities and thus join the ruling class through education is unknown.

Most of the major ceremonial sites had been occupied for hundreds of years before the reigning lords of the Classic Period transformed them into elaborate ceremonial centers. In many areas, a single lord supervised the construction of the great plazas and pyramids we see today—and in the process the destruction of the older, smaller temples that were buried beneath them. Building these centers meant quarrying stone blocks that weighed as much as 65 tons, transporting them despite the lack of wheels and beasts of burden, and hauling huge volumes of earth to fill the pyramids. One can only wonder if these astounding feats were accomplished by conscripted labor, like the pyramids of Egypt, or through religious devotion, like the Gothic cathedrals of France.

The classic Maya civilization, from beginning to end, was set in stone, the most permanent of nature's building materials. As a result, bas-relief sculptures, hieroglyphic inscriptions and astronomical alignments detailing this cultural epoch have survived more than a thousand years of weathering and plant growth. Much of the long-forgotten stonework of the Maya has been discovered; much more has yet to be found.

THE POSTCLASSIC PERIOD (900 to 1525 A.D.)

Just as no one knows what triggered the flowering of Maya civilization, nobody knows what caused its collapse. In fact, scientists know less about the centuries that followed the carving in stone of the final hieroglyph than they do about the years that went before. Most speculate that the Classic Period ended at once throughout the Maya world with the abandonment of the great ceremonial centers, giving rise to a perception that ancient Maya civilization "collapsed" because of some cataclysmic event—war, disease, famine or environmental disaster. The reality may be that to the Maya people themselves it never seemed that their civilization was declining; or perhaps they recorded the fall of the Maya in books that were later lost to posterity.

After the last inscription was carved on a stone monument, Maya priests began writing in books, a major new technology that allowed for the recording in portable form of much more voluminous and detailed information. These priests, as well as the masses, may have seen Postclassic Maya society as more modern and efficient, and the great ceremonial centers as just plain old-fashioned.

Whereas several Maya ruins of the Postclassic Period remain, few have been restored. At Tulum and other, smaller sites along the Quintana Roo coast, visitors can see degenerate examples of Postclassic architecture in the small, often lopsided temples built by the Maya navigators who established trade routes across the Caribbean Sea around 1200 A.D. Five hundred miles to the southwest, the excavated ruins of Zaculeu exemplify the massive, stark fortress cities that Maya warlords built throughout the Guatemalan highlands during the same period.

THE HISPANIC PERIOD (SINCE 1525 A.D.)

The biggest change ever to sweep the Maya world came between 1524 and 1541, when invaders conquered the region on behalf of the Spanish Empire. The horses, armor, steel, gunpowder and other military technology of the Spanish armies proved so overwhelming against the Stone-age armaments of Maya warriors that the people of the Yucatán lowlands either surrendered or retreated deep into the rainforest. The fierce Guatemalan highlanders who stood and fought against the invaders fared no better; entire warlord armies were wiped out in a series of violent sieges and battles that ended in slavery for most Maya people.

In their zeal to Christianize the Indians, the Spaniards crushed Maya culture so thoroughly that the answers to most modern archaeologists' questions were lost forever. All across the Yucatán, pyramids were razed and their stone facings were used to build churches. Thousands of stelae and altar stones were smashed as "idols." Moreover, long before most Maya people even saw their first European, epidemics of smallpox, measles, syphilis and other imported diseases succeeded in wiping out more than half the population. The greatest loss of knowledge came in 1552, when Bishop Diego de Landa ordered the public burning of all Maya books. These books, now called codices, were written on 10- to 24-foot-long strips of pounded bark folded like screens. They contained painted hieroglyphs and illustrations. Each population center in the Yucatán had a library of such books. Yet today only three of these books remain.

The *Codex Dresden*, which was taken to Europe as treasure and kept in Dresden's Royal Library, is the best-preserved of the three. Dated at around 1300 A.D., it contains tables for calculating the motion of the planet Venus, as well as material on childbirth, weaving and floods. Photocopies can be seen in the Anthropology Museum in Mérida, the Popol Vuh Museum in Guatemala City and other museums. The *Codex Peresianus* was found in 1860 among some old papers hidden behind a chimney stone in the Bibliothèque Nationale in Paris. The *Codex Tro-Cortesianus* was also found in the early 1860s—in two pieces that had been hidden in different parts of Spain. It is now in a museum in Madrid. Much of the hieroglyphic text contained in these books has not yet been translated.

Other ancient Maya books escaped Bishop de Landa's bonfire. When conquistadors destroyed the Postclassic capital at Mayapán, the bishop wrote, "The most important possession that the nobles who abandoned Mayapán took . . . was the books of their sciences," which disappeared with them into the deep jungle. As late as 1697, an Itzá Maya chief claimed to have studied the history of the Yucatán "in ancient Indian books."

Additional books survived in translated form. The *Popol Vuh*, written by the Quiché Maya of central Guatemala in the late 1550s from an ancient codex hidden from the Spaniards and since lost, tells the highland Maya creation story and the mythological history of the Maya

---

MODERN MEETS MAYAN

Most large villages have public electricity. Even the most remote communities have at least one television set powered by a gasoline generator. And, since the beginning of the 1980s, villagers in the Yucatán interior have acquired bicycles and bicycle-trucks known as triciclos—*probably the most revolutionary innovation in their recent history.*

world. The *Books of Chilam Balam* also use the Spanish alphabet to transliterate old, banned Maya books. Written in the Itzá Maya language, these reveal a cyclical prophecy/history of the Yucatán based on lost books by a Maya priest named Jaguar Prophet, who is said to have predicted the Spanish conquest. Both the *Popol Vuh* and the *Books of Chilam Balam* are now available in English editions.

THE MAYA PEOPLE TODAY

Travelers who explore the Maya Route soon learn that the indigenous people residing in the region today form a living link to the mysteries of the past. Though governments, religious forms and scientific beliefs have come and gone many times over the past 4000 years, village life among the Maya has changed remarkably little. Maya people today speak the same languages as their ancestors who witnessed the coming of the Spaniards. The hut compounds in which families live and the methods for growing corn and other crops remain similar, as well. Despite nearly five centuries of missionary work by Franciscan friars and U.S.-based evangelical churches, Maya spirituality remains rooted in ancient times.

Living conditions differ dramatically throughout the region. In the Yucatán, once the most economically depressed part of Mexico and the scene of terrible famine as recently as the 1950s, the explosive growth of tourism has brought prosperity and new opportunities. The Mexican government offers education to indigenous children and adults, including all-Maya community colleges and a tuition-free university in Mérida. Although nearly all indigenous people in the states of Quintana Roo, Yucatán and Campeche speak both Spanish and a dialect of the Yucatec Maya language, most job opportunities on the Yucatán Peninsula are now tourist-oriented, so most Maya students also learn English.

In the highlands of Chiapas, where Maya communities are tradition-bound and fiercely independent, the educational opportunities offered by the Mexican government are often rejected. Most children attend public school for only a few years, if at all, and the literacy rate among children and adults is the lowest in Mexico. Agriculture is the economic mainstay, and village lands remain separated by rigid boundaries that date back to ancient times. Villages that control a lot of farmland per capita, such as Zinacantán, are fairly prosperous. Others, such as San Juan Chamula, whose limited landholdings have been over-farmed to near exhaustion, suffer population pressures and dire poverty.

The greatest force impinging on Maya society in the Chiapas highlands today is Christian fundamentalism. Thousands of people have been expelled from their villages because of involvement with the missionaries, known locally as *evangélicos*. These expulsions have created a large class of desperately poor Indians, cast out from their agricultural heritage and unable to find work in modern society.

The present-day plight of the Maya is worst in Guatemala, where they make up two-thirds of the nation's population. The ladino ruling class, fearing the consequences of democracy, denies Indians the right to vote. Public education is unavailable to Indian children, and few villagers learn to speak Spanish. While the literacy rate among ladinos in Guatemala is equivalent to that found in Mexico or the United States, very few Maya people have a chance to learn to read or write. Due to malnutrition and a lack of medical services, the average Maya adult lives only to age 49, which is 27 years less than ladino life expectancy. In addition, most of the nation's farmland is held by ladino landlords and international agribusiness corporations, leaving villagers without enough land for subsistence farming and forcing them to seek jobs on banana and coffee plantations at miserably low wages.

Guatemala's war against communist guerrillas, which began in the 1950s and reached its peak in the mid-1980s, has been used as a pretext to force Maya farmers off their land. More than 500 Maya villages were destroyed by the army. The 40,000 Maya refugees who fled across the border to camps in Mexico began returning to their homeland in large numbers in 1992. Although a cease-fire has been in effect since 1987, peace negotiations between the government and insurgents have remained stalemated over the issue of human rights for the Maya people.

The Maya world once extended across the northern frontiers of Honduras and El Salvador. In Honduras, nearly all Maya Indians have been assimilated into the dominant *mestizo* culture. Less than 2 percent of the population speaks a Maya language or adheres to Maya tradition. This tiny minority is made up mainly of refugees who fled to Honduras from El Salvador during the 1980s, when the government began massacring the Indian population under the auspices of the Salvadoran conflict. An estimated 30,000 Maya villagers were killed— far more than the total number of military casualties on both sides.

In Belize, Maya Indians make up about 12 percent of the population. While some are native to the area, most came as refugees from El Salvador and Guatemala. The relaxed, multicultural society of Belize offers a safe haven from the kind of persecution Maya people have suffered in other Central American countries. They tend to live in farming villages in the northern part of the country.

Altogether, about 5 million Maya people live in Mexico, Guatemala, Honduras and Belize today. They face a host of problems, and for many the conflict between Maya tradition and modern life is as overwhelming now as it was when the Europeans first arrived. As travelers in the Maya world, we feel the deep and abiding rhythms that have carried this ancient race through 4000 years of turmoil, tragedy and triumph. We sense that the mysterious people of Uxmal, Palenque and Tikal still walk among us, carrying secrets we have forgotten or have yet to learn.

FOUR

Quintana Roo

The Maya knew it as a world of haunting beauty, with green seas   **81**
glittering like jade and a sun so radiant they worshipped it as a god. A
thousand years ago, in a place now called Quintana Roo, they built
dazzling pyramids and temples, setting them on wave-lashed bluffs and
the sandy fringes of islands. It was an extraordinary union of humankind and nature.

Today, the union continues. Along this hot, jungle-clad coast of the
Maya Route, now-crumbling pyramids persist along shores of white-
powder sand. Mysterious sinkholes and caves, with pools of an other-
world clarity, reside beneath the limestone earth. Giant masks peer out
of the coastal jungle, their swollen ancient features perfectly preserved.

At the same time, modern magic has turned Quintana Roo into a
kingdom of pleasure worship. This is one of the only places in the
world where you can explore the remnants of a lost civilization and
also get a mean tan. You can peer into a sacrificial well one day and
dive for lobster in a translucent sea the next. You might say Quintana
Roo is where history meets hedonism.

In recent years, this easternmost Mexican coast and its islands have
become an unparalleled mecca for divers and snorkelers. The fabulous
reef system, a fantasyland of fish and undersea flora, darkens the water
for miles just offshore. Onshore, Quintana Roo's beaches rival the
beauty of any beach in the world. The limestone-based sand, rating a
true "10" on a scale of 1 to 10, is perfectly white, always cool (its
particles retain no heat) and is as soft as eiderdown.

Balmy weather also makes Quintana Roo alluring. From November
to April, temperatures hover at 80° to 95° and the area is cooled by

luscious sea breezes. From May to October comes the rainy season, when fewer tourists visit. During autumn months, hurricanes pose an occasional threat. The most recent major storm, Hurricane Gilbert, struck with ferocious intensity in 1988, stripping away much of the coastal vegetation. While it will take years to replace the region's palm trees and flowering plants, most of the damaged buildings were repaired within months of the storm.

Inland, much of the terrain is flat. Moist, low-lying jungles cover the porous limestone topsoil, which erodes into gorgeous cool white sand but makes crop cultivation tough (so much so that thousands of would-be farmers have turned beekeepers and farm honey instead). Rain seeps through the limestone, creating underground rivers and bewitching caverns waiting to be explored.

But Quintana Roo's appeal lies not only in its physical appearance but also in its diversity. For travelers seeking world-class glamour, there is Cancún. Capital of Mexico's Caribbean vacationland and capital of earthly delights, Cancún is renowned for its seductive blend of sand, sea and glitter resorts. The coast south of Cancún to Tulum, now pocketed with quaint beach villages, may soon mirror its northern neighbor. Lately touted as a "Tourist Corridor," the area is due to explode with resorts, restaurants and amusement parks.

The traveler who wants to tune out of civilization and into nature need only look a little farther south. From Tulum all the way to the Belizean border, the coast stretches long and lonely, dotted with an occasional *palapa* hut and washed by the warmth of the Caribbean. Here, the 1.3 million-acre Sian Ka'an Biosphere Reserve shelters a jungle that's home to a spectacular array of wildlife, from howler monkeys and leatherback turtles to pumas and white-lipped peccaries.

Just off Quintana Roo's coast lie two islands, Isla Mujeres and Cozumel, touched by tourism but not overcome by it. Isla Mujeres is the smallest Caribbean resort, just a few miles from Cancún yet eons from the razzle-dazzle. Escapists love its peaceful beaches and picturesque village. Isla Cozumel, originally a sacred Maya site (its name means "island of the swallows"), was the Maya equivalent of the Garden of Eden. It's still just that for active divers, who flock to its fabulous Palancar Reef.

This leg of the Maya Route also offers three great testaments to that ancient world: Tulum, Cobá and Kohunlich. The most-visited Maya site in the entire world, Tulum is a walled city by the sea. Its residents, the seafaring Putún, built a captivating castle on a bluff and worshipped the sun. Inland from Tulum, still shrouded in jungle and barely excavated, Cobá is Quintana Roo's biggest and most mystifying Maya site. In the southern outpost of Quintana Roo, Kohunlich contains big, bizarre and beautiful stucco masks. Little known and rarely visited, it surely will not remain so for long.

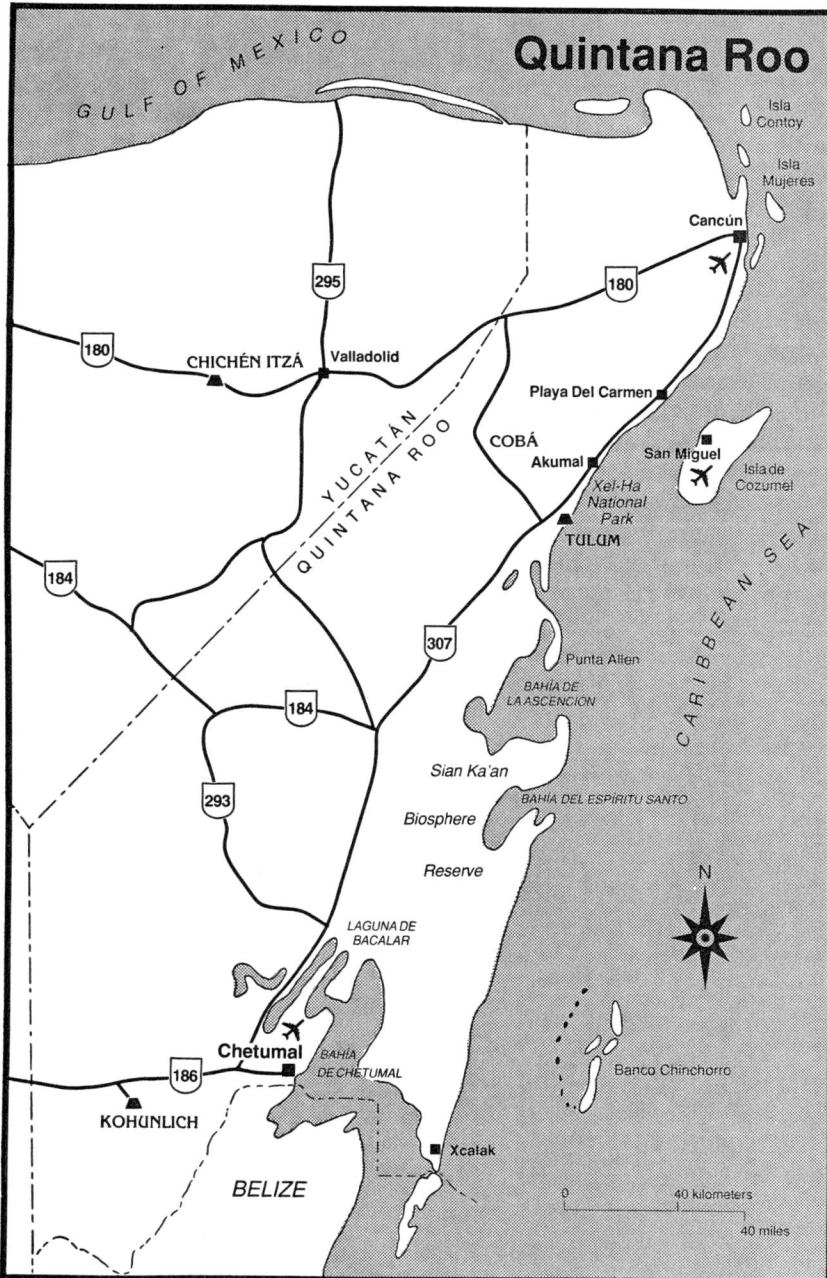

Quintana Roo

GULF OF MEXICO

Isla Contoy

Isla Mujeres

Cancún

295

180

180

CHICHÉN ITZÁ   Valladolid

Playa Del Carmen

COBÁ

Akumal

San Miguel

Xel-Ha National Park

Isla de Cozumel

TULUM

184

307

CARIBBEAN SEA

Punta Allen

BAHÍA DE LA ASCENCIÓN

184

Sian Ka'an

293

Biosphere

BAHÍA DEL ESPÍRITU SANTO

Reserve

N

LAGUNA DE BACALAR

Chetumal

186

BAHÍA DE CHETUMAL

Banco Chinchorro

KOHUNLICH

Xcalak

BELIZE

0   40 kilometers

40 miles

YUCATÁN

QUINTANA ROO

Chetumal, capital of the state of Quintana Roo, is a duty-free port on the border of Belize. Built in 1898 over an old Maya settlement, and rebuilt after a hurricane in the 1950s, Chetumal makes a pleasant stopover en route to Kohunlich and to lakes in the vicinity.

Together, these areas form a region that is both ancient and ageless. For just as throngs of Maya worshipped Kukulcán, god of the sun, so today's millions travel to Quintana Roo to pay homage to this same glorious god. The first stop on their journey is usually Cancún.

Cancún

In just 25 years, Cancún has grown from an anonymous spit of jungle to one of the most famous resorts in the world. Expected to house a half-million residents by 1994, Cancún owes its Cinderella story to a computer that, in 1968, picked it as the ideal place for a vacation. The millions who vacation here each year can testify to Cancún's astounding success. Yet Mexico's "city of the century" bears little resemblance to Mexico. Highrise hotels with familiar American names dominate the lily-white beaches, and all-night discos rock to the latest American beat. The biggest thrill is not bullfighting but bungee jumping, and the hippest pastime is dropping greenbacks at the mall.

But therein lies Cancún's vast appeal. The city created entirely for tourism is indeed a tourist's fantasy, an incredible indulgence of sun, sand and sultry surroundings. Everywhere you look there is dazzling beauty, in the stylized resorts and stylish boutiques, in the flawless bodies lining flawless beaches, and in the sea so intensely green it seems taken from a fairytale.

One of the true geniuses of Cancún is its two-faced design. Half the city forms a mainland downtown area, called **Ciudad Cancún**. The other half, the **Zona Hotelera** (Hotel Zone), sprawls along a wiry island just outside of downtown. With frequent, inexpensive buses canvassing both areas, it's very easy to get around. Nearly 90 fancy hotels preen along the beach, making the Zona Hotelera a sight in itself. To get a good feel for the scope of tourism in Cancún, drive the 23-kilometer length of this island strip. The main drag here is Paseo Kukulcán, aptly named for the Maya sun god.

If you search hard enough, you will find patches of "real" Mexico left in this area. One small but poignant reminder is **Ruinas del Rey** (Paseo Kukulcán, Km. 17; admission), reached by a half-mile walk from the highway through coastal bush. These remains of a Maya city are named for a skeleton ("The King") found on top of the main pyramid. Climb the pyramid steps for a good view of the surrounding green jungle and, just beyond that, Cancún's concrete jungle. Founda-

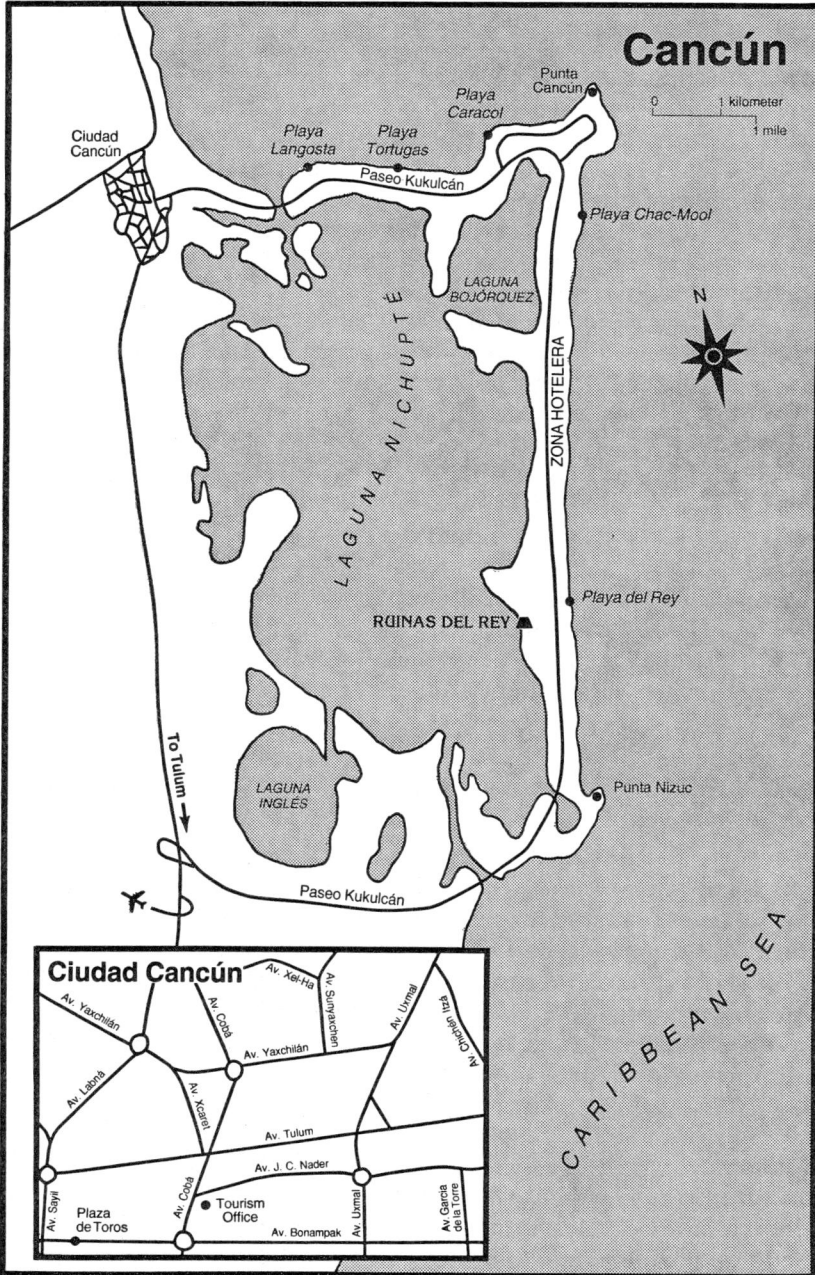

Cancún

Punta Cancún

Playa Caracol

Ciudad Cancún

Playa Langosta   Playa Tortugas

Paseo Kukulcán

Playa Chac-Mool

LAGUNA BOJÓRQUEZ

LAGUNA NICHUPTÉ

ZONA HOTELERA

0   1 kilometer
1 mile

N

Playa del Rey

RUINAS DEL REY

To Tulum

LAGUNA INGLÉS

Punta Nizuc

Paseo Kukulcán

CARIBBEAN SEA

Ciudad Cancún

Av. Xel-Ha

Av. Yaxchilán

Av. Cobá

Av. Sunyaxchén

Av. Uxmal

Av. Chichén Itzá

Av. Yaxchilán

Av. Labná

Av. Xcaret

Av. Tulum

Av. J. C. Nader

Av. Sayil

Av. Cobá

Tourism Office

Av. Uxmal

Av. García de la Torre

Plaza de Toros

Av. Bonampak

Some say the tiny openings in Cancún's Ruinas del Rey suggest they were occupied by aluxes, *bewitched Maya pygmies who stood about 18 inches tall.*

tions, columns, platforms and ancient rubble are spread across cleared, palmy grounds. Eerily, iguanas slither around by the dozens, reminding visitors just who still owns this ancient place.

Probe deeper into Cancún's jungle through **Aqua Ray** (Paseo Kukulcán, Km. 10.5, Zona Hotelera; 83-17-73). The two-and-a-half-hour boat tour ventures through spectacular mangrove canals and stops at a freshwater lagoon for snorkeling. Equipment and refreshments are included. Book one day in advance.

For sheer strolling entertainment, there's no place like **Ciudad Cancún**. With its cobbled sidewalks, grassy medians, crowded shopping stalls, colorful awnings and lively sidewalk cafés, the place is like a nonstop fiesta. Kids with kid-size pushcarts peddle icies on the *zócalo* and mariachi music pours from open windows.

The best source of information on Cancún—and all the rest of Quintana Roo—is available downtown from the **Quintana Roo State Tourism Office** (Avenida Tulum 26; 84-80-73). The office is open from 9 a.m. to 9 p.m., with no siestas!

One of the more popular activities downtown is the Wednesday bullfight at **Plaza de Toros** (Avenidas Bonampak and Sayil, Ciudad Cancún), a small arena where matador meets beast, in true Spanish tradition. Tickets are available at hotels and travel agencies.

CANCÚN LODGING

Few resorts in the world can touch Cancún's hotel scene. Some 88 hotels parade along the sea, their grounds boasting fantasy landscaping and pool areas that are works of art. Guest rooms offer every creature comfort imaginable, and hotel nightclubs lure a jet-set crowd.

The seafront **Club Verano Beat** (Paseo Kukulcán 166; 83-07-22) looks like the least expensive hotel on the strip, youth-oriented and a good bet for apartmentlike quarters with patio and kitchenette. This is nothing fancy, but all spaces are air-conditioned, tiled and tropical-colored. You can enjoy the hacienda-style lobby-bar, quiet beach and private pier. Moderate.

One real bargain hotel on the beach is **Villa Deportiva Juvenil Cancún** (formerly CREA) (Paseo Kukulcán, Km. 3.2; 83-13-37), next to the Club Verano Beat. At this budget-priced youth hostel, you get fan-cooled, eight-bed dormitories and a restaurant. Or, you can pitch your tent on a grassy area adjacent to the sand. Overnight parking is allowed in the front lot, but there are no hookups.

Luxurious in a corporate way, the **Stouffer Presidente Hotel** (Paseo Kukulcán, Lote 7; 83-02-00, reservations: 800-468-3571) is a 294-room extravaganza flanked by a lagoon and the sea. Updated into a first-class property, the good life is made even better here with a beach-front restaurant, swimming pool, club floors, tennis court and an adjacent golf course. Deluxe to ultra-deluxe.

At the northern, action-packed end of the hotel zone, the **Fiesta Americana Coral Beach** (Paseo Kukulcán, Km. 9.5; 83-29-00; reservations: 800-343-7821) rules as queen of Cancún hotels, at least for now. Curving coral buildings, trimmed in emerald balconies and dripping with ferns, embrace a lavish pool area complete with bridges, water slides, swim-up bars and a heart-shaped island for sunbathing. Marble floors, stylish archways and soaring potted palms make the lobby ultra-classy but not overdone. The 602 marble-floored rooms are tropically decorated and feel like suites with their separate sitting areas and terraces overlooking the sea. There are 13 restaurants and bars, indoor tennis courts with stadium seating and a health club. Ultra-deluxe.

Next door, the similarly spectacular **Camino Real** (Punta Cancún; 83-01-00, reservations: 800-228-3000) boasts a natural seawater pool fed by the Caribbean and a gently sloping pyramid design that meshes with sun and sand. The usual assortment of bars, restaurants, nightspots, sea sports and swimming pools is enhanced by lush interior gardens. The 381 rooms have real native charm, with festive furnishings and balconies opening to the sea. In 1990, it added the Royal Beach Club Tower, affording marvelous views, daily continental breakfast and afternoon tea. Ultra-deluxe.

HOW TO BEAT THE HIGH PRICE OF LODGING

*Cancún's hotels are high on glamour, but they're brutal on the budget. Enter Mauricio Almeida, who runs the **Cancún Plaza** (Paseo Kukulcán, Km. 20.5; 85-21-10), a Mexi-Mediterranean condominium right on the beach. Almeida rents Plaza rooms for a fraction of what most beachfront hotels charge. For $35 (summer) to $45 (winter) per night, guests get a spacious, contemporary room with two double beds, kitchenette, air-conditioning, satellite television, and a view of the sea. There's a little beach, two swimming pools, a restaurant and bar.*

To find Almeida, go to room 2107 on the Plaza's tenth floor. If you arrive late at night, go to the condominium's security office and ask for Almeida.

The **Hyatt Regency Cancún** (Punta Cancún; 83-09-66, reservations: 800-228-9000) enjoys the privileged position of being right on the tip of Punta Cancún. Flanked by the sea on three sides, the 14-story, cylindrical hotel features a soaring lobby crowned with glass and balconies strung with flowering vines. Outside, the swimming pool meanders through lush foliage and a glass-walled gymnasium sits near the sea. Activities (wet T-shirt contests, men versus women volleyball) are geared to the young crowd. Ultra-deluxe.

Much classier than the Regency is the **Hyatt Cancún Caribe** (Paseo Kukulcán, Km. 10.5; 83-00-44, reservations: 800-228-9000), a sloping, Maya-style hotel whose terraces overflow with brilliant flowers. The hotel relies not on extravagance but on understated elegance to create a chic, intimate ambience. Completely remodeled in 1989, the rooms are warmly adorned with amber tile floors, tropical prints and oak furniture. Most have seafront balconies; beach-level rooms have spacious garden terraces. *Palapa* bars peek out from the pool area, and a generous swath of beach is marvelous for sunning. Several excellent restaurants provide yet more reasons to stay here. Ultra-deluxe.

Beautiful people check into **Hotel Krystal Cancún** (Paseo Kukulcán, Lote 9; 83-11-33, reservations: 800-231-9860), a place low on glamour but high on energy. Set on a thin stretch of cream-colored beach, the sandstone-and-glass buildings feature 330 tan-toned rooms comfortably appointed with queen-size beds, rattan furniture and pastel decor. The real draw, though, is the sleek young crowd that gathers poolside during the day and at the hotel's wildly popular disco at night. Other amenities include a weight room, sauna, whirlpool and tennis courts. Convenient to shopping malls and restaurants. Ultra-deluxe.

From the boulevard, the **Marriott Casa Magna** (Paseo Kukulcán Retorno; 85-20-00, reservations: 800-228-9290) looks like a plain-Jane. But behind the facade is architectural majesty: massive columns and arches, curving windows and a cupola, and myriads of pale blue ponds that shimmer across the landscape. Wrought-iron chandeliers and Victorian furnishings decorate the lobby, hinting at the hotel's corporate clientele. The rooms, all with a sea or lagoon view, offer more luxury with their marble floors, stuffed chairs and accoutrements such as hair dryers and ironing boards. Ultra-deluxe.

The **Hotel Beach Club Cancún** (Paseo Kukulcán, Km. 11.5; 83-11-77, reservations: 800-346-8225) goes all out to make families feel at home. Here, the young set can join in *Camp de Chamacos* (Camp for Kids), with fun activities like body painting and diving for fake jewels. Parents delight in the family-size suites with marble floors, whirlpool tubs, kitchenettes and separate sleeping nooks for the kids. Three swimming pools, tennis court, fitness center and numerous restaurants (including a family-style deli) round out the amenities. Deluxe.

The **Meliá Cancún** (Paseo Kukulcán, Lote 23; 85-11-14; reservations: 800-336-3542) has, quite simply, Cancún's most smashing lobby. Footpaths wind through lush gardens, streams and gazebos inside this soaring, glass-crowned atrium, and thousands of vines and flowers pour from overhead balconies. It would be enough to spend all day in the lobby, but why not venture to the cool blue swimming pools out back? Just past the pools, a patch of sand is one of Cancún's few topless beaches—evidence of the Europeans who favor this hotel. Every over-sized room features plush carpets, contemporary decor and balconies overlooking the lagoon or sea. Ultra-deluxe.

Families enjoy the Hotel Beach Club Cancún's sister hotel, the **Cancún Palace** (Paseo Kukulcán, Km. 14.5; 85-05-33, reservations: 800-346-8225). The sandstone-and-glass building curves into the beach, sheltering a palmy area with several swimming pools and a big *palapa* bar. Marble floors, peach draperies and cushioned headboards give the guest rooms an air of refinement. Ultra-deluxe.

Of all the fantastic hotels in Cancún, our favorite is **Cancún Puerto al Sol** (Paseo Kukulcán, Km. 20; 85-15-55, reservations: 800-346-8225). Here, at the south end of the hotel zone away from the action, there is little glitz or gimmickry, just total comfort amid sumptuous surroundings. Every room is a primo beachfront suite outfitted with floors of marble and decor the color of the sea. Every marble-coated bathroom has a jacuzzi. Amenities include a spa, indoor and outdoor pools, movie theater, a whirlpool that holds 40 people, and a lovely stretch of white-sand beach. Best of all, the ultra-deluxe price includes all meals, cocktails, watersports and even nighttime shows—definitely a hassle-free vacation.

AN ESCAPIST'S PARADISE

One of the very best places to stay in Quintana Roo is at the charming, secluded **La Posada del Capitan Lafitte** *(Carretera Puerto Juárez, Tulum, Km. 60, Punta Bete; reservations: 800-538-6802 or 303-674-9615 in Colorado). Only 60 kilometers south of Cancún, but worlds away from the crowded resort city, the Capitan Lafitte is an escapist's beachside paradise. Tucked about a mile off the main highway down a dirt road, the hotel rests under low palms and pink bougainvillea. Its 40 stone-and-wood cabanas, with ceiling fans and private terraces, face the turquoise sea. The deceptively simple, sandy grounds contain a dive shop, pool, restaurant-bar and a* palapa *game room with television. The ultra-deluxe price includes breakfast and dinner, taxes and gratuity. If you're looking for something special, this is the place.*

The city of Cancún is shaped like the number "7"

Cancún's least expensive lodging can be found several miles from the beach in downtown. One of the best bargains is **Hotel Margarita** (Avenida Yaxchilán 41; 84-93-33). Opened in 1990, the four-story hostelry has 99 modern rooms with balconies, air-conditioning, televisions, and two double beds. For the moderate rate charged here, you also get a swimming pool and good restaurant.

Slightly more expensive, but still the best little money saver in town, is the charming white pseudocolonial **Hotel Novotol** (Avenida Tulum 75; 84-29-99). The fancier rooms, with air-conditioning, televisions and phones, cost the most. But the cheaper rooms, out back behind the parking lot, are lovely lodgings with red tile floors, fans, brightly tiled baths, dark-wood trim and comfortable beds. There's also a charming lobby café. Moderate.

The **Hotel Plaza Caribe** (Avenidas Tulum and Uxmal; 84-13-77), across from the downtown bus station, has been upgraded somewhat. Surrounding its interior patio and pool are 140 nondescript but clean rooms with air-conditioning, phones (on the blink at times), carpeting and marble washbasins. The lobby-bar show is worth your while. Moderate.

The best of the middle-range downtown hotels is the **Hotel-Suites Caribe Internacional** (Avenida Yaxchilán 36; 84-39-99). The glassy, six-story hostelry contains a lobby-bar, poolside restaurant, hibiscus-filled garden and 80 attractive, air-conditioned rooms with tile floors and marble showers. Moderate.

CANCÚN RESTAURANTS

Gone are the days when you could enjoy superb Cancún cuisine for budget prices. Today, Cancún's whirl of glamorous restaurants boasts lofty surroundings with matching prices. For top dollar, you get catchy themes, splashy decor, and food that's rarely better than average. It's like eating in Disney World every night.

ZONA HOTELERA After shopping in the uptown Plaza Caracol (Paseo Kukulcán, Km. 23), treat yourself at the romantic and award-winning **Casa Rolandi Restaurant** (83-18-17) near the Paseo Kukulcán entrance. The splendid, grotto-like room serves Swiss-Italian specialties and fresh seafood with style for lunch and dinner. Try the black ravioli stuffed with shrimp or the fish baked with squid and shrimp in parchment paper. Moderate.

The ebullient **Carlos 'n Charlie's** (Paseo Kukulcán, Km. 5.5; 83-08-46) is a sprawling waterside restaurant, open and carefree, casting the glow of its yellow lanterns upon Laguna Nichupté. Less manic than other restaurants in this nationwide chain, C 'n C's serves the same humorous "peep, moo, splash, crunch, slurp" menu of fine selections, from French onion soup to barbecued ribs. A lively disco-bar is attached. Lunch and dinner only. Moderate.

The pink Victorian **Bombay Bicycle Club** (Paseo Kukulcán, Km. 6, near Playa Tortugas) is like a wholesome fern bar without the ferns, very deep in brass ceiling fans and stained glass. The huge menu has ribs, pizza, seafood and fine breakfasts, including an anything-goes omelette of your own making. Moderate.

The glamorous **Mediterraneo Restaurant** (Stouffer Presidente Hotel, Paseo Kukulcán, Km. 7; 83-02-00) boasts five dining rooms, each presenting the decor and gourmet cuisine of a Mediterranean country—France, Greece, Italy, Morocco and Spain. Dinner only in a colorful, airy room; deluxe to ultra-deluxe.

Overlooking the Bay of Isla Mujeres, **Calypso Restaurant** (Punta Cancún; 83-01-00) at the Camino Real Hotel is among the best in Cancún. Open for dinner only, it pleases with a blend of Spanish, French, African and East Indian cookery, has brunch on Sunday, live music and the best margarita in town to boot. Ultra-deluxe.

When it comes to atmosphere, few restaurants can match **Bogart's** (Hotel Krystal Cancún, Paseo Kukulcán, Lote 9; 83-11-33). Beautifully appointed with colored fountains, dreamy Moroccan columns and keyhole arches, the place looks straight out of the movies. The bill of fare is not Moroccan but continental, with dishes such as chicken breast stuffed with lobster and roast New Zealand lamb. Deluxe to ultra-deluxe. The Krystal Cancún's other dressy eatery, **Hacienda El Mortero** (83-11-33) is fashioned after a 17th-century colonial house, complete with barrel tile roof, sand-colored stucco and cannons lining the eaves. A mariachi band makes merry while you feast on Yucatecan lime soup (chicken broth simmered with lime, onions and paprika), butterflied shrimp with cactus and chilies, and other tasty regional dishes. Deluxe.

The ultimate trendy, dazzling, multilevel **Blue Bayou** (Hyatt Cancún Caribe, Zona Hotelera; 83-00-44) is Cancún's first tribute to Cajun and Creole cooking. Designed around a huge Maya stela sleek with cascading water, the restaurant spans several floors made grander by vast windows and hanging plants. Live jazz filters over from the bar next door. New Orleans mint juleps and gin fizzes top the menu. Tasty escargot, filé gumbo, jambalaya, andouille and crawfish étouffée are prepared by a French chef. Dinner only. Prices are in the deluxe-to-ultra-deluxe range.

Cancún hosts two million visitors a year—eight times as many as the whole country of Belize!

CIUDAD CANCÚN   For less expensive fare, head for downtown. The refreshingly clean, minimalist, air-conditioned **Cafetería Pop** (Avenida Tulum 26; 84-19-91) has an American-style directness and a lengthy menu of breakfasts, sandwiches, and Mexican plates. The proprietor, Jorge Zaldumbide, speaks English and is a fine Cancún resource. Budget.

One of the nicest downtown sidewalk cafés is **Sea Friends**, or **Amigos del Mar** (Avenida Tulum and Calle Crisántemas; 84-11-99). You can dine on the fan-cooled, open-air patio or in an air-conditioned section behind glass, full of cushioned bamboo chairs and Tiffany lamps. The broad menu ranges from shrimp-stuffed avocado to lobster brochette. A good breakfast stop. Moderate.

Easily Cancún's best Italian restaurant, **La Dolce Vita** (Avenida Cobá 87; 84-04-61) enchants with flickering candles, lacy tablecloths and attentive waiters who speak in deep husky tones. No dish disappoints, from the lobster-studded fettucine and grilled chicken breast with porcini mushrooms and sun-dried tomatoes to the rigatoni swimming in chorizos, mushrooms and chili peppers. Ask for a table in the courtyard, where wild grapes dangle from trellises overhead. Prices are in the deluxe category.

For choice seafood, everyone's rushing to **El Pescador** (Calle Tulipanes 28; 84-26-73). It's a nondescript little indoor-outdoor joint on a side street, cramped with scarlet tables, but the moderately priced fish and shrimp are really great. One drawback: Lately, the time-shares have been giving coupons for El Pescador; hence, long lines. If that's the case, get your seafood fix at **Bucanero** (Paseo Kukulcán 88; 84-22-80), which gets high marks from locals. No wonder, considering the seafood is extra fresh and delightfully prepared, and the grotto atmosphere is *muy* romantic. Cozy booths and oil lamps create a perfect milieu for dishes such as creamy lobster bisque, rich bouillabaisse and snapper *lizianne* (sautéed with tomato sauce and white wine). Deluxe to ultra-deluxe.

Pericos (Avenida Yaxchilán 71; 84-31-52) offers something of the gaudy old Mexican rambunctiousness. Live marimba music bounces off the yellow globe lights and makes the thick walls of the quasi-colonial building vibrate. Dancers in big sombreros shimmy among the pigskin tables, and newlyweds drink from lewd-shaped glasses at the packed bar. Lunch or dinner choices range from juicy shish kebabs to filet mignon. Moderate.

CANCÚN SHOPPING

An easy place to drop a fortune, Cancún bubbles with boutiques and overflows with malls. Even tightwads will succumb to the local buying lust, especially for silver and tropical fashions. But there are no bargains. Ciudad Cancún shops charge as much as the *centro comerciales* (shopping centers) in the Zona Hotelera. Cancún is *the* most expensive resort in Mexico.

ZONA HOTELERA   The empire of shopping malls keeps on growing, though you'd think the market had no room for more competition. One of the newest members of the mall elite is **Plaza Náutilus** (Paseo Kukulcán, Km. 3, next door to the 34-store Plaza Las Velas), distinguished by an egg-shaped outdoor aquarium. Its air-conditioned shops encircle a central café that features live organ music.

Still the plushest shopping arena, air-conditioned **Plaza Caracol** (Paseo Kukulcán, Km. 12) is also the most pleasant place to shop— clean and polished, a fusion of white marble and tinted skylights, run with American efficiency. The 200 shops within feature everything from Kmart quality to Polo and Gucci. Try **Faces** (83-20-52) for elaborate masks, earrings and necklaces; **Keko Tassia** (83-16-96) for upscale Mexican designer dresses and **Mordo** (83-19-31) for leather boots, luggage and fashion belts.

Plaza Lagunas and pink **Costa Blanca** (next door to one another near Plaza Caracol), are outdoor villa-style shopping centers selling beachwear, designer clothes, Maya art and leather.

Plaza El Parian (off Paseo Kukulcán next to the Centro de Convenciones) has shops interspersed with outdoor cafés, so you can both browse and rest. Here, the often overlooked **Anakena** (83-05-39) offers a top collection of Maya temple rubbings and prints, artwork, one-of-a-kind jewelry pieces and pre-Columbian reproductions.

Art aficionados will love the Sergio Bustamante pieces at the **Hyatt Cancún Caribe** (Paseo Kukulcán, Km. 10.5; 83-00-44). At the **Plaza La Fiesta** (83-21-16), across from the Convention Center, the large Mexican jewelry and handicraft market is great for last-minute shopping.

You'll recognize **Flamingo Plaza** (Paseo Kukulcán, Km. 11; 83-28-55) by the giant Gold's Gym filled with muscled bodies pumping iron. Situated lagoonside and one of the newest shopping malls in the Hotel Zone, Flamingo also boasts a handful of interesting shops.

CIUDAD CANCÚN   Avenida Tulum, the main drag, is the hub of the shopping action. One of the better spots is **Sybele** (Avenida Tulum 109; 84-11-81), a classy department store featuring fine clothing for the whole family.

Look for the free Cancún Tips *magazine, available at hotels, which provides detailed information on local happenings.*

Among the city's shopping malls are the **Plaza Centro** and **Pancho Villa Market** (Avenida Tulum) tucked together between Avenidas Tulum and Nadar, where aggressive shopkeepers beckon. For jewelry, check out **Artes Casa Maya** in Plaza Centro or venture upstairs to **La Siesta**, which features Guatemalan and Central American arts and crafts. **Cultura Maya** in Pancho Villa, stalls 20 and 59, is operated by Efrain Herrera, who speaks Maya and sells handpainted vases from Ticul.

Mercado Municipal de Artesanías Kihuic (Avenida Tulum near Avenida Cobá) is the most overpriced circus in Cancún. Stalls sell silver jewelry, horsewhips, blankets and lace tablecloths in an open-armed aura that feels so Mexican, so much the bargainer's bailiwick. Shop around, or you will be stung. Two of the better shops are **Artesanías Xochimilco** (84-11-37), with artistic chess sets, Maya statues and elegant boxes in marble, lapis lazuli and jade; and **Artesanías Cielito Lindo** (84-45-11), with cases of loose gems.

Another downtown find is the aromatic Alondra Lore's complete **Ultra Femme Perfumería** (Avenida Tulum 111; 84-14-02), with its more than 100 quality cosmetic lines. You'll also find soaps and beauty accessories.

CANCÚN NIGHTLIFE

From deafening discos and laid-back *palapa* bars to mini-symphonies in hotel lobbies, Cancún really lights up the night. Nightspots overrun the Zona Hotelera, where every big hotel has its lobby-bar and disco. Ciudad Cancún, too, sizzles after dusk. Expect to pay dearly for drinks ($4 to $6). Cover charges are up to $15 in several top spots.

ZONA HOTELERA   The most popular of all Cancún discos, **La Boom** (Paseo Kukulcán, Km. 3.5; 83-13-72) is Mediterranean-moderne. Housed inside a big white building by the lagoon, La Boom glints with exposed girders, carpets, mirrors, videos and a moving dancefloor. There's a cover.

Palapa-style **Carlos 'n Charlie's** (Paseo Kukulcán, Km. 5.5; 83-08-46), with its elevated dining and pierside dancing along Laguna Nichupté, is a Cancún institution. Great for people-watching. Next door and part of the same chain, **Señor Frog's** (83-29-31) is a wildly popular place featuring live reggae nightly.

The reggae continues at **Jalapeños** (Paseo Kukulcán, Km. 7; 83-28-96), overlooking the hotel zone golf course.

For glamour and special effects, no other disco can touch **Christine** (Hotel Cancún Krystal, Paseo Kukulcán, Lote 9; 83-11-33). A forest of plants under glass extends around the periphery, and overhead the ceiling is crusted with spinning, blinking, rolling spotlights as well as lasers and video screens. Popular and expensive. Cover.

Action central is **Dady'O** (Paseo Kukulcán, Km. 9.5; 83-33-33), which looks and feels like a technicolor cave. Laser lights course through this throbbing disco rotunda, whose theme is: "Life is short. Party Hard." Cover.

Another hot spot for tapping your toes is **Extasis** (Paseo Kukulcán, next to Nautilus Mall). Here, not only do the dancers sway to the beat of the music, the dancefloor actually moves up and down.

Whatever you do, don't miss the outstanding **Ballet Folklórico** (at the Hyatt Regency Cancún, Punta Cancún; 83-09-66). Not to be confused with impostors claiming to be Cancún's "original" folkloric ballet, this authentic performance is pricey but worth it. A fabulous Mexican buffet supper precedes the performance as a live band entertains. The show presents indigenous dances from 11 regions of Mexico, with colorful costumes, high energy, humor and finesse.

CIUDAD CANCÚN   For happy hour, there's no place like **Margarita y Marijuana** (in the Plaza Safa, Avenida Tulum near Crisántemas). Locals and gringos pack the crazy cantina for two-for-one drinks and waiters who plop sombreros on your head and feed you tequila slammers.

The ferns are fake and the wall posters fleshy, but **No Way José** (Avenida Cobá 89) is still downtown's yuppiest bar. A video screen delivers the current American sports, and a deejay delivers the latest American music.

ONE IS ALWAYS ENOUGH

In Texas, it's ten-gallon hats. In Cancún, it's the drinks. Order a cocktail in this tourist town and you get preposterous proportions. Three-pound watermelons hollowed out and filled with three pounds of liquor. Whole pineapples spiked with half-a-dozen potions. Margaritas served in vessels the size of punch bowls. And glasses of beer so tall they come in their own wooden stands.

To check out the big beer scene, stroll the sidewalk bars in Ciudad Cancún. Watch the patrons use two hands to gulp their two-foot-tall beers. And when you get the urge to try one, remember that one is always enough.

A block behind the main drag stands tropical-colonial **Perico's** (Avenida Yaxchilán 71; 84-31-52). With a marimba band, an animated bar complete with saddles for stools and dancing in the aisles, there's never a dull moment.

If you're staying in downtown, drop in to **Bar Alexandar** at the Hotel Playa Caribe (Avenidas Tulum and Uxmal; 84-13-77) for live Mexican music, a tropical show and an all-around good deal.

CANCÚN BEACHES

Some dozen pearly beaches trim the windward side of Cancún. Most are quite narrow, partly because of 1988's Hurricane Gilbert, but mostly because the hotels were built too close to the water. The safest for swimming—the first four listed here—touch the gentle Bahía de Mujeres. The last two, which have some dangerous currents, face the open Caribbean. Camping is not permitted on Cancún beaches.

Playa Las Perlas is the most westerly beach, the first you hit coming from Ciudad Cancún, and one of the most natural beaches in the area. The hard-packed sand, tinted with shadows of surrounding trees, makes a tranquil picnic ground. A pier leads out over the exquisite water. Located in Cancún's Zona Hotelera, Paseo Kukulcán, Km. 2.5.

Playa Langosta, a sandy cove, curves out to a small rocky point and widens into a fuller, softer beach at the feet of the Hotel Casa Maya. This part, scattered with *palapa* shelters, is protected by a small jetty. Located in Cancún's Zona Hotelera, Paseo Kukulcán, Km. 5.

Lovely and undeveloped, with powdery white sand, **Playa Tortugas** could almost be in some backwoods fishing town. A few *palapa*

CRUISING CANCÚN

*To really get into Cancún's festive mood, hop aboard one of the city's **specialty cruises**. Many cruises revolve around pirate or carnival themes, and offer live entertainment, rum drinks and buffet meals. A few of the best include trips to Isla Mujeres aboard the **Aqua II** (Playa Linda Dock; 87-19-09) and the tropical cruiser **Morning Express** (Playa Langosta Dock; 83-14-88). Enjoy Cancún's underwater world aboard the **Nautibus** (Playa Linda Dock; 83-32-16). In the evening, tropical cruises include **Caribbean Carnival Night** (Hotel Club Verano Boat Dock; 84-37-60), **Pirate's Night Adventure at Treasure Island** (Playa Langosta Dock; 83-14-88) and the **Champagne Cruise** (83-03-89) dinner show, which leaves from the pier across from Carlos & Charlie's restaurant. The **Columbus Lobster Dinner Cruise** (83-14-88 or 83-10-21) galleon sails from the Royal Yacht Club.*

shelters and a bamboo lifeguard stand shade the sand. Located in Cancún's Zona Hotelera; take the marked turnoff from Paseo Kukulcán.

Beginning with a rustic picnic shelter and a fishing pier, **Playa Caracol** is a quiet satin beach that gently loops along Bahía de Mujeres to the Hotel Camino Real and a small lighthouse. This is the most easterly beach on the bay before the island makes a 90° turn around Punta Cancún and rolls south along the Caribbean. Located in Cancún's Zona Hotelera, Punta Cancún area. Take the Punta Cancún turnoff from Paseo Kukulcán. Proceed around the *glorieta* (traffic circle) past the Hyatt Regency and turn into the parking lot past the "Archaeological Information" sign.

By no means secluded or untouched by the Midas of tourism, **Playa Chac-Mool** fronts many a hotel and condo. A fabulous walking beach, it stretches from Punta Cancún for about eight kilometers down to Playa del Rey. Its sugary white sand gives you little white slippers as you step out of the crystal tide. The water burns so intensely green it appears to be dyed. Up on a sandy dune, a reproduction of the rain god Chac-Mool surveys the scene. Located in Cancún's Zona Hotelera, Paseo Kukulcán, Km. 13.

The southernmost beach on the island before Punta Nizuc, **Playa del Rey** starts with softly vegetated dunes sloping down into thick, virgin sand that runs along the turquoise sea. This long, unspoiled beach will give you a clue to how Cancún looked prior to its tourist buildup. Not for long, though. Flanked at both ends by construction, this beach will soon feel the crunch of Cancún's growing pains. Located in Cancún's Zona Hotelera, Paseo Kukulcán, opposite the Ruinas del Rey (old Maya ruins).

Isla Mujeres

A speck of land ringed with water the color of apple jade, Isla Mujeres is the jewel of the Yucatán. Incredibly, though it lies only eight kilometers from Cancún, the island manages to maintain a faraway feel. Low jungle bush, brambly bougainvillea and banana plants still claim much of the land. Narrow crumbling roads wend up and down hills, and bristly thatched roofs peek out of the brush. And, at every glance, there is the dazzling green sea.

The island's big action occurs every midday, when hundreds of Cancún day-trippers come to snorkel and shop. Most arrive on one of the double-decker party boats that embark from Cancún's Playa Linda. If rum-infused hordes are not your idea of fun, catch the public ferry from Puerto Juárez, just north of Cancún. The trip costs about US$2 a person (compared to $45 for the party boat!) and has the funkiest entertainment by a little Mexican band. Traveling on your own, you can arrive before the crowds (a must for snorkeling), rent a moped, and really explore the island. Isla Mujeres is just nine kilometers long and has only a handful of roads, so it's easy to get around.

A charming **fishing village**, with its crayon-colored sloops and active town square, greets ferry passengers to Isla Mujeres. The island's hotels, restaurants and shops are concentrated here. Strolling the narrow, balcony-lined lanes here is great fun, but is best done anytime *but* noon to 3 p.m., when day-trippers jam the streets.

Just as today's visitors use Isla Mujeres as a scenic stopover, the Maya rendezvoused here on their way to Cozumel to worship Ixchel, goddess of fertility and the moon. Ixchel got her own temple on Isla Mujeres, the remains of which lie at the southernmost tip of the island, just past the old lighthouse. Climbing the gnarled rocky path to the **temple**, it's easy to see why the Maya chose this spot. The island's most spectacular, it is a bluff that pokes boldly into the sea, its sides deeply carved by eons of wind and water. All that's left of the temple are portions of three walls and several piles of rubble, but the dramatic setting is a fitting testament to the world that was. At sunset, the temple's distorted double arch makes a sensational frame for the land's end cliffs that drop down to the sea. Except for the sun-wrinkled lighthouse watchman, you're apt to be the only one here.

Hundreds of years after the Maya arrived, pirates fell prey to Isla Mujeres' bewitching scenery and charm. Among the rogues who supposedly hid out here was privateer and smuggler Jean Lafitte. In 1841, during his famed travels through the Maya world, John L. Stephens

ISLA CONTOY

*If Cancún is the antithesis of ecotourism, **Isla Contoy** is the paradigm. Tiniest of all the Mexican Caribbean islands, it is inhabited not by humans but by a fantastic array of birds. From common pelicans and egrets to strange brown boobies and flamboyantly colored roseate spoonbills, Contoy is a birder's dream. This National Wildlife Reserve, an hour and a half from Cancún by boat, is also a sunbather's paradise. White crystalline beaches, almost always deserted, line the sliver-shaped island. Snorkelers find plenty to explore offshore.*

A dock and pavilion featuring a display of indigenous marine life constitute the park station on the island's leeward side. Here you can also climb the park tower for a panoramic view of the isle and sea.

Boats leave for Contoy from Cancún, Cozumel and Isla Mujeres. For schedules and prices, check with local marinas or travel agents.

encountered a man on Isla Mujeres who claimed to have been Lafitte's prisoner for two years.

Remnants of the island's illustrious pirate past lie within the **hacienda of Mundaca the Pirate** (off Carretera Garrafón, across from Playa Lancheros). The ruins, a rotting house and arched well that once watered the estate, are slowly decaying in the island jungles. The story behind the ruins far outshines the site itself: notorious Spaniard Fermín Mundaca fell in love with an island beauty, quit his pirating and built a hacienda and fabulous tomb for himself to impress her. For a while it worked. Then she jilted him and eloped with a penniless man. Near the house, a crumbling tombstone with his epitaph says it all: "What I am, you shall be; what you are, I was."

El Garrafón (The Jug) (about seven kilometers from the village on the southwest end of the island; admission) is an underwater national park boasting see-through emerald waters that are a magnet for snorkelers. Sadly, massive snorkeling (sometimes a thousand snorkelers a day) over the past decade has all but destroyed the reef and chased the fish away. Still, the park's grassy hills and complex of shops and restaurants make it a nice spot to sunbathe and relax, as evidenced by the locals who come here. There's a mostly rocky beach, as well as a disappointing "museum" with unspectacular aquariums. If it's underwater wonders you seek, check with one of the dive shops in the fishing village. Locals are happy to take you to a special snorkel or dive spot.

ISLA MUJERES LODGING

Despite its tiny size, Isla Mujeres has much to offer in the way of lodging. Travelers suffering from Cancún burnout come here seeking a slower pace and a less expensive place to sleep, and they find it.

Because there are no car rentals (only mopeds) on the island, taxis are expensive. If you need to be near the action (albeit low-key), choose a hotel in town. If total escape is your goal, plant yourself at the southern end of the island.

The three-story stucco **Posada del Mar** (Avenida Rueda Medina 15; 7-00-44) resembles a plain motel but is ranked among the island's best lodging. The big white rooms enjoy bright views of the village beach and lighthouse, with phones, air-conditioning and fans, balconies and American-style furnishings. A lovely pool, garden and restaurant-bar add to the relaxation. Budget to moderate.

A true sea-worn atmosphere pervades the quaint **Hotel Rocamar** (Avenida Guerrero and Avenida Bravo; 7-01-01), facing a beach just across from the downtown plaza. Its three floors, lined in stone seagull railings, contain slightly funky but very homey fan-cooled rooms (the ones with balconies are a seabreeze heaven). The sea theme appears everywhere, in seashell lamps, giant fish hooks holding up the dressers and polyurethane washbasins inset with shells and seahorses. Budget.

Just up the street stands the **Hotel Isleño** (Avenida Madero and Avenida Guerrero; 7-03-02), near the *zócalo*. Molded cement forms the closets and bedstands in the small white rooms, decorated by little more than cute overhead lamp-fans. There are several rooms per shared bath and some rooms with kitchens and private baths. Budget.

The **Perla Caribe** (Avenida Madero 2; 7-04-44) puts you right on the sea, with a small rocky beach behind its big blue-and-white facade. The little blue-and-white rooms come with ceiling fans or air-conditioning, balconies and plain decor. A new wing contains a cafeteria-bar and pool. This is a pleasant place. Moderate.

Of the many low-cost hotels on the island, the cheapest is **Poc-na** (Calle Matamoros 91; 7-00-90), a pleasant youth hostel with neither age limits nor curfew. Located just a short walk from Playa Los Cocos, the rambling hostelry contains mixed dormitories with woven-hemp bunks, tiny ceiling fans and small communal baths. There's an extra charge for sheets, towels, pillow and mattress. The restaurant on the premises serves breakfast only. Budget.

For bungalows right on the island's nicest beach, check in at **Las Cabañas María del Mar** (Avenida Carlos Lazo 1; 7-01-79). Included among the 45 rooms are five roomy cabañas with outdoor patios and ceiling fans, plus eight smaller rooms in this garden-filled compound. The rooms are cheerfully set up with carved beds, little refrigerators and hammock-slung patios. Budget to moderate.

Set on picturesque North Beach, the pretty, pink-washed **Nautibeach Playa Norte** (Avenida Rueda Medina; reservations necessary: 988-2-02-59 from the United States) satisfies those who need plenty of space. Accommodations in this 1990 condominium feature two bedrooms, a kitchenette, central air-conditioning (rare outside Cancún), and terraces or balconies overlooking the sea. A swimming pool and excellent French-Caribbean restaurant round out the amenities. Jungle landscaping creates an aura of seclusion, though downtown is just a five-minute walk. Deluxe.

Tucked away on the quiet but charming south end of the island, **Maria's Kan Kin** (Carretera al Garrafón; 7-00-15) is a complex of five stucco-and-bamboo rooms set in a garden high above the ocean. Some rooms have air-conditioning, others fans; all have two double beds but are individually decorated. A restaurant, pier and beach complete the picture. Moderate.

Even farther south, but perhaps the best bargain on the island, is **Hotel Garrafón de Castilla** (Carretera Punta Sur, Km. 6; 7-00-19). Opened in 1991, the twin, coral-washed buildings overlook a stunning expanse of aquamarine water. Cancún's highrises loom in the distance.

Isla Mujeres, "Island of Women," was enchantingly named after the statues of Maya goddesses found there by Spanish explorers in 1517.

All 12 rooms feel brand-new, and are fashioned with tile floors, marble vanities, big showers, painted poster beds and matching dressers. For the hotel's moderate price, you also get air-conditioning, good ceiling fans and bottled water. One disadvantage: The tourist boats dock here during midday, unloading hundreds of snorkelers. The rest of the day, it's immensely peaceful.

For other possibilities, check with **Arlene Coates** (May–December 608-244-4341 in Madison, Wisconsin; December–March via telegram to her at Lista de Correos, Isla Mujeres, Quintana Roo, Mexico). Arlene has been booking hotel reservations on the island for more than 15 years and will find what you need from budget to ultra-deluxe. If contacting her by telegram, make sure you include your name, phone and address, as well as a hotel price range.

ISLA MUJERES RESTAURANTS

For breakfast, **Villa del Mar** (Avenida Rueda Medina Sur 1; 7-00-31) hits the spot. Its picture windows gaze out to the sweaty ferry docks, while inside it's clean and air-conditioned. With glass-topped tables and cushioned chairs, the café has no real character but serves a hearty selection of eggs, chicken, meats, Mexican meals and seafood. Budget.

Two doors down, **Mirtita** (Avenida Rueda Medina Sur; 7-02-32) cooks up some of the best hamburgers and steaks in town. This easy-going waterfront restaurant-bar is air-conditioned, with two dining areas as well as a small stage and dancefloor for nighttime entertainment. Budget.

The barely noticeable **Restaurant Miramar** (Avenida Rueda Medina Sur, next to the ferry pier), on the water, is a good place to absorb local life. *Palapa*-roofed and hemmed with a red balcony railing, it's like a backwater stop for gondolas. Some of the island's tastiest seafood is served here, including lobster, succulent garlic shrimp, sopa de lima and fish tacos. Budget to moderate.

A block from the ferry dock, **Guillermos** (Calle Juárez and Avenida Morelos; 7-05-09) is a study in contrasts. The hand-hewn, Daniel Boone-style tables and chairs just don't mesh with the flashy sports paraphernalia, but no matter. Tourists flood the eatery for frosty mugs of beer and fresh seafood such as fish with avocado sauce, ceviche, lobster and grilled shrimp in garlic butter. Unlike most other local eateries, this place is spick-and-span. Moderate to deluxe.

Just off the plaza, **Restaurant Gomar** (Calle Hidalgo; 7-01-42) is a popular meeting ground. Its hacienda-style patio and indoor dining room are fetchingly decked out in striped serape tablecloths, twirling fans and painted tiles. A cool screen of foliage shelters tables from the dust and sun. Good meals, including fresh seafood and meats, are served. Budget.

At night, **La Peña** (Calle Guerrero 5, just off the plaza) offers a breezy seaside picnic ambience under a *palapa* alive with Latin music. Savory pizza (vegetarian to seafood) is the house specialty. There's also chicken, chow mein and conch. Budget.

Ciro's Lobster House (Avenida Matamoros 11) is one of the island's classier seafood houses, with an Americanized wood-paneled look and live music. The food, from shrimp curry to lobster thermidor, is tasty. Moderate.

The island's much-touted house of French haute cuisine is **Maria's Kan Kin Restaurant** (Carretera al Garrafón; 83-14-20 in Cancún). We found the food very ordinary. In mood, it does excel: It's a charming *palapa*-roofed garden restaurant, with dangling seashells and shark jaws, soft lighting and hand-painted burlap menus offering king crab, lobster, shrimp and coconut mousse. Everything is marked in dollars— very overpriced. Moderate to deluxe.

ISLA MUJERES SHOPPING

The village has scattered shops where prices tend to be more reasonable than in either Cancún or Cozumel. When the party boats arrive from Cancún, watch how the guides usher tourists into certain big, expensive shops. One of these, **Rachat & Rome** (Avenida Rueda Medina; 7-02-50) is the most upscale shop on the island. The sunset-pink building, carpeted and air-conditioned, has glass cases full of fine silver, pink coral and gold jewelry.

Nearby, along the pedestrian plaza, **Paulina** has crisp white woven dresses with colorful sashes. **La Sirena** (Avenida Hidalgo and Calle Madero; 7-02-23) has a big inventory of masks, Maya figures, T-shirts, blankets and papier-mâché items.

Down the street, you're apt to observe an artist at work chipping designs in limestone at **Casa del Arte México** (Avenida Hidalgo 6). Besides these superb carvings, there are Maya temple rubbings, batik clothing and images in ivory, obsidian and quartz.

The best shop may be **La Loma** (Avenida Guerrero 6), behind the plaza on the sea. It's a storehouse of treasures: coral jewelry, necklaces of old Maya stones, lacquer trays, delicate knit sweaters and collector's masks.

ISLA MUJERES NIGHTLIFE

On weekends, enjoy the live music and dancing on the *zócalo*. A funky hangout where you can meet the locals is the **Calypso Disco** (they call anything with a dancefloor a disco) near the lighthouse, just past the Posada del Mar.

The best place to watch the sunset, and later hear hot island sounds, is a *palapa* bar called **Jimbo's** (on the north beach, near the end of Avenida Rueda Medina). **La Peña** (Calle Guerrero 5, adjacent to the plaza) is a romantic spot with live music and ocean views.

ISLA MUJERES BEACHES

Isla Mujeres' most beautiful beach, a serene combination of velvety sand and bathtub sea, **Playa Los Cocos** may be the best swimming (or lolling) spot on the whole coast. A continuation of the village beach that begins near the docks and wraps around a point, Cocos runs along the island's northwesterly shore between Nautibeach and El Presidente. The only thing lacking is shade. The island's international set often bathes topless or suns bottomless here. Located on the northwest side of the island and village at the end of Calle Carlos Lazo.

A less-visited, more secluded white-sand beach near the southern end of the island, **Playa Lancheros** has a protected section for gentle swimming. Across the road and down a trail through the undergrowth lie the ruins of Mundaca the Pirate's hacienda. Located along the road from the village to El Garrafón, at the marked turnoff.

Playa del Carmen Area

South of Cancún, Mexico 307, a good paved road through flat and uninspired jungle, follows the Mexican Caribbean's best coastal strip. Inconspicuous roads, often carved in dirt, trail off from the highway toward the sea. These unmarked trails inevitably make for great exploring; generally, the more modest the trail, the better the beach at the end. Some of these beaches are private, so use discretion when deciding whether to set up camp.

About 68 kilometers south of Cancún comes the scenic village **Playa del Carmen**, where the passenger ferry pushes off for Cozumel. Playa, as it's called around town, has grown from a yawning farming and fishing cove to a tourist town in just 25 years. Only eight blocks wide and ten blocks long, the village is a lively place with tumbledown edges. Modest open-air cafés and stores gather along the seafront and down side streets, catering to a steady hum of human traffic. The main action centers around the ferry docks, where locals trying to make a few pesos peddle various goods and services. From here, palm-edged beaches stretch in both directions as far as the eye can see.

Yucatán sand is so cool to the feet that it's called "air-conditioned" sand.

Six kilometers south of Playa del Carmen, a marked turnoff leads to **Xcaret** (admission). Anyone who knew Xcaret (SH-car-et) before 1991 will lament its fate: the development of a $5 million tropical amusement park. This once-secluded cove with bold, brilliant fish and phantom-like waters has been dynamited to make way for a 1700-foot "underground river trip" for snorkelers. Most of the fish are gone, except for the dolphins who have been corralled into a lagoon so humans can swim with them. Pink-and-blue "folk" buses designed just for Xcaret deliver Cancún day-trippers by the hundreds and sometimes thousands. There's a seafood restaurant, bar, watersports center and souvenir shop. Promoters call the transformed Xcaret "Nature's Sacred Paradise."

Chakalal, a lovely turquoise-and-cream lagoon flowing into the sea, is about five kilometers past the beach of Paamul via the turnoff from Mexico 307 marked "Rancho Cuatro Hermanos." Near the west end of the lagoon stands a proud, boxy **Maya temple**. Under the temple winds an underwater tunnel connected to an adjoining lagoon.

Another seldom-visited lagoon, **Yal-ku** is just north of Akumal, reached via a dirt road from the Akumal parking area. Its vivid green water, submarine caves and fish that nibble from your hand make Yal-ku a marvelous swimming and diving hole.

PLAYA DEL CARMEN LODGING

This pretty beachfront town offers unique little tropical inns and one gleaming new hotel. Opened in late 1991, the **Continental Plaza Playacar** (Fraccionamiento Playacar, Km. 62.5; 3-01-00) is draped picturesquely along the sea, a striking sight for arriving ferry passengers. Its sand-colored buildings wend along a pretty beach and a fantasy swimming pool with swim-up *palapa* bar. Gleaming white tile, designer draperies and ethereal shades of blue and green make all 185 rooms look ultra-modern. If you don't mind the ultra-deluxe price tag, this is the place to stay.

One notch down from the Continental, but still offering some creature comforts, is **Hotel Molcas** (next to the ferry terminal; 3-01-34). The slightly worn, colonial-style building features a swimming bar, boutique and popular waterfront restaurant. The 35 rooms are air-conditioned, with tiny balconies, dark Spanish furniture and little Tiffany lamps. Deluxe in price.

For those short on funds, the **CREA Youth Hostel** (four blocks north of Avenida Principal, turn at the Autobuses Turismo and follow the signs) has big, clean dormitories plus several private cabañas for rent with air-conditioning and baths. Budget.

Hotel Copa Cabaña (Calle Cinco, five blocks north of the plaza, one block from the beach), with four rooms and three cabañas, all sparkling clean and set in a quiet garden, is a real find. Its touches include nice tile baths, ceiling fans and dive shop. Budget.

Albatros Royale (five blocks north of the plaza, on the beach; reservations: 800-527-0022) features an eye-catching blend of desert-colored stucco with dramatic *palapa* roofs. Colorful Mexican blankets, ceiling fans (no air-conditioning) and tile floors give each room a cozy feel. The sea lies a few steps out the front door. Ask for a room on the second (and top) floor: the vaulted *palapa* ceilings are extra special. Moderate.

Like some whitewashed haven for shipwrecked souls on a half-forgotten isle, the **Blue Parrot Inn** (six blocks north of the plaza, on the beach; reservations: 800-634-3547) rests among the palms with a semi-Mediterranean laziness. Its 30 rooms with fans, drinking water, good reading lights, mosquito nets, hot water and ice chests make for a relaxed vacation on the beach. You'll also find a dive shop and restaurant, terrific castaway bar, and will get by with English, too. The characters found around this place give it real color. Moderate.

PLAYA DEL CARMEN RESTAURANTS

The reasonable **Restaurant-Bar Pez Vela** (Avenida 5 Norte and Calle 2) is a wild and crazy *palapa* stop for breakfast. T-shirts hang over the bar like faded flags, while salsa music rings out. The tourist special is chili con carne. Budget to moderate.

Across the plaza is the friendly indoor-outdoor **Ristorante Belvedere Pizzeria** with its delicious thin-crusted pizzas and homemade pastas. Two to try: lasagna layered with shrimp and squid à la romana. Fresh fish and happy hour from 1 to 7 p.m. are daily specials. Budget to moderate in price.

Not to be missed is the fancy **Hotel Molcas** (on the beach at the ferry landing; 3-01-34). The big, breezy dining room has a view of the sea and entrées like creole shrimp, beef kebabs, red snapper in tomato sauce and baked pork with Yucatecan spices (guaranteed, says the menu, to be "100-percent Mexican"). Deluxe.

Distinguished along the coast for exceptional dining, **Limones** (Avenida 10A at Calle 2, three blocks north of the ferry dock) is the place for pasta. The owners, natives of Rome, whip up *delisioso* dishes such

---

A shopping tip: Prices everywhere tend to be higher when a cruise ship is in port.

---

as fettucine and veal scallopine, doughy pizza bread and pasta with fresh fish. Dine in a cool courtyard under a ceiling of greenery, or inside under a big *palapa* roof. Flickering candles and strolling guitarists add to the romance. Deluxe to ultra-deluxe.

Down the road, seven blocks from the bus station on Avenida Cinco (turn right at Faces Hotel), you'll find **Ristorante Italiano De Gabi** cooking up fresh seafood and hand-rolled pastas. A shady garden provides a peaceful romantic setting for dishes such as sautéed calamari and fettucine with shrimp and mussels. Bountiful breakfast buffets, featuring eggs, beans and rice and fresh-squeezed juice, are morning highlights. Budget to moderate.

PLAYA DEL CARMEN SHOPPING

You can pick up curios at small shops around the plaza. Most people head for the obvious, nifty shopping mall called **Mercado de Artesanías Xaman Ha**, where 14 shops sell silver, dresses, blankets, hats, serapes, jewelry and T-shirts. Across from the plaza, **Toucan Curios** stocks embroidered bags and beachwear.

PLAYA DEL CARMEN NIGHTLIFE

Playa del Carmen begins jumping at sundown along Avenida Cinco, which is lined with happy-hour restaurants and bars. You'll hear four or five languages and a mix of music.

Ziggy's Disco Bar is upstairs across from the plaza and *the* place to dance. Head for the topside restaurant-bar **El Capitán**, down from the market Kiin (off Avenida 5 Norte), for the latest in sounds.

The **Bar Herman Cortes** at the Hotel Molcas (near the ferry terminal) is a small but fairly swank air-conditioned tavern featuring black leatherette chairs, conquistador decor and an elevated television broadcasting the latest in sports.

Everyone should have a drink at the **Blue Parrot Bar** (Blue Parrot Inn, six blocks north of the plaza). Set outdoors on the beach, the ship-shaped watering hole has swings for seats and crazy characters for patrons. The island music is great, too.

PLAYA DEL CARMEN AREA BEACHES

A wide, clean beach, **Playa del Carmen** seems to rock to a tropical lullaby, soothing and unhurried, sweetened by the rustle of palms. The shore extends for miles both north and south of the ferry pier, where boats push off for Cozumel.

Playa Paamul, a rocky, palm-lined beach, has an intimate feel; it is one of the least trafficked parts of this coast. Marvelous breezes sweep across the aquamarine cove, whose creamy blue waters are darkened by offshore reefs. Rocky platforms intrude upon the cottony sand, but the area is all the more pleasant because it is tucked between two protective points. Camping is allowed. Located about 24 kilometers south of Playa del Carmen; take the marked turnoff from Mexico 307, then follow the dirt road about one-and-a-half kilometers to the beach.

Cozumel

To the Maya, the island of Cozumel was a shrine, a place whose rugged beauty and mystique inspired sacred ceremonies to sensuous gods. As early as 900 A.D., Maya women from across the Yucatán made a pilgrimage here to worship Ixchel, goddess of fertility. They arrived by the hundreds in dugout canoes, praying the island's potent warmth and windy spirit would stir their wombs.

Today's pilgrims come from all over the world to indulge in Cozumel's heady mix of silky beaches, gemlike waters and kaleidoscopic coral reefs. Mexico's largest island, the 45-kilometer-long coral cay is still largely wild and windswept, clothed in shaggy jungle and mangrove swamp. It predated Cancún as the Mexican Caribbean's prime getaway and remains the finest diving site in the country. Despite its international popularity, Cozumel can make you feel like you left civilization—or found it. Ferries to the island leave from Puerto Morelos and Playa del Carmen.

The hub of activity is **San Miguel de Cozumel**, Cozumel's only town, located on the northwest side of the island. This honeycomb of colorful boutiques and lively cafés buzzes around the broad seafront **Plaza del Sol** and extends about 12 blocks along a breezy *malecón*.

Along the plaza, near Avenida 5 Sur, the **Delegación Estatal de Turismo** (2-09-72) provides visitor information. Also, check with the **Cozumel Chamber of Commerce** (Avenida 20 Sur; 2-05-83).

On the *malecón* at Calle 6 Norte is the island's museum, **Museo de la Isla de Cozumel** (2-15-45; admission). Opened in 1987, the pink colonial building houses a worthwhile overview of the island's history and ecology, including striking displays on the spectacular coral reefs. Open Sundays through Fridays from 10 a.m. to 4 p.m. The museum is closed Saturdays.

Farther south, **Parque Laguna Chankanaab** (about nine kilometers south of San Miguel off the coastal road; admission) is unquestionably the gem of the island. The name Chankanaab means "small sea" in Maya, referring to the park's blue lagoon full of parrotfish, barracuda, sergeant majors, octopus and other colorful specimens. The lagoon's beautiful coral is dead, however, and experiments are being conducted to revive it. Visitors may not swim in the lagoon but can snorkel in the even more resplendent sea or roam through the park's **botanical gardens**, which contain more than 2000 species of plants from all over the world. The grounds also contain replicas of a Maya house with backyard elevated farming and a small temple.

No less than 40 ruins testify to Cozumel's importance as a trading center along the Maya Route. Unfortunately, thanks to Hurricane Gilbert and the ravages of time, most are poorly preserved or impossible to reach. At the southern tip of the island, a dirt road turns off the paved highway toward the **Tumba de Caracol** and **El Faro Celerain** (Celerain Lighthouse). The tiny Caracol, a snail-shaped Maya temple dating back to 1200 A.D., resembles a Disney mini-ruin crowned by a small square cupola. It's much too small even for the petite Maya— could it be another haunt of the *aluxes*, those legendary Maya pixies? The road continues to the antique lighthouse at **Punta Celerain**, land's end. If you speak some Spanish and the caretaker likes you, he may unlock the lighthouse and let you climb up for a wild, windy view of Cozumel. You can also negotiate for a boat ride on nearby **Laguna Columbia**.

The **windward shore** of Cozumel is the true escape route: undeveloped and mostly deserted, a coast of scrub jungle and barren beaches, rocks and crumbled ruins. You can drive it in a south-north loop from the leeward highway or cross the island via the Carretera Transversal (which originates in San Miguel as Avenida Benito Juárez) and begin your tour at the beach of Santa Cecilia.

En route, a side road off the Carretera Transversal leads inland to **San Gervasio** (admission), once a Maya governmental center and now Cozumel's best ruins. Less than spectacular, they consist of mediocre stonework nestled in ten acres of bug-bitten jungle. These crumbling altars and shrines, dating from early Classic days to the Postclassic period, were undoubtedly used in ceremonies to Ixchel. Other minor ruins in the early stages of excavation dot the whole northern tip of the island. A 24-kilometer sand track, only suited for motorbikes or jeeps, squiggles north of Santa Cecilia along empty beach to **Punta**

Molas. You pass the small ruined altar and vaulted fortress of **Castillo Real** along the way. Out at the point, a lighthouse shares sea winds with **Aguada Grande**, circular ruins of buildings on platforms.

The drive south along the paved windward highway is very refreshing. Just past Punta Chiquero, pause at **El Mirador** and gaze out from the rocky lookout point to the surging Caribbean.

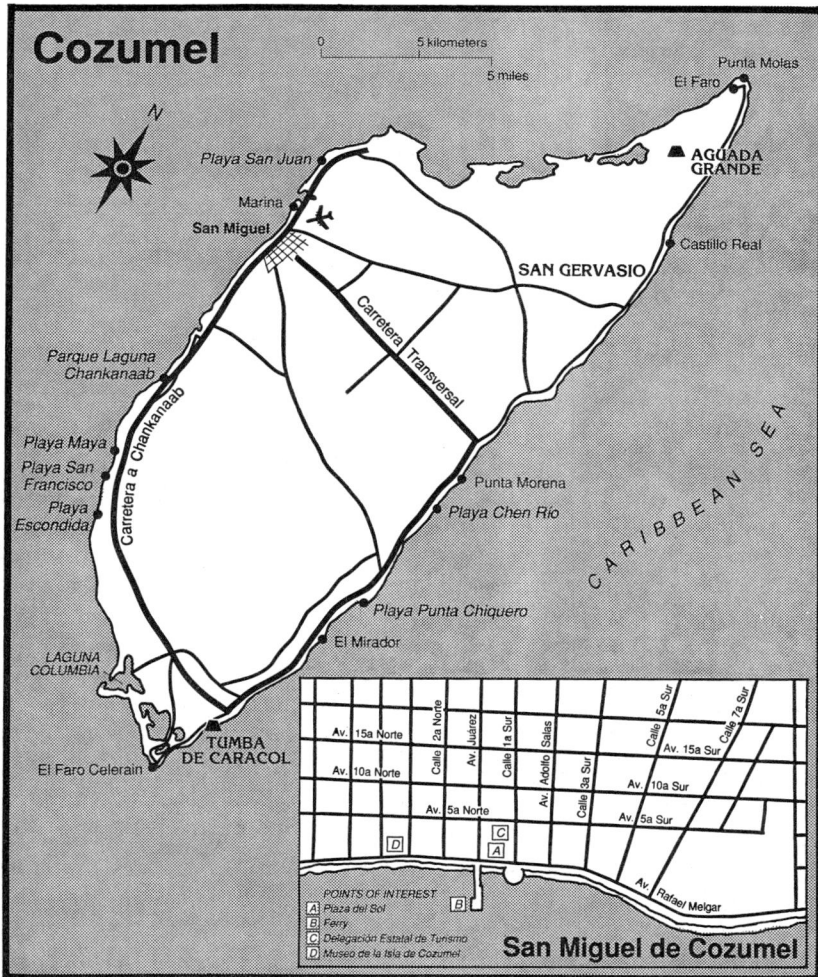

Cozumel

0   5 kilometers
5 miles

N

Punta Molas
El Faro

Playa San Juan

Marina

San Miguel

▲ AGUADA
GRANDE

Castillo Real

SAN GERVASIO

Carretera Transversal

Parque Laguna
Chankanaab

Carretera a Chankanaab

Playa Maya
Playa San
Francisco
Playa
Escondida

Punta Morena

Playa Chen Rio

C A R I B B E A N   S E A

Playa Punta Chiquero

El Mirador

LAGUNA
COLUMBIA

TUMBA
DE CARACOL

El Faro Celerain

Av. 15a Norte
Calle 2a Norte
Av. Juárez
Calle 1a Sur
Calle Salas
Calle 5a Sur
Calle 7a Sur
Av. 15a Sur

Av. 10a Norte
Av. Adolfo Salas
Calle 3a Sur
Av. 10a Sur

Av. 5a Norte
Av. 5a Sur

D

C
A

POINTS OF INTEREST
A Plaza del Sol
B Ferry
C Delegación Estatal de Turismo
D Museo de la Isla de Cozumel

B

Av. Rafael Melgar

San Miguel de Cozumel

Cozumel's Palancar Reef is one of the world's five greatest reef systems.

COZUMEL LODGING

Fancy hotels, many with scuba diving packages built into their prices, line the leeward side of the island. The more modest inns are mostly in the village of San Miguel.

You'll find panache and convenience at the **Hotel Mary Carmen** (Avenida 5a Sur 4; 2-05-81), half a block from the main plaza. Built around a central garden, with chandeliers in the lobby, the Mary Carmen offers 28 small, attractive carpeted rooms containing walnut-veneer furniture and air-conditioning. Budget.

Prefer a sea view? The most reasonable waterfront hotel is the whitewashed, motel-like **Hotel Vista del Mar** (Avenida Rafael Melgar 45; 2-05-45), right on the *malecón* in town. Its three floors all have lounging areas, and its 26 ample, bright rooms with compact refrigerators and balconies are so breezy the air-conditioning is hardly needed. Budget.

A nice compromise between luxury and practicality is the **Hotel del Mesón San Miguel** (Avenida Juárez 2; 2-02-33), the fanciest inn in the village, yet still at a working-class price. Right on the *zócalo*, its easy-going lobby with rattan furniture and spacious, attractive restaurant set the tone for the 97 rooms. Airy and casual, with terraces that overlook the square, rooms have carpets, air-conditioning and phones. Moderate.

An anomaly among Cozumel hotels, **Plaza Las Glorias** (Avenida Melgar, Km. 1.5; 2-20-00, reservations: 800-342-2644) is on the beach *and* within walking distance of town. Fashioned as a Mediterranean villa and painted the prettiest shade of peach, it is one of the island's newest, brightest and best hostelries. In addition to a pool overlooking the ocean, this 171-room, top-of-the-line facility offers several restaurants and bars and a dive shop. Ultra-deluxe.

For extravagant effect, the **Fiesta Americana Sol Caribe** (Carretera a Chankanaab; 2-07-00, reservations: 800-343-7821) takes the cake. Its enormous wooden-roofed lobby soars out over a tropical bar that features waterfalls and live music. Two hivelike highrises shelter a world of tropical lushness: Flower-cloaked trails curl around restaurants, boutiques and a rambling swimming pool punctuated with an island *palapa* bar. The 321 rooms are comfortable, with phones, air-conditioning, color televisions, servibars and carpeting or marble floors. There's a small beach across the street, right next to Cozumel's cruise ship berth. Ultra-deluxe.

The **Stouffer Presidente Hotel** (Carretera a Chankanaab, Km. 6.5; 2-03-22, reservations: 800-468-3571) has remodeled and improved its splendid beach property. The hotel has a breezy, outdoor restaurant and sits next to a perfect snorkeler's cove. The big, brightly colored rooms offer sea views, air-conditioning and large bathrooms. Deluxe to ultra-deluxe.

Amid a welter of hotels catering to scuba divers, the picturesque, villa-like **Galapago Inn** (Carretera a Chankanaab, Km. 1.5; 2-06-63, reservations: 800-847-5708) offers one of the best deals. Set around a fanciful patio, the 58 upbeat stucco rooms blend painted tiles, pigskin furniture and natural light (some have balconies). All are air-conditioned, with refrigerators. The ultra-deluxe price includes three meals daily.

Some of the finest rooms on the island await at the classy **Meliá Maya Cozumel** (Playa Santa Pilar; 2-04-12, reservations: 800-336-3542), a beachfront highrise at the north end of the island. All air-conditioned and carpeted, with lovely sea views and balconies, the 200 rooms have rich tapestry touches: wallhangings, brocade chairs, burlap-shaded lamps. The grounds include two pools, a restaurant, shops and tennis courts. Ultra-deluxe.

COZUMEL RESTAURANTS

The island is drowning in good restaurants. In San Miguel, big, tropical **Las Palmeras** (Avenida Rafael Melgar 27; 2-05-32) is the loveliest place for breakfast. Facing the passenger ferry pier, its open tile and brick interior is fanned by sea breezes that rustle its miniature gardens. Surprisingly prompt waiters bring you steaming omelettes, French toast, seafood, salads, Mexican meals and more. Moderate.

Nearby, the seafront **El Portal** (Avenida Rafael Melgar 2; 2-03-16) is great for breakfast and lunch. The busy, tropical-style room has ceiling fans, tile floor, a small fountain, fast service and a view of the boats. Mexican plates and fresh fish are the specialties. Moderate.

Top honors for elegance go to the upstairs waterfront **Café del Puerto** (Avenida Rafael Melgar 2; 2-03-16). Bamboo-and-gourd tropical lamps float from the natural straw ceiling and polish the coppery tile floor with soft lighting. The moonlit sea shines through the tall windows. A piano tenders soft ballads as waiters serve sumptuous portions of meats and seafood like *parriada mixta* (mixed seafood) and *langosta diabla* (lobster in a flaming pineapple). Dinner only. Moderate.

The Renaissance-style **Donatello** (Avenida Rafael Melgar 131; 2-25-86) announces its waterfront presence with coral rock columns, arched windows and sloping tile roof. Ultra-chic and romantic, the inside shimmers with pale pink walls and huge Old-World paintings. From lobster, scampi and veal to fettucine with clams, mussels and shrimp, the dressy eatery excels in the art of fine Italian cooking. Dinner only. Deluxe.

Pizza Rolandi (Avenida Rafael Melgar 23; 2-09-46) has a romantic, hideaway garden patio where guests can listen to classical music while enjoying a pitcher of sangria, homemade pastas, thin-crusted pizzas baked in a wood-fired oven and attentive service. Ask for the pizza-crust garlic bread. Budget to moderate.

If you feel homesick or just want to catch the latest NFL game, **The Sports Page** (Avenida 5a Norte and Calle 2a; 2-11-99) is Cozumel's spotless, red-white-and-blue corner of Americana, with nonstop televisions showing the latest sports events. Walls and ceiling are plastered with football banners and team shirts. Burgers and fries are big here, plus seafood, steak and excellent breakfasts. Budget to moderate.

Believed by many to be the island's best, **Pepe's Grill** (Avenida Rafael Melgar and Calle Adolfo Salas; 2-02-13) is a smart, slightly snobbish upstairs-downstairs restaurant on the *malecón*, shimmering with candlelight and live piano music. Such flaming specialties as shrimp jovial and brandy-laced drinks light up the aisles like a magic show. Exotica like tomato stuffed with baby eels and conch chowder share menu space with delicious Mexican meals and meats. Dinner only. Deluxe.

Enjoy a cool drink or meal at the open-air **Plaza Leza** (Calle 1a Sur 6; 2-10-41). Its umbrella-shaded outdoor tables are sheltered by little shrubs, while the raised interior is top-heavy with Spanish-style furniture and travel posters. Mexican dishes dominate the menu. The Spanish omelettes and coconut ice cream with Kahlua are tops. Budget to moderate.

A find is the family-run **La Choza** (at the corner of Calle Salas and Avenida 10 Sur; 2-09-58). A *palapa* room with crude wooden chairs, this eatery caters to the locals and serves the best Mexican food in town. At least one Yucatecan dish is whipped up daily, though the rest of the day's entrées depends on what the cook has in mind. Ask for the daily special. Moderate.

The rich, dark-wood **Morgan's** (Avenida 5a and Calle Juárez; 2-05-84), all in imported pine, resembles a West Indies townhouse, with an outer veranda and patio, and lush island melodies lilting inside. Named for English pirate Henry Morgan, this chic, air-conditioned restaurant presents a treasure chest of entrées, from flaming crepes to Spanish *zarzuela* (seafood in tomato stew) to conch steak. Lunch and dinner. Moderate.

Ernesto's Fajitas Factory (Zona Hotelera Sur, near Hotel Sol Caribe; 2-31-52) may be Cozumel's most distinctive eatery—an open, round *palapa* on the roadside, ringed in stools that are usually crowded with fajita fans. Fajitas are a kind of Tex-Mex taco with spicy beef, chicken or shrimp inside. You can also order all-American breakfasts, nachos and hamburgers. Moderate.

COZUMEL SHOPPING

Shopping is terrific in San Miguel de Cozumel. Starting at the *zócalo* where it faces the *malecón*, several mega-shops hold court with catchalls of crafts. **Opus** (Avenida Rafael Melgar; 2-13-95) is one such, an air-conditioned zoo of brass animals, wooden toys, clowns, sunglasses and T-shirts. **Las Campanas** (Plaza del Sol; 2-07-72) is another curio outlet with good prices. The more sophisticated **Bali-Hai** (Avenida Rafael Melgar 25; 2-02-60) wows visitors with its expensive collection of brass buckles and tropical jewelry made with shells, coins and tassels.

Moving north along the *malecón*, posh **Casablanca** (Avenida Rafael Melgar 33; 2-11-77) resembles a colonial art gallery with cases and niches filled with Maya art, jewelry and silver sculptures. **El Paso** (Avenida Rafael Melgar 21; 2-13-13), one of Cozumel's first shops, sparkles with silver and a large onyx collection.

Xamanek (Avenida Rafael Melgar 149; 2-09-40), named for the Maya traveler's god, is a narrow, alleylike store packed with dangling birds and beasts in ceramic and leather.

Bazaar Cozumel (Avenida Rafael Melgar 23; 2-00-85), in business for more than 30 years, has the finest art items on the island, including signed Felguerez' sculptures, Chaman masks, tin figures from Michoacán and pre-Columbian reproductions.

The newer **Villa Mar** (Avenida Juárez 2) houses unique stores carrying everything from silver, leather and Guatemalan weaves to batik and artwork.

Los Cincos Soles (Avenida Rafael Melgar 27; 2-01-32) is a wander-through complex of surprises, from wooden puzzles and papier-mâché fruits to a back gallery full of temple rubbings and antiques.

COZUMEL NIGHTLIFE

The after-dark scene on Cozumel ranges from spirited sports bars and lively discos to cozy waterfront *palapas*. The proximity of everything creates a neighborly atmosphere.

The hot spot downtown is **Carlos 'n Charlie's** (Avenida Rafael Melgar, near the pier; 2-01-91), maybe the best in the chain. Noisy and crazy, with a volleyball court, beer guzzling contests and gobs of great graffiti, it doesn't skimp on the atmosphere or drinks.

The disco king is **Neptuno** (Avenida Rafael Melgar; 2-15-37), across from the Restaurant Acuario. The room heats up with videos, laser lights and a late happy hour, and is often filled with a young international crowd on the prowl.

Shift into sports gear for a drink at the all-American **Sports Page** (Calle 2a and Avenida 5a Norte; 2-11-99). A television tuned eternally to the latest game and the bar's air-conditioned comfort make it a welcoming venue for game talk and beer.

Action central in these parts is a place called **Scaramouche** (Calle Adolfo Salas and Calle 11a Sur), a contemporary club-disco that draws an energized crowd.

Begin the evening at **Ernesto's** (Carretera a Chankanaab, next to Hotel Fiesta Americana Sol Caribe; 2-31-52). The place jumps with live music as sunburned visitors sit at the *palapa* bar and drink from plastic cups. The service can be erratic, but it's worth it.

Quietude comes more naturally at the dramatic **Lobby Bar Chac-Mool** (in the Fiesta Americana Sol Caribe; 2-07-00). Under the soaring wing of a cantilevered roof, this patio bar spreads out beneath a replica of the Maya god Chac-Mool and a series of cascading fountains. Mariachis and other musicians perform nightly. The big event here, though, is the weekly **"Viva Mexico,"** featuring a Mexican buffet and live show spotlighting the country's music and dance. Call ahead for reservations.

COZUMEL BEACHES

Cozumel is crusted with beaches on both its leeward and windward shores. Since the waters surrounding the island are part of an underwater nature park, shore fishing is not permitted. Following are some of the best beaches.

Playa San Juan (also called Playa Azul) is a friendly, family-oriented beach covering the northern hotel strip from the Meliá Maya Cozumel Hotel to Puerto Abrigo. Its best section fronts the Hotel Playa Azul. Here, windsurfers skim the soft waves, shade trees rustle and tiny black-and-yellow birds flit down to the local restaurant and perch on your chair. Located toward the northwestern end of Cozumel; turn off the paved road at Hotel Playa Azul.

A seaside crystalline lagoon twinkling with colored fish, **Laguna Chankanaab** stands alongside a botanical garden and manmade beach with full facilities. The meadow of sand, small but lovely for sunbathing, faces the island's prime snorkeling turf just offshore—a giant jewel box of tropical sea life. Located about ten kilometers south of San Miguel; there's a marked turnoff from the main coastal road.

Playa Maya, a quiet sandy beach with a few *palapa* umbrellas and plastic reclining seats in the sand, lacks the sizzle of the more popular spots but exudes instead a feeling of dreamy relaxation. Backed by low-lying jungle, the beach forms scallops around soft points to the south. The sand is scattered with white coral and broken conch shells.

Despite its small-town feel, over 90 percent of Cozumel is still smothered in jungle.

Located about 15 kilometers south of San Miguel; take the marked turnoff from the main coastal road.

Cozumel's number-one beach, **Playa San Francisco** is anchored by the San Francisco Beach Club, one of the island's oldest restaurants. Here, lunch and early dinners are enjoyed under a *palapa* on the beach. The splendid beach runs along the crystal clear sea and is where narcissistic, bikini-clad sunbathers sip piña coladas. Beach play includes wave runners and snorkeling trips to Colombia reef. To get to the northern beach, travel 15 kilometers south of San Miguel, just past Playa Maya; take the marked turnoff from the main coastal road. For the southern beach, located about one-and-a-half kilometers farther south, take the marked turnoff from the main coastal road.

In a hushed jungle at the end of a bumpy road, **Playa Escondida** flows out of the shadows and wanders for several miles along limpid and motionless water. Tin-and-thatched shacks half-buried in shoreline vegetation send little smoke signals into the air as fish sizzle on outdoor grills. More of a sanctuary for natives than tourists, this may be Cozumel's best escapist beach. Located about 19 kilometers south of San Miguel along the coastal road; look for the marked turnoff.

A pretty, wild beach on Cozumel's windward shore, **Punta Morena** winds down from a small settlement of huts and palms where fishermen gather to barbecue fresh fish. Seaweed and interesting rock formations lie along the beach. One sculpted rock, reached by a little wooden bridge, is called *Copa de Piedra* (the stone cup). An overhanging grotto with a sandy floor, called *Cueva del Amor*, is reached by crude rocky stairs. Located along the windward road just south of Santa Cecilia, Km. 45.

Another pretty beach is **Playa Chen Río**. Located in a cove protected by a wall of rocks, this crescent of sand slides along the somnolent turquoise water. Very quiet and private, with a few *palapa* umbrellas for shade. Located along the windward road just south of Punta Morena, Km. 42.

Punta Chiquero is the most beautiful beach on Cozumel's eastern coast, perhaps on the entire island. Protected by a tousled green headland, the sugar-white shore clings to a sheltered cove, then ventures south for a kilometer or so along the open sea. Cages holding parakeets dangle from the eaves of the quaint thatch-roofed restaurant, and playful coatimundis nuzzle their pointy noses into your sandals for attention. There's good camping. Located off the windward road south of Chen Río, Km. 37.

Akumal Area

Back on the mainland at Playa del Carmen, travel about 37 kilometers south until you reach Akumal. Akumal is not really a town, but a handful of charming hotels and *palapa* cabanas strung along a palm-speckled cove. This little paradise by the sea enjoys a delightfully slow pace and a refreshing lack of crowds. Right on the beach, where several shipwrecked Spanish sailors washed ashore in 1511, stands a hand-sóme bronze **statue of Gonzalo Guerrero** dressed as an Indian, with his Maya wife and children. Guerrero fathered the first Euro-American family and later fought against the Spanish when they tried to conquer the Yucatán.

Four kilometers south of Akumal, the sign on the highway says "La Playa Más Bonita en el Mundo" (The Most Beautiful Beach in the World). It is no empty claim. Here at **Playa Chemuyil**, coconut palms and thick jungle tumble down to white sand that's as soft as talcum powder. Little screened jungle huts, perfect for beach camping, line the cobalt sea, and a big *palapa* bar is usually attended by eccentric characters—making this idyllic spot all the more interesting.

A little farther south, the crystal lagoons at **Xel-Ha National Park** (admission) attract everyone who ever wanted to don mask and flip-pers. Sometimes called "the world's biggest natural aquarium," Xel-Ha (SHELL-ha) is one of the Yucatán's major attractions. As you enter the park, the first lagoon is closed to swimmers, but the shallow seaside lagoon swarms with snorkelers exclaiming over the flashing rainbows of fish. There are several restaurants and places to rent dive gear, kayaks and glass-bottom boats. The entrance to the complex contains the **Museo de Rescates Subamaticos** (admission), a small museum show-ing crusty items rescued from shipwrecks by Mexican divers. The park also has a small zoo with one painful sight: a pen where several spider monkeys are tied to a tree by leashes. Perhaps the park staff, realizing this is not ecotourism, will eventually untie the poor creatures!

Across the highway from the lagoons, the **Xel-Ha ruins** (admission) are gradually being dug out of the jungle. So far, these temples are mostly rubble heaps bearing faint frescoes. Nearby lies a leaf-strewn *cenote*.

The most glaring example of mass development along the coast is **Puerto Aventuras**, about seven kilometers north of Akumal. Billed as "the new Maya civilization," this slick mini-city sprawls along 980 acres and boasts 30 tennis courts, a 230-slip marina, championship golf, shopping mall, numerous bars and restaurants, and nearly 2000 condominium and hotel rooms, many still under construction. With its ersatz Mexi-Mediterranean architecture and flawless Disney-like design, it looks about as Mexican as the Eiffel Tower. Hardly a "Maya civilization," new or old.

Xel-Ha is the largest freshwater creek on Mexico's Caribbean coast.

AKUMAL AREA LODGING

The biggest time-share game south of Cancún, **Puerto Aventuras Resort** (seven kilometers north of Akumal, off Mexico 307; 2-23-00; reservations: 800-451-8891) also offers 309 hotel rooms. The pseudo-Mexican planned community, with its golf course, tennis courts, marina and chic shops, could be anywhere. Accommodations are ultramodern and cushy, featuring soft pastel decor and wall art made with Cancún sand. Each room has a kitchen with microwave. Ultra-deluxe. (*A word of caution*: The resort's time-share salespeople, who work at locations along Mexico 307, may say anything to lure you here. We were told Puerto Aventuras was only a hotel, not a time-share, and that the resort "tour" would take 15 minutes. It turned out to be a one-hour sales pitch. Worse yet, after the sales pitch, we were told there was no hotel—only time-share rooms we should buy.)

The scenic, away-from-it-all beach community of Akumal is an oasis of quaint bungalows and hotels. In the center of Akumal "action," offering the most character for the least money, is the **Hotel Club Akumal Caribe Villas Maya** (reservations: 800-351-1622 or 915-584-3552 in Texas). Rooms here are in a beachfront hotel and a sprinkling of villas. The three-story hotel demonstrates real Mexican flavor in its white stuccoed walls, arched doorways trimmed in pink, and tile floors that shine like glass. Each room overlooks the sea and Z-shaped pool, and has air-conditioning and a kitchenette stocked with purified water. A few steps away in the sand, the villas are tucked in a tangle of brilliant bougainvillea and palm trees. Slightly smaller and more rustic that the hotel rooms, the villas do have air-conditioning, fans and beds so comfortable you'll forget you're away from home. Moderate to deluxe.

For a budget price, you'll get bungalows with no air-conditioning but with tile floors, double beds, drapes and showers (usually cold). Inquire at **Restaurant Zacil and Bungalows** (2-33-57).

Down the beach, the **Hotel Akumal Cancún** (Carretera Puerto Juárez-Tulum, Km. 104; 2-24-53) has 91 rooms, all with air-conditioning and sunny terraces. Also featured are a disco-bar, restaurants, dive shop and tennis. Moderate.

Remote, picturesque and luxurious, **Villas Flamingo** (reservations: 800-351-1622 or 915-584-3552 in Texas) is a five-minute drive farther down the beach on a wind-swept crest of Half Moon Bay. Architecturally stunning, the pink Moorish Mediterranean villas are decorated with domes and arches, clay-tiled awnings and pillared terraces, and a stairway that curls like a serpent's tail. The four apartment-size units—each with two floors—have kitchens, living rooms and spacious bedrooms. A fish-filled lagoon provides splendid snorkeling. A must for escapists. Ultra-deluxe.

Half Moon Bay is rimmed with low-slung condominiums built in recent years. The **U–Nah–Kin** (reservations: 409-935-4475 in Georgia) has contemporary beachfront condo units with air-conditioning and satellite television, priced in the moderate range. If bookings are slow, however, the owners will make you a budget-priced deal.

Just south of Akumal, on its own private beach, **Club Aventuras Akumal** (Fraccionamiento Aventuras Akumal, Km. 251; 4-23-03, reservations: 2-28-87 in Cozumel) presents an all-inclusive, modern beach resort with high energy and an appealing dive program. Each room bears a plaque with the name of a Mexican diver, and the diving focus is clear in the well-equipped dive shop. The hotel is a playground of rusty ballast balls, ship's ropes and horns, nets and shells around its pool, restaurant and bar. Ultra-deluxe rates include all meals, cocktails and watersports.

About two kilometers farther south, basking in a crescent of powdery beach, you'll find **Chemuyil Hotel** (Playa Chemuyil, off Mexico 307; 2-01-72). Opened in 1991 and the only noncamping accommodations in this location, the white, two-story building sits near the campground and houses seven basic rooms with kitchenettes and air-conditioning—much appreciated during the sweltering summer. Prices are moderate.

BEWARE THE TIME-SHARE

The timeshare salesman has become as much a part of Mexico's Caribbean as blood-thirsty mosquitoes in the jungle. He lurks everywhere—on the beaches, the sidewalks, even in the national parks—waiting to whisk you to a concrete highrise. If you go, you will meet another salesman who will give you a slick sales spiel. He will show you a dazzling room that, for six months' salary, can be yours today. He will point out sketches of grand things to come, things like yacht-filled marinas, golf courses and maybe even a pool where you can swim with dolphins—things that denote "progress." After two hours, he will lead you to a smoke-filled room where you will be pumped with liquor and pressured to buy now. If you decline to buy, he will try very hard to make you feel bad. Bad for not liking his time-share, bad for wasting his time, bad for ever going with that time-share salesman in the first place.

Akumal, Mayan for "place of the turtle," was named for thousands of turtles who used to bury their eggs on the beach.

AKUMAL AREA RESTAURANTS

There are several fine spots to eat in Akumal. The best is the open-air **Lol-ha (Flor de Aqua)** (Playa Akumal), where colorful piñatas and hammocks dangle from a soaring *palapa* ceiling. This, and a perennial breeze rustling its potted plants, make Lol-ha a relaxing place to dine. For breakfast, there's tasty bacon and eggs; for dinner, an extensive lineup of seafood, meat, chicken and make-your-own tacos. No lunch. Moderate to deluxe. The attached **Pizzeria Lol-ha** is a cozy, glass-walled room serving good Italian pies and the latest American sports on television. Moderate.

A brief stroll from Lol-ha, **Restaurant Zacil** (Playa Akumal) sits under a cavernous *palapa* roof, alive with spinning fans. Its circular glass walls look out to the beach, inviting fine views of the sea. You can choose from Caesar salad, steak, chicken and a seafood plate. Moderate to deluxe.

At Playa Chemuyil, about four kilometers south of Akumal, the lively little **Restaurant-Bar Marco Polo** is a hammock-draped beach café-in-the-round whose bar stools are always full of interesting characters. Fishermen, sailors, divers and campers all tend to congregate here. The fish and chicken dinners are *muy sabrosas* (very tasty). Dine at the bar or on the beach at a cozy table overlooking the horseshoe bay. Budget in price.

AKUMAL AREA SHOPPING

The resorts here have limited shopping. Akumal has two shops with crafts and clothes near one another right on the beach. At the entrance to Xel-Ha, there's a row of crafts shops with beachwear and blankets.

AKUMAL AREA NIGHTLIFE

A sprinkling of sleepy beach bars barely keeps the coast awake at night. Everyone gathers around the **Snack Bar Lol-ha** (Playa Akumal) for drinks, day and night. The big beachside *palapa* bar attracts the most interesting characters.

During the winter high season, enough people fill the Hotel Akumal Cancún to liven its **Disco Arrecife** (Mexico 307, Km. 104). Really just a *palapa* bar, it features dancing in the sand.
   Restaurant-Bar Marco Polo (off Mexico 307, Playa Chemuyil) is
a great little thatched-roofed watering hole-in-the-round, wide open,
right on the beach and often crowded. Try the "Chemuyil Special," a
delicious blender drink of Kahlua, milk, rum, vanilla, coconut crème
and ice served in half a gourd.

AKUMAL AREA BEACHES

A relaxed little tourist colony, **Playa Akumal** seems to have emerged
almost organically among the palms. Through the fronds shines the
opal-blue sea, and along its edge curves a stretch of alabaster sand—it's
a dream come true. The swimming is sublime, and dive shops here
offer gear, lessons and trips to offshore reefs.
   Though the palm tree blight and Hurricane Gilbert have taken their
toll, **Playa Chemuyil** is still a bona fide Eden. The horseshoe-shaped
beach, drenched in long shadows, pillowy white where the sun streaks
through, with caressing breezes to turn the pages of your bestseller just
at the crucial moment, Chemuyil leaves no want un-met. The soft
sand shines like crystals in the sun, and verdant jungle and swaying
palms line the shore. The little screened jungle huts under the palms
give camping a Congo edge with civilized conveniences. Located four
kilometers south of Akumal off Mexico 307; watch for the sign that
says "La Playa Más Bonita en el Mundo" (The Most Beautiful Beach in
the World).
   Another vision of loveliness, **Playa Xcacel** is a fresh little beach
facing the open sea with waves just strong enough for body-surfing.
The thick white sand runs down from a still palm grove to a row of
palapa shelters. A shipwreck is visible from the shore. Camping is great
under the palms. Located 12 kilometers south of Akumal, off Mexico
307.
   Beautiful in its own right, **Playa Aventuras** lacks palm trees and is
somehow left a little wanting despite its smattering of *palapa* shelters.
Backed by a lowrise hotel and time-sharing complex at its northern
end, the beach moves beyond a protecting point of land into a wilder
open area, quite empty and isolated. A pier near the hotel accommo-
dates boat traffic. Little globs of petroleum washing ashore from offshore oil tankers can blacken your feet. Located about seven
kilometers north of Akumal on Mexico 307, at the turnoff for Hotel
Aventuras Akumal or Playa Aventuras.

Tulum to Boca Paila

A fabled fortress by the sea, **Tulum** (admission) is the Maya world's most visited site and surely its most disarming. Silvery temples and columns gather on a rocky bluff lashed by transparent green waves and skirted by an apron of white beach. There is a brooding, almost Machiavellian feel to this setting of salt-beaded limestone walls, steamy jungle and pounding sea. No wonder explorer John L. Stephens, when staying here in 1842, felt compelled to look "out upon the boundless ocean."

Tulum, whose Postclassic buildings date to 1200 A.D., means "City of the New Dawn," perhaps because of the fantastic sunrises that bathe the buildings. Created in honor of Kukulcán, god of the sun, the architecture reveals obvious Toltec influences with its platforms and sloping terraces and balustrades fashioned as plumed rattlesnakes. Though Tulum lacks the grand pyramids of Chichén Itzá and Uxmal, it more than makes up for it with its stylized designs and unparalleled seaside setting.

Tulum is not large. The walled compound contains but 60 buildings, thought to be about ten percent of its original size. The ruins are easily seen in just two hours, preferably with one of the many guides on hand.

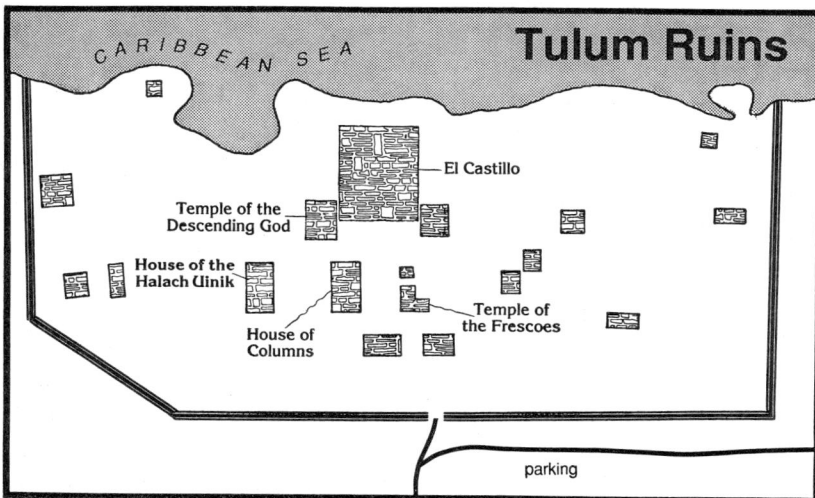

In its heyday, Tulum was home to only a few hundred permanent residents, most of them seafaring Putún. But its 20-foot-thick walls often provided temporary refuge for those escaping warring tribes. Tulum was also the official starting point for funeral processions, which, accompanied by impassioned singing and praying, departed in canoes bound for Campeche.

Besides its compelling surroundings, Tulum enjoys another distinction: It was the only Maya city still inhabited when the Spanish arrived in 1518. The expedition, led by Juan de Grijalva, encountered brilliant red and white and blue buildings stretching so far down the coast they appeared as big as the Spanish city of Seville. Approaching by ship, the conquistadors were no doubt most overwhelmed by the sight of the lovely **Castillo** looming atop the only rocky promontory in Quintana Roo. Built in two main phases, the castle is crowned by a temple whose columns are wrapped in carvings of plumed rattlesnakes, symbols for Kukulcán. In front of the temple rests an altar where, during elaborate ceremonies, victims would have their hearts torn out. Recently, the Mexican government has prohibited visitors from climbing the castle to help preserve what's left of this marvelous building.

Most significant of all Tulum's temples is the **Temple of the Frescoes**, an observatory that reveals the Maya genius in measuring days. With perfectly placed columns and porticoes, the Maya used the size of the sun's and moon's rays to figure hours of day and night. Inside the temple is another brilliant find: paintings and murals whose colors and ornamented figures are still quite vivid. Use a flashlight to best see the frescoes, which portray the Maya zest for life in flowing pictures of tropical flowers and fruits and through depictions of local farming and offerings of food, including maize, to the gods.

ANCIENT REEF RELIEF

In the days of the Maya, the reef off Quintana Roo was famed for shredding any boat that dared approach the shore. But safe passage lay in the secret of Tulum's Castillo. High in this castle by the sea are two small windows that, when illuminated by lanterns, send beams of light across the water. At precisely the spot where both beams can be seen is a natural opening in the reef.

Naturally, the lanterns were off duty one fateful day in 1511, when a Spanish ship struck the reef and sank. Of the 17 sailors who survived, 15 died of disease or were sacrificed by the Maya. The remaining two became slaves—the first European residents of Quintana Roo.

Just north of the temple, the L-shaped **House of Columns** is also called the Great Palace because it was the city's largest dwelling. Indeed, its rooms and galleries are spacious, despite their flat roofs. A departure from typical Maya vaulted roofs, flat roofs were popular in Tulum. Unfortunately, their inferior design brought them tumbling down much sooner. A short stroll north, the **House of the Halach Uinik** is an astronomer's dream. Here, inside a columned solar sanctuary, myriads of drawings and sculptures proclaim the intricacies of the solstices and equinoxes. A pair of plumed serpents, for example, arch together to show the daily journey of the sun.

Tulum's trademark is the **Temple of the Descending God**, whose guardian, with his feet in the air, head pointed down and body encased in plumed phallic symbols, is a fitting deity for divers. Mysteriously, as the sun emerges from the horizon each morning, its first rays illuminate the feet of the figure. Then, for one fleeting moment, the entire god is lit by the sun.

As recently as the 1960s, the only way to reach Tulum was by boat. But the paving of a road from here to Cancún has put Tulum on the map in a big way. This means hundreds, sometimes thousands, of Cancún day-trippers arrive by bus every day. Clad in swimsuits and armed with cameras, they pour across the ruins and jockey for good camera angles—a sight that would horrify Tulum's ancient residents. To skip the midday crush, catch a public bus or drive your own car and arrive early (around 8 a.m.) or late (3 p.m.). Another tip: The guides here are expensive (about US$20 per hour), so it's best to share a guide with other visitors. Finding the other visitors will be your job. If you're lucky, you can hook up with a group tour in progress and then just tip the guide. Most guides are locals whose Maya stories may or may not be entirely accurate, even if they are told with great enthusiasm.

Like many other ancient Maya sites, Tulum is a paradox. Right at the entrance to this age-old compound is modern-day capitalism: rows and rows of vendors hawking everything from muy cheapo T-shirts to pricey carved masks. Just south of the ruins down a crumbly road is the actual **pueblo of Tulum**, a drab eye-blink off the highway, with a few stores, a taco shop and a *palapa*-roofed church blending Maya and Catholic traditions.

South from here is a traveler's tropical dream: nine kilometers of lonely beach, scattered with coconut palms and weathered cabanas, looking like something out of *Robinson Crusoe*. This idyllic, largely undiscovered finger of coast is a favorite of backpackers and campers, who fasten their hammocks to coconut trees and sleep under the stars. The coastal road is only partly paved and winds through shaggy rainforest to the outpost of **Boca Paila**, and beyond this secluded point to the lobster fishing village of **Punta Allen**. Both villages lie within the

Sian Ka'an Biosphere Reserve, where large-scale development is banned and ecotourism programs encourage new ways of fishing. In Punta Allen, for instance, fishermen no longer use traps to catch lobster. Instead, they create artificial homes where the lobsters must grow to a certain size before they are harvested. There's no public transportation to this area, so drive your own car or thumb a ride, which is relatively easy on this patch of backroad peninsula.

For *cenote* fans, cool clear **Cenote Salvaje** hides deep in the jungle via a muddy trail inland from Rancho San Eric. With diving gear, you can explore its dropoffs into black abysses.

TULUM TO BOCA PAILA LODGING

If you just want to see the ruins, the new **Hotel "Acuario"** (Carretera Puerto Juárez–Tulum, at the crossroads for the Tulum turnoff from Mexico 307; 84-48-56 in Cancún) has 15 rooms, ceiling fans, mini-refrigerators, hot water, marble floors, television and a pool. The owner is a character. Budget.

The badly paved road south of Tulum to Boca Paila cuts through the tropical bush of Sian Ka'an Biosphere Reserve and is dotted with primitive but personalized bungalow inns. These beach camps with

---

WHERE THE SKY IS BORN

Across the heart of Quintana Roo lies a vast coastal wilderness, pitted with sinkholes and scattered with patches of tropical forest, mangroves and grassy savannas. At the edge of this wilderness, where soft sand dunes meet the shimmering sea, the sky is born. Sian Ka'an, Mayan for "the sky is born," is what the Mayas called this coastal kingdom teeming with wildlife. Jaguars and pumas, fleeting white-tail deer and gangly jabiru storks, screeching howler monkeys and slow-going manatees—they all share this fragile world.

*Today, 1.3 million acres of this wilderness make up the **Sian Ka'an Biosphere Reserve**, where several hundred wildlife species, including many on the endangered list, are hopefully protected from the human species. Stretching south from Tulum for more than 97 kilometers, the tropical reserve offers unparalleled insight into Quintana Roo. All-day adventure treks are offered by Amigos de Sian Ka'an (Apartado Postal 770, Cancún, Quintana Roo, C.P. 77500; 84-95-83 in Cancún). Outings are limited to a maximum of nine people, and feature a three-hour boat trip, snorkeling in a cenote and splendid peeks at Quintana Roo's real wildlife.*

their palm-thatched cabins line the coast; but you have to like slumming it to tolerate the facilities (wells for washing, latrines, etc.), or lack of them.

The one exception is several kilometers down the road at **Osho Oasis** (Carretera Tulum-Boca Paila; 415-381-9861 in California). A unique, tropical-style hamlet, it is truly an oasis. The kitchen is rebuilt, modern and hygienic, featuring its own water purification. The 21 spacious, round cabañas have delightful suspended beds with mosquito nets and either stone or ceramic tile floors. Several have private baths with hot water. Meditation sessions are held on the beach every morning, and innovative vegetarian cuisine is served three times a day under a large *palapa* roof. Budget to moderate.

Farther along lie the dunelike, palm-spotted grounds of **Cabañas Los Arrecifes** (Carretera Tulum–Boca Paila), where 13 bare-bones cabañas are sprinkled inside a walled compound on a swath of white beach. The bigger cabañas come with electricity, private baths, stone walls inset with shelves, front porches and shuttered windows. Smaller huts have only a bed and mosquito nets. Take a look at the rooms before you choose; some are cleaner and brighter than others. Budget in price.

The weatherworn **Cabañas Tulum** (Carretera Tulum–Boca Paila) rises out of the palms like a caricature. What is this big, well-lit building, with 18 stone cabañas half sunk in drifts of sand, doing on this skinny jungle backroad? Just relaxing and waiting for people like you. It's one of those hip hangouts only the offbeat-elite really appreciate. There's erratic lighting, a good restaurant and a beach to make your heart sigh. Rooms are battered but tolerable, like mini-hurricane shelters. Budget.

The paved but pothole-studded road deteriorates to dirt as you continue to Boca Paila. Here the better of two luxurious fishing camps is the **Boca Paila Fishing Lodge** (Carretera Tulum–Boca Paila; reservations required: 800-245-1950). This expensive mecca for bonefishing in the nearby lagoon has eight large, attractive cabañas with electricity, ceiling fans and private baths, all facing a heavenly beach. Ultra-deluxe rates include all meals plus a daily boat and fishing guide. The lodge also arranges tours to the Sian Ka'an alligator farm and to the ruins at Tulum and Cobá. Four-day stay required in low season; seven days in high season.

TULUM TO BOCA PAILA RESTAURANTS

There's something to work up an appetite over around here. **El Faisán y El Venado** (crossroads of Mexico 307 and the Tulum turnoff) has a

> *The longest surviving* sacbé, *or ancient Maya highway, runs for nearly 100 kilometers from Cobá to the town of Yaxuna, near Chichén Itzá.*

fresh kitchen and dishes up everything from chicken to coconut ice cream. The **Restaurant El Crucero** across the street is cheaper and serves tasty food, but it is not as nice. Both budget. Some small hotels to the south have restaurants, as well.

About three kilometers south of Tulum toward Boca Paila, **El Pairiso** (2-36-36) feels like the end of the world. Propped on a pretty deserted beach, the big round, concrete-floored restaurant is wrapped in jalousie windows to catch constant sea breezes. Pork chops, fried chicken, broiled grouper and hefty breakfasts of hot cakes and eggs rancheros headline the Mexi-American bill of fare. Budget.

TULUM TO BOCA PAILA SHOPPING

Tulum has the best shopping along the coast south of Cancún. Stall after stall fills the parking area just outside the ruins, and haggling brings prices down to very attractive levels. Silver, onyx, masks, blankets, hammocks—the full lineup can be found here.

TULUM TO BOCA PAILA BEACHES

Playas Tulum, the site of the ruined Maya fortress, has only a minuscule patch of beach. South of Tulum, however, the beach runs wild for 24 kilometers down to Boca Paila on a pristine, still untamed peninsula. Random rustic hotels, fishermen's shacks, hidden cenotes, tangled jungle, furtive wild birds, lagoons and a flourishing mosquito population color this coast, explorable via a narrow, unpaved road. The long, silent beaches have a savage sort of timelessness that is almost mystical. Beyond the Boca Paila bridge to Punta Allen, there's another 32 kilometers of solitary sand, jungle and palms. It is all set aside as an biosphere reserve called Sian Ka'an, closed to future commercial development. There's great camping here. To get there, take the marked turnoff for the Tulum ruins. From the ruins, continue on the road for Boca Paila south of the ruins. Almost any seaward turnoff will lead to the beach.

Cobá

Spread across 80 squares miles, riddled with lakes and ancient lime-stone roads and swallowed in undergrowth, Cobá is the most mysteri-ous Maya site in the Yucatán. For many explorers, it is also the most exhilarating, for here rose one of the largest, grandest cities of the Maya world. A mind-boggling 20,000 structures testify to Cobá's greatness as a heart of commerce, worship and Classic Period living. At one time, archaeologists believe, some 40,000 people lived here.

Situated about 40 kilometers northwest of Tulum, past jungle ham-lets and hidden *cenotes*, Cobá is slowly being resurrected from the jun-gle. Less than five percent has been excavated, yet it is possible to spend days exploring the broad causeways, shady leaf-floored paths, hidden caves, and temples that hover high above the treetops. The soaring pyramids and intricate stelae found here are reminiscent of the ruins at Tikal in Guatemala's Petén jungle. Most of Cobá's construction, however, lacks the elegance and refinement of Tikal. Archaeologists speculate

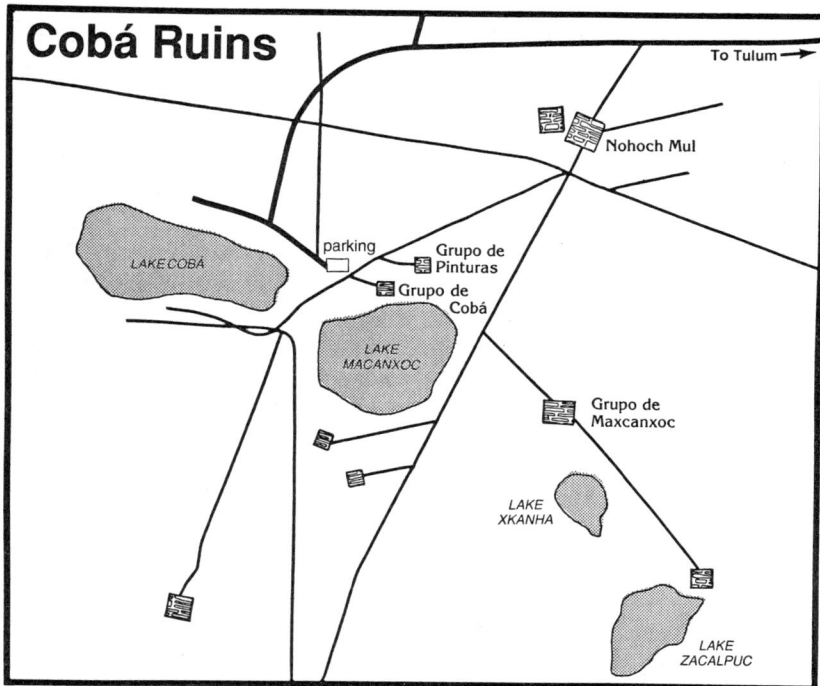

Cobá Ruins

To Tulum →

Nohoch Mul

parking

Grupo de Pinturas

Grupo de Cobá

LAKE COBÁ

LAKE MACANXOC

Grupo de Maxcanxoc

LAKE XKANHA

LAKE ZACALPUC

Several of Cobá's stelae appear to portray women rulers from Tikal who married Cobá rulers—a logical link between two great cities.

that perhaps Cobá's designers didn't enjoy the *haute école* talents of their southern neighbors. Or maybe, in an effort to impress those neighbors, they simply built too fast to worry about the finer points of construction.

Cobá rests amid five rippling lakes, a fitting setting for a place whose name means "ruffled water." During its heyday from 600 to 900 A.D., thousands of small houses were sprinkled around the lakes and through the forest, and 20 courtyards provided social hubs for an elite society. An intricate network of *sacbes*, or ancient Maya highways, radiated out from Cobá toward other settlements. Today, over 45 *sacbes* survive. Also called "white roads" because their white rock finish glows at night, the *sacbes* were probably more ceremonial than functional, since the Maya had no pack animals to carry their goods along these avenues.

Because of the distance between ruins, and because very little is unearthed, it's best to start with a guide. Several are available, for a fee, near the Cobá entrance. From here, trails wind through the rainforest to marked ruins, many mere rubble heaps. Off the main trail, the first set of buildings is the **Grupo de Cobá**, fashioned around a sunken patio. Here stands the crumbly **Iglesia**, or church, pyramid with its rounded corners and superimposed platforms. At 78 feet, it is Cobá's second-highest building. If you're skilled at climbing steep steps, ascend to the top for a jungle panorama. Back on terra firma, slip through the vaulted rock tunnel that heads off south from Iglesia.

Farther down the main trail, a side trail leads to the **Grupo de Pinturas**, or paintings group, named for the drawings and hieroglyphs painted in a riot of colors. Thought to be from Cobá's last period, most are now badly faded, thanks to centuries of sun, rain and looters. Here, a four-tiered pyramid is topped by a little temple with sun-bleached murals and inexplicable Postclassic inscriptions. A short stroll from here, the **Maxcanxoc Group** rewards with stelae carved with detailed portraits and inscriptions.

Cobá's most striking site is the 140-foot **Nohoch Mul** pyramid (located about a half-mile northeast of Iglesia), the tallest in northern Yucatán, rising like an island out of a sea of trees. Its creators were obviously thinking of Tikal's pyramid when they dramatically placed 120 steps down the face of the building. However, instead of crowning it with a grand Tikal-style temple, they settled for a small, squat temple. At the entrance to the temple are carvings of the same upside-down, descending god found at Tulum. The jungle view from up here is mood-heightening.

Unlike Tulum, which is cooled by sea breezes, Cobá gets numb-ingly hot. Try to visit in the morning or late afternoon. No matter when you arrive, you'll feel like you have the place to yourself. The solitude here only adds to the sense of otherworldliness.

COBÁ LODGING

To truly immerse yourself in the mood of Cobá, stay at **Villa Arqueo-lógica Cobá** (reservations: 800-258-2633). Parked at the entrance to these fascinating ruins and offering the only good accommodations for miles around, the charming, two-story villas are a splendid choice for Mayaphiles. There's a library well-stocked with books and videos on the Maya world, and 40 air-conditioned guest rooms designed with real local flavor: woven hemp blankets, red tile floors, and white stucco walls worn to a perfect Mexican patina. And though they're small, the rooms aren't stuffy. Owned by Club Med, the lodge also offers a good restaurant, swimming pool and tennis court. Moderate to deluxe.

COBÁ RESTAURANTS

Only a handful of restaurants provide dining near the ruins. In the village of Cobá, **El Bocadito** ("Little Mouthful") has budget-priced sandwiches and beef and chicken dishes that, though average-tasting, will boost your energy for climbing pyramids. The quaint eatery also serves up indigenous surroundings with its ragged thatched roof, red tile floors and jungle bouquets set on linen tablecloths.

If you're serious about a good meal, or just want to overhear the latest Cobá gossip, dine at Club Med's **Villa Arqueológica Cobá**,

---

THE CHICLEROS OF QUINTANA ROO

Until tourism came to Quintana Roo, local business mainly centered around chicling. Chicle is the gooey sap of the sapodilla tree that's extracted by workers called chicleros and used to make chewing gum. Since the turn of the century, the Maya have been skilled chicleros, though business really picked up after World War I when everyone started chewing gum (remember Chiclets?).

Getting to the sap is not easy, since a chiclero must climb 40 to 60 feet up the tree, then, working his way back down, use a machete to slash deep zigzags along the trunk. The sap slowly zigs and zags down the tree and into a bag at the base of the trunk. The chicle is boiled down, formed into blocks and shipped to North America. While searching the Yucatán wilds for sapodilla trees, many a chiclero has happened upon ancient Maya cities that now, thanks to tourism, are world-famous ruins.

located next to the ruins entrance. Archaeologists, Mayaphiles and other experts trade stories in this spacious, formal dining room. To match the conversation, the international cuisine features a choice of chicken, beef or seafood dishes. Moderate to deluxe.

Chetumal Area

Chetumal, set on the edge of Belize and the capital of Quintana Roo, is probably Mexico's nicest border town. Throwing off its shady past as a smuggler's haven and its former isolation, the town has grown into a modern free port, importing all sorts of foreign goods and exporting hardwoods from the peninsula's jungles. Chetumal's 190,000 inhabitants include many professionals, who give the city a corporate edge and provide the daily downtown hustle and bustle.

At the end of busy, store-lined Avenida de los Héroes, the beautiful bayside **Plaza Cívica** and **Parque Central** have colored fountains, grand monuments and live folkloric performances on weekends. A lovely **malecón** curves along Boulevard Bahía, following the contours of the bay. A **balneario**, or bathing resort, northeast of the square provides facilities but no beach. In a town full of statues, the most arresting is the **Alegoría de Mestizaje** (Avenida de los Héroes near Avenida Mahatma Gandhi), a sculpted saga of the offspring of an Indian woman and a Spanish man.

Along the Parque Central, the **Tourist Information Office** (second floor of the Government Palace, Avenida de los Héroes; 2-08-55), can help you get around the area. Open until 9 p.m. weekdays, the office has helpful, English-speaking staff.

Few travelers stay long in Chetumal, preferring to see the real wonder of south Quintana Roo: **Kohunlich**. This marvelously obscure Maya city lies 70 kilometers west of Chetumal off Mexico 186, where a side road tunnels through the jungle to the ruins. Little publicized and least visited of all Yucatán ruins, Kohunlich presents a long-forgotten world, half-consumed by Edenic forest and hills of brush. Built during Classic times, from 300 to 600 A.D., it harbors one of the Yucatán's oldest ball courts as well as a fantastic hydraulic system that channeled rainwater into a huge reservoir. Two hundred mounds of rubble and several stelae dot this wooded wonderland where lizards flit among ferns and orchids and bromeliads hang from trees like giant Christmas ornaments. Cohune palms, sacred to the Maya for their healing oils, fan out across the landscape like nature's giants.

Deep in the palm forest stands Kohunlich's crowning glory, the **Pyramid of the Masks**, whose stairway is carved with huge and im-

Kohunlich is so rarely visited that there's no public transport to the ruins.

peccably detailed masks of Maya gods. A thrill for any Mayaphile, the stucco masks stand about six feet high, their bulging tongues, handlebar mustaches and saucer eyes forming a haunting picture. Different from Maya masks found anywhere else, these are the faces of Kinich Ahau, the sun-eyed lord, worshipped by the people of Kohunlich. Across his eyes are the hieroglyph for kin, meaning sun, day or time.

How fitting that the modern-day discoverer of Kohunlich should be a distant kin to those original residents. In the 1960s, Maya Ignacio Ek uncovered the ruins while hunting one day. Ronald Wright, in his book *Time Among the Maya*, tells how Ek's dogs chased a *tepeizquinte* (a piglike creature) down a burrow in a mound covered with cohune palms. Ek enlarged the hole with a stick and "saw the giant face of an ancient god, hidden by the jungle for more than a thousand years." Archaeologists excavated the masks and some of the buildings, and left Ek as caretaker and guide, which he remained until he retired in 1991. Now Ek's son, Francisco Ek, watches over Kohunlich. He will tell you much about this mystical place, and about the Maya of today and yesterday.

Driving your own car is by far the best way to get to Kohunlich (you'll have plenty of time to listen to Ek). You can hire a taxi from Chetumal, but drivers charge about US$80 for an all-day trip, so find some comrades to split the fare. There's a small admission charge.

Due east of Chetumal, about 30 kilometers offshore, lies **Banco Chinchorro**, the ship-eating shoal of reefs every diver dreams of exploring. Skiffs can be rented at the dozing pueblo of Xcalak, about 180 kilometers southeast of Chetumal (via Mexico 307 and a desolate unpaved coastal road).

Laguna de Bacalar, about 40 kilometers northwest of Chetumal off Mexico 307, is called "The Lagoon of Seven Colors" and "The Place Where the Rainbow Is Born." It boasts pure, clear, placid water, streaked with flamboyant blues that resemble strips of satin. A *balneario*, or bathing resort, provides bathroom facilities, a restaurant and pier. Little open-air restaurants line the shore. **Fuerte San Felipe Bacalar**, built in 1729 to fend off pirate attacks, peers out from a hillside near the *balneario* and contains a small museum of regional artifacts.

The lakelike **Cenote Azul**, located off Mexico 307 at Km. 34 just south of Laguna de Bacalar, forms an immense circle edged in jungle growth. Its inert blue-black waters, the color of India ink, give you an eerie feeling as you swim out and peer down into unknown depths. A tropical restaurant with a menagerie of exotic birds overlooks the *cenote*.

Pretty and peaceful **Laguna Milagros**, little sister of Bacalar and about 12 kilometers west of Chetumal off Mexico 186, lies fringed in lazy restaurants and grassy, palm-shaded shores.

CHETUMAL AREA LODGING

Unless you're a fan of hot, bustling cities, you probably won't want to stay in Chetumal. For those who do need a bed for the night, there are several low-cost, no-frills hotels. No matter what time of year you visit, Chetumal is steamy, so go for a room with air-conditioning.

By far the best place to hang your hat is the classy **Los Cocos** (Avenida Héroes 138; 2-05-44), formerly Hotel Del Prado. The peaceful interior garden, with its swimming pool and gardens dotted with white furniture, gives a sense of having left the city. Good-sized and air-conditioned, the 80 rooms have been redone with tirol (textured) walls, contemporary decor, televisions, phones, small terraces and seating areas. Moderate to deluxe.

Not far from Central Park, in the heart of the restaurant and hotel district, **Jacaranda** (Avenida Alvaro Obregón 201; 2-14-55) offers bare-bones accommodations at rock-bottom prices. The midrise hotel's 46 rooms have blank walls and clean sheets, and welcome breathing space. Fluorescent lights blink in the hallways. The rooms with air-conditioning keep city noise and heat at bay. Budget

Chetumal's oldest hostelry and one of the least expensive is the motel-style **Hotel El Dorado** (Avenida Cinco de Mayo 42; 2-03-15), near the plaza. Its 27 rooms are air-conditioned and have been renovated. Ask for an upstairs room with balcony. Budget.

A pleasant alternative is the reasonably priced **Hotel Caribe Princess** (Avenida Alvaro Obregón 168; 2-09-00), a few blocks off the main drag. Its ugly concrete-molded exterior belies a comfortable, friendly interior of plain, air-conditioned rooms with carpets, phones and balconies. Budget.

The **Hotel Continental Caribe** (Avenida Héroes 171; 2-11-00) looks strangely out of place with its stark modern facade wedged between chaotic storefronts. Inside, things brighten up with a lush atrium decorated with fountains and swimming pool. The 61 rooms are sterile but thankfully clean and air-conditioned, with servibar and television. Moderate.

About 40 kilometers north of Chetumal on brilliant Laguna de Bacalar is a wonderfully peaceful spot to stay, the quiet **Hotel Laguna** (Mexico 307, Cenote Azul turnoff; 2-35-17 in Chetumal). Rising three stories, it reveals a turquoise-and-white facade nestled in shade trees and reflecting the jeweled sheen of the lagoon. The spacious, pale-blue guest rooms, freshened by breezes and expansive terraces, have ceiling fans and shell lamps. A shimmering pool, patio-bar and restaurant overlook the water. Budget.

CHETUMAL RESTAURANTS

There are lots of choices here and you'll find restaurant prices overall quite reasonable. Start with **Restaurant La Ostra** (Calle Efraím Aguilar 162; 2-04-52), off Avenida Héroes near the Aqua Potable Tower. Air-conditioned and clean, it serves typical Mexican dishes and a hearty breakfast. Budget.

A pleasant spot for breakfast or evening coffee, **Café Pérez Quintal** (Edifio 7 de Deciembre 4 and Calle 22 de Enero) adjacent to the Government Palace is an open-air café facing the tree-filled Parque Central. Here you'll find delicious omelettes, seafood, sandwiches, fruit salads and meats. Budget.

For pizza, you cannot go wrong at popular, attractive **Sergio's Pizza** (Avenida Alvaro Obregón 182), where the excellent service is second only to the crisp crust. Air-conditioned and sparkling like an English bistro, it is adorned with beautiful stained glass, wood paneled walls and bottles of pricey liquor lining the bar. Sergio's also features a salad bar, cheese fondue, barbecued ribs and a respectable wine list. Lunch and dinner. Budget to moderate.

Next door, same ownership, is the modern and elegant **Maria Restaurante** (Avenida Alvaro Obregón; 2-04-91), a splendid room with open kitchen, polished tile floors, beamed ceilings and wooden tables and chairs. It serves the best pasta in Chetumal, as well as delightful bean soup charros, tacos, seafood, steaks and giant goblets of fruity sangria. Budget to moderate.

You can watch your chicken baking through the window of **Pollo Brujo** (Avenida Alvaro Obregón 208; 2-27-13), where choices include baked, roasted or barbecued chicken, usually wrapped in a steamy tortilla. Budget.

A traveler's friend is the **Super & Restaurant Arcadas** (corner of Avenida Héroes and Calle Zaragoza). Open 24 hours, Arcadas' open walls, ceiling fans and breezy ambience make it feel like a sidewalk café and attract the local crowd. A large selection of Mexican-style sandwiches is on hand, but the menu is in English. Budget.

About 40 kilometers north of Chetumal near Laguna de Bacalar, **Restaurant Cenote Azul** (turnoff from Mexico 307, Km. 34, Bacalar) is a junglelike, *palapa*-roofed restaurant hovering on the edge of the inky blue Cenote Azul. Caged parrots line the entryway, and wicker arches define the window openings. Besides seafood and barbecued sheep, ask for deer and wild boar (not on the menu). Breakfast and lunch only. Budget to moderate.

If camping or parking for the night on a private beach, ask permission from the land-owner. You'll make a friend.

CHETUMAL SHOPPING

Unless you plan to stock up on Danish ham, Planter's peanuts or Japanese calculators, most of the import shops along Avenida de los Héroes won't interest you. But the **Mercado Municipal** (Avenidas Insurgentes and Lazo) probably will, especially on Sundays. Everyone who hasn't skipped off to one of the blue lagoons is here, fingering mounds of gaudy plastic jewelry or listening to cheap, pirated cassettes of Mexican hits. Clothes, hammocks, suitcases, dolls—a vibrant variety of sweet nothings make for a good spree.

CHETUMAL NIGHTLIFE

It's slow. You can do some footwork at crowded **Antares Disco** (Boulevard Bahía near Calle Esmeralda), but if you're over 30 you'll feel every inch an oldster. All the teens in town congregate here. Cover. In the same building is **La Mancha**, featuring a live band, singers, a clever emcee and lots of zest, energy and color. The entertainment begins at 11 p.m. and continues until 5 a.m. (or sunup).

Switch Bar in the Hotel Continental Caribe (Avenida Héroes 171; 2-11-00) mixes live Latin tunes and music videos in a mature environment where you can converse without shouting.

The Sporting Life

CAMPING

Many marvelous camping spots lie along the Caribbean coast. Developed resort areas on Cancún and parts of Cozumel are off-limits to campers, but that still leaves miles of beaches to the south, many with palm-shaded campgrounds right on the sea.

You can expect to deal with *muchos* mosquitoes and sandfleas, especially during the May-to-October rainy season. Bring repellent and mosquito nets.

Camping supplies and sporting goods can be found in Cancún at **Supermarket San Francisco de Asís** (Avenida Tulum next to Mercado Kuhuic); on Isla Mujeres at **Super Betino** (Avenida Morelos 5;

2-01-27); on Cozumel at the **Conasupo** (Avenida 10 in San Miguel); and in Chetumal at **Mercado Lázaro Cárdenas** (Calzado Veracruz and Segundo Circuito Periférico).

FISHING AND BOATING

Caribbean waters teem with sailfish, marlin, bluefin tuna (March through May) and kingfish and wahoo (May through September). Coastal lagoons excel in fishing for bonefish and pompano. In addition to the following outlets, major hotels can arrange fishing trips.

Cancún has a mind-boggling variety of facilities for lagoon fishing and deep-sea fishing. Check with **Marina Del Rey** (Paseo Kukulcán, Km. 15.5; 83-17-48), **Aqua Tours** (Paseo Kukulcán, Km. 6.25; 83-04-00), **Aqua Ray** (Paseo Kukulcán, Km. 10.5, in front of Continental Villas Plaza; 83-30-07), and **Royal Yacht Club** (Paseo Kukulcán, Km. 16.5; 85-06-41). Many other marinas also offer full- or half-day fishing trips.

On Isla Mujeres, sportfishing can be arranged through **Sociedad Cooperativa de Transportación Turística de Isla Mujeres** (Avenida Rueda Medina and Calle Madero; 7-02-74) or **Mexico Divers** (Avenida Rueda Medina near the ferry dock; 7-01-30).

On Cozumel, fishing headquarters is the marina at **Club Abrigo Nautico de Cozumel** (Puerto de Abrigo, north of San Miguel, near the airport; 2-10-24). You can also try **Carlos Vega at Aquarius Travel** (Calle 3 Sur #2; 2-10-92) or **Fantasía Divers** (across from Hotel Sol Caribe; 2-12-58). For boat rentals, call **Adolfo Garcia** (2-17-57).

South of Cancún, you can plan fishing trips in Playa del Carmen by contacting **Arturo's Dive Shop** (Calle 8, half a block from the beach and five blocks from the plaza). In Akumal, try **Kapaalua Dive Shop** (Playa Akumal). Playa Chemuyil's **dive shop**, directly on the beach, also offers trips.

TESTING THE WATERS

For the most part calm and splendid, swimming in certain parts of the Caribbean can be tricky. Beware of riptides along the Cancún shoreline from the Hotel Camino Real to the Club Med. These sudden, strong currents can drag you out to sea. Don't panic or swim straight for shore. Instead, escape the current by swimming parallel to the shore, then swim in diagonally.

South of Tulum, at Boca Paila, two fishing camps feature flats-fishing in Bahía Ascensión: **Boca Paila Fishing Lodge** (2-00-53 in Cozumel) and **Pez Maya Fishing and Beach Resort** (2-04-11). For fishing around Chetumal, try skiff rentals at the village of Xcalak.

Sailboats, kayaks, catamarans, motorboats, broncos and canoes are available at the Caribbean resorts.

In Cancún, there is a good selection of boats for rent at most of the marinas in the Zona Hotelera: **Marina Aqua Ray** (83-30-07), **Aqua Tours** (83-04-00) and **Royal Yacht Club** (85-03-91).

On Isla Mujeres, hobie cats and kayaks are for rent at **Water Sports Center-Tarzan** (Playa Los Cocos).

On Cozumel, there are sailboats and kayaks for rent at **Stouffer Presidente Hotel** (Carretera a Chankanaab, Km. 6.5; 2-03-22) and **Sociedad Cooperativa de Servicios Turísticos** (municipal pier, San Miguel).

For information about pleasure cruises, see the "Sightseeing" sections in this chapter.

THE CARIBBEAN'S MAGIC GARDENS

One of the world's premier barrier reef systems stretches some 400 kilometers from Isla Contoy north of Cancún all the way down to the speckled cayes of Belize. These undersea zones resemble a silent, blossoming dream or dazzling hallucination. To dive them is to enter another planet.

The reefs, though they look like inanimate rock, are actually living colonies of polyps that absorb food from the nutrient-rich Gulf Stream and have slowly grown into a coral jungle as complex as the Amazon. Finger coral, elkhorn, mountainous star, brain coral, purple leaf and orange tube, precious black coral with sepia age rings, plus green stinging coral and red fire sponges, which burn when touched, are just a few of the species that bloom to towering heights on the ocean floor. Hewn into breathtaking landscapes, this coral world is dappled with vivid sea fans, treelike gorgonia, prickly sea urchins, sea whips and lush anemones.

Throughout this subterranean garden are brilliant schools of fish and myriad other sea creatures: gaudy parrotfish, candy bass, spotted scorpionfish camouflaged in the mottled sand, coral crabs skittering sideways like moving shards of reef, turquoise angelfish, flamefish and starfish, colossal sea turtles and manta rays—an astonishing visual symphony rippling by, beautiful beyond belief.

But not all is harmonious beauty. Inside crevices, where you should never poke a prying hand, live moray eels, whose saw-toothed fangs hold decayed food particles that can fatally poison the eels' victims. And just off Isla Mujeres lie the bizarre caves of the sleeping sharks—the only place in the world where you can stroke a shark as it dozes in a stupor brought about by this area's low salinity.

WINDSURFING

The waves along the gulf and the Caribbean won't support surfing, but are ideal for windsurfing. Sailboard rentals and lessons are widely available along the Caribbean.

In Cancún, nearly every beach has a marina offering windsurfing lessons. The premier windsurfing school is at the **Hotel Camino Real** (Zona Hotelera; 3-01-00). For sailboards, try **Aqua Tours** (Zona Hotelera; 3-04-00), **Hotel Fiesta Americana** (Zona Hotelera; 3-14-00), **Club de Vela** (Hotel Playa Blanca, Paseo Kukulcán; 3-04-44) and **Cancún Deportes Acuáticos** (Hotel Calinda, Paseo Kukulcán; 3-16-00). On Isla Mujeres, check at **Water Sports Center** (on Playa Los Cocos) for rentals and lessons. Ask for Tarzan, a local character who is the owner and an excellent instructor. On Cozumel, try **Sol Cabañas del Caribe** (Playa San Juan; 2-00-72), **Marine Sports Hotel Fiesta Inn** (Carretera Sur, Km. 1.7; 2-28-11) and **Stouffer Presidente Hotel** (Carretera a Chankanaab; 2-03-22).

Where are the tamer dive sites? Near Isla Mujeres, Manchones Reef provides calm depths for beginning divers, and El Dormitorio is a graveyard of 16th-century pirate ships. Cancún shares with Isla Mujeres a group of lovely shallow reefs (40-foot depths), including Cuevones Reef (full of small caves), fish-rich La Bandera Reef and the ornate reefs off Punta Nizac.

As for Cozumel, its riches surpass description. The most popular spots include the sea off shimmering Laguna Chankanaab, La Ceiba Reef with its sunken plane, the precipitous Santa Rosa Wall, Columbia Reef with its mountainous columns and pinnacles, and the mighty Palancar Reef, six miles long and plunging 3000 feet, containing easily half-a-dozen kingdoms of labyrinths, caverns and ravines.

South of Cancún, there's fantastic diving around Akumal, where objects from old Spanish galleons have been recovered, and great snorkeling in the lagoons at Xel-Ha, where kaleidoscopic fish eat from your hand. Farther south, some 32 kilometers offshore from the village of Xcalak, stands the notorious Banco Chinchorro, whose jagged reefs have sent hundreds of ships to an early grave—a diver's happy hunting ground.

Strangest of all is to dive a cenote, the region's remarkably deep natural wells. Many of these wells are swirled with murky waters, where blind fish wriggle through the darkness. But other cenotes have water as clear as liquid air, making them marvelous for diving. Dive shops can point you to the best cenotes. Archaeological sites are off-limits because of lootings at cenotes.

Whether in a cenote or in the sea, the water remains near body temperature all year round and is especially pleasant in the summer. Diving lessons and excursions are not cheap, but if you savor beauty and mystery, skip a few movies back home and catch this show.

SNORKELING AND SCUBA DIVING

The Yucatán's Caribbean coast has the best scuba diving in Mexico and some of the most fabulous underwater scenery in the world. Countless dive shops crowd the resorts and beaches (most hotels have their own). Some shops feature *cenote* and cave diving. Lagoon snorkeling is entrancing for beginners.

In Cancún, a good place for instruction is **Scuba Cancún** (across from Casa Maya Hotel, Paseo Kukulcán; 83-10-11). Equipment and lessons are also available at **Aqua Tours** (Paseo Kukulcán, Km. 6.25; 83-04-00), **Marina Aqua Ray** (Paseo Kukulcán, Km. 10.5 at Lorenzillo's restaurant; 83-30-07) and **Cancún Deportes Acuáticos** (Hotel Calinda, Paseo Kukulcán; 83-16-00).

On Isla Mujeres, diving instructions and gear are provided by **Tienda de Buceo El Garrafón** (Carretera Garrafón, Km. 6), **Bahía** (Avenida Rueda Medina 14; 7-03-40) and **Mexico Divers** (Avenida Rueda Medina and Avenida Madero; 7-01-31). Mexico Divers offers trips to the sleeping shark caves.

South of Cancún, you'll find gear and lessons in Playa del Carmen at **Arturo's Dive Shop** (Calle 8, half a block from the beach).

Cozumel, the *corazón* of Caribbean diving and home of the Palancar Reef, has more dive shops than restaurants. Some of the best are **Cozumel Equalizers** (Aldolfo Rosado Salas 72; 2-33-41), **Dive Paradise** (601 Avenida Rafael Melgar, on the waterfront; 2-10-07), **Deportes Acuáticos** (Avenida Rafael Melgar and Calle 8a Norte; 2-06-40), **Blue Bubbles** (Calle 5 South 298; 2-18-65) and **Fantasía Divers** (in front of the Fiesta Americana Sol Caribe, Carretera a Chankanaab; 2-07-00). **Buzos Profesionales del Caribe** (2-10-80) has three locations on the island.

On Playa Akumal, equipment is available at **Kapaalua Dive Shop**, which also provides cave and *cenote* diving. At **Aventuras Akumal** (off Mexico 307 just south of Playa Akumal), the Club of Explorations and Water Sports of Mexico (CEDAM) dive shop is a center for recovery of sunken treasure and runs trips to remote Banco Chinchorro. At crystalline Laguna Xel-Ha to the south, snorkeling gear is for rent.

MISCELLANEOUS WATER SPORTS

Cancún offers a cascade of offbeat water sports, from jetskiing to seaplaning. You can do some plain old waterskiing at **Cancún Deportes Acuáticos** (Hotel Calinda, Paseo Kukulcán; 83-16-00) and **Aqua Tours** (Paseo Kukulcán, Km. 6.25; 83-04-00). Seaplane rides, offering panoramic views of the coast, are available from **Avioturismo**

(Paseo Kukulcán, Km. 5.5, Laguna Nichupté; 83-03-15). Jet skis are for rent at **Marina Aqua Ray** (Paseo Kukulcán, Km. 10.5, 83-30-07), where you also can arrange snorkeling, waterskiing, fishing, cruising and water fun with wave runners. Marina Aqua Ray is a certified dive center. Snorkel and scuba with bilingual instructors are available.

GOLF

A golf course is located in Cancún at **Pok-Ta-Pok Golf and Tennis Club** (Paseo Kukulcán, Km. 7.5; 83-08-71). Along the coast, you can tee off at **Puerto Aventuras Resort** (96 kilometers south of Cancún, off Mexico 307; 2-23-00).

TENNIS

Most big resort hotels have their own tennis courts. You will also find courts in Cancún at **Pok-Ta-Pok Golf and Tennis Club** (Paseo Kukulcán, Km. 7.5; 83-08-71) and **Paradise Beach and Racquet Club** (Zona Hotelera, next to Hotel Fiesta Americana; 83-14-03); and in Chetumal at the **Club Campestre** (Avenida López Mateos).

MOTORBIKING

In Cancún, mopeds (*motos*) can be rented at various beachside hotels. Try the **Hotel Carrousel** (Paseo Kukulcán, Zona Hotelera; 83-05-13), **Casa Maya Hotel** (Paseo Kukulcán, Zona Hotelera; 83-05-55) and **Franky's** (next door to the Krystal Cancún, Paseo Kukulcán; 83-11-33).

For a small island like Isla Mujeres, *motos* are the perfect way to get around. Rental outfits are ubiquitous, as are the diligent salesmen who meet you at the ferry dock, promising the best and cheapest. If you'd rather shop on your own, check out **Ciro's** (Avenida Matamoros 11; 7-01-02), **Kankín** (Calle Abasolo 15), **Kin-ha** (Avenida Rueda Medina next to the Pemex station; 7-00-86) and **Moto Rent Cárdenas** (Avenida Guerrero 105-A; 7-00-79).

On the island of Cozumel, *motos* are equally popular. Many hotels offer scooter rentals, but it's usually cheaper to rent from a dealer. Try **Ruben's** (Calle 1a Sur and Avenida 10a; 2-02-58) or **Rentadora Cozumel** (Avenida 10 Sur 172; 2-15-03).

BICYCLING

Cancún Bicycle Club (at the Hotel Sierra Radisson Plaza and Hotel Plaza Las Glorias, Zona Hotelera; 84-32-99) has beach cruiser bicycles for rent in Cancún.

For bicycles on Isla Mujeres, see **Rent Me Sport Bike** (Avenida Juárez and Calle Morelos).

Bike rentals on Cozumel are offered by many hotels, but as with motor scooters, it's usually cheaper to rent from a dealer. Try **Ruben's** (Calle 1a Sur and Avenida 10a; 2-02-58) or **Rentadora Cozumel** (Avenida 10 Sur 172; 2-15-03).

Transportation

BY CAR

Both **Mexico 180** and **Mexico 186** enter Quintana Roo from the southwest, connecting the state of Campeche with neighboring Tabasco and Chiapas. You may also enter from the country of Belize via Chetumal. From a point directly north of the Belize border, Mexico 186 heads west across the bottom of Quintana Roo and **Mexico 307** shoots north toward beaches, hugging the state's Caribbean coast. A good road system unifies Quintana Roo, connecting all major towns, ruins and beaches.

BY AIR

Cancún International Airport, located about 13 kilometers south of downtown Cancún and 24 kilometers from the heart of the hotel zone, is the major airport of Quintana Roo. Service from major cities in the United States is provided by Aeroméxico, American Airlines, Continental Airlines, Mexicana Airlines, Northwest Airlines and United Airlines.

Few hotels provide free airport transfers. Mini-vans are the least expensive way to get to and from the airport, charging about US$3 per person. Taxis charge about US$18 from the airport to the hotel zone, and about US$11 from the hotel zone to the airport.

If driving to Cobá, make sure you have plenty of gas. The only station is on Mexico 307, near the Cobá turnoff.

Mexicana Airlines offers nonstop service from Miami to **Cozumel International Airport**. Mexicana and Aerocaribe fly between Cancún and Cozumel.

Aerocaribe also provides infrequent service between Cancún and **Chetumal International Airport**. Most people, however, travel between these two cities by deluxe express bus (see below).

BY BUS

Daily bus service connects all cities and major ruins in Quintana Roo. The key bus lines are **Autotransportes de Oriente (ADO)** and **Autotransportes del Caribe**, both with first- and second-class coaches. Local service is provided by **Autobuses de Progreso, Unión de Camioneros de Yucatán** and **Batty Bus**. Main information numbers and bus stations are as follows:

Cancún: ADO (84-13-78), Autotransportes del Caribe (84-13-65), and Lineas del Sol (84-54-34), all at Avenida Tulum and Avenida Uxmal, Ciudad Cancún.

Playa del Carmen: ADO and Autotransportes del Caribe (both across from Plaza Central).

Chetumal: ADO, Autotransportes del Caribe and Batty Bus all use the same terminal (Avenida Insurgentes). The four-hour express bus to Cancún is quite fancy—complete with air-conditioning, restrooms, movies (in English with Spanish subtitles) and attendants who serve drinks and snacks.

BY BOAT

Cruise ships often anchor off Cancún and Cozumel as they voyage through the Caribbean. Companies that serve this area include **Carnival Cruise Lines** (800-327-9501), **Norwegian Caribbean Line** (800-327-7030), **Royal Caribbean Cruise Line** (800-327-6700), **Dolphin Cruise Lines** (800-222-1003) and **Costa Cruise Lines** (800-462-6782).

There is also **ferry service** from the Cancún area to Isla Mujeres. Most visitors take the passenger ferry from Puerto Juárez, three kilometers north of Ciudad Cancún, which leaves several times daily.

Crossings to and from the island are cheap, but lines may be long and schedules change. Check with the tourist department for the latest hours.

Three kilometers farther north, a car ferry leaves from Punta Sam. Both ferry trips take about 40 minutes.

Cozumel is connected to the mainland by regular passenger ferries to and from Playa del Carmen, about 64 kilometers south of Cancún. The ferries are actually private boat companies who earnestly compete, each claiming to be "*los más rápidos,*" the fastest boat to Cozumel. There is in fact an on-again-off-again waterjet service (2-15-08 or 2-15-88) that costs a few dollars more per person—worth it in rough seas.

Vehicle ferries, with highly erratic schedules, sail to and from Puerto Morelos, a village about 32 kilometers south of Cancún. The dock here was severely damaged during Hurricane Gilbert, however, and at this writing there is only one ferry a day, departing at the ungodly hour of 6 a.m. Worse yet, passengers must arrive two hours early, and then, supply vehicles have priority. For current information, call the terminal in Cozumel (International Pier across from Fiesta Americana Sol Caribe; 2-09-38) or go directly to the Puerto Morelos terminal (no phone) and ask.

CAR RENTALS

Cancún is rental car headquarters for Quintana Roo. The ubiquitous Volkswagen Beetle (manual transmission and no air-conditioning) is least expensive at about US$50 a day, including mandatory insurance. If you haven't driven one since when, you'll have loads of fun buzzing up and down the skinny coastal road with dozens of other tourist-filled Beetles. Cancún rental agencies abound in hotel lobbies, along Avenida Tulum in Ciudad Cancún, and around the international airport. Car companies include **Budget** (84-02-04), **Hertz** (84-46-92), **National Inter-Rent** (84-99-08), **Thrifty** (84-36-26), **Econorent** (84-18-26) and **Dollar** (84-20-39).

Car rentals are also available on the island of Cozumel. Try your luck at **Hertz** (2-10-09), **Budget** (2-09-03), **Econorent** (2-06-55) or **National Inter-Rent** (2-32-63).

PUBLIC TRANSPORTATION

Good local bus systems and taxis galore make Quintana Roo very easy to navigate. Public buses run up and down Mexico 307, the coastal road, although schedules are sometimes erratic.

Cancún has a terrific bus system. Main routes are Avenida Tulum in Ciudad Cancún to the Zona Hotelera along Boulevard Kukulcán. Some buses go as far down the beach as the Club Med. Others go to Puerto Juárez and Punta Sam for the Isla Mujeres ferries. Though there are designated bus stops, you can easily flag down a bus most anywhere. Fares are less than US$1.

On Cozumel, buses run from San Miguel (in front of Las Palmeras Restaurant) to southern beaches.

FIVE

Yucatán and Campeche

As you travel west from Cancún along the main highway to Mérida in search of adventure-filled days and romantic tropical nights under a Maya moon, it doesn't take long before you begin to feel like you're in a very different land. Along this section of the Maya Route, towns like Nuevo Xcan and Chemax introduce a world where things happen at a slower pace. Maya women, in white embroidered dresses that miraculously always seem to look spotless, stroll through the village streets. Children chase turkeys or sit by the roadside watching with big eyes as tourists drive by. Old men trudge along the highway carrying loads of cooking firewood on their backs.

White churches with grand facades built from the rubble of Maya temples tower over rounded, thatch-roofed huts of a style that the local people have been living in since ancient times. Magenta splashes of bougainvillea burst through the low, thick Yucatecan forest surrounding the villages. The jungle is home to wild boar, white-tailed deer, wild turkeys, ducks, rabbits, pumas and even a few surviving jaguars.

Throughout the Yucatán, you will see stately old plantations that now stand abandoned and overgrown, a new generation of ruins. Until the mid-20th century, this was a wealthy region where a handful of plantation owners exploited the Indian population to produce most of the world's henequen (sisal), a fiber that comes from large yucca-like plants and was once used to make rope. As synthetic fibers replaced henequen after World War II, the big plantations shut down and the rural people of the region returned to subsistence sharecropping. The Yucatán remained the poorest region of Mexico until the late 1960s, when the resort of Cancún was created. Today, tourism is by far the biggest industry in the area.

Each year, North Americans and other visitors are drawn to the Yucatán in ever-increasing numbers to see the great Maya ruins. Chichén Itzá, strongly influenced in its day by newcomers from central Mexico, recalls in its art the Toltec traditions of military might and human sacrifice. Uxmal speaks eloquently to us of balance and elegance and wisdom through its ancient architecture. Mayapán, for centuries the greatest capital of the Yucatán, has vanished almost completely, but Uxmal and Chichén Itzá have been restored and now attract millions of visitors annually.

Travelers who come from all over the world to walk among the ruins of a once-great civilization may wonder how a simple farming culture suddenly flowered into a great empire with magnificent pyramid temples, elegant works of art and libraries, an advanced calendar system and amazingly precise knowledge of astronomy. Or why, after six centuries, it suddenly ended, to be replaced by a militaristic system of feudal city-states ruled by warlords.

Even though the Maya civilization flourished just a few hundred miles from what is now the United States, and ended only a few centuries ago, we know much less about it than we do about ancient Egypt, Greece or Rome. Many clues were intentionally destroyed by European invaders, and many others were lost to the jungle and the ravages of time. Today, experts armed with computers are devoting in toto millions of hours to unlocking the secrets of the ancient Maya. New discoveries and new theories are revealed every year. New mysteries appear faster than the old ones are solved. As for us curious amateurs, we approach the great Maya ruins of the Yucatán with boundless curiosity and an overwhelming sense of awe. We come away trying to explain their existence with scientific theories, or with old legends, or simply with our innermost spirits.

If the big-name ruins whet your enthusiasm for the mysteries of the ancient Maya past, rent a car and discover the wealth of other Maya ceremonial centers scattered around the peninsula. There are many such places—Labná, Dzibilchaltún, Edzná, the ceremonial caverns at Loltún and scores of other sites where tour buses seldom go. Some are slowly being restored, others are in much the same condition as when explorers first rediscovered them, and undoubtedly there are still others that have not yet been found.

As you explore this enchanting corner of the tropics, go ahead and succumb to the charms of the Yucatán's 450-year-old Spanish colonial cities—Valladolid, Campeche and particularly Mérida, the colonial capital of an area now divided into three Mexican states. It is a city of stately mansions and loud, labyrinthine markets, of restful parks and plazas, of artists and street hustlers, a once-white city in need of fresh paint, proudly Yucatecan. Listen closely and you'll hear echoes of the region's unique cultural heritage in the rhythms of Yucatecan life today.

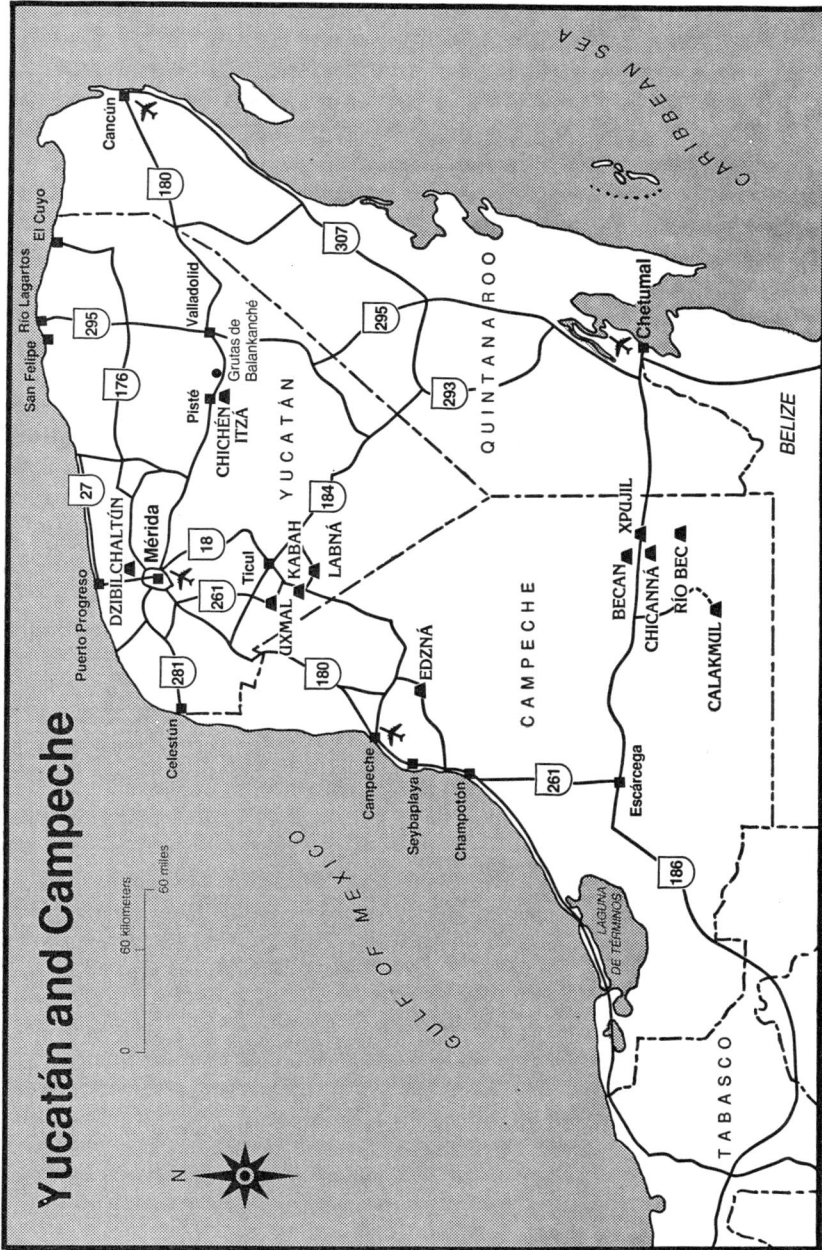

Yucatán and Campeche

Valladolid Area

Valladolid is the first major town you come to after crossing from Quintana Roo to the state of Yucatán on Route 180, the Cancún-Mérida Highway. This quiet colonial town of 100,000 people was founded by upper-crust Spaniards in 1543. It bore the brunt of the Yucatecan Caste War as, in 1847, Maya warriors massacred the town's non-Indian residents, triggering the Maya people's violent but futile struggle for independence from Mexico.

The oldest church buildings in the Yucatán can be found here. The massive **Church of San Bernardino de Siena** and adjoining **Ex-Convent of Sisal** are located six blocks west of the *zócalo*, behind thick fortified walls that defended them against frequent Indian attacks during the Caste War. All of the church's art and ornamentation was looted during that war and a later Indian uprising in 1910, leaving the interior simple and austere to this day. The resident statue of the Virgin of Guadalupe is believed to work miracles.

In recent years, Valladolid's fortunes have brightened as its location, 90 minutes from Cancún and just 47 kilometers from Chichén Itzá, has made for a steady stream of tourist traffic through the center of town. Most visitors still find little reason to stop in Valladolid, though for budget-minded travelers it does offer the best low-end lodging prospects in the Chichén Itzá area.

As is true of virtually all colonial cities on the Yucatán Peninsula, a pre-Hispanic Maya center formerly existed on the site of modern-day

---

THE YUCATÁN AND THE TEXAS NAVY

The Yucatán and its people seem very different from mainstream Mexico, and it's no wonder. Through three centuries of Spanish colonialism, Yucatán was a separate captain-generalcy, independent of both New Spain (Mexico) and Guatemala. After winning freedom from Spain in the early 1800s, Yucatán joined the newly formed Republic of Mexico—but soon came to regret it.

In 1840, revolution broke out and Yucatán tried to secede from Mexico and form an alliance with the newly independent Republic of Texas. A deal was struck whereby Yucatán would share the cost of creating the Texas Navy, and together the two new nations would control the Gulf of Mexico.

When General Santa Anna, already infamous in Texas for the massacre of the Alamo's defenders, subdued the rebellion and restored Mexico's power over Yucatán, he divided the peninsula into three territories (now states)—Quintana Roo, Yucatán and Campeche—to decentralize the power of local politicians.

Besides Chac, the Yucatecan rain god, and Chac-mool, the bloodthirsty, humanlike sacrificial figure imported by the Toltecs, there was also a King Chac, who built the Palace of Governors at Uxmal.

Valladolid and was destroyed to provide building materials for the Spanish settlement. The ancient name was Zací, and its water supply was the **Cenote Zací** (Calle 36 between Calles 39 and 37; admission), located in a park three blocks east of Valladolid's main plaza. The *cenote* is a huge pool, formed when part of the roof collapsed in an underground river. Its green waters plunge nearly 400 feet, shadowed by a stalactite-studded cavern, which you enter via a narrow, slippery stairway. Boys dive for tips from the overhanging precipice. Swimming is allowed, but is not a very appealing idea because of the fuzzy, gooey growths of algae.

To find a *cenote* that's good for swimming, head seven kilometers west of town, watching for the marked turnoff from Route 180 for **Cenote Dzitnup** (admission), the best freshwater swimming hole on the Yucatán Peninsula. Cool, crystalline, the pool glows soft blue where the sun streams through a hole in the ceiling a hundred feet above, then fades into blackness in the depths of a cavern dripping with limestone curtains and crystals. Absolutely irresistible on a hot Yucatán afternoon.

From Valladolid, you can take a side trip north to the Gulf Coast by following Route 295 a distance of 103 kilometers to **Río Lagartos** (the name means Alligator River), a small fishing village in a swampy region of lagoons. Few alligators remain. The big attraction in this wildlife preserve area appears from April through early July, when the mudflats blush with hordes of pink flamingos. To see them, hire a boat in town (fishermen may wave you down as you drive along the water-front). The two-hour trip takes you through marshlands as soupy green as a Louisiana bayou, rich with ducks, herons, pelicans and egrets. Finally, you enter **Orilla Emal**, the muddy shallows where an estimated 15,000 fluorescent-pink flamingos nest and feed, always gracefully taking wing before you get close enough for a photo. The best time to view them is early morning or late afternoon. Their nesting grounds, a network of estuaries, extend west beyond San Felipe and east past El Cayo. Rangers from the Mexican Ministry of Ecology patrol to make sure that visitors don't get too close to nesting areas.

VALLADOLID AREA LODGING

The best accommodations in town are at the **Hotel El Mesón del Marqués** (Calle 39 No. 203; 6-20-73). This colonial hotel on the *zócalo* in a 17th-century hacienda lost none of its cool, thick-walled magic in the transition to an inn. To its 34 old-fashioned, yellow-walled rooms with beamed ceilings and heavy wooden furniture, the hotel has added 16 new guest rooms. Most rooms have bathtubs, a rare luxury in Mexican hotels. The windows in the old section open onto a balcony overlooking the pool. At the entrance is a garden, fountain, lovely gift shop and colonial restaurant. Incredibly priced in the budget range.

The inexpensive, but rather plain **Hotel San Clemente** (Calle 42 No. 206; 6-22-08), located on the corner of the plaza in Valladolid, has 64 guest rooms, as well as a restaurant and bar. Budget.

If you opt to spend the night in Río Lagartos, which lets you take advantage of dusk and dawn opportunities for birdwatching in the flamingo preserve, the only lodging in town is the faded **Hotel María Nefertity** (Río Lagartos, 14-78). Inside the slumping, sea-eaten building stands a bust of the Egyptian queen Nefertiti in a fountain full of melancholy turtles. Around the patio are 20 small pink rooms with ceiling fans, cement floors and screened windows. Budget.

VALLADOLID AREA RESTAURANTS

The finest restaurant in Valladolid is the **Hosteleria del Marqués** (Calle 39 No. 203; 6-20-73) in the Hotel El Mesón del Marqués, facing the main plaza. Prices are in the moderate range, the decor is luxurious, and the service is first-rate. Specialties include chicken Valladolid-style, in a tangy tomato sauce, and fresh lobster from Río Lagartos.

Another exceptional Valladolid restaurant, **Casa de los Arcos** (Calle 39 between Calles 38 and 40; 6-24-67), one block east of the *zócalo*, serves regional cuisine such as *poc-chuc* (pork filets in an orange and

---

THE CASTE WAR

After Mexican independence, the revolutionary army of the Yucatán recruited Maya soldiers and trained them in modern warfare. It was a big mistake. In 1847—an apocalyptic time, the Maya calendar and books of Chilam Balam predicted—the native people, who had been treated with no more respect than domestic animals by the Spanish-speaking colonists, rose up in anger and tried to drive their ladino oppressors out of the Yucatán. The destruction of colonial Valladolid signaled the start of a bloody Indian war, which lasted for years before the Mexican army succeeded in brutally "pacifying" the Maya. Many people were killed on both sides, and many more fled to become refugees. By the end of the Caste War, the population of the Yucatán had fallen from 500,000 to 200,000 people.

onion sauce) and *pollo pibil* (chicken barbecued in banana leaves). A combination plate offers samples of the most popular Yucatecan dishes. The two dining rooms are spacious but rather plain. Moderate.

Río Lagartos has several small hole-in-the-wall restaurants that serve simple, inexpensive meals like fish tacos and spaghetti. For somewhat more elaborate fare, try the **Restaurant los Flamingos** (Río Lagartos, 14–78), set under a huge thatched roof at the back of the Hotel María Nefertity.

VALLADOLID AREA BEACHES

A handful of minor, out-of-the-way beaches stipples the Gulf of Mexico north and northeast of Valladolid and Tizimin. The beaches themselves are far less interesting than the flamingos, and a bit remote.

Playa Río Lagartos is not on the mainland but on the protective peninsula across the water at Punta Holohit. There are more than five miles of sand, which shifts from drab and narrow to broad and shell-packed—a beachcomber's heaven. There are no facilities here. Camping is very private, and no shelter is provided, but swimming and shell-collecting are great. To get there, take a boat from Río Lagartos across to the "island."

Like Río Lagartos, the gulfside village of San Felipe has no mainland beach. However, an island beach called **Playa San Felipe** is accessible by a ten-minute boat trip. The crumbly, thin sand curves around a soft point where the shallow water is a gorgeous reminiscence of the Mexican Caribbean. There are no facilities, the sand is uncomfortable for camping, and there is no shelter. Swimming, however, is excellent—ideal for children. To get there, take a boat to the island from the main pier at the fishing village of San Felipe, ten kilometers west of Río Lagartos.

Chichén Itzá

Each year, three million people visit **Chichén Itzá** (admission plus parking fee), the best-known of all ancient Maya ruins. Located just off the main highway midway between Cancún and Mérida, the ruins can be reached from either city in about two hours. It is the top guided-tour destination in the Yucatán; in fact, tour buses usually outnumber private cars in the archaeological zone's parking lot. To appreciate this ancient ceremonial center free from polyglot throngs of fellow tourists, it's best to visit before 10:00 a.m., when the buses start rolling in. As at all Mexican archaeological zones, admission is free on Sundays and the ruins are extremely crowded then.

Chichén Itzá is unique among Maya ruins. Its meticulously restored structures feature many columns, inviting comparison with ancient Rome. Here, too, stands the largest blood sport stadium ever built in pre-Hispanic America. Elaborate bas-reliefs and sculptures memorialize warriors of old, while carved stone murals, still bearing traces of paint after a thousand years, depict gruesome scenes of human sacrifice. None of the features that form Chichén Itzá's awe-inspiring, somewhat macabre character are common to other archaeological sites in the Yucatán; they more closely resemble those of Toltec sites a thousand miles away in central Mexico.

Chichén Itzá was founded in the year 495 A.D. by the Itzá Maya people, who migrated from small communities on the island of Cozumel in Quintana Roo. The name "Itzá" is often translated as "water sorcerers," referring to priests who divined the wishes of the gods from the waters of *cenotes* (limestone sinkholes). One of these is the famous Sacred Cenote at Chichén Itzá, which was used for ceremonies and, some say, human sacrifices.

The Itzá Maya occupied the original community of Chichén Itzá for about 200 years. In 692 A.D., they abandoned the site and moved south into the Petén rainforest. About 300 years later, in 998 A.D., their descendants returned to Chichén Itzá to restore the city's former glory. It became a part of the powerful triumvirate of Postclassic Maya cities known as the League of Mayapán, which reigned supreme in the Yucatán until 1204 A.D., when it was destroyed by civil war. The Itzá people then retreated into the Petén jungle for the final time.

Because the art and architecture of Chichén Itzá appears influenced by the Toltec people of central Mexico, some archaeologists believe that the Itzá Maya had previously mixed with the Toltecs before founding the city. Others believe that in its heyday, Chichén Itzá had established trade relations with the Toltec city of Tulá, hundreds of miles to the west on the far side of the Gulf of Mexico.

At the entrance to the Chichén Itzá ruins area is a large, modern **visitors center** featuring a relief map that gives visitors an overview of the ruins as they must have looked in ancient times, with large structures stuccoed and brightly painted and roofs intact. There is also a museum that has preserved some of the site's best sculptures. Chichén Itzá is one of a very few sites where sculptures and artifacts are displayed in a museum adjoining the ruins. Visitors to Maya ruins are sometimes disappointed to find that the best statues, stelae and bas-relief carvings have been removed to museums in other parts of the world. Yet artworks that have been left in place among the ruins are being destroyed by acid rain. At the museum you'll also find photographs documenting early archaeological expeditions and excavations at the site. Look at a photo that shows the condition in which the Pyramid of

Kukulcán was discovered and you will get some idea of the years of painstaking tree-chopping, digging and sifting and organizing chunks of rubble-like pieces of a giant puzzle that went into restoring the ruins to the condition in which we see them today.

Inside the ruins area, the first structure to catch your attention, straight ahead as you walk along the pathway from the visitors center, is the **Pyramid of Kukulcán**, also called **El Castillo** ("the castle"). This magnificent stepped pyramid, purely Toltec in its design, rises to a height of 79 feet. The main stairway, flanked by giant stone serpent heads, faces the path to the Sacred Cenote. Only two of the four sides have been fully restored, so that future archaeologists can look at the other two sides and see the condition in which the pyramid was originally found. The facade of the temple at the top is adorned by a giant mask of Chac, the Maya rain god, as well as representations of the plumed serpent Kukulcán or Quetzalcóatl. The pyramid was built over an earlier, lower temple mound, and a narrow stairway from the top, open to the public during limited hours, leads down into the older temple in the heart of the pyramid, where you'll find a Chac-mool and a throne in the shape of a jaguar.

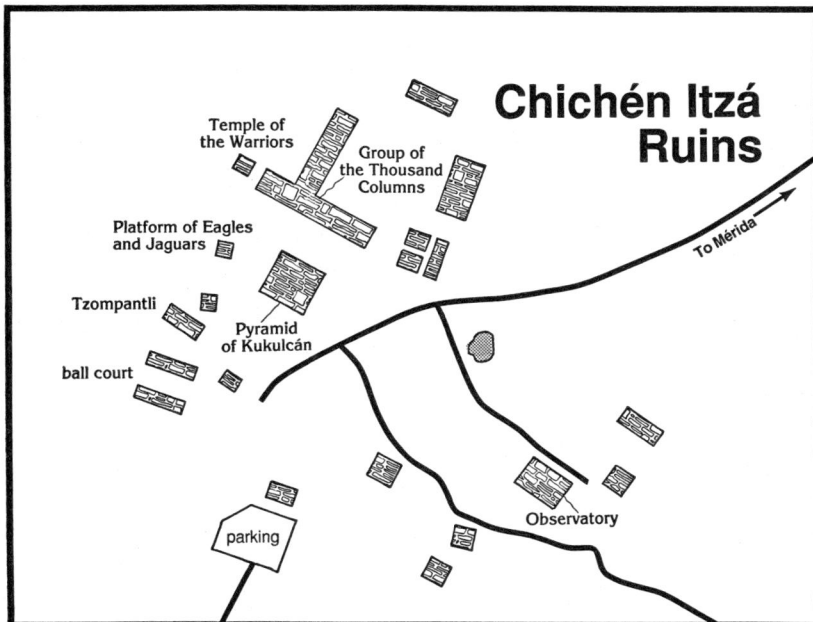

Chichén Itzá Ruins

Temple of the Warriors

Group of the Thousand Columns

To Mérida

Platform of Eagles and Jaguars

Tzompantli

Pyramid of Kukulcán

ball court

Observatory

parking

"Atlantean figures" are statues that support altars. The name comes from Atlas, the Greek titan who carried the heavens on his shoulders, and bears no relation to the mythical kingdom of Atlantis.

The **Temple of the Warriors**, due east of the Pyramid of Kukulcán, originally had a roof made of wood and stucco. While it, too, contains rain god and plumed serpent figures, the temple was apparently dedicated to Chac-mool, the semireclining, humanlike sculpture at the top of the steep stairway. Rarely seen in Maya culture, Chacmool is found more often in central Mexico, where in latter centuries he was associated with human sacrifice. With his distant, perhaps psychopathic countenance, this mythical being held a bowl ready to receive from the priests the heart ripped still beating from the sacrificial victim. There is no direct evidence that the same kind of ritual was practiced at Chichén Itzá, however, and many experts contend that this Chac-mool may have been used as a place to leave other types of religious offerings or to hold an oil torch.

Another unusual feature of this temple is the altar located toward the back, supported by 19 Atlantean figures. The many unique Atlantean figures found here and elsewhere at Chichén Itzá were each individually designed. The figures wear many different kinds of apparel and appear to have different racial characteristics. It is not clear whether they represent real persons, or whether their design reveals some inexplicable Maya awareness of humankind's incredible diversity.

The Temple of the Warriors was named for the grid of some 200 square columns that stand in rank and file at the foot of the main stairway. Each is carved in low relief, with a different Toltec warrior on each side. On some of the columns, traces of the paint that once brought them to life can still be seen. The warriors' eyes were originally inlaid with pearlescent shells. More rows of columns fill the colonnades on the west side of the temple, bringing the total to 1000 columns, which probably once supported a thatched roof. Many archaeologists believe that the colonnades were used as a public marketplace, while others think they housed small chapels or shrines.

A long *sacbé*, a causeway that was paved with limestone in ancient times, leads to the **Sacred Cenote**, a large natural sinkhole fed by an underground river, which provided the main water supply for the city of Chichén Itzá. The circular *cenote* is about 197 feet in diameter, with a sheer vertical drop of 73 feet from the rim to the surface of the water. The water itself is about 57 feet deep, with a layer of muck at the bottom that is too deep to measure.

Dredging operations undertaken by American treasure hunter Edward Thompson in 1901 turned up the bones of 50 human beings, giving rise to the legend of virgins being sacrificed in the Sacred Cenote. The tale provides a popular motif—pagan priests preparing to hurl a beautiful young woman into the murky deep—for restaurant murals and kitsch tourist art all over the Yucatán. There is little, if any, truth to the sensationalist legend. Most of the skeletons found in the *cenote* were those of young children, who may have fallen in and drowned by accident over the five centuries that Chichén Itzá was inhabited. Some sort of religious ceremonies undoubtedly took place on the brink of the Sacred Cenote, since there is a sweat lodge of the type used by ancient Maya priests for ritual purification, but many archaeologists doubt that human sacrifice was involved. Why, they ask, would the people intentionally pollute their water supply with corpses?

The **ball court** at Chichén Itzá is the largest in the Maya world. While other Maya ball courts, such as the ones that have been restored at Uxmal and Palenque and the eight smaller courts in unexcavated areas of Chichén Itzá, are similar in area to a tennis court, this one is longer than a football field—545 feet—from end to end, with goal rings 20 feet above the ground. No one knows for sure why this court was built on such a grand scale that it must have been difficult to play the Maya ball game here. Some archaeologists suggest that the game provided a substitute for war, and that this may have been the site of a kind of ancient "Superbowl" where disputes between city-states of the Yucatán were settled. Bas-relief sculptures along the side walls depict players of a winning team holding the severed, gushing head of a losing team member. (Those who contend that human sacrifice was

---

RAIDERS OF THE SACRED CENOTE

In 1901, Edward Thompson, the United States Consul to Mérida, bought the ranch on which the unexcavated ruins of Chichén Itzá were located for $500 and proceeded to dredge the bottom of the Sacred Cenote for treasure. His efforts over several summers yielded an amazing array of artifacts that had apparently been thrown into the cenote *as offerings to the rain god, Chac. The items included jade jewelry, metal and rubber balls, pottery, wooden and wax figurines, mirrors, sandals and incense. Some of the objects came from as far away as Panama and perhaps Columbia. Most of Thompson's loot was sent to Harvard University, in whose museum it remains today. Thompson's original dredge is on display near the restrooms at the Chichén Itzá visitors center, alongside a plaque in Spanish that condemns Thompson for stealing Mexico's treasures and Harvard for refusing to return them. Even today, some Maya people who make pilgrimages to Chichén Itzá thrown small fetishes or figurines into the* cenote *as prayer offerings for rain.*

A human face peering out of the jaws of a serpent, the Maya symbol for astronomers, is a common motif in sculptures throughout Chichén Itzá and shows the reverence in which stargazers were held.

not practiced at Chichén Itzá suggest—unconvincingly—that the beheadings depicted here may have been merely symbolic.)

Adjacent to the ball court, the grim **Tzompantli** ("wall of skulls") is a low platform, similar to sacrificial platforms found in the Toltec cities of central Mexico, covered with carvings of hundreds of human skulls. It also has sculptured panels of armed warriors and eagles devouring human hearts, as well as another panel that shows a winning ball team decapitating the loser, similar to the ones in the ball court. All these clues suggest that the Tzompantli was where sacrifices were carried out in connection with the ball games. Right next to the Tzompantli, the small **Platform of Eagles and Jaguars** is exquisitely decorated in motifs associated with a powerful military order from the Toltec city of Tula.

The Northern Group also includes a number of lesser structures, some of them completely ruined and unreconstructed. One of them, the **Ossuary**, a collapsed temple on a burial mound about ten meters high, has an opening in its center that descends into a natural cave beneath the mound.

The Central Group is generally believed to be older than the Northern Group. Most buildings in this group, such as the Nunnery and the Temple of the Deer, are typical of Maya ruins found elsewhere in the Yucatán and show much less Toltec influence than do the structures in the Northern Group. Recently, some archaeologists have found evidence that the structures in both groups were actually built around the same time, suggesting that more than one subculture may have occupied or used Chichén Itzá simultaneously.

The most remarkable structure in the Central Group is the **Observatory**, also called **El Caracol** ("the snail") because of the spiral form of its inner stairway. This round tower was designed to track celestial movements. The partly crumbled upper room, which is not open to the public, contains windows aligned with the positions of the setting sun at the equinoxes and the summer solstice, as well as others marking the four cardinal directions. Archaeoastronomers have also found sightlines between other windows and doorways in the building relating to cycles of the moon and the planet Venus.

Although experts disagree on how much of the observatory was built by early Maya people and how much reflects later Toltec influence, there is no doubt that this was one of the most important structures at Chichén Itzá, where religion and the science of astronomy were inseparable. The large incense burners in the shape of human heads placed all around the edges of the observatory platform indicate that major ceremonies were held here. Celestial movements provided Maya priests with their only accurate measure of the flow of time, the essence of Maya religious beliefs, and this observatory may have helped make Chichén Itzá one of the most important cities in the Yucatán.

In the woods beyond the Central Group, trails lead to various sites in the South Group, which consists of about 15 structures in an advanced state of ruin. The largest is the **Temple of the Tree Lintels**, reminiscent of the architectural style of Uxmal. Nearby, the **Temple of the Initial Series** has hieroglyphs on a doorway lintel representing the only "long count" Maya calendar date found at Chichén Itzá, corresponding to the year 879 A.D. In another crumbled structure, the **Temple of the Phalluses**, giant stone phallic monuments found in several rooms are typical of a Gulf Coast fertility cult, and are quite unusual in either a Maya or Toltec ceremonial center.

Large and impressive as Chichén Itzá is, the structures we see at this site are only a sampling of what lies hidden in some six square kilometers of land still overgrown with jungle. Every hill around the ruins is actually a manmade mound or unexcavated ruin. There is much left for future generations of archaeologists to unearth. Future digs may reveal answers to some of the puzzles that surround Chichén Itzá. More likely, however, they will disclose still more mysteries to tantalize our imaginations.

ARCHAEOASTRONOMY 101

Every year at the spring equinox (March 20) and the autumn equinox (September 21), at about 3:00 in the afternoon, a strange phenomenon can be seen on the balustrade of the north staircase on Chichén Itzá's Pyramid of Kukulcán. The shadow of the pyramid's northwest edge aligns precisely with the balustrade to cast an undulating pattern of light that joins the serpent head at the base of the stairway to become the body of the serpent descending the pyramid. On these days, many thousands of spectators come to Chichén Itzá to witness the event—travelers from around the world, as well as Yucatán Maya people who come to lay hands on the statues of the plumed serpent as a way of gaining personal power. The equinox phenomenon is one of the best-known examples of the ancient Maya people's sophistication in astronomy, and proves that they planned this giant structure according to precise calculations of the sun's path. Since a Maya groundskeeper at Chichén Itzá first noticed the phenomenon in the 1940s, a whole new field of study, called archaeoastronomy, has emerged. Today, hundreds of scientists devote their careers to studying the relationships between Maya structures and celestial bodies.

Leaving Chichén Itzá, be sure to tour the **Grutas de Balankanché** (about eight kilometers east of Chichén Itzá off Route 180; admission), or you will miss one of the most mysterious places of worship in the Chichén Itzá area. The caves, shut up for more than 500 years, were discovered in 1959 by a tourist guide. Today, local guides take small groups down into the electrically lit corridors, which narrow into passageways so tight and twisting you have to writhe through like a snake. Suddenly, a wondrous chamber opens up, with a massive stalagmite rising from the floor like a mystic tree and sparkling stalactites encrusting the ceiling like leaves.

All around the chamber's base, carved faces stare up from Maya pots, which are believed to be thousand-year-old offerings to the gods who lived in the cave. Another crouch-down passageway leads to an underground pool as still as glass, with more pots peering out of the crannies, one even sitting on its own small island in the water. The oxygen gets thin very fast, so the tour does not last long. Check the current schedule at the display in the Chichén Itzá visitors center and arrive punctually. A regional botanical garden surrounding the parking area and cave entrance building provides a pleasant, peaceful environment in the event you have to wait for your tour. Tours in English and Spanish alternate hourly.

West of Pisté, an expensive toll road ambitiously named the **Cancún-Mérida Autopiste** promises to link the capital with the Caribbean some day. Meanwhile, it merely provides a welcome break from narrow roads and speed bumps for 49 kilometers. The only scenery worth mentioning along this tree-lined, four-lane limited-access highway is the strange series of rockpiles, each painted a different bright color, that decorates the center median.

THE ILIAD—*YUCATÁN STYLE*

One legend about the fall of Chichén Itzá that you will hear repeatedly throughout the lowland Maya country is that of the romance between Sac-Nicte, the daughter of Lord Hunac Ceel of Mayapán, and Canek, the young lord of Chichén Itzá. Unfortunately, Sac-Nicte was pledged to marry the older, wealthier lord of Uxmal. Canek attacked the wedding celebration and carried Sac-Nicte off to share a honeymoon exile in the Petén, never again to be seen in the Yucatán.

This outrage started a war that put an end to the great Maya empire of the Yucatán, as the combined armies of Uxmal and Mayapán wiped out the Itzá armies and drove the surviving residents of Chichén Itzá deep into the rainforest. Later, the Itzá would take their revenge by totally destroying the city of Mayapán, but Chichén Itzá would never be reoccupied.

The older, more leisurely **Route 180** parallels the new toll highway, and you can take it for free. You can also take a side trip to the town of Izamal, 18 kilometers north of Route 180 via a paved two-lane road that turns off at the little village of Kantunil.

Izamal (population 40,000) embodies both the collision and synthesis of cultures that shaped the Yucatán. It was a royal court of the Itzá Maya people hundreds of years before the Spanish Conquest, as the surviving pyramid—the third-largest in Mexico—in the center of town attests. Another pyramid was located where the **Convento de San Antonio de Padua** stands today. The temple was razed and its platform became the foundation for the huge cathedral, monastery and atrium.

Not only the church buildings but also most of the structures surrounding the central plaza were built with stones from the ancient ceremonial center. The entire **town center** is painted yellow, a tradition that has persisted since ancient times, when all the Maya cities were painted in bold hues. Traditional Yucatán huts surround the town, and one can easily feel that life hasn't changed very much for the people who have occupied this area since Izamal was at the height of its pre-Hispanic glory.

CHICHÉN ITZÁ LODGING

Within walking distance of the ruins at Chichén Itzá, several "archaeological hotels" offer the closest thing in the area to real luxury. Top of the line—and closest to the ruins—is **Mayaland** (Chichén Itzá; phone 25-21-22 in Mérida for reservations). The guest rooms in the main hotel building, which dates back to 1923 and was recently refurbished, are spacious and air-conditioned, and most have balconies. The rustic Yucatán-style huts set alongside bougainvillea-shaded footpaths amid 100 acres of lush grounds cost more and have no air-conditioning, only ceiling fans, but plenty of comfort and character. All guest rooms have showers, telephones and satellite television. The hotel has a large swimming pool, a bar and several restaurants. Other amenities include horse rentals and tennis courts. Deluxe.

The **Hacienda Chichén** (Chichén Itzá; phone 24-87-22 in Mérida for reservations), on the same road, is under the same management as Mayaland and offers slightly lower rates. Construction of the main building was begun in the late 1500s using stones from outlying temples of Chichén Itzá. The hacienda was burned during the Caste War in the mid-1800s. Fifty years later, U.S. Consul Edward Thompson bought the abandoned house and its land, which included the archaeological zone of Chichén Itzá, for a few hundred dollars. Thompson was later deported for looting the site and smuggling the spoils out of

Mexico to the Harvard Museum, and the hacienda was seized by the Mexican government. Archaeologists used it as a base of operations while restoring Chichén Itzá, building the cottages that serve as guest rooms today. The rooms are large, airy and simple, with ceiling fans but no air-conditioning. There are also no televisions or phones. There is, however, a swimming pool surrounded by tranquil gardens. Moderate.

The **Villa Arqueológica** (Chichén Itzá; 6-28-30) is one of a chain of hotels located at ancient ruins all over Mexico, managed by Club Med. Rooms, though small, are air-conditioned and fairly luxurious. There are no double beds. The hotel has tennis courts and a pool surrounded by pretty gardens. The public areas of the hotel display an impressive collection of Maya sculpture and artifacts, and there is an extensive library of books on Maya archaeology, about half of them in English. Moderate.

Located two kilometers east of the Chichén Itzá archaeological zone, the **Hotel Dolores Alba** (Route 180; phone 21-37-45 in Mérida for reservations) offers 18 small, clean rooms with private baths in an attractive country house. There is a small swimming pool. The management can provide transportation to the ruins, though you will have to take a taxi back. Rates are in the budget range, but meals for two in the hotel dining room can set you back more than the cost of the room, and there are no other restaurants close by.

About four kilometers west of Chichén Itzá, the moderate-priced **Pirámide Inn** (Route 180, Pisté; phone Pisté Exchange No. 5) is our favorite among the numerous motels in the town of Pisté. Rooms are dark but pleasant, with air-conditioning and satellite television offering a limited number of U.S. channels. The grounds surrounding the swimming pool are nicely landscaped with palms and flowering plants, as well as a small shrine, a model of a Maya Pyramid, an artificial waterfall and a genuine Maya burial mound—a reminder that the site of modern-day Pisté was part of the greater Chichén Itzá metropolitan area a thousand years ago. Explore the back streets of town and you will find other small Maya sites dating from ancient times. On the second floor above the lobby is an extensive and fascinating display of photos and maps, developed over the years by the Explorers' Club, covering all the major archaeological sites along the Ruta Maya.

The most luxurious accommodations in Pisté are at the **Misión Inn Chichén Itzá** (Route 180, Pisté; phone 23-95-00 in Mérida for reservations), one of a regional chain of modern, upscale hotels and motor inns. The 48 cheery, air-conditioned rooms feature bright bedspreads, print drapes and fancy wall tiles. A restaurant and bar adjoin the nice, private swimming pool surrounded by lush vegetation. However, the location cannot compare to similarly priced lodgings within walking distance of the ruins. Deluxe.

CHICHÉN ITZÁ RESTAURANTS

A small cafeteria-style restaurant in the visitors center complex at Chichén Itzá serves sopa de lima and luncheon entrées ranging from hamburgers to pollo pibil. Moderate.

For a more luxurious intermission from exploring the ruins of Chichén Itzá, try a restaurant in one of the hotels within walking distance of the ruins. They are located outside the south gate, west of the Observatory. While the main dining room at Mayaland is historic and full of rustic elegance, the menu is more interesting in the restaurant at the Villa Arqueológica, which offers a full range of French, Maya and Mexican menu selections. Both hotel restaurants deluxe-priced.

In Pisté, the gaudy **Restaurant Fiesta** (Route 180) caters mainly to bus tour groups. The typical Yucatecan cuisine served here—sopa de lima, cochinita pibil, pescado à la Veracruzana—is well-prepared, prices are moderate and service is efficient, but the most notable feature of this restaurant is its murals. Two walls are painted with the artist's concept, based loosely on temple art, of each major god in the Maya pantheon. Another wall is decorated with a lurid portrayal of an attractive young woman, presumably virginal, about to be sacrificed in Chichén Itzá's Sacred Cenote.

Authentic regional food costs less at **El Carrousel** (Route 180), set under a huge thatched roof in the center of town. Decor is utilitarian, and the tablecloths are Mexican blankets. The pollo pibil here is excellent. The restaurant's clientele is made up mostly of day-trippers from Cancún or Mérida, so it closes early in the evening, before the traditional Mexican dinner hour. Moderate.

A MYSTERY OF MAYA ART

Here's something to wonder about as you view the finely detailed sculptures both in the Chichén Itzá museum and among the ruins: In the natural environment of pre-Hispanic Yucatán, limestone was the hardest substance known. The Maya had no metal tools. How did they achieve the smooth, delicate stone carvings that have endured over the centuries? Some archaeologists doubt that this sculptural work could have been done by chipping stone against stone. They suggest that the Maya people may have used a solution from some forest plant to soften the limestone so it could be worked more easily. As logical as this theory sounds, no one has yet discovered any substance in the Yucatán forest that would soften the stone. How the ancient artists carved limestone remains one of the many mysteries that still surround the ruins at Chichén Itzá.

The finest restaurant in Pisté is the **Restaurant Xaybé** (Route 180), across the road from the Misión Inn. Seating is in lush tropical gardens around a swimming pool, which restaurant patrons are welcome to use. This is one of the very few restaurants between Cancún and Mérida that does not specialize in Yucatecan regional cuisine. The Xaybé features such fare as steaks and spaghetti. Moderate.

CHICHÉN ITZÁ SHOPPING

The **visitors center complex** at Chichén Itzá has a camera shop, a fine jewelry store and a branch of Librería Dante, the Yucatán's major bookstore chain, which carries a large stock of books about the Maya, including many in English, French, German and Japanese.

Across the parking lot from the visitors center is a big **open-air market** filled with curio stands. Vendors seduce, cajole and implore tourists ("Sprechen Sie Deutsch? No? You speak English, my friend? Come see what I have for you—almost free!") to examine their wares, which range from many, many T-shirts to Chac-mool keychains and ash trays to regional products like hammocks, Panama hats and colorful machine-embroidered white *huipiles* of the type that Maya women wear throughout the Yucatán. Prices and selection are nowhere near as good as you will find in Mérida, but better than in Cancún.

CHICHÉN ITZÁ NIGHTLIFE

A **Sound and Light Show** is staged at Chichén Itzá twice nightly—one show in Spanish and the other in English—every night of the year. Check for times at the visitors center or any hotel in the area. Though the show's theme is a corny mix of pageantry, mythology and misinformation about ancient Chichén Itzá, the lighting special effects are impressive, and the show is certainly the most exciting thing going on around here after dark.

THE STREETS OF MÉRIDA

Mérida is an easy city to navigate once you catch on to the eccentric street-numbering system. Even-numbered calles (streets) run north and south, with street numbers increasing as you go west. Odd-numbered calles run east and west, with street numbers increasing as you go south. Most places give their addresses in the form "Calle 57 x 58" (that is, the corner of 57th Street and 58th Street) or "Calle 57 between Calles 58 and 60." Street address numbers, used for receiving mail but not very helpful in locating the place, are sometimes given but more often nonexistent. When used, they always follow the street number, as "Calle 57 No. 421."

Mérida

With a population rapidly approaching one million, Mérida is the largest city in the Yucatán and the second-largest on the Ruta Maya (only Guatemala City is bigger). Yet this comfortable city feels much smaller than it is. The colonial downtown area is compact enough to invite sightseeing on foot, and the city's other visitor attractions are close enough to go there in a *calesa* (horse-drawn carriage). An unusual transportation option, these are the real thing—charming old open-air buggies that have been on the streets of the city since before there were automobiles. Nowadays they look sort of beat-up and their wheels wobble a bit, but they still take passengers through the city's narrow streets at the same plodding pace as motor vehicle traffic. Rates run slightly higher than those of taxis.

Being without a car is an advantage during a stay in Mérida, because all streets in the downtown area are one-way and very narrow. It is not safe to park a car on the street overnight. Guarded off-street parking lots are small and privately operated but not very expensive.

Start your walking tour of downtown Mérida at the **Plaza de la Independencia**, the central *zócalo*, which is bounded by Calles 60, 61, 62 and 63. In Latin America, the plaza serves an important social purpose. It's *the* place one goes to meet people. Visitors and residents alike hang around on its long, long benches and people-watch. You can, too. If you're willing to try out your Spanish, you'll find plenty of locals, not all of them selling anything, happy to converse with you. Strolling mariachi bands play in the late afternoon, as lovers whisper on *confidenciales*, the S-shaped loveseats unique to Yucatecan parks.

The plaza was formerly the ceremonial center of a Postclassic Maya city called T'ho. Mérida was founded in 1542 by Francisco Montejo under a charter from the king of Spain granting him the exclusive right to exploit the Yucatán Peninsula at his own expense. The Montejo name is still prominent in Mérida—on everything from the city's most exclusive boulevard to a popular local brand of beer. Francisco Montejo ordered the pyramids and temples of T'ho destroyed; then he used some of the ancient stones to build his home, **Casa Montejo** (Calle 63), located on the south side of the plaza. It was refashioned into a bank in 1984. Walk in and enjoy the patio while imagining how the grandees lived at the time when Spain was growing fat on Mexico's riches. At the entrance, check out the Montejo coat of arms, which depicts Spanish conquistadors crushing Maya heads underfoot. It was carved by the Maya slaves whose labor built Casa Montejo. The building is open to the public on Sundays.

Built on the exact site of the main temple in ancient T'ho, the **Mérida Cathedral** (Calle 60) looms over the east side of the plaza.

It is generally safe to walk the streets of Mérida day or night. Be alert for pickpockets in the market area, the bus terminal and any other crowded places.

Designed to double as a fortress against any native people who might resent the Spanish presence, it was constructed between 1561 and 1598 using the stones of the Maya temple. It is considered one of Mexico's purest examples of 16th-century architecture. A relic called El Cristo de las Ampollas (Christ of the Blisters) has its own side altar. Legend says this cross was carved from a flaming tree that remained unscorched. The cross was merely blistered from a later fire that destroyed the church where it hung. Now an annual celebration in Mérida commemorates this miracle. Mérida's most wretched beggars huddle in the church entranceway. Give alms, if you would.

On the north side of the plaza, the **Palacio de Gobierno** (Calle 61) is the executive headquarters of the state of Yucatán. Mural-size paintings, some as large as 432 square feet, symbolically depict the struggle between Spanish conquerors and ancient Maya forefathers for the Yucatecan body and soul. The murals are part of a series of 27 contemporary paintings done in the early 1970s by regional artist Fernando Castro Pacheco to present fresh interpretations of Yucatán's cultural heritage. More are displayed in the ballroom-like Hall of History on the second floor. The high doorways and balconies of the Hall of History afford a fine view of the Plaza de la Independencia.

The **Palacio Municipal** (city hall) (Calle 62) stands on the west side of the plaza. Here the local government posts its last quarter's financial statements, showing how much it received in taxes and how the funds were spent, along with photographs of public events and projects the city has sponsored recently.

The center of the **Mercado Municipal** (public market) is two blocks east and two blocks south of the Plaza de la Independencia. It is bounded by Calles 56, 65, 54 and 59. Mérida used to have five separate markets in the adjoining district—some for produce, meat and fish, others for handicrafts and household goods. As the city's population has skyrocketed, the several markets have sprawled together into a somewhat disorganized maze of vendors' stalls, hole-in-the-wall retail shops and colorful crowds filling several blocks. Take a look at the exotic selection of tropical fruits offered for sale—ciruela Maya, manililla, mamey, lima, mango Indio and papayas the size of watermelons. Here, too, lots of fresh flowers and live birds are sold. There is a tourist-oriented artesanía section on the second floor. Another arts and crafts market, the **Mercado Garcia Rejon**, is nearby at Calles 65 and 62.

A block north of the central Plaza de la Independencia, **Parque Hidalgo** (Calles 60 and 59) is a busy little plaza. The sidewalk cafés here are a popular gathering place for foreign travelers, as well as for hawkers selling hammocks and Panama hats. There are **two statues** in the park: one of the heroic Father Hidalgo, who launched Mexico's War of Independence, and one of General Cepeda Peraza, who fought with Benito Juárez against Porfirio Diaz in 1873.

Alongside this park rises the old **Iglesia de Jesús** (Calle 59), a Jesuit church where Mérida's bluebloods congregate. Adjoining the church on the other side, the peaceful little **Parque de la Madre** features a marble replica of a French mother-and-child sculpture. Next to Par-

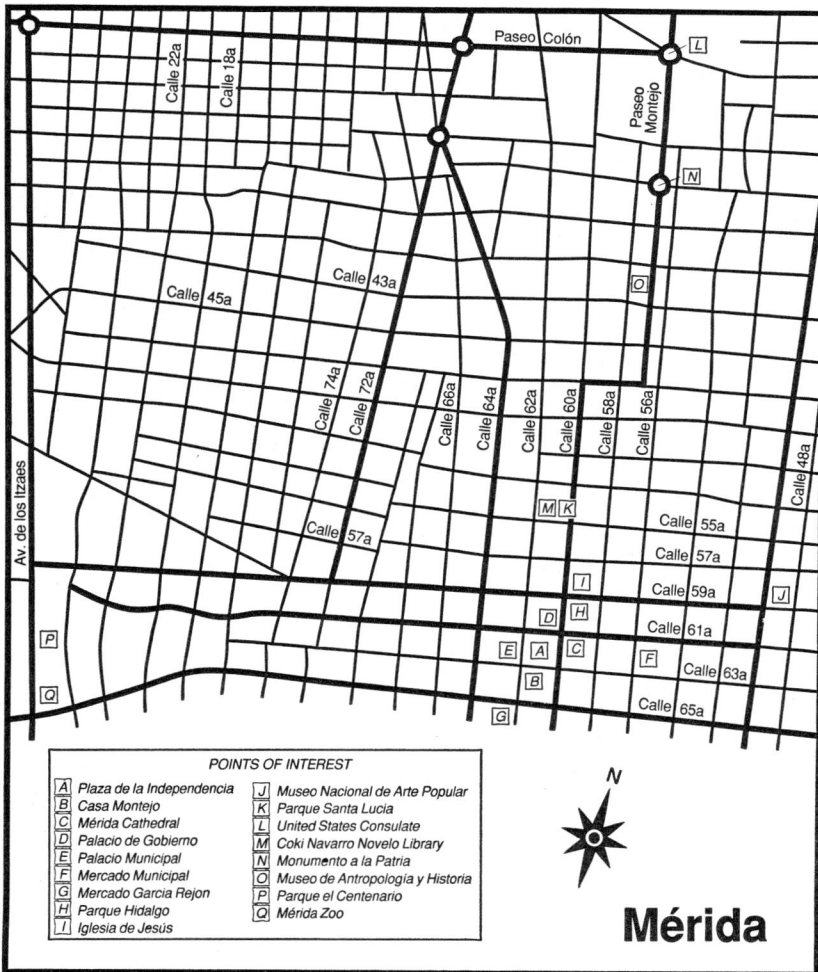

POINTS OF INTEREST

A Plaza de la Independencia	J Museo Nacional de Arte Popular
B Casa Montejo	K Parque Santa Lucia
C Mérida Cathedral	L United States Consulate
D Palacio de Gobierno	M Coki Navarro Novelo Library
E Palacio Municipal	N Monumento a la Patria
F Mercado Municipal	O Museo de Antropología y Historia
G Mercado Garcia Rejon	P Parque el Centenario
H Parque Hidalgo	Q Mérida Zoo
I Iglesia de Jesús	

N

Mérida

que de la Madre stands the **Teatro Peón Contreras** (Calles 60 and 57), a half-block-long cultural center of Italian design, full of fin-de-siecle flourishes. Many theater and dance performances are staged at this theater, which was named for a local poet.

Also across from Parque Hidalgo, the **Pinocoteca Juan Gamboa Guzman y Museo Gottdiener** (Calle 59 between Calles 58 and 60) presents a well-kept, starchy collection of old Yucatecan and European oil paintings, with a more contemporary sculpture gallery attached.

About six blocks east of Parque Hidalgo, the **Museo Nacional de Arte Popular** (Calles 59 and 50), located behind the Mejorada Church, pays tribute to the wild Mexican imagination in displays of handiwork by *indígenas* (native people) of the 32 Mexican states. Situated in a vast, decrepit-looking old colonial building with 20-foot-high ceilings, the museum also displays maps showing local arts and crafts of various villages throughout the Yucatán Peninsula. The museum shop offers a selection of fine artesanía, including beautifully embroidered women's dresses priced in the hundreds of U.S. dollars.

Parque Santa Lucia (Calles 60 and 55) was a slave market and a terminal for horse-drawn carriages in centuries past. Today, it features informal art exhibitions and, every Thursday evening, Yucatecan folk dancing. **Iglesia de Santa Lucía**, facing the park, was built in 1575 and served as a church for blacks and mulattos. Until 1821, its churchyard contained the municipal cemetery.

Just past the Parque Santa Ana, a seven-block stroll or a brief, entertaining horse-drawn taxi ride north from the main plaza, Calle 60 bends into the broad **Paseo de Montejo**, named for the city's founder. This grand boulevard, with its sidewalk cafés and roundabout monuments, was inspired by the Champs-Elysées and was once lined with French-style mansions—the spoils of rich henequen landowners who tried to give Mérida a Parisian accent. Sadly, many of these little castles are being replaced by modern construction, while others are becom-

WHERE TRAVELERS PRAY

*Five blocks southwest of the zócalo, you'll find the tiny 18th-century **Ermita de Santa Isabel**. This traveler's chapel, wedged between Calle 66 and Calle 64 at the corner of Calle 77, has a walled garden full of Maya sculptures. If you walk there along Calle 64, you will pass through the ornate old gate that was once the entrance into the walled colonial city.*

The corridors of Mérida's city hall are often the site of book fairs, art exhibitions and other local happenings.

ing bank buildings. Banks along Paseo de Montejo certainly are easier to find and less crowded than those downtown. The **United States Consulate** is located on this boulevard, where it intersects Avenida Colón. At the same intersection, a sculptural tour de force, the **Parque de las Américas**, covers four square blocks, with a different landmark at each corner. The park is planted with trees from every nation in the Americas. Two blocks farther north on Paseo de Montejo, the **Monumento a la Patria** (Monument to the Nation) presents a magnificent sculpture-in-the-round by Rómulo Rozo depicting the history of Mexico, Maya style.

Located at the south end of Paseo de Montejo, the **Museo de Antropología y Historia** (Paseo de Montejo and Calle 43; 233-05-57; admission), is located in the spacious, high-ceilinged Palacio Cantón, a former governor's mansion, and displays the finest collection of Maya artifacts in the Yucatán. Exhibits cover all facets of pre-Hispanic Maya life. You'll learn about the complex Maya calendar system and see replicas of pages from the few Maya books that survived the Spanish invasion. You'll find out about Maya "beauty" practices such as setting precious stones in their teeth and flattening the craniums of newborn babies. You'll find information about many lowland Maya sites and see firsthand the fine sculptures that were discovered at these ruins. The exhibit captions are in Spanish, but freelance English-speaking guides may approach you as you enter the museum. There is also a good bookstore that sells museum guides in English, French, German or Japanese.

A moderate taxi or *calesa* trip from downtown, **Parque El Centenario** and the free **Mérida Zoo** are located on Mérida's west side along Avenida Itzaes, the *periférico* that becomes Route 180 south to Uxmal and Campeche. Most of the city's largest park is filled with children's playground equipment, fanciful statues and shady trees under which parents rig their hammocks to relax while the kids play. There are refreshment stands and a miniature train. The zoo, though rather small and old-fashioned, has lions and tigers as well as regional wildlife such as the endangered tapir and the tepezcuintle, a greenish-furred, cat-sized nocturnal rodent that is a favorite meat in the Yucatán, Belize and Guatemala. You'll also find an impressive collection of sheep and goat species from around the world. The centerpiece of the zoo, opened in 1992, is a big, wooded walk-in aviary full of regional birds.

MÉRIDA LODGING

The largest hotel in Mérida is the deluxe-priced **Holiday Inn** (Avenida Colón No. 498 at Paseo de Montejo; 25-68-77), next door to the United States Consulate. This fashionable, modern hotel has a swimming pool, tennis courts and one of the most upscale discos in town, as well as clothing boutiques and other pricey shops off the lobby. Rooms have air-conditioning, minibars and satellite television featuring all the most popular English-language cable networks from the United States. If fact, if you stay here you can quickly forget that you're not in the United States. Due to the distance from downtown, the Holiday Inn is only a viable option if you have a car or, better yet, lots and lots of small bills for taxi fares.

Another very attractive Paseo de Montejo hotel is the **Montejo Palace** (Paseo de Montejo No. 483; 24-76-44). Offering somewhat lower rates than the Holiday Inn, but still in the deluxe price range, this hotel couldn't be better located—on the city's classiest boulevard, a block from the anthropology museum. What this hotel makes up for in location, it lacks in character. It's a pretty bland hostelry in a city full of hotels that fairly ooze colonial charm. Guest rooms have white walls, traditional Spanish-style furniture and balconies overlooking the courtyard. Facilities include a swimming pool, a rooftop nightclub and room service. It is possible to walk to the downtown *zócalo* from here, though you may be worn out by the time you get there. Taxis and *calesas* wait beside the museum.

Inconspicuously situated on a quiet downtown side street midway between Parque Hidalgo and the Museo Nacional de Arte Popular, the **Calinda Panamerica** (Calle 58 No. 45 at Calle 52; 23-91-11) is one of the plushest hotels in Mérida. The front part of the hotel includes a

---

LITTLE-KNOWN MÉRIDA MUSEUMS

Mérida has some hidden little museums that stand as monuments to private individuals' personal enthusiasms—interesting if you're interested in them. Coins and currency are the focus of the **Coki Navarro Novelo Library** *(Calle 55 No. 510 A, upstairs) near Parque Santa Lucia. Besides a collection of old and foreign money, the library has a collection of books on the subject in English and Spanish. Chronically short-staffed, this privately financed library is open erratic hours. If you find it closed, drop by later. The* **Museo Alcocer**, *a private museum open by appointment only, displays musical instruments of the Indians and mestizos of Mexico. It is located in Colonia Aleman, a suburb of Mérida, at Avenida 36 No. 299-B at Calle 21.*

English-speaking guides at the Anthropology Museum, as at Maya ruins, are self-employed, not paid staff members. They will expect a tip for their services.

vast tiled courtyard lobby dating back to the turn-of-the-century Porfirio Diaz era. The ornate opulence of that bygone era is kept alive in the hotel's common area, featuring Corinthian columns that were imported from Europe. In stark contrast is the sleek, modern highrise building behind the old part of the hotel. It is here that most of the 106 guest rooms are located. There is a fine restaurant, as well as a bar and a nightclub that has fiestas on weekend nights, folk dancing performances on other nights. Other guest facilities include a swimming pool and gift shop. Rooms are big and have every amenity, including room service and satellite television with most U.S. cable networks. Deluxe.

The **Hotel Misión Mérida** (Calle 60 No. 491 at Calle 57; 23-95-00) is a complete resort in a hacienda package, with lobby-bar, restaurant, pool, disco and shops set amid potted plants, beamed ceilings, fountains, urns and columns. The Spanish influence disappears in the 150 carpeted, contemporary rooms with demure color schemes, phones, air-conditioning, satellite television and lovely views of the town. An impressive piece of Maya sculpture from the ancient city of T'ho, which stood where downtown Mérida is located today, was discovered by workmen digging the foundation for this modern 11-story hotel. It is now on display near the front entrance. Deluxe.

Next door to the Misión Mérida, the **Casa del Balam** (Calle 60 No. 488 at Calle 57; 24-88-44) was formerly the mansion of the Barbachano family, pioneers in developing the Yucatán's tourist industry back in the 1930s. Today, it is one of the city's most elegant vintage hotels. Wrought iron, fancy tilework and a courtyard fountain accent the colonial flavor of the common rooms, while the 54 guest rooms have been renovated to the highest standards of contemporary comfort. Amenities include a pool, sun deck, restaurant, two bars and a gift shop. Ultra-deluxe.

Posada Toledo (Calle 58 at Calle 57; 23-26-90), a longtime favorite among Yucatán travelers in the know, was also the former home of a prominent Mérida family. It is smaller than the Casa del Balam—just 20 rooms—and not nearly as luxurious, but its quiet, homelike feel makes it special. Guest accommodations are on two-and-a-half floors surrounding a romantic tropical courtyard that overflows with flowering plants. Be sure to look at your room first. The quality of the guest accommodations varies from room to room a lot more than the rates do, from high-ceilinged, antique-filled suites with spectacular decor to small, dark rooms devoid of charm. Some rooms have air-conditioning. No television. Rates range from budget to moderate.

Geckos, little lizardlike creatures that make chirping noises at night, often wander hotel walls. They eat mosquitoes and are considered good luck.

The delightful old **Hotel Caribe** (Calle 59 No. 500; 24-90-22) occupies a balcony-laced colonial-style building overlooking Parque Hidalgo. The beam-ceilinged lobby, where a suit of armor is on display, opens into a courtyard restaurant. The 56 dark but comfortable rooms have tiled floors, phones, simple furnishings, ceiling fans, televisions and balconies. Air-conditioned rooms are available at higher rates. Moderate.

Just on the other side of the movie theater from the Hotel Caribe, also facing Parque Hidalgo, stands the **Gran Hotel** (Calle 60 No. 496; 24-77-30). Dating back to 1894, Mérida's oldest hotel has five stories of guest rooms opening out onto a tropical deco courtyard full of columns and plants. Some rooms are air-conditioned, and televisions are available upon request. Moderate.

Casa Mexalio (Calle 68 No. 495; 21-40-32) is a unique bed-and-breakfast inn concealed in a pleasant residential neighborhood on Mérida's west side. Developed by a partnership of Mexican and norteamericano innkeepers, it features extravagant decor blending elements from around the world—French tapestries, oriental rugs and dark, massive rustic furniture. The five rooms have loft sleeping areas. There is a central sitting room with a television, hammock and small library. Rates are in the deluxe range.

The most offbeat and entertaining hotel in Mérida is the **Hotel Trinidad Galería** (Calle 60 at Calle 51; 23-24-63). It's in the same artsy-ritzy neighborhood as the Hotel Misión Mérida and Casa del Balam but in an extremely different price range. Rooms here are small and dark. Fans and private bathrooms make them a bargain at their very budget rates. Some rooms have phones, and there are a none-too-clean swimming pool and a wildly overgrown central courtyard. The lobby, courtyard and common rooms are decorated with an amazing array of paintings, sculptures and found objects, including broken mannequins and colonial-era statues painted in bright colors. A life-size cutout of Charlie Chaplin stands beside the homemade fountain to greet guests as they enter the lobby, where the walls are filled with art by resident painters.

MÉRIDA RESTAURANTS

A leisurely breakfast spot is the outdoor **Cafetería El Mesón** (Calle 59 No. 500; 24-92-32) in Parque Hidalgo, a popular gathering place for international travelers. Enjoy an omelette, an enchilada or a fruit salad at umbrella-shaded wrought-iron tables while you try to resist the moneychangers and hammock and Panama hat vendors who work the park day and night. Budget.

The classic coffeehouse and hangout for locals and foreign visitors alike is bustling, high-ceilinged **Restaurant Express** (Calle 60 No. 502 at Calle 59; 21-37-38). A delightful spot to nurse a coffee, watch the people pass in the Parque Hidalgo across the street or write postcards under the whirling ceiling fans, the Express also has good food, from yogurt to Maya-style chicken. Budget.

A great little vegetarian café in downtown Mérida is **Restaurante Andana Maya** (Calle 59 No. 507 between Calles 60 and 62). Set in a sunny white open-air courtyard away from the street noise, it attracts a steady clientele of international travelers with its health-conscious, budget-priced dishes such as pastas, veggieburgers and enchiladas made with textured soy protein. Salad vegetables served here are organically grown and washed using purified water. A bulletin board carries notices for private classes and services available in Mérida's small but active New Age scene.

Dine inside in an air-conditioned colonial salon or outside on a starlit patio at **Portico del Peregrino** (Calle 57 No. 501; 21-68-44), a sweet old-fashioned restaurant near the university. Selections on the international menu include seafood zarzuela, beef filet in mustard sauce and baked eggplant. Moderate.

La Belle Epoca (Calle 60 No. 497; 28-19-28), upstairs in the Hotel del Parque, serves regional and international cuisine such as châteaubriand with béarnaise sauce, eggplant parmesan and grilled beef à la Yucateca in a lavish atmosphere of ornate 19th-century elegance. Deluxe in price.

One of Mérida's finest regional restaurants is **Los Almendros** (Calle 50 No. 493 between Calles 57 and 59; 21-28-51), a higher-priced big-city spin-off of the little eatery in the Maya town of Ticul some 60 kilometers south of Mérida where they invented poc-chuc. Los Al-

---

A SIDE TRIP TO HAVANA?

*Have you ever wished you could visit Castro's **Cuba**? From Mérida, you can. Travel agents at many hotels here offer three- to five-day package tours to Cuba at surprisingly low prices. Most people who take these trips are tourists from the United States. Trade sanctions that have been in force against Cuba since the early 1960s prohibit U.S. citizens from spending any money whatsoever in Cuba. But if you pay a Mexican tour organizer and he arranges Cuban food, lodging and transportation for you, it's legal!*

A traditional Yucatecan breakfast is huevos motuleños, *a fried egg served over refried beans and a tortilla, heaped with tomato salsa, peas, chopped ham and shredded cheese, with fried bananas on the side.*

mendros enjoys a wide reputation for serving the best Yucatecan cuisine anywhere. The spacious, air-conditioned, cheerful, turbulent restaurant buzzes with employees in regional costumes. Menus include photos and translations of all selections. A specialty of the house is *pollo ticuleño*, breaded chicken in a special sauce. Moderate.

Los Flamboyanes (Paseo de Montejo No. 374 between Calles 31 and 33; 44-09-88) is a modern, air-conditioned restaurant where they serve a wide choice of Yucatecan dishes, including many using turkey, which is rarely seen in restaurants even though it is one of the most common meats in Yucatecan homes. Try the turkey in black chile sauce, or even the pickled turkey. Moderate.

If you're ready for a break from regional cuisine, dip into some zesty Italian cooking at charming **La Casona** (Calle 60 No. 434; 23-83-48). Occupying a fine old restored house with a lush interior garden near Paseo de Montejo, La Casona serves homemade pasta, steaks, seafood and soups. Try the manicotti, osso buco or spinach calzone. Moderate.

For a special splurge, dine at French-accented **Le Gourmet** (Avenida Pérez Ponce No. 109-A; 27-19-70). This deluxe-priced restaurant has a classy, air-conditioned allure and a superb menu. An awning-covered portico introduces a series of carpeted dining rooms with cane-backed chairs and excellent service. Start with an appetizer of *mousse de alcachofa* (artichoke pâté), then move on to shrimp stuffed with crab meat, chicken crepes or—our favorite—venison Le Gourmet-style.

Mérida has a large Lebanese subculture, and some of its finest restaurants feature cuisine from Lebanon. **Alberto's Continental** (Calles 64 and 57; 21-22-98) serves specialties such as shish-kebab, hummus, tabouleh and fried kibi, as well as other choices ranging from spaghetti to sea bass, in a beautiful white colonial building erected in 1727 over the rubble of a Maya mound. Old statues, lamp-lit eaves and a courtyard full of antiques give it the air of an enchanted monastery. Deluxe in price.

The Yucatán is less than 400 miles from Cuba, so Cuban expatriates are a major influence in both the art and restaurant scenes around Mérida. A good, authentic, moderately priced Cuban restaurant in the downtown area is **La Giraldilla** (Calle 60 No. 484 between Calles 55 and 57; 24-23-23). The air-conditioned restaurant features specialties like roast suckling pig, sleeping black beans, green banana fisticuffs and Mojitos cocktails.

La Cartelera (Calle 10 No. 50; 21-33-28), located in the eastside suburb of Colonia Lázaro Cárdenas is a budget-priced restaurant that doubles as an art gallery. Here you can eat pasta amid local artists' works in an ever-changing exhibition that the owners cultivate like a garden. Artists and art lovers gather here on Sunday afternoons.

MÉRIDA SHOPPING

Souvenir and gift items typical of the Yucatán include *guayaberas* (pleated men's dress shirts), *huipiles* (beautifully embroidered native dresses), hammocks (the world's best and brightest) and Panama hats, and are available all over Mérida. With a little negotiating, prices are much better than in Cancún or around Chichén Itzá. In the *zócalo* and Parque Hidalgo, hat and hammock sellers of all ages are drawn to foreign travelers like flies to honey. The two main retail shopping districts are the public market area and the shops, galleries and boutiques north of the *zócalo* along Calle 60.

The **Mercado Municipal** (Calle 65 and Calle 56) is the nucleus of a rambling four-block area bursting with bohemian madness. Hammock vendors will attach themselves to you like long-lost friends. Children will dog your footsteps and beggars will put demands on your generosity. Mosquito coils, toothbrushes, bouquets of radishes and pyramids of grapes swell the outdoor aisles. The indoor stalls are packed with huaraches, sombreros, guitars and exquisitely embroidered *huipiles*, as well as exotic items like live scarab beetles bedecked with costume jewels (people wear them). Two large gift shops among many in the bazaar are **Curios Lucy** (Calle 56; 23-74-91) and **Bazar de Artesanías Mexicanas** (Calle 56). Besides locally made items, a lot of shops sell clothing and rugs from the state of Oaxaca and silver from Taxco in Guerrero. These and other items that are not made in

---

HOW ABOUT A HAMMOCK?

Visitors who buy hammocks from street vendors are likely to overpay. The municipal market is the place to get the best hammocks. Village people all over the Yucatán spend their days weaving hammocks and sending them to the Mérida marketplace for sale. It seems amazing that there could be buyers for all the hammocks here, but they are not just for the tourist trade. Hammocks are the main item of "furniture" in every Yucatecan hut, and more people possess hammocks than own shoes. The two factors that determine a hammock's quality are its size and the thickness of the strands. The cotton ones are cheaper, but nylon is finer.

Peel any fruit or vegetables you buy in the market—they've probably been rinsed in water that might not agree with the gringo digestive tract.

the Yucatán are quite expensive—often costing as much here as they would in the United States. Taxco silver costs more in the market than it does in retail stores along Calle 60.

A quieter place to browse, the government-run **Casa de los Artesanías** (Casa de la Cultura de Mayab, Calle 63 No. 503; 23-53-92) gathers Christmas ornaments, ceramic devils, painted urns, straw bags and crafts from all over Mexico under one roof.

One of the best places to buy hammocks is **Tejidos y Cordeles Nacionales** (Calle 56 No. 516-B; 21-33-68), a cooperative shop with 10,000 hammocks to choose from. Two other good hammock stores are **El Hamaguero** (Calle 58 No. 572) and **El Campesino** (Calle 58 No. 543), both between Calles 69 and 71. The shops, which are also family factories, have rooms where you can try the hammock before you buy. Bargaining is in order at both stores.

Shops along Calle 60 range from blatantly tourist-oriented curio shops to fine art galleries. Snazzy **Galería Mexicana** (Calle 60 at Calle 59; 24-52-11) stocks exquisite vases and smashing jewelry, along with toys, books and art postcards. Next door, **El Paso** (Calle 60 No. 501; 21-28-28) has bright batik blouses, handblown glass and wooden *santos* (statues of saints). Up the street, colonial-style **Fernando Huertas** (Calle 59 No. 511; 21-60-35) shines with unusual jewelry, sculptures and women's fashions displayed in antique armoires. **Jack** (Calle 59 No. 507; 21-59-88) has good-quality *huipiles*. The shop also carries cool, stylishly tailored *guayaberas*.

Mexico Lindo (Calle 60 No. 486; 21-01-26), next door to the Hotel Casa de Balam, dazzles with Taxco silver jewelry. A fascinating antique shop featuring colonial furniture, clocks and mirrors, with a few museum-quality pieces, is **Antiguedades Imporio** (Calle 60 No. 455 at Calle 51; 21-01-26). Across the street, the **Galería Manolo Rivero** (Calle 60; 21-09-35) showcases modern art from all over the world. For the best in local art, search out **Galería de Arte** (Calle 53 No. 502, between Calles 60 and 58), which exhibits reasonably priced paintings, engravings and sculptures by Yucatecan artists.

On Parque Hidalgo, a **Librerías Dante** (Calle 60 at Calle 57; 24-95-22) store has a great selection of maps and books on the Yucatán's ancient Maya sites available in English, Spanish and other languages. This and most other bookstores in the Yucatán are owned by the region's largest publishing house, Editorial Dante, which puts out everything from college textbooks to tourist-oriented comics.

MÉRIDA NIGHTLIFE

Mérida's municipal government sponsors nightly entertainment in public places around the city. All weeknight performances are free and start at 9:00 p.m. year-round. The biggest event of the week is on Sunday, from 9:00 a.m. to 9:00 p.m., when the streets surrounding the Plaza de la Independencia are closed to motor vehicles. Concerts ring out from the adjoining municipal buildings as street theater and sidewalk vendors fill the city center with a festive atmosphere. Don't miss the **flea market** in Santa Lucia Park (Calles 60 and 55), where artisans, hobbyists and local cooks show off their talents to visitors.

Every Monday evening, the plaza in the **Palacio Municipal** (Calle 62) on the west side of the *zócalo* is the scene of a regional *vaquería*, a Mexican cowboy fiesta with traditional dress and dancing that recalls the era of the great haciendas.

On Tuesdays, a **Musical Memories concert** features big band music of the 1940s—Glenn Miller and Benny Goodman with a Mexican accent—in Parque Santiago (Calles 59 and 72) in front of the Rex movie theater. Another popular Tuesday night event is the **Ballet Folklórico** of the University of Yucatán, which performs at the Teatro Peón Contreras (Calles 60 and 57; admission).

On Wednesdays, the **Casa Cultural de Mayab** (Calle 63 between Calles 64 and 66) hosts string quartets and piano concertos.

Thursday evening's event, "**La Serenata**," is the most popular of all the city's concerts, drawing a large crowd of both locals and visitors to

---

HUIPILES AND GUAYABERAS

One of the embroidered white huipiles that the village women wear might make a great souvenir or gift. Maya women have worn these dresses ever since the Church came along in the 1500s preaching modesty. Modern Mérida women wouldn't be caught wearing huipiles, which are viewed as low-class, countrified garb. Back in the United States, though, these dresses become stunning. Commercial huipiles are usually made of synthetic fabrics and embroidered using a sewing machine. Fine hand-embroidered, 100-percent cotton huipiles can be found if you search diligently. They cost much more.

For men, guayaberas—four-pocket dress shirts decorated with elaborate double-stitching and lots of little buttons that don't fasten to anything—are the tropical equivalent of a coat and tie. A guayabera will satisfy the dress code in the fanciest restaurants in the Yucatán. Unless you live in Miami, however, you may not have much occasion to wear it back home.

Mother-and-child sculptures are common in the Yucatán, where motherhood is revered. You'll find such a statue in every town, no matter how small.

view outstanding Yucatecan folk dancing performances. It is held in Parque Santa Lucia (Calles 60 and 55).

When Friday night rolls around, the central courtyard at the University of Yucatán (Calles 57 and 60) becomes the romantic setting for the **University Students' Serenade**, blending chorale music with lots of youthful public displays of affection.

On Saturday evenings, the public event is a 6:00 p.m. mass held in English at **Santa Lucia Church** (Calles 60 and 55), directly across from the park of the same name. Later on Saturday evenings, people pack the discos.

Mérida has a fairly sophisticated nightclub scene. Soak yourself in sentiment at **El Trovador Bohemio** (23-03-85) and **Salón Piano Peregrina** (23-93-76), both near Parque Santa Lucia. These piano bars feature delightful singers of the Mexican moonlight-and-roses genre, Mérida's forte. El Trovador is very dim and crowded, with more professional performances. Peregrina, however, gives a more varied show, with trios and bongos and old standard tunes. The informality encourages the audience onto the dancefloor. Both places have cover charges.

Several nightclubs offer tourist-oriented Maya shows with extravagant costumes and mock sacrificial rituals. The most elaborate is at **Los Tulipanes** (Calle 42 between Calles 43 and 45; 27-20-09). This pricey supper club under a giant *palapa* roof has its own *cenote*, where a human sacrifice is simulated. Nightly performances on a gaudily lit stage come with mediocre dinners—order the minimum. The dances are slick and flashy. There's a cover charge. Wear mosquito repellent.

The rooftop **Nightclub Aloha** (Hotel Montejo Palace, Paseo de Montejo 483-C; 24-76-44) features both a late-night dynamic floorshow and live dance music. Cover.

Pancho's Restaurant-Bar (Calle 59 No. 509; 23-09-42) looks small but actually extends back into a series of lantern-lit patios and a tree-filled garden where after-hours drinks are served. Despite the disco music, the mood caters to soft conversations. Even the dancefloor is dark and intimate.

If you crave bright lights and chic pandemonium, go and get it at **La Trova** (Hotel Misión Mérida, Calle 60 No. 491; 23-95-00) or **Zero Disco** (Holiday Inn, Avenida Colón at Calle 60; 25-68-77). Both have cover charges. La Trova has a happy hour.

Day Trips from Mérida

Three relatively short drives or bus rides from the city will take you to a variety of little-known spots including gentle Gulf Coast beaches, wildlife preserves frequented by flamingo flocks, and all that is left of some of the Yucatán's most important ancient Maya cities.

MAYAPÁN   Twenty kilometers southeast of Mérida on Route 18, the small town of **Acancéh** is one of many Yucatán settlements that have been inhabited more or less continuously since the classic Maya era. What makes this town unusual is the large **pyramid mound** that stands between storefronts on the main street, facing out on the dusty plaza. Stripped of most of its stone facing, the pyramid endures as one of the tallest and most imposing landmarks in town.

From Acancéh, continue for another 20 kilometers south on Route 18 to reach the almost vanished ruins of **Mayapán** (admission), the last Postclassic Maya capital of Yucatán. It is about 2 kilometers west of the main road on an unpaved, not very well-marked side road from the tiny village of Telchaquillo. (Note: The ruins of Mayapán are not to be confused with the village of Mayapán 40 kilometers to the south.) Rarely visited by tourists these days, Mayapán was the capital of the Yucatán Maya during the Postclassic period, which lasted for six centuries from about 900 A.D. to the Spanish Conquest. For more than two centuries, the League of Mayapán, a three-way alliance between Mayapán, Chichén Itzá and Uxmal, stood as the most powerful force in the Maya world.

The preoccupation with war is evident from the fortification wall that surrounded Mayapán. Other Postclassic Maya centers such as Tulum also had fortresslike walls. Also like Tulum, Mayapán was built in what archaeologists term a "decadent" archaeological style, striving to recapture the grandeur of Classic Maya ceremonial centers like Uxmal, but never quite succeeding. In a rebellion in 1441 A.D., Mayapán was completely destroyed, leaving only what we find there today: heaps of rubble where great pyramids once stood; *cenotes* choked with algae and water lilies; fragments of the ancient castle within whose walls 12,000 people lived. Today, most of the city site, which covered several square miles, is overgrown with low, tangled jungle. In short, there is nothing much to see at Mayapán, but for visitors who are sensitive to echoes of the dim past, it can offer an eloquent nothingness.

DZIBILCHALTÚN AND PUERTO PROGRESO   Another good short excursion from Mérida takes you to visit the scant remains of what was formerly one of the most important cities in the Maya empire, then continues north to Yucatán state's main seaport. Drive 17 kilometers

The name Dzibilchaltún means "place of inscriptions on flat stones." One of the stelae, or sculptured monument stones, found in the park is on exhibit in front of the visitors center.

north of Mérida on Route 261, a continuation of Paseo de Montejo also known as the Mérida-Progreso Highway. Located about seven kilometers east of the highway on a marked, paved side road that runs past the small Universidad Mayab campus, **Parque Nacional Dzibilchaltún** (admission) preserves all that's left of a site the Maya people occupied continuously for over two thousand years, from 800 B.C. to 1250 A.D. The city of Dzibilchaltún was one of the largest on the Yucatán for much of that time, and many experts believe it served as the peninsula's capital city. Archaeologists have identified the foundation mounds of more than 6000 residential structures on the 19-square-kilometer site.

After you stop in the park's **visitors center**, which contains small artifacts and interpretive exhibits, the first large structure you will notice as you walk along the dirt trail into the ruins area was not built by the Maya. It is an old **Spanish mission church** built of stones that were salvaged from ancient Maya temples. You'll recognize the church by its large round arch, an idea that Maya architects never thought of. Today, the church ruins have crumbled enough to blend in with the much older Maya ruins that surround it.

The stones of Dzibilchaltún have been a handy source of building material for centuries. Huts in the nearby village that bears the same name and walls around local farmers' fields contain blocks of limestone quarried 1500 years ago to build pyramids and temples to the old Maya gods. The old *sacbé* formerly used for ceremonial processions serves today's villagers as a bicycle route and cowpath. As for the ruins themselves, most are now little more than steep hills, mounds and ridges breaking the otherwise flat, scrubby Yucatán lowlands.

The main restored Maya structure at Dzibilchaltún stands at the east end of a long *sacbé* running east from the church. Known as the **Temple of the Seven Dolls**, it has a stairway leading up to a square tower-like temple with a unique pyramidal roof comb. In the visitors center you can see the dolls that were found in the temple and gave it its name. Each doll has a different physical defect, suggesting that the temple may have been used for healing ceremonies.

The most popular spot at Dzibilchaltún is the sacred *cenote* called **Xlacah**. Shallow enough to wade among the water lilies at the east end, 40 meters deep at the west end, it is a popular local swimming hole where Maya kids from miles around congregate on hot days (which, in this region, means most days). Archaeologists who dredged the bottom of this *cenote* found some 30,000 artifacts that had been thrown into the water over the centuries, probably as offerings to the god of rain. Unlike at Chichén Itzá, no human skeletons were found in this *cenote*.

Follow Route 261 north for about another 16 kilometers and you'll arrive at **Puerto Progreso**, the shipping port and beach resort for Mérida. Although its emerald green, often surfless, shallow water (you can wade out into the Gulf of Mexico practically beyond sight of land and still stand on the sea floor) will never rival the Caribbean shores at Cancún, its long, palm-lined *malecón* (promenade) and endless stretches of sandy beach make for pleasant walking or sunbathing. The three-kilometer causeway that extends out into the gulf is a pier where Yucatecan items such as honey, cement, henequen products and fish are exported to the world, and imports, primarily corn, are brought in. At the far end of the pier, the water reaches only 20 feet in depth, and a project is underway to extend the pier for another three kilometers out to sea.

A coastal highway, still Route 261, extends east and west from Puerto Progreso, following the beach for 60 kilometers and running through several small, nondescript fishing villages. At the end of the

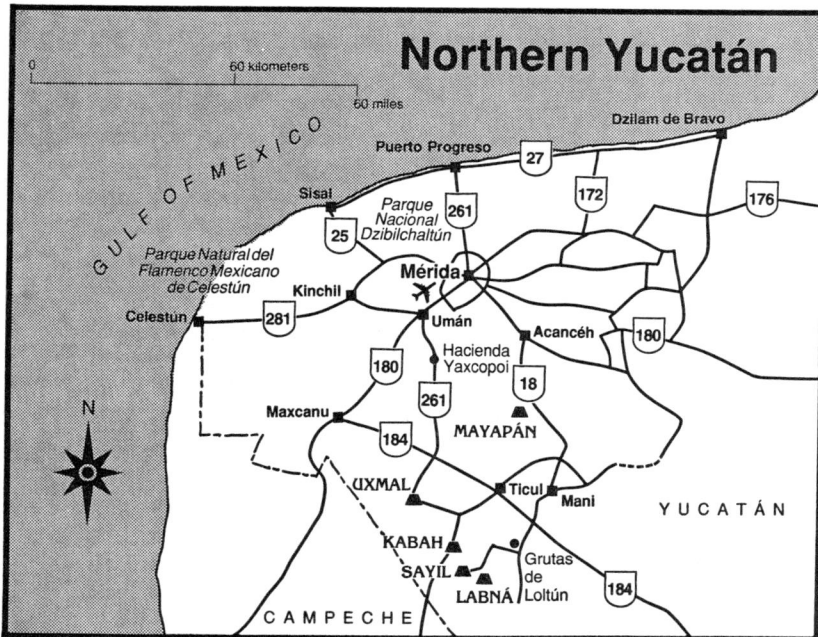

Northern Yucatán

line to the east, **Dzilam de Bravo** is a gathering place for pink flamingos and the final resting place of buccaneer Jean Lafitte, whose grave is on the beach.

CELESTÚN   A third day-trip possibility is **Celestún**, 90 kilometers west of Mérida on Route 281. Take the same road out of the city that you would follow to go to Uxmal (see below), but turn west at the complicated highway junction in central Umán. Celestún is an isolated fishing village where Mérida residents often go to lie on the beach. North of town, an unpaved road that gradually deteriorates into a soggy jeep trail leads through the **Parque Natural del Flamenco Mexicano de Celestún**, the largest of the natural wetland areas along the Yucatán Gulf Coast that have been set aside to protect flamingos. You can watch flocks of them in and over the large estuary just north of the village during the nesting season, April through June. Early morning is the best time to see them in flight.

DAY TRIPS FROM MÉRIDA LODGING

If you want to stay longer than just a day trip, Puerto Progreso offers a growing number of sleek, modern, expensive resort facilities along with older, more run-down budget-priced inns. There is not much in the way of midrange accommodations.

Top of the line is the new **Fiesta Inn Mérida Beach** (Calle 19 No. 91, Puerto Progreso; 5-05-00), a two-story stucco complex with a

---

THE LORDS OF MAYAPÁN

Legend has it that the god-king Quetzalcóatl/Kukulcán built Mayapán in 1007 A.D. The most famous of the city's rulers, though, was Hunac Ceel, the father of Princess Sac-Nicte, whose illicit romance with the king of Chichén Itzá caused the collapse of the League of Mayapán, the fall of Chichén Itzá and the end of the classic Maya era in the Yucatán.

Hunac Ceel was born a commoner. As a young man, he joined a religious pilgrimage to the Sacred Cenote at Chichén Itzá. There he hurled himself into the water and resurfaced with a vision. The gods, he announced, had ordained that he, Hunac Ceel, would be the Lord of Mayapán and ruler of all the Yucatán. He asserted his claim with the help of non-Maya mercenary warriors from central Mexico and founded the hybrid Cocom dynasty, the ruling power in the Yucatán for more than two hundred years.

lively pool area next to the beach. There are also tennis courts, a marina and bicycles for rent. Guest rooms—modern and bright, strikingly decorated in a blue-green and peach color scheme—have satellite television and private balconies. Rates are ultra-deluxe.

Another new beach resort hotel on the outskirts of Puerto Progreso is the **Paraíso Maya** (Telchac Puerto; for reservations call 28-13-51 in Mérida). This huge (more than 500 rooms) resort has spacious, air-conditioned rooms with kitchenettes, balconies and satellite television. Some rooms are privately owned as condominiums. There is a beachfront swimming pool, and concessionaires rent everything from sailboards and snorkeling gear to sports cars and motorcycles. Prices are in the deluxe range.

At the other end of the spectrum, the budget-priced **Tropical Suites** (Avenida Malecón and Calle 23; 5-12-63) offers clean guest rooms as well as apartments with kitchenettes—and hammocks!

Just across the street and also located on the water, the small, cheerful **Real del Mar** (Avenida Malecón and Calle 23) has nine rooms, all at budget prices.

DAY TRIPS FROM MÉRIDA RESTAURANTS

In Puerto Progreso, try the big, budget-priced seafront **Capitán Marisco** (Calles 60 and 62 on the *malecón*; 5-06-39), with its central skylight, draped fishing nets and outdoor patio. All sorts of seafood are served. The restaurant closes early in the evening.

In Celestún, budget-priced seafood restaurants can be found all along the beach. A typical, decent place is **Restaurant Lupita** (Calles 10 and 7), which serves tasty shrimp plates in a very unpretentious setting.

DAY TRIPS FROM MÉRIDA BEACHES

Just east of Puerto Progreso, restful little **Playa Chicxulub Puerto** launches a stretch of sand that wanders through coastal towns for about 80 kilometers, all the way east to Dzilam de Bravo. The same half-forgotten, careless air resides in all. Small vacation homes, patches of palms and sun-bleached skiffs line the narrow shores along an increasingly vivid blue gulf. There are small restaurants and stores. Camping is possible away from the private cabanas. Swimming, windsurfing and fishing are good. Skiffs are for rent on the beaches. The best beach areas east of Chicxulub Puerto are at San Crisanto and Chabihau, both tiny tropical villages. Chicxulub Puerto is one-and-a-half kilometers east of

Progreso on Route 27. San Crisanto is about 50 kilometers farther east, past Telchac Puerto, and Chabihau about six kilometers more.

Playa Progreso and **Playa Yucalpetén** are cut from the same cloth. These nice white beaches scattered with small shells provide two kinds of lounging. Progreso offers pretty sand, palms and restaurants, backed by Puerto Progreso's quaint ten-block *malecón*. Seven kilometers west of town, Yucalpetén's tidy patch of sand has a *balneario* (bathing resort) with restrooms and showers. Speedboats and waterskiers from the nearby marina streak the blue-green waters. Both beaches are good for picnicking. Camping would be mosquito-plagued and public at Playa Progreso; it is prohibited at Yucalpetén. The swimming at both beaches is very pleasant, with clear, calm water most of the year. Windsurfing is good. Snorkelers and scuba divers go to the **Alacrán Reef** (the name means "scorpion") to the northwest. Fishermen can rent boats at the marina in Yucalpetén.

Serving another holiday village, **Playa Chelem** scallops the gulf in neat scoops of shell-scattered sand and is overlooked by little stucco cottages. The fusion of the Gulf of Mexico and the Caribbean sea here yields lovely blue water pocked with the stumpy remains of wooden piers. Swimming is very pleasant. Windsurfing and fishing are good. Camping would be cramped with no privacy. To get there, take Route 261 west from Puerto Progreso for 13 kilometers.

Twenty kilometers west of Puerto Progreso, long, lazy **Playa Chuburna** slopes down from shrub-covered dunes crested by little beach houses and shady palms. Serving a sandy-trailed beach community, the narrow beach continues for about 50 kilometers west along the gulf to the once-bustling port of Sisal, where henequen was shipped by the ton. Do not attempt the rollercoaster sand road from Chuburna to Sisal in a passenger car. Playa Chuburna has small restaurants. Camping is possible there, but cramped and rather public. The beach camping situation is better a few kilometers down the beach. Windsurfing and fishing are good, and swimming is very good in the beautiful turquoise water.

Fronting the dusty fishing village of Celestún, about 100 kilometers west of Mérida, **Playa Celestún** is a long white beach flowing north along the Gulf of Mexico toward the flamingo sanctuary. Along the village beach stand armadas of little fishing boats bristling with *jimbas* (cane poles) used to catch the local specialty, octopus. Hurricane season brings a brisk north wind; otherwise, the sand, sea and palms sway in a pleasant lull. The village is full of zesty little restaurants. Camping is good north of the village. Swimming is lovely in the opaque green water. Windsurfing, boating and fishing are great. To visit the flamingos, rent a fishing boat from fishermen in the village or at the bridge over the estuary. The north end of the beach is best for shell collecting—small shells and big conches.

Uxmal and the Puuc Zone

"Puuc" means "hills" in the local Maya language, and the Puuc Zone is a hilly region that fills the western interior of the otherwise flat Yucatán Peninsula between Mérida and Campeche. Ever since 800 B.C., this rolling terrain has been the best farmland in the Yucatán because earth washes down from the forested hilltops to collect as rich topsoil in valleys below. Yielding two corn crops a year, the Puuc Zone still supplies most of the grain for Maya Mexico.

The only problem with living in the Puuc hill country, then as now, is the lack of water. There are no lakes or running streams in these hills, and no *cenotes* like those that supplied water for Chichén Itzá and Dzibilchaltún. The ancient occupants of Uxmal and other Puuc centers dug huge underground cisterns called *chaltunes* to catch and hold rainwater, and they irrigated their farmlands with a network of reservoirs and canals. Even today, the chronic water shortage keeps villages small throughout the hill country.

To tour Uxmal (pronounced "Oosh-MAHL") and the other Puuc Maya sites, head south from Mérida on Route 180. The highway is an

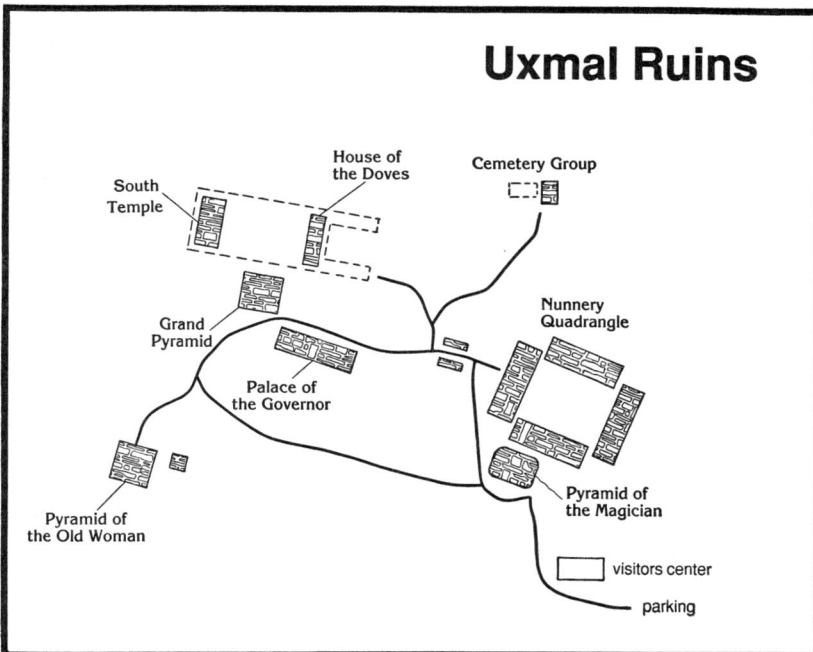

Uxmal Ruins

extension of Avenida Itzaes, the *periférico* that goes around the western perimeter of Mérida. Once you get past the town of Umán, where the highway branches three ways in a confusion of signs at the central plaza, Route 261 to Uxmal is easy to follow. If you come to **Hacienda Yaxcopoil** (admission), an old henequen plantation that is now open to the public as a museum, you'll know you're on the right highway.

Uxmal (admission) is considered by many ruins buffs to be the finest, most purely Maya site in the Yucatán. Although, like Chichén Itzá and other centers in the region, it was occupied for much of its history by people of Toltec descent, its ornate facades covered with complex geometric patterns and graceful sculptures of finely cut stone blocks bear little resemblance to the grandiose and somewhat sinister designs of Chichén Itzá. If Chichén Itzá seems to invite comparison to the ruins of ancient Rome, Uxmal is more often likened to the city-states of classical Greece because of the subtle perfection of its architectural proportioning and the fine balance between simplicity and complexity in its ornamentation. Unlike Chichén Itzá, nothing at Uxmal suggests militarism, human sacrifice or other dark forms of blood lust. Uxmal, one cannot help but feel, must truly have been a place of intellect and ceremony, of science and spirit, just as local legend suggests.

Almost nothing is known about Uxmal's early history except that it was founded in the 7th century A.D., at the height of the Classic Period. In those days, the educated ruling class of priests and noblemen extracted taxes in the form of agricultural products and labor from the uneducated peasant farmers and erected ceremonial centers that grew to become the central plazas of Maya cities. One of the largest cities in the Yucatán, Uxmal had about 25,000 residents in its heyday.

Uxmal's ancient temples continued to be used by the local Maya people for secret religious ceremonies even after the Spanish Conquest. Centuries later, when explorer John Lloyd Stephens first visited Uxmal in 1841, he recorded that the local people would not stay at Uxmal after dark because, according to local legend, the snakes and gods on temple facades came to life at night.

Grouped on a broad plateau, the ruins of Uxmal cast a low silhouette above a flat jungle landscape—not the towering rainforest you will encounter to the south in the Lacandón and Petén regions, but a tangle of undergrowth so dense that not even trees can pierce it to reach full height. Iguanas of impressive size can often be seen basking among the ruins.

Upon entering Uxmal, you come first to the **Pyramid of the Magician**. This unique, oval-shaped pyramid measures 117 feet in height and 178 feet wide at the base. The main stairway to the upper temples is exceptionally steep, and most people who climb it cling to the chain that was originally fastened to the center of the stairway as a handhold for the convenience of Empress Carlota, the wife of Emperor Maximilian of Mexico, upon her visit in 1865. Looking at the Pyramid of the Magician from a distance, you can see how newer temples were built over older ones. The pyramid actually contains five temples, constructed at different times—one at ground level, three more on a platform two-thirds of the way up the pyramid, and a fifth one at the top. The name Uxmal, from Maya words meaning "built three times," probably refers to the three levels of temples here. Despite the legend that it was magically built in a single night, it is clear from the number of successive temples that the Pyramid of the Magician was constructed little by little over a period of about 400 years. According to another legend, the Toltec-Maya leader Quetzalcóatl-Kukulcán, after rebuilding Chichén Itzá and founding Mayapán, ended his life at Uxmal and is buried beneath the Pyramid of the Magician. So far, however, archaeologists have found no tomb in this pyramid. The first archaeological project undertaken at Uxmal, the Pyramid of the Magician was restored in the 1940s by the late Franz Blom, the explorer

THE PLUMED SERPENT

Every Mexican schoolchild knows the story of **Quetzalcóatl**, *the Plumed Serpent, a mythical godlike leader who taught the indigenous people of Mexico all their arts and sciences. Quetzalcóatl first appeared in Teotihuacan Toltec legend as a leader much like Britain's King Arthur. The founder of the Toltec civilization, he fell into disgrace for violating his own laws and set himself on fire, vowing that he would be back one day as he rose to become the planet Venus.*

Thereafter, the Toltec head priests of this cult were given the title Quetzalcóatl. One of them, a messiahlike figure named Ce Acatl Topiltzin, proclaimed in himself the second coming of Quetzalcóatl and became king of the Toltecs in 968 A.D., reigning for decades and building the Toltec capital of Tula. Finally, his opponents deposed him and drove him from the city. Quetzalcóatl sailed away into the east on a raft of snakes, vowing like his namesake that one day he would return.

This time, Quetzalcóatl's raft carried him straight across the Gulf of Mexico to land on a Yucatán beach. By coincidence, the Maya people were also expecting the return of the Plumed Serpent, whom they knew as Kukulcán. Topiltzin-Quetzalcóatl-Kukulcán became the king of the Itzá Maya. He revived and rebuilt the ancient capital at Chichén Itzá, where massive sculptured stone heads representing the Plumed Serpent were placed throughout the city in his honor. Later, his enemies deposed him once more. He went to Uxmal, where he committed suicide and was buried under the Pyramid of the Magician.

whose headquarters, Casa Na-Bolom, you'll want to visit if your travels take you to San Cristóbal de las Casas, Chiapas (see Chapter Six).

Directly past the pyramid, swallows who live in the surrounding dark, vaulted rooms dart ceaselessly back and forth across the enclosed main plaza, known as the **Nunnery Quadrangle** because an early Spanish explorer thought it looked a lot like a Spanish convent. Actually, nobody is quite sure how the buildings surrounding the plaza were used. The 74 cell-like rooms are too cramped to have been the homes of nobility, and there are too many to have been quarters for resident priests. Some archaeologists theorize that the Nunnery Quadrangle was actually a sort of university campus as the old legend claims—perhaps a military academy, seminary for priests or school for the children of the ruling class. Others think it may have provided housing for visiting dignitaries participating in ceremonies in the central quadrangle.

The ornamentation on the Nunnery Quadrangle facades includes some of the most magnificent stonework in the Maya world. The **North Building** is the oldest, and the intertwining stone rattlesnakes that decorate it were probably ancestors of the plumed serpent Kukulcán. Long before Quetzalcóatl crossed the Gulf of Mexico to the Yucatán, the rattlesnake symbolized divinity and power to the Maya. The masks that cover much of the facade are of Chac, the rain god, who is an overwhelming presence in all of the Puuc Zone ruins. A curious feature is the series of seated human figures, bound like prisoners.

The **South Building**, lowest in elevation and second oldest, is simpler, its facade dominated by a geometric lattice design. Look over the eight interior doorways for stone carvings of Yucatán huts, looking just as they do today. This decorative device seems to have been the rage for a few years back then. Red handprints, perhaps the signature of the architect, can still be seen on the ceilings of two rooms.

The **East Building**, also subdued in its decoration, is the best preserved of the four. The owl-head motif at the roofline is usually understood by Maya archaeologists to symbolize death. What it means in this context is a mystery.

The ornamentation on the **West Building** is grandiose. Besides the lavishly rendered giant snakes, it features male nudes. A throne with a feather canopy is carved over the middle doorway. Seated on the throne is an old man with the body of a turtle. This may have symbolized the same lord whose residence, the House of the Turtles near the Palace of the Governor south of the ball court, had a row of turtles carved on the facade.

The Uxmal structure most admired by archaeologists is the **Palace of the Governor**, which most experts believe was built at the height of Uxmal's splendor as the home of a ruler who was also a master astronomer. Ninety-six meters in length, it contained 24 rooms. The frieze on the upper part of the palace was constructed in three layers—a latticework background made from 20,000 identical carved stones, an overlay of geometric fretwork, and a third layer of sculptures depicting persons, gods and animals. Over the central doorway is an empty headdress of long plumes; the face of the ruler who wore them crumbled or was destroyed long ago. It is one of five rulers memorialized on the frieze. Other sculptures on this amazing facade include personifications of the planet Venus, and others glorifying astronomers. Modern archaeoastronomers have discovered that the palace was precisely aligned with the path of Venus so that at the bright planet's southern solstice, it aligned perfectly with the central doorway of the palace, the jaguar throne in the courtyard, and a temple on a hilltop eight kilometers away.

Southeast of the Palace of the Governor is the most recently excavated structure at Uxmal, the **Grand Pyramid**. The temple on top of this pyramid is known as the Temple of the Guacamayas because of the many unusual stone blocks carved to represent parrots. Maya builders of the Classic Period had filled the temple with rubble in preparation to bury it and raise the pyramid to a higher level, which would have made it taller than the Pyramid of the Magician. For some unknown reason, construction was abandoned. When archaeologists cleared the rubble away, they found the giant Chac mask that you can see in the back room of the temple.

THE DWARF-KING OF UXMAL

According to a tale first recorded by John Lloyd Stephens in the 1840s and still told by tour guides today, Uxmal was built by a dwarf with magical powers. A curandera, the spiritual mother of all Yucatecan healers today, hatched the dwarf boy from an egg she had bought from some magical beings of the night. One day the boy struck a forbidden gong, and it upset the lord of the town tremendously. A prophesy foretold that when the gong sounded, the ruler would be replaced by a boy "not born of woman."

The lord condemned the dwarf boy to death but offered a reprieve if the boy could accomplish three seemingly superhuman tasks—of mathematics, sculpture and architecture. One of them was to build a great pyramid, now called the Pyramid of the Magician, in a single night. The boy passed all three tests, yet the lord decided to have him beheaded anyway. Through trickery, the boy contrived to have the old lord executed in his place. The dwarf boy them became the new lord of Uxmal and built the city whose ruins we see today.

*Although Kabah may seem deceptively small, archaeologists have determined that
there are at least 80 unexcavated structures at the site.*

Two other large pyramids stand at Uxmal—the partly restored
Cemetery Group Temple, with its strange skulls-and-bones ornamentation, to the north of the Grand Pyramid, and the unexcavated
Pyramid of the Old Woman, the oldest pyramid in the area, to the
southeast.

Perhaps the strangest-looking structure at Uxmal is the **House of
the Doves**. Once a ruler's residence, it has collapsed completely, leaving only a bridgelike support wall and the lofty, jagged remnants of a
roof comb. This palace formed one side of a separate ceremonial plaza.
The unexcavated ruins of the other buildings that surrounded the
plaza are in poor condition.

Beyond Uxmal, you can continue down the highway following the
"Ruta Puuc" signs to reach a series of smaller Maya ruins—Kabah,
Sayil, Labná and the cave at Loltún—that date back to the same era as
Uxmal. Some structures at each site have been nicely restored since the
area was opened to tourism with the paving of the road in 1978.

Kabah (admission), just 32 kilometers by road from Uxmal, is
thrown in as an added attraction on most guided tours that run from
Mérida. Expect to encounter other visitors here, sometimes by the
busload. Thanks to its newfound popularity, the site is undergoing
extensive restoration. In fact, on our last visit it seemed as if entire
buildings had suddenly sprung up where only grassy knolls strewn
with stone rubble had been before. Workmen were scrambling everywhere in the ruins. Roof combs were appearing on buildings that
hadn't even had roofs a few years ago. New stone is being quarried to
rebuild undecorated walls, and the incongruity of fresh-cut masonry
in a site more than a thousand years old makes for a somewhat artificial
first impression. Kabah's restored area is sure to keep growing in the
years to come.

The most impressive building at Kabah is the **Palace of the Masks**,
whose facade is entirely covered with about 250 representations of the
hook-nosed rain god, Chac. Each mask is made up of 30 individually
shaped blocks of cut stone—a massive monument to the force that has
always meant life or death to the people of the Yucatán. Indentations
on both sides of the nose of each mask may have been for burning
incense or holding torches.

On the other side of the highway from the ruins entrance, a road
leads back past the lofty, rubbled remains of the Great Temple to the
Arch of Kabah, the gate to the city in ancient times. From the foot of

the steps on the far side of the arch, a raised *sacbé* paved with white limestone once ran straight through the forest for a distance of 15 kilometers to Uxmal. The road continued for another ten kilometers to Labná. Now the ancient road runs about 600 meters to a small, plain ruined temple. Beyond that point, the forest has overgrown everything. A sometimes-faint foot trail continues to trace the old *sacbé* route. If you follow it for a ways into the forest, you will gain a deeper appreciation of how much work it must have been to construct and maintain these roads. The Maya people had no beasts of burden or wheeled vehicles, so the main reason for these roads must have been to keep a clear route through the jungle for religious processions and commerce.

Follow the "Ruta Puuc" sign, taking the east (left) fork in the highway five kilometers beyond Kabah. Another five kilometers will bring you to Sayil. It's ten kilometers more to Labná. Both Sayil and Labná are beyond the reach of most tour buses and vans. You need a car to get there. This means you will encounter few other tourists there. You may even find that you have the ruins all to yourself.

The beautiful reddish-orange hue of the stonework at both Sayil and Labná was not the natural color of the limestone, nor did the Maya paint the structures that color. Iron oxide in the dirt stained the ruins as they lay buried over the centuries before excavation began in the 1950s.

At **Sayil** (admission), only a couple of structures have been restored out of 75 known to lie hidden under tree-choked earthen mounds at the site. The main restoration is **El Palacio** (The Palace), an exquisite three-story building. It has 50 double-chambered rooms, as well as patios, porticoes and galleries. Sculptures of mythological beings on the cornices of El Palacio include a huge Chac mask—complete with teeth—and several "diving gods."

Behind the palace, you can see a catch basin, which was designed to funnel rainwater into an underground *chultun* (cistern). Farther along,

---

MYSTERY OF THE ANCIENT DIVERS

The significance of the "diving god" at Sayil is the subject of endless speculation. The same motif is found at Tulum, built 500 years after Sayil on the other side of the Yucatán Peninsula; it is not found elsewhere in the Puuc Zone. Ufologists point to this landlocked diver as "evidence" that humanoid extraterrestrials visited the ancient Maya people—diving down to earth from the sky. A more conventional explanation is that "diving gods" were people who, like Mayapán founder Hunac Ceel, dived into the depths of sacred cenotes seeking enlightenment.

you will find a small, ruined pyramid called **El Mirador** (The Look-out), topped by a temple with a tall, intact roof comb. Stay on the foot trail that continues beyond the pyramid and you will come to a big sculpture of a nude male figure with exaggerated genitals, thought to be a fertility idol used in Postclassic Putún Maya rituals.

Labná (admission), when we have visited, has proved to be the most peaceful and contemplative of the Puuc Zone ceremonial centers. The **Palace of Labná** is similar to the one at Sayil but longer. Its most remarkable sculpture is a serpent head holding a human face within its jaws. Many experts think it symbolizes astronomy, the art of the scientist-priests who dominated Maya culture during the Classic Period. Another interpretation is that the gruesome reptilian jaws are those of the crocodile that symbolizes the underworld where ancient Maya leaders were believed to go when they died. The Chac mask flanked by human figures on the palace facade is one of the largest masks of the Maya rain god ever discovered. Over the central doorway of the palace is a hieroglyphic date: 869 A.D.

A restored *sacbé* leads from the palace to the **Labná Vault**, the largest and finest example of a Maya arch ever found. Over the entrances to the rooms on each side of the arch are sculptural representations of Yucatecan huts like the ones the Maya people of the region still live in today. Fragments remain of the elaborate roof comb that topped this grand gateway. Through the arch is **El Castillo** (The Castle), a steep pyramid with a temple on top. One half of the temple is crumbled to rubble, while the other half is miraculously intact right up to the lofty roof comb.

To reach **Grutas de Loltún** (admission), continue on the Ruta Puuc highway for 15 kilometers past Labná and turn left onto the four-kilometer entrance road to the caves. The network of *grutas* (caves) forms a long cavern the limits of which have not been fully explored. The largest known limestone cavern in the Yucatán, it has been used by the Maya people since before the dawn of history. Evidence has been found that cave-dwelling ancestors of the Maya lived here at least 4000 years ago. Among the items discovered in the caves are a giant stone head and a mastadon skeleton. During the Classic Period, chambers were used for rituals to establish contact with the underworld. As recently as 1850, Maya people of the area lived in the caves to hide from Spanish soldiers during the Caste War.

The cavern displays plenty of stalactites, stalagmites and other strangely shaped minerals as it leads room by room to a "lost world," where daylight pours through a hole in the ceiling and vines drip down from the earth's surface high above. The palpable sense that people have been using the place since Old Testament times gives the place a haunted feeling, and explorers who have ventured deeper, beyond the big room where tours turn back, have returned claiming that a mysterious force seems to guard the cavern's innermost recesses. Visitors are only allowed into the caves with a tour guide. Regularly scheduled tours run about every 90 minutes from 9:30 a.m. to 3:30 p.m. Guides are usually available to take you on a private tour at other times for a more substantial tip. The guides work for tips only, so plan to pay yours a few pesos in addition to the charge for admission to the caves.

Most visitors to the Puuc Zone turn around after visiting Grutas de Loltún and retrace their route back to Route 180. Finding your way through the Maya towns in this area can be difficult. Roads lead to the town plaza and leave you there without a hint as to how to find the road to the next town. There are few road signs or highway numbers. You will find it necessary to ask directions frequently. Hardly anyone understands English in these parts, and even travelers who are fluent in Spanish may have trouble with the local dialect. Navigation problems, together with livestock, playing children and *triciclos* in the roadway, make travel in this area very slow. On our most recent trip through the hill country, it took a full day of practically nonstop driving to make our way from Ticul to Chichén Itzá, a distance of 200 kilometers. Still, glimpses into the everyday lives of rural Maya people made the trip worthwhile.

For an easier way to see a modern Maya town, take the short detour just before the turnoff to Grutas de Loltún and stroll or at least drive through the stony streets of **Yaaxhon**, where turkeys and pigs wander nonchalantly in and out of whitewashed Yucatán huts and men dressed all in white pedal along with women, children and bundles of firewood balanced on the rear fenders of bicycles. Then, after seeing the Grutas de Loltún, turn around and backtrack the Ruta Puuc highway to rejoin Route 180 at Kabah, either to head back to Uxmal or Mérida for the night or to continue your journey along the Maya Route to Edzná and Campeche.

MONUMENTAL INDECENCY?

When she visited in 1865, the Empress Carlota of Mexico expressed shock at all the phallic symbolism at Uxmal—and she wasn't the only one. For example, a group of more than a dozen giant stone monuments that may have symbolized psychedelic mushrooms or phalluses used to stand not far from the Palace of the Governor. An old photo of the giant mushrooms can be seen in the Explorers' Club exhibit upstairs in the Pirámide Inn in Piste, near Chichén Itzá. In the 1940s, the monuments were pulled from the ground and dragged into the woods in response to tourists' complaints that Uxmal contained far too much indecent art. Vandals later destroyed them.

UXMAL AND THE PUUC ZONE LODGING

Several upscale "archaeological hotels" near Uxmal provide the only tourist accommodations in the Puuc Zone. Closest to the ruins is the **Villa Arqueológica** (24-70-53). Run by Club Med, this is one of a chain of identical hotels at major ruins that the Mexican government built in the late 1970s. There are none of the games and organized activities that Club Med is known for. The hotel presents an audio-visual show about Uxmal and has a good library of books in English about the Maya and other pre-Hispanic Mexican civilizations. Other facilities include a courtyard swimming pool and tennis courts. Guest rooms are bright, modern and air-conditioned. All are furnished with twin beds, not double beds, making the Villa Arqueológica a dubious option for honeymooners and the romantically inclined. Deluxe.

In the same price range as the Villa Arqueológica, the older **Hacienda Uxmal** (23-25-97), situated across the highway from the ruins entrance, is full of colonial elegance. Guest rooms are large and old-fashioned, with massive hand-carved furniture and ceiling fans. Some have bathtubs. Outside the rooms, tiled verandas set with divans and plants overlook the beautiful swimming pool.

A kilometer or so north of the ruins, the **Misión Inn Uxmal** (24-73-08) is situated so that each room has a panoramic view of the Pyramid of the Magician and other Uxmal structures rising above the forest in the distance. The rooms are large, attractive and ultramodern, with ceiling fans and big private balconies. Palms and a pretty lawn surround the swimming pool. Moderate.

Budget-priced accommodations can be found four kilometers north of the ruins at **Rancho Uxmal** (2-10-80). Guest rooms have private baths, hot water and ceiling fans.

The easiest plan is to use your Uxmal hotel as a home base while exploring the Puuc hill country. Tourist facilities are almost nonexis-

---

HOW THE PUUC MAYA VANISHED

All along the Ruta Puuc from Uxmal to Grutas de Loltún, there are hardly any signs of modern-day inhabitants. It's easy to see how early explorers in these hills could have formed the erroneous belief that the people who built the cities and ceremonial centers of the Puuc Zone later vanished mysteriously. The truth is that within a generation after the Spanish Conquest, an estimated 90 percent of the Maya population of the hill country died from European diseases to which they had no natural immunity, such as smallpox, influenza and measles. The few survivors regrouped in Ticul and other towns and villages a short distance to the north.

Postclassic Maya priests wrote enough books to fill entire libraries. But at his headquarters in Mani, Bishop Landa publicly burned them all. Only a few fragments of Maya books have survived.

tent in the towns and villages beyond Labná and Loltún. For visitors who seek really cheap lodging, Ticul, a mainly Maya town of 40,000 people, has the only hotels in the area. The best accommodation there is at the **Hotel-Restaurant Cerro Inn**, about three kilometers from the center of town on the highway to Mérida. The grounds are nicely shaded with palm trees. The guest rooms are motel-style units minimally furnished with double beds and absolutely nothing else, but they have private baths and ceiling fans. Room rates are in the very low budget range. The two hotels in the town center of Ticul are not as nice.

UXMAL AND THE PUUC ZONE RESTAURANTS

In the visitors center at Uxmal, the full-service **Restaurant Yax Beh** serves sandwiches and light meals during the hours when the ruins are open. Prices are higher than you'd pay in Mérida but lower than at restaurants in the neighboring hotels. The three upscale archaeological hotels offer guests a choice of rates—European Plan (without meals) or Modified American Plan (including dinner and breakfast). Their restaurants are open to the public, too. The excellent restaurant at the **Villa Arqueológica** (24-70-53), generally considered the best of the hotel restaurants, specializes in Continental cuisine prepared for the palates of European visitors. Prices range from moderate to deluxe.

At the **Hacienda Uxmal** (23-25-97), the restaurant features a varied menu including Yucatecan specialties as well as American and Continental selections. The hacienda ambience couldn't be more romantic. Deluxe.

The moderately priced restaurant at the **Misión Inn Uxmal** (24-73-08) offers limited menu options, which change often—usually a choice of chicken, pork or fish prepared in regional style.

Under a big thatched roof, the restaurant at the **Rancho Uxmal** (2-01-80) serves a similar selection of chicken, pork or fish entrées à la Yucateca at prices in the budget range.

Visitors passing through Ticul will want to try **Los Almendros** (Calle 23 between Calles 24 and 26), famed throughout Mexico for its excellent Yucatecan cuisine. The restaurant has now been franchised in Mérida and Cancún, but this is the original. Poc-chuc, the orange-and-onion pork fillets popular throughout the Yucatán, were invented in this unpretentious, budget-priced, family-run restaurant.

UXMAL AREA SHOPPING

Shopping opportunities are few and far between in the Puuc hills. Tourist shops are beginning to spring up along Route 261 between Umán and Uxmal. While there's nothing special about the curios on sale at the roadside **Mercado Central de Artesanías los Pájaros,** the shop has a large private zoo out back with cages of regional birds like pheasants, toucans, parrots and loros, as well as a tame javelina. A little farther south in the village of Muna, a **women's cooperative** has set up a market for locally made *huipiles* of white cotton with elaborate embroidery.

The archaeological hotels around Uxmal have shops where local craftsmen sell high-quality, pricey handcrafted items. Carvers sell beautiful wooden replicas of sculptures from all over the classic Maya world at the **Misión Inn Uxmal,** while at the **Villa Arqueológica,** modern sculptors create exquisitely detailed stone reproductions of Maya art.

At the Uxmal visitors center, you will find a Mexican government **gift shop** that carries fine arts and crafts from all over the country, as well as a branch of the **Librerías Dante** bookstore chain stocked with a large selection of books on the Maya people and Yucatán's ancient ruins in Spanish, English and other languages. Outside by the parking lot, a number of vendors sell T-shirts and other low-priced souvenir items.

A large part of the Maya population in the Puuc region earns money by making tourist goods such as hammocks and Panama hats, but these items are all taken to Mérida for sale, so it takes a lot of searching and bargaining to buy them locally. **Ticul** is the center for two manufacturing industries that supply the whole Yucatán Peninsula—ceramic kitchen pottery and shoes. Stroll around town and you'll find more *zapaterías* (shoe shops) than any other kind of store.

PANAMA HATS DON'T COME FROM PANAMA

The best Panama hats come from the tiny village of Becal, located just off the main highway, midway between Mérida and Campeche. They are handcrafted underground in caves, where cool temperatures and steady humidity make the fibers more pliable as the hat is being shaped and woven. This is why you can wad the hat up, cram it into your pocket, backpack or suitcase, and, when you pull it out later, it will spring right back into shape. Although the hats are Yucatecan, they became known as Panama hats because American fortune seekers bound for the gold fields of California bought these hats to keep the tropical sun at bay on the overland trek across the Isthmus of Panama.

Imagine what Edzná must have looked like when the walls of its temples were covered with ornate stucco sculpture and painted in bright hues of red, yellow, blue and brown.

Edzná

If you treasure solitude among the ruins, or if you want to visit a major Maya city that nobody back home has ever heard of, Edzná is one of the best options. Thanks to its out-of-the-way location, 50 kilometers northeast of the untouristy city of Campeche, few travelers visit Edzná. To get there from Uxmal, drive south from the Kabah junction on Route 261. After you cross the state line, 25 more kilometers will bring you to **Grutas de Xtacumbilxunaan** (admission), a cave that contains no ceremonial chambers. It does have a waterhole in its depths that been used as an emergency water source during dry spells since ancient times.

After traveling a total of 94 kilometers on from Kabah, you will intersect Route 188 at the archaeological zone of Edzná. Dating back to the Late Classic Period, around 633 to 810 A.D. (based on hieroglyphic dates carved on stelae), **Edzná** (admission) was a large, prosperous center ideally located at the crossroads between trade routes from the Puuc hill country, the Petén and the southern lowlands. If Edzná had been located much nearer to Cancún, or even Mérida, it would now be overrun with tourists.

The name Edzná means "house of grimaces," referring to the masks that once graced the roof comb of the **Temple of Five Levels**, the largest pyramid at Edzná. Though the best masks have been removed to museums, leaving a rather plain facade with badly weathered remnants of jaguar and serpent motifs on each level, the temple's height and steepness make it impressive. It stands 39 meters high, overlooking a broad acropolis. It is unlike other Maya temple pyramids in that the lower four levels each contain a series of rooms that appear to have been used as residences by rulers or priests. A passageway runs beneath the stairs on the first level to an inner temple within the pyramid. Mysterious hieroglyphs carved into several steps on the broad central stairway are still legible, if not translatable. The roof comb on top of the rather plain temple at the pyramid's apex is similar to those seen on some temples at Palenque.

In front of the Temple of Five Levels, the **Plaza Central of Edzná** covers an area of 16,000 square meters—three times the size of a football field—and is elevated seven meters above ground level. As a feat of earth-moving, the raised plaza was a more formidable project even than construction of the pyramid. In the center of the plaza is a ceremonial platform, and on the far side of the plaza a grand stairway 100 meters wide goes up the side of a long pyramid crowned by what was probably a government administration building, now called the **Temple of the Moon**. Unlike those at most ancient Maya sites in the Yucatán, the buildings at Edzná did not have stone roofs. Instead, the original roofs were thatched—big-scale versions of the palm-thatched roofs still used today on traditional Yucatán huts. Two other structures, known only as the **Southwest Temple** and the **Northwest Temple**, mark the corners of the plaza.

The restored part of Edzná was once the center of a city that covered more than two square kilometers. At least five smaller complexes, including a recently discovered ball court, await excavation on the outskirts of this major site. Several stelae carved with hieroglyphs have been found around these outlying sites, though the ones that have not been removed to museums are broken or so badly weathered that they cannot be read. Another feature of Edzná that interests archaeologists is the extensive system of Maya irrigation canals and reservoirs that surround the center. Little by little, future archaeologists will reveal more of this ancient city. Meanwhile, we must be content to ponder the scrub-covered manmade mounds throughout the area and wonder what new mysteries they conceal.

Campeche

The wonderfully historic port of **Campeche** (pop. 175,000), capital of the state of the same name, originated as the Maya village Ah Kim Pech, meaning "tick of the serpent." After the Spanish landed in 1517, the city became an important outlet for exotic woods used as dyes. As it grew and became more vulnerable to pirate attacks, a massive wall was erected in 1686 for the then-staggering sum of $3300. The **Puerta de Mar** ("door of the sea") and **Puerta de Tierra** ("door of the land"), a pair of huge stone portals at opposite ends of Calle 59, are the most poignant remnants of the wall, which was torn down after several centuries to let the stifling city breathe again.

The **waterfront area** bounded by Circuito Baleartes and Avenida 16 de Septiembre was the site of the old walled city. Walk the narrow streets, alluringly lit at night with Spanish lanterns, and explore the ponderous *baluartes* (bulwarks) and pretty plazas. Start at the **Baluarte de San Carlos** (Calle 8 and Calle 65), the first fort built in Campeche, erected in 1676. Proceed down to the **Baluarte de la Soledad** (Calle 8; 6-81-79), a fort converted into a tiny museum for ancient art from Isla de Jaina, a sacred Maya burial island 40 kilometers offshore. Unfortunately, you can't visit the island, but the delicate figurines excavated there are unmistakable.

The old fort **Baluarte de Santiago** (Calle 8 and Calle 49; 6-68-29) now contains a lovely botanical garden, Xmuch' Haltun, full of hummingbirds and stone pathways. A few blocks west stands the rambling Parque Principal in the shadow of the moldy 16th-century **Catedral de Campeche** (Calle 10 and Calle 55). Have a look at the amazing sarcophagus near the altar, encrusted with silver bells, angels and a figure of Christ.

With its many churches, the town seems to have one foot in Heaven. One interesting church is the old **Iglesia de San Francisco**, where conquistador Hernán Cortes' son was baptized, located along the *malecón* at Calle Mariano Escobedo.

Downtown Campeche

POINTS OF INTEREST

A Puerta de Mar
B Puerta de Tierra
C Baluarte de San Carlos
D Baluarte de la Soledad
E Baluarte de Santiago
F Catedral de Campeche
G Museo de Campeche
H Museo Regional de Campeche
I Parque Alameda
J Palacio de Gobierno and
    Congreso del Estado

The **Museo de Campeche** (Calle 10 and Calle 63; 6-14-24) occupies the former cathedral of San José. This hulking weather-streaked stone shell now shelters a display of artisans' work.

A better exhibition resides at the **Museo Regional de Campeche** (Calle 59 and Calle 14), colonial home of the Spanish king's lieutenant in 1790. Its rooms surround a central courtyard and contain contemporary art and a fine collection of Maya artifacts, including outstanding jade masks from ancient tombs.

It's a short walk from the museum to the delightful **Parque Alameda** (Avenida República and Calle 55), a triangular garden just beyond the Baluarte de San Francisco. Surrounded by castlelike ramparts and posts, Alameda welcomes strollers with its molded benches and shade. Puente de las Mercedes, at the north end, is a small, white bridge guarded by snobbish stone dogs with their noses in the air.

For novelty, walk down Avenida 16 de Septiembre past the **Palacio de Gobierno** (Government Palace) and **Congreso del Estado** (State Congress), nicknamed "The Jukebox" and "The Flying Saucer," respectively, because of their sci-fi architecture.

On the southern outskirts of town, the impressive **Fuerte de San Miguel** (ascend Carretera Escénica from Avenida Resurgimiento) leans out over a hillside and is rimmed by moats once filled with skin-seering lime. Dating from 1700, the fort now houses a museo arqueología that includes marvelous ship replicas, pirate lore and Maya art. The view from the parapets alone is worth the trip.

Near the southern entrance to town on Route 180, a huge stone figure, called **Monumento Resurgimiento** (Revival Monument), rises between the lanes—a torso with a torch held high for democracy, a Latin statue of Liberty.

CAMPECHE'S SECRET MAYA RUINS

Travelers in search of truly unknown Maya ruins can turn off at the little village of Hopelchén onto the paved side road that runs for about 50 kilometers to the village of Dzibalchén. Near the village, the ruins of **Hochob** *are completely unrestored and mostly uncleared, but have a well-preserved temple with a huge Chac mask for a facade, its doorway a gaping mouth. An unpaved side road from Dzibalchén runs through the scrub forest to the next village, Iturbide, where the unexcavated ruins of* **Dzibilnocac** *feature an unusual rounded temple that also contains a big, fearsome Chac mask. Return to the main highway the same way you came. Be sure you have at least half a tank of gas before undertaking this side trip. The nearest Pemex station—or hotel or restaurant—is in Campeche.*

CAMPECHE LODGING

Old hotels fill the city of Campeche. The best are along the waterfront. For comfort, the 103-room **Hotel Baluartes** (Avenida Ruiz Cortines; 6-39-11) takes top billing. Modern and square, set in an unexciting parking lot with its back to downtown and its face to the *malecón*, the Baluartes has ample, gold-hued rooms with hanging wicker lamps, carpets, color televisions and big picture windows with views of the gulf. For extras, there's the restaurant-bar, nightclub, pool, café and terrace. Moderate.

Right next door, the **Ramada Inn** (Avenida Ruiz Cortines No. 51; 6-22-33) offers affordable luxury. The U.S.-based Ramada chain has taken over the former El Presidente, part of the now-defunct chain that used to set the standard for luxury accommodations in Mexico. With spacious rooms, modern decor and balconies overlooking the water, it has much to offer at moderate rates. The amenities include a swimming pool, restaurant, bar, playground and even a popular disco.

The newest of the waterfront hotels is the **Alhambra** (Avenida Resurgimiento No. 85; 6-69-88) at the southern end of the *malecón*. This big pink hotel has 100 modern, air-conditioned rooms with satellite television. There is a swimming pool as well as a restaurant, bar and disco. The hotel is right across from Campeche's public bathing beach and a block away from an historic hilltop fortress, the Fuerte de San Miguel, an ideal spot from which to watch the sunset. Moderate.

The best of the numerous low-cost inns in town is the **Hotel López** (Calle 12 No. 189; 6-33-44). Built around a narrow courtyard, its 39 rooms are saved from being drab by the pink tile walls, high ceilings and colorful tile floors. All are air-conditioned and have fans and telephones. Budget.

CAMPECHE RESTAURANTS

Campeche is a shrimp boat port, so *camarones* (shrimp) and other seafood specialties abound here. The local seafood institution, **Restaurant Miramar** (Calle 8 and Calle 61; 6-28-83) faces the Puerta del Mar. This old colonial building is full of romantic touches: black Spanish lanterns, golden glass doors laced with grillwork, beamed ceilings. Its atmosphere outshines its cuisine, which includes the popular *congrejo moro* (stone crab), fish soup and squid. Budget to moderate.

One of the most attractive eateries on the Yucatán coast is the shiny, colonial **Restaurant Marganzo** (Calle 8) in the middle of the block near the *zócalo*, across from the castle. Marganzo features regional dishes in a setting accented by black-and-white tile, arches and ceiling fans. There is a nightclub upstairs. Moderate.

The downtown **Restaurant del Parque** (Calle 8 at Calle 57; 6-02-40), facing the well-lit Parque Principal, attracts a lively local crowd. With colored lights and ceiling fans, it's breezy and upbeat. The menu is highlighted by seafood, assorted meats, salads and Mexican plates, but service can be slow. Budget to moderate.

Our favorite all-night café (open only from sundown to sunup) is the indoor-outdoor **Cafetería Le Jardín Hotel Baluartes** (Avenida Ruiz Cortines; 6-39-11). Locals and international travelers alike gather in air-conditioned coolness around the white wrought-iron tables to sip coffees, nibble pastries and lick ice creams. Budget to moderate.

An inexpensive stop is the **Restaurant López** (Calle 12 No. 189; 6-31-20) upstairs in the López Hotel. Simple, basic and budget-priced. Try the huevos típicos or the camarones with salsa.

CAMPECHE SHOPPING

Not a great shopping town, Campeche does have a row of shops along Calle 8 where souvenirs are peddled. Two good shops are **Artesanía Típica Naval** (Calle 8 No. 259; 6-57-08), which carries bottled exotic fruits like nance and marañón, and **El Coral** (Calle 8 No. 255; 6-32-85), which has Maya replica figurines.

Another collection of shops, **Exposición y Venta Permanente de Artesanías** (Avenida Circuito), occupies the old Baluarte San Pedro. Locally made craft items—indigenous dresses and hammocks, as well as baskets and Panama hats woven from jipijapa palm fronds—are for sale.

YUCATECAN CUISINE

Yucatán has the most distinctive regional cuisine to be found anywhere in Mexico. Chicken and pork are its mainstays. One of the most common regional dishes is pollo pibil, *chicken marinated in a sauce of achiote, seville orange and spices, then barbecued in banana leaves. The same dish made with pork is called* cochinita pibil. *Another dinner entrée served just about everywhere is* poc-chuc, *pork fillet cooked in a tangy sauce of seville orange and pickled onions.* Puchero *is a stew made of chicken, pork, carrots, squash, cabbage, potatoes, yams and bananas, traditionally served on Sundays in Yucatecan homes.*

For lighter fare, the best bet is sopa de lima, *a soup made with chicken, fried tortilla pieces and a slice of lime. (The large, sweeter Mexican lime, or* lima, *is not the same fruit known in the United States as a lime, which Mexicans call a* limón.) *Yucatecan tacos, called* salbutes *or* panuchos *depending on how the tortilla is cooked, are made with shredded turkey, pickled onion and avocado. A popular vegetarian dish is* papadzules, *chopped hard-boiled eggs rolled up in tortillas and served in a pumpkin seed sauce.*

Beware the man-o-war, a poisonous blue jellyfish that sometimes drifts into the waters around Campeche in large numbers, especially in the summer. Its burning sting can be soothed with ice water, calamine lotion or ammonia mixed with water.

Powerful odors assail the senses at the **Mercado Municipal** (Avenida Gobernadores), a labyrinth of indoor stalls tumbling with food, baby chicks, good luck soaps, handicrafts and posters of pop personalities and Jesus.

CAMPECHE BEACHES

One of the only strands worth mentioning in the area is **Playa Bonita**. This narrow beach on a small cove is a local weekend hangout. It's friendly but lacks beauty. Backed by a line of palms and a big recreational pavilion, the thin sand is littered with bottle caps and stones. Facilities include lockers, showers and baths, refreshments and *palapa* shelters. Camping is not safe. Swimming is calm and gentle, but there is possible contamination from the nearby thermoelectric plant in Lerma. A seaside trail leads south for several kilometers to a nicer, less accessible beach called San Lorenzo. To get to Playa Bonita, take the marked turnoff 13 kilometers south of Campeche on Route 180, just before the town of Lerma.

Route 180 runs along the sandy shore from Campeche to Champotón. Thirty-three kilometers south of Campeche, the traditional fishing village of Seybaplaya occupies one of the most attractive locations along this part of the Gulf Coast. The waterfront of the village itself is smelly and full of dead fish parts, but **Balneario Payucan**, the small, secluded swimming beach north of town is idyllic. To get there, follow the unpaved road at the far north end of the bay.

Río Bec Area

Many visitors choose not to continue on the Ruta Maya through Chiapas and Guatemala for various reasons—not enough time, no passport, or the impossibility of crossing into Guatemala with a rental car. If this describes your situation, for a complete "grand tour" of the Yucatán Peninsula, you can follow the Gulf of Mexico's sandy shoreline on Route 180 for 65 kilometers to Champotón, then head due south on Route 261 for 80 kilometers to Escárcega, a dusty, unappealing crossroads town. From Escárcega, Route 186 runs just about due east for a distance of 270 kilometers to Chetumal, Quintana Roo, the southernmost town on Mexico's Caribbean coast, just across the river from Belize. From there, you can work your way back up the coast to Cancún (see Chapter Four for complete details).

Midway along the route from Escárcega to Chetumal, you'll come to a group of little-known Maya ruins that represent the Río Bec Maya culture. They are considered important by archaeologists, but since they are not restored or developed, travelers don't go out of their way to visit them.

The first ruin eastbound travelers reach on Route 186 is **Chicanná**, 500 meters south of the highway. One structure, the **House of the Serpent Mouth,** has been excavated, revealing a front doorway surrounded by a serpent mask representing Itzamná, the Maya sun god. Archaeological digs are still in progress at Chicanná, and other nearby buildings that are being unearthed also have portals in the form of animal masks.

Becan, two-and-a-half kilometers east of Chicanná, was inhabited from 550 to 1000 A.D. Temples at Becan once stood as much as 35 meters (117 feet) high. Some long stairways survive. The site was entirely surrounded by a meandering moat two kilometers long, which you can still see today. All the Río Bec communities were built with defensive features much like those of medieval European castles, suggesting that this region was plagued by wars during the Classic Period.

The village of **Xpujil,** six kilometers east of Becan, has been occupied by the Maya people continuously since around 400 A.D. The ancient ceremonial center of Xpujil is on the outskirts of the present-day town. Its triple towers are visible from the highway. Two inlaid masks adorn the back side of the towered structure. Not much else has been excavated at the site.

The site of **Río Bec,** well-preserved but not excavated or restored, is located about 15 kilometers south of Xpujil, off a four-wheel-drive road through the jungle. If you want to go there, hire a guide at Xpujil. The archaeological zone sprawls over 50 square kilometers, completely overgrown by jungle, and the ruined structures can be difficult to find.

SAVING THE YUCATÁN'S ENDANGERED RAINFOREST

The area immediately surrounding Becan and Chicanná includes a narrow strip of protected rainforest that connects the two vast expanses of the **Calakmul Biosphere Reserve** *a few kilometers north and south of the highway. The reserve is intended to save a portion of the Petén rainforest on the Mexican side of the border, where so much of it has been burned off for farming. Established under the UNESCO Man and the Biosphere program, the reserve adjoins Guatemala's Maya Biosphere Reserve north of Tikal National Park and Belize's smaller, hard-to-reach Río Bravo Conservation Area on the northwest border. Supporters of the Ruta Maya concept envision the three reserves as a single international park, which they refer to as the Maya Peace Park.*

If you buy a hammock to use for camping on this trip, get a mosquitero para ham-
aca *(mosquito net), too. Many small stores around Mérida's market sell them.*

The **Calakmul Biosphere Reserve** is named for the ancient Maya
city of Calakmul, located about 55 kilometers southwest of Río Bec in
the heart of the reserve, reached via a rocky unpaved road. Calakmul is
reputed to have been one of the largest Maya cities, with a population
of more than 60,000. A pyramid here that covers five acres at its base
may have been the most massive structure in the ancient Maya world.
Archaeological projects are going on at a furious pace. Calakmul will
be a fascinating, hard-to-reach Maya site, much as Tikal and Yaxchilán
are today. If you want to mount an expedition to Calakmul right now,
though, you should start by obtaining permission and information from
the Instituto Nacional de Antropología e Historia in Mexico City.

RÍO BEC AREA LODGING

The nearest food and lodging to the Río Bec area is at Escárcega.
Rooms in this small town are cheap and very basic. The finest hostelry
in town is the **Hotel Escárcega** (Route 186; 4-01-86). It has clean
rooms with private baths and ceiling fans, some of them set by a small
garden away from the noisy street. Budget.

The Sporting Life

BICYCLING

The flat terrain of the Yucatán makes it an incomparable place for bike
touring—if you don't mind the hot climate. Strangely enough, while
many more people ride bicycles than drive cars, we have not been able
to find a single place in Mérida or elsewhere in the Yucatán that rents
bicycles. However, just about anything can be arranged informally.
Tell your hotel manager or any local travel agent a day or two in advance that you'd be interested in renting a bicycle and chances are
good that they'll be able to find someone who would like to rent one
out to a rich gringo.

CAMPING

Many marvelous camping spots, some shaded by palm trees, lie along
the Gulf Coast. You can expect to confront mosquitoes and sand fleas,
especially during the May-to-October rainy season. Bring repellent

---

Scuba enthusiasts shun the Yucatán's freshwater cenotes. Diving there can mean trouble with local authorities, who are always on the lookout for illegal Maya artifact hunters.

---

and mosquito nets. Camping supplies and sporting goods can be found in Mérida at **Supermaz** (Calle 59 No. 514) and **Deporterama** (Calle 59 No. 508; 23-63-07) and in Campeche at **Superdiez** (Area Akim-Pech off Malecón Miguel Alemán near Avenida Francisco Madero).

FISHING AND BOATING

Gulf waters swarm with tarpon, grouper, red snapper and sea bass. North of Mérida, a few kilometers west of Puerto Progreso, **Servicios Acuático en la Peninsula de Yucatán** (at the harbor in Yucalpetén) provides boats and fishing tips. Fishermen in most of the little villages along the coast, such as Río Lagartos and Celestún, are eager to guide you in their boats to the best fishing areas, since tourist charters pay better than catching fish. In Campeche, make fishing arrangements at the **pescadería** (fish market) at the end of Avenida Francisco Madero along the *malecón*.

SNORKELING AND SCUBA DIVING

Do your diving before you leave the Caribbean coast. The Gulf of Mexico shoreline along the north and west coasts of the Yucatán Peninsula is a shallow shelf of limestone reaching miles out into the gulf under often murky water. Visibility is best from June through September. Some people enjoy snorkeling and diving around the Alacrán Reef northwest of Progreso. (*Alacrán* means "scorpion"; think how cool that will sound back home.) Small rock formations that extend from the beach east of Puerto Progreso at San Miguel and Uaymitún are also suitable for snorkeling.

GOLF AND TENNIS

There is an 18-hole championship golf course just outside Mérida at the **Club Deportiva La Ceiba** (Route 261; 24-75-25), 16 kilometers north of the city, about halfway to Puerto Progreso. The sporting club also has tennis courts. Other Mérida area tennis courts can be found at the **Club Campestre de Mérida** (Calle 30 No. 500; 7-11-00) and the **Holiday Inn** (Avenida Colón No. 498 at Paseo de Montejo; 25-68-77).

Transportation

BY CAR

Route 180 runs east and west between Cancún and Mérida, passing through Valladolid and Pisté (near Chichén Itzá). Beyond Mérida, Route 180 continues to Campeche and down the Gulf Coast.

Route 261 splits away from Route 180 at Umán south of Mérida and goes to the ancient Maya sites of Uxmal, Kabah and Edzná, rejoining Route 180 south of Campeche. Continuing south, Route 261 goes to the crossroads town of Escárcega.

From Escárcega, **Route 186** runs east to Chetumal on the Caribbean coast of Quintana Roo and southwest to Palenque in the state of Chiapas.

All three major routes through the Yucatán are paved, two-lane highways with lots of *topes* (speed bumps) to slow cars down through each tiny roadside village. When driving, expect to average about 55 kph (33 mph).

BY AIR

Licenciado Manuel Crescencio Rejón International Airport, serving Mérida, is located seven kilometers southwest of the city. The only international flights that still land at the airport are twice-daily Aeroméxico from Miami. Mexicana and Aeroméxico both have frequent flights to and from Mexico City. Aero Cozumel and Aerocaribe offer service between Mérida and the region's other major airports—Cancún, Chetumal, Villahermosa and Tuxtla Gutiérrez. Aeroméxico also serves the small Campeche National Airport.

BY BUS

Buses are the public transportation mode of choice throughout the Yucatán Peninsula. First-class buses, though not as luxurious as in other parts of Mexico, are quiet, comfortable and reliable—and cheap. Second-class buses tend to be sort of folkloric—good practice for the bad buses in Guatemala.

Mérida's **Union de Camioneros de Yucatán** (Calle 69 between Calles 68 and 70; 24-83-91) is the hub for all bus travel in the Yucatán interior. Autobuses de Oriente Mérida-Puerto Juárez operates frequent bus service to Chichén Itzá, Valladolid and Cancún, as well as to Tzimin and Playa del Carmen. Autobuses de Oriente (ADO) has long-distance buses to Campeche and Palenque and also to other regions of Mexico. Autotransportes del Sureste en Yucatán runs buses to Palenque and Tuxtla Gutiérrez. Autotransportes del Sur operates buses to Uxmal, Kabah and Campeche. Autotransportes del Caribe has frequent buses to Ticul, in the heart of the Puuc hill country, and Caribbean coast destinations including Chetumal and Tulum. Autotransportes Peninsulares provides first-class bus service to Chetumal.

In Campeche, buses depart from the **Terminal de Autobuses de Oriente** (ADO) (Avenida Gobernadores No. 289), one-and-three-fourths kilometers from the city center. Autotransporte del Oriente buses run to Mérida, Escárcega, Palenque, San Cristóbal de las Casas and Tuxtla Gutiérrez, as well as to other destinations throughout eastern Mexico. Autotransportes del Sur operates buses to Kabah, Uxmal and Mérida.

Escárcega, a small town south of Campeche, is at a busy crossroads where many travelers change buses. There are two separate bus terminals. **Terminal de Autobuses de Oriente** (ADO), the larger of the two, has service to Campeche, Mérida, Cancún, Chetumal, Palenque, Tuxtla Gutiérrez and Villahermosa. **Terminal de Autobuses del Sur** has buses going to Campeche, Mérida, Chetumal, Xpujil, Palenque, San Cristóbal de las Casas and Tuxtla Gutiérrez.

BY TRAIN

Ferrocarriles Nacionales de Mexico, Mexico's government-owned rail system, has passenger stations in Mérida (Calle 55 between Calles 48 and 50; 23-59-44) and Campeche (Avenida Héroes de Nacozari; 6-51-48). One train daily in each direction links these cities with Palenque. The same trains serve Veracruz and Mexico City. First-class train tickets are extremely inexpensive. Many, though not all, of the "first-class" train coaches on this route are nearly 100 years old and quite run down, with disgusting restrooms. There are no private compartments and no place to lock up baggage on the train. Midnight thefts of sleeping tourists' luggage on the overnight trains are common enough to prompt official warnings. Still, the trains are perhaps the most exciting mode of travel between Mérida, Campeche and Palenque, traveling through some backcountry far away from highway routes.

CAR RENTALS

Mérida has dozens of car rental agencies, while other towns in Yucatán and Campeche states have virtually none. The price of renting a car in Mérida is about the same as in the United States and much lower than in Cancún. Rental rates double during July and August, the peak tourist season when most European travelers visit. Most rental cars in the Yucatán are new-model Volkswagen Beetles, which are more popular here than in the rest of Mexico.

In Mérida, as in most Mexican cities, hotel managers like it if you book your rental car through them. They get a commission from the rental agency, and it costs you no more than if you dealt directly with the agency. Larger hotels have travel agent desks that will help you arrange car rentals or guided tours.

There are several rent-a-car agencies at the Mérida airport, including **Algo Rent S.A. de C.V.** (24-99-66), **Autos Modelos del Mayab Dollar Rent a Car** (24-02-80), **Rent A Matic Itzá S.A.** (24-70-68) and **Renta Ejecutiva Mérida S.A. de C.V.** (24-51-96). Among the rental agencies conveniently located in the downtown area are **Cosmopolitan Rent A Car de Yucatán S. de R.L. de C.V.** (Calle 58 No. 487-4; 23-57-35), **Auto Renta Económica de Yucatán S.A.** (Calle 57 No. 500-4) and **Alquiladora Caribe S.A.** (Calle 62 No. 488-3; 24-97-91).

PUBLIC TRANSPORTATION

Taxis and tour vans dawdle in the parking lot at Chichén Itzá until about 2:00 in the afternoon. They provide local transportation to the station in Pisté for people who are traveling by bus and serve the hotels in the area. The taxi drivers will also cheerfully offer to drive you all the way to Mérida or Cancún. That's because they know foreign tourists have lots of money. (The fare is higher than the cost of a car rental.)

In Mérida, buses, taxis and other conveyances are freelance operations charging rates that are regulated by the government. Public buses go all over town at frequent intervals—every 20 minutes on most routes during daylight hours. Buses will stop for you at any marked bus stop, and there is one on just about every block. Fares are absurdly cheap.

Taxis operate from stands near the *zócalo*, the Market, Parque Hidalgo and other spots around downtown and Paseo de Montejo. Agree on the fare before you ride. *Combis* (VW shuttle buses) are midway between buses and taxis. They depart regularly from between the *zócalo* and the public market and take fixed routes to suburban areas and outlying villages.

Campeche has regular buses around town circulating out of the market district (Avenida Gobernadores and Avenida Circuito), but most of the interesting sites can be seen on foot.

SIX

Chiapas

Mexico's remaining rainforest, cool pine-clad mountain highlands and Pacific beaches lie within a few hours' drive or bus ride of each other in Chiapas. This Mexican state at the southern edge of Mexico, bordering Guatemala and the Pacific Ocean, is a land of dramatic contrasts. For visitors, the two key destinations are Palenque in the lowlands and San Cristóbal de las Casas in the highlands. From these twin bases, travelers can make side trips to waterfalls and caves, ancient ruins and present-day villages of the Tzotzil Maya, a people linked more closely to the ancient past than to the modern world just down the road.

Chiapas boasts the finest Maya ruins in Mexico—Palenque and Yaxchilán. They were once part of a network of resplendent ceremonial centers that formed a jungle kingdom stretching some 400 kilometers from Palenque to Tikal. Now, their overgrown walls and exquisite sculptures pocked with age lie within the fast-shrinking rainforest domain of the Lacandón Indians, sometimes romantically called the "last lords of Palenque."

The elegant hillside ruins at Palenque, where the richest of all Maya tombs was discovered in the 1950s, are attracting burgeoning numbers of foreign visitors. Even on busy weekends, though, the crowds at this popular national park are nothing like the throngs that pack Yucatán ruins like Tulum and Chichén Itzá. While the local hotel and restaurant industry has not yet taken on the trappings of a tourist mecca, it is easy to imagine that Palenque's popularity will continue to grow, for these incomparable ruins possess all the magic you could hope to find in any ancient ceremonial center.

The town of Palenque is also the jumping-off point for trips to Bonampak and Yaxchilán—truly lost cities deep in the Lacandón rain-forest. They can only be reached by a long trip through the jungle on a dirt track that follows the Guatemalan border at a discreet distance. Then, to get to the magnificent ceremonial center at Yaxchilán, you take a boat down the river that marks the border. Now undergoing restoration, Yaxchilán is destined to become a 21st-century tourist attraction when the government paves the road. In the meantime, this "undiscovered" site belongs to the few travelers intrepid enough to get there.

The state is home to at least five major language groups of Maya Indi-ans—the Tzotzil, Tzeltal, Lacandón, Tojolabal and Chol—who make up the majority of the population and follow a tradition-bound way of life similar to that of other highland Maya groups living across the Guatemalan border. Chiapas resembles Guatemala more than it does either main-stream Mexico or the Yucatán Peninsula, and for good reason. Chiapas was part of Guatemala from Spanish colonial times until 1841, when its leaders seceded from Central America (the stillborn nation of which Gua-temala was a part) to join Mexico for economic reasons. The Maya people had no regard for the international boundary until the 1980s, when Guatemalan military attacks on Maya villages drove tens of thou-sands of people across the border to refugee camps in Mexico. Some of the refugees have now been relocated to other parts of Mexico, while many others have been returning voluntarily to Guatemala.

Today, most of the Maya people indigenous to Chiapas live in isolated communities and homesteads situated among the cool pine forests of the highlands—fairytale villages of colorfully dressed women walking bare-foot, balancing heavy loads on their heads or weaving their fine, warm clothing on backstrap looms. At these altitudes, the pigs grow shaggy to ward off the night chill and sheep are held sacred for their warm wool.

San Cristóbal de las Casas is a Spanish colonial capital that has been largely bypassed by modern times. Surrounding the old city is the land of the highland Maya, deeply traditional people struggling to cope with the recent arrival of the rest of the world. Glimpses of their way of life gleaned from a few days' exploration in villages like San Juan Chamula, Zinacantán and Tenejapa may haunt you for a lifetime.

If you thought the tropics were always hot, San Cristóbal de las Casas will surprise you. Daytime temperatures are moderate to cool, and even on summer evenings you'll want a sweater or jacket. The thermometer can drop below freezing on winter nights, though the climate is dry in that season—it never snows. The height of the tourist season is in July and August, when San Cristóbal's cool mountain setting offers a respite from the stifling heat of lower elevations like Palenque and the Yucatán. Since the peak season coincides with the time most Europeans can travel, San Cristóbal hosts many more European visi-

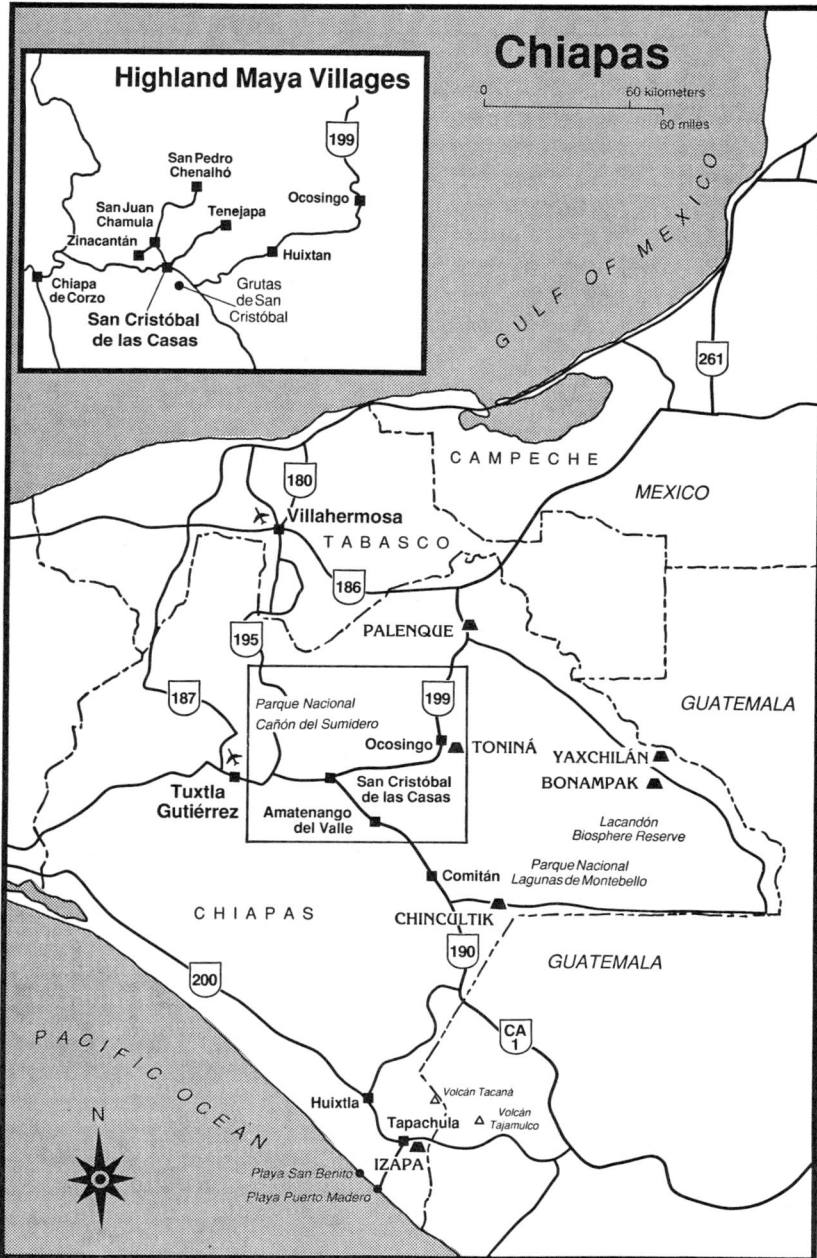

Chiapas

Highland Maya Villages

San Pedro Chenalhó

San Juan Chamula

Zinacantán

Tenejapa

Ocosingo

Huixtan

Chiapa de Corzo

San Cristóbal de las Casas

Grutas de San Cristóbal

199

0   60 kilometers

60 miles

GULF OF MEXICO

CAMPECHE

MEXICO

261

180

Villahermosa

TABASCO

186

195

PALENQUE

Parque Nacional Cañón del Sumidero

187

199

GUATEMALA

Ocosingo   TONINÁ

YAXCHILÁN

BONAMPAK

Tuxtla Gutiérrez

San Cristóbal de las Casas

Amatenango del Valle

Lacandón Biosphere Reserve

Comitán

Parque Nacional Lagunas de Montebello

CHIAPAS

CHINCULTIK

190

GUATEMALA

200

CA 1

PACIFIC OCEAN

N

Huixtla

Volcán Tacaná

Tapachula   △ Volcán Tajamulco

IZAPA

Playa San Benito

Playa Puerto Madero

Some Olmec art depicts two separate races—one with Polynesian characteristics, the other with Semitic features and beards. The true origins of the Olmec people are lost in the dim past.

tors than Americans. The slang word the local Indians call foreigners is not *gringo*, but *alemanteca* (German).

As you travel between these major milestones along the Ruta Maya, side trips will beckon, offering opportunities to swim among the wonderful waterfalls at Agua Azul, poke around the practically unknown Maya ruins at Toniná, cruise through the 4000-foot-deep Cañón del Sumidero or see what the beaches look like at the southern end of Mexico's Pacific coast.

Villahermosa

Most air travelers headed for Palenque from the United States, Mexico City or Mérida land at the Rovirosa Airport in Villahermosa (population 400,000), capital of the neighboring state of Tabasco. The city is situated just 140 kilometers west of Palenque in the heart of Mexico's oil-producing region. Too commercial to be charming, Villahermosa is nevertheless graced with wide boulevards and a modern park with a unique Olmec sculpture garden.

Parque La Venta (off Paseo Tabasco and Boulevard Grijalva), a beautiful park that weaves along La Laguna de los Illusiones, has bridges, lookout points, a columned promenade, a zoo and an unusual **outdoor museum** (admission) that resembles a sculpture garden. Three massive heads stare eerily out of thickets of tropical foliage. The Olmec people believed the head was a great source of power. The thick lips, broad noses and oriental eyes of these images lead some experts to speculate that the Olmecs may have had Polynesian roots. The 25-ton heads were hewn out of basalt dragged 160 kilometers from the nearest mountains to La Venta, an Olmec ceremonial center, more than 3000 years ago. Other Olmec monuments in the outdoor museum include stelae, altars and a tomb. All were discovered in an oil field in the Tonalá Swamps 129 kilometers northwest of Villahermosa.

Another Villahermosa must is the **Museo Regional de Antropología Carlos Pellicer Camara** (Malecón Carlos Madrazo; admission), one of Mexico's finest museums. Poet Carlos Pellicer Camara organized its fine collection of Olmec, Totonac and Maya artifacts. The museum also contains representative pieces from Aztec, Mixtec, Teotihuacán, Totonac and Zapotec cultures, as well as from archaeological sites in the states of Colima and Nayarit.

VILLAHERMOSA LODGING

The award-winning **Hotel Maya Tabasco** (Boulevard Adolfo Ruiz Cortínez No. 907 and Boulevard Grijalva; 2-18-25) is a contemporary five-story hotel with 160 large, comfortable rooms. Each is appointed with red carpets, colonial furniture and blue-tiled bath. The staff is exceptionally friendly. Moderate to deluxe.

An admirable remodeling job has made the **Hotel Don Carlos** (Avenida Francisco Madero No. 416; 2-24-92) in El Centro one of the Villahermosa area's better midrange accommodations. Rooms are clean and have televisions and telephones. The lobby-bar swings with live music nightly, and the hotel has a pool and restaurant. Moderate.

Downtown, also on the pedestrian mall, is the 68-room **Hotel Miraflores** (Calle Reforma No. 304; 2-00-54). Its modern rooms, though not especially attractive, have all the trimmings: phone, television, air-conditioning. Give the popular lobby-bar a whirl. Budget.

VILLAHERMOSA RESTAURANTS

With its checkerboard floor and cheerful service, the **Restaurant Oriente** (Avenida Francisco Madero No. 423; 2-11-01), on the edge of the downtown pedestrian mall, is the perfect place for breakfast.

THE LEGACY OF THE OLMECS

*The origin of the Maya civilization is connected with an even more ancient group, the **Olmec** people. Some anthropologists believe that the first Maya were direct descendants of Olmecs who migrated from Veracruz to colonize Chiapas and the Yucatán Peninsula. Others think the Maya civilization resulted from the influence of Olmec ideas on more primitive Maya people living along the Pacific coast of Chiapas and Guatemala.*

Exactly who the Olmecs were is one of the great mysteries of New World archaeology. Their civilization appeared suddenly around 1200 B.C. and lasted until 400 B.C. No Olmec burial remains have ever been found, and their dwellings were swallowed up by swamplands millennia ago. All that is known about the Olmec people comes from their art, which includes giant stone heads, round clay pyramids, sculptured altars and finely carved jade jewelry. The jaguar god, later revered by the Maya as the symbol of earth and night, first appeared in Olmec art. The Olmecs developed a form of writing and the foundation of the calendar system later used by the Maya and other Mexican cultures.

The ancient Maya did not fire their ceramics, but simply air-dried and painted them. The Maya pots, urns and effigies in the Villahermosa anthropology museum are so fragile that their survival is nothing short of miraculous.

Besides eggs and cereals, this busy café serves sandwiches, chicken, seafood and steaks. Budget.

Another downtown prize eatery is the sparkling, air-conditioned **Restaurant-Café Madán** (Avenida Francisco Madero No. 408; 2-16-50). The booths and carpet are part of its Americanized look. The menu features banana splits and hamburgers, plus Mexican dishes—and the food is good. Budget to moderate.

The seafood house **Restaurant-Bar Club de Pesca** (Avenida 27 de Febrero No. 812; 2-21-97) will satisfy your craving for paella and fresh fish creatively prepared, accompanied by live music nightly. Budget to moderate.

Out by the bullring on the south side of town, big bad **Carlos 'n Charlie's** (Plaza de Toros; 3-42-60) holds forth with the gags and charm typical of this Mexican chain: a bull's head wearing sunglasses in the bar, a fully set table and chairs glued upside down to the ceiling, a tropical trio playing romantic tunes. The food, from spicy shrimp consommé to *sábana invierno* (thin filet covered with beans and cheese) is delicious. Moderate.

Small but elite, **El Guaraguao** (Calle 27 de Febrero No. 947; 2-56-95) specializes in *empanadas pejelagarto* (empanadas filled with alligator fish) as well as other regional dishes from Tabasco. The few tables fill quickly in this popular spot, so go early or make a reservation. Moderate to deluxe.

VILLAHERMOSA SHOPPING

For browsing, the downtown **pedestrian mall** (along Avenida Francisco Madero) has attractive boutiques, though not many crafts. For indigenous art, try the **artisan's shop** at the Museo Regional de Antropología Carlos Pellicer Camara (Malecón Carlos Madrazo).

VILLAHERMOSA NIGHTLIFE

A good bit's stirring here after sundown. **Studio 8** (Hotel Maya Tabasco, Boulevard Ruiz Cortines No. 907; 2-18-25) is a good disco with a lobby-bar show. **Snob Disco** (Excelaris Hyatt Hotel, Avenida Benito Juárez No. 106, Colonia Linda Vista; 3-44-44) is a hopping deluxe club that draws a young crowd.

If a jazzy drink is enough action, saunter over to **Carlos 'n Charlie's** (Plaza de Toros; 3-42-60) and enjoy live tropical music amid bullfight decor. Check with the tourist department on seasonal bullfights at the neighboring bullring.

The most romantic place to relax after dark is **Los Guayacanes** (Malecón Carlos Madrazo; 2-92-85), a lovely bamboo-roofed restaurant-bar attached to the Museo Regional de Antropología and overlooking the Río Grijalva.

VILLAHERMOSA BEACHES

For a side trip to the beach, drive 108 kilometers northwest of Villa-hermosa to **Playa Paraíso**. Appropriately named, this beautiful beach is the Gulf Coast's own little piece of paradise. Sixteen kilometers long, with sand almost white against a dark forest of towering coconut palms, it stands at the end of a very circuitous route north of the delightful tropical village of Paraíso. A large, modernistic pavilion dominates the sand like a ladino Sydney Opera House, bouncing with salsa tunes on Sundays. You won't find many tourists here. Camping is good, except for nightly mosquitoes. Swimming is good, but shallow. There are launches for rent. You can also find good fishing here.

Palenque

At **Palenque** (admission), you'll find a compact array of architectur-ally exquisite temples surrounding a 1300-year-old royal palace, one of the most remarkable structures in the Maya world. Elaborate stucco sculpture was a specialty of Palenque's artists, and well-preserved examples can be found both inside and outside of several structures, along with traces of the bright red paint that once set off the city against the deep green walls of jungle.

Tucked into a pocket on the side of the Tumbala Mountains, which rise suddenly from the flatlands to the cool, remote high country, this most sacred of ancient Maya ceremonial centers consists of three com-pact clusters of buildings, some of which have been restored, and a number of other mounds on the edges of a jungle clearing. In ancient times, the temple complex of Palenque extended for at least six kilometers up and down the banks of a small river, now known as the Río Otolum.

Although Palenque's existence was known long before most other Maya ruins, it remains one of the Ruta Maya's most mysterious "lost cities." Much of Palenque's mystique comes from the overabundance of theories about its origins. The pagodalike architecture of the palace and artistic similarities to temple friezes in Cambodia have led some to see a link between Palenque and the Buddhists of Southeast Asia. Others have convinced themselves that Palenque was inspired by the Egyptians, Greeks, Hebrews or Romans. More recently, researcher Erich von Däniken has asserted that the relief sculpture on Lord Pacal's stone sarcophagus depicts an "ancient astronaut," supporting his theory that the Maya world was inspired by visitors from outer space. Somehow, explorers have often felt uncomfortable with the obvious truth that the Classic magnificence of Palenque was first conceived in the minds of "primitive" forest people.

Travelers who come to Palenque after visiting other major Maya sites such as Chichén Itzá and Uxmal will see the differences in art, architecture and environment immediately. The more you travel in the Maya world, the clearer it becomes that each ancient Maya ceremonial center was unique, displaying the singular genius of a great leader or dynasty. Most rulers, like the dwarf magician of Uxmal or the god-king whose plumed serpent emblem appears everywhere in Chichén Itzá, remain cloaked in legend. At Palenque, however, archaeologists know exactly who built the palace and temples, including exact dates of birth and death and even what they looked like and how they dressed.

Although small temples at the Palenque site were used for worship as early as 400 A.D., this remote outpost of Maya civilization only became a major ceremonial center in the year 615 A.D., when Lord Pacal, one of the greatest charismatic leaders in Maya history, ascended the throne at the age of 12. Under the rule of Pacal and his two sons, Chan Bahlum II and Kan Xul II, Palenque bloomed for a hundred years and then vanished as jungle overran its temples, pyramids, palace and ball court. By the year 720 A.D., all construction had ceased, and by 800 the city had been abandoned forever. Yet the Lacandón people, Maya descendants who live deep in the rainforest of western Chiapas, still make religious pilgrimages to hold ceremonies in these temples.

Today, the ruins at Palenque are a favorite tourist destination. While they receive only a small fraction of the number of vacationers that descend on Chichén Itzá or Tulum each day, the ruins can be quite crowded. Especially on Sundays, when admission is free, you may find yourself standing in line to descend into Lord Pacal's tomb or climb the palace tower. The most congestion-free time to visit, and perhaps the most beautiful, is in the early morning, when a soft jungle mist drifts ghostlike through the ruins.

The **Temple of Inscriptions** stands to your right as you enter the ruins area. Seventy-five feet high, it is the tallest structure at Palenque. The roof comb, now nearly gone, is thought to have added another 40 feet to its height. Although this stepped pyramid set into the hillside is no rival in size for the grand pyramids at Chichén Itzá and Uxmal, it holds a couple of surprises that have made it one of the most famous ancient Maya structures. Climb the steep stairway to the top. From there, you can see a great distance over the lowlands to the north and get the best view of the labyrinthine palace directly below. On the front of the long temple are a series of carvings that depict a Maya nobleman in formal dress holding a child. They probably represent Lord Pacal and his heir, prince Chan Bahlum II.

Inside the temple, the walls are filled with three huge panels of hieroglyphs. They are not very legible today. Fortunately, even though they doubted that anyone would ever be able to make sense of the Maya glyphs, American explorer John Lloyd Stephens and his artist companion, Frederick Catherwood, painstakingly recorded them all in 1841, before time, tourism and air pollution had taken their toll. Many archaeologists have dedicated their lives to translating these particular inscriptions, and today they are understood to contain a genealogy of Lord Pacal and a history of the major events during his reign.

Another secret of the Temple of Inscriptions remained hidden for more than a century after Stephens and Catherwood surveyed Palenque. In 1948, Mexican archaeologist Alberto Ruz Lhuiller chanced to notice that the floor inside the temple was slightly higher than the platform outside. Searching for an explanation, he discovered that one

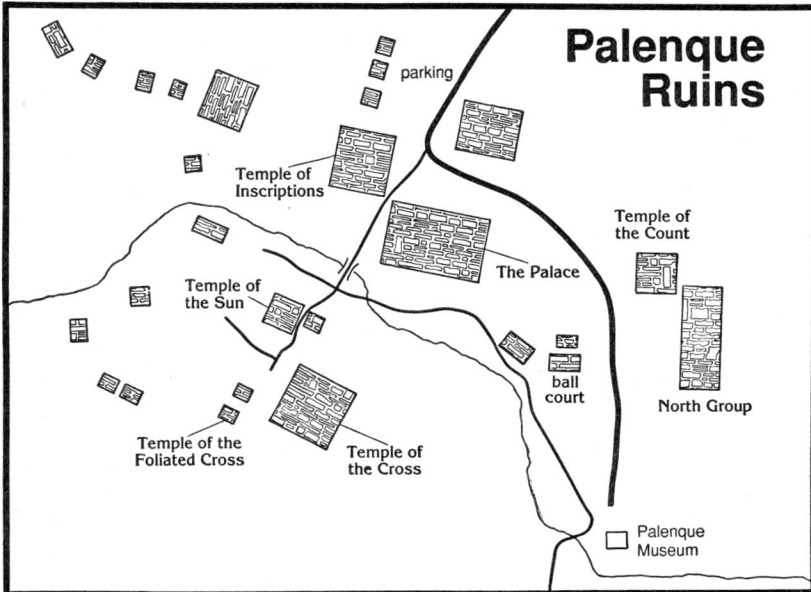

Palenque Ruins

Stucco, used to create elaborate sculpted friezes such as those found at Palenque, was made from powdered limestone. It was quite similar to modern concrete.

of the floor flagstones had holes in it that could be used to lift it. Under the stone was an opening filled with rock and rubble that turned out to be a secret stairway.

Lhuiller spent four years hauling rocks out of the stairway. When he finally reached the bottom, which was lower than the ground level on which the pyramid stood, he found eight corpses. They were young men, buried there to guard the mortal remains of Lord Pacal himself, who lay dressed in ceremonial garb and jade ornaments in a sarcophagus under a five-ton slab of rock. Carved on the slab was one of the most spectacular bas-relief sculptures ever found in the Maya world.

The bones and treasures were taken to the National Museum of Anthropology in Mexico City, but the sarcophagus can still be seen by descending the steep, slippery stairway down close green-walled passageways to the tomb. According to experts, the bas-relief depicts Pacal descending into the underworld on a "foliated cross," a powerful symbol from Classic Maya times that is still a common sight in the highland villages of Chiapas. Believers in the "gods from outer space" theory could be right: if you squint your eyes, it *does* look a lot like an ancient astronaut.

Pacal's tomb was the first royal Maya burial discovered by modern archaeologists. Since then, others have been found at Tikal, Guatemala, and Copán, Honduras, while at Palenque more than a thousand burials of lesser personages have been discovered within the ceremonial complex. But no other Maya tomb yet found can rival the splendor of Lord Pacal's.

Past the Temple of Inscriptions is Palenque's most fascinating building, known simply as the **Palace**. It was built one addition at a time over more than a century as the royal residence of Lord Pacal and his clan, who are represented in stucco friezes throughout the complex. It is an intricate maze of a ruin, with inner courtyards, dank vaulted galleries, porticoes, underground passageways, a five-story tower and pagodalike roofs. You can spend an hour or more just poking around in this structure.

Many archaeologists believe the tower of the Palace was built as an astronomical observatory. The tower was situated so that on the winter solstice the sun when viewed from it sets directly behind the Temple of Inscriptions—into the tomb of Lord Pacal.

The Palace contains 176 separate fragments of painting and sculpture. Most of the sculpture at Palenque, except for hieroglyphs, was done in stucco, which the artist made by mixing finely powdered limestone with water to make a paste similar to modern concrete. It allowed the artists to do more elaborate high-relief work than was possible with limestone. Unfortunately, the jungle dampness destroys stucco quickly, leaving modern visitors to marvel at the remaining fragmentary examples and speculate on what the city must have looked like when all the sculptured friezes were intact and painted bright yellow, blue and green against the city's red walls. What has endured at Palenque and especially on the Palace is considered to be the finest decorative architecture of pre-Hispanic America. The delicately rendered facial expressions in the friezes speak to us today with all the power and passion their creators put into them.

Following the main footpath beyond the Palace takes you past Palenque's small, partly buried **ball court** and a multilevel cluster of little buildings known as the **North Group**. Just west of the North Group is the **Temple of the Count**, where Austrian artist Jean-Frédéric Maximilien, Comte de Waldeck, lived while working on his romanticized paintings of Palenque during the 1830s. You will understand why the count chose this structure to call home when you see the picture-perfect view of the main ruins from its doorway.

At the end of the main trail, just beyond the North Group, is the **Palenque Museum**. The central exhibit is a huge tablet of hieroglyphs originally found in the Palace. At the top of the tablet, a relief carving shows Lord Pacal, his wife, Ahpo-Hel, and their second son Kan Xul—a 7th-century family portrait that was probably made when Lord Kan

---

STEPHENS "DISCOVERS" PALENQUE

Palenque was "discovered" by gentleman adventurer John Lloyd Stephens during his first expedition to Central America in 1837. Actually, for nearly 70 years before Stephens' arrival, Palenque had been known to Spanish explorers, who had removed some of the best sculptures and hieroglyph panels and sent them to King Charles III of Spain. It was Stephens, however, who captured the public imagination with a series of books recording his adventures.

Stephens astonished the reading public with his bestselling two-volume work, Incidents of Travel in Central America, Chiapas and Yucatán *(1841). The climax of that book was a detailed 90-page description of the wonders of Palenque— and Stephens' attempts to buy the site. The 35 detailed drawings of Palenque by Stephens' illustrator companion, Frederick Catherwood, are widely reproduced as prints and sold in tourist shops along the Ruta Maya today. The book and its sequel have stayed in print for more than 150 years and still make for entertaining reading.*

Although the ancient Maya did not use gold or other precious metals, they were adept at carving gemstones, including jade, crystal, turquoise, amethyst and emerald. Shields, helmets and breastplates were often covered with mosaics of precious stones.

Xul ascended the throne long after his parents' deaths. The museum also contains stucco sculptures, jade jewelry and the only stele found at Palenque.

Across the river, to the east of the Temple of Inscriptions, a group of three temples stands out against the surrounding forest. These are the **Temple of the Cross**, the **Temple of the Foliated Cross** and the **Temple of the Sun**. From a distance, the three structures appear to be rather small. The two lofty and delicate-looking roof combs that remain intact seem larger than the temples they crown. It is only as you walk into the plaza between the temples that you realize their massive scale. They are set on high pyramids that were once stuccoed and painted but are now buried and covered with grass. All three temples, representing a "holy trinity" of gods who were believed to be the ancestors of Palenque's royal family, were built simultaneously in honor of Lord Pacal's successor—his older son, Chan Bahlum II—when he ascended the throne in 683 A.D.

The eastern temple group has provided speculative thinkers with clues hinting that foreigners from across the ocean might have influenced the building of Palenque. Relief sculptures in the Temple of the Foliated Cross are strikingly similar to some found at Angkor Wat in Cambodia. Flower motifs in the temple sculptures resemble nothing so much as the lotus, an Asian plant that was unknown in ancient Mexico. Large, sculptured stone crosses found inside two of the temples even provided evidence that led some early scholars to believe Palenque was built by medieval Christian missionaries.

A relief panel to the right of the doorway to the Temple of the Cross is the oldest known picture of a person smoking a cigar—just like the hand-rolled ones used today among the Lacandón Indians, descendants of the people of Palenque.

It is worth your time and energy to venture into the backcountry of **Palenque National Park** during your visit. Although the park is not large, it preserves the only remnant of virgin rainforest in Chiapas that is accessible by paved road. The main route into the forest is a trail that follows the west side of the river from one park boundary to the other. If you take the trail downriver past the museum and staff residences, you will come to a series of waterfalls with idyllic little pools for swimming. After a couple of steep descents down rock faces, the trail meets the main road near Mayabel Campground. For a longer hike, take the trail that runs south along the hillside above the river for about six kilometers to an Indian village where local people live by subsistence farming on fields they created by slashing and burning the rainforest, much as farmers did during Palenque's heyday. The Palenque backcountry, with its towering ceiba trees and hanging vines, is one of the last places in Mexico where the throaty cries of endangered black howler monkeys still ring through the forest.

The ladino town of **Palenque** (population 30,000) near Route 186, about seven kilometers from the archaeological site, was called Santo Domingo until the ruins became a famous tourist destination with the discovery of Pacal's tomb. Its name has been changed to Palenque on maps and train and bus schedules. Locals still use the old name, and you can quickly win new friends with remarks like "*Mucho gusto Santo Domingo*" ("I like Santo Domingo a lot"). To avoid confusion with the ruins and respect local tradition, many people refer to the town as "Santo Domingo Palenque."

The western side of town, where the bus stations and most hotels are located, has only a few streets. Along a rugged ravine called *La Cañada* that fills the northwest quarter of the town, many of the houses have no road access and are reached by steep footpaths. Proceed west along Avenida Juárez to reach the long, narrow concrete plaza in front of the church. Past the plaza, the upper end of town is residential in character. Stroll through a few back streets to see all the little urban farmsteads teeming with pigs, turkeys, goats and even burros, right in the middle of town.

COUNT WALDECK AT PALENQUE

Jean-Frédéric Maximilien, Comte de Waldeck, a gentleman artist from Austria, lived among the ruins of Palenque from 1832 to 1835, several years before the Americans Stephens and Catherwood "discovered" the site. Waldeck, who was 64 years of age when he arrived, lived with his local Indian mistress first in the small temple now called the Temple of the Count and later in a compound of huts below the Temple of the Sun.

Waldeck's many paintings of Palenque, always depicting the ruins in a romantic golden glow, were captivating but wildly inaccurate. Eager to support his conviction that the Maya culture had its roots in the ancient civilizations of the Mediterranean, Waldeck filled his paintings with stylistic details borrowed from ancient Egypt and Greece. He also imagined Hebrew, Hindu and Roman artistic influences.

The eccentric count left Palenque to retire in Paris, where in 1838 the publication of the illustrated book of his discoveries in the Maya world caused great excitement and made him a celebrity.

PALENQUE LODGING

Palenque National Park does not have any luxury tourist accommodations within walking distance of the ruins the way Chichén Itzá, Uxmal and Cobá do. The only place to sleep at the park is the funky **Camping Mayabel**, which has tent and RV campsites, *palapas* for hammock campers and a few very basic motel-style rooms, as well as a small restaurant. The hillside campground is surrounded by rainforest on three sides, and a trail leads to nearby waterfalls and small Maya ruins.

The nearest jungle lodge to Palenque National Park is **Centro Turístico-Cultural Chan-Kah Resort Village** (Km. 3 Carretera a las Ruinas; 5-03-18). The resort is midway between the ruins (too far to walk up the steep road, though it's a nice sunset walk back down) and the town of Palenque. Minibuses run back and forth along the ruins road constantly, so you will never have to wait more than a few minutes for a ride either to town or to the ruins. The charge is just a few cents. Guest accommodations in the resort are spacious, modern duplex units scattered throughout the lush, landscaped grounds around a series of river-fed swimming pools. The management claims that the water comes from a mountain spring that was sacred to the ancient Maya for its miraculous restorative properties. The huge, thatch-roofed, open-air main building houses the lobby, restaurant and spacious sitting areas. Rates range from moderate to deluxe. The same owners also operate the **Hotel Chan-Kah Centro** (Hidalgo 15; 5-03-18), a newish hotel near the main plaza in Santo Domingo Palenque. The bright, modern rooms have ceiling fans and private baths, and there is a large second-floor terrace. Rates are low-moderate.

In the countryside on the outskirts of the town of Palenque, you'll find the area's most luxurious lodging, the **Hotel Misión Palenque** (Route 199; 5-02-41). This recent addition to the familiar chain of upscale Yucatán hotels offers guest rooms with televisions, phones and air-conditioning. Facilities include a swimming pool and tennis courts. The hotel provides free shuttle service to the ruins for guests. This is also the largest hotel around, with 160 rooms. Deluxe.

Another interesting lodge in the Palenque area is the **Hotel Nututún Viva** (Km. 3 Carretera Ocosingo, 5-01-00), located a short distance out of town on the road that goes up the mountains to Agua Azul, Misol-Ha and San Cristóbal de las Casas. This moderate-priced 60-unit motel is a real bargain. The air-conditioned guest rooms have phones and satellite television. There are landscaped gardens as well as a natural, inviting river swimming area. It is only practical to stay here if you have a car, since local public transportation along this road is unpredictable at best. Taxis can take you between the hotel and the town of Palenque for a few dollars each way.

There are dozens of smaller hotels in the commercial district and west side of the town of Palenque. Those on the main streets offer low rates but generally spartan accommodations and can be noisy. If you wish to stay in town, your best bet is the **Hotel La Cañada** (Calle Cañada; 5-01-02), secluded in a forest setting just a few blocks from the center of town. Guest accommodations are in cottages that were originally built for archaeologists during the restoration of the Palenque ruins. Most have air-conditioning and bathtubs. Moderate.

PALENQUE RESTAURANTS

Visitors to the Palenque ruins have two options for lunch or dinner nearby. The budget-priced option is the small thatch-roofed restaurant at **Camping Mayabel** just inside the national park entrance. The simple, filling fare features tacos, pizza and such, along with delightfully cold soft drinks and beer. Halfway between town and the ruins, the full-service restaurant at **Chan-Kah Resort Village** (Km. 3 Carretera a las Ruinas; 5-03-18) offers well-prepared chicken and fish dishes in a quiet, casual atmosphere with a touch of tropical elegance. Prices, in the deluxe range, are much higher than the same meal would cost in town.

In the town of Palenque, one of our favorites is **Restaurant Girasoles** (Avenida Juárez No. 189; 5-03-83), an unassuming checkered-tablecloth café that offers a good selection of conventional Mexican dishes. This is about the only restaurant in Palenque that opens before 8:00 in the morning, and breakfast specialties include *chilaquiles* (leftover tortillas cooked with chile, chicken and cheese—a tasty Mexican favorite) and the best cup of coffee in town. Budget.

Across the street, **Restaurante Montes Azules** (Avenida Juárez No. 20) features an all natural wood decor and a lovely view of the *cañada* that runs through the lower end of town. Food here is just plain good. A typical *comida corrida* (daily special) consists of fried catfish served with carrot salad, chicken soup and rice, coffee or tea and, for dessert, flan. Budget. Late in the evening, musicians play the marimba here—just about the only entertainment possibility in a town that is devoid of nightlife.

Probably the nicest restaurant in the town of Palenque is **La Selva** (Calle Hidalgo; 5-03-63), next door to the Hotel La Cañada. Hidden in a junglelike setting within walking distance of Avenida Juárez and the *zócalo*, this place offers fine dining in a self-consciously tropical atmosphere. Waiters dress in flamboyant regional style and ceiling fans spin incessantly. Try the fajitas. Deluxe.

PALENQUE SHOPPING

The most distinctive souvenir items sold around Palenque are the hand-made arrows of the Lacandón Indians who live in the surrounding rainforest. The arrows have brightly colored tail feathers and assorted styles of chipped stone and sharpened bone tips. When they are used for hunting, the tips are dipped in poison. Sets of arrows that have actually been used (though probably not poisoned) sell at a higher price than those originally made for the tourist trade, though they don't look much different. The arrows are usually sold in splays of from 5 to 15 that can be folded for carrying, then fanned out to hang on your wall back home. White-garbed Lacandones sell them by the parking lot at Palenque ruins and at the Agua Azul waterfalls.

Several shops and vendors' stalls in the town of Palenque offer reproductions of Lord Pacal's sarcophagus and other sculptures from the Palenque ruins in a variety of media from leather burnings and plaster-of-paris castings to wood carvings and limestone sculptures. Palenque is full of highly skilled craftspeople who have been making these reproductions for years, and the workmanship is often quite fine.

Bonampak and Yaxchilán

Many ruins enthusiasts say that Yaxchilán is their favorite Maya site—better than Palenque, Copán or Tikal. Yaxchilán is the Maya ceremonial center most recently opened to public view. The adventure of getting there, of discovering as if for the first time the ruins of a once-great city deep in the jungle, makes a trip to Yaxchilán and the smaller outlying site of Bonampak one of the most memorable experiences on the Maya Route.

Situated deep in the Lacandón rainforest on the Guatemalan border, Bonampak and Yaxchilán were accessible only by private-charter bush planes flying out of Tuxtla Gutiérrez and Villahermosa until 1985. That was the year the Mexican government responded to worsening social violence in Guatemala (which had driven more than 40,000 Maya villagers over the border to refugee camps in Mexico and erupted in clashes with Guatemalan soldiers on the Mexican side of the Usamacinta River) by building a 463-kilometer unpaved *carretera frontera* (border highway) along the entire border between Chiapas and Guatemala. The road also served to open the border region to settlement. Today, visitors who go to Yaxchilán by plane see a dramatic border panorama—pristine, impenetrable rainforest on the Guatemala side; cleared agricultural lands on the Mexican side.

Animals depicted in ancient Maya paintings such as those at Bonampak include owls, cougars, serpents, monkeys, tapirs and a variety of birds.

The border "highway" makes it possible to travel most of the way to Bonampak and Yaxchilán by minivan tour or private car. Reasonably priced overnight tours run regularly from Palenque. You spend the night in a hammock in a Quonset hut dormitory—the only tourist accommodation around. Inquire in Santo Domingo Palenque at Viajes Toniná (Avenida Juárez No. 105; 5-03-84). The unpaved road is good enough for passenger cars as far as the trailhead for Bonampak and all the way to Corozal, the departure point for the boat downriver to Yaxchilán. One-day airplane tours, which are very expensive, can be arranged at the airport in either Santo Domingo Palenque or San Cristóbal de las Casas.

A road is under construction that will someday take tourist traffic right up to both Bonampak and Yaxchilán. In the meantime, whether you get there by private car, tour van or flightseeing plane, the trip to Bonampak involves ten kilometers on a rough road that often washes out, followed by a hot hike through the jungle. To reach Yaxchilán, you must park in the little river port of Corozal (also called Echeverría) and take a power launch downriver to the ruins. The boat trip takes about 45 minutes to get there, but the return trip against the current takes twice as long.

Bonampak is set in the foothills of the mountain range that separates the Lacanja and Usamacinta river valleys. The tropical rainforest that shrouds the hills gives the ruin an atmosphere of mystery and great age. The site is made up of a small plaza surrounded by a group of buildings, most of them crumbled into mounds of stone rubble. When archaeologists "discovered" it in 1946, Bonampak was still being used ceremonially by the Lacandón Indians who lived in the surrounding forest, descendants of the people who built the temples between 200 and 900 A.D. Archaeologists found elaborately carved stelae and charted all the structures at the site except one, which was so hidden by tangled greenery that early expeditions overlooked it, even though it was in the heart of the complex. Later the same year, United Fruit Company photographer Giles G. Healy found his way into the hidden building, which was dubbed simply **Building 1**. The works of art concealed inside would revolutionize scientists' ideas about the ancient Maya civilization.

Three chambers inside Building 1 contain panels of frescoes. Painted on surfaces of wet limestone cement, the whole array containing some 270 human figures was completed in just 48 hours. Now, 1200 years later, the frescoes are by far the best-preserved examples known of Maya painting. Once brilliant in their hues, they have faded badly since their discovery, but reproductions have been installed for comparison. (Other copies of these famous paintings can be found in the Museum of Anthropology in Mérida, the Regional Museum of Anthropology in Villahermosa, the National Museum of Anthropology in Mexico City and the Hotel Bonampak in Tuxtla Gutiérrez.)

The Bonampak frescoes tell the story of a raid and sacrificial ceremony. In the first room, nobles dressed in jaguar-skin robes and elaborate headdresses, carrying richly decorated scepters, organize their warriors for battle as musicians and masked dancers perform a processional that may have been a kind of war dance. The painting in the central room shows the raid itself, as armed warriors of Bonampak swoop down on a rival village. Despite the bloodthirsty brutality evident in the painting, the limited weaponry of the Maya army suggests that the main purpose of the raids was to maim and take prisoners, not to kill. A smaller painting in the same room shows a group of prisoners being led before the lord of Bonampak for judgment. In the third room, we see one of the prisoners being sacrificed on the temple steps while his fellow prisoners plead for their lives. The favored method for killing prisoners of war appears to have been hacking off their heads with a big stone knife.

Before the paintings were found, experts and laymen alike generally believed that the Maya were a peaceful, morally superior people who lived under the benign rule of philosophers and found spiritual guidance by studying the mysteries of time and the universe. Any evidence of human sacrifice at other sites, especially Chichén Itzá, could be explained away as evil influences imported from central Mexico by the Toltecs. But now, deep in the rainforest where no Toltec ever ventured, the Bonampak frescoes revealed a savage world where warlords ruled over a rigid caste system and slaughtered neighboring communities to enhance their own prestige—in other words, a society not much different from the one Cortez found in the Aztec empire some 700 years later.

Since the discovery of the Bonampak murals, archaeologists have found other evidence of warfare among the Maya cities in Classic times. Experts in reconstructing Maya history from hieroglyphs have learned, for instance, of a long-running conflict between Tikal and its neighboring city of Uaxactún that reshaped the power structure throughout the Petén every time a general devised a new combat tactic. What nobody knows is whether mass violence was widespread in ancient Maya society or limited to a few anomalous times and places.

After all, the Bonampak murals were painted in 48 hours out of the 700-year history of this small, remote settlement on the western outskirts of the vast Maya empire. Few other artworks of the Classic Pe-

Priests' visions were central to ancient Maya religion. Depicted as curling, smokelike rays in friezes at Palenque and Yaxchilán, the visions were induced by psychoactive plants and self-inflicted pain.

riod in Maya history deal with military subjects. Could Bonampak have been some kind of outlaw stronghold when the paintings were made? Or could Building 1 have been a temple of some strange religious sect? Once, hundreds of temples throughout the Maya world must have contained such murals, now lost to the ravages of time. Would they have corroborated the Bonampak view of Maya civilization, or would they have shown us that the Maya world was one of greater cultural diversity than we realize? As is usually the case in Maya archaeology, the discovery of the Bonampak frescoes raised more questions than it answered.

When you return from Bonampak to the main road, you're less than 20 kilometers south of Yaxchilán as the crow flies. But to get there, you need to drive east for an hour to **Corozal** (Echeverría), a small port across the Usamacinta River from a remote area of the Petén in Guatemala. Van tours and independent adventurers traveling by car spend the night here. (Bring your own food and camping equipment. Tourist facilities are probably inevitable in Corozal's future, but today they do not exist.) In the morning, visitors take a motorized launch from Corozal to Yaxchilán, about a 45-minute trip down a river that flows smooth as glass and deep green with algae between solid walls of jungle.

Yaxchilán was a major ceremonial center during the same period as Palenque to the north and Tikal to the east. Building began here around 200 A.D. The city reached its highest development under two lords, Jaguar Shield and his son Bird Jaguar, in the 700s. Although Yaxchilán was deserted around 900 A.D., like other lowland Chiapas sites it is still used for religious rituals by the Lacandón Maya people who inhabit the surrounding rainforest. According to anthropologist/photographer Gertrude Blum, who spent years among the Lacandones, they believe that their chief god, Hatchak'yum, lives in the ruins of Yaxchilán.

Although we think of Yaxchilán today as one of the loneliest places along the Ruta Maya and one of the hardest to reach, 1200 years ago it was a big, busy port city. Boats were the fastest and easiest transportation mode in the ancient Maya world, and the Usamacinta was its longest navigable river. Yaxchilán's strategic position made it a key commercial center from which trade routes reached to the Petén, the Maya highlands and the lowlands around Palenque.

For more than a decade, the Mexican government promoted a plan for a series of dams on the Usamacinta River that would have flooded Yaxchilán. The plan has been abandoned (for now).

Disembarking by the **main plaza**, which is set along the river's edge, visitors will find it easy to imagine the clamor and commotion that must have characterized the busy, colorful waterfront in bygone days. Adjoining the plaza are two ball courts, several low platforms that may have been marketplaces and the ruins of structures that were probably residences and warehouses.

The ruins of Yaxchilán cover a larger area than those at Palenque, though only a few structures have had any restoration work so far. A total of 86 stone buildings have been identified at the site. The dense tangle of giant trees and choking vines has been cleared away to expose the tops of about 40 structures whose foundation mounds remain buried—manmade hills in the forest floor.

Yaxchilán is unusual in that the surrounding terrain along a gooseneck in the river prevented it from being organized in a square, oriented to the paths of planets, as are most other Classic Maya sites. Instead, the city is built up from the main plaza in a series of terraces.

A long stairway climbs more than 200 feet from the main plaza to the site's showpiece ceremonial temple, called **Structure 33**, the dominant temple at Yaxchilán, with its long roof comb decorated with a sculpture of a seated god. From that level, another stairway to the south continues even higher—to **Structure 41**, on a hilltop 360 feet in elevation, making it much higher than any manmade pyramid in the Maya world. The third major area is **Structure 44**, on a separate hilltop to the west. This unexcavated ruin was a complex labyrinth of rooms and courtyards similar to the Palace at Palenque or the North Acropolis at Tikal. A series of five monumental stelae stands in front of Structure 44. Some of the best examples of the sculpted lintels for which Yaxchilán is famed can be found over three doorways, and the doorsteps are carved with rows of hieroglyphs.

The art of Yaxchilán rivals almost anything at Palenque, and the secluded rainforest setting far from the roar of tour buses makes it all the more magical. At Yaxchilán, limestone lintels, stelae and interior and exterior walls all were carved with hieroglyphic inscriptions, portraits of royalty and many dramatic scenes that seem to be windows into the dark side of the ancient Maya spirit. Warfare, captivity and ritual bloodletting are common themes, as are symbolic representations of sacred visions. Unlike any other known Maya center, many relief sculptures are of women, suggesting that they may have been rulers or priests. One such lintel sculpture depicts a woman driving a stingray spine through her tongue in a ceremony designed to induce visions, symbolized by the smokelike patterns coming from her head. Was Yaxchilán known in the Maya world as a place of prophecy, as tour guides claim?

Sculpture, in fact, seems to be strewn everywhere in Yaxchilán in broken fragments so alien and fraught with symbolism as to defy 20th-century understanding. Our only regret at Yaxchilán is that there is never enough time to spend poking around in the hills and ravines for more artistic enigmas to puzzle over. As long as the only access to Yaxchilán is by hired boat and there is no place to stay in the vicinity, visits are limited to a few brief hours. Some day, when the road to Yaxchilán is completed and archaeological hotels begin to spring up nearby, future travelers will be able to linger at Yaxchilán for days on end—but never again with the solitude that can be experienced there today.

NOTE: Although a glance at the map makes following the border "highway" beyond Yaxchilán all the way to Lagunas de Montebello and Comitán look like an intriguing plan, it is only feasible if you have a high-clearance vehicle and several extra five-gallon cans of gasoline. The journey cannot be made in a single day, and there is no food, lodging or designated camping anywhere along the route. Beyond the tiny settlement of Boca Lacantun, the "highway" through the jungle becomes sort of vague and theoretical in places.

Ocosingo Area

Less than an hour out of the town of Palenque on the Carretera Ocosingo, a good, recently paved road that climbs up the mountains to San Cristóbal de las Casas, you will come to **Misol-Ha** (admission), a waterfall that plunges 100 feet into a picture-perfect pool. Here you can enjoy a swim in an idyllic rainforest setting. Farther up the Ocosingo road from Misol-Ha, the waterfalls at **Agua Azul** (admission) are spectacular not for their height but for their number and expanse. More than 500 falls spill between large limestone pools that comprise this, the most popular swimming spot in Chiapas. Especially on hot, sunny weekends, you'll find hundreds of bathers from as far away as Tuxtla Gutiérrez enjoying the cool mountain water. In the dry season, it has a brilliant azure hue. When the rains come, the water turns muddy, but the power of the falls during the wet season is impressive enough to merit a visit even then. A trail leads upriver for about two kilometers to a small village.

If you are driving from Palenque to San Cristóbal de las Casas in your own vehicle or a rental car, it's easy to stop at either or both swimming spots en route. Non-drivers can reach Agua Azul by taking

one of the second-class buses that run between Santo Domingo Palenque and San Cristóbal de las Casas six times a day. Ask the driver to let
you off at Agua Azul Crucero, where the rough road to Agua Azul
leaves the highway. It is a four-and-a-half-kilometer hike from the
highway down to the falls. You'll have to climb back up to the highway
and catch another second-class bus back to Santo Domingo Palenque
or onward to San Cristóbal de las Casas before about 4:00 p.m. An
easier way to reach both Misol-Ha and Agua Azul is to take one of the
colectivos (minibuses) that leave Santo Domingo Palenque every morning between 9:00 and 10:00, returning in midafternoon. The fares are
quite low, but you may find the stop at Misol-Ha far too brief. Guided
tours that stop for a full hour at Misol-Ha and two hours at Agua Azul
can be arranged in Santo Domingo Palenque through Viajes Toniná
(Avenida Juárez No. 105; 5-03-84).

Midway to San Cristóbal de las Casas, the highway passes through
Ocosingo. The majority of the 20,000 inhabitants in this plain, poor
town are Tzeltal Maya. If you are driving, you can make a detour here
to visit the little-known Maya ruin of **Toniná** (admission), located 14
kilometers east of town. From the *zócalo*, five blocks east of the main
highway, turn south on Calle 1 Oriente Sur, the street that runs in
front of the main church. Watch closely for signs that mark the way to
Toniná at each fork in the road.

Toniná, a large ceremonial center built on seven levels up a terraced
hillside, was inhabited at the same time as the great ceremonial centers

---

PROTECTOR OF THE INDIANS

Bartolomé de las Casas, *for whom San Cristóbal de las Casas was partly named,
came to the Americas as an* encomendado—*a possessor of Indians "given" to him
sight-unseen by the king of Spain—within ten years after Columbus landed. As he
came to know "his" Indians in the Caribbean, he had a spiritual enlightenment
and began complaining to the king about the brutal mistreatment of the Indians.*

*Las Casas renounced his grant from the king to become a priest at age 36. His
missionary work in Venezuela, Guatemala and Peru earned him the title of Protector of
the Indians, as well as the enmity of both the military and slave owners. At the age
of 70, he was appointed to serve as the first Bishop of Chiapas in the recently
founded capital, San Cristóbal. Three years later, he was recalled to Spain to answer
charges trumped up by his enemies. In his own defense, he informed the king that
15 million Indians had died in the half-century since Columbus landed and went on
to argue that Indians were people and therefore entitled to basic human rights—a
revolutionary idea in 1544! Las Casas was acquitted of all charges and returned to
San Cristóbal, where he spent his remaining years among the Maya people.*

at Palenque and Yaxchilán. The highest of eight temples at the site, a huge pyramid that stands 200 feet above the main plaza, was excavated by a French government expedition. As for the rest, so little excavation or restoration work has been done at Toniná that it takes a lot of imagination to visualize the city that once filled this valley.

Toniná does have a lot of well-preserved sculptures and hieroglyphs. The decoration shows artistic influences not only from Palenque and Yaxchilán but also from as far away as the Puuc hill country around Uxmal in western Yucatán. The best example is the shrine to Chac, the rain god, on the fourth level. While several theories have been proposed that would account for the presence of the Puuc style here, it lends credibility to the old legend that Uxmal was an ancient "university" from which ideas were exported to distant parts of the Maya world.

The best of Toniná's stelae, altars, calendar stones, jade carvings and other sculptures have been gathered in a **museum**, which is the most interesting place to see at the site. One sandstone panel depicts Lord Kan Xul II of Palenque bound as a prisoner. Royal burial chambers have also been unearthed high on the hillside, and a dubious local legend has it that a highly ornamented underground chamber once formed the entrance to a cave leading all the way from Toniná to Palenque—75 kilometers away!

OCOSINGO AREA LODGING

For a town of 20,000 people, Ocosingo has quite a few hotels. Foreign tourists are a rarity here, however, and most accommodations cater to Mexican low-budget travelers who wish to avoid the tourist-zone prices in Palenque and San Cristóbal de las Casas. The best hotel in town is the **Hotel Central** (Avenida Central 1; 3-00-39), facing the *zócalo*. This colonial-style hotel has bright, airy rooms with private baths and ceiling fans. Some even have satellite television. The budget rates are so reasonable that there is no reason to settle for one of Ocosingo's cheaper, noisier, bathroom-down-the-hall hotels.

OCOSINGO AREA RESTAURANTS

The **Restaurant La Montura** (Avenida Central No. 5), on the plaza next door to the Hotel Central, serves tasty baked chicken dishes and other conventional fare at open-air tables ideal for observing life in the heart of this small mountain town. Prices, which range from budget to moderate, are higher than you would find elsewhere in town, but the sidewalk setting is worth every peso.

If you're up for something a little more adventurous, walk one block west of the *zócalo*, where the **Restaurante San Cristóbal** (Avenida

Central No. 22) offers a limited menu with changing daily specials, such as delicious chicken mole, at low budget prices. The, uh, "interesting" decor, typical of Guatemalan jungle restaurants but quite unusual for Mexico, consists of an amazing clutter of bad taxidermy—wild animal skins, armadillo shells, dried bats and stuffed birds—peering at you from dimly lit corners. Ask and the owner might tell you the stories behind the dead animals while you eat.

San Cristóbal de las Casas

The transition from Palenque to San Cristóbal de las Casas (population 100,000) couldn't be more dramatic. From the steamy jungle heat of the lowlands, a few hours' drive or bus ride takes you to cool pine forests 7000 feet above sea level. San Cristóbal is situated in the center of a broad valley, surrounded by high mountain peaks. Wood smoke from thousands of fireplaces drifts in the crisp early morning air at any time of year. In winter, when the Yucatán Peninsula fills up with *norteamericano* refugees from the snow and ice back home, San Cristóbal has freezing nights and snow may dust the surrounding mountains. In the summer months, when so much of Mexico swelters under stifling heat, humidity and incessant rain, San Cristóbal's mild climate seems a lot like paradise.

San Cristóbal de las Casas was the capital of Chiapas from its founding in the 1500s until 1892. At that time, 50 years after Chiapas broke its ties with Guatemala and became a Mexican state, the national government decided that it was too hard to get to and moved the capital to Tuxtla Gutiérrez. Today, all of San Cristóbal has been declared a national historic district to preserve and protect its traditional character, its stately old colonial architecture and narrow, colorful streets.

The elusive, magical character of San Cristóbal invites comparison to other destinations—none of them in Mexico—that share a certain distinctive allure. It is like Santa Fe, New Mexico, sophisticated and timeless, surrounded by Indians, provincial and proud of it. It is like Antigua Guatemala, a bastion of the past where American and European expatriates, Mexico City refugees and soul-saving missionaries to the native people together hold the excesses of the modern age at bay.

The people who write official tourist brochures for the state of Chiapas claim that San Cristóbal's central **zócalo** area is like the Paris of an earlier century. Except for the Indians, they may be right. The city center looks mountain-rustic, as ornate as you'd expect a Spanish colonial capital city to be, and very old. Park pigeons abound. Unlike elsewhere in Mexico, this plaza is busiest in the afternoon and almost deserted after dark.

Check the bulletin board in front of the **tourist office** on the south-west side of the plaza. San Cristóbal, more than any other place on the Ruta Maya, supports independent, culturally sensitive and environmentally aware tour guides who will show you insights into village life that you would have a hard time discovering on your own. Guides known only by their first names—Mercedes and Alejandro are legendary—post flyers without phone numbers on this bulletin board telling where to meet in the morning.

For an overview of the city, climb the long, long stairway that starts at four blocks south and two blocks west of the *zócalo* at the corner of Allende and H. Dominguez, 266 steps up to the hilltop **San Cristóbal Chapel**, dedicated to Saint Christopher, the patron saint of the city and of Columbus and all travelers since. Except for a lifelike statue of the saint carrying young Jesus on his shoulder, the interior of the chapel is quite plain. You may hear prayers in the strange, loud style of the Maya people. Walk around behind the chapel to see the huge sculpture of Christ on the cross—made entirely of old license plates.

Back at the *zócalo*, walk six blocks north on Utrilla to reach San Cristóbal's colorful public market. Midway along, you'll come to **Santo Domingo Church**, a formidable edifice that dates back to 1547. The facade, added a century later, incorporates the coat of arms of the Spanish king along with nearly full-sized statues of apostles. The interior is dazzling with gold leaf and often thick with copal, the sacred incense of the Maya.

Behind Santo Domingo Church is the showroom of **Sna Jolobil Weavers' Cooperative**. The cooperative represents more than 600

OUTCASTS OF THE CHIAPAS HIGHLANDS

In San Cristóbal de las Casas, you see more beggars and colorfully dressed, desperately poor trinket vendors than anywhere else in Maya Mexico. Thousands of rural Maya people wander the pavement of San Cristóbal, refugees in a quiet religious war that has been sweeping through the Maya highlands of Chiapas and Guatemala since the 1970s. Most of them have been expelled from the surrounding villages.

Full participation in the religious life of communities like Chamula, Zinacantán and Tenejapa is mandatory. People who get involved with evangélicos (missionaries, usually from the United States) are banished forever from the village and its lands—along with their entire families.

The small city of San Cristóbal cannot hope to absorb such large numbers of homeless people. The only place for the exiles is out past the city limits in makeshift communities of tiny clapboard shacks like La Hormuga ("the anthill"), where there is no electricity, drinking water or plumbing.

weavers from 20 villages in the mountains that surround San Cristóbal. Its purpose is to preserve and revive traditional weaving methods of the region. Only natural dies and fibers are used in making the *huipiles* and other traditional clothing offered for sale here. The quality of weaving displayed in the co-op showroom is the highest in town, and the prices run accordingly steep. In the large, open courtyard that surrounds the church, dozens of women display literally thousands of lower-priced clothing items, some made locally and some crafted in Guatemalan refugee camps or imported from Guatemalan villages by *evangélico* groups. Most outdoor vendors at the church, as elsewhere in the city streets, have been banished from San Juan Chamula or other mountain villages for associating with evangelist missionaries and depend for their survival on selling their wares to tourists.

About three blocks north of Santo Domingo Church is San Cristóbal's colorful **public market**. The large market consists mostly of produce stalls that show off the amazing variety of crops the Maya people grow. You'll find live chickens, ground seeds, candied fruits, giant carrots and tiny new potatoes, along with a profusion of fresh cut flowers, the biggest cash crop of Zinacantán. The flowers, as well as the large sacks of pine needles, are used for weddings, festivals and other celebrations. Other oddities to be found in the market—raw black wool, love and domination powders, several types of copal incense—make unusual souvenirs.

A ten-block walk or quick taxi ride east from Santo Domingo Church, through narrow, walled residential streets, will bring you to

---

MR. AND MRS. BLOM

Danish mapmaker **Frans Blom** *came to Mexico as a young man to work on oil company surveys. He soon changed career goals and ultimately became the 20th century's greatest archaeologist of Maya civilization. He excavated Palenque and Uxmal, served as director of Tulane University's Middle American Research Institute and led many archaeological expeditions into remote areas in search of undiscovered ruins.*

Blom at first refused to take Swiss photographer Gertrude Duby along on an expedition, claiming that it would mean bad luck. He relented and let her join his 1943 archaeological trek, where he fell ill with a tropical fever. Ms. Duby stayed with Blom for ten days until medical help arrived. She soon returned to the rainforest to live among the Lacandón Indians, the only outsider ever allowed to photograph them.

Gertrude Duby and Frans Blom were married in 1950. Together, they founded the Center for Scientific Studies at Casa Na-Bolom, still an essential stop for every Maya enthusiast.

Casa Na-Bolom (Avenida Vicente Guerrero No. 33; 8-14-18; admission), the home of the late anthropologist Frans Blom and his widow, photographer-turned-anthropologist Gertrude Duby Blom. It now operates as a private museum and research center of the Maya culture. Throughout the hacienda-style house and grounds of this peaceful forest oasis set in the midst of a San Cristóbal residential district, visitors find relics collected over a lifetime of archaeological digs, as well as unique photographs taken by Mrs. Blom among the Lacandón people of the deep rainforest, Spanish colonial religious artifacts surreptitiously acquired during a time when private chapels were briefly declared illegal in Mexico, paintings and sculptures created by a long line of artists-in-residence who have sojourned at Casa Na-Bolom over the years and a host of other wonders. Casual visitors can discover why Na-Bolom is one of the most special places along the Maya Route by taking one of the late-afternoon tours conducted daily by volunteers who live and work at the research center.

Serious students of the Maya world, ancient or modern, should allow time in their journeys to linger and browse at length in the library at Na-Bolom, one of the finest collections on earth of information on the subject, with over 11,000 books about the Maya culture and related topics in English, Spanish, German, French, Swedish and other languages, as well as 4000 magazines and manuscripts fully indexed and cross-referenced on computer. Volunteer staff members are happy to help you navigate through the library materials in search of a solution to any Maya mystery, big or small.

SAN CRISTÓBAL DE LAS CASAS LODGING

San Cristóbal's modern, full-service hotels are located out on the edge of town along the Pan American Highway (Route 190). They are not within comfortable walking distance of the city center. If you are driving, you will find parking much easier at lodgings along the highway. If you are traveling by bus, you will find it much easier and more interesting to stay in one of the hotels near the *zócalo*, where colonial charm more than makes up for anything that may be lacking in the way of modern conveniences.

One of the best choices along the Pan American Highway is the **Maya-Quetzal San Cristóbal** (Carretera Panamericana Km. 1171; 8-11-81), a U.S.-style motor inn that has 50 comfortable, modern rooms with telephone and television. Common areas include a restaurant, bar and discotheque. There is plenty of parking, a rare luxury in this city of narrow streets that predate the automobile by 400 years. Rates are moderate.

Also on the Pan American Highway is the **Hotel Bonampak** (Calzada Mexico No. 5; 8-16-21), another 50-room motel with phones and satellite televisions. It doesn't have a disco but does have an indoor-outdoor pool, a tennis court, a miniature golf course and a children's playground. Moderate.

Visitors who prefer a country setting might like the **Molino de la Alborada** (Periferico Sur; 8-09-35), a group of nine rustic rental cottages, all with fireplaces, among tall pine trees not far from the airport. Guests can rent horses and explore trails that plunge deep into the mountains. The owner provides transportation to San Cristóbal's downtown historic district. There is a small restaurant on the premises. Rates are moderate.

To really appreciate the unique ambience of San Cristóbal de las Casas, there's no substitute for staying in the old city center. The most luxurious downtown hotel is **Hoteles Diego de Mazariegos** (5 de Febrero No. 1 and Maria Adelaida Flores No. 2; 8-18-25). It occupies two grand old colonial mansions on opposite sides of Utrilla a block north of the *zócalo*. Its twin addresses appear to be on different streets because the street changes its name as it crosses Utrilla. Rooms have been renovated in keeping with the 18th-century charm of the mansions, with tile floors, beamed ceilings and wrought-iron window frames. Some rooms have fireplaces. Moderate.

The **Hotel Español** (1 de Marzo 15; 8-00-45) is a colonial charmer located two blocks north of the *zócalo* and priced at the low end of the moderate range. All rooms have fireplaces, private bathrooms with showers, and telephones. Ask to see your room before renting it, as some are beautifully restored while others, for the same rate, may be a bit too folkloric for some tastes. The peaceful courtyard, ablaze with bougainvillea around a lovely fountain, is the best thing about this hotel.

On the southeast corner of the *zócalo*, the **Hotel Santa Clara** (Avenida Insurgentes No. 1) was built as the mansion of Captain Diego de Mazariegos, the founder of San Cristóbal, in 1531. It has been renovated and offers guest rooms around a courtyard with a fountain, a cage of bright-hued, noisy loros and macaws and outdoor café seating for patrons of the hotel restaurant. The second-floor terrace has pleasant guest sitting areas. The rooms are adequate but variable in quality. Ask to see yours before you rent it. For families and those traveling in groups, some rooms available here are quite large and have three or four beds. There is a swimming pool in a separate courtyard adjoining the hotel. All rooms have phones, and some have cable televisions. Rates are in the low-moderate range.

Two doors down from the Santa Clara, the **Hotel Ciudad Real** (Plaza 31 de Marzo No. 10; 8-01-87) also has an ideal location right off the *zócalo* and just about the same low-to-moderate rates. The rooms

A corn liquor called posh, *a holy sacrament among the Tzotzil, is used in all religious ceremonies. It is risky to refuse a drink of* posh *if one is offered, since abstinence is sometimes thought to be a mark of the devil.*

are small but nicely appointed, with carpeting and televisions. They surround a cozy, covered courtyard with restaurant seating and a huge fireplace along one side.

If you are able to make reservations far in advance, by far the most fascinating accommodations in San Cristóbal, and quite possibly in the whole Ruta Maya region, are to be found at **Casa Na-Bolom** (Avenida Vicente Guerrero No. 33; 8-14-18). This endlessly intriguing old hacienda turned museum and study center used to—and sometimes still does—host visiting archaeologists and anthropologists from around the world. For the most part, the comfortable, old-fashioned guest rooms are now used as bed-and-breakfast accommodations for tourists. At the high end of the moderate price range, the rooms are expensive by San Cristóbal standards (though a bargain compared to lodging in the Yucatán), and well worth it if you've ever wondered what it's like to live in a museum. They are also the only guest rooms in San Cristóbal with bathtubs. Cottages toward the back of the property are reserved for families of Lacandón Indians, who stay there whenever they visit the city.

SAN CRISTÓBAL DE LAS CASAS RESTAURANTS

Our top suggestion for dinner in San Cristóbal is the most unusual and memorable. At **Casa Na-Bolom** (Avenida Vicente Guerrero No. 31; 8-14-18), dinner for 40 has been a tradition since the 1950s, when Franz and Trudi Blom's dining room was the scene of nightly multilingual discussions among the world's leading Maya archaeologists and explorers. The tradition continues, though today the long wooden table is more likely to be lined with tourists in the know, together with staff members of the study center (generally student volunteers from the United States) and sometimes Lacandón Indians visiting the city. The dining room is filled with art and artifacts. Excellent, imaginative vegetarian dinners are served. The fixed price is moderate. Dinner starts at a set hour, and reservations are essential.

Highland cuisine cannot rival the wonderful regional dishes of the Yucatán. In fact, after scouting out a number of San Cristóbal restaurants, you may reasonably conclude that the most typical local food is spaghetti. The indigenous population of highland Chiapas and Guatemala lives almost entirely on corn tortillas and black beans, which are offered in some restaurants as *desayuno chapin*, the cheapest item on the menu. (Add a chunk of grilled meat and it becomes *comida chapin*.) The influx of foreign visitors to San Cristóbal has fostered the development of many small restaurants that serve American and Continental dishes, as well as specialty dishes from other regions of Mexico.

Perhaps the fanciest dining spot in town, and certainly the most touristy, is the **Fogón de Jovel** (Avenida 16 de Septiembre No. 11, 8-11-53), a spiffy courtyard restaurant with spotless tablecloths and non-Indian waiters dressed in a glamorized version of native *traje*. The menu features a good selection of dishes from other parts of Mexico, notably Yucatán and Oaxaca. A marimba band and folk dancers perform in the evening. Though prices are moderate, this is about as close as you can come to a splurge in San Cristóbal.

On Avenida General Utrilla, which runs north from the *zócalo* toward the market, are several restaurants that specialize in vegetarian cuisine, as well as some fun little art gallery-cafés. One of the best is **Barra Vegetariana Samadhi** (Calle 28 de Agosto at Utrilla), a hole-in-the-wall place specializing in tofu dishes with a Mexican flair. Budget.

A venerable American expatriate hangout in San Cristóbal is **Unicornio** (Insurgentes No. 35), on the way from the *zócalo* to the bus terminal. A pizza or burger and fries in this plain little budget-priced restaurant is many people's idea of a homesickness remedy. It is most popular on Sundays, when the special is paella.

For a good steak, your best bet is **La Herradura** (Calle León No. 7D; 8-40-88), a clean, comfortable restaurant two blocks south of the *zócalo*. They serve American-style steaks—T-bones, ribeyes and sirloins, as well as Mexican style—*arrechería* or *filete*. Prices are moderate. If seafood is more to your taste, try **La Langosta Restaurante** (Calle Madero No. 9; 8-22-38), where you can listen to marimba music while you dine on Yucatán lobster. Moderate.

The modest wood-paneled **Malclovio Restaurant** (1 de Marzo No. 5; 8-07-18) offers an assortment of uncommon Mexican dishes such as *chilaquiles*, *pelliscadas* and *sincronizadas,* as well as more familiar fare. The specialty is hamburgers and french fries. Budget. Another good little budget-priced local restaurant is **Normita II** (Avenida Juárez No. 6), where you can get excellent *posole, pancita* and *burritas norteñas* at very low prices.

SAN CRISTÓBAL DE LAS CASAS SHOPPING

Of all the arts of the ancient Maya, none has lived on like weaving. You can see it in the distinctive *traje*, or traditional clothing, of the highland Maya today. Just like their distant ancestors, village women today make clothing that is often colorfully decorated in brocade, the designs

Wool is so central to the highland Maya way of life that sheep are held sacred. They wander where they please in villages like San Juan Chamula; to sell or slaughter one would be unthinkable.

worked into the warp of the material while they weave on backstrap looms. Colors and patterns have special symbolism—for example, designs on *huipiles* might signify the sun and moon, mountains, the rain or a language. Each Tzotzil and Tzeltal village has its own colors and style of women's *huipiles*, serving almost as a uniform to help people identify each other on market days. The San Cristóbal region is one of the few places in Mexico where men, as well as women, still wear *traje*.

For a look at the highest quality weaving in Chiapas, go to **Sna Jolobíl** (which means "Weaver's House" in Tzotzil) at the side of Santo Domingo Church facing Avenida Juárez. This nonprofit shop showcases the work of a weaver's cooperative made up of nearly 700 Tzotzil and Tzeltal women from 20 villages in the surrounding mountains. All the work for sale here is finer than any you are likely to find elsewhere. The best *huipiles* can cost hundreds of dollars and represent months of work. There are also more affordable gift items for sale, as well as hard-to-find books on highland Maya culture, including some books on weaving techniques with translations into Maya dialects.

You will find moderately priced local *traje* for sale in most of the villages around San Cristóbal. The best selection, though not the best prices, is available on market days. Sunday is the market day at most villages in the area. Tenejapa also has a market on Thursday.

Some culturally aware travelers contend that tourist dollars spent in Indian villages like San Juan Chamula do more harm than good, as cash quickly erodes traditional lifestyles. An alternative is to buy from the women who display their wares on the ground in front of Santo Domingo Church. Most of these women have been expelled from nearby villages and now depend on their sales to feed themselves and their children. Some items they sell are handmade by them or others in their community. Many others are imported from Guatemala by *evangélicos* who maintain missions on both sides of the border. If you are going to Guatemala, you will find prices for the same items *much* lower there. If not, San Cristóbal de las Casas provides an opportunity to buy Guatemalan clothing and accessories direct from highland Maya women at a fraction of U.S. prices. Price negotiating is in order. You can expect to pay about 50 percent less when buying from the vendors at Santo Domingo Church than the same item costs in one of the retail shops that line Utrilla on the way to the church and the market.

Amber is another specialty of the Chiapas highlands. The Maya of ancient times used amber for adornment, worship, barter and burial.

Today, many continue to believe that wearing amber promotes health, wards off the "evil eye" and relieves the discomforts of fever and allergies. This semiprecious stone, actually the petrified resin of evergreen trees that lived 50,000 years ago, is mined by hand in the surrounding mountains. (There are some amber diggings near the side of the highway as you leave San Cristóbal en route to Comitán.) You can see an amazing collection of carved amber jewelry and figurines, much of it in Maya motifs, at the **Museo de Ambar** (Avenida Utrilla No. 10), which also has a beautiful selection of jewelry for sale. Indian vendors all over town sell strings of beads purported to be amber. Caveat emptor. Most "amber" sold on the street is plastic, glass or even copal incense.

SAN CRISTÓBAL DE LAS CASAS NIGHTLIFE

The recommended after-dark activity in San Cristóbal de las Casas is to curl up by the fireplace at your hotel with a good book. Nothing much happens here at night. The streets are practically deserted by 8:00 in the evening. There are no bars in town, and only one movie house. Live music can be found between 8:00 and 10:00 p.m. at some of the more tourist-oriented restaurants, at least on Friday and Saturday nights. The most exciting entertainment event of the week is the traditional Sunday evening *paseo*, when young men and women dressed in their finest clothes stroll formally around the *zócalo*, sometimes under the watchful eyes of adult relatives, but these days more often to the scrutiny of giggling peers, and the air is charged with mariachi music and romance.

Highland Maya Villages

The other must-see destinations of the Chiapas highlands are in the countryside just a few minutes by paved road from downtown San Cristóbal. Visits to the outlying Tzotzil and Tzeltal Maya villages around San Cristóbal de las Casas can show you the closest thing in today's world to the spiritual drive that led to the creation of the ancient Maya ceremonial centers. While much has stayed the same in Maya life since before Columbus dropped anchor, so, too, has everything changed—not once but many times—as new rulers, new priests and gods and temples and new technologies have swept away the old ones every few centuries.

To form an idea of why the great Maya pyramids and palaces were built and how they were used from the everyday lives of Chamulans and Zinacantanas today would be like trying to understand the faith that raised Gothic cathedrals by observing life on the main street of a modern farming village in the south of France. And yet, the highland

Maya today meet threats of overpopulation, soil depletion and the whole range of problems a community faces when it clings to ancient ways within walking distance of a major highway with the deep, slow, impassioned rhythms of spiritual commitments already ancient when the first Spanish priest set foot in these remote mountains.

The most accessible of the many Maya villages that surround San Cristóbal de las Casas are Zinacantán and San Juan Chamula. Both are Tzotzil-speaking villages, situated in neighboring valleys just a few kilometers apart, but their customs and dialects are so different that residents of the two villages can only communicate in Spanish. Even though large numbers of foreign tourists visit both villages, the residents are wary of outsiders, and no ladino or foreigner is ever permitted to spend the night in either village under any circumstances. As soon as you arrive in the village, you must go to the administration building and pay the permit fee, plus an additional fee if you wish to enter the church (as you definitely should).

Visitors are subject to a number of strict regulations. The toughest rule relates to the use of cameras. If you carry a camera at all, you will be met with suspicion and outright hostility. Photographing churches or religious ceremonies is treated as a serious crime. Whether or not the rumors about tourists who have been killed for picture-taking are true, unauthorized photography is sure to mean destruction of your camera, and you could spend the rest of your vacation in the village jail. All in all, the best plan is to leave your camera at home when visiting highland Maya villages.

MEXICO'S LAST WILD PEOPLE

The **Southern Lacandón Indians**, who live deep in what remains of Chiapas' lowland rainforest, are the last nomadic, unchristianized tribe in Mexico. They fled into the jungle 400 years ago to save their independence and have avoided contact with Spanish colonial and ladino influences ever since. Though there are only about 400 living Lacandones, their numbers have not declined during the 20th century.

They are probably descendants of the people who built the magnificent ceremonial centers of Yaxchilán and Palenque. Many experts believe that studies of Lacandón spiritual practices—as described by archaeologist Gertrude Duby Blom, who lived among the forest people for extended periods of time—offer a unique window into the belief system of the ancient Maya.

Sadly, the world that the Lacandones have known for more than a millennium has nearly vanished as population pressures, slash-and-burn farming techniques and timber operations are destroying the rainforest in Chiapas at an alarming rate.

Churches without clergy are the most striking aspect of village life among the Tzotzil and Tzeltal Maya. Especially in their religious practices, the native people who live around San Cristóbal have always been fiercely independent. More than once in centuries past, they have risen up against authority. The conflict was a religious one: While devoutly Catholic, the highland Maya often experienced miracles, mystical visions and appearances of saints, which both church and state saw as dangerous heresy and suppressed brutally. In 1712, a Tzeltal and Tzotzil uprising against the power of Spain resulted in a siege against San Cristóbal de las Casas and the slaying of hundreds of people on both sides.

The situation came to a head in 1869, when an adolescent girl in San Juan Chamula, who came to be called Santa Rosa, announced that some magical stones had fallen from heaven and that they talked to her. Excitement over the talking stones sent shock waves of religious fervor through the highland villages and aroused government fears of a repeat of the "caste wars" that had ripped the Yucatán apart twenty years before. Finally, Spanish soldiers massacred many hundreds of unarmed men, women and children in San Juan Chamula while they were praying. While the slaughter put an end to any possibility of armed Indian revolt, it also marked the beginning of the end of the Catholic presence in the Maya villages. For more than a century, no priest has set foot in the church at Zinacantán, and priests have only been allowed in San Juan Chamula once a year to perform baptisms on the feast day of St. John the Baptist, Chamula's patron saint.

A visit to a Maya church like the ones at San Juan Chamula and Zinacantán makes for an unforgettable experience. The churches contain no representations of Christ on the cross. In the Tzotzil "folk Catholic" religion, a strange blend of amateur Catholicism and ancient Maya tradition, the belief is that Christ rose from death to become the sun, while the Virgin Mary rose to become the moon. They are worshipped in the heavens, not inside the church.

As you enter the church at **San Juan Chamula**, you will find the air thick with the scent and smoke of copal, an incense made from tree sap. In Maya tradition, copal smoke carries prayers to the heavens. There are no pews, only a broad floor covered with pine boughs so that each footstep releases a fresh forest scent. Life-sized statues of saints line the walls. A mirror hangs from the neck of each statue in the belief that it lets the saint see the person whose image is reflected there.

Supplicants light long, slender candles on the floor before the saints—black candles for death or birth; green, yellow and orange for different crops; red for harmony with family members or authority figures, white for any prayer. Villagers working on hands and knees constantly scrape the deposits of old candle wax off the floor.

Alcohol is sacred to the highland Maya people, who use it to induce visions during religious ceremonies. Whatever a person does under the influence of alcohol is believed to be divinely inspired.

Individual prayers are chanted aloud, and lucky visitors may witness one of the elaborate ceremonies performed by the village *mayordomos*. Followed by women bearing huge *incensarios* filled with glowing copal, accompanied by musicians with guitars, accordions and harps, punctuated by bursts of fireworks, the village elders chant complex prayers that resound out of the dim past.

Only about 300 people live within the village of San Juan Chamula. Most Chamulans—16,000 of them—live on small farms throughout the valley. The same arrangement characterized the great "cities" of the ancient Maya, where peasants lived in huts dispersed over a large area and came together for prayer and politics in ceremonial centers. Chamulans live under the feudal *cacique* system that most Maya communities have used since the 1200s. A few powerful individuals within the tribe own most of the land in the valley, while the poorer people work as sharecroppers.

As health care has improved in recent years, the Chamula population has exploded far beyond the traditional economy's capacity to sustain it. Now much of the farmland is eroded and worn out. Even the lofty pine trees have been denuded of branches nearly to their tops for firewood and ceremonial boughs. As the land slips deeper into poverty, the people are forced more and more into the cash economy of the outside world—changing their fiercely independent way of life beyond recognition. Today, the largest house in San Juan Chamula belongs to the village Coca-Cola distributor.

Strolling around the village, you will see other links between the Maya people today and their ancient ancestors. Blue-green, six-foot-tall wooden crosses stand everywhere, decorated with circles that mark the four directions and stylized corn symbols. They are said to represent the Tree of Life. Similar crosses carved from stone were found inside two temples at Palenque. The sweat baths behind many Chamula houses, used by women to prepare for childbirth and sometimes by men for healing rituals, are like the ones built a thousand years ago at Chichén Itzá.

Not far from San Juan Chamula is the village of **Zinacantán**, reached by taking the other fork in the road and driving into the next valley. Although both Chamula and Zinacantán are Tzotzil Maya villages, there is such a difference in dialect that residents of the two cannot understand each other's speech. Zinacantán feels much different from Chamula—more cheerful. Their land grant is larger and their

Remember, tempting though it may be, that photography is absolutely prohibited anywhere in or around Zinacantán, and penalties are severe.

population smaller, and most land is farmed communally. In brilliant contrast to the austere black-wool tunics of the Chamulans, the men of Zinacantán wear flamboyant pink-and-red *traje*. Zinacantán's major cash crop is flowers.

Though the village is dominated by a big new administration building, the true center of community life is the priestless church. As in San Juan Chamula, the church at Zinacantán contains no Christ on the cross, though a Christ figure dressed in traditional pink village clothing lies in state in a large coffin at one side of the church.

While San Juan Chamula and Zinacantán are the villages most foreign travelers choose to visit because they are the closest to the city, many other equally fascinating Maya communities are scattered through all the mountain valleys around San Cristóbal. You could easily spend weeks exploring them all.

If you continue on the road through San Juan Chamula, you can reach as many as six other Tzotzil villages, each unique in its dress and customs. Of particular interest is **San Pedro Chenalhó**, 37 kilometers from San Cristóbal and a two-hour trip over increasingly rough roads. It is the only Tzotzil village that accepts outsiders as overnight guests. Inquire at the tourist office in the village administration building about accommodations.

A road that winds into the hills east of San Cristóbal goes to a park where a natural limestone arch known as **El Arcotete** spans the river, a popular local picnic spot. Past the arch, the road climbs near **Cerro Tzontehuitz**, the highest point in the Chiapas highlands at 9700 feet, and then descends gradually to the village of **Tenejapa**, one of the most colorful Tzeltal villages. Here, the men wear long black *túnicas* and ribbon hats, while women wear fancy *huipiles* heavily embroidered in bright hues. Except during Sunday and Thursday markets, villagers are less tolerant of foreigners here. Dress modestly and follow tribal rules. Tourists reportedly have been assaulted for taking illegal photographs.

Following Route 190, the Pan American Highway, for nine kilometers south of San Cristóbal will bring you to **Grutas de San Cristóbal** (admission), a large cavern with spectacular stalactite formations. The cave is about three-and-a-half kilometers long, but only the first kilometer is illuminated for tours. Drivers may wish to take a short side trip from the cave along Route 199 in the direction of Ocosingo. The paved road passes through **Huixtán**, an old village that was the ancestral home of the Tzotzil Maya before the Spanish arrived in the region. The main place of interest in town is the church, one of the oldest in Chiapas.

Volkswagen minibuses called combis run back and forth from the public market in San Cristóbal and virtually all of the villages during daylight hours. Many non-Indians ride the *combis* on Sunday, which is market day in most villages.

Tuxtla Gutiérrez Area

An hour's drive west of San Cristóbal de las Casas on Route 190, **Chiapa de Corzo** (population 50,000) is one of the oldest continuously occupied townsites in Mexico. Founded in 1528 on a riverbank where Olmec, Maya and Zapotec communities have stood since 1500 B.C., it was the first Spanish settlement in Chiapas. Chiapa de Corzo still retains a good bit of colonial charm. Among the city's notable works of art and architecture is the **Mudejar Fountain**, locally known as *La Pila* (The Basin). It was built in 1565 in a design that re-creates on a massive scale the crown of King Carlos V of Spain. The **Church of San Dominico de Guzman**, southeast of the *zócalo*, is built entirely of brick and has three naves and six domes. The enormous bell in the main tower is one of the oldest in the Americas.

Chiapa de Corzo is the departure point for boat excursions into spectacular **Parque Nacional Cañón del Sumidero**. Outboard motor launches, which are inexpensive if you gather a party of six or more passengers, take sightseers on a 47-kilometer cruise down the Grijalva River through the deepest part of the canyon, where the river runs 500 feet deep and cliffs rise 4000 feet above its surface. At the entrance to the canyon is an ancient Chiapaneco ceremonial center, which was dedicated to Nandada, the god of water. The canyon's depths are a secluded bit of tropical paradise alive with water birds, turtles, iguanas, raccoons and alligators. Gliding across the bright green water smooth as plate glass, you'll see the grand cascade of the Arbol de Navidad waterfall, the Cueva de Colores and El Chorreadero, where an underground river springs to the surface in a deep *cenote*. The boat tour takes about two hours, turning around at Netzahualcóyotl Dam. The dam makes the water run deep through the canyon; without it, power boats could not run on the river. The water that spills over the dam runs the largest hydroelectric plant in Latin America. The Cañón del Sumidero can also be viewed from the rim at five overlooks off Calle 11 Oriente Norte on the outskirts of Tuxtla Gutiérrez.

Most travelers only find reason to visit **Tuxtla Gutiérrez** if they are making a plane or bus connection here en route to San Cristóbal de las Casas from central Mexico. This modern city of 300,000 people, the capital of Chiapas, has excellent hotels and restaurants but not much in the way of sightseeing. The local economy is built around coffee and

The state takes its name from its first two Spanish towns—both named Chiapa.
Chiapa de Corzo was one; the other was San Cristóbal de las Casas, originally
called Chiapa de los Españoles.

tobacco production. Like so many Chiapas town names, Tuxtla Gutiérrez is a synthesis of two names from different cultures. "Tuxtla" came from the Toltec name for the old Zoque Indian settlement that originally occupied the site. It means "Place of Many Rabbits." The "Gutiérrez" is for Don Joaquín Miguel Gutiérrez, the local hero who caused Chiapas to join Mexico.

The top Tuxtla sightseeing highlight is the **Miguel Alvárez de Toro Zoological Gardens** (nicknamed ZOO-MAT), located on the south side of the city off Calle Libramiento Sur. A shuttle bus goes there from the corner of Calle 1 Oriente Sur and Avenida 7 Sur Oriente. It is generally considered to be the finest zoo in Mexico. Set in a natural rainforest, the zoo houses animals native to the amazingly diverse environments of Chiapas in spacious habitats landscaped with flora from the animals' places of origin. The wildlife on exhibit includes jaguars, ocelots, macaws, wild boar and lots of snakes.

Another place worth visiting in Tuxtla Gutiérrez is the **Museo Regional de Chiapas** (Calle 11 Oriente Norte at Avenida 5 Norte Oriente), located in the **Parque Madero** in the northeast part of town. The ground floor of the museum displays one of the finest collections of ancient Maya artifacts in the world, containing outstanding pieces from Palenque, Yaxchilán and other Chiapas sites. Upstairs are Spanish colonial antiques and exhibits on the crafts and culture of the highland Maya today. Nearby in the same park are shady botanical gardens where young lovers stroll past little signs designed to help visitors identify the myriad trees and plants of the Chiapas forest.

TUXTLA GUTIÉRREZ AREA LODGING

The better hotels in Tuxtla Gutiérrez are away from the downtown area. You'll find most of the foreign travelers in town on any given day either staying, eating or just hanging out at the moderate-priced **Hotel Bonampak** (Boulevard Dr. Belisario Domínguez No. 180; 3-20-50), located toward the west end of town. This was the old-time luxury hotel in town, and while it is not exactly colonial (Tuxtla Gutiérrez is only a century old), the hotel has a mellow feel plus a special attraction: exact reproductions of the murals of Bonampak, brighter and clearer than the originals and much easier to get to. Rumor has it that the postcards of the Bonampak murals that are for sale just about everywhere along the Ruta Maya were actually taken here. The hotel has a swimming pool, a sauna and a tennis court. The recently refurbished guest rooms have satellite television, phones and air-conditioning. Moderate.

The top of the line in Tuxtla accommodations, and the largest lodging facility in town, is the **Hotel Flamboyant** (Boulevard Dr. Belisario Domínguez Km. 1081; 2-92-59), an 118-unit motor inn transformed through lavish decoration and lush landscaping into a pseudo-Arabian fantasyland. The colorful, brand-new-looking guest units surround a central lawn and swimming pool area with a single tennis court. Amenities include phones and satellite television. Moderate to deluxe.

If you prefer to stay downtown near the *zócalo*, you'll find nice, modern accommodations in the nine-story **Gran Hotel Humberto** (Avenida Central Poniente No. 180; 2-20-80). Located just a block west of the central plaza, the hotel has 112 bright, spacious guest rooms with air-conditioning, phones and satellite televisions—a bargain at the low end of the moderate price category.

For budget-priced accommodations in downtown Tuxtla, try the **Hotel San Marcos** (Calle 2 Oriente Sur No. 176; 3-19-40), a block south of the central plaza. Some rooms have air-conditioning, and all have phones and hot water. Don't be put off by the rather dreary lobby; the rooms are cheerful and clean, and the location makes it one of the quieter downtown hotels.

Chiapa de Corzo has only one hotel: the **Hotel Los Angeles** (Calle Julián Grajales No. 2; 6-00-48) just off the town plaza. It is plain and devoid of amenities but nice enough as small-town Mexican hotels go.

TUXTLA GUTIÉRREZ AREA RESTAURANTS

Las Pinachas (Avenida Central Oriente No. 857; 2-53-51), in Tuxtla Gutiérrez eight blocks east of the *zócalo*, is a dream come true—a rather chic thatch-roofed restaurant with a voluminous menu that offers a complete survey of southeastern Mexico specialties including antojitos, juicy grilled meats and sweet tamales. A marimba group plays in the afternoons and evenings. Budget to moderate.

Tuxtla Gutiérrez has a small but visible Chinese community and a remarkable number of Chinese restaurants. Perhaps the best of them is **La Gran Muralla China** (Avenida 2 Norte Poniente No. 334; 3-08-99), a moderately priced dinner place that is rather exclusive by Chiapas standards. Both the food and the decor are 100-percent Cantonese, synthesizing strangely with the Mexican music that's played loudly through speakers in the corners of the ceiling. Imported oriental wines are available.

The opulent 1950s-era dining room in the **Hotel Bonampak** (Boulevard Dr. Belisario Domínguez No. 180; 3-20-50) serves beef steaks and seafood at moderate prices in a romantic setting. Quicker and more affordable is the hotel's cafeteria-style coffee shop, where regional and international dishes (which is to say, grilled chicken and spaghetti) are the order of the day.

Restaurante Vegetariano Na-Yaxal (Calle 6 Poniente No. 724, with a second, smaller location just off the central plaza near the cathedral) offers all the ambience of a fast-food joint, but the menu features what many travelers crave after a few weeks on the road—elaborate vegetable salads, great smoothies and fruit plates smothered in yogurt and granola. Budget.

In Chiapa de Corzo, upscale, tourist-oriented restaurants line the east side of the plaza. The best is **Jardín Turístico** ("Tourist Garden"). The name says it all. Typical roast chicken dinners are priced in the moderate range. If you're looking for something a little more offbeat, head down to the waterfront, where *palapa* restaurants like **Restaurant Nancy** serve budget-priced seafood cocktails, chicken and fish.

TUXTLA GUTIÉRREZ AREA SHOPPING

In Tuxtla Gutiérrez, weaving, amber jewelry, wood carving and pottery from all over Chiapas are displayed for sale at the **Bazar Ishcanal** and **Instituto de la Artesanía Chiapaneca** (Boulevard Dr. Belisario Domínguez No. 950), both located on the ground floor of the building that houses the state tourism office, across the street from the Hotel Bonampak on the west side of town.

Chiapa de Corzo is famous for lacquerware—elaborately decorated boxes, serving trays and even furniture. A lacquer museum just off the *zócalo* traces the art from its Spanish Colonial origins to the present day, and contemporary pieces are for sale all over town. Ornately lacquered gourds are a popular souvenir item. Wood carving is another Chiapa de Corzo specialty. This is also a good place to look for dance masks and handmade musical instruments.

TUXTLA GUTIÉRREZ AREA NIGHTLIFE

Disco Shiek (Boulevard Dr. Belisario Domínguez Km. 1081; 2-92-59), the discotheque at the Hotel Flamboyant, is the chic nightspot in Tuxtla Gutiérrez, a city with more discos than anyplace else on the Maya Route west of Cancún. Young professional people dress to the hilt to come here on Thursday, Friday and Saturday nights. The recorded music is trendy international Eurotechnopop. Cover. The **Night Club El Mirador** (Avenida Central Poniente No. 180; 2-20-80) on the ninth floor of the Gran Hotel Humberto is also a happening spot on weekends. Another popular disco, **Altaluz 2001** (Prolongación 3 Poniente Sur) is open every night except Sunday and Monday.

City-sponsored concerts featuring traditional music performed by brass-and-string bands are held on Sunday evenings in the central plaza.

The Ancient Maya made music with an early form of marimba as well as with drums, maracas, wooden flutes, conch shell trumpets and whistles made from deer bones.

Comitán Area

Travelers en route to Comitán and the border crossing at Ciudad Cuauhtémoc via Route 190 from San Cristóbal de las Casas pass through **Amatenango del Valle** after 37 kilometers. One of the most accessible Tzeltal villages, Amatenango is famous for its animal-shaped pottery, which is still fired the old-fashioned way inside the open wood fires located throughout the village streets and courtyards. Here, you'll find everything from fanciful figurines to whole fireplaces shaped and painted to look like grinning Cheshire cats.

Comitán (population 60,000) is the last town of any size before you reach the border with Guatemala, 85 kilometers to the east via Route 190. (Ciudad Cuauhtémoc, on the border, is not really a town at all, just a customs and immigration station, a handful of tiny restaurants and a few very basic hotel rooms.) The main reason travelers stop in Comitán is to visit the **Guatemalan Consulate** (Avenida 2 Poniente Norte 28; 2-26-69). For tourists from the United States and most other industrialized nations, crossing the border is no problem. You must stop at the consulate to get a visa in advance, however, if you are traveling on a passport issued by a nation that is associated with terrorism or drug trafficking or one that does not give Guatemala full diplomatic recognition. For instance, citizens of Ireland and Israel are required to apply for visas in advance. You'll also need to apply in advance for a visa if you plan to stay longer than 30 days in Guatemala or if you want a multiple-entry permit.

You may wish to exchange Mexican pesos for Guatemalan quetzales at the **Bancomer** on Comitán's *zócalo*. The exchange rate is not good, but it is better than you'll get from moneychangers at the border. Beyond the border zone, it is very difficult to convert pesos into quetzales, though U.S. dollars and traveler's checks are easily convertible everywhere. Wherever you change money, get enough quetzales to pay fees to border officials, ride the bus to Huehuetenango, buy a meal and rent a room for the night. About Q200 (US$40) per person should cover everything.

Known to the ancient Maya as Balum Canán ("Nine Stars"), Comitán, at its cool, mile-high, elevation is said to have the most pleasant climate in the state of Chiapas. A great variety of flowers brighten its boulevards and main plaza year-round. Comitán is the birthplace of two famous figures in Mexican history—Rosario Castellanos, one of Mexico's greatest writers, and Dr. Belisario Domínguez, a martyr of the revolution whose house is now the **Casa Museo Dr. Belisario**, a museum of the Mexican Revolution located half a block south of the plaza on Avenida Central Sur.

Comitán is the jumping-off point for a side trip to **Parque Nacional Lagunas de Montebello**, 60 kilometers out of town on the Guatemalan border. The park covers an area of 150,000 acres and contains 68 lakes—each one with water of a different hue. The variety of color is caused by oxides in the water and by different depths. Among the most beautiful of the lakes are Tziscao, Agua Tinta ("Dark Water"), Pojol, San Lorenzo, Bosque Azul ("Blue Forest"), Esmeralda ("Emerald"), Ensueño ("Dream") and Montebello. The lake district is famed for orchids and birds, including the quetzal, Guatemala's nearly extinct national bird.

Ten kilometers west of Lagunas de Montebello on the road back to Comitán is the Maya archaeological site of **Chincultik**. The small ruin lies three kilometers off the main road on an unpaved side road. Its name means "Terraced Well" in the local Maya tongue, and the ceremonial center here reached its height between 400 and 600 A.D. Chincultik consists of two plazas. On the higher one stands a pyramid with two altars and some small temples perched on top of a hill from which you get a panoramic view of the Montebello lake district and Chincultik's sacred *cenote*. The lower plaza contains a ball court, a cemetery and several stelae.

Buses and *combis* run frequently from Comitán to Lagunas de Montebello and Chincultik, a two-hour trip. Tours to the lakes can also be arranged from San Cristóbal de las Casas through PoSeTuR, a travel agency located at 5 de Febrero No. 1; 8-07-25.

COMITÁN AREA LODGING

The hotel scene in Comitán has little to offer the discriminating traveler. A lot of guest rooms are available, since the town is a natural stopover for people traveling to and from Guatemala, but most are cramped, tattered accommodations without private baths and often without windows. The best hotel in town is the **Hotel Robert's** (Avenida 1 Poniente Sur No. 5; 2-10-94), where the 38 clean, modern, almost bright rooms have satellite television. The town's only disco is on the ground floor. Moderate.

COMITÁN AREA RESTAURANTS

A good sidewalk café for people-watching in Comitán is the budget-priced **Café Casa de la Cultura** on the plaza in the small auditorium and art gallery next to the 16th-century Santo Domingo Church. For more formal dining, one good option is the **Nevelandia** (Calle Central Norte No. 1; 2-00-95), where the waiters wear crisp starched uniforms and the *comida corrida* is a bargain in the moderate price range. It is located across from the northwest corner of the plaza. Hotel Robert's **El Excovés Restaurant** also offers a satisfying lunch or dinner at a moderate price.

The Pacific Coast

Most travelers following the Maya Route overland from Mexico to Guatemala cross the border at Ciudad Cuauhtémoc and proceed to Huehuetenango. An alternative for travelers curious to see what the Pacific Ocean looks like along Mexico's southernmost coastline is to continue south for 165 kilometers to Tapachula, a Chiapas border town near the seashore and the Maya ruins of Izapa.

At the foot of an extinct volcano, the busy frontier city of **Tapachula** (population 150,000) buzzes with commerce—and political unrest. This shipping center for the southwest agricultural zone is also a major conduit of traffic to and from Guatemala. The volcano north of Tapachula is **Volcán Tacana**. Across the border rises a sister volcano, **Volcán Tajamulco**.

North of Tapachula off Route 200 are the scattered ruins of **Izapa**, dating back 1000 years to an Olmec-Maya culture. Marked by a pyramid sign, a small ceremonial site along the roadside contains restored pyramids, an altar stone and stelae with hieroglyphs, as well as a ball court (probably built later, when the community was past its prime). This is a Preclassic site, occupied from 200 B.C. to 200 A.D. Izapa is of special interest to archaeologists as a "missing link" between the Classic Maya culture and the mysterious Olmec people who came before them and developed the first high civilization in Mexico and Central America.

A more secretive site a a few kilometers south of Izapa (back in the direction of Tapachula) is concealed on the opposite side of the road, reached by a path through a cocoa plantation. There is no sign. If in doubt, ask locals about **Las Esculturas Escondidas** ("The Hidden Sculptures"). Children may lead you to a green field ringed in eroded stelae and chipped figures of a smiling frog and a tree of life. Beyond an unexcavated hill near a fast-running stream, a fantastic stone serpent rears up out of the banana trees with a man in its mouth. No doubt many more treasures wait here to be unearthed by future generations of scholars.

You can also dip into local history at Tapachula's little **Museo de Antropologia** (Parque de Exposiciones, Route 225 Km. 2). The museum houses a fine collection of Maya pieces, including a ritualistic urn with the original paints on its totemic faces and a turquoise-studded skull.

If you drive 25 kilometers south of Tapachula, you will reach the Pacific coast at **Puerto Madero**. Near this quiet little fishing village lie narrow black-sand beaches that are considered to be the best in Chiapas. For details, see "Pacific Coast Area Beaches" below.

PACIFIC COAST AREA LODGING

In downtown Tapachula, near the main plaza, you can't go wrong at the comfortable **Hotel Fénix** (Avenida 4 Norte No. 19; 5-07-55). Its parking area faces an interior garden. The rooms are cozy and small, with double beds, ceiling fans, phones and worn furniture. Budget.

You will pay more for the comparative luxury of the hilltop **Loma Real** (Route 200 Km. 244; 6-14-40), one of the town's oldest and best hotels. Designed to meet businessman standards, the Loma Real features 86 rooms carpeted in royal blue with leather easy chairs, executive desk ensembles, phones, air-conditioning and big color televisions with cable. There are also a restaurant-bar and a disco. Moderate.

If you want to enjoy a first-class stay, indulge yourself at the lovely **Hotel Kamico** (Prolongación Central Oriente, Carretera a Guatemala; 6-26-40), just over 14 kilometers from the border. Its 92 quiet rooms radiate from a well-tended garden containing a pool, patio and restaurant-bar. The ample units are painted in warm autumnal hues and feature king-sized beds, terraces, televisions, phones and air-conditioning. Moderate in price.

PACIFIC COAST AREA RESTAURANTS

Big, shady Parque Hidalgo, Tapachula's central *zócalo*, is rimmed with fetching indoor-outdoor cafés serving inexpensive meals and snacks. At one corner stands **Los Comales** (Portal Perez, corner of Avenida 8 Norte), open to the plaza with rattan chairs and bright tablecloths. The menu marches through fruits, ice creams, seafood, eggs, Mexican dishes, sandwiches and cappuccinos. Budget.

Just across the street, lively and tropical **La Parrilla** (Avenida 8 Norte No. 20, Tapachula; 6-40-62) stays open 24 hours a day and offers bargain meals. When we stopped there, its *comida corrida* (meal of the day) featured soup, rice, a meat entrée, beans, dessert and a soft drink at a very reasonable price. You can order everything from beef brochettes to cheese sandwiches à la carte. Budget.

A new kid on the block in this bustling city is the attractive **Restaurant Hostal Del Rey** (Hotel Fénix, Avenida 4 Norte No. 17, Tapachula; 5-07-55), an oasis of red tile floors, ceiling fans, adobe walls, rattan furniture and chicken tacos. Budget.

Many coffee plantations around Tapachula are owned by people of German origin whose ancestors moved from Guatemala to escape anti-German persecution during World War I.

For more elegant dining in Tapachula, both the **Hotel Loma Real** (Route 200 Km. 244; 6-14-40) and the **Hotel Kamico** (Prolongación Central Oriente, Carretera a Guatemala; 6-26-40) have attractive restaurants open for all meals. In the Loma Real, the view is pleasant and the service excellent. The fish *veracruzana*, cooked with tomatoes, chilies, onions and bay leaf, is highly recommended, as is the *sopa de tortilla* (tortilla soup), and for dessert, the scrumptious flan Loma Real. Prices at both restaurants are moderate.

Located 25 kilometers south of Tapachula, Puerto Madero is a bit of a culinary wasteland, but you can munch on fresh seafood at budget prices and enjoy the crash of the waves at **Restaurant San Rafael** (Calle 3 Poniente). Try the mullet eggs. Or saunter up the dirt road to **Restaurant Costa Azul** (Calle 3 Poniente) and see the open kitchen that serves up fresh fish on crude wooden tables. Budget.

PACIFIC COAST AREA BEACHES

For the most part, the Pacific coast of Chiapas is a disappointing region of mud flats on the Mar Muerto—the Dead Sea, a king-sized stagnant puddle, almost totally landlocked, with swampy brown beaches and haggard villages—one of the most joyless seashores in all Mexico. In the final stretch before the Guatemala border, the luxuriant Sierra de Soconusco rears up and rescues the coast with some tropical backbone.

Near easygoing Puerto Madero, a bedraggled seaside pueblo 25 kilometers south of Tapachula on Route 200/225, you'll find **Playa Puerto Madero** and **Playa San Benito**. These rocky shores, some forming breakwaters against the surging brown surf, breed narrow beaches with volcanic black sand. At the southern end of town past the lighthouse, Playa Puerto Madero loops around open seas and fronts a quiet cove behind the lighthouse. A more attractive beach, Playa San Benito, sweeps the northern edge of town. Beginning near a small, sandy cemetery, its gray sand, backed by *palapas*, curves for several kilometers along the open sea.

Currents are dangerous for swimming near town, safe off the cove around the lighthouse and near the protective rocks at the cemetery end of San Benito. Stay close to shore—sharks reportedly lurk here.

Puerto Madero has no decent hotel, and it's not safe to camp on the beach. Spend the day and drive back to Tapachula for the night.

The theatrical arts of the ancient Maya featured elaborate costumes and pageantry. No original Maya plays have survived, but early Spanish priests wrote descriptions of performances and transcribed one play, the Rabinal-Achi, in its entirety.

The Sporting Life

SWIMMING

The hot lowlands of Chiapas boast several places where people come from all over the region to take the plunge and cool off. After sampling the small, secluded waterfalls and pools near the campground in **Palenque National Park**, you may find it hard to resist the grand-scale falls and pools at **Agua Azul** and **Misol-Ha** described in the "Ocosingo Area" section in this chapter.

If you're spending any time around Chiapa de Corzo and Tuxtla Gutiérrez, you might want to check out the waterfall **El Aguacero**, reached via a dirt road off Route 190, 53 kilometers west of Tuxtla. This is a very popular spot with the locals on weekends, but it's off the beaten tourist path, so on a weekday afternoon you may find that you have the place all to yourself.

HIKING

Palenque National Park has one long hiking trail, which runs about six kilometers up the side of a narrow river valley to a small Indian farming village at the edge of the park. It offers the most accessible close-up view of a remnant of Chiapas' once-fabulous rainforest, teeming with monkeys and tropical birds.

The mountains around San Cristóbal de las Casas are full of walking trails, thoroughfares for Maya farmers who live far from any road. Popular hikes include the network of trails through the **Reserva Ecológica Huitepec**, an expanse of uncut "cloud forest" or mountain evergreen forest managed by the Mexican environmental group Pronatura. Trips guided by Pronatura can be arranged through local travel agencies. The trailhead is about three kilometers out of town off the road to San Juan Chamula and Zinacantán.

Another very popular trek is the seven-kilometer trail between **Zinacantán** and **San Juan Chamula**. The trail traverses the high ridgeline that separates the valleys where the two villages are situated for a magnificent overview of the Maya landscape. A lot of people, both local Indians and foreign visitors, use this trail, and it is quite safe. A maze of other trails runs throughout the highlands, but local authorities warn that remote areas are not safe. The attitude of some Tzotzil people toward foreigners is ambivalent at best, and hikers who are inexperienced at communicating with the people of the highlands should stick to the main trail.

Two other popular hikes are the six-kilometer trip along the banks of the Río Fogatico from a trailhead off San Cristóbal's periferico to **El Arcotete**, a popular recreation area, and the steep climb to the summit of **Tzontehuitzl**, the highest mountain in the area at at 9700 feet. There are also some pleasant nature trails at **Grutas de San Cristóbal**, ten kilometers out of San Cristóbal on the road to Amatenango and Comitán.

HORSEBACK RIDING

There are enough horseback rides to keep you saddlesore for weeks in the mountains around San Cristóbal de las Casas. Besides the trails listed under "Hiking" above, the 14-kilometer backcountry trail that leads from the outskirts of San Cristóbal along a pretty mountain stream to the village of **San Juan Chamula** is a favorite all-day trip on horseback. Horse rentals and guided trips of anywhere from a few hours to several days duration can be arranged through PoSeTuR (5 de Febrero No. 1; 8-07-25) in the Hotel Diego de Mazariegos or at any hotel travel agency in San Cristóbal.

Guided horseback rides through the jungle lowlands can be arranged with the help of Viajes Toniná (Avenida Juárez No. 105; 5-03-84) or any other travel agency in Palenque.

Transportation

BY CAR

The Maya Route follows **Route 186** to Palenque from Escárcega (see Chapter Five). From there, this paved two-lane highway continues westward to Villahermosa, Tabasco, the nearest city to Palenque.

Chiapas's two top tourist destinations, Palenque and San Cristóbal de las Casas, are linked by an unnumbered highway called the **Carretera Ocosingo**. This wide, recently paved two-lane road climbs through the mountains in many spectacular switchbacks.

At San Cristóbal de las Casas, the Carretera Ocosingo joins **Route 190**, better known as the Pan American Highway. Taking this highway to the west will bring you to Chiapa de Corzo, Cañón del Sumidero and the state capital, Tuxtla Gutiérrez. Proceeding eastward on the Pan American Highway will take you to Comitán and the turnoff to the Guatemalan border at Ciudad Cuauhtémoc.

The Pan American Highway does not actually cross into Guatemala at Ciudad Cuauhtémoc. Instead, it veers south and meanders along the border, all the way to Tapachula, near the Pacific coast, before crossing the border.

BY AIR

Most people traveling by air to Palenque will fly into **Rovirosa Airport** in Villahermosa, the capital of the neighboring state of Tabasco, about 140 kilometers to the west, and rent a car there. Aeroméxico and Mexicana have several flights daily to Villahermosa from Mexico City and Mérida. There is no direct flight from Villahermosa to Palenque. Aviasca flies daily from Tuxtla Gutiérrez to Palenque, the only regularly scheduled passenger flight that lands at Palenque's small airstrip.

San Cristóbal de las Casas has no scheduled passenger service. Travelers wishing to reach San Cristóbal by plane fly into Tuxtla Gutiérrez's **Aeropuerto San Juan**, actually located 22 kilometers west at the little town of Ocozocoautla. Mexicana flies daily between Tuxtla and Mexico City. Smaller commuter planes fly out of the **Aeropuerto Terán**, on Tuxtla Gutiérrez's western outskirts, where Aviasca provides service to and from Palenque, Villahermosa, Tapachula and Oaxaca, while Aerocaribe flies to and from Mérida and Cancún.

BY BUS

First-class overnight express buses from Mérida via Campeche to Palenque are operated by Autobuses de Oriente (ADO). Other buses run between Campeche and Villahermosa almost hourly and can drop you off at Catazaja, the turnoff to Palenque, where *combi* transportation into town is usually available.

Omnibus Cristóbal Colón operates daily first-class buses between Palenque and San Cristóbal. These are new, luxurious buses, complete with a video system that plays old Cantinflas movies during the four-hour trip.

From San Cristóbal de las Casas's ADO/Cristóbal Colón bus terminal (8-02-91) on the Pan American Highway at Avenida Insurgentes, eight blocks due south of the *zócalo*, first-class buses run daily to destinations throughout southeastern Mexico, including Tuxtla Gutiérrez, Tapachula, Palenque and Ciudad Cuauhtémoc, the border crossing point to the Guatemalan Highlands.

In Tuxtla Gutiérrez, the Cristóbal Colón bus terminal (2-16-39) is conveniently located just two blocks from the *zócalo* at Avenida 2 Norte Poniente and Calle 2 Poniente Norte. Buses run from there to Comitán and the Guatemalan border crossing at Ciudad Cuauhtémoc, as well as to San Cristóbal, Palenque, Tapachula and other destinations throughout southeastern Mexico. ADO has a separate terminal (Calle 9 Poniente Sur at Avenida 5 Sur Poniente; 2-87-25) with service to Mexico City and other points west.

BY TRAIN

Ferrocarrilles Nacionales de Mexico operates daily trains between Mexico City and Mérida, which stop in Palenque. Other stops on the route include Veracruz, Villahermosa and Campeche. The journey from Mexico City to Mérida by train takes almost two days, so a rest day in Palenque will seem more and more like a great idea. This train route is wonderful. The train itself leaves much to be desired, as discussed more fully in Chapter Five.

CAR RENTALS

Rental cars are few and far between in both Palenque and San Cristóbal de las Casas, and in high season (winter in Palenque, summer in San Cristóbal) there may be none available closer than Villahermosa or Tuxtla Gutiérrez. Even so, the travel agencies in major hotels can often order cars brought in from the larger cities. In Palenque, the local car rental agency is **Leon Tovilla Mario** (Calle Hidalgo No. 46; 5-03-01). In San Cristóbal, it is **Auto Rent A Car Yaxchilán S.A.** (Diego de Mazariegos No. 36; 8-18-71).

Tuxtla Gutiérrez rental agencies include **Autos de Renta Gabriel** (Boulevard Dr. Belisario Domínguez No. 780; 2-24-51), **Budget-Tuxtla Rent A Car S.A.** (Boulevard Dr. Belisario Domínguez No. 2510; 2-55-06) and **Estafetas de Chiapas S.A.** (Calle 13 Oriente Norte No. 310; 3-0465).

In Tapachula, rental cars are available at **Auto Rentas Renovales S.A.** (Avenida Central Sur 3; 6-54-03).

PUBLIC TRANSPORTATION

Combis (also called *colectivos*), Volkswagen buses that can carry eight to ten passengers, are the main form of local transportation everywhere in Chiapas. In Palenque, *combis* run up and down the road from town to the ruins in such numbers that you will rarely have to wait more than five minutes for one. In San Cristóbal de las Casas, *combis* run back and forth between the public market and most of the neighboring Indian villages almost constantly. Fares are minimal. Palenque, San Cristóbal, Tuxtla Gutiérrez and Tapachula also have plenty of private taxis, which cost more.

SEVEN

Guatemala

Guatemala, the heart of the Maya world, presents travelers with formidable challenges and rewards them with memorable adventures. It is in
Guatemala that the most exotic places on the Maya Route are to be
found. Foremost among these is the lost world of Tikal, the most
splendid of all ancient Maya cities, hidden deep in North America's
largest rainforest. Another great Maya city, Copán—the site of un-
equaled Maya stone sculptures and hieroglyph carvings—lies in ruins
in a remote corner of Honduras, so close to the border that it is generally regarded as a Guatemalan travel destination.

In Guatemala, you'll also find other extraordinary places such as the
Río Dulce, one of the last fragments of "undiscovered" tropical paradise
in the Caribbean; Antigua Guatemala, an early Spanish colonial capital
twice toppled by earthquakes but now revived as an historic district
that brings the 18th century closer than the sprawling metropolis of
Guatemala City just over the mountain; and Lake Atitlán, surrounded
by volcanoes, Maya villages and the resort town of Panajachel, a low-
rent rendezvous for adventurous travelers, old-time hippies and foot-
loose expatriates from all over the world. Terrain and climates vary
dramatically, from the looming peaks of the western highlands, where
the weather is cool year-round, to the jungle lowlands of the east and
north, where it is always hot. This astonishing range of landscape and
lifestyles lies within the borders of a nation no larger than the state of
Ohio. Guatemala is all the more appealing because prices for food,
lodging and transportation are some of the best travel bargains on the
North American continent, less than half of what comparable accommodations cost in Mexico.

Guatemala has the largest population of any Central American country—twice as large as Panama and Costa Rica combined. Two-thirds of the people are Maya Indians. It is the only North American nation in which the majority of the population is traditional Indian and the only Central American country where the indigenous people have not been fully assimilated or exterminated. Village life throughout the western highlands has changed little since the first Spanish conquerors arrived nearly five centuries ago. The people wear brightly colored traditional clothing that signifies the wearer's village, speak to each other in ancient tongues and worship the old gods at forest shrines, along with Christian saints in churches.

A visit to Guatemala is sure to evoke ambivalent feelings in any traveler. Along with its incomparable cultural heritage and magnificent natural beauty come darker realities. It is one of the poorest nations in the Western Hemisphere. The average income of Guatemalans is only about one-third that of Mexicans. Poverty is so severe that half of all Guatemalan families cannot get enough food to meet minimum nutritional needs. Compared with Mexico, life expectancy is ten years shorter, infant mortality is 50 percent higher, and there are only half as many hospital beds per capita. Forty-five percent of the population, including most indigenous people, cannot read. Only recently has the nation emerged from thirty years of civil war and brutal military repression into a new and tenuous spirit of freedom.

Tourism, though still in its infancy, is Guatemala's fastest-growing industry. Revenue from tourism has more than quadrupled since the formation of the new democratic government in 1986, and tourism is now seen as the country's best hope for economic recovery. The government's desire to develop an eco-travel industry patterned after the La Ruta Maya Conservation Foundation plan, and proven successful in Belize and Costa Rica, has brought unprecedented measures to protect Guatemalan wildlife and even, sometimes grudgingly, to improve the situation of the Maya people. It also translates into friendly, hospitable and protective attitudes among the local people toward foreign visitors.

After a couple of relaxing weeks in Mexico, traveling in Guatemala may give you occasional jolts of culture shock. At such times, the company of fellow travelers becomes vitally important. Then, too, once you wander away from the well-trodden path, there's not much lodging or food to be found. For these reasons, even the hardiest travelers prefer Guatemala's well-established tourist route.

Plan to center your Guatemala explorations around three main hubs—Lake Atitlán and Antigua Guatemala in the south and Tikal National Park in the north. Other great places, such as traditional Maya villages, wildlife reserves and the ruins of magnificent ceremonial centers at Quiriguá and Copán, lie along the route that links these

three destinations. As you follow the Maya Route through Guatemala, you'll marvel at the abundance of bright color: macaws and parrots in the skies, flowers that bloom all year, native women in lavishly embroidered *huipiles* and men in pink-striped pants. You'll hear the music of marimbas, the whispers of waves lapping on lakeshores, the din of jungle birds and beasts. You'll find opportunities to wander through labyrinthine public markets where incense, spices and a cacophony of strange native languages assail the senses, to scale lofty, smoldering volcanoes and to hike trails through cloud forest and deep jungle. Most of all, you'll experience the timeless Maya spirit that built a sophisticated and complex civilization in ancient times only to witness its collapse and ruin, to suffer conquest, exploitation, slavery and persecution, and still to endure.

Huehuetenango

Most travelers who enter Guatemala by road from Chiapas, Mexico, make their first night's stop at **Huehuetenango**, the first large town. Visitors who arrive in Guatemala by air rarely go near the place—and don't know what they're missing. Although Indian and ladino alike are poor in this remote mountain state—it was a guerrilla stronghold in the 1970s and early 1980s—on our recent visit there was no slightest hint of political unrest or even random lawlessness—just some of the most cheerful and friendly people in Guatemala. Huehuetenango has several language schools, and its popularity as a place to study Spanish is growing because, unlike Antigua Guatemala where language instruction has become a major industry, little English is spoken anywhere in Huehuetenango.

Huehuetenango (population 50,000), commonly called "Huehue" (pronounced "WAY-way"), is the capital of the department (like a state) of the same name. The 88-kilometer trip from the border to town on paved Route 1, climbing from 2500 to 6300 feet in elevation, unveils dry, dusty, played-out hillside farms in the claustrophobic valley of Río Selegua. Foot trails disappearing up into ravines barely hint at the grand mountain ranges just a few kilometers away.

Your first impression on arrival in the town of Huehuetenango may well be of a place in hopeless disorder and disrepair, of brightly painted buildings peeled until they are half-gray and battered old cars and trucks, many pocked with bullet holes, chugging through the streets as if each trip might be their last. Small people, exotically dressed in colorful clothing, walk barefoot down the middle of narrow streets roughly cobbled with round rocks, carrying improbable burdens like four-by-eight-foot sheets of tin roofing and net bags full of live baby chicks, or

In Guatemala, the town plaza is usually called a parque, *not a* zócalo—*just one of many vocabulary differences between Guatemala and Mexico.*

sit in open doorways and curbs of crumbling sidewalks gazing fixedly with black, unreadable eyes at any foreign traveler who may wander past.

All second-class buses (and all buses from the border *are* second-class) let you off on Avenida 1 near the **public market**. The market itself is inside a dim old building between Avenidas 1 and 2 and Calles 3 and 4, but the local color spills out into all the surrounding streets, for this is the center of town as far as the Indians are concerned. You'll find produce, clothing, low-priced cookware and hardware, and even livestock for sale in the market, along with prayer candles, used bottles and green (unroasted) coffee beans.

For the ladino population, as well as for travelers, the center of town is the concrete **plaza** or *parque central*, located four blocks west of the market between Avenidas 4 and 5 and Calles 2 and 3. A ponderous old colonial-style cathedral with a façade full of decorative columns looms over the plaza, but the main point of interest is in the middle of the park, a giant relief map of the Department of Huehuetenango painted with vegetation zones and roads, with flags marking the locations of major villages. As you can see from the map, the 12,800-foot high point in the Cordillera de los Cuchumatanes, the highest mountain range in Central America, looms in the center of the department just above the village of Todos Santos Cuchumatán, 54 kilometers from the town of Huehuetenango.

Seventy percent of the population of the town of Huehuetenango and the surrounding villages is Maya Indian. Almost all are descendants of the Mam Maya, whose rugged domain at the time the Spanish first arrived had almost exactly the same boundaries as the Department of Huehuetenango today. There are about 30 major Maya villages in the department of Huehuetenango, some of them almost as large as the capital town. The easiest Indian villages to visit are Chiantla and Aguacatán, both on a wide, rocky, hard-packed road that runs north and then east of Huehuetenango. Chiantla is just about 4 kilometers out of town, and Aguacatán 18 kilometers farther on. You can easily make a round-trip by bus to both villages in a single day.

Chiantla is most famous throughout the Maya highlands as a religious center. It is widely believed that the image of the Virgin Mary kept here possesses miraculous healing powers, and the faithful from all over the region make a pilgrimage here on February 2 each year. The main industry in the village of Chiantla is cattle grazing, and leather goods are a specialty.

Aguacatán is a unique village whose people speak a language unlike any other in the Maya world. The people, who are unusually small even by Maya standards, wear some of the most distinctive *traje* (traditional native clothing) in the Maya highlands, especially the women's blouses of white satin festooned with glittery ribbonwork and simple, symbolic embroidered figures. The village is so rural in character that there hardly seems to be a town center. The main cash crop is avocados. A visit is most interesting on market days, which in Aguacatán are twice weekly—on Sundays and Thursdays. The unexcavated ruin of Chalchitán lies buried near the banks of the Río San Juan, about 2 kilometers north of the village.

By far the most memorable of the Maya villages in Huehuetenango is a lot harder to reach. **Todos Santos Cuchumatán**, a true Central American Shangri-la in the heart of Guatemala's proposed Los Cuchumatanes National Park, is set at the 8200-foot elevation in a valley within shouting distance of a craggy peak that towers above the village. There was no road access to Todos Santos until the 1970s, and even today visitors are likely to feel that they have stepped back into medieval times. Lingering memories of the Postclassic Maya world are still strong here. Recent anthropological studies claim that Todos Santos is one of the few places where the 260-times-365-day "short-count" calendar of the ancient Olmec, Maya and Toltec civilizations is still in use. To confirm this fact for yourself, you would probably have to engage in lengthy discussions in the Mam language. Another remnant of ancient times is more tangible: a series of burial mounds from the Preclassic ceremonial site of Tecumanchún can be seen by looking south up the ridgeline from the center of town.

The men of Todos Santos, who stand taller and seem prouder than the residents of other highland villages, dress in a style unique to this valley, with red-and-white striped trousers, homespun shirts with crimson collars, and warm black-wool cloaks and leggings. They are often seen in Huehuetenango, while men from other villages, dressed in remarkably different *traje* and carrying bundles of trade goods on their backs, trek in and out of Todos Santos on a daily basis.

Todos Santos is a 54-kilometer trip from Huehuetenango, but the journey can take almost half a day, since the road is as bad as any that visitors are likely to find themselves on anywhere in Guatemala. You would not want to drive your own vehicle or dare to drive a rental car there. Two beat-up second-class buses a day—one before dawn and the other shortly after noon, with additional buses for the Saturday market—leave from Huehuetenango's market area, reaching Todos Santos in the late afternoon. They do not start the return trip until the next morning, so any outsiders who visit Todos Santos must be prepared to spend the night. Accommodations are in two primitive guest houses.

You will want to bring camping gear—preferably a sleeping bag. Chill air pours down from the mountaintops at night, dropping temperatures in Todos Santos perilously close to the freezing mark almost every night of the year.

Other villages of special interest in the highlands around Huehuetenango include **San Juan Ixcoy**, 64 kilometers from the capital over the crest of the mountain range, where they specialize in growing temperate-zone fruits such as apples and cherries, which are rare and expensive delicacies in the tropics; **Santa Eulalia**, 84 kilometers by slow paved road, where shrines and ceremonial caves are maintained just outside the village; and **San Mateo Ixtatán**, 112 kilometers away, the farthest place in the Cuchumatán Mountains that can be reached by road, where mineral salt from a local spring is believed to have magical powers.

About four kilometers out of Huehuetenango is the closest thing to a tourist attraction in the area—the more-or-less restored ruins of **Zaculeu** (admission), which was the Mam Maya capital of the region until Spanish *conquistadores* arrived in the year 1525. It is generally considered to be one of the worst restoration jobs in the history of archaeology. The United Fruit Company, which virtually owned Guatemala for much of the 20th century, rebuilt Zaculeu as a set for publicity photos in 1946 and 1947, hastily slathering over the old walls and temple mounds with concrete. Even the ball court was completely paved, creating an entirely different impression than other ball courts found along the Ruta Maya. Today, the concrete is as cracked and cockeyed as the sidewalks of Huehuetenango, and a streaky gray patina of not-so-great age has settled over the ruins. The stark, streaked planes of Zaculeu pose a wonderful challenge for photographers. Put a human subject in

---

A DIFFERENT KIND OF MAYA RUIN

Zaculeu *is one of only two restored Postclassic Maya sites. (The other is Tulum, at the opposite extremity of the Ruta Maya.) It has absolutely no paintings, sculpture, hieroglyphs, stelae, arches, roof combs or any of the other artistic and architectural features that capture our imagination about the Maya world. This is not, as many people think, because of the heavy-handed United Fruit Company restoration. The fact is, when the Spanish arrived, they found a ceremonial center that looked very much as it does today. The highland Maya of Postclassic times (950 A.D. to 1525 A.D.) did not bother with art. Theirs was a society ruled by military warlords. The buildings were not beautiful, but they were massive.*

Slate plaques covered with shiny pyrite were made in Zaculeu and traded throughout the Maya world. Although no one knows for sure, they may have had the same significance as the mirrors that hang around saints' necks in Maya churches today.

bright-colored clothing anywhere within these ruins and you can't help but take an unusual and dramatic picture.

Many Maya buffs dismiss Zaculeu as a downright boring place to spend an afternoon. But we've found it well worth visiting (once, anyway), for its historical interest, as well as for the dramatic visual effect of its square, unadorned contours set against a backdrop of Guatemala's highest mountains. As a series of paintings and interpretive displays in Spanish in the museum at the site recounts, Zaculeu was the last bastion of the highland Maya people against Spanish soldiers led by Gonzalo de Alvarado, younger brother of the conqueror of Guatemala. Its location on a bluff flanked by deep ravines made it unassailable, and it finally took a six-month siege to starve the Mam people into submission and finish the fall of the Maya empire in 1525.

It is a long, gradual uphill walk, which takes slightly more than an hour, from the plaza in Huehuetenango to the Zaculeu ruins, but we would not recommend it to anyone who has doubts about asking and understanding directions in Spanish, because the route has several forks and intersections. Taxi fares are quite reasonable around Huehue, and a shuttle bus runs back and forth on the road past the ruins periodically. The same route is much easier to follow on the way back to town. The people who live along the road, several of whom you will undoubtedly meet if you walk, are remarkably open and friendly toward strangers.

HUEHUETENANGO LODGING

The best lodging in Huehuetenango is the **Hotel Zaculeu** (Avenida 5 No. 1-14; 64-10-86), a comfortable lowrise hotel just a block from the central plaza. Don't expect American-style amenities like television, in-room phones or air-conditioning; aside from a handful of international-class hotels in Guatemala City, technological conveniences like these are virtually unheard-of in Guatemalan accommodations. Instead, this hotel has quiet, cozy rooms with bright-colored bedspreads, private bathrooms with reliable hot water and a lovely, peaceful interior courtyard with a big fountain and lots of flowers. The Hotel Zaculeu is similar to many of our moderate-priced hotel recommendations in Mexican towns like Mérida and San Cristóbal de las Casas, but because of the weakness of Guatemalan currency against the U.S. dollar, this hotel falls into the low end of the budget price range.

If the Hotel Zaculeu is full, the best alternative is the **Hotel Central** (Avenida 5 No. 1-33) across the street. Rooms here are big but dark, baths are down the hall and the courtyard is bare and paved with concrete, but this bare-bones lodging is a cut above the other hotels in town. Most guests here are young American and European budget travelers. Rates are so close to the bottom of the budget range that rooms seem almost free.

If you are driving your own car or a rental, staying downtown can pose a serious parking problem. The best alternative is the **Centro Turístico Pino Montano** (Carretera Panamericana Km. 259; 53-13-94), a rather run-down roadside motel on Route 1, two kilometers northwest of the turnoff to Huehuetenango. The 20 guest rooms are in bungalows in a pleasant-enough landscaped setting. There is a small, none-too-clean unheated swimming pool. Rates, in the budget range, are about the same as at the nicer Hotel Zaculeu in town. As those touring Guatemala by car will soon discover, this is actually one of the better motels to be found along the highways of Guatemala, a nation where so few people have automobiles that the whole concept of motels doesn't make much sense.

In the village of Todos Santos Cuchumatán, where visitors by bus have no choice but to spend the night, very basic lodging is available at two guest houses—the **Hospedaje La Paz** and the **Pensión Lucía**, both near where the buses stop. You get a mattress and a roof over your head but no indoor plumbing. The cost to stay is minimal.

HUEHUETENANGO RESTAURANTS

Huehuetenango has nothing even close to a fancy restaurant. It's no problem at all to eat cheaply in Huehuetenango; eating well is more challenging. The best meal bargain in town is at the plain, simple restaurant in the **Hotel Central** (Avenida 5 No. 1-33), where fixed menus offer *comida corrida* meals, typically including fruit, a beverage, roast chicken, spaghetti, potatoes, a vegetable, plenty of handmade tortillas and dessert, all for less than you'd pay for a "quarter pounder with cheese" back in the United States.

The nicer **Hotel Zaculeu** (Avenida 5 No. 1-14; 64-10-86) across the street also has a restaurant, but it seems to be empty most of the time. The decor is intriguing—a big mural of Maya huts in the highlands on one wall dominates the room—but the food is just okay and the prices, while still in the budget range, are outrageously high by Huehuetenango standards.

A place where a lot of foreign visitors in the know hang out is **Pizza Hogareña** (Avenida 6 No. 4-45), an unpretentious establishment that looks like a hole-in-the-wall from the street, but which has a huge back room. Besides pizzas, the menu includes sandwiches, *churrascos* and a wide variety of spaghetti dishes. The same management operates a similar eatery, **Restaurante Rincón** (Avenida 6 No. 7-21) three blocks farther south. Prices are in the budget range at both places.

Visitors who have just arrived in Guatemala should rest assured that they will find much better restaurants in other parts of the country where more tourists stay.

HUEHUETENANGO SHOPPING

Weaving is the preeminent craft throughout the Guatemalan highlands, dating back all the way to the ancient Maya civilization through an unbroken chain of mothers and daughters. In and around Huehuetenango, you can find some of the best buys in native *traje*, or distinctive village clothing, though it takes a little looking.

Commercial Guatemalan clothing is available in several shops around Huehuetenango. There is an unusually nice selection of blouses, *huipiles* and bags of all sizes at **Artesanías Ixquil** (Avenida 5 No. 1-30), next door to the Hotel Zaculeu and half a block from the central plaza. For the most part, however, you'll find a much better

---

THOSE WONDERFUL GUATEMALAN CLOTHES

Textiles and clothing make up the fastest-growing sector of Guatemala's economy today. This clothing, exported to every corner of the industrialized world, is made by Guatemalan women, Indian and ladino alike, who own hand looms or sewing machines and work in their own homes. They can make as much as US$1.50 a day, which is considered a good wage for women in Guatemala. This low labor cost, together with favorable foreign currency exchange rates, makes Guatemalan clothing an incredible bargain.

There is a big difference between commercial clothing products and traje, or traditional village clothing. Each village throughout central and western Guatemala has its own style and pattern of clothing, which is unlike that of any other village. Although at first glance all traje of a particular village looks alike, small differences in detail make each garment unique in the eyes of other village women. Unlike in most indigenous villages of Mexico, in Guatemala both men and women wear traje. Designs woven or embroidered into the clothing symbolize anything from animals and rivers to mountains and Maya gods; in many cases the original meaning of a stylized design has been lost to memory. Careful craft goes into each garment, and a single huipil with a cash value of US$30 or $40 can take several months to make.

When it comes to village traje, *or native clothing, Huehuetenango and the surrounding villages are some of the best places in Guatemala to shop.*

---

selection at equally good prices in tourist centers like Lake Atitlán and Antigua Guatemala.

In the **Huehuetenango public market**, you can find *huipiles* and other *traje* from every village in the department if you ask around. Indian women trade both newly made and used *huipiles* to market vendors and shops for sewing supplies or household goods. A good plan is to look at the clothing that Indians wear to market and, when you see a style you like, find out what village it comes from. Then ask around to find out who has it for sale.

Of course, you'll get a better price and a better story to go with it if you buy *traje* in the village where it was made. Beat-up old buses that leave from Avenida 1 near the market serve all major villages in the mountains around Huehuetenango. Market days are Saturday in **Todos Santos Cuchumatán** and Sunday in **Chiantla, Aguacatán, Santa Eulalia, San Mateo Ixtatán** and **Barillas**. Both Aguacatán and San Mateo Ixtatán hold a second market day on Thursday.

Quetzaltenango (Xela)

Travelers are most likely to find themselves passing through **Quetzaltenango** (population 100,000) on a side trip to the Maya ruins around Retalhuleu and the Pacific coast at Champerico. The main reason to stop is that the city has more and better hotels and restaurants than either of the latter towns. Quetzaltenango has little to offer in the way of sightseeing, and it is easy to bypass by simply staying on the highway from Huehuetenango to Los Encuentros, which passes 11 kilometers north of town. (Note: Both the highway from Ciudad Cuauhtémoc, Chiapas, through Huehuetenango and the one from Tapachula, Chiapas, through Quetzaltenango are designated as Route 1, and both are commonly called the Carretera Panamericana.)

The trip from Huehuetenango to Quetzaltenango is 69 kilometers on a paved mountain highway and makes for a scenic two-hour drive or a wild three-hour bus trip. As you reach the Quetzaltenango Valley and near the turnoff for the city, you pass through the town of San Cristóbal Totonicapán. From there, an unpaved road leads to **San Francisco el Alto**, where the Friday market is the biggest village market in Guatemala. Fifteen kilometers farther on the same road will bring you to **Momostenango**, where they weave the thick, warm wool used here and elsewhere to make blankets, ponchos and jackets. There are several hot springs in the hills around town, including **Palá Chiquito**, the popular local bathing spot about six kilometers up the road. Try to get one of the persistent youngsters who follow visitors around offering guide services to take you to the altar mounds on **Chuitmesabal**, a hill about two kilometers out of town. The altars are part of a strange highland Maya tradition that is still practiced around Momostenango. On "Eight Monkey," the New Year's Day of the 260-day Maya religious calendar that has been in use since ancient times, the people of the village leave pieces of pottery that has broken during the year as offerings to the old gods. Outsiders are not allowed at the ceremonies, but you can see the mounds that have built up over centuries of ceremonies. For nondrivers, buses run regularly from the Templo de Minerva in Quetzaltenango to both San Francisco el Alto and Momostenango.

Quetzaltenango is the second-biggest city in Guatemala, though its population of roughly 100,000 is only one-twentieth that of Guatemala City, the nation's capital. Although the city has been officially named Quetzaltenango since the beginning of the Spanish colonial era nearly five centuries ago, everybody who lives here calls it Xela (pronounced "SHAY-la"), the Quiché name for the ancient Maya city that once occupied the site. The old name has stuck thanks to the most important historical event that ever took place here: the defeat by Spanish *conquistador* Pedro de Alvarado of the great Quiché Maya hero Tecun Umán in 1524, which opened the route from Mexico to the Guatemalan interior and spelled the beginning of the end for the Maya people as an independent race.

Quetzaltenango's central plaza, called the **Parque Centroamérica**, is surrounded by gray neoclassical buildings with Greek columns made of concrete. Other huge columns stand alone as monoliths around the plaza. Though the architects sought to imbue the city center with a colonial feeling, all the buildings—many of them banks—are actually of recent origin, as the city was destroyed by an earthquake in 1902. On the south end of the plaza, the **Casa de Cultura del Occidente** (Calle 7) contains the **Museo de Historia Natural**, a packrat hodgepodge of curiosities ranging from examples of pre-Hispanic pottery, village *traje* and documents from various revolutions to bad taxidermy and such bizarre curiosities as a human brain in formaldehyde. Downstairs in the Casa de Cultura is an excellent exhibit of highland Maya dance masks and musical instruments. There is also a gallery where paintings by regional artists are sometimes shown. On the second floor is an office of **INGUAT**, the Guatemalan government's tourism bureau.

Quetzaltenango's second-best point of interest, located on the northwest side of town about 1 kilometer from the central plaza along Calle Rodolfo Robles, is the **Templo de Minerva**. This concrete

At a shrine in Zunil, it is customary to make offerings to Maximón, a seated mannequin dressed in a stylized Spanish suit, a cowboy hat, sunglasses and many scarves, by blowing cigar smoke in his face and pouring liquor down his throat.

replica of an ancient Greek temple dedicated to the goddess of learning, built in the early years of the 20th century by Manuel Estrada Cabrera, Guatemala's "education president," is one of the largest among several such temples that he built all over the country, few of which are still standing. It is said that Estrada Cabrera built more Roman temples than schools. Near the temple is the **Parque Zoológico**, a depressing little zoo and children's playground.

Ten kilometers south of Quetzaltenango on Route 9S, **Zunil** may be the most colorful village in the Guatemalan highlands. The village women dress in *huipiles* and long shawls in a full range of pink, red and purple hues. The village church has an ornate old white façade and, inside, an altar made of pure silver. For a firsthand look at one of the strangest aspects of highland Maya folk religion, walk up to the small house behind the church, which serves as a shrine to Maximón. Also called San Simón or Alvarado, this effigy does not live in the church because he is considered by the Catholic clergy to be an "evil saint" and perhaps a manifestation of Judas Iscariot. The local people see him as an incarnation of the ancient Maya god Mam and believe that he has the power to heal the sick and answer prayers for money. Visitors are expected to make small offerings of cash. Buses to Zunil run regularly from Quetzaltenango.

From the highway near Zunil, a rugged nine-kilometer unpaved road leads to **Fuentes Georgina** (admission), a beautiful hot-springs spa owned by the Guatemalan government. It has a pool and a restaurant, along with a few budget-priced cabins, in a setting that couldn't be more idyllic. Sulfurous steam drifts through a landscape of cedars and giant ferns scattered with fountains and statues of unclad women. The spa is set on the edge of a precipice overlooking a cool pine forest valley.

If you continue down Route 9S for another 31 kilometers, you'll come to an intersection called El Zarco where the highway crosses Route 2, the *Carretera al Pacífico* (Highway to the Pacific). If you turn west on this highway, a drive of about 12 kilometers will bring you to the turnoff to the archaeological site at **Abaj Takalik**, reached on a 9-kilometer road that is paved as far as the village of El Asintal and then gradually deteriorates into a dirt track. The site is now being excavated to reveal giant stone heads in the Olmec style that date back some 4000 years. Scientists hope that Abaj Takalik may provide clues about the earliest origins of the Maya civilization.

If you stay on Route 9S and keep going south from El Zarco, you will almost immediately find yourself in **Retalhuleu**, a ladino town of 50,000. Its warm climate makes it a popular weekend getaway for businessmen and plantation owners from the chilly, often gray highlands around Quetzaltenango, so there are better hotels and restaurants than you would expect, but nothing much to see in town. Another 38 kilometers on Route 9S brings you to the Pacific coast and the shantytown has-been coffee port of **Champerico**. The few visitors who venture down this way find long but not very appealing brown beaches and, for the truly intrepid outdoorsperson, boatmen willing to take fishermen or sightseers up the coast to **Reserva Natural El Manchón**, a vast, isolated, rarely seen wetland inhabited by myriad birds, alligators and mosquitoes. If all you want to do is see the ocean, though, you might wait and go to Likín, a resort community on the coast south of Antigua and Guatemala City, where you can sightsee in more pleasant surroundings.

QUETZALTENANGO LODGING

A stay at the **Pensión Bonifaz** (Calle 4 No. 10-50; 61-42-41) will spirit you back to an earlier era of elegance. This 62-room hotel facing the central plaza is divided between two buildings—the original turn-of-the-century hotel and a modern annex. Rooms in the old section have been refurbished recently, and some have balconies overlooking the plaza. All the rooms are large, all have private bathrooms and many have tubs. There are no in-room televisions or telephones, but the central TV lounge is a popular gathering place. Rates are in the moderate range for both rooms and suites.

For drivers, the **Hotel Del Campo** (Camino a Cantel at Las Rosas Junction; 61-20-64), the largest lodging establishment in Quetzaltenango with more than 100 rooms, is located a long way from the city center but close to where Routes 9S and 2 intersect. Rooms are modern and carpeted, with furnishings comparable to those in good motor inns in the United States. It has an indoor heated swimming pool. Prices are at the high end of the budget range.

A good bet for lower-priced rooms is the **Hotel Modelo** (Avenida 14-A No. 2-31; 61-27-15), located five blocks from the central plaza, around the block from the pizzerias Pastelería Bombonier and Pizza Ricca. The guest rooms here are small but colorfully decorated, all with private bath. If you've never huddled around a big fireplace in the tropics before, the best place we can think of to try it is in the cozy lobby of this family-operated hotel, a favorite with Guatemalan businessmen and families. Budget.

QUETZALTENANGO RESTAURANTS

The best restaurant in Quetzaltenango is at the **Pensión Bonifaz** (Calle 4 No. 10-50; 61-42-41), facing the Parque Centroamérica. This old-fashioned grand hotel has three dining rooms, all with the same menu. The cuisine is continental, with selections that range from spaghetti to filet mignon. The colonial-style decor features heavy wooden furniture and lots of wrought iron, and the staff dresses in traditional highland Maya *traje*. In the afternoon, the last of Quetzaltenango's German coffee-plantation high society congregates around the fireplace. It's one of the most elegant places in Guatemala, and prices are in the budget range.

A more modest place—where you can sample an assortment of regional foods at a low budget price—is the **Cafetería El Kopetin** (Avenida 14 No. 3-31; 61-24-01). The specialty at this modern family-style restaurant is the *parillada* (barbecue), a platter of five different meats with all the trimmings. Other entrées run the gamut from cheeseburgers to seafood. Budget.

Pizza places are special in Guatemala. They're where local families eat out on special occasions and foreign travelers hang out to lose those culture shock blues. Quetzaltenango's two popular pizzerias, which also serve burgers and fries and such, are neighbors two blocks west and two blocks north of the Parque Centroamérica. **Pizza Ricca** (Avenida 14 No. 2-52; 61-81-62) has wooden booths and pizza bakers in white, and low budget prices. Nearby **Pastelería Bombonier** (Avenida 14 No. 2-20; 61-62-25) has equally good food at even lower prices, but is quite small, with seating for only three parties at one time.

QUETZALTENANGO AREA SHOPPING

The old **Mercadito** (Little Market) off Quetzaltenango's central plaza still operates on a small scale. It is mostly tourist-oriented, with a fair selection of commercial-quality clothing and jewelry. The larger public market is **La Democracia** at Avenida 16 and Calle Rodolfo Robles in Zone 3, ten blocks northwest of the city center. This is the place where the locals go for food and furniture, kitchenware and bolts of blue denim, imported all the way from the United States.

Every Friday, **San Francisco el Alto** hosts the largest village market in Guatemala. Unlike such well-known weekly markets as the one at Chichicastenango, this is mainly a genuine Indian market with few concessions to tourism. You'll find lots of pigs for sale, as well as fruits and vegetables from all over the country, handwoven and imported fabrics, strange herbs and more. Blankets and all kinds of woolen goods are an excellent buy here. It starts early, with some vendors doing business by candlelight before dawn, and by noon it's all over.

If you can make it to **Momostenango** for the Sunday market, you'll find the best buys imaginable on wool blankets, a challenge to carry back home but worth it for their warmth. There is a second market day on Wednesday. If you go to this village on any day other than market day, you'll find that most of the places in Momostenango that represent themselves as blanket factories are actually retail stores with hefty markups. For the best selection and prices, visit the cooperative in the center of town or the *fábrica de chamarras* (the real blanket factory) on the outskirts of town.

Lake Atitlán Area

Lake Atitlán is Guatemala's leading beach resort. For international travelers, the area offers a mixed bag of just about everything one goes to Guatemala to see. The big, beautiful lake—20 kilometers long, 10 kilometers wide and 320 meters deep—wraps around the bases of a group of volcanoes that reach up to 3500 meters (11,700 feet) into the clear blue highland sky. Along the lake shore stand a dozen traditional villages, many of them only accessible by boat or by foot trail. These villages are home to three distinct language groups of Maya Indians.

That Lake Atitlán should be a beach resort at all is curious, for the beaches, even in front of the best hotels, are narrow and rocky. The water is chilly for swimming, and pollution may pose health risks since raw sewage drains into the lake, which has no outlet. Yet the lake does have a lively beach scene, especially on weekends, when Guatemalans flock here from the city. The rest of the week, the waterfront around the town of Panajachel is one of those rare places where you can while away hour after hour just staring in wonder at the water and the vast, mysterious volcanic landscape beyond.

The distance to Los Encuentros Junction, where the road to Lake Atitlán turns off from Route 1, is 97 kilometers from Huehuetenango or 70 kilometers from Quetzaltenango. Panajachel, on the shore of Lake Atitlán, is 15 kilometers to the south of Los Encuentros. The road from the Pan American Highway (Route 1) to the lake is also designated Route 1. It passes through the department capital, Sololá (population 10,000), set on a mesa with a spectacular view of the lake, and then descends abruptly into Panajachel on the shoreline.

Panajachel (population 5000) is the only developed tourist resort area along the shore of Lake Atitlán, though much of the east side of the lake is filling up with the big, walled villas of Guatemala's moneyed

The words atitlán *("lake") and* tenango *(town), are Nahuatl, the language of Aztec slaves who came to Guatemala with the first Spanish conquistadores.*

elite. Almost completely swallowed up by modern commercial development, the original town dates back to the year 1567, when Franciscan missionaries built a church and monastery at the site of a makeshift Spanish fort that had been established to wage war against the local Tzutuhil Maya population. The original church façade still stands, though the church building behind it was replaced after an earthquake. The church is just about the only sightseeing highlight in town. Nearby, an unabashedly tourist-oriented public market features perhaps the widest array of *típica* (traditional) clothing to be found at any permanent market in Guatemala. While it operates every day, Sunday is the big market day.

Panajachel presents one of the most unusual cross-sections of humanity in Guatemala. Indians from the dozen Tzutuhil, Quiché and Cakchiquel villages around the lake come to Panajachel to sell things to tourists and shop at the grocery stores and pharmacies. Prominent businessmen from Guatemala City bring their mistresses here. Young ladinos, including lots of self-styled gangsters, are drawn here by Pana's reputation as an international jet-set hotbed of drugs, sex and rock-n-roll. In fact, Panajachel is one of the few places in Guatemala where marijuana and other drugs are readily available, though dealers are outnumbered by rip-off artists and plainclothes Guatemalan policemen. While there's nothing particularly sexy about this scene by United States or European standards, in a country where people keep their skin under wraps from neck to ankle, the prospect of bodies on the beach in bathing suits may be excitement enough.

In Panajachel, you will encounter a sizable percentage of all the foreigners in Guatemala at any given time, including bus tour groups and backpackers from every part of the industrialized world, more middle-aged hippie dropouts than most people realize are still on the face of the planet, and a handful of older North American expatriates who have found that retirement checks go a long way in this funky corner of paradise. It is rare, here or elsewhere in Guatemala, to meet anyone who will admit to actually liking Panajachel. It is fashionable to refer to the town by its disparaging nickname, "Gringotenango." Yet every visitor to Guatemala comes here, and while they are here they all appear to be enjoying themselves. It makes a comfortable home base for a wide range of explorations in the heart of the highlands. And let's admit it: in Guatemala it can be comforting sometimes to surround oneself with other tourists.

The traditional villages situated on other parts of Lake Atitlán's shoreline are pure highland Maya. They seem to have been established on the lake almost by coincidence, for most village people here do not catch fish from the lake or depend on canoes for transportation, preferring to carry their burdens along the rough dirt tracks that link the villages; nor do they know how to swim.

The largest village on the lake, three times the size of Panajachel, is **Santiago Atitlán**, the home of the Tzutuhil Maya people since pre-Hispanic times. The usual way to get there is to take one of the motor launches that leave Panajachel in the morning and return in the early afternoon. The boat trip, one hour each way, is lovely, particularly on the approach to Santiago Atitlán, with its spectacular setting at the foot of **Volcán Atitlán** and **Volcán San Pedro** across the narrow bay.

Santiago Atitlán is the commercial center for all the Indian villages around the lake, and every day is market day. Fridays and Tuesdays are the busiest. When boatloads of tourists are in town—roughly from 10:00 in the morning to 1:00 in the afternoon, the hawking of *típica* and curios reaches a fever pitch all the way from the boat landing to the market on the north side of the town plaza. The selection and prices are not much different than you would find in Panajachel.

A HEROINE FOR THE MAYA PEOPLE

*In October 1992, exactly 500 years after Columbus first set foot on an American beach, the Nobel Peace Prize was awarded to a Maya woman of humble origin, **Rigoberta Menchú Tum**. The daughter of a village healer and midwife, Ms. Menchú grew up in the highland department of Quiché, one of the most violent areas during the civil war of the 1980s. In 1981, her father was among 39 protestors burned to death in the Spanish Embassy in Guatemala City while demonstrating for human rights. Soon afterwards, her mother and younger brother were arrested by the military and tortured to death. Ms. Menchú fled to Mexico, where she wrote a book, I, Rigoberta, about her family's ordeal and the plight of Guatemala's Maya people. Published in 1983, the book is in print in Spanish, English and nine other languages.*

Rigoberta Menchú worked with other refugees along the Guatemalan border throughout the 1980s and now speaks out for the rights of native people throughout the Americas. The Guatemalan military filed a protest when her Nobel Prize was announced, charging that she was a spokesperson for a leftist guerilla group to which several of her relatives belonged. At the time, peace negotiations between the government and the guerillas were deadlocked because of a single issue—the government's refusal to recognize human rights for Guatemala's Indians. When the honor bestowed on Ms. Menchú was greeted with unanimous praise in the world press, the Guatemalan government withdrew its protest. She is the only Guatemalan ever to have received a Nobel Prize.

The big white church has stood facing the town plaza since 1568, when it was built as the headquarters for Franciscan missionary efforts in the region. As elsewhere in the highlands, this church reveals a strange fusion of Catholic and pre-Hispanic Maya religious beliefs. Besides the saints dressed in village *traje*, signs of ancient influences include carvings of the corn god Yum-Kax on the pulpit and throne. Santiago Atitlán is another of the highland villages where Maximón, the reprobate saint who represents a synthesis of Judas Iscariot, Spanish *conquistador* Pedro de Alvarado and the old Maya god Mam, is worshipped. Unlike at Zunil, visitors are not allowed to see the effigy of Maximón except during Holy Week, when he steals the show. On a more contemporary and sobering note, a plaque behind the altar commemorates a village priest who was assassinated by a government death squad in 1981 during Guatemala's civil war.

After the day's last excursion boat leaves, the people of Santiago Atitlán settle back into the ancient language and stately rhythms of everyday life in one of the world's most isolated and beautiful spots. To experience this peaceful village without the selling frenzy, plan to spend a night here (see "Lake Atitlán Area Lodging").

While Santiago Atitlán is the native town most tourists visit during their Lake Atitlán stay, other villages on the lakefront are also well worth seeing. **San Pedro la Laguna**, a Tzutuhil-speaking community around the other side of the San Pedro volcano from Santiago Atitlán, is a good place to experience the rhythms of modern village life with its somewhat less traditional but much less touristy atmosphere. *Evangélico* church influence is very much in evidence here. Boats make a circuit of the lake daily in each direction, stopping at San Pedro la Laguna, Santiago Atitlán, and the Cakchiquel Maya villages of **San Luis Tolimán**, a commercial center for area coffee growers, and **San Antonio Palopó**, a peaceful little adobe town where the main industry is cultivating onions.

A popular side trip from Lake Atitlán is to **Chichicastenango** (population 9000), the most famous of all highland Maya villages in Guatemala. Chichicastenango is just 32 kilometers to the north of Panajachel, crossing the Pan American Highway at Los Encuentros. Buses run frequently between the two towns. Go there on a market day—Thursday or Sunday—to see one of the biggest and most colorful public markets in Guatemala. Specialties of the village, besides the beautiful hand-embroidered *huipiles* made by the village women, include masks and carved wooden boxes. Because of the market's enormous popularity, vendors from all over the country—ladino as well as Maya—come here to sell, and asking prices for many items run higher than in Panajachel or Antigua. It is not the goods for sale but the sheer spectacle of so many people in bright-hued *traje* from all over Guatemala that makes market days in "Chichi" so special.

The **Church of Santo Tomás** on Chichicastenango's plaza dates back to 1540. As in many other highland village churches along the Ruta Maya, this one is used constantly for prayers and ceremonies that involve offerings of incense and candles, liquor and flowers, but no priests. What is unusual about this church is the presence of *chuchkajaues*, native prayer men who know the exact words and phrases that will most effectively invoke a saint's help. Instead of speaking directly to the saints as in most other Maya churches, the people hire one of the chuchkajaues who wait at the front door of the church to speak for them. This church is where, in the early 1700s, a priest discovered the *Popol Vuh*, the sacred book of the Quiché, which remains the best source of insights into the pre-Hispanic past of the highland Maya.

The **Museo Regional**, on the south side of the plaza, features artifacts from around the department of Quiché, including pottery, stone points and other relics from Iximché and Utatlán. The museum's primary exhibit is the Ildefonso Rossbach jade collection, consisting of carvings given by villagers to the accountant-turned-priest, who resided in Chichicastenango for 50 years until his death in 1944. Ceremonial offerings are still held at Rossbach's large tomb, which dominates the town cemetery.

Much of the spiritual life of Chichicastenango takes place outside the church and without the slightest veneer of Christianity. Ask one of the ubiquitous child tour guides to show you the way down the hill to the shrine of **Pascual Abaj**, where an ancient stone head stands above a group of altars and incense burners. Besides the usual offerings—candles, flowers, Pepsi Cola—*chuchkajaues* sometimes sacrifice live chickens here in elaborate rituals.

The ruins of one of the most important pre-Hispanic cities in Guatemala lie on the outskirts of **Santa Cruz del Quiché** (population 15,000), 33 kilometers north of Chichicastenango. Buses run regularly between the two towns, and the ruins are a short taxi ride or a long walk from the town center. The ruins have two names: **Utatlán** (admission), the Aztec name given by early Spanish conquerors, is the name used on maps, while the locals know it by its Maya name, Cumarcaj. It was the short-lived capital of the Quiché Maya, a warrior society of Mexican Toltec origin that conquered the Guatemalan highlands in the 1300s. Today, there is not much to see at Utatlán, but the site is worth a visit for the almost palpable specters of historical events that loom over it. Because the city was at the height of its splendor at the time of the Spanish conquest, and because the record of the Quiché empire was recorded at length in the *Popol Vuh*, more is known about the history of Utatlán than any other Maya site.

Time and looting have reduced what was once the greatest city in Guatemala to a handful of grass-covered mounds. John Lloyd Stephens' account of his 1839 expedition through the Maya world, *Incidents of Travel in Central America, Chiapas, and Yucatán*, tells us that some stairways and smooth-cut stone facing, as well as paintings on stucco walls, still survived at the site when he visited. Now virtually all of the stonework has been taken away and used as building material elsewhere, leaving only faint echoes of past greatness. A model at the small visitors center shows what Utatlán looked like during its heyday.

Utatlán is best visited as a day trip from Lake Atitlán or Chichicastenango, since the town of Santa Cruz del Quiché was a center of Guatemala's guerrilla conflict until quite recently and still lacks accommodations for travelers. However, Utatlán is one of the few Maya ruins where camping is allowed.

Another important Maya ruin, **Iximché** (admission), is located 5 kilometers south of the town of **Tecpán Guatemala** (population 6000), a village that served briefly as the first capital of Guatemala in 1524. Iximché was the short-lived capital of the Cakchiquel Maya, the enemies of the Quiché at Utatlán, from its founding in 1470 to the arrival of the Spanish army 54 years later. At the southeasternmost reach of the Aztec Empire, the Cakchiquel people of Iximché paid tribute to the Mexicans and adopted Aztec customs, notably mass human sacrifices of prisoners of war. Like the other major highland Maya ruins at Zaculeu and Utatlán, Iximché even in its heyday was unimpressive compared to fabulous lowland ceremonial centers such as Uxmal, Palenque, Copán and Tikal. The largest temple pyramids were only nine meters in height and devoid of sculpture. The ceremonial center appears to have been extraordinarily spacious and open, with temple mounds and altars graded from the hilly natural landscape around four large plazas. Several temples and one of the two large ball courts at Iximché are better preserved than anything at Utatlán, however, and visitors can see from faint remnants of paintings on two of them that the walls of the ceremonial center were once covered with bright-colored murals inside and out. Iximché, perhaps better than any other highland ruin, imparts a feel for the warlord era that marked the declining Maya civilization in the last centuries before it fell to Spanish invaders. Tecpán Guatemala and the ruins of Iximché are just off the Pan American Highway, 48 kilometers from Panajachel on the way to Antigua Guatemala and Guatemala City.

LAKE ATITLÁN AREA LODGING

The finest hotel on the lake is the **Hotel Atitlán** (Sololá Road, Panajachel; 62-14-29), situated on the edge of a coffee *finca* (plantation) one-and-a-half kilometers north of town. This beautiful colonial-style hotel, full of fancy tilework and carved hardwood trim, has 44 guest

In contrast to other Latin American countries like Mexico, which has been ruled from a single capital since long before the Spanish conquest, Guatemala's capital has changed again and again.

rooms on three floors. The rooms have private baths (though hot water is sporadic), twin beds and balconies overlooking the lake with fantastic views of the volcanoes. The grounds blaze with colorful tropical flowers and overflow with magenta cascades of bougainvillea. There are a swimming pool and a guests-only beach. Deluxe.

The other expensive hotel in town is the **Hotel Del Lago** (Calle Rancho Grande; 62-15-55). Operated by the Biltmore International hotel chain, this six-story highrise tourist facility lacks the lush colonial atmosphere of the Hotel Atitlán, but makes up for it with a perfect location on the waterfront just down the hill from town. With 100 guest rooms, the hotel has nearly half of all the tourist beds in Panajachel and often fills up with tour groups. The rooms are fairly lavish, with bathtubs and marble fixtures, as well as balconies overlooking the lake. The hotel's dock is where the boats leave for Santiago Atitlán and other villages around the lake. Deluxe.

Very nice accommodations, almost on the beachfront, are available at the small **Hotel Visión Azul** (Sololá Road; 62-14-26), located less than one-half kilometer from town where the Hotel Atitlán entrance road forks off the Sololá Road. The 24-room white stucco hotel, nestled on a hillside amid banana trees and bougainvillea, features a swimming pool, a riding stable and the best beach on Lake Atitlán. All guest rooms are large and sunny, with private baths and terraces facing the lake across a grassy pasture. Rates are moderate.

Another pleasant midrange hotel, closer to the center of things, is the **Cacique Inn** (Calle Embarcadero; 62-12-05) on the waterfront between Calle Principal and Calle Santander. Each of the 33 large rooms, decorated with native weavings, has its own fireplace and private bath. The rooms are in a compound of pseudo-rustic buildings with Mediterranean-style tile roofs surrounding a beautifully landscaped courtyard with a small swimming pool. Budget.

A pleasant hotel near the center of town, the **Hotel Regis** (Calle Santander at Calle 14 de Febrero; 62-11-49) consists of 14 guest rooms in duplexes and bungalows set around an attractive colonial-style main building, which houses a lobby area and dining room adorned with local arts and crafts. Each guest room has a private bath and a veranda that looks out on a green lawn landscaped with palm trees. Some rooms have kitchenettes, and televisions are available at an additional charge. For children, there is a playground with a wading pool, swing and slide. Rates are in the budget range. The hotel is across the street from the Guatel office, where you can phone home. (An international long-distance call costs substantially more than does a night's stay at the Hotel Regis.)

There are also quite a few cheaper hotels in Panajachel, but you'll find better bargains in the low-budget range, as well as an environment that is at once more peaceful and more memorable, on the far side of the lake in the Maya village of Santiago Atitlán. The better of the two lodgings in town, the **Hotel Chi-Nim-Ya**, located on the lakefront, has 12 rooms with very basic furnishings. One, at a slightly higher rate, has a private bath, while the others share the same bathroom. **Pensión Rosita**, facing the village square, costs about the same and has more primitive plumbing. The guest rooms offer a bed and nothing else. Adventuresome travelers should look at a stay in this or any other Indian village as a cultural experience, bearing in mind that even the crudest accommodations are a cut above the conditions in which the local villagers spend their whole lives.

GUATEMALA'S ILL-FATED CAPITALS

When the first conquistadores rode eastward from Mexico into the Maya highlands, the region was ruled by Quiché warlords whose court was in the city of **Cumarcaj**. *(Today the ruins of this capital are also known as Utatlán). When Pedro de Alvarado and his army conquered the Quiché and Cakchiquel people and destroyed Cumarcaj, he established his first capital at* **Tecpán Guatemala**, *near the Maya city of Iximché in 1524. Alvarado reigned there for only three years before a Cakchiquel uprising forced him to withdraw to a safer location.*

Alvarado established his second capital, Santiago de los Caballeros de Guatemala, at the foot of Volcán de Agua. He ruled from that city until his death fourteen years later, in 1541. Upon his death, his widow Doña Beatriz declared herself Guatemala's new ruler and, as her first official act, ordered that the entire cathedral be painted black in mourning for Alvarado. Legend holds that this command offended God and doomed the city. Within a matter of days, an earthquake struck, bursting a natural dam that contained a lake in the crater of Volcán de Agua, and water and mud surged down the volcano's steep slope to virtually wash away the capital city, drowning Doña Beatriz. The site is now called **Ciudad Vieja** *("old city").*

A second Santiago de los Caballeros de Guatemala was built at a more discreet distance from the volcanoes. Known today as **Antigua Guatemala**, *it stood as the greatest city in Central America for more than two centuries before it was virtually destroyed by an earthquake. In 1775, the king of Spain ordered the capital moved to its present site.* **Guatemala City** *lasted almost as long as Antigua Guatemala had but was ruined by an earthquake in 1976. A massive international relief effort helped to rebuild the capital city on the same site.*

Improbably enough, Chichicastenango has one of the finest hotels in all of Guatemala, the **Mayan Inn** (Calle 8 at Avenida 3; 56-11-76). This 30-room colonial-style hotel three blocks west of the village square has antique furnishings, lush gardens and lovely views. The guest rooms, set around beautifully landscaped courtyards, have massive hand-carved furniture, fireplaces and handmade textiles everywhere you look. Rates are deluxe, and the American plan (meals included) is worth considering since the village has little to offer in the way of restaurants.

Chichicastenango has no accommodations in the moderate price range. If you're visiting on a budget, head for the **Maya Lodge** (56-11-67) facing the central plaza. The ten rooms, low-budget priced, are simple, with just a bed, a table, and a chair. A few rooms have private baths and fireplaces. Staying here puts you right in the middle of the action on market day: when you leave the hotel, you immediately find yourself elbow-to-elbow in the frenzied crowd. Meals in the hotel's tiny restaurant are also in the low-budget price range.

LAKE ATITLÁN AREA RESTAURANTS

Panajachel is full of restaurants. Very few have telephones, and reservations are unheard of. In Panajachel, there's no such thing as street addresses, but you'll have no trouble finding any of the places listed here.

Probably the most elegant restaurant in town is **Casablanca**. Located on Calle Principal near the town center, it's open for dinner only. The two-story dining area has big picture windows overlooking the main street, hanging plants and paintings by top local artists on the walls. The fare consists primarily of steaks and seafood, and you'll find the lobster a real bargain. Salads and sandwiches are also available. This restaurant seems to be a favorite of German tourists. Moderate.

Most of the other casually fancy, tourist-oriented restaurants in town are affiliated with the bigger hotels. One of the best is the dining room at the **Hotel Atitlán** (62-14-29), one-and-a-half kilometers out of town on the road to Sololá. Floor-to-ceiling windows provide diners with a panoramic view of the lake and the volcanoes. The menu, which changes seasonally, features an international assortment of beef, chicken, pork and shrimp dishes, as well as fresh-caught bass broiled to a turn. Moderate.

La Laguna (Calle Principal at Calle Los Arboles) offers indoor or outdoor dining. The indoor seating area is elaborately decorated with native arts and handicrafts, and one wall is muraled with the best map in town of Lake Atitlán, while the outdoor patio faces a nicely landscaped front yard. The menu offers a good selection of native and foreign dishes, from black bean soup to pepper steak. This is a good place to try *pepian de pollo*, the national dish of Guatemala. Most entrées are priced in the budget range.

One of the several places in Panajachel where North American expatriates hang out is **Al Chisme**, one block off Calle Principal on Calle Los Arboles. The restaurant is plain, and so clean it gleams. There are tables on a streetside patio, as well as indoors. The menu consists of an eclectic assortment of international dishes—crepes, Belgian waffles, borscht, lasagna, shrimp scampi, stuffed breast of chicken and lots more. Service is on the slow side, but there are piles of vintage American and German magazines to keep you occupied while you wait, and this is probably the best place in town to ask around for hiking and sightseeing suggestions, and also get up-to-date info on your next destination. Budget to moderate.

Near the public market and the post office, the **Comedor Hseih** is another expatriate favorite. The menu at this tiny vegetarian restaurant features a wide selection of soups, salads, sandwiches, pasta dishes and pizzas at very low budget prices. But the best pizzas in town (some say in all of Guatemala), also budget-priced, are to be found at the **Flyin' Mayan Yacht Club**, on Calle Principal at Calle Santander next to the Mayan Palace, right in the center of town.

For native food at very low prices, head for **Ranchón Típica**, on Calle Santander across the street from the Hotel Regis. The specialty at this dark, candlelit, rustic-style place is black bass fresh from the lake, served with a full complement of Guatemalan staples—fat, handmade corn tortillas, rice, black beans, and *plántanos fritos* (fried bananas). They also serve grilled beef or chicken. Many patrons linger over dinner for three or four hours to enjoy the nightly live folk music. Budget.

LAKE ATITLÁN AREA SHOPPING

You'll find mind-boggling arrays of *típica* clothing in the markets at Santiago Atitlán and Sololá on Fridays and Tuesdays, with plenty of street vendors on other days, and at Chichicastenango on Thursdays and Sundays. Panajachel also has a lot of street vendors and small, nameless shops selling *típica*. Asking prices are on the high side in all three places, though still incredible bargains by U.S. standards. Price negotiation is appropriate and expected, and these vendors drive hard bargains. Chichicastenango is the only place we've found where if you walk away from a deal (either as a bargaining strategy or just to think it over), when you return you'll find that the price has been *raised* especially for you.

Other art-and-craft specialties in Panajachel include wood carving and leatherwork by native artisans, along with hand-painted T-shirts, landscape paintings and silver jewelry made by North American and

European expatriates who make their homes around Lake Atitlán. Another phenomenon seen in small shops around Panajachel (though you'll find much more of it in Antigua) is high-fashion clothing handmade by local Indian seamstresses from designs created by American emigrés who live in the area.

LAKE ATITLÁN AREA NIGHTLIFE

The sizable American expatriate community in Panajachel has given rise to an odd phenomenon—the video bar. These are small theaters where *gringos* sit on folding chairs in the dark around a big-screen television and watch recent English-language movies on videotape. Three different videos are shown each afternoon and evening, repeating in a different order every week until the owner takes a trip back to the United States and buys some more. Video bars come and go; the longest-established one is the **Café Xocomil** on Calle Santander next to the El Patio restaurant.

The best spot in town for dancing is the **Chapitol** on Calle Los Arboles, where a mixed crowd of locals and foreign visitors mingles to live, loud Latin music most evenings. Just down the street, **Nuan's Dance Bar**, the only discotheque in Panajachel, has a deejay armed with a solid international selection of rock, world beat and salsa records. On some evenings, you'll find live jazz or blues on Calle Santander at the **Circus Bar**, a rustic saloon with circus posters on the walls. Also on Calle Santander is **The Last Resort**, where a lot of expatriates go to waste away the late evening in this remote corner of Margaritaville.

LAKE ATITLÁN AREA BEACHES

The chilly water off Panajachel's rocky **public beach**, where the Panajachel River flows into Lake Atitlán, is noxious, evil smelling and disturbingly unsanitary. Locals do their laundry, wash their trucks, and clean fish there. Untreated sewage drips into the water upriver. There is a lot of social sunbathing on the beach, making it a fun place to spend the morning—as long as you don't go in the water. The camping policy varies: sometimes whole colonies of tents line the beach on both sides of the river, while at other times the police rust campers and may search them for drugs. A cleaner beach, at the **Hotel Visión Azul** off the Sololá Road north of town, is open to non-guests for a nominal fee, and camping is also permitted there.

Antigua Guatemala

Antigua Guatemala (population 30,000) is one of the world's truly unique places. The town is a fragment of the old Spanish empire, preserved as if in a museum within the natural fortress formed by the three huge volcanoes that surround it: Volcán de Fuego, which still smolders with sulfurous fumes; solitary Volcán de Agua, which once destroyed an older Spanish city; and the highest, 13,250-foot Volcán Acatenango. Antigua's stately old buildings, chic shops, colorful native markets and nearly constant celebrations and processions makes it a world apart from nearby Guatemala City—or anywhere else.

Antigua was Guatemala's capital city through most of the Spanish colonial era, from 1543 to 1773—longer than Washington has been the capital of the United States. Known then as Santiago de los Caballeros de Guatemala, it was one of the most elegant cities of the Spanish empire, rivaling Mexico City or Lima. With more than twice its present-day population, it had 38 Catholic churches, one of the first universities in the Western Hemisphere, and one of the first newspapers. Noble families born to wealth and power, as well as those who had grown rich exploiting the people and resources of the Americas, held court in private palaces impressive in their grandeur.

Hardly any architecture remains from the 16th and 17th centuries because the capital was ruined by an earthquake in the year 1717. Following the earthquake, Antigua's residents immediately began to rebuild it, using the architecture we see in Antigua today: low Baroque-style structures of massive adobe walls and arches reinforced with thick, squat pillars, designed to survive any conceivable earthquake. But then, 56 years later, following a year-long series of warning shocks, a mammoth quake rolled through the capital in 1773, laying waste to its great churches and palaces. Disaster relief to Guatemala became a hotly contested issue between the pope in Rome, who wanted to see the capital restored, and the king of Spain, who wanted to move it elsewhere. The people of the city huddled among the crumbling walls and collapsed roofs for three years before the dispute was settled and the king ordered Santiago de los Caballeros de Guatemala (thereafter called Antigua Guatemala) abandoned. All the building materials and works of art that could be salvaged from the ruins were to be carried 47 kilometers over a mountain range to the new capital, Nueva Guatemala de la Asunción (now Guatemala City).

Despite miserable living conditions and the ravages of epidemic diseases, and in defiance of the king's commands, residents refused to leave the bleak remains of what had been Central America's grandest and most beautiful city. Antigua was never entirely abandoned, though it remained in a woeful state of decay and disrepair for nearly two centuries as coffee plantations took over the surrounding countryside.

British author Aldous Huxley visited in 1934 and reported to his English-speaking readership, "There is nothing grand at Antigua; but there is much that is charming; much that is surprising and queer; much—indeed everything—that is picturesque and romantic in the most extravagantly 18th century style." His description turned Antigua into a tourist destination and attracted the founders of Antigua's expatriate community. Today, hundreds of American, Canadian, British and South African immigrants make their permanent homes in Antigua, while hundreds of other Anglos are in town for weeks or even months at a time to study Spanish.

The sizable English-speaking presence helps make Antigua a major travelers' destination. Just a 45-minute drive from Guatemala City and within day-trip distance of other key tourist spots like Chichicastenango and Lake Atitlán, Antigua is perhaps the most comfortable and friendly place in Guatemala to use as a base camp for explorations to other parts of the country. Here, you'll find colorful markets where Indians in village *traje* sell beautiful textiles and handicrafts. You'll find time-honored folk rituals and echoes of grandeur from the Spanish empire. But you'll also find televisions featuring CNN and HBO in English, almost-current editions of the *Miami Herald* and sympathetic Americans knowledgeable in the ways of Guatemala who are happy to share words of caution and encouragement with anyone who is truly interested in understanding this small and surpassingly strange country.

In the past decade, as Guatemala City's crime and congestion problems have made it into a more and more unpleasant place to live, wealthy Guatemalans have also begun to move to Antigua. The result is that the town is becoming one of the most chic neighborhoods in Guatemala, with a growing number of residents commuting to the city in long black chauffeur-driven limousines. Yet a feeling lingers that the prosperous Guatemalans are somehow outsiders in a solid community of Anglo expatriates and Indians, an accidental community that has no economy except tourism and no reason for its existence except an ideal climate and an eccentric sort of charm.

Nothing in the city is more than two kilometers from anything else or about eight blocks from the central plaza. All over Antigua Guatemala are many crumbling remains of grandiose structures, most of them stabilized and propped up with reinforcing buttresses since the most recent major earthquake in 1976. There are narrow, stone-cobbled streets that feel very much like the 18th century, and the unexpected can lie around any corner, as Antiguans love public celebrations of all kinds. Almost every late afternoon sees a school marching band parade, a birthday party erupting with fireworks in the streets or a religious procession of the faithful walking beside a pickup truck that carries a life-sized statue of a saint.

Start your explorations at the **Parque Central**, the graceful and busy town plaza also known by its colonial name, the Plaza de Armas. Here, park benches set amid flower gardens and shaded by trees trimmed to circular perfection surround a fountain (c. 1936, reconstructed after the 1738 original) adorned by a bevy of female statues gushing water. The central plaza is one of the great spots of the world for people-watching, offering a daily kaleidoscope of beggars and vendors, village peasants and wealthy businessmen, soldiers and nuns, elderly people and little children, not to mention travelers from all parts of the globe.

Historic buildings face the Parque Central. On the east side of the plaza, the **Church of San José** was built around two chapels, all that remained after the 1773 earthquake of the Cathedral de Santiago (c. 1669), which had been the largest cathedral in Central America. Ruins of the rest of the cathedral can still be seen behind the present-day church. Conquistador Pedro de Alvarado and his wife, Doña Beatriz, lie buried beneath the floor of the old cathedral. Along the plaza's

Antigua Guatemala

CHURCHES
A San José
B Compañía de Jesús
C San Augustín
D San Jerónimo
E La Recolección
F La Merced
G Santa Catalina
H Santa Teresa
I Las Capuchinas
J Nuestra Señora del Carmen
K Santo Domingo
L Santa Rosa de Lima
M La Candelaria
N Nuestra Señora de la Concepción
O San Francisco
P San José el Viejo

Semana Santa (Holy Week) is the biggest festival of the year in Antigua Guatemala.

south side, the **Palace of the Captain-Generals** (c. 1764) was the nation's capitol building for less than ten years before the earthquake ruined it. The stately old building once housed government offices, the treasury and the state ballrooms. Today, a portion of it is used as the offices of Guatemala's tourism agency, **INGUAT**, where you won't find much printed visitor information but, if you speak Spanish, the staff is ready to answer your questions. Visitors can also enter the courtyard and climb to the second floor for a view of the plaza, but most of the palace is in ruins. On the north side of the plaza, the **Ayuntamiento** (c. 1740) still serves as Antigua's city hall after more than 250 years. It also contains two small museums, the **Museo de Santiago**, which exhibits antiques from the colonial era, and the **Museo del Libro Antiguo**, where old books and historical documents are on display.

Antigua Guatemala is laid out on a completely square grid. All streets have both a number and a long name left over from the colonial era; an intersection may be marked with one or the other, neither or both. For example, the Parque Central is located in the exact center of the city between 4 and 5 calles and 4 and 5 avenidas, or to put it another way, between Calle del Ayuntamiento/Calle de la Concepción, Calle de la Polvora y Landivar/Calle de la Universidad, Calle del Obispo Marroquin/Calle del Conquistador, and Calle de Santa Catalina/Calle de la Sin Ventura. The number system is much simpler. Just remember that numbered *calles* run east and west, the numbers go up as you go south—toward the Volcán de Agua—and the word *poniente* (west) or *oriente* (east) tells which direction you are from the central plaza; *avenidas* run north and south, the numbers increasing as you go west—toward the Volcán Acatenango and its steamy, nearly hidden companion, Volcán de Fuego—and the word *norte* (north) or *sur* (south) tells which way you are from the plaza.

From the Parque Central, the first place to explore should be the **public market**. Many travelers make their arrival there, as all buses pick up and let off passengers at the row of stores directly in front of the market. You'll find a wonderful maze of stalls both mundane and exotic in Antigua's market, including a wide selection of *típica* from all over the country along with everything from shoe repairers and onion vendors to medicine women who sell herbs to heal every ailment. Cardamon and other spices, which have recently become major cash crops in this part of Guatemala, are also displayed in abundance. To get to the public market, follow either 4 Calle Poniente or 5 Calle Poniente westward for three blocks.

Along the way, 4 Calle Poniente takes you past the ruins of the **Church and Convent of Compañía de Jesús** (c. 1626), also the site of an early Jesuit college. The king of Spain expelled the Jesuits from his empire 150 years later, and shortly after that the massive church was completely ruined by the great earthquake, leaving only a crumbled façade and some broken statues to hint at its former glory. Today, it is filled with stalls of *típica* clothing and jewelry vendors. The Jesuit college was the home of Rafael Landívar, whom scholars consider to be the finest poet in Spanish colonial literature. Notwithstanding that he wrote his poetry in Italy after being expelled from Guatemala along with the other Jesuits, he is commemorated in the **Monumento a Landívar**, a little park with a series of five arches on the south side of the main public market. Nearby, on 5 Calle Poniente, the ruin of the **Church of San Augustín** dates back to 1615, making it one of the oldest structures in Antigua.

A walk through the northwest side of town on 1 Calle Poniente will take you past the walls of the abandoned **Church of San Jerónimo** (c. 1757) to the ruins of **La Recolección** (c. 1708), formerly a monastery where colonial Central America's largest church library was housed along with a collection of oil paintings on sacred themes. Today, La Recolección has been reduced to a few still-standing columns and arches that invite comparison to ruins of ancient Rome. Farther east on 1 Calle Poniente, between 6 Avenida Norte and 5 Avenida Norte, **La Merced Church** (c. 1552) may be the most striking example of colonial architecture in Antigua. The church was spared any serious damage in the great earthquake, a fact that was briefly seen as a miracle until the church was damaged by a smaller quake a few months later. Churrigueresque ornamentation—complex patterns of stucco vines, birds and flowers—covers the entire pink church façade, whose massive columns and niches hold brightly painted saints. The church has been mostly restored and is now used for regular services. The four-ton statue of the Black Christ in the church is carried through the streets annually as a centerpiece of Antigua's lavish Semana Santa observances. Adjoining La Merced, the **Convent of Santa Clara** contains what must have been a beautiful fountain before the statuary was removed to Guatemala City. Other historic ruins in this part of town include the **Church and Convent of Santa Catalina** (c. 1606), a half-block south on 5 Avenida Norte, and the **Church and Convent of Santa Teresa** (c. 1675), two blocks east on 1 Calle Oriente.

Farther east, on 2 Calle Poniente at 2 Avenida Norte, is the **Church and Convent of Las Capuchinas** (c. 1736), one of the city's most interesting ruins. Of the many convents in Antigua, where young women retreated after failures in love or were sent by irate parents after becoming pregnant, this was the most luxurious. Although the convent cells in the unique, circular *torre de retiro* (tower of retreat) are tiny, just four feet by eight feet, each had its own private bathroom with running water, an extravagance practically unheard of in those days. Below ground level, a huge round vault with a single massive column flaring from the center to form a continuous arch with the outer walls is considered to be one of the architectural wonders of the Spanish empire. It was probably used as a cooling cellar for perishable foods, though tour guides like to suggest that it was a torture chamber.

Between the central plaza and Las Capuchinas, on 3 Avenida Norte near 3 Calle Oriente, is the small, charming **Church of Nuestra Señora del Carmen** (c. 1686, mostly rebuilt in 1728). In the extreme northeast corner of the city, off 1 Avenida Norte, are a group of other old ecclesiastical buildings—the **Church and Convent of Santo Domingo** (c. 1553), of which little but rubble remains though it once housed some of the greatest artworks and treasures in the empire, as well as the first public clock in Guatemala. Other colonial churches in the same neighborhood are the pretty little **Church of Santa Rosa de Lima** (c. 1570) at the end of 1 Calle Oriente and, two blocks farther north on 1 Avenida Norte, the hopelessly ruined **Church of La Candelaria** (c. 1550).

A stroll east from the Parque Central along 5 Calle Oriente first takes you past the sole remaining building of the **Royal University of San Carlos de Borromeo**, which has suffered very little earthquake damage since its construction in 1760. In colonial times, teaching prelates from the Jesuit, Dominican and Franciscan orders held classes here in law, theology and medicine, as well as such unusual subjects as the Cakchiquel language. The university building now houses the **Museo Colonial**, where exhibits depict everyday life and learning in 18th-century Guatemala. Especially good are the collection of religious oil paintings and saints carved from wood and the restorations of colonial classrooms. Two blocks farther east, the **Díaz del Castillo House** is open to the public. Far from elegant, this old house is historically noteworthy because its original owner, Bernal Díaz, a retired Spanish foot soldier who became a founding father of the town and a city councilman of Santiago de los Caballeros de Guatemala (now Antigua Guatemala), wrote the classic *History of the Conquest of New Spain* while living here. This definitive eyewitness account of Cortés' victories in Mexico is still in print in ten languages after nearly 450 years. Up the block and across the street at the corner of 1 Avenida—known in Spanish colonial times as Calle de la Nobleza, which means Street of the Nobility—the more imposing **Casa Popenoe** (admission) was the finest mansion in the city when it was built in 1636. It was reduced to rubble by the 1773 earthquake. In 1931, U.S. agricultural advisor Dr. William Popenoe bought the wreckage and spent a fortune restoring it to its former glory with careful attention to detail and 17th-century authenticity. Fully furnished with the finest in Spanish colonial antiques, the mansion is open for midafternoon tours daily except Sunday.

A block north and a block east of the mansion, on 4 Calle Oriente, are the ruins of the **Temple and Convent of Nuestra Señora de la Concepción** (c. 1578), the oldest convent in the city. Although little remains except fragments of collapsed walls, the convent holds a special place in Antigua history. Sor Juana de Maldonado, the daughter of one of Guatemala's wealthiest families, retreated here after an unhappy love affair to live, despite a vow of poverty, in a huge private apartment lavishly decorated with Spanish artworks, lace, gold and jewels. Thanks to her father's influence, she was made abbess of the convent in disregard of older and more devout nuns. Public anger over the appointment embroiled the whole city in turmoil and sporadic violence. In later years, however, Sor Juana distinguished herself as one of Guatemala's greatest poets.

Two blocks south of Casa Popenoe, at 1 Avenida Sur and 7 Calle Oriente, the **Church of San Francisco** (c. 1543) has been restored and is once again used for church services. Four blocks to the west on 8 Calle Oriente, **San José el Viejo** was built by a crew of devout volunteers without permission from the king of Spain, who ordered the church demolished. Local residents refused, resulting in a 25-year

---

STUDY SPANISH IN ANTIGUA

Language schools are everywhere in Antigua Guatemala. Many American college students come here to gain practical experience in speaking Spanish, and long-term travelers come to brush up on their language skills before proceeding to other parts of Latin America. Guatemalan language schools place students with local families, where they receive room, board and twenty hours a week of individual instruction in Spanish. Prices are extremely low. Some schools also have classes for children as young as age six.

Prospective language students will want to meet their instructors and look at the living accommodations before signing up, but may wish to contact schools in advance to ask about availability. Among the most reputable language schools in Antigua Guatemala are **Monja Blanca** (6 Avenida Norte No. 41; 32-25-48), **Nahual Academia de Español** (6 Avenida Norte No. 9; 32-25-48), **Centro de Español Don Pedro de Alvarado** (1 Calle Poniente No. 24; no phone), **Centro Lingüístico Maya** (5 Calle Poniente No. 20; 32-06-56), **Tecún Umán School of Spanish** (6 Calle Poniente No. 34; no phone) and **La Alianza Spanish School** (1 Avenida Sur No. 20, no phone).

standoff before the church was finally allowed to open its doors. From here, the Parque Central is three blocks north along 5 Avenida Sur.

Some of the most rewarding short side trips from Antigua Guatemala are to villages on the slopes of Volcán de Agua. Six kilometers south of the city on Route 14 lies **Ciudad Vieja**, the capital of Guatemala before it was destroyed by floods in 1541 and the government moved to what is now Antigua. The town was washed away so completely that archaeologists are unsure where the original plaza, palace and cathedral were located. Today, visitors to this coffee-growing community of about 10,000 people will find plenty of guides eager to tell the tragic story of the old capital for a modest *propina*, but there really isn't much to see. A kilometer or so to the north on a side road that leaves the highway at Ciudad Vieja is the Cakchiquel village of **San Antonio Aguas Calientes**, renowned for some of the finest traditional backstrap weaving in Guatemala. Although the beautiful *huipiles* for sale in stalls on the plaza can also be found for about the same price in Antigua's public market, there is a certain appeal to buying them in the village where they are made, and visitors often have a chance to watch the women weaving.

Twelve kilometers south of Antigua on a different road, an extension of 1 Avenida Sur, the Cakchiquel village of **Santa María de Jesús** is a colorful community of thatch-roofed huts where the women wear lovely purple *huipiles* and some men still wear traditional red shirts lavishly embroidered with flower designs. The view from this village high on the northeast slope of the volcano is spectacular. Santa María is the starting point for hikers to climb Volcán de Agua (see the "Hiking" section at the end of this chapter).

ANTIGUA GUATEMALA LODGING

Antigua's lodging scene offers an extraordinarily wide range in terms of price and class. While there are a number of very inexpensive hotels that host mainly students, several of the better accommodations rank among the most luxurious in the country. Rates vary greatly depending on the season, peaking during Christmas and Semana Santa. At other times of the year, room prices are often a small fraction of the maximum authorized rate, which the government requires be posted (in dollars!) on room doors.

Look for quality lodgings on Antigua's chic shopping and restaurant street at the **Posada de Don Rodrigo** (5 Avenida Norte No. 17; 32-02-91). This inn, originally a colonial mansion known as Casa de los Leones, has been so beautifully restored that it is worth visiting as a sightseeing highlight even if you're not staying there. It fills an entire city block near La Merced church and an ornate old city gate that arches over 5 Avenida. The 40 guest rooms are set around two open courtyards, each with gardens. The rear courtyard has a large fountain surrounded by restaurant tables, where musicians play the marimba in the afternoons. Each room is individually decorated and furnished with Spanish colonial antiques. While all rooms have private baths and phones, other amenities vary tremendously, so be sure to look at the room before renting it. Some have fireplaces or views of the volcanoes. Rates range from moderate to deluxe depending on the season.

A smaller, less expensive but still very comfortable downtown lodging that also offers wonderful colonial charm is the **Hotel Aurora** (4 Calle Oriente No. 16; 32-02-17), just east of Doña Luisa's Restaurant and several blocks east of the central plaza. The oldest hotel in Antigua, it has been operating continuously since 1923. The 16 large rooms, which have very high ceilings and heavy, rustic wood furnishings, are situated around a courtyard with a carefully tended lawn and flowering trees and shrubbery. There is a gracious sitting room with a fireplace and a television. Breakfast is included in the moderate room rates.

The finest hotel in town—indeed, one of the finest in all of Guatemala—is the **Hotel Antigua** (8 Calle Poniente No. 1; 32-03-31), located on the south side of the city near the historic Church of San José and just four blocks from the Parque Central. This exclusive 60-room hotel caters to Guatemala's wealthy class, offering every imaginable amenity, such as a fireplace, bar, cable television and two double beds (a rarity in Guatemala hotels) in each guest room. Accommodations are in a series of low buildings with furnished porticoes around lovely courtyard gardens. The hotel also has a heated swimming pool and off-street parking. Deluxe.

Two blocks south of the Hotel Antigua, colonial charm comes with a much lower price tag at **El Rosario Lodge** (5 Avenida Sur No. 36; 32-03-66). At the pavement's end, surrounded by shade trees, the lodge is the former main house of a coffee plantation. It offers more in the way of peace and quiet than any other hotel in Antigua. Though the ten guest rooms are spare and functional, they are brightened by colorful locally woven textiles and all have private baths. El Rosario is only a 15-minute walk from the center of town, but guests are advised not to stroll after dark in this isolated neighborhood. Rates are a great bargain in the budget range.

Finally, we must mention Antigua's largest and most expensive hotel, the **Ramada Antigua** (9 Calle Final at Carretera Ciudad Vieja; 32-00-11). This modern 156-room hotel on the outskirts of town along the road to Ciudad Vieja is totally devoid of the colonial ambience our other hotel suggestions offer in abundance. Instead, it offers an array of resort-style amenities including three pools, tennis courts, saunas, a workout room, a children's playground, bicycle rentals, and a restaurant, bar, disco and shopping complex. The rooms are impressively large, bright and contemporary, with fireplaces, bathtubs, and balconies with spectacular volcano views. Rates, in the deluxe range, are a little less than you would pay for comparable accommodations in the United States.

ANTIGUA GUATEMALA RESTAURANTS

Even more than in other Guatemalan cities, Antigua's restaurants shun anything resembling regional cuisine in favor of food with an international flair intended to attract foreign visitors. The only problem with dining out in Antigua is choosing between the many outstanding restaurants in town. Our personal favorite is **Sueños del Quetzal** (5 Avenida Norte No. 3, upstairs). This all-vegetarian restaurant under English-speaking management, with seating on a balcony overlooking the street, is probably the healthiest place to eat in all of Guatemala. The voluminous menu, featuring unusual casseroles and imaginative stir-fry dishes made with fresh produce from the country's first organic farm, draws a mostly young clientele of Americans and Europeans. Prices are budget.

Next door, the **Fonda de la Calle Real** (5 Avenida Norte No. 5, upstairs) is where students at Antigua's dozens of language schools congregate. The large, rather plain restaurant has a friendly, though almost completely Spanish-speaking, atmosphere and features live music on weekends. House specialties include fondue and *caldo real* (royal soup), a rich chicken soup with lots of trimmings. There is also a full menu of more substantial chicken, pork and beef entrées. The budget prices are set with students in mind, though the portions tend to run smaller here than at other restaurants nearby, making this place a dubious bargain for anyone with a big appetite.

Across the street, **Café Café** (5 Avenida Norte No. 14) serves some typically Guatemalan dishes such as pepián and stuffed peppers, as well as a predictable array of international fare, in a covered courtyard bedecked with potted palms and flowers and flanked on both sides by rows of fashionable boutiques. An upscale shoppers' favorite, it is liveliest in the afternoons. As the name suggests, this is a good place for hot coffee and multilingual conversation; however, patrons who stop in at breakfast time will find that the bright red tablecloths used the night before are not changed until later in the day, giving the place an unkempt and bleary look first thing in the morning. Prices fall in the budget category.

A great place for truly hungry travelers, the **Restaurant Katok** (4 Avenida Norte No. 7) is loud, funky and full of that tattered-yet-dignified ambience that is peculiarly Guatemalan. Old photos on the walls show Antigua as it was in the early decades of the 20th century. The food selection consists of various *carnes parilladas* (grilled meats) including beef, lamb, rabbit, sausage and ham. The best bet is a platter for one or several people containing a substantial portion of each meat along with salad, potatoes, beans and fried bananas. Budget.

The traditional gringo hangout in Antigua is **Restaurant Doña Luisa Xicotencatl** (4 Calle Oriente No. 12), generally called just "Doña Luisa's," a few blocks east of the Parque Central. Travelers gather at tables in the open-air courtyard to exchange new discoveries and words of encouragement, and often to arrange ride-sharing for excursions to other parts of Guatemala. The English-language bulletin board here is the town's largest, and there is a fair-sized lending library of paperbacks in English. CNN news broadcasts play constantly on the television in the room behind the courtyard. There are other, more secluded dining areas upstairs. Breakfast options include a heaping fruit salad of pineapple, mango, banana and assorted melon slices served with yogurt and granola on the side. The coffee, from locally grown beans, is some of the best in town. Lunch and dinner entrées include Reuben sandwiches, Texas-style chile con carne, and stuffed baked potatoes. The best take-out bakery in town is at the front of the restaurant. Budget.

For a big splurge, the place to go is **El Sereno** (6 Calle Poniente No. 30; 32-00-73), one block south and three blocks west of the Parque Central. Often rated as the finest restaurant in Guatemala, this colonial-style mansion offers a choice between dining outdoors on a patio amid tropical flower gardens around a fountain or indoors, where beamed ceilings, a large fireplace, mahogany furnishings, oil paintings and classical background music set the stage for a romantic candlelight dinner. Typical of the classic French fare is baked ham in a rich crème de cassis et moûtard sauce, served as the main event in a multicourse feast with potato soup, a salad du jour, exquisitely prepared steamed vegetables and a choice of fine wines, with a chocolate mousse for dessert. Prices, in the deluxe range, are extremely expensive by Guatemalan standards but, thanks to the U.S. dollar's high buying power, really about the same as you would pay for a soup and salad at a Cancún beach hotel or a steak in the States. This is the only restaurant we've found in Guatemala that accepts advance reservations.

ANTIGUA GUATEMALA SHOPPING

The public market in Antigua is one of the best around. It combines the same kind of wide selection of *típica* clothing and other handicrafts as you would find in Panajachel or Chichicastenango with the cornucopia of produce and down-to-earth native household items available in the market at places like Huehuetenango. Located four blocks west of the Parque Central, the covered market sprawls over an area of about six square blocks and operates every day. Saturday is the busiest market day. Unusual souvenir and gift possibilities here include incense, green (unroasted) coffee beans and many kinds of dried spices. (Although you cannot bring fresh produce back to the United States, dried plant products pose no problem.) Other places in Antigua where many vendors sell *típica* clothing from all over Guatemala include the old public market site in the ruins of the **Church and Convent of Compañía de Jesús** on 4 Calle Poniente and the center median of 8 Calle Oriente near the **Church of San Francisco.**

Antigua is also noteworthy for its designer shops. Dozens of residents, most of them foreign expatriates, are in the business of creating original clothing and accessory designs and hiring local women to make them. While much of the apparel made this way is exported to stores in the United States and Europe, a fair sampling is displayed in boutiques around Guatemala. One of the best of the breed is **Katz,** which deals in chic black-and-white clothing. It is one of several fashionable shops around the covered café courtyard in **La Casa de las Gargolas** (5 Avenida Norte No. 14). Other stylish shops can be found farther along 5 Avenida Norte. For one of the most interesting selections of women's clothing and accessories made from handwoven native fabrics, check out **Under the Volcano** (5 Calle Poniente No. 13).

Some of the hardest, finest-quality jade in the world is mined in Guatemala. The art of jade cutting has been passed down through the centuries, and today several companies in Antigua operate jade mines, factories, and showrooms that are the most elegant stores in town. Just east of the Parque Central is the ritzy **Casa de Jades** (4 Calle Oriente No. 3), where, in addition to luxury-priced jewelry, the stock includes more modest gift items such as cassette tapes of Guatemalan Maya music. A little way up the street at the oldest and largest of the jade factory/showrooms is **Jades, S.A.** (4 Calle Oriente No. 34; 32-07-52), where the showpieces are magnificent and exorbitantly expensive replicas of royal burial masks like the one found in King Pacal's tomb in Palenque. Perhaps the most interesting jade factory to tour is **Jades J.C.** (9 Calle Oriente No. 2-A), operated in a family home on the outskirts of town; their showroom is at 5 Avenida Sur No. 6; 32-06-77. *Jades* is pronounced "HA-days" in Spanish.

Specialty food shops are good to know about, especially if you are packing a picnic lunch for a volcano climb or preparing for a trip to the eastern part of the country, where restaurants are few and far between. Several places in Antigua deal in cheeses and wines, gourmet items, and commonplace American foods, which are sold here as cures

---

Jade was the most precious of all treasures to the ancient Maya people, who believed that it possessed the power to stop pain and prevent or heal injuries.

---

for homesickness. When students have been away from the States for a month or so, their eyes can grow misty at the sight of a box of Triscuits. The most American-oriented of these places, with English-speaking management, is **Deliciosa Delicatessen** (4 Avenida Norte No. 10-D). Other good food shops are **Supermarket Aylin** (6 Avenida Norte No. 1; 32-02-16) and **La Cava del Marqués** (3 Avenida Norte No. 11).

ANTIGUA GUATEMALA NIGHTLIFE

Antigua's usually sedate nightclub scene can become lively when a lot of visitors are in town. Most clubs have a distinctly American ambience, with hardly a marimba in sight. The **Mistral Bar and Lounge** (7 Calle Oriente No. 4) is a meet-you-there-later sort of place where people congregate to watch CNN at happy hour and HBO after dinner. The claustrophobic disco **Moscas y Miel** (5 Calle Poniente No. 5) is the hub of the town's partying singles scene—such as it is. The name means "Flies and Honey." Live music can be found at a number of small dance clubs and bars around town on Friday and Saturday nights. **Bianco's** (6 Avenida Norte No. 17; 32-07-27) is the place to go for rock and reggae, and **El Tarro** (4 Calle Oriente No. 12) has blues.

Video bars showing English-language movies on big-screen televisions are popular in Antigua. There are two in town, and they are practically identical: **Cine-Café Oscar** (3 Avenida Norte No. 2) and the **Frisco Video Bar** (1 Avenida Sur No. 15). Each of them shows three different movies daily, repeating about once a week, with little overlap in selection between the two theaters. Schedules for both video bars are published weekly in the *Antigua Weekly Classifieds*.

Homesick Europeans and other travelers with a taste for the improbable may wish to stop for an afternoon or late-night snack at the **Café Opera** (6 Avenida Norte No. 15), an elegant little café that serves coffee, wine and croissants. Run by Italian expatriates, it is decorated with opera posters and programs. Verdi arias emanate from the stereo speakers. All this, in spite of the fact that there is no opera house anywhere in Guatemala and no opera performance has taken place here in nearly a century.

Guatemala City

Contrasting completely with the rest of the country, the capital city of Guatemala has become a low-budget, landlocked version of Los Angeles, full of cheap concrete-block buildings, traffic snarls, smog and street crime. If there were any practical way to avoid the city while touring the fascinating country of Guatemala, we would recommend it. Unfortunately, there is not.

Don't get us wrong. Guatemala City does have some good sightseeing attractions. Its museums are the finest in Central America, the ruins of a great Maya ceremonial center lie hidden in the suburbs, and the giant relief map of the country in Parque Minerva offers an overview that enhances any traveler's perception of Guatemala. Yet, with all this, Guatemala City is a stressful place to visit. In planning your travel itinerary, it is best to minimize your time in the capital in favor of gentler destinations.

Inevitably, you will visit Guatemala City at least once on any trip to Guatemala. Travelers who come by air will arrive at the international airport in the southern part of the city. Those who are going by bus will arrive from the western highlands and change buses in Guatemala City to continue their trip into the eastern or northern part of the country. As for driving, all roads in Guatemala lead to the capital, and en route from the western highlands to any other part of the country there is no way to avoid a hair-raising spin on the *periférico* (freeway) that winds crazily through the city.

One might expect Guatemala City, founded in 1776 after the abandonment of the ruined capital at Antigua Guatemala, to have fine old colonial buildings. Literary travelers from John Lloyd Stephens and Anthony Trollope in the 19th century to Aldous Huxley in the early 20th century described Guatemala City in glowing phrases, holding it up as the most magnificent city in Central America, in many ways the equal to any European capital.

Sadly, the last vestiges of colonial architecture were smashed by a violent earthquake that struck Guatemala City in its bicentennial year, 1976. It was the third major quake to wreak havoc on the city, surpassing others that had struck in 1830 and 1917–18, and this time shattered neighborhoods were apparently rebuilt as plainly and cheaply as possible, abandoning the illusion that any structure could be permanent here. An exploding population has also tarnished the capital's former charm. As Guatemala City has grown to over two million in population, the former farmland at the outskirts has become a boundless sprawl of slum housing that scrambles up mountainsides and spills off into deep gorges. In the poor neighborhoods, modern urban life is uneasily mar-

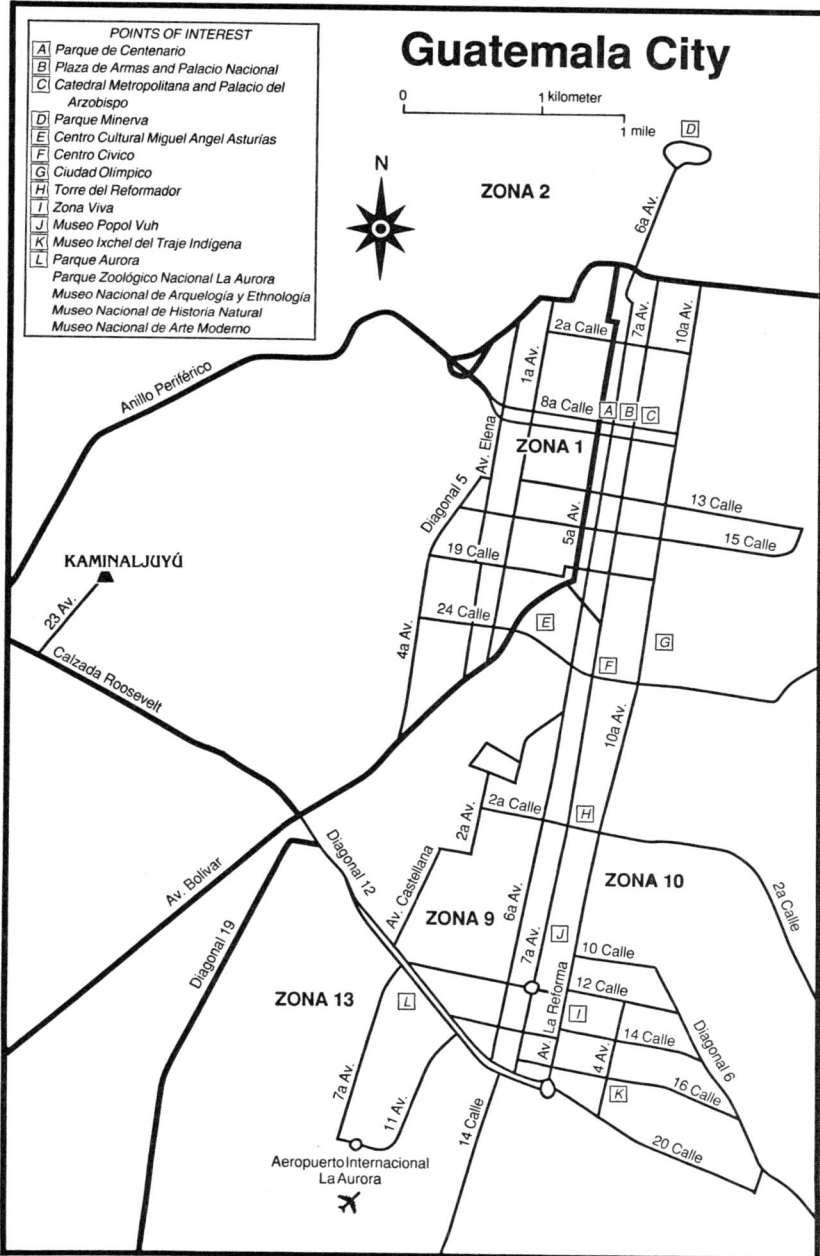

Guatemala City

POINTS OF INTEREST
- A Parque de Centenario
- B Plaza de Armas and Palacio Nacional
- C Catedral Metropolitana and Palacio del Arzobispo
- D Parque Minerva
- E Centro Cultural Miguel Angel Asturías
- F Centro Cívico
- G Ciudad Olímpico
- H Torre del Reformador
- I Zona Viva
- J Museo Popol Vuh
- K Museo Ixchel del Traje Indígena
- L Parque Aurora
- Parque Zoológico Nacional La Aurora
- Museo Nacional de Arqueología y Ethnología
- Museo Nacional de Historia Natural
- Museo Nacional de Arte Moderno

0   1 kilometer

1 mile

N

ZONA 2

6a Av.

Anillo Periférico

2a Calle

7a Av.

10a Av.

1a Av.

8a Calle A B C

Av. Elena

ZONA 1

Diagonal 5

13 Calle

15 Calle

5a Av.

19 Calle

KAMINALJUYÚ

23 Av.

Calzada Roosevelt

24 Calle

4a Av.

E

G

F

10a Av.

2a Calle

2a Av.

H

Av. Bolívar

Diagonal 12

Av. Castellana

ZONA 9

6a Av.

ZONA 10

2a Calle

Diagonal 19

7a Av.

J

10 Calle

Av. La Reforma

12 Calle

ZONA 13

L

I

14 Calle

Diagonal 6

7a Av.

11 Av.

4 Av.

K

16 Calle

14 Calle

20 Calle

Aeropuerto Internacional
La Aurora

ried to ancient village ways. It is not unusual to see men on bicycles herding flocks of goats down the freeway.

The last hints of old Guatemala City are to be found in the city center, around the central plaza. Situated in Zona 1 between 6 Calle and 8 Calle, the plaza consists of two adjoining parks—the **Parque de Centenario** on the west side of 6 Avenida and the **Plaza de Armas** (also called the Plaza Mayor) on the east side. The Plaza de Armas, which had been left in ruins through most of the 20th century after the 1917 earthquake, was excavated after the 1976 earthquake to make an underground parking garage. Today, the park is a bare expanse of concrete providing plenty of open space but not much in the way of beauty. The Parque de Centenario, however, remains a small gem of a park with shade trees, a big old-fashioned bandshell and benches where a full array of Guatemala City's people can be found chatting, reading newspapers or otherwise whiling away the day.

On the east side of the plaza, the huge **Palacio Nacional** (National Palace) was built between 1939 and 1943 in neo-classical style with a huge portico supported by many pillars. It is the "White House" of Guatemala, where the president of the country and his executive staff have their offices. The palace is open to the general public—don't be intimidated by the armed guards. Just say *"Estamos turistas"* and walk into the central courtyard to see the murals by Guatemalan artist Alfredo Galvez Suárez re-creating the nation's history from ancient Maya times through Central American independence in 1821. On the second floor, historical scenes are also the subjects of elaborate stained-glass windows in the vast *sala de recepción* where presidential receptions are held. Notice the stuffed quetzal, the national bird, an official example of the Guatemalan enthusiasm for wildlife taxidermy, in the coat of arms behind the row of flags at the end of the room.

One of the oldest buildings in the city, the **Catedral Metropolitana**, was originally built between 1782 and 1815. Its squat, thick walls were engineered to withstand earthquakes. Extensive restoration efforts followed the 1830, 1917 and 1976 earthquakes, and today, two centuries later, the cathedral still stands on the east side of the central square. Along with the adjoining **Palacio del Arzobispo** (Archbishop's Palace), it is the capital city's last remnant of Spanish colonial architecture. Inside the cathedral, many of the saint figures and religious relics graced the churches of Antigua Guatemala before the old city was abandoned and they were moved. While some of the altars along the sides of the cathedral radiate with gold leaf and fine artwork, the main church is surprisingly austere, evidence of the Guatemalan government's ambivalence toward the Catholic faith from the first years of independence to the present day.

Drive or take a taxi about three kilometers north along 6 Avenida, beyond the *periférico*, to **Parque Minerva** in Zona 2 and you'll find the most remarkable sight in Guatemala City—the **Mapa en Relieve**. This huge relief map of the country was sculpted from concrete in 1905 and is repainted annually. It fills an area of 40 meters by 80 meters—nearly the size of a football field! Water runs in the rivers, and major roads and towns are shown. Viewing the vast map from an observation tower, visitors sense the complexity of Guatemala's mountain ranges and understand how, in a little country the size of Ohio, large areas—the western highlands, the Petén jungle—can be so completely isolated from the mainstream of society as represented by Guatemala City. Trace your travel route around the country and let your imagination take wing.

For a different kind of bird's-eye view, head 12 blocks south of the central plaza on 6 Avenida or 7 Avenida, the main downtown thoroughfares, to a cool, nicely landscaped park that is the setting for the strangely shaped blue-and-white **Centro Cultural Miguel Angel Asturias** (24 Calle 3-81, Zona 1; 2-40-41), a complex of three theaters looming among the battlements of an old hilltop fortress. The theater building is usually open to the public, and its round windows provide the best views of Guatemala City's downtown area. The building also houses the bizarre, self-congratulatory **Museo Militar** (Military Museum). The theater overlooks the **Centro Civico**, a group of buildings that contain municipal and national government offices, including the headquarters of **INGUAT** (7 Avenida 1-17; 31-13-33), the Guatemalan government tourist office, which has maps and tourist information galore. From the hilltop, you can also see the new downtown commercial district and the **Ciudad Olímpico** (Olympic City), a sports complex that includes the national soccer stadium, an indoor arena, a gymnasium, tennis courts and a swimming pool.

Another 12 blocks south on 7 Avenida, at the corner of 2 Calle in Zona 9, the **Torre del Reformador** (Tower of the Reformer) is dedicated to the memory of President Justo Rufino Barrios, the "liberal" dictator who, during his 1873-to-1885 reign, revolutionized the nation's caste system by including both elite *creolos* (of Spanish heritage) and Hispanicized *mestizos* (people of mixed Spanish and Indian blood) in a new social caste known as ladinos, allied to repress, exploit and pity the Maya people. This two-tiered caste system remains strong today, and Barrios is remembered—by ladinos, anyway—as one of the nation's greatest leaders. The tower, a downscaled replica of the Eiffel Tower in Paris, is visible from most parts of the city. The bell at the top is rung just once a year, on the June 30 anniversary of the revolution that brought President Barrios to power.

From the Torre del Reformador, sightseers can jog two blocks east to Avenida La Reforma and head south along the avenue through the **Zona Viva**, the city's chic international district, with its upscale restaurants, nightclubs and hotels. Along Avenida La Reforma is one of Guatemala City's finest museums, the **Museo Popol Vuh** (Avenida La Reforma No. 8-60, Zona 9; 34-71-21; admission). The museum is operated by a private college, the Universidad Francisco Marroquín, which received the outstanding collection of pre-Hispanic Maya artifacts it contains from a wealthy benefactor in 1977. The Popol Vuh Museum, named for the mythic history of the Quiché Maya (the manuscript is *not* in this museum), exhibits Maya artworks from all parts of Guatemala—Kaminaljuyú in suburban Guatemala City, the great Quiché, Cakchiquel and Mam cities of the western highlands, Quiriguá in the east, and Tikal and the other great centers in the Petén far to the north. While the collection of Maya pottery is said to be the best on earth, the most striking exhibit is a display of mannequins representing masked and costumed dancers in a Quiché reenactment of the Spanish conquest.

From the south end of Avenida La Reforma, the **Museo Ixchel del Traje Indígena** (4 Avenida No. 16-27; 68-07-13; admission) is just two blocks east. Ixchel was the only female among the pantheon of ancient Maya gods. The goddess Ixchel represented the moon and is still revered throughout the Maya world in the form of the Virgin of Guadalupe (thus the crescent moon on which Latin America's dark-skinned Virgin Mary stands). According to legend, Ixchel originated the art of weaving, so hers is a fitting name for a museum exhibiting the best collection on earth of traditional Maya clothing and textiles. The museum, in a two-story mansion, shows in great detail the meth-

---

THE SACRED BOOK OF THE QUICHÉ MAYA

*The greatest of the Maya books that have survived to modern times is the **Popol Vuh**. Written around 1550, it is a comprehensive history and mythology of the Quiché Maya. Equal in scope to the Old Testament of the Bible, the Popol Vuh describes how the world was created by K'ucumatz (the Quiché name for the Plumed Serpent). It tells how the first race of humans was created from mud but washed away, how the second race of humans was made from wood but would not worship the gods and so were destroyed except for a few who became the monkeys of the jungle, and how finally the race of humans that inhabits the earth today was fashioned from maize—which explains why people now eat corn instead of mud or wood. The book goes on to tell of the creation of the sun and moon, the origins of sacrificial rites, and the history and genealogy of Quiché rulers beginning with their departure from the Toltec city of Tula and continuing through the arrival of the Catholic church a thousand years later.*

ods and meanings of native dress, with examples of the evolution of village *traje* to that seen in markets and villages today. In front of the museum, Maya women offer handmade apparel for sale. Interpretive plaques at this museum are in English, as well as Spanish.

A few blocks west of Avenida La Reforma (take 14 Calle) is the city's largest park, **Parque Aurora**, which contains the zoo and most of Guatemala's government-run museums. The **Parque Zoológico Nacional La Aurora** (7 Avenida Zona 13; 72-05-07), like most in Latin America, is cramped and a little sad, but it does have an interesting newer exhibit area featuring the animals of the Petén rainforest—armadillos, coatimundis, tepescuintles, jaguarundis, spider monkeys and even endangered Petén crocodiles.

The most respected of the museums is the **Museo Nacional de Arqueología y Etnología** (La Aurora, Zona 13 Salón 5; 72-04-89; admission), which houses the largest collection in the world of Guatemalan Maya sculpture, together with ancient pottery, jewelry and masks. Here you'll find stelae from the ruins of Kaminaljuyú and a massive throne from the hard-to-reach site of Piedras Negras, north of Yaxchilán on the Guatemalan side of the border with Chiapas. Besides antiquities, the museum has an ethnology hall with 150 fine examples of village *traje* and displays on traditional ways of life among the highland Maya.

Also in the park is the modest **Museo Nacional de Historia Natural** (La Aurora, Zona 13 Salón 4; 72-04-68), where stuffed bird and beast specimens are displayed in dioramas that simulate natural habitats in various regions of the country—good preparation for a journey to Tikal National Park and other areas in the Petén where wildlife abounds. The third museum, the **Museo Nacional de Arte Moderno** (La Aurora, Zona 13 Salón 6; 72-04-67), features a well-focused selection of Guatemalan "modern" art spanning two centuries, from the end of the Spanish colonial era to the present day, and including works by the country's best-known painter, Carlos Mérida.

From Parque Aurora, it is relatively easy to visit the ancient ruins of **Kaminaljuyú** (admission) in the city's northwestern suburbs. Buses go there, and drivers can simply head west on Diagonal 12, which becomes Calzada Roosevelt, to 23 Avenida, which runs north to the site.

Kaminaljuyú is one of the oldest major ruins in the Maya world. It was originally built in the Preclassic area, about 300 B.C. by a farming people known as the Miraflores. Unlike later highland Maya cities, Kaminaljuyú was built on an open plain without defensive fortifications. The city existed in peace for six hundred years before it was conquered by Toltec invaders from the central Mexican capital of Teotihuacan around 300 A.D. The synthesis of Toltec and Maya influences seen in the art of Kaminaljuyú's Classic Period, which is on display in both the Popol Vuh Museum and the Museo Nacional de

---

Kaminaljuyú was the largest center for jade mining and carving in the ancient Maya world.

Arqueología y Etnología, is hauntingly similar to that of Chichén Itzá in the Yucatán several centuries later, and stelae found here rank as the oldest known Maya glyph carvings. Kaminaljuyú continued to reign as the greatest city of the Guatemalan highlands throughout the Classic Maya period, enjoying trade relations with Tikal and other cities of the Petén, as well as with Copán, until it was destroyed in a war around 900 A.D.—the same time that Tikal, Copán and other cities all over the Maya world collapsed.

Although Kaminaljuyú was one of the largest Maya cities, with a population of 50,000 people, few traces of its architecture remain today. The temple and palace walls were made from light volcanic pumice mortared and stuccoed with adobe, materials that eroded back into earth soon after the buildings were abandoned, leaving the bare fields and grassy mounds we see at Kaminaljuyú today. Much of the area covered by the original city has been bulldozed for suburban residential development, and much of the site has been dug up over the years by looters in search of pre-Colombian pots and jade jewelry. Archaeologists are studying the sadly neglected site with new interest, exploring the city's foundations through underground tunnels. The Guatemalan government has undertaken a plan to restore Kaminaljuyú in hopes of enhancing tourist interest.

GUATEMALA CITY LODGING

Guatemala City's most sophisticated (and expensive) hotels are located in and around the Zona Viva, the city's sleek international district of exclusive restaurants and nightclubs and high-fashion boutiques flanking the east side of Avenida La Reforma between 12 Calle and 16 Calle in Zona 10. This is the most convenient hotel area to the airport. All of the Zona Viva hotels are huge highrises with hundreds of rooms. The top of the line is the **Hotel Camino Real Guatemala** (Avenida La Reforma at 14 Calle, Zona 10; 68-14-71), a ten-story, 400-room megastructure that offers every conceivable amenity including a fully equipped gym and health spa, tennis courts and swimming pools, a beauty shop, 24-hour room service and same-day dry cleaning. The guest rooms are large and tastefully decorated, though with no hint of distinctively Guatemalan character, and have telephones, air-conditioning, minibars and satellite television showing most U.S. networks. The rates, in the ultra-deluxe range, are about the same as for comparable accommodations in most United States cities, and give the Camino Real and other hotels of its ilk a certain air of privilege and elitism. A night's stay here costs more than the average Guatemalan citizen earns in two months!

Also in the Zona Viva area, the **Hotel Guatemala Fiesta** (1 Avenida 13-22, Zona 9; 32-25-72) has 240 rooms and suites in a 16-story building. We mention this place because it is where the airlines put up passengers stranded for the night by flight cancellations or reroutings, which are quite common in Central America. The hotel's kitchen also prepares the in-flight meals for all commercial planes departing from La Aurora International Airport. The ultra-deluxe rates are nearly as high as at the Camino Real, but the rooms seem a little frayed around the edges, and the loud orange color scheme makes this a place where you wouldn't want to wake up with a hangover. Rooms have telephones, satellite television and air-conditioning. The hotel's best feature is its extensive array of indoor and rooftop sports facilities, including swimming, tennis, racquetball, squash, volleyball, soccer and a complete gym and spa.

The big Zona Viva hotels are flawlessly designed for business travelers, but may prove a bit of a bore for more adventuresome or romantic souls. To find a wider selection of more unusual accommodations, head for Zona 1 and the noisy, congested heart of downtown Guatemala City. You can sample opulence left over from an earlier era at the **Hotel Ritz-Continental** (6 Calle A No. 10-13, Zona 1; 8-08-99), an old-fashioned grand hotel that was the height of luxury around 1950. The 202 guest rooms have been refurbished with wood floors, ornate hand-carved moldings and furnishings and marble bathroom fittings. All rooms have telephones, air-conditioning and satellite television, as well as balconies overlooking the downtown streets. The hotel has a swimming pool, and just like the National Palace a few blocks away, the lobby has a stuffed quetzal. Moderate.

A much smaller hotel than the Ritz-Continental, the **Hotel Pan American** (9 Calle No. 5-63, Zona 1; 53-59-91) also offers a touch of Art Deco class at affordable rates in the middle of downtown. The 60 guest rooms are high-ceilinged, old-fashioned and still elegant. The rooms are clean and well kept, and the original 1930s-vintage furnishings have been in use for so long that the rooms now qualify as "antique-furnished." All rooms have color television, telephones and private bathrooms with tubs, and some have balconies overlooking the stately interior courtyard with its soothing fountain. The lobby decor features fine examples of Maya weaving, and some staff members wear colorful village *traje*. Moderate.

Guatemala City, about the same size as Philadelphia, is the biggest city between Mexico City and Medellín, Colombia.

On a quiet side street toward the southeast corner of downtown, the **Posada Belén** (13 Calle A No. 10-30, Zona 1; 53-45-30) is a homey ten-room *pensión*—like an English or American bed and breakfast—decorated with native handicrafts and houseplants. The clean, simple rooms, each with private bath, surround a courtyard brightened by parrots and lots of tropical flowers. Although the Posada Belén is far enough from most of Guatemala's tourist attractions that you might want to take a taxi, the peaceful location in a nice older residential neighborhood is worth it. Rates are moderate, and reservations are essential.

You'll also need to call ahead if you want to stay at the **Hotel Chalet Suizo** (14 Calle 6-82, Zona 1; 51-37-86), a low-priced place that has enjoyed a near-legendary reputation among international backpack travelers for decades. Some of the 25 rooms have private baths, and all are budget-basic. Some are more comfortable than others. Be sure to ask for one on the side of the building away from the noise of the street. The decor in the common areas consists of a veritable jungle of potted plants and some travel posters of Switzerland, but the real ambience of the place comes from its guests—as youthful, sociable and energetic a crowd of foreign visitors as any you'll find in Guatemala. Prcies are budget.

GUATEMALA CITY RESTAURANTS

Guatemala City prides itself on its international array of restaurants—from American fast-food places to extravagant French establishments, and everything in between. The city's two **McDonalds** (10 Calle No. 5-30, Zona 1, and 14 Calle at 7 Avenida, Zona 9) are enormously popular, though as symbols of the United States, they have occasionally been targeted by terrorist bombers. At the other end of the spectrum, **La Fonda del Camino** (Avenida La Reforma at 14 Calle, Zona 10; 68-14-71), in the Hotel Camino Real Guatemala, is the city's most elegant French restaurant. This is the place where Guatemala's privileged class goes to savor *haute cuisine* in an atmosphere of candlelit underground intimacy. The prices, which range from moderate to deluxe, offer wonderful bargains compared to similar restaurants in the United States or Europe.

Just north of the Zona Viva, **Nim-Guaa** (Avenida La Reforma at 8 Calle, Zona 10) is one of our favorite restaurants for regional cuisine served in an honest atmosphere of rough-hewn wood paneling and handwoven tablecloths. Short but savory, the menu features carne a la parilla, enchiladas and Guatemalan-style tamales. Service is leisurely but enthusiastic, and prices are in the budget range.

You'll find wood-paneled walls, rustic tables and good beefsteaks grilled over an open fire as you watch at **El Rodeo** (7 Avenida No. 14-84, Zona 9; 31-49-28). The meals are served American-steakhouse style, with baked potatoes, salad and garlic bread on the side. Service here is prompt, portions are huge, and prices are moderate. In the evening, you can catch the marimba band while you eat.

For something really different, try the **Samba Restaurant** (1 Avenida at Calle 13, Zona 10), a small place with a romantic garden for dining al fresco. Situated amid dozens of international eateries in the Zona Viva, this is Guatemala's only Brazilian restaurant. Shrimp, lobster and chicken are served in gently spiced sauces that will intrigue even the most jaded palate.

Downtown, the dining room in the grand old **Hotel Pan American** (9 Calle No. 5-63, Zona 1; 53-59-91) is a special place to eat. Its decor features arts and crafts from the Maya highlands, and the waiters wear *traje* from Chichicastenango. The menu, which changes daily, features Guatemalan regional dishes, as well as American-style sandwiches and full dinners. Prices are moderate for dinner and well down in the budget range for the generous fixed-price luncheons.

You can watch tortillas being made by hand while you eat at **Los Antojitos** (15 Calle 6-28, Zona 1; 51-11-67), a casual, very popular downtown restaurant specializing in native Guatemalan food. Big picture windows let you watch the throngs of people who pack the sidewalks outside as you listen to marimba music and savor a variety of light dishes (*antojitos* means "appetizers") or a full meal of grilled meat with fried plantains, black beans and tortillas. Prices start in the budget range and vary widely.

Spanish cuisine is featured at **Altuna** (5 Avenida No. 12-31; 51-71-85), a large restaurant lush with potted plants and full of Old World charm, from its massive, hand-carved, dark-finished wooden tables and chairs to the cool, dignified serving staff. The restaurant is known for its numerous shrimp dishes. It also offers an array of Iberian dishes from paella to roast dove. Moderate.

El Gran Pavo (13 Calle No. 4-41, Zona 1; 51-09-33) is Guatemala City's best Mexican restaurant—not the sort of piñata-festooned tacos-and-tostadas place that most Americans think of as a Mexican restaurant, but a huge complex of plain, bright dining halls in an old house. Designed with Mexican visitors in mind, the menu features specialties

---

East from Guatemala City, Route 9 is generally known as the Carretera Atlántica, even though its eastern terminus actually fronts the Caribbean Sea and not the Atlantic Ocean.

---

from every region of Guatemala's big neighbor to the north—pocchuc, pescado veracruzano, enchiladas suizas, pollo en mole and lots more. Budget. There is a second El Gran Pavo location near the Zona Viva district at 12 Calle No. 6-54, Zona 9, 32-56-93.

GUATEMALA CITY SHOPPING

The **Zona Viva** section of Paseo La Reforma is lined with stylish boutiques and jewelry shops, but it's not exactly a world-class shopping district. In fact, most wealthy Guatemalans fly to Miami for their serious spending sprees. But a little browsing along this stylish street will give you a good idea of what Central America's high-fashion designers are up to these days—often surprising bursts of creativity.

Downtown, a block from the central plaza and directly behind the cathedral, the **Mercado Central** was Guatemala City's main public market before the 1976 earthquake destroyed it. The recently rebuilt market, underground beneath a parking lot, has two floors of vendors' stalls each a full city block in area. The bottom level has food and the level above it has textiles, leather goods, pottery, incense, and other handmade items. Prices at the Mercado Central run somewhat lower than at the more touristy markets in Antigua, Panajachel and Chichicastenango, and you may find very good buys on handwoven cloth. Be alert. Pickpockets and pack slashers abound in Guatemala City's public markets, and foreign visitors are their favorite targets.

Today, the Mercado Central has been eclipsed as an everyday shopping place for locals by the new **public market** adjoining the second-class bus "terminal" in Zona 4, which is easier for most city residents to reach. Bounded by 1 Avenida, 1 Calle, 4 Avenida and 7 Calle, this huge market overloads the senses with its noise, smells and crowds. Most vendors sell fresh produce, meats and household goods. You won't find much in the way of souvenir or gift items here—or many tourists—but if you want to immerse yourself in one of the biggest, brashest and most raucous marketplaces in Latin America, this is the place.

At the **Mercado Artesanía** in Parque Aurora, you'll find a good selection of *típica* and *traje* clothing, leather goods, and other handicraft items. Prices tend to run higher than at the Mercado Central downtown, and much higher than at village markets in the western highlands.

GUATEMALA CITY NIGHTLIFE

In case your travels in other parts of the country have led you to the conclusion that there is no life after dark in Guatemala, an evening in Guatemala City will dispel that notion once and for all. Here, you'll find real nightclubs with a touch of glitz and "beautiful" people in evening dress.

In the Zona Viva, **Dash Disco** (12 Calle No. 1-25, Zona 10; 35-27-12) used to be the hottest dance club in Guatemala City a few years ago. Though now considered a bit déclassé by local trendsetters, it still has one of the best sound systems and light shows in town and a big library of international disco tunes.

The chic spot in the Zona Viva lately is **El Jaguar Discotheque** (Avenida La Reforma at 14 Calle, Zona 10; 68-14-71) in the Hotel Camino Real Guatemala. Small but completely paneled with mirrors that make it seem vast, this place draws a fashionable clientele and can be hard to get into on weekends.

For live music, one of the top Zona Viva clubs is **Kahlua** (1 Avenida No. 13-29, Zona 10), which features Guatemalan rock-and-roll and a reggae-like Caribbean style of dance music known as *punta* that comes from the east coast.

Downtown in the Hotel Ritz Continental, you'll find **Brasilia** (6 Calle A No. 10-13, Zona 1; 8-08-99), a glitzy *salsa* club that seems to be right out of the 1950s. Sip a drink with fruit floating in it in a hotel bar version of tropical ambience and join suave men and glamorous women as they rhumba across the tiny dancefloor.

Guatemala City's oddly old-fashioned **red light district**, one of the most notorious in Central America, is a dangerous place to walk around after dark—as is everyplace in Zona 1. And yes, there is AIDS (called "SIDA") in Guatemala City. But anyone curious about Third World sleaze can lock the car doors and cruise past to see how sex is sold in this rather prudish country. The action is along 18 Calle in Zona 1, centered around 9 Avenida.

The city also hosts virtually all the cultural events staged in Guatemala. The **Instituto Guatemalteco-Americano** (Ruta 1 and Via 4, Zona 4; 31-00-22), where Guatemalan students go to learn English, often presents live theater performances and films in English. The theater is also used for dance performances.

Guatemala's national theater, the **Centro Cultural Miguel Angel Asturias** (24 Calle 3-81, Zona 1; 2-40-41), presents a wide variety of live performances. It actually consists of three theaters—an outdoor concert stage, a 2000-seat indoor playhouse and a small, intimate theater designed for chamber music concerts.

Day Trips from Guatemala City

MIXCO VIEJO AND BIOTOPO DE QUETZAL   A better-preserved Maya ruin than Kaminaljuyú, **Mixco Viejo** can be visited on a day trip north from Guatemala City on Route 5. It is a 25-kilometer drive along the paved highway, among verdant hill country and through the colorful, infrequently visited Cakchiquel Maya villages of San Pedro Sacatepéquez and San Juan Sacatepéquez, where cut flowers are the main cash crop, to the roadside hamlet of Montúfar and the turnoff to Mixco Viejo. From there, it is another 16 kilometers on a rough dirt road to the hilltop ruins site with its spectacular 360-degree view. This was the capital of the Pokomam Maya from the 1200s to 1525, when conquistador Pedro de Alvarado captured it and relocated the entire population to Mixco Nuevo, now a western suburb of Guatemala City.

The architecture of Mixco Viejo looks very much like that of Zaculeu, another Postclassic highland Maya stronghold. It is austere in appearance, without sculpture or other ornamentation. Some of the original plaster-covered walls have survived the centuries, and many of the main structures were restored by a team of French archaeologists in the 1950s, but the site was badly damaged by the 1976 earthquake, leaving some of the restoration work as dilapidated as the old walls. The most striking features of Mixco Viejo, besides its magnificent location, are two large ball courts.

Past the turnoff to Mixco Viejo, the pavement ends but Route 5 continues over the mountains to Salamá (population 11,000), capital of the department of Baja Verapaz, a distance of 88 kilometers that takes three hours to drive. The route passes through the orange-growing town of **Rabinal** (population 6000), founded in 1537 by Fray Bartolomé de las Casas, who was known in Guatemala and Chiapas by the honorary title Protector of the Indians. As bloody Spanish conquests decimated other Maya tribes throughout the Guatemala highlands, de las Casas persuaded Pedro de Alvarado, captain-general of Guatemala, to let him prove that he could pacify the Rabinal Indians in five years through gentle Christian persuasion. His approach worked, largely because the people who were unwilling to accept foreign domination and a new religion were moved out of the district to a relocation camp that eventually became the village of San Lucas Sacatepéquez near Antigua Guatemala. The successful conversion of the Indians who stayed set the example for a new strategy of nonviolence in the Spanish conquest and provided the name for the departments of Baja Verapaz and neighboring Alta Verapaz. The word "Verapaz" means "True Peace." Rabinal has a beautiful colonial church, and just outside of town are the unrestored ruins of **Cahyup**, an unexcavated Postclassic

Maya fortress-city that probably looked a lot like Zaculeu before time crumbled and buried it.

From Salamá, take paved Route 17 east for 13 kilometers to the intersection with Route 14, and then go north for 34 kilometers to the village of Pantín and the entrance to the **Biotopo de Quetzal Mario Dary Rivera** (admission). This magnificent stand of ancient forest is the last remaining habitat of Guatemala's national bird. The best time to see these elusive birds is at dawn. (Overnight camping is permitted in the reserve.) Later in the day they are hard to find, but the reserve is worth a visit anyway. The reserve is a mountainside wooded in primeval "cloud forest"—high-altitude rainforest—lush with orchids, air ferns and bromeliads that thrive in the damp, cool microclimate under a dense forest canopy. Nature trails take you through the cloud forest and along the Río Colorado as it tumbles down the steep slope. Bring a jacket.

An easier and slightly faster return route from the Biotopo de Quetzal to Guatemala City is via Route 17 and then Route 9, a total distance of 167 kilometers, all paved. From the junction of routes 17 and 9, Copán is as close as Guatemala City, so it is possible to work in a visit to the quetzal reserve on a trip east to Copán, Quiriguá, the Río Dulce and Livingston. The only problem is where to spend the night. Lodging is hard to find along Route 9. For adventuresome travelers, camping at

---

GUATEMALA'S ENDANGERED SYMBOL OF FREEDOM

The image of the **quetzal**, *Guatemala's national bird, is everywhere—woven into the patterns of típica clothing, sculpted in bright-painted clay figurines, printed on tourist brochures and posters, incorporated into the national seal. The main unit of currency is called the quetzal. The highest honor the government can bestow is admission to the Order of the Quetzal.*

Reverence for this green and bright red bird with its long, flowing tail feathers is rooted deep in Maya tradition. Stelae at the ruins of Tikal, Copán and Quiriguá show noblemen or priests bedecked in huge headdresses of quetzal feathers, and it is the quetzal that provided the plumage for the Plumed Serpent, known variously as Quetzalcóatl, Kukulcán or Gucumatz, whose legend spread through the ancient Maya and Toltec world.

The quetzal was chosen as the national symbol because it cannot survive in captivity. To the Guatemalan people, its image means "Live free or die." Ironically, it is this same trait that may doom the quetzal to extinction, for it only nests in the trunks of wild avocado trees that grow in a unique high-altitude forest zone known as the cloud forest, an environment that is also, unfortunately, perfect for growing coffee beans.

the reserve and rising at dawn to watch the flight of the quetzals before heading on to Copán may be the perfect solution.

LA DEMOCRACIA, SANTA LUCÍA AND THE PACIFIC COAST   Another good side trip from Guatemala City is the drive south on Route 9 (follow Avenida Bolívar from the vicinity of the National Theater) through Amatitlán and Escuintla to the only part of Guatemala's Pacific coast that has been developed as a beach resort. The 108-kilometer drive takes about two hours nonstop, but you may wish to take time for sightseeing along the way.

Amatitlán, a town of 20,000 people on the shore of a large lake of the same name near the foot of still-active Volcán de Pacaya, rivals Panajachel as a lakeside resort for Guatemalans, though it sees little international tourism. It must have been idyllic in an earlier era, though today the area is plagued by crime problems, air pollution from a power plant and water pollution from the many vacation homes that line most of the lake shore. A scenic road loops around the lake, and an aerial tramway takes visitors up to **Parque Naciones Unidas** (United Nations Park) on the volcano's slope for a great view of the lake.

The lowland town of **Escuintla** (population 40,000) has agricultural processing plants and oil refineries, but not much to attract visitors. It is here, though, that travelers can turn west on Route 2 to visit several extraordinary archaeological sites. The small village of **La Democracia,** 25 kilometers west on Route 2 and then ten kilometers south, has a museum exhibiting stone artifacts found at nearby Finca Monte Alto. The most remarkable of the Monte Alto finds are a group of giant stone head sculptures set around a towering ceiba tree in La Democracia's central plaza. The heads, along with those discovered at Abaj Takalik and other sites in the area, so closely resemble the famed Olmec heads of southern Veracruz, Mexico (many of the Mexican Olmec heads are larger, however), that some archaeologists now believe the oldest civilization in Mesoamerica might trace its roots to Guatemala's Pacific coastal lowlands. Many of the mysterious stone heads in this area date back nearly a thousand years and are among the oldest large sculptures in the Maya world.

More Olmec-like sculpture carved from volcanic rock has been found all around the town of **Santa Lucía Cotzumalguapa** (pop, 15,000), which is located 33 kilometers west of Escuintla. Archaeologists find this area interesting not only because of the mysterious Olmec link but also because of the broad array of artistic styles. Some incorporate designs and motifs that also appear in Mexican Toltec or Yucatecan Maya sculpture; others, including some that contain non-Maya glyph inscriptions, are unique to the countryside around this town. Several archaeological digs have been undertaken around Santa Lucía, reveal-

On weekends, the beach at Puerto San José is packed shoulder-to-shoulder with sun-seekers from Guatemala City, but on weekdays it is almost empty.

ing pottery and tools, but the artifacts have provided scant clues about the people who built a civilization here centuries before the emergence of the Classic Maya culture.

Santa Lucía's central park contains replicas of several strange stone monuments found in the area. Many of the originals stand in the fields of nearby *fincas*. The plantations have grown mostly coffee until recently, and the mysterious stone carvings are still being unearthed as new lower fields are cleared to expand sugarcane production. One of the main archaeological sites, **Bilbao**, is located on a small dirt road at the north end of town near the start of 4 Avenida (a southbound street). Several foot trails lead off this road to clearings in the cane fields where the ancient sculptures stand. By continuing west on the Bilbao road, turning right on a wider road and right again on the road to Ingenio Los Tarros, you'll come to **Finca El Baúl**, where many of the monuments found on the plantation have been moved to a small open-air museum not far from the main house. **Monument 13** at El Baúl, one of the most puzzling, is a giant head with a full beard. Scientists have long puzzled over bearded figures depicted in ancient artwork not only here but also at Copán and Quiriguá and in the Olmec region of Veracruz, Mexico, since most Indians today cannot grow such beards. Ask at Finca El Baúl for directions to other sculpture groups and temple mounds concealed by the El Baúl cane fields, especially the haunting visage of Monument 3.

From Escuintla, Route 9 continues south for 48 kilometers to reach the coast at **Puerto San José** (population 10,000), which was Guatemala's largest shipping port in the 19th century, but no longer sees many ships. Now the town's main attraction is the long, white beach, which is on the other side of the intracoastal canal. Boats are waiting to take you there.

If you have a car, you can reach more secluded beaches nearby. **Balneario Chulamar** five kilometers to the west, is wider and quieter than Puerto San José. A similar distance to the east is **Balneario Likín**, a planned community of posh vacation homes owned by Guatemala's moneyed elite. Another seven kilometers to the east, the laid-back village of **Iztapa** (population 2000) was Guatemala's first seaport, established by Pedro de Alvarado in the mid-16th century and used for 300 years before Puerto San José was built. Although tourism is also the main industry here, it is much less developed than Puerto San José and enjoys a mellower atmosphere, though the mosquitoes are fierce at times.

DAY TRIPS FROM GUATEMALA CITY LODGING

Guatemala's beach resorts cater to two kinds of visitors—day-trippers and vacation-home owners. Hotel accommodations are minimal. Both Chulamar and Iztapa have clusters of very basic cabanas for rates that are shockingly high compared to lodging costs in any other part of Guatemala. Thatch-roofed huts without private baths run in the deluxe-price range. Iztapa also has two funky little hotels that rent budget-priced rooms. The **Hotel Brasilia** is a simple, johns-down-the-hall place, while the nearby **María del Mar** has small, dark concrete-block rooms with private baths arranged motel-style around a swimming pool.

DAY TRIPS FROM GUATEMALA CITY RESTAURANTS

Guatemala's Pacific beach resorts have no real sit-down restaurants. All of the beaches from Chulamar to Iztapa have food stands that sell fruit, fish tacos and whole fried fish at very budget prices. Wise travelers stock up on picnic supplies before embarking on a trip south from Guatemala City.

Copán

Copán (admission) ranks along with Chichén Itzá, Uxmal, Palenque and Tikal as one of the most exciting sites of the Maya world. Copán is off the beaten path, down a long dirt road and across the Honduras border, so fewer travelers go there than to the other great sites. Yet the unique stone sculptures of Copán are so striking—indeed, haunting—that visitors agree unanimously that it's well worth the trip.

You can still feel the magic that inspired American explorer John Lloyd Stephens to write in 1841, "The beauty of the sculpture, the solemn stillness of the woods, disturbed only by the scrambling of monkeys and the chattering of parrots, the desolation of the city, and the mystery that hung over it, all created an interest higher, if possible, than I had ever felt among the ruins of the Old World."

To reach Copán, you leave Route 9 at the Río Hondo crossroads, 130 kilometers east of Guatemala City, and proceed south on Route 10 for 44 kilometers, past the town of Zacapa, to the Vado Hondo intersection. Turn left there onto an unpaved road and continue for a very slow 48 kilometers. You will arrive at a tiny border crossing called El Florida. The border is open from 7:00 a.m. to 6:00 p.m. Copán is just 11 kilometers on the other side. Minibuses putt back and forth frequently along the road from the border to the village and ruins.

If you are driving—the only easy, reliable way to get to the Honduras border unless you take one of the package tours that are organized on an irregular basis through travel agencies in Guatemala City and Antigua—you will want to leave your vehicle on the Guatemala side of the border and take public transportation to the ruins. Rental cars cannot be taken across the border, and if you take your own car across, you'll have to wait while Honduran authorities fumigate it to kill fruit flies. It's hardly worth the hassle. Crossing the border as a pedestrian is fairly easy, especially if you take minimal luggage. You must clear both Guatemalan and Honduran authorities each direction and pay fees in the US$5 to $10 range each time. Telling the border guards of both countries that you are only visiting the ruins saves time and trouble. The Honduran authorities will issue a frontier pass that eliminates the need to apply for a visa in advance. The Guatemalans will save your tourist card (the paper stapled to your passport), cancel the exit stamp when you return and let you back into the country on the same document, avoiding the technicality that would otherwise bar travelers without multiple-entry visas from reentering Guatemala for 72 hours.

The shuttle vans go both to the village of Ruinas Copán and to the ruins one kilometer away. It is an easy and pleasant walk between the village and the ruins visitors center on a pretty forest trail that parallels the road and leads directly to the **Great Plaza** of ancient Copán. Also known as the Plaza of Red Plaster, this broad ceremonial courtyard now covered with lawn was entirely paved during Copán's days of glory. It contains the most remarkable sculptures found anywhere in the Maya world. While the major features of Copán—the great statues and the hieroglyphic stairway—are right on the plaza, visitors who walk from the village to the ruins soon realize that the ancient city

---

THE BEARDED KINGS

*Facial hair was apparently in fashion for rulers of Copán. Art found elsewhere in the Maya world suggests that beards were very rare in ancient times, as they are among Maya Indians today, leading some to speculate that the lords who reigned over the Motagua River Basin may have been of a different race from another part of the world. At Copán, the personage on the west side of **Stela C** has a full beard. Those on **Stelae B** and **D** have goatees, and **Stela F** has one with a moustache. Archaeologists have theorized that the figure on **Stela H** may have been a woman. If so, she would be the only known woman ruler in the ancient Maya world. Gender, however, was not part of the information carved on the stelae in hieroglyphs, and some contemporary experts assert that Stela H shows a king wearing unisex clothing.*

American explorer John Lloyd Stephens was so impressed with Copán that he bought the lost city from a local farmer—for $50.

---

covered a large area and that impressive stelae and unexcavated temple mounds can be found along a number of trails through the forest.

Set on the bank of the Río Amarillo, Copán dominated a vast series of valleys upriver to the east. Though it is one of the most remote and undeveloped parts of Honduras today, the valleys and forests around Copán were a densely populated region in ancient times. The city itself had a population of about 10,000, and most of the jungle in the valley had been cleared for agriculture. Today, the area has grown back in a wild tangle of hardwoods and vines, out of which archaeologists have reclaimed the ancient city's central plazas. Beautifully carved stelae, which may mark astronomical alignments, stand on several hilltops reached by one- to two-kilometer foot trails from the main center, and if you take time to walk up to one of them, particularly **Stela 12**, you will be rewarded with a stupendous view of the ruins and the river valley over which the lords of Copán reigned. Carved on the stela is the most complete genealogy anywhere of a Maya royal family.

Carved from massive blocks of a fine-textured stone called andesite, the stelae of Copán stand about ten feet tall. Unlike the relief stelae sculptures of human forms seen at other sites like Chichén Itzá, Palenque and Tikal, the stelae of Copán are carved almost completely in the round. There are a dozen stelae in the Great Plaza. All portray rulers of Copán, and each statue is decorated with hieroglyphs that record the lineage, birth, death and marriage dates, and major accomplishments of the lord it represents. The headdresses, too, bear amazingly detailed ornamentation of stylized human and animal forms with symbolic meanings.

The stelae were originally painted bright red. **Stela C**, the only one in the plaza with faces on both sides, had fallen over and lain with one side protected from the weather for centuries, and so still shows traces of the paint. Each of the stelae has a cross-shaped underground vault at its base. Some of the vaults have been excavated to reveal objects such as knife blades, pottery, animal bones and even, in the vault below **Stela H**, pieces of gold imported from South America. The vaults are unique to Copán, and their exact meaning remains a mystery.

In front of several stelae are strange "zoomorphic" altars carved in highly stylized animal shapes—frogs, jaguars, giant snakes and more fanciful forms—patterned with hieroglyphs and sacred signs. The altars were used for religious offerings, including animal sacrifices. They may also have been used as thrones for priests. Near Stela H are two altars in the shape of plumed serpents and a third showing men's faces peering from the open jaws of a two-headed snake. The two-headed snake, **Altar G**, bears the latest date hieroglyph found at Copán—800 A.D.

On the south side of the Great Plaza, just past the largest and most impressively decorated of ancient Copán's several ball courts, a group of low, broad stepped pyramids and ceremonial platforms surrounds two smaller plazas designated the **East Court** and the **West Court**. By the entrance from the Great Plaza into this complex stands the most spectacular structure in Copán, Building 26, home to the **Hieroglyphic Stairway**. Rising between two balustrades decorated with serpent motifs, the stairway is made from 2500 blocks of stone—each carved with hieroglyphs. The longest inscription found anywhere in the Maya world, it appears to be a comprehensive history of Copán up to the stairway's dedication date, 763 A.D. On this masterpiece, as John Lloyd Stephens mused a century and a half ago, the rulers of Copán "published a record of themselves, through which we might one day hold conference with a perished race." More than a few archaeologists have dedicated their whole lives to deciphering the message of the Hieroglyphic Stairway and, today, with the aid of computers, they have translated roughly a third of it.

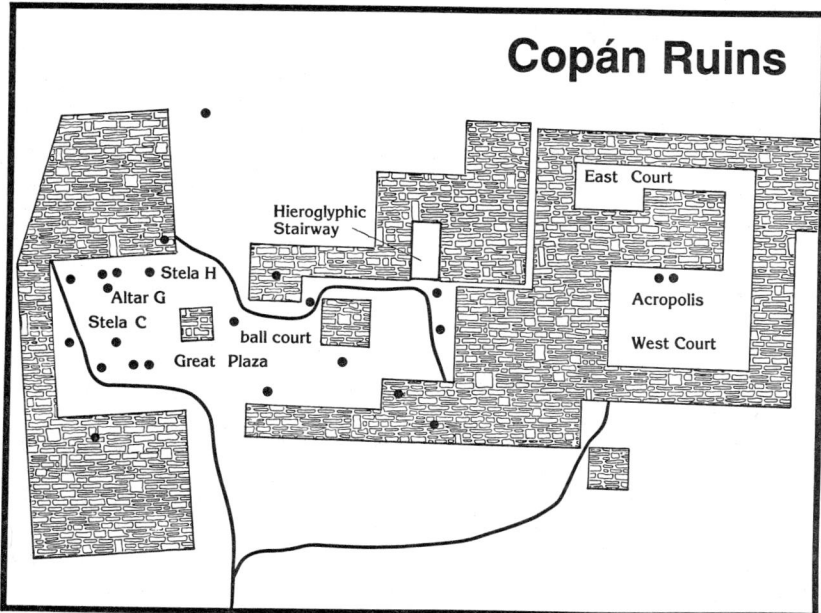

Copán Ruins

East Court

Hieroglyphic
Stairway

• Stela H

Altar G

Stela C

ball court

Great Plaza

Acropolis

West Court

In 1989, members of the Copán Acropolis Archaeological Project tunneled 56 feet in from an entrance beside the Hieroglyphic Stairway to discover a large burial vault containing the remains of a noble personage believed to be a son of Copán's greatest king, Smoke-Imix, and brother of the next king, 18-Rabbit. Buried with him were some of the most exquisite jade carvings and jewelry that archaeologists have ever found at a Maya site.

Many of the artifacts found during excavations of the ancient city are exhibited at the **Museo Regional de Arqueología**, facing the central plaza in the village of Ruinas Copán. In ancient times, the finest pottery in the Maya world—notably polychrome pieces decorated with elaborate ceremonial scenes—was made at Copán, and some of the finest examples are on display in the museum along with jade masks and jewelry, tools and sculptures in clay and stone. Some hieroglyph panels have been moved to the museum for protection from wear and erosion, while replicas have been installed at the ruins. Included among the exhibits are the complete contents of the tomb of a priest or sorcerer, found in a section of the archaeological zone now called Las Sepulturas ("The Tombs") and dated to about 450 A.D.

COPÁN LODGING

Spending the night on the Honduras side of the border affords you the opportunity to visit the ruins in the cool, misty hours just after dawn, when you may find that you have the mystery-laden site all to yourself. There are several small hotels in the village of Ruinas Copán. Electricity at the better hotels, which comes from gasoline generators, is turned on at 6:00 p.m. and stays on until about 9:30. Advance reservations are

LORDS OF ANCIENT COPÁN

Archaeologists know a lot about the history of Copán because of the detailed records carved on the city's famous monuments. Copán was ruled by a single, unbroken dynasty of lords for four centuries, from the ascension of the legendary god-king Yax-Kuk-Mo' in 426 A.D., through 17 generations of lords, to the death of U-Cit-Tok (whose mother was a princess of the royal family at Palenque) on February 10, 822. The city thrived all through the 8th century, but civilization began to collapse at Copán around the year 800 and the city was gradually abandoned. During its heyday, Copán produced the greatest sculptural accomplishments of the ancient Maya world, as well as the most ambitious hieroglyphic records.

unheard of, but travelers arriving by early afternoon usually have no problem finding a room.

The best is **Hotel Maya Copantl**, on the town square. Behind its flashy multihued pastel paint job, the hotel offers decent rooms with modern furnishings and private baths, as well as a courtyard so overgrown with flora that guests feel like they are staying in the jungle, not in town. Budget.

Nearby, also on the main plaza and in the same price range, the **Hotel Marina** also offers guest rooms with private baths. It may be more old-fashioned and a bit threadbare and musty, but the laid-back tropical ambience—screened porch and colorful bird mascots—makes it a reasonable choice in the budget range. The Hotel Marina also has an annex around the corner that offers very cheap rooms with shared baths down the hall, and several other little places around town offer similar rudimentary accommodations.

COPÁN RESTAURANTS

The best place to eat in Ruinas Copán is the plain-looking dining room at the **Hotel Maya Copantl**, where generous multi-course set meals are priced in the budget range. You can get a good, basic *comida chapín*, a workingman's meal of beans, rice, fried plantains and fat little corn tortillas along with a tiny chunk of meat or chicken, at the **Mini-Hotel Paty**, a short walk from the plaza on the way to the ruins, or a plate of spaghetti at the nearby **Tunkul Restaurant**. Both places charge low, low budget prices. The village also has a small public market with food stalls. You'll also find a **cafeteria** at the ruins.

Quiriguá and Río Dulce Area

The straight-line distance from Copán to **Quiriguá** (admission) is a mere 48 kilometers. Traveling as the macaw flies between the region's two great ancient city sites would carry you above a formidable mountain ridge, skimming the canopy of luxuriant, impenetrable rainforest as you glided over the international border. By road, however, the distance is more like 170 kilometers, and the trip, including the wait for shuttle buses to and from the border and the formalities of reentering Guatemala, takes half a day. Quiriguá is just off Route 9 where the highway descends along the Río Montagua from its steep-flanked valley into the broad, hot, moist delta that is Guatemala's major banana-growing region. It is 200 kilometers east of Guatemala City and 90 kilometers from the Atlantic coast.

Quiriguá was Copán's main rival for several centuries, from about 600 to 900 A.D. Archaeologists have devoted much energy to unraveling the true relationship between the two cities. Hieroglyphic records seem to suggest that the royal families of Quiriguá and Copán were related by marriage. An inscription at Copán reveals that one of its greatest rulers, Lord 18-Rabbit, was captured by soldiers from Quiriguá and later beheaded. Some experts also think that Copán captured Quiriguá earlier in 18-Rabbit's reign. While most of the stelae at Quiriguá were done in a style much different from that of Copán, the first stela erected there—**Monument 8**, which bears an inscription dating it to 751 A.D.—is so similar in style to those at Copán that many archaeologists believe the lords of Quiriguá hired artists from Copán to create it.

Quiriguá is situated in the middle of a vast banana plantation formerly owned by the United Fruit Company, which controlled Guatemala through the first half of the 20th century. Although Quiriguá was a small city, it covered a much larger area than the restored site would suggest today. Most of the city's temple mounds were razed and obliterated to plant banana trees. But the Great Plaza, with its huge, unique

---

HONDURAS

Honduras resembles Guatemala in many ways. It is almost exactly the same size as its neighbor to the north. Its economy offers average Hondurans the same low standard of living, and Gross National Product per capita is about the same. As in Guatemala, the top exports are coffee and bananas. The literacy rate, too, is about the same—60 percent—although the Honduran government spends three times as much on education. Military spending is also three times as high in Honduras as in Guatemala. Military aid from the United States skyrocketed during the 1980s, when its strategic location bordering Nicaragua, El Salvador and Guatemala made Honduras an island of pro-U.S. sentiment amid the region's hottest trouble spots, and the military remains central to Honduran society.

Honduras has only half the population of Guatemala, mainly because Honduras has no Indians. Most of the country's indigenous people died from diseases or were exterminated, and the survivors were assimilated into the ladino-mestizo rural culture. Many small, unexcavated Maya ruins dot the valleys of northwestern Honduras, but only spectacular Copán—the country's principal tourist attraction—hosts any visitors other than archaeologists. In fact, Honduras only receives one-fifth as many foreign visitors as Guatemala, and the majority of them come solely to see Copán. The La Ruta Maya Conservation Foundation and the Mundo Maya coalition envision development of other Maya sites in Honduras as a means of promoting future tourism.

stelae and zoomorphic altars, was so remarkable that United Fruit hired a team of archaeologists in 1934 to restore it and set aside a tiny parcel of the once-magnificent jungle surrounding it. To get to Quiriguá from the main highway, you need to go about three kilometers south on a wide unpaved road used by fleets of huge trucks that carry away unimaginable quantities of still-green bananas in a virtually nonstop tropical harvest. A quick look at a working plantation may change the way you look at bananas in the supermarket back home.

The original layout of Quiriguá, much of it now concealed by a thousand-year overgrowth of rainforest, was a lot like that of Copán. The only structures that have been cleared and excavated at Quiriguá, however, are the small, plain temples surrounding the **Acropolis**, a sunken ceremonial plaza flanked all around by stone steps like the antithesis of a pyramid. Even more than Copán, Quiriguá is architecturally unimpressive but redeemed by its artwork. Towering stelae statues, the tallest in the Maya world by far, line the **Great Plaza**. The zoomorphic altars are also the largest found anywhere. The free-flowing, abstracted features, symbols and hieroglyphs of these imaginative giant frog and cockroach figures create a counterpoint to the rigid, formal statues.

Each of the statues and altars was carved from a single large slab or boulder of a peculiar reddish sandstone. It came out of the quarry soft, damp and easy to carve, but dried harder than concrete, so tough that statues made from it have survived a thousand years of abandonment and neglect in surprisingly good condition. Bringing the massive stones from the quarry five kilometers away was a remarkable feat. No one knows for sure how it was done. The tallest of the sculptures, **Monument 5**, stands 35 feet high and was carved from a single 43-foot stone monolith that weighed 65 tons.

All of the Quiriguá stelae were erected during the 64-year period from 746 to 810 A.D. For half of that period, Quiriguá was ruled by a single leader, Cauac Sky. Hieroglyphs on one stela record that earlier in his reign, in 737, Lord Cauac Sky waged war against Copán and put its leader to death. Although little is known of the history of Quiriguá before Cauac Sky ascended the throne, most experts believe that Quiriguá's independence from Copán was won in this war, and that the giant stelae were erected at Quiriguá after independence in order to establish that the city was every bit as magnificent as its rival to the south. Fully half of the stelae in Quiriguá's Great Plaza portray Lord Cauac Sky at different times during his reign. They include, in chronological order, **Monuments 8, 10, 6, 4, 5, 1** and **3**. (The stelae and zoomorphs are numbered according to their positions around the plaza, not the order in which they were made.) Hieroglyphs on **Monument 11** record his death. After his death, the statues of subsequent rulers were smaller and more modest, and most of the creative energy of

Quiriguá's sculptors went into fantastic zoomorphic altars instead. At Quiriguá, as at Copán, many of the statues have beards. Lord Cauac Sky apparently introduced the fashion around 761 A.D., when Monument 6 was erected, and the style continued for 12 years after his death. The long goatee-style beards look remarkably like the ornamental chinpieces of ancient Egyptian pharaohs, and we can only speculate whether the lords of Quiriguá and Copán grew real beards or donned artificial ones.

It is best to visit Quiriguá late in the day or when the weather is overcast, since in bright sunlight the thatched roofs that protect the huge stelae and zoomorphic altars cast shadows that make photographing them almost impossible.

Continuing east along Route 9 for 41 kilometers will bring you to a road junction where Route 13 heads north to Castillo San Felipe, a distance of 34 kilometers, while Route 9 continues east to Puerto Barrios, 51 kilometers away. **Puerto Barrios** (population 25,000), a hot, charmless town full of railroad tracks, used to be the United Fruit Company's shipping port. Today, bananas still travel by boat, but most set sail from the giant new dock complex at Santo Tomás de Castilla on the southern tip of the bay. Puerto Barrios has an evil reputation as a town of tough waterfront dives, drugs and prostitutes. Except for those seeking cheap and potentially dangerous thrills, there is really not much to attract visitors. You can catch a launch here to Livingston and Parque Nacional Río Dulce, but a better plan is to take a launch from Castillo San Felipe *down* the river to Livingston.

Castillo San Felipe (admission), a small stone fort complete with lookout towers, a drawbridge and cannons on the ramparts, was built in 1686 to guard the mouth of Lake Izabal from British privateers like Sir Francis Drake. The fort, which is reached via a four-kilometer unpaved road from the north side of the toll bridge, has a shady picnic area and a swimming beach. Car travelers who plan to catch a boat to Livingston and perhaps spend a night or two there, will find guarded parking lots under the Castillo San Felipe bridge.

Lake Izabal, the largest lake in Guatemala, is about 20 kilometers wide and 45 kilometers long. Its waters reach a depth of 18 meters (60 feet). The lake's shoreline, dotted with more than a dozen fishing villages, is virtually inaccessible by land. The largest village, El Estor, can be reached by a grueling 140-kilometer unpaved road that leaves the highway midway between the Biotopo Mario Dary Rivera quetzal sanctuary and Cobán, and takes all day to drive. The other villages can only be reached by boat. Fishing is the main pastime on the lake, and motor launches with pilot can be hired at the Castillo San Felipe bridge or any of the resort hotels nearby.

Downriver from the Castillo San Felipe bridge, **Parque Nacional Río Dulce** is truly one of Guatemala's most magical spots. Less than 40 kilometers long, the river flows from the mouth of Lake Izabal to Livingston with just enough force to keep the salt water of the Gulf of Honduras from encroaching upstream. A boat trip down the Río Dulce takes you first past a scattering of expensive vacation homes and several marinas full of mostly American yachts and sailboats, then across a broad expanse of open water called **El Golfete**, where local fishermen cast their nets from hand-hewn dugout canoes called *cayucas*.

Much of the north shore of El Golfete is protected as the **Biotopo Chacón Machaca**, a wildlife sanctuary for the endangered West Indian Manatee. Guides claim that jaguars and tapirs also still roam the deep forest along the north shore. Downriver, El Golfete narrows abruptly into a steep canyon whose walls, dripping with lush jungle vegetation, reach hundreds of feet above the water. Egrets peer from every tree, pelicans glide by just inches above the water, turtles sun themselves along the riverbank. Here and there a cluster of thatch-roofed huts nestles between the cliffs and the water. People who live along the Río Dulce—mothers with infant children and bundles of groceries from Livingston, even unaccompanied young children—paddle their cayucas up and down the river in the kind of uncompli-cated purity that daydreams are made of.

The remote tropical paradise feel of the Río Dulce is in part illu-sory, for the boundary of the national park is defined by the top rim of the gorge. Just beyond it are endless banana fields and the shacks and

---

THE OCTOPUS

The United Fruit Company, a United States-based corporation that had a monopoly on tropical fruits imported to the United States, first moved into Guatemala in 1901. It started out buying land on which to grow bananas and soon became the country's largest landowner and employer. The company built and at one time owned all railroads, shipping ports and public utilities in Guatemala. As World War II began, the company persuaded Guatemala's president to expel Guatemalans of German descent, who owned most of the coffee plantations, and place the plantations under United Fruit Company control. So widespread was the company's power that it came to be nicknamed El Pulpo (The Octopus).

villages of some of the poorest country people in Guatemala. Yet within the park, you can experience one of the last fragments of primeval America, much of it practically unchanged since the days of Columbus.

At the mouth of the Río Dulce, where the gorge spills into the Gulf of Honduras, the southwesternmost corner of the Caribbean Sea, lies one of Guatemala's most unusual little towns. Isolated by unbridged river, roadless forest and the Belizean border just a short way up the coast, **Livingston** (population 3000) is Guatemala's only Garifuna community. The "Black Carib" residents claim descent from the fierce "Red Carib" Indians who made their home on the Caribbean island of St. Vincent and accepted into their tribe Africans who had escaped from slavery. They were deported from their island by the British after an uprising in 1795 and now live up and down the Mosquito Coast from southern Belize to Honduras. Most people in Livingston are multilingual, speaking Spanish and English as well as the African-based Garifuna patois.

Livingston's brightly painted wooden houses and storefronts run uphill from the docks along a single main street, which is paved although there is not a single motor vehicle in town—a fact to which the town owes its timeless tropical charm. In a few hours, you can stroll every street in town, visit the simple Catholic church with its ebony-skinned Jesus and Virgin of Guadalupe, then walk over the hill and up the narrow, hard, brown beach where Livingston's dreadlocked youth can usually be found savoring reggae and ganja, to the far end, where a trail leads up to **Siete Altares**, a series of waterfalls and pools just right for bathing. Hire a local to guide you there; a few tourists have been robbed at the falls.

Beyond that, there's not much for either visitors or locals to do in Livingston. For both, people-watching is a major pastime, and the most rewarding time to do it is on weekends, when settlers paddle to town from fishing camps up the coast and emerge from the jungle via foot trails to attend church services. No cars, no televisions, no soldiers or armed guards, and nothing at all to do. If you spend a night or two, you may find in Livingston one of the most relaxed and relaxing places on the continent, a welcome respite from some of the more nerve-jangling aspects of travel in Guatemala.

QUIRIGUÁ AND RÍO DULCE AREA LODGING

Surprisingly enough, there are no roadside motels along Route 9 east from Guatemala City all the way to the Atlantic coast. Local people often know someone who is willing to rent travelers a room for the night, especially around the Quiriguá turnoff, but the accommodations are likely to be quite primitive.

The closest comfortable lodging to Quiriguá is to be found at the upper end of the Río Dulce near the Castillo San Felipe Bridge. Our favorite is the **Hotel Catamaran** (32-48-29), a complex of bungalows set on an island downriver from the bridge. There is an inexpensive guarded parking lot under the bridge, and motor launches—often the same ones that go downriver to Livingston in the morning—wait nearby to take you across to the hotel. Guest accommodations, set along the shore and around grounds bursting with colorful flowers with a cage of parrots and a swimming pool in the middle, are rustic and simply furnished but quite large and airy, with private baths, screens to keep the mosquitoes out and balconies overlooking the water. The river gently lapping outside the window assures guests a sound night's sleep. Moderate.

Another resort complex in the best sense of the word, the **Hotel Izabal Tropical** (47-84-01) is situated on the shore of Lake Izabal about four kilometers down a dirt road from Castillo San Felipe. Fourteen thatch-roofed bamboo-and-stucco guest cabanas are scattered across a hillside overlooking the lake. Each has a ceiling fan and a private bathroom with shower. The hotel has both a children's and an adults' swimming pool amid beautiful gardens that bloom year-round. It also has its own boat dock, and you can usually find boats for hire there with or without a pilot. Rates are moderate.

An anomalous 45-room resort hotel tucked off the main street about a block above the docks in Livingston, the **Hotel Tucán Dugú** (48-15-88) offers bright, modern rooms and suites in a huge thatch-roofed building with a swimming pool. Prices are moderate for regular rooms in the main building and deluxe for the more private bungalows along the walkway that leads down to the hotel's private beach.

Practically across the street from the Tucán Dugú, you'll find a completely different kind of Caribbean charm at the **Hotel Río Dulce** (48-10-59), a plain but picture-perfect little blue two-story inn with a white picket fence, flower gardens, a big front-porch perfectly situated for main-street people-watching, and basic shared-bath rooms at a very low budget price. Youthful backpackers find their way here from all over the world.

If you choose to stay in Puerto Barrios (as you might if you plan to catch a bus to Tikal or a boat to Punta Gorda, Belize), the town's best accommodations are at the **Hotel Puerto Libre** (Carretera Atlántica Km. 292; 48-04-47), an American-style motel with air-conditioning, a swimming pool and satellite television. Rates are moderate. Located out of town at the junction with the road to Santo Tomás de Castillo, the Puerto Libre can present a problem for those who are traveling by public transportation. In town, the **Hotel Del Norte** (7 Calle at 1 Avenida; 48-00-87) is a partly renovated, Caribbean-style wooden inn on the waterfront. Shuttered doorways open out onto private balconies with views of the bay. Only two of the bright, simply furnished rooms have private baths. Budget.

QUIRIGUÁ AND RÍO DULCE AREA RESTAURANTS

Aside from a few small food stands along the highway, there are no restaurants in the vicinity of Quiriguá. Boys often hang around the parking lot at the ruins selling big bunches of small, sweet bananas to visitors for a few pennies.

In the Río Dulce resort area around the bridge at Castillo San Felipe, the best meals are served in restaurants at the various hotels along the river. The **Hotel Catamaran** (32-48-29) has a thatch-roofed open-air restaurant built out over the water. The menu includes most of the standard Guatemalan restaurant items—fruit salads, *desayuno chapín*, roast chicken, spaghetti, local fish—and you can watch big luxury sailboats with American names glide past as you eat. Prices are moderate. Hours of service are limited. Accessible by dirt road instead of by boat, the **Hotel Izabal Tropical** (47-84-01) also has a restaurant built over the water, with a range of menu choices and prices similar to those at the Catamaran.

Food stands clustered around the Castillo San Felipe bridge sell fish—most likely perch or tarpon—freshly caught from the lake, grilled with spices and served with tortillas and rice on the side. Try **Mary's**, a tiny place at the end of a dock just east of the bridge. Prices are in the low budget range.

Livingston has several modest restaurants that cater to the low-key lunchtime tourist trade, since the locals generally catch their own meals. The **Restaurante Tiburongato**, a clean place with checkered plastic tablecloths and an open-air latticework façade that looks out on the town's main street, is typical. Menu items include ceviche and a local seafood stew called *tapado,* which is made with coconut and plantains. Budget.

If you're spending the night in Livingston, your best dinner bet is the amazing **African Place**. Designed and built by an immigrant from Spain, it is an authentic Moorish-style stone castle in miniature, patterned after those of southern Spain, with archways, ornate tilework and wrought-iron grillworks accenting windows that peer out into the jungle. Wonderfully imaginative seafood dishes such as shrimp in garlic sauce and curried fish are moderately priced.

Puerto Barrios has no restaurants special enough to search out. The restaurant at the **Hotel Del Norte** (7 Calle at 1 Avenida, 48-00-87) with its no-nonsense ambience and predictable menu of fish and chicken dishes, is reputed to be the best in town.

QUIRIGUÁ AND RÍO DULCE AREA SHOPPING

Souvenir and gift shoppers will want to save their money for another time as they relax along the Río Dulce. A few roadside stalls near the Castillo San Felipe bridge offer limited selections of the same kind of *típica* clothing found all over Guatemala, at prices considerably higher than you'd pay in the western highlands where it is made. A hut near the pool at the **Hotel Catamaran** houses a small gallery where members of a cooperative of American artists—who live on boats nearby—show their work.

Many of the storefronts that line the main street of Livingston offer various handcrafted goods. Prices are very high for clothing brought in from other parts of Guatemala, but occasional locally made gift items such as coconut carvings and Afro-Caribbean paintings may bring a smile to your face as they tug at your billfold.

Tikal National Park and El Petén

A visit to **Tikal** makes the perfect climax to any tour of the Maya Route. Tikal is one of the true wonders of the world, a must-see destination, even if you don't plan to venture into any other part of Guatemala. No other Maya ruin can compare to it for majestic architecture and a setting that captures the imagination and won't let go. And if you want to experience primeval rainforest close up, Tikal is one of the best places on earth to do it.

Tikal was the greatest capital of the ancient Maya world. Founded as early as 600 B.C., it reached a peak population of about 50,000 a thousand years later and was one of the two largest cities in the Western Hemisphere during the Classic Period, along with Teotíhuacan in central Mexico. Tikal was situated in the exact center of the Maya land, equidistant from Copán in the south, Uxmal in the north, and Palenque in the west, and had close cultural ties to all parts of the region. Many experts believe the knowledge and ideas that shaped the classic Maya civilization originated in Tikal around 250 A.D., and the abandonment of Tikal around 900 A.D. coincided with the collapse of the high Maya civilization everywhere.

One aspect of Tikal's magic is that it is so hard to reach. What was once the wealthy and populous centerpiece of the ancient Maya world is now a remote frontier backwater surrounded by millions of acres of almost impenetrable rainforest. There is no easy way to get there overland. A notoriously bad road runs 205 kilometers north from the Castillo San Felipe bridge on the Río Dulce to Flores, capital of the vast, wild department of Petén and gateway to Tikal. The last 167 kilometers are unpaved and very rough. The distance may not sound daunting, but the grueling trip takes about twelve hours by second-class bus or private high-clearance vehicle. Another unpaved road runs from the border with Belize.

A decade ago, Guatemala's military government of the time received international aid to widen and pave the road to the Petén, but the funds were diverted by corrupt leaders and the road never got built. More recently, in connection with the Guatemalan government's agreement to set aside a large part of the Petén rainforest as a UNESCO Man and Biosphere Reserve, the World Bank pledged new funding to improve the road and stimulate tourism in the Petén—but the money will not be released until Guatemala convinces the bank that it will take all necessary measures to protect the Petén rainforest from pioneers flocking there to build new settlements and destroy the forest. In the meantime, the trip to Tikal is a battering, bruising, bone-jarring, muscle-wracking test of endurance.

The bus trip to Tikal from Belmopan, Belize, is shorter—52 kilometers by paved highway from the Belizean capital to the border and another 65 kilometers on an unpaved road from the border to the intersection with the isolated stretch of highway that connects Flores and Tikal National Park. However, the hassle and delay of crossing the border and changing buses, along with persistent reports of bandit activity along this road, make it a trip that's certainly not for the faint-hearted.

The simple way to get to Tikal is by plane, a surprisingly short hop—less than an hour—from Guatemala City. There are also a few sporadic flights each week from Belize City and Cancún. Flying over the Petén during daylight hours, you can see vividly the deforestation that is currently taking place in this environmentally delicate region. Dense rainforest still blankets the ridgelines and hilltops, but each valley is cleared for crops and livestock grazing as fast as a narrow dirt jeep road can penetrate it.

Passenger planes land at the airport near **Santa Elena** on the south shore of Lake Petén Itzá, about an hour's trip by shuttle bus from Tikal National Park. Most of the population of El Petén today lives in Santa Elena (population 10,000) and the contiguous town of San Benito (population 15,000). Together, the two towns form a frontier boom-town sprawl laced with open sewers and rattling with gas-powered electrical generators. While a modest tourist trade provides income for some area residents, more of them harvest renewable forest products such as chicle gum and pepsin leaves or join crews for oil exploration, the newest threat to the rainforest.

The capital of El Petén, **Flores** (population 1500) is built on a small island in the lake and is reached by a long earthen causeway from Santa Elena. A quintessentially quaint little town with an Old World feel to its tangled, claustrophobic streets, Flores is built on the site of Tayasal, the last ancient Maya stronghold to fall to the Spanish Empire. Tayasal was visited by Hernán Cortés, conqueror of Mexico, in 1525, but endured unmolested for nearly two centuries before a military expedition captured and razed it in 1697. You can walk all over town in less than an hour. The La Ruta Maya Conservation Foundation and George Washington University's Institute of Urban Development Research have developed plans that would encourage the cultivation of Flores as a tourist center complete with houseboat tourist accommodations on Lake Petén Itzá, a regional museum in the abandoned prison building facing the hilltop town square, and even a sewage treatment plant. All this is years in the future, though. For now, Flores is one of Central America's more low-key and isolated frontier towns.

Ask at any restaurant or hotel in the Flores-Santa Elena area and they can probably put you in touch with a guide who will take you on an inexpensive three-hour boat tour of the islands near Flores. Stops on the tour include a group of small temple mounds—all that remains of the old Maya fortress city of **Tayasal**—as well as a spot called **La Garrucha**, where you can climb a tall tower, hang from a cable and zip above the water to land on another island nearby, then climb another tower there and zip back. The final stop on most boat tours is **Petencito** (admission), a zoo occupied exclusively by animals native to the Petén rainforest, including many rare or elusive species—jaguars, cougars, marmosets, tepezcuintles—that visitors are unlikely to spot in the wild. If you thought the cable slide at La Garrucha was fun, give the very scary 300-foot concrete water slide at Petencito a try!

WILDLIFE OF TIKAL

The rainforest of the Petén supports the richest array of wildlife to be found anywhere on the North American continent. Mammals that live in the forest include several species of predatory cats—margays, jaguarundis, ocelots, cougars and jaguars—as well as other uncommon species such as anteaters, kinkajous and tapirs. Visitors are unlikely to see any of these rare, elusive animals in the wild, but there are other jungle creatures that most visitors to Tikal National Park can expect to see. Foremost among them are spider monkeys, easy to spot because of the rattling, crashing noises they make as they leap from branch to branch. Black howler monkeys, reportedly common throughout the Petén just a few years ago, are still spotted once in a while. Armadillos, tepezcuintles and coatimundis may be seen in the underbrush toward dusk, as are javelinas (also called peccaries), a small piglike beast. Visitors often catch glimpses of silver foxes, known to the locals as "gatos de la selva" ("forest cats") gliding through the ruins of Tikal. Other forest denizens include weasels, opossums, porcupines and deer.

At Tikal, recent acid rain has all but obliterated many stela carvings and temple inscriptions that had lasted a thousand years or more.

The 63-kilometer stretch of wide blacktop highway that runs between Santa Elena and Tikal National Park is the only pavement in the northern half of Guatemala. For much of the distance, the road runs past a huge but not very active army base left over from Guatemala's long civil war, during which rebel guerrillas are said to have operated within the national park and throughout El Petén. Midway along the highway, at the eastern tip of Lake Petén Itzá near the intersection with the road from Belize, a dirt road turns off and follows the north shore of the lake all the way back to San Benito. A few kilometers from the main highway on the north shore road brings you to the **Biotopo Cerro Cahui**, a 1600-acre reserve set aside to protect a last fragment of natural habitat for several endangered wetland species—the Petén turkey, the Petén crocodile and the tapir. Explore the network of trails through the luxuriant forest of the reserve. You'll spot bright tropical birds and maybe javelinas, armadillos and spider monkeys.

Tikal National Park (admission) is a different kind of experience from other major Maya ruins like Chichén Itzá, Uxmal, Palenque or Copán, in part because the archaeological site is so big. Most visitors find that trying to see everything at Tikal in a single day is too exhausting and that three days is just about right to fully appreciate the park.

There are two museums near the entrance to the ruins area. The **Tikal Museum**, located near the Jungle Lodge, contains many of the best small artifacts that have been found among the ruins, including pottery painted with elaborate scenes of ancient Maya life and polished bones etched with pictures of gods, demons and warriors. The highlight of the museum is a replica of the tomb of Lord Ah Cacau, the greatest ruler of Tikal, containing his bones, eight pounds of jade jewelry, incense pots and other treasures positioned as archaeologists originally discovered them in a vault below the Temple of the Great Jaguar. On the other side of the parking lot, a new building houses the **Visitor Center and Stelae Museum**. Although the Petén rainforest seems far removed from the industrial world, within the past few decades acid rain has seriously damaged many stelae, making it necessary to move the best ones indoors for protection. Outside the visitor center is a huge model, about 10 meters square, showing what Tikal looked like 1100 years ago.

From the parking lot near the hotels and museums, a rocky causeway, or pedestrians-only road built by the ancient Maya and restored by modern archaeologists, cuts through the dense forest for one-and-a-half kilometers to the central Plaza Mayor, the heart of ancient Tikal. From there, a triangular loop trail takes you through the Mundo Perdido complex, to lofty Templo IV, then to clusters of nondescript structures, called simply Complex M, Complex P, Group H and Complex Q, before returning to the Plaza Mayor. A separate trail leads to the solitary Temple of the Inscriptions. Park rangers have placed small concrete water basins beside the causeways at several points to attract monkeys and birds. A full circuit of the main ruins involves a hot, fairly strenuous hike of some 10 kilometers through the rainforest.

At the center of the Tikal ruins area is the meticulously restored group of buildings flanking the four sides of the two-acre **Plaza Mayor** (Great Plaza). Now covered with neatly mown grass, the whole square was paved with stucco in ancient times and resurfaced about once every century-and-a-half. The plaza was in use as early as 150 B.C. The first layer of pavement has been dated to about 100 A.D. and the final layer to 700 A.D.—a generation before any of the temples that now surround the plaza were completed. All of the structures at Tikal were painted bright red, with colorful bas-relief murals on the huge roof combs.

Along the north side of the plaza stand two rows of tombstone-shaped **stelae** with round altars in front of them. Other, similar stelae are set near the stairways of the various structures around the plaza. Most of the stelae are carved with the images of Tikal's noblemen in ceremonial garb with elaborate plumed headdresses, and many have hieroglyphs carved along the sides. As you explore outlying parts of the ruins, you will see dozens of massive stone stelae like these scattered throughout the forest. On some, the relief carving has been obliterated by time; others were quarried but never carved or erected, or smashed on purpose as the leaders they glorified fell into disrepute; and the best-preserved still invite us to wonder about the meanings of the messages so painstakingly inscribed and dispatched across the centuries to us, the people of the future. The oldest dated stela at Tikal was erected in 292 A.D., and the most recent in 771 A.D.

At the east and west ends of the plaza stand two of the extremely tall, stepped pyramids unique to Tikal. On the east end, **Temple I**, sometimes called the "Temple of the Great Jaguar," is the taller. It towers 170 feet high with its lofty, crumbling roof comb. It is the only pyramid we've seen anywhere in the Maya world that the public is not allowed to climb. A sign on a chain across the narrow stairway says that it is closed temporarily for restoration, but tour guides claim that it has been closed indefinitely since a tourist fell down the steep stairs to his death in the early 1980s. The tomb of Ah Cacau, the most important of ancient Tikal's leaders, was discovered at the foot of this pyramid. He reigned during the early part of the 8th century A.D., and his name translates as "Lord Chocolate." His remains, along with artifacts from his tomb including priceless jade jewelry, can be seen in a replica of the burial vault at the Tikal Museum. Just to the south of Temple I is the main **ball court**, surprisingly small for such an important ceremonial center as Tikal.

Directly across the plaza, on the west side, is **Temple II**, also known as the "Temple of the Masks." It is squat and wider than Temple I, with three levels to Temple I's nine. The top level's broad walkway around all sides of the temple offers good views of the Plaza Mayor, the acropolises and the surrounding forest canopy. Temples I and II were built at the same time and are thought to represent the male and female principles. Carvings on the lintels and walls of the temple chambers on top suggest to some archaeologists that Temple II was a burial pyramid for the wife of Ah Cacau, who was buried under Temple I. This is mere theory, however, as her tomb has not been found.

While the **North Acropolis** may lack the dramatic architecture of the pyramids, it is by far the more interesting structure to explore. It is a broad mound with a number of separate temples, apparently dedicated to different gods, and a tricky labyrinth of stairways and passages to reach them. Eight temples made up the acropolis in the 8th century, when Tikal's great pyramids were built. Archaeological digs have revealed that the mound on which the temples stand contains older temples built upon the ruins of yet older ones, dating back to 400 B.C. One excavation of the facade of a buried temple contains a huge stucco mask, taller than a person, of a fierce-eyed rain god with a bulbous, warty nose, perfectly preserved by earth and rubble while the stucco sculptures on the exposed buildings of Tikal were being obliterated by the rainforest climate. To the right of the giant mask, a dark, vaulted passageway leads into the pyramid. Feel your way through the darkness to the end, then strike a match and you'll find yourself face-to-face with another gargantuan god mask.

The **Central Acropolis** covers an area of four acres. It is believed to have been the royal palace of Tikal, a complex of spacious multistory residences built around six separate courtyards. Only the front part of the palace, facing the plaza, has been completely excavated; the back part merges gracefully into the forest. The majestic roof comb that breaks the skyline behind the Central Acropolis is the top of **Temple V**, the second-tallest pyramid at Tikal at 56 meters in height. Still unexcavated and shrouded by trees, it shows what all five of the great temple pyramids at Tikal must have looked like when early archaeologists came to explore and photograph the site at the end of the 19th century. A narrow foot trail from the east end of the Central Acropolis leads into the rainforest to Temple V, then returns to the main trail near Mundo Perdido.

The **Mundo Perdido** ("Lost World") complex, which lies southwest of the Plaza Mayor, presents a sharp contrast to the central ruins area. The massive **Main Pyramid** at the center of a group of 38 structures was built at least 500 years before the pyramids of the Plaza Mayor, suggesting that this area may have been the main ceremonial center for much of Tikal's history. Unlike the main plaza with its formal, landscaped feel, the Mundo Perdido complex has been excavated with an eye toward minimizing the impact on the surrounding forest, so the lower structures lie nestled among the roots and trunks of forest giants. From the top of the great pyramid, you can see the summits of Temples I and II on the Plaza Mayor, just the roof combs rising face-to-face, sun-and-moon, he-and-she through the canopy of a rainforest that rolls unbroken, astonishing in its vastness, all the way to the distant horizon. East of the pyramid and north of a small plaza with seven temples, is a **triple ball court** thought to be the only one of its kind in the Maya world.

At the westernmost end of the ruins area, **Temple IV**, known as the Temple of the Double-Headed Serpent, is the tallest manmade structure at Tikal. At 228 feet in height, this pyramid was also the second-tallest structure in the ancient Maya world. It was believed to be the tallest until one pyramid at El Mirador, 70 kilometers straight-line distance to the north across the roadless depths of the Petén rainforest and

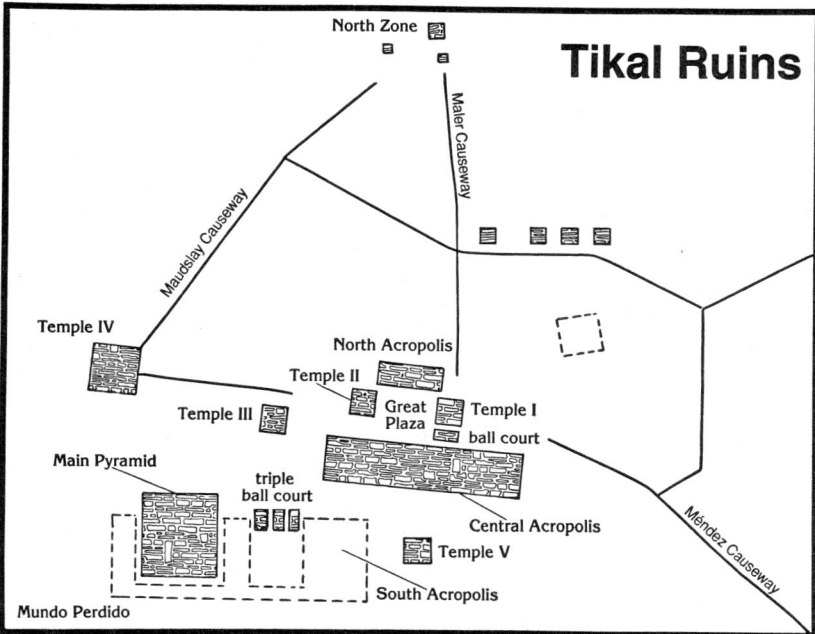

Tikal Ruins

North Zone

Maler Causeway

Maudslay Causeway

Temple IV

North Acropolis

Temple II

Temple III

Great Plaza

Temple I

ball court

Main Pyramid

triple ball court

Central Acropolis

Méndez Causeway

Temple V

South Acropolis

Mundo Perdido

presently inaccessible to sightseers, was measured at about a meter taller. Temple IV has been cleared but not excavated, so instead of a very steep stairway to the top, there's a very steep foot trail. As you reach the summit, a metal ladder affixed to the temple wall lets you climb all the way up to the roof comb. Near Temple IV are a parking lot, reached by a road that circles around the archaeological zone, and a group picnic area, so it is common to find busloads of school children swarming up and down the pyramid.

On the other side of the main ruins area, the Méndez Causeway branches away from the main trail and leads in a straight line through the forest for one kilometer to the **Temple of the Inscriptions,** a large, solitary temple on the outskirts of the ancient city. Covering the entire surface of the roof comb, you can still make out the only major hieroglyphic inscription found at Tikal. The temple is so far removed from the main ruins of Tikal that it was not discovered until 1951. Why this unusual and impressive temple should be set apart by both distance and architecture from the rest of the city is unknown. The stela that stands in front of the temple was intentionally smashed, probably by the people of ancient Tikal.

Visitors are not allowed to spend the night in the ruins area. Rangers check to see that everybody is out before dark. They explain that jaguars and other dangerous beasts roam the forest at night, and if pressed ("But I thought jaguars were almost extinct. . . .") admit that it is other, supernatural beings that make the ruins a place to be avoided at night. Outsiders doubt it, they say, but everybody around there knows it is true.

No night watchman will stop you from walking to the ruins after midnight. Dawn as experienced from the ruins at Tikal is an ultimate travel experience, absolutely worth the inconvenience of rising before first light. Early-to-bed, early-to-rise is less of a hardship here than it would be most places because the electricity shuts off at 9:30 p.m. in the national park hotels.

A mist as thick as ocean fog shrouds Tikal in the hours before dawn. As the sun rises, the mist glows first pink and then golden. For a moment, you can glimpse the glory of Tikal in ancient times. Then the ancient temples, shadows at first, turn to stone as the mist burns away. The forest comes alive suddenly with the cries of monkeys and birds and the throbbing drone of insects, and the heat of the day begins. A dawn tour led by freelancing off-duty park rangers is well worth the small fee. The rangers, many of whom were born and raised on the edge of the Petén rainforest, are amazingly knowledgeable about the diversity of plant and animal species found in the park. You can also walk into the park on your own as early as you like, and young travelers staying at the campground organize informal 4:00 a.m. expeditions to the pyramids most mornings.

At any time of day you choose to walk among the various outlying ruins of Tikal, they quickly become a mere excuse for venturing deeper into the rainforest. At every turn, a smaller trail beckons you off into the deep jungle for a spontaneous visit to some half-buried temple or hidden forest glade. Monkeys create dins of excitement as you enter their territory. Colorful toucans scatter from the trees in front of you. The diversity of plant and animal life in the Petén jungle means that around every bend in the trail you discover something new—a tree full of orchids, a strange fruit, a kaleidoscopic butterfly swarm, a line of leafcutter ants marching in single file for as far as you can see. Jungle trails have a way of tempting people onward. Use good judgment. There is a risk of getting lost in this terrain.

Tikal National Park covers a forested area of 575 square kilometers (222 square miles). During Tikal's heyday, the whole area was cleared for small suburban farms where peasants grew maize, beans and tomatoes both for themselves and for the priests and rulers who lived in the great city center. Anywhere you go in the backcountry of Tikal National Park, you will find low mounds and tumbled-down stone walls that remain from these ancient homesteads—even in places that are almost inaccessible today. Archaeologists will never excavate all of the sites in the jungle of Tikal National Park, and visitors will always be able to wonder what undiscovered treasures may lie hidden there.

Despite its size, Tikal National Park protects less than two percent of El Petén, the largest contiguous expanse of rainforest on the North American continent. The northern third of the Petén rainforest—all the land north of Tikal to the northern, eastern and western borders of Guatemala, has been designated as the Maya Biosphere Reserve, a unit of the UNESCO Man and Biosphere program that protects inhabited wilderness areas, allowing some economic use of the forest in a buffer zone around a protected core area. The Maya Biosphere Reserve, en-

---

THE AGE OF THE RAINFOREST

Most of the rainforest around Tikal is almost certainly less than a thousand years old. Using satellite mapping to reveal the outlines of ancient farmers' fields, archaeologists have determined that virtually all the land within a 100-kilometer radius of Tikal had been cleared for cultivation 1100 years ago. After the abandonment of the city began, around 900 A.D., it is difficult to estimate how long it took for the lofty ceiba, mahogany and sapodilla trees to take root among the ruins. The jungle existed in something like its present form when Spanish conquistador Hernán Cortés visited the region in 1525.

The national park rangers at Tikal are paid only the equivalent of about two dollars a day, so some of them "moonlight" as tour guides to lead visitors on jungle hikes at dawn for a unique opportunity to witness the awakening of the forest.

compassing an area of 13,600 square kilometers (5400 square miles), is one of the most ambitious efforts to save the rainforest anywhere in the world. La Ruta Maya Conservation Foundation, armed with a large grant from the MacArthur Foundation, hopes to go one step further, merging Guatemala's Maya Biosphere Reserve with Mexico's Calakmul Biosphere Reserve and Belize's Río Bravo Conservation Area to form the Maya Peace Park, a huge international park that would span the three nations' often-troubled borders and allow cooperative ecotourism development in the region.

At least 25 other major ceremonial centers have been found in the Maya Biosphere Reserve and another dozen along the Río Pasión in the southwestern part of the department of Petén. Of those in the biosphere reserve, most are accessible only by very primitive four-wheel-drive tracks that can only be used during the dry season, and several are located in terrain so impassable that archaeologists can only reach them by helicopter. None are currently open to the general public, though proponents of the Maya Peace Park plan hope that **El Mirador**, site of a large ceremonial center whose temples include the tallest known Maya pyramid, will someday be opened to tourists by shuttle bus or even monorail.

At present, the only ruin in the Maya Biosphere Reserve that casual visitors can get to from Tikal is **Uaxactún**, located 20 kilometers north of the Tikal ruins and just a short distance outside the north boundary of the national park. For centuries, Uaxactún was a rival city to Tikal. Nothing about these partially excavated but unrestored ruins suggests that this ceremonial site even came close to achieving the grandeur of Tikal, but inscriptions on Tikal's temples and stelae reveal that the two cities fought bloody wars and that, at least once, the army of Uaxactún conquered Tikal. Some backpackers hike from Tikal to Uaxactún. Camping equipment is a must, since even strong hikers find it impossible to walk there and back the same day. Or a local guide can take you there in a four-wheel-drive vehicle, a rough one-hour trip each way.

The biggest problem facing visitors who would like to explore more remote areas of the Petén is lack of transportation. Very few travelers come to Tikal in their own vehicles, and public transportation is quite limited. A few enterprising guides, who don't advertise but can be found by word of mouth through any hotel or restaurant operator or shuttle van driver, run tours from Flores and Tikal to other Maya ruins in the Petén—especially **El Ceibal**, which can also be reached by public transportation. The trip involves traveling 60 kilometers by car or bus on a good dirt road to the jungle village of Sayaxché and hiring a boat there to take you 18 kilometers down the Río Pasión to the ruins. The ruins can also be reached by a new four-wheel-drive track, but the jungle boat trip is more fun. El Ceibal is noted by archaeologists as having the only circular temple in the entire Maya world. It also has 56 carved stone stelae, including one that certainly seems to depict a Maya warrior talking on the telephone! The stelae, altars and stone walls at El Ceibal are covered with a bright orange lichen, creating a dramatic contrast to the amazingly lush rainforest that constantly threatens to swallow the ancient city once more.

TIKAL NATIONAL PARK AND EL PETÉN LODGING

Staying at Tikal National Park is best because there is too much in the park to experience in a single day, and the shuttle trip between Flores/ Santa Elena and Tikal, an hour each way, costs more than a hotel room does. Staying in the park also lets you spend the night surrounded by the sounds of the jungle and visit the ruins in the eerie dawn mist.

There are three hotels in Tikal National Park, totalling 49 rooms between them. Because of development restrictions imposed by the Guatemalan government when the Maya Biosphere Reserve was created, no new hotels can be built. Sometimes, tour groups fill them to capacity and other times they are almost empty. You don't know until you go there, because it's not easy to make advance reservations and none of the hotels has a telephone. The men who drive shuttle vans between the airport at Santa Elena and the national park may know about room availability. Otherwise, the best plan for travelers arriving on the morning plane is just to go to the park by noon and see whether you can find lodging. If you can't get a room, you'll have time to return to Flores by midafternoon and find one there.

Our favorite hotel at the national park is the 15-room **Tikal Inn**, a classic jungle lodge that consists of an attractively rustic main building, where you'll find the dining room, lobby and four rather elegantly decorated guest rooms with four-poster beds, as well as a row of thatched-roof cabanas along one side of a broad expanse of lawn with a swimming pool in the center and dense rainforest around the perimeter of the grounds. The cabanas have complete modern conveniences, including electric light from 6:00 to 9:30 p.m. and private bathrooms with running water that is warm late in the day. The hotel's mascot ocelot lives in a large enclosure in the jungle nearby, screams hauntingly in the night, and sometimes is let loose on the grounds to romp with cat-loving guests. Reservations can only be made by sending a letter to "Tikal Inn, Tikal, Petén, Guatemala" telling what dates you want,

Since most Santa Elena and Flores hotels have no telephones or reservation systems, the managers meet arriving planes at the Santa Elena airport to drum up business.

then sending payment in full after you receive confirmation. Moderate; modified American plan available.

The largest hotel at Tikal is the 32-room **Jungle Lodge** (send reservation requests to 29 Calle No. 18-01, Zona 12, Guatemala City or call 76-02-94 in Guatemala City). It was originally built in the 1930s to house archaeological teams working at Tikal. A recent remodeling has converted the rustic old cabins into spacious, pleasant cabanas with tin roofs that are noisy in the rain and private baths with reliable hot water. The moderate rates are higher than at the Tikal Inn.

The third option, the **Jaguar Inn**, next door to the Tikal Museum, has just two guest rooms in simple thatched-roof cottages with private baths. During the dry season, several large, furnished tents are also rented out as guest accommodations. The food here is not very good, so it is better to opt for a room only, without meals, and eat across the road at the campground. Moderate.

The most luxurious accommodations in the Petén are at the **Hotel Camino Real Tikal** (El Remate; for reservations call 33-46-33 in Guatemala City), outside the national park near the intersection where the road from Belize intersects the highway between Santa Elena and Tikal. All 120 rooms have private baths, air-conditioning, and satellite television complete with remote control—shamelessly self-indulgent amenities in a region where most of the local people live without running water or indoor plumbing. Guest facilities include a swimming pool, a lakefront beach, tennis courts, restaurants, a bar and a disco. Ultra-deluxe.

In Santa Elena, one of the better hotels is the **Hotel Maya Internacional** (81-12-76; for reservations write 2 Avenida No. 7-78, Zona 10, Guatemala City, or call 36-39-09). This compound of 20 rustic rooms in duplex bungalows on stilts over Lake Petén Itzá used to be the top of the line in the Petén region, but has lost most of its formerly landscaped grounds to the rising water lever of the lake over the past few years. Nature lovers can watch from the bungalow porch as multitudes of egrets, herons and other wading birds fish among the water lilies just a few feet away. Rooms have private baths. Be careful of the electric water-heating shower heads, common in hotels around Santa Elena and Flores, but said to be dangerous because of the possibility of electrocution. Moderate.

Of numerous small lodgings in the island town of Flores, the modern **Savanna Hotel** (81-12-48) is our favorite simply because of the view. Unlike most of the other hotels, which are located near the causeway, this one is on the far side of the island overlooking the full expanse of Lake Petén Itzá. Of the 23 rooms, the ones at the back have the best lake views. The four-story hotel has nothing in the way of decor to spruce up its plain, concrete block architecture, but the grand panorama from the second-story patio makes up for it. Moderate.

TIKAL NATIONAL PARK AND EL PETÉN RESTAURANTS

At Tikal, each of the hotels has its own small restaurant serving a set menu at set hours, with the price of breakfast and dinner included in the "modified American plan" room rate. The only alternatives are a series of *comedores* situated down the road from the campground, serving basic food at budget prices. The restaurant at the campground itself is the largest in the area and serves a low-priced selection of soups, sandwiches and spaghetti.

Flores has a number of rustic-but-nice restaurants that offer entrées of local game from the Petén rainforest, typically including alligator, venison, tepezcuintle, armadillo, wild turkey, pheasant and rabbit. This is the traditional food of the region, and travelers who feel queasy about dining on freshly killed jungle animals may have to subsist on fruit salads. More conventional meats such as chicken and pork are only found in the dining rooms of better hotels. The town's best restaurants are in a cluster along Calle Centroamérica, the main street one block north of the island end of the causeway.

Our favorite restaurant in Flores is **La Mesa de los Maya** (Calle Centroamérica; 81-12-40). The servings are generous and the cuisine is out of this world. Handwoven tablecloths and wall hangings brighten the two cozy, plain-but-honest little dining rooms, as does the friendly pet toucan. There is a full bar on the premises, though a drink costs much more than a dinner does.

A block down the street, **Restaurant La Jungla** (Calle Centroamérica) is overgrown with jungle plants like a fern bar run amok. Inside, the decor consists of boa constrictor skins, jaguar heads, stuffed birds and other trophies. The food and service are okay, but all that taxidermy is enough to make you feel as if the rest of your dinner entrée were watching over your shoulder. Budget.

Around the block, facing the waterfront about a block west of the causeway, **El Faisan** (Flores) is another small restaurant and bar serving a similar selection of grilled wild animal meats. Rough wood paneling decorated from floor to ceiling with photos, drawings and maps of Tikal create an archaeology ambience that sets it apart from the other restaurants nearby. It is open later in the evening than most of the others, too. Budget.

TIKAL NATIONAL PARK AND EL PETÉN SHOPPING

The souvenir industry in Flores and Tikal is in its infancy. A cluster of four shops near the Tikal Museum and the entrance to the ruins area has a high-priced selection of *típica* clothing from other parts of Guatemala that is worth looking at only if you are not planning to visit the highlands on your trip. It also has lots and lots of Tikal T-shirts. Other makeshift shops along the narrow streets of Flores also stock limited selections of *típica*. The best souvenirs of Tikal we've seen are a videotape with aerial footage of the rainforest and the ruins and an audio tape of jungle sounds recorded at Tikal.

The Sporting Life

BICYCLING

By renting a bicycle in Panajachel at **Hotel del Lago** or **Los Geranios Turicentro**, both on the waterfront, you can spend the day exploring the back roads that connect the villages along the shores of Lake Atitlán.

At **Antigua Mountain Bike** (5 Avenida Sur No. 36 Apt. #9) in Antigua Guatemala, you can arrange guided tours in English, Spanish, French or German, ranging from part-day trips around nearby coffee fincas to three- to five-day trips around Lake Atitlán, including all meals and van transportation.

BOATING AND FISHING

Several Panajachel hotels, including the **Hotel Atitlán** and the **Hotel Vision Azul**, offer rental motorboats so you can explore Lake Atitlán on your own. Rowboats and canoes, as well as fishing tackle, can be rented on the beach at **Lake Recreation Services**. Fishermen will find that the native fish of Lake Atitlán have all been displaced by black bass, which were introduced by the government as a sport fish during the 1980s.

HIKING

Volcano climbing is popular among visitors to the Guatemalan highlands. South of Quetzaltenango, the **Volcán Santa María** reaches an elevation of 12,375 feet and commands a view of all of Guatemala's highest mountains, including the Cuchumatán Mountains above Huehuetenango and the volcanoes around Lake Atitlán and Antigua, as well as the lowlands that spill south to the Pacific coast. A lower crater known as **Santiaguito**, standing at the 8166-foot elevation on the big volcano's south slope, has been steadily active since 1902 and continues to spew forth ash and noxious fumes fairly regularly. A very steep seven-kilometer trail climbs to the Santa María summit from the village of Llano del Pinal on the north slope, which can be reached by local bus. The distance may not sound like much, but it is a difficult all-day round-trip to the top of the volcano and back.

The three volcanoes around Lake Atitlán that comprise Parque Nacional Atitlán are probably the most-often hiked peaks in Guatemala. The easiest climb is **Volcán San Pedro**, 9900 feet high, the only Lake Atitlán volcano that can be climbed up and back the same day. The nine-kilometer trail starts at the village of San Pedro La Laguna. The six- to eight-hour trek to the summit of **Volcán Toliman**, 10,280 feet high, is considered the most difficult climb, and **Volcán Atitlán**, the highest of the three volcanoes at 11,600 feet has a hut on top where climbers can spend the night. The trails to both volcanoes start on the south shore of the lake at the village of San Lucas Tolimán, where hikers' maps of the national park are sold at the American Pie restaurant.

Near Antigua, the most popular volcano climb is on **Volcán Agua** south of town. The six-kilometer climb from the village of Santa María de Jesús to the summit of the 12,350-foot volcano can easily be done up-and-back in a single day. The smoking, rumbling **Volcán Fuego** west of town, standing 12,350 feet high, can also be climbed in a day, while nearby **Volcán Acatenango**, at 13,040 feet in height, takes two days for a round-trip and has a hikers' hut at the summit. The shortest trails up both volcanoes start at the village of Yepocapá on the west slope. Information on guide services and current safety bulletins are available at the INGUAT office in the Palacio de los Capitanes-Generales on the south side of the Parque Central in Antigua. The **Asociación Andinismo** (6 Avenida Norte No. 34) in Antigua organizes hiking trips in the region, and the **Casa Andinista** (4 Calle Oriente No. 5-A) sells trail maps and guidebooks for hikers.

A U.S. State Department advisory warns against hiking on **Volcán de Pacaya**, the closest volcano to Guatemala City, where there is said to be a serious bandit problem, and where even large organized groups have been robbed.

For a gentle walk through the cloud forest, visit the **Biotopo de Quetzal Mario Dary Rivera**, where there are presently two nature trail loops. One is three kilometers long, and the other is half that. Both are steep in spots. Of the reserve's 2849 acres, only 62 acres are accessible to hikers. Additional trails were under construction the last time we visited, and more of this unique reserve will gradually be opened to the public.

Tikal National Park is a great place for rainforest hiking, with an extensive network of well-worn trails. The ultimate hike is to the ruins of **Uaxactún**, located 20 kilometers north of the Tikal ruins and just beyond the north boundary of the national park. It is a two-day round-trip along a rough jeep trail through the jungle.

HORSEBACK RIDING

In Antigua Guatemala, horses can be rented for private rides or guided tours to the volcanoes at the stables of **R. Roland Pérez** (San Pedro El Panorama No. 228; 32-28-09).

WINDSURFING

Lake Atitlán is *the* place for windsurfing and morning is the time to go. There is almost always a breeze. However, in the afternoon, an unpredictable wind known as *el xocomil* can make both canoeing and windsurfing quite dangerous. Sailboards are rented on the beach at **Lake Recreation Services.**

Transportation

BY CAR

The main highway through Guatemala is **Route 1,** the Pan American Highway. The Guatemalan portion of this international highway starts at the border station of La Mesilla, where it enters Guatemala from San Cristóbal de las Casas and Comitán in the Mexican state of Chiapas. Route 1, a well-maintained two-lane paved highway, takes you on a winding, mountainous trip past Huehuetenango, Quetzaltenango, Lake Atitlán and Antigua Guatemala before arriving in Guatemala City. From the capital, the Pan American Highway veers south into El Salvador.

The main highway to eastern Guatemala destinations such as the Río Dulce, Quiriguá, and the turnoff to Copán, Guatemala, is **Route 9,** known as the Carretera Atlántica, or Atlantic Highway. Two-lane, paved Route 9 twists up and down mountains for the first 100 kilometers, then descends into the Montagua River Valley and follows the river all the way to the sea.

Getting to Tikal by car is a formidable challenge. Unpaved, mountainous **Route 5** north from Guatemala City takes forever and should only be attempted by adventurous souls in high-clearance vehicles. A shorter and easier way is to drive to the Río Dulce area and take **Route 13** north past Castillo de San Felipe. The first one-third of this route is paved, but the last 168 kilometers is a rocky dirt road that is very rough in spots. Start with a full tank of gas and allow at least eight hours to drive the unpaved portion of this route. Few travelers opt to go to the Petén by car, and for good reason.

BY AIR

La Aurora International Airport is perched on the edge of a gorge in the southern part of Guatemala City, on the boundary between Zona 9 and Zona 13. Most flights from the United States, Europe and other parts of the world connect through Miami, Houston, Dallas/Fort Worth or Los Angeles. They include American, Continental, Air France, British Airways, Iberia, Japan Air Lines, KLM Royal Dutch Airlines and Lufthansa. Guatemala's recently privatized national airline, Aviateca, has flights from Los Angeles, Houston, Miami, Cancún and Mérida. Other Latin American airlines that fly into Guatemala City include Aeroquetzal (Guatemalan), Aerocaribe and Mexicana (Mexican), Aeronica (Nicaraguan), COPA (Panamanian), LACSA and TACA (Costa Rican) and SAHSA (Honduran).

There are scheduled flights to the **Santa Elena Airport**, near Flores and less than an hour by shuttle van from Tikal National Park, from Guatemala City every morning on Aviateca, as well as flights several days a week from Belize City on Aerovías and from Cancún on Aeroquetzal or Aviateca. Additional flights are announced intermittently, and flights in and out of Santa Elena are routinely cancelled whenever there are too few passengers. A flexible attitude is essential. If your flight cancels and you can't get on another one the same day, the airline is required by international conventions to provide you with a hotel room and meals until the next available flight.

BY BUS

Guatemalan towns and cities have no central bus terminal buildings. Second-class buses, which can take you virtually anywhere in Guatemala, always originate in streets or open lots around the public market. Drivers shout their destinations. In Guatemala City's chaotic outdoor marketplace/terminal, where fifty or more buses may be loading at one time, the uproar can be overwhelming. To ride a second-class bus, whether you board at the market or flag one down along the road, just find a place to sit or stand. After a while, the conductor will clamber back to sell you a ticket for a few quetzales.

A few comfortable, reserved-seat first-class buses operate out of individual garages hidden away on side streets of some larger towns. In Huehuetenango, **Transportes Los Halcones** (7 Avenida No. 3-62 in

Huehuetenango; 7 Avenida No. 15-27, Zona 1 in Guatemala City; 8-19-97) runs daily buses to Guatemala City and connects with second-class buses to Quetzaltenango, Lake Atitlán and Antigua Guatemala. **Rutas Orientales** (19 Calle No. 8-18, Zona 1, Guatemala City; 53-72-82) operates first-class buses to Esquipulas near the Honduran border and can let you off at Chiquimula, where you can catch a minibus to the border crossing for the Maya ruins of Copán. **Transportes Litegua** (15 Calle 10-40, Zona 1, Guatemala City; 53-81-69) has daily buses to Puerto Barrios that connect with shuttles to the Lake Izabal/Río Dulce resort area. **Transportes Fuente del Norte** (17 Calle No. 8-46, Zona 1, Guatemala City; 51-38-17) operates first-class buses to Santa Elena, near Tikal National Park.

BY TRAIN

Government-operated passenger trains run twice a week from Ciudad Tecún Umán on the Mexican border south of Tapachula, Chiapas, to Guatemala City and from there to Puerto Barrios on the Caribbean coast. They are surely among the worst trains in the Western Hemisphere, so unreliable, unsavory and decrepit that if you ride one (and survive), you'll have a great story to tell in years to come.

GUATEMALAN BUSES

Visitors experiencing Third World travel for the first time will find Guatemala's public buses appalling, and even the most seasoned of globetrotters will find them by turns frustrating and hilarious. With increasing tourism, some comfortable first-class buses can now be found operating out of little garages hidden away on side streets of larger towns, but trips to most places in Guatemala—including such popular tourist destinations as Panajachel, Antigua, Chichicastenango and Tikal—involve riding second-class buses.

A typical second-class bus is of the same type as old school buses. Independently owned and operated, many are 30 to 40 years old and may have rust holes in the floor or broken-out windows. They pick up passengers at the public market and leave whenever all the hard bench seats are full, then drive around town picking up more passengers from streetcorners until the aisles are also full. Once on the road, they stop to load and unload passengers at every tiny crossroad. Baggage, from slabs of sheet metal roofing and baskets full of live chickens to your suitcase, are thrown onto a luggage rack on top of the bus. If the inside of the bus gets too crowded and claustrophobic, most drivers will let you ride on the roof, too.

CAR RENTALS

The major international car rental agencies with booths at La Aurora International Airport in Guatemala City include **Avis** (31-00-17; also at 12 Calle No. 2-73, Zona 9; 31-69-90), **Hertz** (31-17-11; also at 7 Avenida No. 14-76, Zona 9; 32-22-42), **National Inter-Rent** (31-83-65; also at 4 Calle 1-42, Zona 10; 68-01-75), **Dollar** (31-71-85; also at Avenida La Reforma No. 6-14, Zona 9; 34-82-85) and **Budget** (31-02-73; also at Avenida La Reforma No. 15-00, Zona 9; 31-65-46). Guatemala's largest car rental agency is **Tabarini Renta Autos** (La Aurora International Airport; 31-47-55; also at 2 Calle A No. 7-30, Zona 10; 31-61-08). Motorcycles, as well as cars, are for rent in Guatemala City at **Rental Moto-Car** (11 Calle 2-18, Zona 9; 34-14-16).

Antigua Guatemala also has a branch of **Avis** (5 Avenida Norte No. 22; 32-02-91). Cars can also be rented through the English-speaking travel agency **El Tecolote Travel Services** (6 Avenida Norte No. 59-A; 32-07-84).

In Santa Elena, you can rent a four-wheel-drive vehicle or microbus at **Koka Rent Autos** (Santa Elena Airport; 50-12-33).

PUBLIC TRANSPORTATION

In Guatemala City, run-down and usually very crowded city buses serve most parts of the city. Bus number 82 runs between the center of downtown and the Zona Viva. In addition, minibuses known as micros run up and down practically every street in the city. You'll find plenty of taxis around La Aurora International Airport, the Zona Viva, and the Parque Central.

Daily shuttles run from Antigua Guatemala to the airport in Guatemala City for a few dollars, but most leave Antigua during the predawn hours. Reservations are required. For a current schedule, call 32-03-56 or inquire at **Viajes Tivoli** (5 Avenida Norte No. 10-A; 32-30-41) above the bookstore on the west side of the *parque central*. The cost of taking a taxi between Antigua Guatemala and the airport in Guatemala City is around US$20.

You'll also find plenty of private taxis in Huehuetenango, Quetzaltenango and Panajachel. Typically, they are old cars so beat up that it's a wonder they run at all. Some we've ridden in even had bullet holes. But the fares are low. (Be sure to agree on the price of the trip before getting into the taxi.)

Minibuses provide transportation between Santa Elena and Tikal National Park. Most of them leave Santa Elena between 8:00 and 9:00 a.m., or whenever the morning plane from Guatemala City arrives, and leave the ruins around 2:00 p.m. for the return trip.

EIGHT

Belize

Ask most people where Belize is and they will ask for a map. Little   **347**
wonder the tiny country is such a secret, wedged as it is between
formidable Guatemala and the vast Yucatán Peninsula, a morsel of
jungle confronting two giants. Facing out to the Caribbean, Belize
seems ready to break from land and drift out to sea.

But Belize was no secret to the Maya. Like the Morocco of the
Western Hemisphere, this region overflowed with sophisticated trade
and profound culture, mystical religions and mighty kingdoms. Great
rulers and priests lived here, and so did artists, writers and aristocrats.
One city, the jungle-veiled Caracol, boasted nearly 200,000 residents—
more than live in today's Belize. Two thousand years ago, Caracol crushed
its big neighbor, Tikal, Guatemala, and ruled the Maya world for more
than 100 years.

Today, remnants of that lost world are slowly waking from their
jungle slumber. Whole cities, some only discovered in the last 40 years,
are being resurrected by teams of archaeologists. Each day's excavations reveals physical wonders offering few explanations and many
mysteries, beckoning outsiders to come ponder Belize's ancient treasures.
Toothy pyramids loom on mountain ridges, and three-story-high masks
stare out from jungle haunts. Elaborate networks of reservoirs, causeways
and *sacbes*, or ancient roads, link age-old cities. The tallest building in
modern-day Belize is a Maya pyramid, and so is the second highest.

Along with these ancient marvels come an array of natural wonders.
Indeed, this country the size of Massachusetts harbors the world's second-
longest barrier reef (behind Australia's), where a thread of unspoiled
isles are washed by the Caribbean Sea. Here also is the world's only

Belize has preserved more than 80 percent of its original forests. By contrast, its neighbor El Salvador has saved only 2 percent.

jaguar preserve, the longest chain of caves in the Western Hemisphere, and the seventh-highest waterfall in the world.

Wild animals come in a splendorous array of shapes, sizes and names, from spiny anteaters and spider monkeys to kinkajou bears and bare-throated tiger herons. Fishing and scuba diving are so outstanding, their praises are whispered so as not to spoil their secrets.

Belize's 190,000 residents are themselves a phenomenon, an improbably diverse blend of Creoles and Maya, Mennonites and Chinese, Arabs, mestizos (Spanish-Indians) and Garifunas (Black Caribs). English is the country's first language, but there are five other major languages, including Maya. Belize history speaks not only of ancient Maya civilizations but of New World outlaws—British pirates and black loggers, escaped East Indian slaves and Yucatán refugees from the Caste War—who gave the little country a tenacious pioneer mentality. The same frontier mentality permeates today's Belize, which is fittingly called "The Adventure Coast."

Within that rugged coast are five distinct regions—the Cayes, Belize City, Northern Belize, Western Belize and Southern Belize. Of course, the Cayes actually extend off the coast, forming a thread of islands trimmed in coral rock and mangroves. Only about a dozen are inhabited and only two, Ambergris Caye and Caye Caulker, possess villages. Right on the coast, covering a finger of land, is Belize City. Belize's only real city, it is the country's center of business.

North from the city, Northern Belize presents a lush, lonely landscape harboring the powerful ancient ceremonial center of Lamanai and the peaceful Altun Ha, where fantastic jade artifacts have been found. Western Belize attracts chic adventurers who stay in charming jungle lodges and explore Maya medicine trails and the popular ruins at Xunantunich. The west is also home to Caracol, a great Maya city swallowed in jungle, hours from civilization. Southern Belize is where hard-core explorers go to see what few travelers have seen: primitive Maya villages and the profound ruins at Lubaantun and Nim Li Punit.

Throughout these regions, travelers will find few creature comforts. Instead, they will discover a land that still belongs to the rainforest and to the sea, not to the frills of tourism. Indeed, this country where the per capita income is only $1100 a year is waging an intense campaign to save its environment. More than 25 wildlife and archaeological preserves have been set aside, including the 100,000-acre Cockscomb Basin, the world's only jaguar sanctuary. Jaguars have been wiped out of other

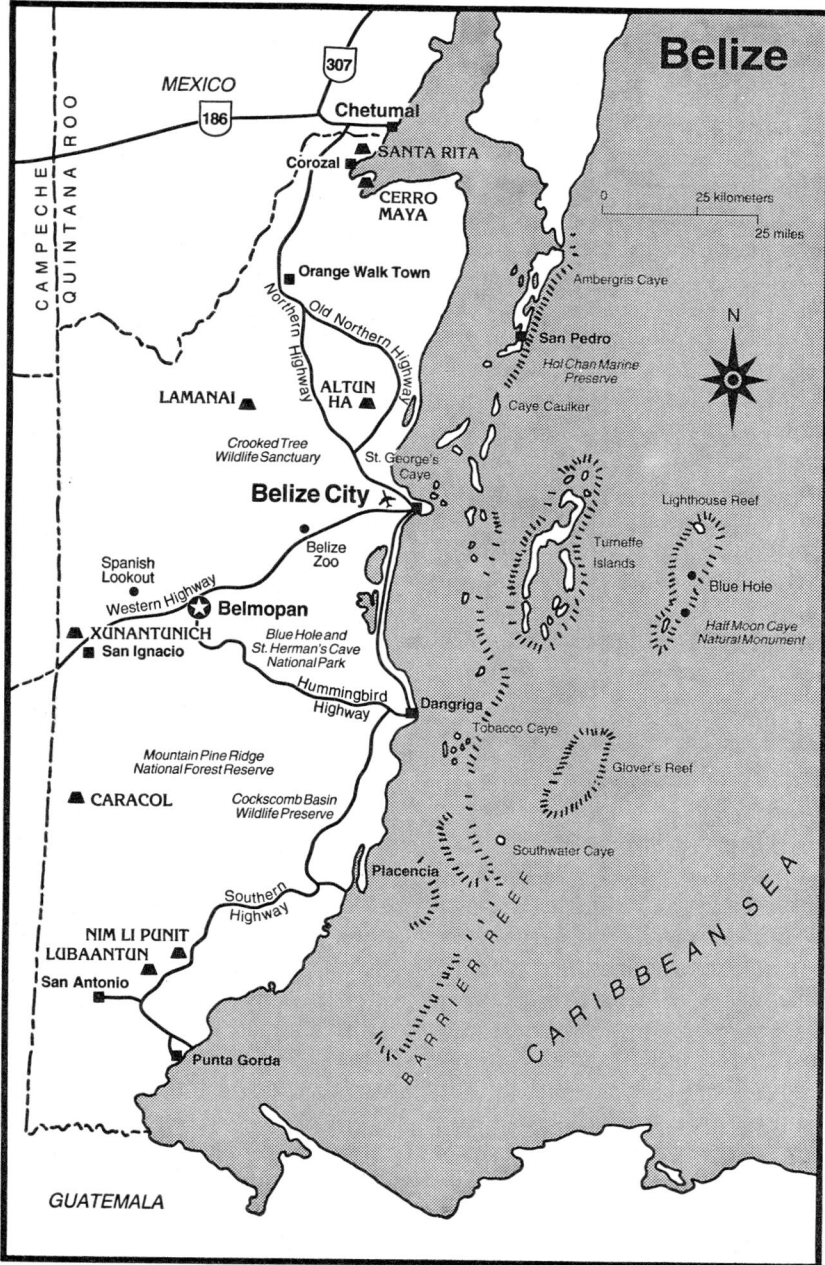

Belize

MEXICO

307

186

Chetumal

Corozal • SANTA RITA

CERRO MAYA

CAMPECHE

QUINTANA ROO

Orange Walk Town

Ambergris Caye

0   25 kilometers

25 miles

San Pedro

Hol Chan Marine Preserve

N

Northern Highway

Old Northern Highway

LAMANAI

ALTUN HA

Caye Caulker

Crooked Tree Wildlife Sanctuary

St. George's Caye

Lighthouse Reef

Belize City

Belize Zoo

Turneffe Islands

Blue Hole

Spanish Lookout

Western Highway

Belmopan

Half Moon Caye Natural Monument

XUNANTUNICH

San Ignacio

Blue Hole and St. Herman's Cave National Park

Hummingbird Highway

Dangriga

Tobacco Caye

Mountain Pine Ridge National Forest Reserve

Glover's Reef

CARACOL

Cockscomb Basin Wildlife Preserve

Southwater Caye

Placencia

Southern Highway

BARRIER REEF

NIM LI PUNIT

LUBAANTUN

San Antonio

CARIBBEAN SEA

Punta Gorda

GUATEMALA

Each year, more tourists visit Ambergris Caye than visit the whole rest of Belize!

parts of Central America, where rainforests are ravaged every day. Belizeans point to this devastation, as well as over-development in the Caribbean and Florida, in the crusade to save their country. Bumper stickers proclaim their love for wild animals, and local gossip is laced with the latest ecotourism news.

There is a certain innocence in Belize, a simple existence where the rigors of life have not yet slipped in. Events here often seem surreal: rabbits hop around a restaurant floor, a monkey joins you for breakfast, and toucans fill the garden where you're having a jungle massage. Women wash their clothes in the rivers and cook iguanas on their wood-fired stoves. No one wears shoes on the islands, but why should they? The streets are made of sand.

After a while, when you begin thinking Belize might be a little too primitive, too far out there, something Belizean happens. Like a destitute farmer donating his land to save the animals. Or a Maya villager taking time to show a stranger how to grind corn. Or a wild dolphin taking you for a swim off an isolated island. And then you fall in love with Belize all over again.

Belize is just like that. In no time, it burrows deep into your consciousness. And before you know it, you find yourself humming a Garifuna tune, listening for the howl of a monkey, searching the horizon for the familiar site of a Maya village.

The Cayes

The Belize Cayes stretch eastward from the mainland, a sprinkling of coral rock isles basking in the fabulous blues and greens of the Caribbean Sea. They range in size from tiny mangrove specks inhabited only by seabirds to substantial islands with thriving fishing villages. Their first inhabitants were the Maya, who established intricate island trading routes during the Classic Period, from 250 to 900 A.D. Seven hundred years later, British pirates used the isolated, scrubby isles to stash the treasure they had plundered from Spanish galleons. Today, little evidence exists of either the Spanish or the Maya, but the islands remain pristine and isolated.

The cayes (pronounced "keys") are why most visitors come to Belize, for here can be found some of the best diving and fishing in the world. Along this 200-mile-long barrier reef—the longest in the Western Hemisphere—is an underwater Eden of animated sea creatures and wildly colorful coral. Minimal human intrusion has preserved the beauty under water, and preserved the old ways on land.

The pace of life is slow in the Cayes. There are no paved roads—only sand streets—and electricity is often provided by a generator. Many cayes have only one or two hotels, and are accessible only by chartered plane or boat.

Only **Ambergris Caye**, has succumbed to real tourism. Twenty-eight miles long, the country's biggest island boasts the most and best resorts and the finest array of restaurants, shops and bars in all of Belize. Yet Ambergris is where people still go to get away, whether it be hippies escaping to a secluded campground or the rich and famous retreating to Journey's End, a posh resort literally at land's end.

Situated northeast of Belize City, about a one-and-a-half-hour boatride away, Ambergris Caye is actually closer to Mexico than Belize. Only a skinny channel separates the north tip of the island from the Yucatán Peninsula. But most of Ambergris' activity is concentrated near the island's south end, in the seaside village of **San Pedro**. Home to about 2000 residents, the village is a busy little place, with golf carts buzzing up and down the sand streets and punta rock music drifting from outdoor bars. Wobbly docks loaded with boats are strung along the seafront, and old clapboard buildings huddle against new concrete condominiums. Unlike anywhere else in Belize, San Pedro has a definite feel of American influence, from the stark new buildings financed by American companies to the American-owned hotels, restaurants and bars. Yet, for now at least, Ambergris Caye is still a place

---

YESTERDAY'S BRITISH HONDURAS

Belize owes its English influence to 17th-century British settlers, an uncanny lot of loggers, Puritans and pirates, who established outposts along the coast. Over the next 200 years, the Spanish tried repeatedly to conquer the area. But the British won out and, in 1862, the region became the colony of British Honduras.

But it wasn't until 1981 that the colony declared itself the nation of Belize. That's because, under British rule, the Belizeans felt protected from neighboring Guatemala. Like the Spanish before them, Guatemala has long laid claim to the colony and even today Guatemalan maps don't recognize Belize. To thwart aggression, British troops maintain a strong military presence in Belize. You'll see battalions at the international airport, in the cayes, and along the Belize-Guatemala border.

Hopefully, the situation will improve soon. In early 1993, Guatemala and Belize were negotiating a treaty to give Guatemala limited access to Belize waters. In exchange, Guatemala would relinquish its claim. In the meantime, both nations continue to work in harmony to promote their shared treasure: the Maya Route.

where visitors aren't subjected to the rigors of mass tourism. Locals frequent the same restaurants and shops as tourists, and everyone is treated with the usual brand of Belizean hospitality.

If you're lucky enough to be in San Pedro on a Saturday night, you'll see local families gather in the town square for their weekly get-together. It's a festive occasion, with folks cooking dinner on make-shift grills and kids playing basketball. Small children come all dressed up, then promptly get dirty playing in the sand streets.

South of town, off the southern tip of the island, the **Hol Chan Marine Preserve** is a five-square-mile underwater park accessible only by boat. Overfishing in the early 1980s nearly destroyed the area's fragile reef system, and drove most of the sea life away. In 1987, the Belizean government made it a national preserve, and installed buoys for boats to tie to, thereby avoiding anchoring on the reef. Today, the reef is thriving again, and snorkelers can admire its brilliant coral and sea fans. Most fascinating, though, are the green moray eels that live in the walls of the preserve's 30-foot-deep channel. Snorkeling excursions can be arranged with one of the many boats at the San Pedro docks, or through most hotels.

Just 20 scenic minutes by boat from Ambergris Caye is **Caye Caulker**. Despite its designation as the second-most populous caye in Belize, Caye Caulker hasn't changed much since the 1960s. Electricity did arrive in the mid-1980s, but there are still only a handful of old cars that cruise the sand streets. Life here feels like a slow-motion film, with dogs lazing everywhere, rickety picket fences running in all directions, and rows of battered clapboard homes tilting ever so slightly to the wind. Barefoot children tote tubs of bananas on their heads, and fishermen wrestle conch meat from their shells along crooked docks. Caye Caulker is still very much a fishing village; every afternoon along the seafront, crayon-colored sloops arrive laden with snapper, grouper and, in season, bright pink lobsters. If some boats have dual purposes, their owners don't try to hide it: Notice the sloops named "Suspect," "Miss Conduct" and "Bong." Right next to the main fishing docks is the tiny island cemetery, overgrown with weeds.

Spanning about five square miles, Caye Caulker is mostly swamp. The town itself is only four streets wide and about ten streets long, all sand, of course. Lodging on the island ranges from modest accommodations to bare-bones; the best hotel is the Tropical Paradise, though whose idea of paradise could well be a point of debate. But the traveler looking for a slice of yesterday, in an unhurried pace, will find Caye Caulker a paradise.

Caye Caulker's 800 residents are ever protective of their little island paradise. When local officials announced plans to open an airstrip, residents rallied against it, saying it would bring too much tourism. Visitors can learn about the island, and Belize's fragile reef system, in a slide show offered most weeknights at **Sea-ing is Belizing** (near the soccer field, toward the north end of town; 22-2189; admission), a photo gallery and book exchange. The slides are taken by gallery owner James Beveridge, an underwater photographer and Belize conservationist. Other than the slide show, nighttime activities are pretty much limited to dining on catch-of-the-day, drinking rum at a tiki bar, or gazing at the stars.

During the day, snorkeling, scuba diving and fishing are top pursuits. Several boats offer excursions, but by far the most popular trips are with **Chocolate** (for reservations, call 22-2151 in Belize City), the island's most famous boat captain. Chocolate lives in a thatched-roof house along the seashore with his partner, aptly named Annie Seashore.

Farther out to sea lie three atolls, ringlike bands of coral isles surrounding lagoons. From the air, they appear stunning oddities, as the calm emerald waters of the lagoons seem corralled by the blustery blue waters of the sea. On land, the scenery is just as compelling. The secluded coral isles that make up **Lighthouse Reef, Glover's Reef** and **Turneffe** atolls are the quintessence of tropical paradise: white sand beaches studded with swaying coconut palms and washed with warm, shallow waters. Only three resorts—one within each atoll—are found here, offering visitors to these isolated isles a true castaway experience.

Within the Lighthouse Reef atoll is the famous **Blue Hole**, explored in the 1970s by Jacques Cousteau. Actually an ocean sinkhole, it spans a spectacular 1000 feet across and plunges 480 feet down from the atoll's ten-foot-deep lagoon. Riddled with stalactites and stalagmites and pitch-black caves, the Blue Hole is difficult to reach (on a calm day, it's two hours by boat from Belize City), but that only adds to its mystique. Several dive operators offer one-day trips, but dedicated scuba divers should consider staying at **Lighthouse Reef Resort** (800-423-3114), which includes a trip to the Blue Hole in its one-week package. The resort also offers excursions to **Half Moon Caye Natural Monument** (for information, contact the Belize Audubon Society; 2-77369 in Belize City) at the southeast corner of Lighthouse Reef. The 45-acre sanctuary, Belize's first national park, is home to about 4000 red-footed booby birds, which are very rare. Among the other fascinating creatures living here are mangrove warblers and frigate birds, wish-willie lizards, and loggerhead and hawksbill turtles, who lay their eggs on the sandy eastern beaches. Arrive at dusk and

The transparent waters around Half Moon Caye Natural Monument reach an amazing visibility—to a depth of 200 feet.

you may catch one of nature's intense shows: aerial bird fights between the frigates and boobies.

Other secluded cayes, including **St. George's Caye, Southwater Caye** and **Tobacco Caye**, possess only one or two lodges each, offering that rare opportunity to stay at a near-deserted island. Getting to these isles takes some doing (usually a two- to four-hour boat ride or a small chartered plane), but the lodges can arrange transportation. Most people find the journeys not only adventurous, but a marvelous window to the unspoiled Caribbean of Belize.

CAYES LODGING

Cayes lodging ranges from charming seaside motels and thatched bungalows on the beach to fishing cabins on a secluded island. The only true upscale accommodations are on Ambergris Caye, and those are not ultra-luxurious. In fact, most of the cayes' hostelries are what you'll soon come to know as funky-Belizean: full of charm and personality, but lacking in creature comforts. Only the expensive few offer air-conditioning, but sea breezes are adequate on all but the muggiest of summer days.

On Ambergris Caye, budget and moderate accommodations can be found in the town of San Pedro, while deluxe resorts tend to be on the north and south ends of the island. Lodging on the north end is accessible only by boat—something to consider if you plan to spend a lot of time in town. Hotels there do provide ferry service to and from San Pedro, though the schedules are infrequent. If you stay on the south end of Ambergris, you'll need a bicycle or golf cart (available from most hotels) to get to town.

One of the southernmost hostelries is also one of the most engaging. Nestled on a sublime stretch of beach, the **Victoria House** (about two miles south of San Pedro, Ambergris Caye; 26-2067 or 800-247-5159 in the United States) boasts 29 rooms spread among a delightful Victorian plantation house, several row houses, and Mexican-style *casitas*. Most desirable are the *casitas*, wrapped by spacious porches and warmly adorned with Mexican tile floors, hardwood furnishings, high-beamed ceilings and Belizean paintings. Rooms in the houses, though slightly smaller, are attractively appointed with white wicker. All rooms have small refrigerators. Complimentary bicycles, as well as van service to town throughout the day, are included in the ultra-deluxe rate.

For contemporary, condominium-style accommodations, check into **Caribbean Villas** (about one-and-a-half miles south of San Pedro, Ambergris Caye; 26-2715). The white stucco buildings, resting right on the beach, feature fashionable rooms and apartments with plenty of privacy and space. There's no restaurant, but most rooms have well-stocked kitchenettes, and all come with complimentary bicycles for getting back and forth to town. Deluxe.

Situated along a curving, palmy beach, **Ramon's Village** (just south of San Pedro, Ambergris Caye; 26-2071, or 800-624-4215 in the United States) enjoys the liveliest atmosphere of any island hotel. The sands are alive with volleyball games, the saltwater pool is always filled with people, and the outdoor bar stays busy from morning till late night. Accommodations are in 60 *palapa*-style cabanas, squeezed together along the sand, with louvered windows, wood or tile floors, ceiling fans (but no air-conditioning) and comfortable furnishings. The ultra-deluxe price buys atmosphere, not cushy rooms.

With its sea-weathered white clapboard, faded gingerbread and dormer windows, the **Barrier Reef Hotel** (Barrier Reef Drive, San Pedro, Ambergris Caye; 26-2075) looks perfectly Belizean. This friendly seaside guesthouse is also a good buy. The ten moderate-priced rooms, with white plaster walls and Belizean tile floors, are basic but comfortable. Seven rooms have air-conditioning. There's a good restaurant and popular lounge.

Lily's (Barrier Reef Drive, San Pedro, Ambergris Caye; 26-2059) is a friendly, tumbledown sort of place, with myriads of levels and cluttered rooftops. Wood-paneled walls, vinyl floors and ceiling fans are standard decor in the ten bare but clean rooms, all priced in the budget range. By far the best rooms are the three that face the sea. The owners, long-time residents of San Pedro, also offer delicious home cooking in a tiny restaurant.

Luscious landscaping on a generous expanse of sugary white beach make the **Paradise Resort Hotel** (on the north end of San Pedro, Ambergris Caye; 26-2083 or 800-223-9832 in the United States) instantly appealing. To match the surroundings, 15 palm-thatched cabanas are outfitted with straw mat floors, bamboo closets and wood shutters. Four have air-conditioning; the rest come with ceiling fans. For those who crave less indigenous quarters, there are four contemporary villas and two condominiums—all right on the sea. Prices are in the deluxe-price range.

For those who yearn for the comforts of home, **Rock's Inn** (just north of San Pedro, Ambergris Caye; 26-2326) boasts some of the most modern, spacious rooms in all of Belize. Facing the sea, with a tiny beach, the white Mediterranean building houses 14 air-conditioned apartments with comfortable beds, sofas, dinettes, kitchens and big windows wrapped in pretty drapes. Deluxe.

Like some sanctuary for shipwrecked souls, **Captain Morgan's Retreat** (on the north end of Ambergris Caye; 26-2567 or 800-447-2931 in the United States) is stashed on a deserted stretch of beach, accessible only by boat. The 21 simple, thatched-roof *casitas* virtually disappear into the palm trees, and the bamboo restaurant and sand-floored bar look like they were built by Captain Morgan himself. Furnishings in the *casitas* are simple but tasteful, with louvered wood windows, plank floors, vaulted ceilings with fans (but no air-conditioning) and roomy porches facing the sea. A favorite of honeymooners, and others who really want to escape. Ultra-deluxe.

Robin Leach, on his "Lifestyles of the Rich and Famous" television program, has extolled the virtues of **Journey's End** (on the north end of Ambergris Caye; 26-2173), a dream getaway resort that ranks among Belize's finest. Indeed, this sprawling, secluded retreat would seem to have it all: a fantasy palm-speckled beach, stylized swimming pool with nude sunbathing deck, small casino, lovely beach cabanas and modern hotel rooms with televisions (rare in Belize!), along with a staff that sees to your every need. The restaurant's accomplished chef turns out daily gourmet delights, as well as twice-weekly beach barbecues that are culinary shows. Besides all this, there's complimentary boat service to and from San Pedro (the resort is reached only by boat) several times daily. Ultra-deluxe.

If modest, back-to-nature accommodations are more your style (and budget), check into a room on Caye Caulker. Most lodging here is a notch above camping, with clean, nondescript rooms that have ceiling fans and hot water that is more or less dependable. The water on Caye Caulker is not purified, so use *only* bottled water for drinking and brushing your teeth.

Oddly, the best place to sleep is next door to the cemetery, at the **Tropical Paradise Hotel** (seafront on the south end of town, Caye Caulker; 22-2124). Here, rooms are available in a hotel building or along two rows of tiny, tin-roofed, plywood cabanas parked next to the beach. The cabanas, by far the best choice, feature vinyl floors, wood-paneled walls and newly remodeled bathrooms. Four cabanas have wall unit air conditioners—offering the only air-conditioned lodging on the island. Budget, with moderate rates for air-conditioned rooms.

Next door, the **Seabeezzz** (seafront on the south end of town, Caye Caulker; 22-2176) really is a breeeezzy place to stay. Constant tradewinds cool three small clapboard buildings, where six tidy rooms provide clean, comfortable lodging. Best of all, the rooms open onto

*The knotted rope speed bumps and "Go Slow" sign on Caye Caulker's sand
street—who are they meant for, the island's four cars?*

an immaculate courtyard brimming with tropical plants and exotic
fruit trees. Open from November through April. Budget.

Deisy's Hotel (south end of town, Caye Caulker; 22-2150) resembles a spiffy boarding house. All 12 rooms are newly painted and neat
as a pin. Unfortunately, the community bathrooms are not as pleasant.
Ask for a room with ceiling fan. Budget.

Vegas Far Inn (seafront near the middle of town, Caye Caulker;
22-2142) has a handful of tidy rooms for rent, as well as a lovely camping area right on the sea. The hot showers are the indoor-outdoor
kind, but things seem private enough. The local family who owns the
place treats the guests like family, and cookouts are quite common.
Prices are budget.

For rock-bottom rooms at rock-bottom rates, check into **Riva's
Guest House** (north end of town, Caye Caulker; 22-2127). You'll
sleep above a Chinese restaurant, but you'll have clean sheets and generally clean surroundings. The bathroom's down the hall. Budget.

The prettiest pastel buildings on the waterfront can be found at the
Rainbow Hotel (north end of town, Caye Caulker; 22-2123). Inside
the 16 rooms are attractive green tile floors, battered dressers and mat-
tresses that range from firm to slightly lumpy. For television lovers, the
cable televisions in each room are a real find. Budget.

Belize's out-island lodges are most popular with anglers and scuba
divers who prefer nature over civilization. Lodge owners take ecotourism quite seriously, sometimes even limiting the number of anglers
allowed per week. Depending on how "out" the island is, you may be
required to stay at least a week. Any less would be impractical, since
getting there requires a lengthy boat trip (four hours, in some cases) or
chartering a small plane.

Some islands have only one resort with the restaurant that provides
daily meals (usually very good) for guests. The bar is often run on the
honor system—no problem if there are only 20 people on the whole
island.

The idyllic caye that's home to **Saint George's Lodge** (St. George's
Caye; for reservations, call 2-44190 in Belize City or 800-678-6871 in
the United States) is only 180 feet wide and one-and-a-half miles long. It's
only 20 minutes from Belize City by boat, making day trips to the
mainland quite easy. The area offers sensational diving and fishing, but
what's really special are the six stilt cottages perched over the sea.
There are also ten rooms in a main building, a family-style restaurant

with superior local fare (including good vegetarian menus), and a little beach. There's no bar, so guests should BYOB. Electricity is provided by a windmill. Ultra-deluxe rates include all meals and boat transfers from Belize City.

The most popular out-island resort is **Turneffe Island Lodge** (Caye Bokel, in the Turneffe Islands atoll; for reservations, call 800-338-8149), situated on a private 12-acre caye. A cluster of charming frame bungalows, swallowed in palm trees, line the sandy shore and offer comfortable rooms with private baths and views of the sea. Guests spend most of their time in the sea, either diving the fabulous reef or fishing the flats. The waters around Turneffe are renowned for bone-fish. To help keep them that way, the lodge limits the number of anglers to six per week. Minimum stay is one week; all meals and round-trip air transportation from Belize City included. Rates fall in the ultra-deluxe-price range.

Lighthouse Reef Resort (on Northern Caye, in the Lighthouse Reef atoll; for reservations, call 800-423-3114) resembles a tropical illusion: a castaway island, ringed in coconut palms and powdery white sand, with just ten lovely cabanas tucked along the beach. Offshore, the underwater panorama is no less spectacular, which explains why so many scuba divers stay here. Dives are offered several times a day and at night, including trips to the famous Blue Hole. Accommodations are casual and roomy; every cabana has air-conditioning, modern decor and porches with rocking chairs. The restaurant serves unusually good food, and there's a real feeling of camaraderie among guests. But perhaps the best part of staying here is arriving. After your plane bumps to a halt on the rocky airstrip, you'll be greeted by the friendly, always-barefoot manager named Dennis, wearing a parrot on his shoulder. Weekly packages only; all meals and air transportation from Belize City included. Ultra-deluxe.

On a secluded little island off the coast of Dangriga, the **Blue Marlin Lodge** (Southwater Caye, east of Dangriga; for reservations, call 800-798-1558) is named for the large fish caught offshore by lodge owner Mike Zabaneh. He and his wife, Rosella, offer ten rustic rooms and three concrete cabanas for guests who'd like to try their own luck with a hook and line. Scuba divers can enjoy fantastic reef panoramas, including an unusual dome-shaped cavern near the lodge. There's a lovely sand beach here and a thatched-roof restaurant and bar. Minimum stay four nights. Ultra-deluxe rates include all meals and transportation from Belize City.

With only six cabanas and four hours by boat from the mainland, **Manta Resort** (Glover's Reef atoll; for reservations, call 800-342-0053) is a seclusionist's paradise. Around the lodge are 12 palmy acres to explore, and beyond that, an oval necklace of coral isles surrounding an 80-square-mile lagoon. Nothing fancy, the thatched-roof cabanas are made of mahogany and feature solar-heated showers and tiny porches over the sand. Among the splendid dive sites nearby are five English merchant ships, sunk in the 18th century. Ultra-deluxe rates include all meals.

CAYES RESTAURANTS

Cayes eateries possess those typical Belizean elements: funky decor, sand floors and fascinating characters hailing from all corners of the earth. Few restaurants keep "official" hours, but you'll always find something open to suit your needs. Besides the Belizean staple of rice and beans (which can be quite tasty), expect plenty of fresh seafood when dining on the islands. Here is a good place to try your first Belikin beer, Belize's ubiquitous national brew, which, by the way, happens to be very good beer.

In a lovely South Seas-style building that looks across the beach, **Jade Garden** (a half-mile south of the airstrip, San Pedro, Ambergris Caye; 26-2506) invites with its polished wood floors, soaring wood ceilings and pink and white linens. The Chinese fare does not shine as much as the decor, but it is a welcome change of pace. Chop suey, chow mein, sweet and sour and foo yong dishes are available, as well as American specials such as ribeye steak and seafood kebabs. Prices range from moderate to deluxe.

GIBNUT, BAMBOO CHICKEN AND THE WORLD'S HOTTEST PEPPER

One reason people come to Belize is for adventure. That's why you should try gibnut, bamboo chicken and the world's hottest chile pepper. Gibnut, or paca, is a large nocturnal rodent whose tender white flesh is considered tastier than steak. Bamboo chicken is the nickname for iguana, which, when fried or grilled, does taste a lot like chicken. If you're a little apprehensive about these culinary adventures, start with a swig of Belize's own Caribbean white rum. The slightly sweet, smooth-as-silk elixir is soothing on sultry jungle nights.

For nonalcoholic sizzle, try a dab of Melinda's Hot Pepper Sauce. It's made with habañeros, the world's hottest peppers, which measure between 200,000 and 300,000 on the Scoville Chart, the Richter scale of chile peppers (jalapeños measure 5000). Melinda's is fused with shredded carrots and other vegetables that temper the habañero heat and create an addictive sauce (after visiting Belize, we can't live without a bottle of Melinda's in the fridge).

Elvi's Kitchen (Pescador Drive, San Pedro, Ambergris Caye; 26-2176) has sand floors, long picnic tables and a tree growing up through the middle—the perfect venue for trading tall tales. The food plays second string to the atmosphere, but it's filling fare nonetheless. Choose from burgers, fish sandwiches and other fish dishes, steaks and rice. Popular for breakfast, too. Budget to moderate.

The Hut (south end of San Pedro, near the airstrip, Ambergris Caye) looks just like it sounds: a hunching old clapboard building, buried along a side street. But inside is a cozy little dining room, adorned with colorful tablecloths, wood beams and plenty of potted plants. The blackboard menu features fresh seafood and produce, with specials such as shrimp curry, roast pork with creole gravy, stone crab claws and fish in wine with dill sauce. Moderate.

Mary Ellen's Little Italy (Barrier Reef Drive, San Pedro, Ambergris Caye; 26-2866) is an immensely romantic seaside venue with a touch of Southern charm. The latter comes from Mary Ellen, a former attorney from Tennessee. Classical music and sea breezes stream through the dining room, decorated with red-and-white checked tablecloths, flickering red candles and tropical flowers. Here also is the island's best Italian cuisine, from bubbling deep-dish pasta to chicken and pork dishes smothered in garlic and wine sauce. Moderate.

If you arrive at San Pedro by boat, you'll immediately spot **Fido's** (Barrier Reef Drive, San Pedro, Ambergris Caye; 26-2409). The big and breezy marketplace, crowned with a giant thatched roof, is the place for burritos, burgers, buffalo chicken wings, pizza by the slice and other quick bites. Budget.

Lily's (Barrier Reef Drive, San Pedro, Ambergris Caye; 26-2059) is widely known among locals for its hefty home-cooked portions. For breakfast, there's huevos rancheros and shrimp omelettes; for lunch, try the fried shrimp or fish simmered in Mexican barbecue sauce. The surroundings—battered rattan chairs, laminated wood clocks and turtle shells parked on the walls—are perfectly Belizean. Prices are in the budget range.

Caye Caulker's eateries are offbeat, super casual (don't mind the cats or dogs) and full of strange possibilities. A hippie will serve you tonight, but tomorrow night's waiter may be a moonlighting preacher or even a kid from down the street. Chairs and tables never match—that would be boring—and hours are apt to change with boating conditions.

Considering the norm, then, the restaurant at the **Tropical Paradise Hotel** (south end of town, Caye Caulker; 22-2124) seems almost formal. Red and blue starched linens cover every table, and the service is dependably good. The breakfast, lunch and dinner fare isn't spectacular, but most meals are under $5. Fresh fish and shellfish, fried chicken, burgers and creole dishes are available. Budget.

To really get into the Caye Caulker mood, walk up into the **I & I Upstairs Café** (south end of town, a block from the Tropical Paradise). The outdoor terrace is as funky as can be, with haphazard tables, plants potted in plastic buckets, and the owners' pet rabbits hopping around the floor. The menu, scrawled on notebook paper, features three or four fresh tasty seafoods of the day, usually grilled or baked, plus a hearty fish soup. For romantic dining, ask for one of the two tables on the rooftop—the best view in Caye Caulker. Budget.

Pinx Restaurant & Bar (seafront, near the middle of town, Caye Caulker) is the spot for cheap, creole-style chicken and seafood, and the island's best pies (try the key lime, coconut or banana cream). Dine inside a little pink clapboard building, or outside on picnic tables overlooking the sea. Budget.

Paper lanterns, Mennonite mahogany tables and sea views lure diners to the **Sand Box** (facing the sea on the north end of town, Caye Caulker). Once you're there, the talented chef and owner, a woman from South Florida, treats you to fresh, inventive pasta and seafood dishes. Top choices are shrimp lasagna, conch fritters, and snapper stuffed with spinach, shrimp and mushrooms. Easily the island's best food. Budget.

Expatriates gather at **Aberdeen** (north end of town, Caye Caulker; 22-2127) for fried rice, curries, chop suey, chow mein and other Oriental fare. Or, if you crave plain old American-style food, go for the T-bone steak or baked lobster. Budget.

CAYES SHOPPING

Don't count on any shopping sprees in Belize. The few stores here import virtually everything from the United States, Guatemala and Mexico, at higher prices, of course.

On the cayes, several shops do offer something different: Belizean art. The largest selection is at **Iguana Jack's** (on the main street, San Pedro, Ambergris Caye; 26-2767). The cozy seaside gallery displays original paintings and color prints, painted clay vessels and exotic jewelry.

Belizean Arts (in Fido's marketplace, San Pedro, Ambergris Caye; 26-2638) also carries original paintings of Maya and island scenes, as well as artsy T-shirts.

Next door to Belizean Arts, the **Salty Dog** has Guatemalan woven satchels and wallets.

The Guatemalan shorts and wristbands at **Regine's Gift Shop** (near the middle of town, Caye Caulker; 22-2167) are a bit pricey, but the books on Belize are worth a look.

CAYES NIGHTLIFE

San Pedro, on Ambergris Caye, has the best nightlife in Belize, with possibilities ranging from intimate seaside bars to over-the-water pubs and sand-floored discos. Knowing these possibilities, the British sailors and pilots stationed in Belize flock to San Pedro, adding an uproarious nighttime dimension.

Big Daddy's (seafront, toward the south end of San Pedro; 26-2052) is the last word on disco around these parts. Nothing fancy, the bamboo shanty on the beach rocks until the wee hours of the morning. Bands play on Saturday nights. Cover.

The obvious choice for a pub is the ever-popular, sand-floored **Tackle Box Bar** (at the Coral Beach Hotel, on the main street, San Pedro; 26-2001), perched over the water at the end of a pier. Sadly, the owners have corralled numerous sea turtles outside the bar and called it a tourist attraction. Perhaps as more travelers become ecotourists, they will complain, and the poor creatures will be set free.

For a before- or after-dinner drink, nestle up to the long padded bar at **The Pier Lounge** (seafront, near the center of San Pedro; 26-2002). On weekends, there's live blues and folk music.

The tiny **Purple Parrot Bar** (seafront at Fido's marketplace, San Pedro) draws big crowds with occasional reggae and punta rock bands. On off nights, it's a quiet spot for a drink.

Sandals (on the main street, near the north end of San Pedro; 26-2281) is the local pool joint, with sand floors, recorded reggae and dusty sandals parked on the walls.

The one and only true watering hole on Caye Caulker is **The Reef Bar** (seafront, on the north end of town; 22-2196), a bamboo hut with sand floors and dart boards. Recorded blues and reggae entertains nightly crowds, many of whom heed the bar's sign that says "No Shoes, No Shirts, No Problem."

CAYES BEACHES AND PARKS

The choicest beaches are on the out islands, and so not within easy reach of the average visitor. On Ambergris Caye, there is no official public beach, but good beaches can be found behind hotels on the north and south end of San Pedro. On Caye Caulker, **The Cut** was created in 1961, compliments of Hurricane Hattie. It's now the place to hang with locals, who cool off in the air-clear aquamarine channel and warm up on little sun docks. The "public beach" is really a small patch of dirt with palm trees. There's a couple of marooned boats, and a popular tiki bar that looks like it may topple over any day now. Located at the northernmost tip of town.

If you're on Antelope, Iguana or Armadillo Street, you must be in Belize City.

Belize City

Belize City is the place most travelers to Belize see first, after arriving at the international airport. Unfortunately, it is not the best introduction. Sweltering hot all the time, it is crowded with crumbling streets, tin-roofed shanties and British colonial buildings that have seen better days. Murky Haulover Creek slices through the center of the city, bubbling with sailboats and makeshift skiffs and fed by open sewage canals that line the streets. The 60,000 people who live and work here create a continuous grind of activity—quite unlike the rest of the country, where life is slow and the land virtually empty. Built on swamps and wracked by hurricanes through the years, Belize City seems to lead a teetering existence.

But the city has its high points, not the least of which is the people. Like all Belizeans, city residents are gregarious, laid-back and ever helpful to newcomers. Some are too helpful, though, as they hustle visitors to lend pocket change, buy drugs or join them in finding "some action." But visitors who stick to the better neighborhoods, and avoid venturing out alone at night, will find Belize City safer than big cities back home. At night, the infamous scene of petty crime is the Swing Bridge; avoid walking it from dusk to dawn, no matter how many people you're with.

The very best neighborhood is the **Fort George neighborhood**. Draped across the tip of a peninsula, on the northern side of Haulover Creek, the area is sprinkled with big whitewashed homes trimmed in filigree and framed by white picket fences. Here, along the waterfront Fort Street and Marine Parade, is **embassy row**, where several countries have picturesque buildings among the palm and poinciana trees. At the tip of the peninsula stands the stately **Radisson Fort George Hotel**, whose name is a misnomer since it was never a fort. Built in 1953 as a hotel, it once boasted the only swimming pool in Belize. But times have changed, and now there are more than a dozen.

A block from the Fort George Hotel are the **Baron Bliss Memorial** and the **Fort George Lighthouse** (Marine Parade). The memorial is dedicated to the Englishman who bequeathed his $2 million fortune to the people of Belize. North on Marine Parade and facing the sea, **Memorial Park** is a rambling grassy area with a tin-roofed gazebo, amphitheater and obelisk honoring the 40 Belizean men who died in World War I.

Nearby, the **Market** (Front Street) is rundown, even as outdoor markets go, but it's still a good lesson in Latin American foods. Dozens of baskets contain a cornucopia of produce, from glassy red scotch bonnet peppers and shaggy boniato (a tuber) to silky red beans and juicy passion fruit. The friendly Belizean women, anxious to make a sale, will tell you how to prepare each item. Remember: Buy only what you can peel yourself, and wash everything in purified water.

Around the bend is the headquarters for information on Belize. The **Belize Tourist Bureau** (89 North Front Street; 2-77213) has helpful employees and excellent maps and guides.

From here, you can spot the **Swing Bridge** and its constant hum of activity. The city's geographic frame of reference, the bridge crosses Haulover Creek and swings open at 5:30 a.m. and 5:30 p.m. daily, causing instant gridlock. On the south side of the bridge lies the heart of the city, centered around Albert and Regent streets and the Southern Foreshore. Here, buildings crowd shoulder-to-shoulder and street vendors hawk baskets of bread and icies flavored with tamarind, banana and papaya. Bicyclists, pedestrians with parasols, and rickety old school buses compete for the same narrow stretch of pavement. At high noon, the roadside park benches get so hot they burn right through your jeans.

Strolling the area, you'll instantly recognize **St. John's Cathedral** (corner of Regent and Albert streets; 2-72137) by its manicured lawns and dignified red-brick facade. The oldest Anglican church in Central America, it was built by slaves from 1812 to 1826. Down the way stands the white clapboard **Supreme Court** (Regent Street across from Central Park) with its four-sided clock tower and filigreed iron balcony, the prettiest balcony in town.

Belize City's most flamboyant personality can usually be found at his **Admiral Burnaby's Art Gallery and Coffee House** (9 Regent Street; 2-77453). But his name isn't Burnaby; it's Emory King. The cigar-smoking, panama-hatted man-about-town is a writer, lecturer, real estate salesman, tour guide and self-proclaimed expert on antique bottles. The American expatriate ended up in Belize in 1953 after his boat, the *Vagabond*, got snagged on some coral offshore. By the time his boat was fixed, King had already fallen for Belize. He never went home. If you don't catch him at his coffee house, you can see him in the 1986 movie *Mosquito Coast*, where he played a bit part with Harrison Ford.

For a real slice of Belize City life, wander the side streets between Regent Street and Southern Foreshore. Under the canopies of shady poinciana trees, brilliant parrots squawk from cages and women scrub their wash in big tubs. Children tote heavy strings of fish, fresh from the painted wood sloops bobbing in the nearby harbor.

Continue north along the water and you'll soon find the **Bliss Institute** (1 Bliss Promenade; 2-77267), a weathered white concrete edifice and center of Belize culture. Inside, there's the extensive National Library and a few permanent exhibits, including limestone altars uncovered from the Maya city of Caracol. Traveling exhibits, sponsored by the resident Belize Arts Council, feature bamboo crafts and paintings by Belizean and international artists.

BELIZE CITY LODGING

For the most part, accommodations in Belize City are extremely basic, with four walls, hot water and a bed, plus a ceiling fan if you're lucky. Considering the often suffocating heat and the nagging problem of street hustlers, we highly recommend you take a room in or near the Fort George neighborhood, where several lovely hotels offer air-conditioned rooms.

The city's most distinguished establishment is the **Radisson Fort George Hotel** (Marine Parade; 2-77400), whose 76 air-conditioned rooms are among the plushest in Belize. Favored by business travelers, its lush, walled grounds with brick lanai and swimming pool seem worlds away from the bustling street life. Rooms in the main building

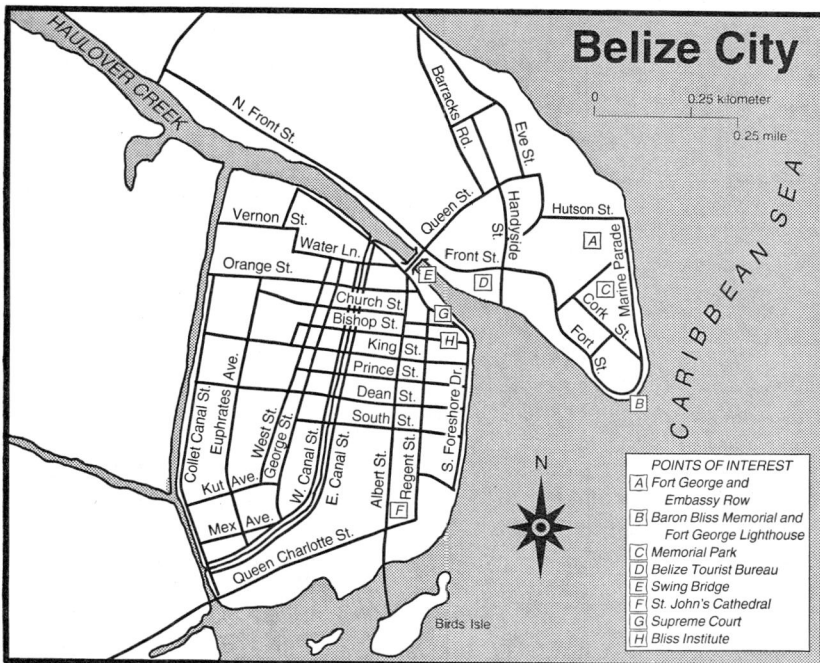

Belize City

POINTS OF INTEREST
A Fort George and Embassy Row
B Baron Bliss Memorial and Fort George Lighthouse
C Memorial Park
D Belize Tourist Bureau
E Swing Bridge
F St. John's Cathedral
G Supreme Court
H Bliss Institute

supply commanding views of the sea, and are furnished with teak-wood armoires, marble baths and that Belize rarity, cable television. Near the gardens, rooms take on a tropical flavor, with vivid green-tile floors, sea-blue bedspreads and louvered shutters. An excellent restaurant and lounge round out the amenities. Ultra-deluxe, but worth it.

A 1991 remodeling gave the **Holiday Inn Villa Belize** (13 Cork Street; 2-32800) a bright, contemporary ambience. Everything in the lobby is vivid and tropical, from the green wicker settees to the shiny ceramic floors. Of the 41 rooms, 30 offer splendid sea views, and all have air-conditioning, island prints and light oak furnishings. Add to that a helpful staff, top-notch restaurant and its location in the Fort George neighborhood, and you have a fine place to stay. Prices range from deluxe to ultra-deluxe.

Undoubtedly the best bargain in town, the 1930s' colonial **Colton House** (9 Cork Street; 2-44666) invites with its front porch with double swings, polished pine floors, lacy draperies and shelves lined with good books. Alan and Ondina Colton are congenial innkeepers, making sure guests are comfortable in the four spacious bedrooms. There's no air-conditioning, but each room has a ceiling fan, as well as pine floors, plush carpets and a private entrance. Two have private baths. Located in the Fort George neighborhood. Budget rates include complimentary coffee.

If the Colton House is booked, try the **Fort Street Guest House** (4 Fort Street; 2-30116). It's not as classy, but the six budget-priced bedrooms are quite cozy with their tongue-in-groove ceilings and floors, woven Guatemalan rugs and battered assortment of furniture. Unfortunately, the beds take up most of the room. There's a shared bath and ceiling fans, but it gets hot in the summer.

THE FAMOUS BARON BLISS OF BELIZE

*One man who fell in love with Belize never set foot in the country. In 1926, Englishman Henry Edward Ernest Victor Bliss, known as **Baron Bliss**, sailed into the harbor at Belize City. Sick with food poisoning contracted in Trinidad, he was unable to leave his boat. For the next few months Bliss lived on board, fishing and trying to recover from his illness. He never recovered, but he did befriend many Belizeans, who brought him food and took care of him. When he died, he left a $2 million trust to the people of Belize.*

The Baron's generosity made him a national hero and paid for numerous public buildings, including health clinics and schools and the Bliss Institute museum. And though he never walked on Belize in life, he is buried in a tomb in Belize City, right where the land meets the water.

The stately white **Château Caribbean** (6 Marine Parade; 2-30800) is showing some wear, but it still imparts an island charm. Overlooking the sea, with a large swimming pool encased in palmy grounds, the colonial mansion offers 23 pleasant, air-conditioned rooms with private balconies and cable television. Deluxe.

Just outside the Fort George neighborhood, but in the same class with the Radisson Fort George, is the **Ramada Royal Reef** (Newtown Barracks; 2-32670). The best choice for young couples and families, the attractive teal building is set along the Caribbean Sea and boasts a fantasy pool (the best in Belize) with swim-up bar. There are 113 air-conditioned rooms, each with a sea view and decor that's contemporary but tropical: textured concrete walls, cane headboards and striking tones of plum, teal and auburn. Besides cable television, amenities include a hair salon, marina and several good restaurants and bars. Ultra-deluxe.

If you have to stay downtown, the best choice is the **Bellevue Hotel** (5 Southern Foreshore; 2-77051), whose two-story brick facade with arched windows curve along the seafront. It's a charming place with a little garden, a wedge-shaped swimming pool and a bar called the Maya Tavern. All 37 rooms are carpeted and air-conditioned, and feature cable television, small dressers and pretty bedspreads with seashell designs. Deluxe.

Reminiscent of a youth hostel, **Seaside Guest House** (3 Prince Street; 2-78339) has dormitory accommodations plus two single and three double rooms, all with twin beds and shared baths. Seabreezes help cool things down, but it's still hot and noisy. Hot breakfasts are US$1. Clean but funky. Budget.

BELIZE CITY RESTAURANTS

Despite its reputation as a rice-and-beans country, Belize has much to offer in the way of skillfully prepared seafood dishes and gratifying home cooking. In Belize City, fine dining exists in hotel restaurants, while soulful fare can be found in seedy diners tucked here and there.

The menu's pricey, but the fresh, inventive seafood preparations at **Radisson Fort George Hotel** (Marine Parade; 2-77400) are designed to please travelers. Situated along the sea, with pink starched linens and vases brimming with tropical flowers, the small dining room purveys dishes such as grouper filet with shrimp and white wine sauce, bouillabaisse and stuffed baked stone crab. Breakfast and lunch are on par. Ultra-deluxe.

Top of the Town (at the Holiday Inn Villa Belize, 13 Cork Street; 2-32800) holds the designation as the restaurant at the highest elevation in all of Belize. As you might expect, it also dispenses terrific city and harbor views. The cuisine, a medley of lobster, shrimp creole, conch ceviche and Oriental stir-fry is average to very good. Early American woods, draped with linens, create a warm, classy aura. Deluxe.

Glimmering oil lamps, brilliant tropical flowers and white eyelet tablecloths make **Fort Street Guest House and Restaurant** (4 Fort Street; 2-30116) an intimate place to dine. Set in a big whitewashed colonial house, the piped-in blues and Bogey and Bacall decor give a feeling of bygone days. The chalkboard menu is read tableside, listing five or six items the cook has prepared for the evening. Cajun shrimp, kingfish with sour cream and pineapple, and snapper tic tick (baked in foil with onions and peppers) are a few possibilities. Moderate to deluxe.

Visitors inevitably ask: "How do we get to **Mom's**?" (11 Handyside Street; 2-45523). It's a little tough to find, tucked as it is along a crowded side street. But find it you should, since you won't want to miss the crisp-fried chicken and mashed potatoes oozing with thick, peppery gravy. Or the stew chicken, slow-cooked until the chicken falls apart. Wash it down with sweet, pulpy limeade, then finish with creamy bread pudding or banana cake. For lighter appetites, there are BLTs and burgers; for breakfast, fat omelettes with refried beans and johnnycakes. Headquarters for Belize City comings-and-goings, Mom's is dearly loved by American and English expatriates. Budget.

The Grill (164 Newtown Barracks; 2-45020) has a reputation as an on-again, off-again establishment, but when we tried it, we found it exceptionally good. Fresh seafood, beef and chicken, grilled or bathed in light sauces, are served in a seafront room framed by candlelight and white linens. Tables are well-spaced for privacy, and the service is above par. Moderate to deluxe.

The restaurant at the downtown **Bellevue Hotel** (5 Southern Foreshore; 2-77051) boasts one of the most extensive and highly acclaimed dinner menus in the city. For starters, try the smoked Belizean blue marlin, then move on to entrées such as pork oscar, brandy peppersteak, menage a trois (sautéed snapper, lobster and shrimp) or rock fish olé (stuffed with capers, olives and onions and topped with spicy tomato sauce). It all tastes as good as it sounds, and it's served in an elegant dining room that faces out to sea. Deluxe.

Around the corner, on the first floor of a delightful whitewashed building, **GG's Café & Patio** (2B King Street; 2-74378) serves down-home Belizean fare like stewed pork, beef or chicken, pork steaks and burgers slathered with hot sauce. Nothin' fancy, the inside is a mishmash of nautical and south-of-the-border decor. Or, dine out on the patio. Budget.

Dit's (50 King Street; 2-73330) is as Belizean as they come: friendly and uproarious, with plastic tables and local artwork, and Campbell's soup cans sold at the cash register. Choose from meat pies, "fry" chicken, *garnaches* (fried tortillas stuffed with tomatoes and onions), and rice and beans with stew chicken, beef or fish. Budget.

The funkiest diner in town, **Macy's** (18 Bishop Street; 2-73419) became famous in the late 1980s when England's Queen Elizabeth dined here on gibnut (a large rodent considered a local delicacy). Now the rodent has been elevated to "royal gibnut" on the menu. Right there beside it is oxtail soup, and more traditional offerings like stew rice and beans, grouper and snapper—pan-fried for lunch, steamed for dinner. Budget.

BELIZE CITY SHOPPING

A little coffee with your art? **Admiral Burnaby's Art Gallery and Coffee House** (9 Regent Street; 2-77453) will serve you a cup, while you peruse Belizean watercolors, wood carvings and Guatemalan woven fabrics, right alongside jeans and baseball caps made in the United States.

The pleasant, colorful **Go Tees** (23 Regent Street; 2-74082) purveys tropical clothing, wood jewelry, postcards by Belizean artists and books on Belize.

The **Belize Bookshop** (corner of Regent Street and Rectory Lane; 2-72054) stocks everything from coloring books and tattered, third-generation paperbacks to excellent books on Belize.

If you'd rather slum it for bargain prices, walk along King Street between Albert and Canal streets. The narrow stores here are jammed with electronics, sneakers, cosmetics, lingerie and T-shirts.

PUNTA ROCK, BRUKDOWN AND JUMPUP

*The sound is loud, throbbing and rhythmic, resounding from car radios, bars and eateries, and windows of homes. The **punta rock** music that Belizeans love sounds part reggae, part disco and part rock 'n roll. It owes its reggae influence to the Garifuna, Black Caribs who immigrated to Belize from St. Vincent and other isles.*

*Slightly less pervasive but still popular is **brukdown** music, born in last century's mahogany camps. Around nighttime campfires, loggers would pound rhythms on wood blocks, glass bottles and the jawbones of asses. Someone would play a harmonica and a guitar, and sometimes even a banjo. Over time, bass drums and accordions were added to create a sound called "boom and chime."*

*Belizeans celebrate their passion for music with **jumpup** street dances. These are festive events, with food and rum flowing freely. As one local notice put it, the party "starts around dusk and continues until food gone, rum gone and people gone."*

There are only 21 people per square mile in Belize.

BELIZE CITY NIGHTLIFE

Most local bars are seedy joints and not places for tourists. Stick to the hotel bars, such as the Radisson Fort George's **Paddle Lounge** (Marine Parade; 2-77400), where a big- screen television shows the latest American sports.

With its rambling tiled terrace overlooking the sea, **The Lighthouse** (at the Holiday Inn Village Belize, 13 Cork Street; 2-32800) offers romance with its drinks.

Settle into a cane-back chair and watch the big screen television or gaze at the pool at the **Blue Hole Lounge** (Ramada Royal Reef Hotel, Newtown Barracks; 2-32670). Punta rock and popular American tunes are generated by a stereo, and there's happy hour nightly.

The **Hard Rock Café** (35 Queen Street; 2-32041) is a pirate of the international chain, despite the ubiquitous T-shirts that claim otherwise. But the third-floor perch is wildly popular with young foreigners, including British military men, who drink and dance to punta rock music.

The Belize Arts Council sponsors occasional theater and dance performances at the **Bliss Institute** (1 Bliss Promenade; 2-72458). The talent is both national and international.

Northern Belize

From Belize City, the Northern Highway wends 100 miles to the Yucatán border, past two magnificent and mysterious Maya cities, Altun Ha and Lamanai, as well as endless remnants of stone houses, walls and other testaments to Maya greatness. Traveling this northern corridor, you are constantly reminded of the ancient Maya civilization, whether it's the house mounds at one's jungle lodge or the 1000-year-old well near a swimming hole.

Just three decades ago, this region was a no man's land choked by dense jungle and pocketed with swamps, and the highway was a pot-holed trail that rarely got you from here to there without some calamity. Today, the road is smooth and lined with small villages, fields of shaggy sugarcane, and ponds populated by wood storks and egrets. Of course, the jungle retains its hold—thanks to conservation efforts by Belizeans—and "highway" traffic is just as likely to be a sprinting Jesus Christ lizard as a car.

Out here in the bush country, everything is measured in mile posts (you'll see the small signs along the road). Near Mile 14 on the Northern Highway, the turnoff for the village of Burrel Boom will take you nine miles down a dusty, rocky trail to the **Community Baboon Sanctuary** (admission). There's no phone here, and hardly anyone around, but a sign proclaims that the area has just received "24 Hours Electricity." No doubt it propels the fans that whir inside the sanctuary's little museum, where there are absorbing exhibits on the endangered black howler monkeys, also known in Belize as baboons. Black howlers, who are found only in Belize, Southern Mexico, the Yucatán and northern Guatemala, are instantly endearing with their cherub faces, beseeching eyes and tiny hands and feet. Their narrow throats magnify their roars—often mistaken for jaguar screams—so they can be heard more than a mile away.

You may hear the baboons at the museum, but to see them, you'll have to take a walk in the jungle. If you don't have a guide, a museum attendant will go to the nearby village and fetch you one. Local guides are infinitely versed on the native flora, pointing out the spiny bamboo, red ginger, bromeliads and guanacaste trees that line the trail and the Belize River, which flows through the sanctuary. Spiny bamboo, one learns, protects the riverbanks from erosion, and red ginger is called "forest Visine" because its juice takes the red out of irritated eyes. The petals of the bromeliads can store up to two gallons of water and provide a home for 12 species of insects, and the trunk of the guanacaste tree was used by the Maya to make dugout canoes. Here also are many mapola trees, whose canopies are loved by howler monkeys. On most days, you'll spot families of monkeys scurrying through the treetops. The babies are not much bigger than your hand.

Of course, the monkeys are just some of the thousands of jungle residents. Foot-wide butterflies dance in and out of forest shadows and red-eyed tree frogs emit flashes of color. We even encountered a boa constrictor, all seven feet of him, stretched across the footpath.

Unlike most reserves, which are government-owned and run, this 20-square-mile sanctuary is run as a grassroots cooperative: The land is owned by 125 villagers, mostly farmers and ranchers, who have agreed to protect the wildlife habitat. When the sanctuary was founded in 1985, there were about 500 howler monkeys here. Today, there are more than 1400.

Back on the Northern Highway, about 19 miles farther north, lies a sanctuary for birds. At the 3000-acre **Crooked Tree Wildlife Sanctuary** (admission), you'll encounter the fascinating and formidable jabiru stork. The Western Hemisphere's largest flying bird, it boasts a wing span that can reach 12 feet. Arrive during the dry season (November through March is the best time), when the storks and thou-

---

The temple depicted on the Belikin beer label is Altun Ha's Temple of the Sun God.

---

sands of other birds create a flurry of activity. The winged creatures who live here range from purple gallinules and ruddy crakes to social flycatchers and lesser yellowlegs. Explore the paths along the lagoons for close-up views of these ever-entertaining birds. One of the most fascinating is the anhingha, which swims underwater, then dries his water-gorged wings on a tree branch. Locals rent boats and offer guided boat trips, but they're expensive (up to US$80), and the scenery is much the same. When the rainy season starts, the sanctuary floods and many birds leave. Before you visit, call the Belize Audubon Society (2-77369 in Belize City) to check current conditions.

Just south of the sanctuary is a fork where the Northern Highway meets the **Old Northern Highway**. Formerly *the* highway in northern Belize, this delightful sliver of lonesome, well-worn pavement bumps and turns for 40 miles past cohune palms, thick bush and a scattering of clapboard houses. It is so narrow, a taxi driver points out, that when he meets a car, "we play chicken."

The road is the reason **Altun Ha** (Old Northern Highway, 31 miles north of Belize City; admission) was discovered. In 1957, quarriers looking for stone to build the road selected some 2000-year-old specimens at this Maya site. As they dug, they uncovered more than just rock mounds. There were 13 structures surrounding two plazas, including one 60-foot temple now called **Temple of the Sun God**. Several years later, as archaeologists did their own digging at the temple, they made a thrilling find: the head of Kinich Ahau, the sun god, carved from a single piece of jade. The largest carved jade artifact ever discovered on the Maya Route, it weighs nearly ten pounds and is beautifully sculpted. What made it even more spectacular was that the stone was located next to the remains of a priest. Rarely did the Maya bury their dead in temples, so what was the significance? The excavation team, led by Canadian archaeologist David Pendergast, never reached a conclusion. What they did find, however, were six more priests entombed in the temple.

A Classical city, Altun Ha was a link in the Caribbean trade route that ran north through the Yucatán. It was a minor ceremonial center, lacking any stelae, yet Pendergast found remnants of jade and copal tree resin obviously used in rituals—a practice rare among the Maya. Many of the fragments were found on the round altar atop the Sun God temple, located in **Plaza B**. Like many Maya structures, this temple was constantly being improved on; Pendergast noted eight separate construction periods. And while the Sun God Temple was obviously the premier building, Altun Ha boasts five additional temples, surrounding **Plaza A**. Four are dedicated to the forces of nature—the sun, rain, wind and moon—while the fifth, the **Temple of the Green Tomb**, held human remains and hundreds of pieces of jade jewelry, some quite elaborate.

Away from the plazas, a quarter-mile trail through the jungle leads to a misty, lime-colored reservoir. Called **Rockstone Pond**, the clay-lined, spring-fed basin was enlarged by the Maya, as evidenced by the sharp stone blocks—probably digging tools—found around the shore-line. At the south end, they built a dam of stone and clay to keep the water from seeping into surrounding swamps. The reservoir is surrounded by house mounds, the remains of waterfront residences.

Altun Ha is one of Belize's most popular Maya sites, mainly because of its proximity to Belize City. But except for the occasional mid-morning and mid-afternoon tour buses, there are no crowds. Sightsee at your leisure, exploring the ceremonial structures and house mounds sprinkled around the lush jungle clearing.

The modern-day hub of northern Belize lies 37 miles north of Al-tun Ha along the Old Northern Highway. You'll know you're getting close to **Orange Walk Town** when you see the old trucks stuffed with

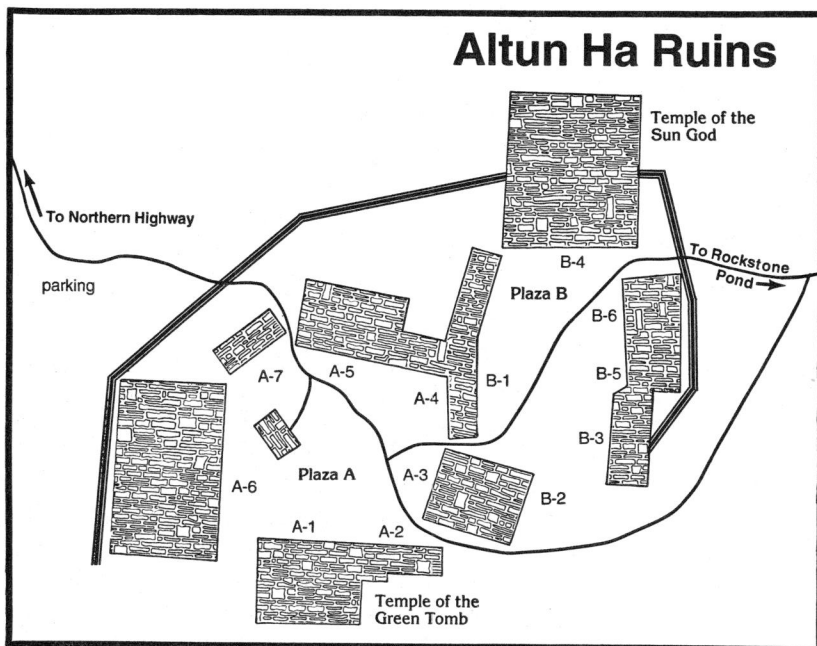

Altun Ha Ruins

cut sugarcane, and notice a sweet molasses smell in the air. Sugarcane is the number-one business in this working town, where a rich ethnic mix includes Chinese, Hindu Indians, Maya and Mexicans. The downtown is edged with tired cinderblock buildings, tortilla bakeries, ice factories and a string of churches. But the number-one reason to come to Orange Walk is Lamanai.

The Maya would no doubt be pleased with the modern-day way to arrive at **Lamanai**—a two-hour, backwater boat trip. After all, Lamanai means "submerged crocodile," a name befitting a city sprawled on the jowls of a gorged lagoon. The trip starts near Orange Walk, on the New River, which winds southward past an old rum factory, slash-and-burn farms, and Mennonite villages. Guatemalan women wash their clothes in the clear warmth of the water, and long-nose bats sleep in hollow tree trunks above the river. The narrow water eventually opens onto the broad lagoon, a wide yawn in the river.

Approaching Lamanai by boat, you first see a gathering of thatched buildings left over from the days of archaeologist David Pendergast, who excavated the area during the 1970s and 1980s. Maya caretakers now live here, while excavations and restorations continue on several of the 720 Maya structures that lie shrouded in 950 acres of jungle. Leaf and rubble paths curl between the buildings, which tower above the trees and form a mystical maze. A guide is necessary to navigate the largely unmarked area.

Wandering around the hulking stone structures, it is difficult to imagine that this great ceremonial center was begun around 1500 B.C. Even more astounding, it was still inhabited in the 19th century, making it one of the longest occupied Maya sites. The Spanish came to Lamanai and built two Christian churches, whose remains exist today. But far greater than those houses of worship are the Maya ceremonial structures. The one known as Lag, or structure N10-43, rises to 112 feet and is the largest Preclassic building on the Maya Route. A sturdy flight of stairs runs up the front, depositing visitors on a platform that looks across the pastoral Maya lowlands and slow, sinuous New River. It is on this platform that the Maya likely performed complex religious ceremonies. Among the more bizarre, the men pierced their penises with stingray spines, while the women dragged strings of thorns across their tongues.

Lag faces a good-sized ball court, where Maya athletes played *pok-ta-pok*, a basketball-style sport using a small rubber ball. Nearby is the **Jaguar Temple**, built in the 6th century and wildly decorated. One massive mask here shows a Maya man inside the mouth of a crocodile wearing a plumed headdress, a sign of the sun god, Kukulcán.

There are numerous other masks and stelae, and buildings containing flint and pottery, at Lamanai. In fact, it takes at least four hours to explore the two-square-mile city center—with a guide, of course. But don't count on finding any at Lamanai; it's best to hire a guide a day before you plan to visit. Boats leave from various points around Orange Walk Town for the four-hour round-trip ride to the ruins. One of the more popular launch spots is Jim's Cool Pool, at the Northern Highway toll bridge south of Orange Walk. Brothers Joel and Anthony Armstrong, who live in an old yellow school bus along the river, will usually take you to Lamanai in their motorboat. An excellent Lamanai tour is offered by the owners of **Maruba Resort** (Old Northern Highway; 3-22199), who provide a gourmet picnic lunch atop one of the pyramids.

If you've been amazed by the brilliant butterflies weaving around the Belize forests, don't miss the **Shipstern Nature Reserve and Butterfly Breeding Centre** (about an hour's drive from Orange Walk). Here, on a sunny day, butterflies are so thick they appear a constant whirlwind of color (they hide in the foliage on cloudy days). More than 200 species reside within a mesh enclosure that resembles a mini-forest. Visitors can wander through, learning about the butterflies' breeding cycles and extensive research being done here. Of course, many more creatures reside within this 22,000-acre reserve. Wading birds find the miles of salt lagoons and mangrove marshes safe places to raise their young, and white-tailed deer, brocket deer and tapir take shelter in the vast hardwood forests. Botanical trails offer peeks at these animals; guides are available at the reserve's visitors' center. Tours to the reserve are offered by **Maruba Resort** (Old Northern Highway; 3-22199). Or check with **Tony's Inn** (south end of Corozal; 4-22055).

North of here, the last real town before the Mexico border is **Corozal**. Curving along a pale blue, blustery sea, with a shore saturated in coconut palms, Corozal is scenic and peaceful. The expensive homes sprinkled along the water hint that this is a town with money, albeit mostly foreign money. Wealthy Belizeans do own vacation homes

---

SPOTTED PEOPLE, DOG-EATING ANTEATERS AND A VAMPIRE NAMED OLE HEG

Maya folklore is so firmly etched in Belize life that the Belize Postal Service publishes a booklet on some of the myths. One myth says that people who eat baby tapirs, who have spots, will become spotted, too. Another says that anteaters will poke their tongues up a dog's nose and yank out his brains. And children in rural villages still mark bridges and doors with chalk to ward off Ole Heg, a vampire woman said to suck the blood of people in impoverished communities.

Many Belizeans take these myths very seriously, and visitors should respect their beliefs. After all, strange stories are just one more alluring feature of the mystical Maya experience.

here, but it's the Americans and Europeans who fuel much of the real estate market. Local pride shines through in the picturesque **central park** (1st Street North, one block from the sea) with its pretty fountains and canopies of poinciana trees. Around town, you'll also notice the hand-written signs, tacked to electric poles, that read: "Don't Be Mean. Keep Corozal Clean."

On the outskirts of Corozal, two minor Maya sites offer interesting side trips. It's best to take a boat to **Cerro Maya**, located south of Corozal, near where the New River empties into Corozal Bay. Boats leave from downtown Corozal; or, check at **Tony's Inn** (south end of town; 4-22055). Cerro Maya, meaning "Maya Hill," is spread across more than 50 acres of forest, though the city center—resting on a gentle hill—is easily explored in an hour. Several plazas are surrounded by pyramids, including one that's 72 feet tall. Like these buildings, the ball courts and artifacts found here date from 400 B.C. to 100 A.D.

Archaeologists believe **Santa Rita** (off the Northern Highway, just north of Corozal) was the Maya city of Chetumal, located about 35 miles south of today's Chetumal, Mexico. Situated on Corozal Bay, near the New River and Río Hondo river, Santa Rita likely controlled the trade arteries that funnelled cacao, honey and vanilla from Belize to the northern Yucatán. The city was discovered around the turn of the century by Thomas Gann, amateur archaeologist and Corozal's town doctor. Gann uncovered fantastic Mixtec-style frescoes, jade jewelry and pottery, though the frescoes have since been destroyed. Today's site will not impress visitors as it did Gann. Only one structure survives: a Classic building, riddled with doorways and connecting rooms, including a main room where burnt offerings were made.

For eight miles from Corozal to the Mexico border, the Northern Highway yields rural vistas of wide open pastures, scrub forest, and fields swelled with corn, bananas and sugarcane. There are a few eye-blink towns, including the pueblo-like Santa Clara and Santa Elena Concepción, that look more like Mexico than Belize. Mexico officially starts at the bridge spanning the Río Hondo river. The **border crossing** is quick and simple on the Belize side, long and often complicated on the Mexican side, especially if a public bus has just disgorged its riders. American citizens, who need a passport, will be issued a Mexican tourist card. The card will be reclaimed by the border officials upon reentering Belize. Most people crossing into Mexico are taking a day trip to **Chetumal** (see Chapter Four for more information), mainly to shop the crowded, inexpensive markets. Buses are the cheapest way to go, costing about US$1.25 each way. Taxis are extremely expensive; the one-way trip is about $20. One exception is taxi driver **Anibal Orellana** (4-23456 in Corozal), who will take you to Chetumal for about $6.

NORTHERN BELIZE LODGING

A soothing body massage, given in the warm, damp embrace of the jungle, is just one reason to stay at the secluded **Maruba Resort & Jungle Spa** (on the Old Northern Highway in Maskall Village, 40 miles north of Belize City; 3-22199, or 713-799-2031 in Texas). There are many others, such as the peaceful, luscious grounds with pineapple orchard, coconut-lined paths and myriads of hummingbirds. And the big jacuzzi, swirling under the cashew trees, and swimming pool where water gushes from rocks. The 15 rooms are all different, from the chapel room with stave doors and bottle wall to the spacious jungle penthouse with sensuous wood art. But the resort specialties are massages, seaweed body wraps and other blissful body treatments, given by Chicagoan Alexandra Wendling, an Olympic track medalist whose family owns the resort. There are no restaurants nearby, but delicious meals are provided by the resort. Don't be surprised if a monkey joins you for breakfast. Ultra-deluxe.

A ROOM WITH A TEMPLE VIEW

*For the ultimate Maya experience, spend the night in a 1700-year-old Maya city. It's possible at **Chan Chich Lodge** (for reservations call 25-2321 in Belize City or 800-343-8009 in the United States), whose lovely thatched bungalows rest atop a Classic plaza encased in temples and burial mounds. Buried in Northwestern Belize and surrounded by 250,000 acres of virgin rainforest, the lodge offers a window on the wildlife of Belize. Howler and spider monkeys navigate the trees overhead, toucans color the sky, and curassows and ocellated turkeys nest in the nearby bush.*

Lest you think building a lodge on a Maya ruin is sacrilege, owner Barry Bowen points out that since he opened, previous problems with looting and marijuana growing have ceased. He still has his opponents, but Bowen is known as an ecotourism advocate, taking care to protect the ruins while visitors enjoy them. In fact, the lodge is favored by birdwatchers, naturalists and lovers of archaeology. Guided tours of the ruins, including burial chambers painted with friezes, are offered by caretakers Tom and Josie Harding. Horseback riding, canoeing and local sightseeing excursions are also available.

Accommodations are in 12 bungalows, fashioned from local woods, with hot showers, ceiling fans and wrap-around verandas. There's a restaurant where everyone meets for meals, as well as a congenial bar. Because of its extreme remoteness, the lodge provides charter flights in small planes from Belize City to the nearby outpost of Gallon Jug—a marvelous way to see the wilds of northern Belize. Deluxe prices include all meals and complimentary beer.

By far the best choice for Corozal lodging is **Tony's Inn** (south end of town; 4-22055), which feels like an upscale motor court. The crisp white, two-story buildings enjoy a breezy seaside locale, complete with outdoor palapa bar and precious patch of white beach. The rooms are big and modern, with tile floors and ceiling fans. Some even come with air-conditioning and satellite television. Moderate to deluxe.

If you're short on cash, check out the **Hotel Maya** (south end of Corozal; 4-22082), situated across from the sea. The 17 rooms are very clean, but the dressers are beat up and the draperies look like sheets. The owners are a friendly local family. Budget.

Tucked on a finger of sandy, windy beach that juts out to sea, **Adventure Inn** (seven miles north of Corozal, Consejo Shores; 4-22187) looks like a castaway's hideout. The 21 stilt cabanas are basic island digs, with hardwood floors, white stucco walls and waves splashing near the front doors. All have ceiling fans and some have air-conditioning (the inn just received electricity in 1992). Several have outdoor showers. At moderate prices, this is a splendid lodging choice.

NORTHERN BELIZE RESTAURANTS

The fare is not spectacular, but **Tony's Inn** (south end of town; 4-22055) easily wins as Corozal's top restaurant. Choose from a variety of seafood dishes, baked, broiled or fried, as well as pork chops, fried chicken, and rice and beans. Linens cover the tables, and jalousie windows funnel in seabreezes. Breakfast and lunch are also available. Moderate to deluxe.

With only four tables, the **Hotel Maya** (south end of Corozal; 4-22082) feels like someone's private dining room. In a way it is, since it belongs to a family who prepares homestyle meals for a loyal local following. The menu changes depending on what's fresh each day, but entrées might include fried chicken or T-bone steaks. Breakfast features omelettes and eggs with refried beans. Moderate.

Of the many Chinese restaurants in Orange Walk, **Lee's** (11 San Antonio Road; 3-22174) stands out. The interior is cool, clean and modern, if not utilitarian, and the portions generous and tasty. Besides the traditional sweet and sours, chop sueys and chow meins, there's baked fish and grilled pork chops. Budget to moderate.

It's out in the middle of nowhere, but worth a drive to **Adventure Inn** (seven miles north of Corozal, Consejo Shores; 4-22187) to soak up the time-forgotten island atmosphere. The floor is concrete and the bar U-shaped, and the patrons look like they sat down several years ago and settled right in. Grilled fish with garlic butter, seafood kebabs, beef tenderloin and liver pâté are a few specialties of the creative chef. Breakfasts are extra special. Moderate.

NORTHERN BELIZE NIGHTLIFE

There's not much. Your best bet is an after-dinner drink at your hotel bar (your only choice if you're staying in the jungle). The seafront bar at **Adventure Inn** (seven miles north of Corozal, Consejo Shores; 4-22187) is a local watering hole full of character and characters.

Western Belize

The Belize cayes may offer a window to the world at sea, but barely an hour away, Western Belize opens onto a world of luscious jungle, forest-clad mountains and mighty temples shrouded in mystery. The gateway to this world is the Western Highway, which runs 82 paved miles from Belize City to the Guatemala border. Heading west from the city, the landscape is at first lonely and rugged, with scrub palmetto, mangrove swamps, and a few clapboard homes on stilts. Then mountains are slowly etched on the horizon, jagged summits with intense green forest cascading down their slopes.

Like the Northern Highway, this western route is measured in mile posts. When you reach Mile Post 30, you'll see a small sign for the **Belize Zoo** (admission). A wonderful introduction to Belize's wildlife, the zoo is home to Rambo the toucan, Balboa the boa constrictor, Pete the jaguar, April the tapir (Belize's national animal) and many other rare and colorful creatures. It seems inaccurate to call it a zoo, since the 100 species of animals do not occupy cages. Instead, they dwell in patches of forest veiled in wire mesh. Their spaces are so big and private that, if an animal is so inclined, he or she can hide from visitors, reiterating that this is *their* world.

Sprinkled around the grounds are hand-hewn signs that speak to visitors: "I'm a great black hawk, but guys who take shots at me are Great Big Turkeys," says the sign where a black hawk lives. And at the spider monkey home: "Listen! We make bad pets! We would much rather spend time with other monkeys than with human primates!"

The clever signs are the work of Sharon Matola, an American biologist who founded the zoo in 1983 after several animals were abandoned by a wildlife filmmaker. Since then, the zoo has gone from a funky little place with a few pens to one of Belize's shining ecotourism stars. And the former lion tamer, circus showgirl and fungi specialist has become Belize's own star, a Belizean version of Dian Fossey (portrayed in *Gorillas in the Mist*), receiving publicity from *Sports Illustrated*, *National Geographic* and numerous other magazines. Today, Matola lives in a thatched jungle bungalow, about a mile from the zoo.

About 22 miles west from here is **Belmopan**, the capital of Belize since 1961, when Hurricane Hattie devastated Belize City, the then-capital. Though the government was moved, residents were slow to follow, preferring to live in Belize City even though they worked in Belmopan. In fact, the town was so desolate at night it was called the "City of Sadness." But Belmopan is slowly attracting new residents, and today it is home to 5000.

It takes about five minutes to see the entire city, a cluster of uninspiring cinderblock buildings surrounded by chainlink fence. Within this complex is the **Archaeology Department** (8-22106), which houses a small collection of Maya relics. Tours are offered Monday, Wednesday and Friday from 1:30 to 4:00 p.m.; call ahead for reservations.

South of Belmopan, the **Hummingbird Highway** is a part-paved, part-potholed path that resembles a collapsing sidewalk through the jungle. Not only is it extremely scenic, it will take you to the **Blue Hole and St. Herman's Caves National Park** (see "Western Belize Beaches and Parks" below).

West of Belmopan, the Western Highway rises and falls through pine-clad mountain ridges and rocky pasturelands speckled with modest villages. This is the heart of **Cayo Country**, a region once rich with logging and chicle farming. Today, it boasts citrus groves and cattle ranches and an ever increasing ecotourism trade. The pulse of Cayo, as it's called around Belize, is **San Ignacio**, located 20 miles west of Belmopan. Extending along the banks of the Macal River and ringed with hills, San Ignacio is filled with restaurants, shops, businesses and nearly 9000 people who keep the town bubbling along. San Ignacio has long attracted a vast spectrum of humanity, from Maya, mestizos (Spanish-Indians) and Guatemalan refugees to Lebanese entrepreneurs, Mennonite farmers, and adventure-seeking Americans and Europeans. Watching the various walks of life and listening to jungle tales told around town, one gets the distinct feeling that something exciting is about to happen at any time.

After a stroll around town, you may want to have a look at the minor ruins of **Cahal Pech** (Buena Vista Road; take the trail leading away from Cahal Pech Disco). Though not initially impressive, wander the forested grounds and you'll find the Preclassic city quite extensive. There are seven courtyards and 34 structures, including several temples, two ball courts and a sweathouse, sprinkled across two acres. The largest ceremonial structure is 77 feet high, with sharply tiered steps running up its face. Sadly, several buildings have been layered with concrete to slow down erosion.

San Ignacio is the headquarters for booking tours to surrounding Maya ruins and various sights, and for arranging horseback riding and hiking in the hills. It is also the place to arrange a canoe trip to **Ix Chel**

Farm and the **Panti Medicine Trail** (check with Eva's restaurant, 22 Burns Avenue, San Ignacio; 92-2267). On the crest of a hill, amid five cleared acres of high bush country, the farm is owned by Americans Rosita Arvigo and Gregory Shropshire. The couple call it Ix Chel, after the Maya goddess of healing and of rainbows. On many summer afternoons, after the rain-gorged clouds have unleashed their showers on the forest, rainbows arch across the hilltop farm.

For several years, Arvigo and Shropshire have been collecting and researching the jungle vegetation that lies at their back door. So far, the husband and wife team have collected over 750 plant species, which are being catalogued by the New York Botanical Garden. The garden, along with the National Institute of Health, Metropolitan Life Insurance and other organizations, have provided grants for research at the farm. Already, the world's jungles have produced treatments for ovarian cancer (a substance called taxol, derived from the yew tree) and Hodgkin's disease (substances from the periwinkle). It is hoped that the forest holds cures for other cancers and for AIDS.

The Panti Medicine Trail, which begins near the couple's house, helps visitors learn about their research. You can take a self-guided tour, but it's far more enjoyable to hire a bush guide, available daily from 7 a.m. to 5 p.m. With his descriptions of jungle healing secrets, a guide makes the trail come to life. The trail is named for Don Eligio Panti, one of Central America's most revered bush doctors. Now in his mid-90s and nearly blind, the Maya shaman still practices natural healing in a nearby village. For several years, Arvigo has been Panti's apprentice—a rarity, as she puts it, "for a gringo and a woman."

BELIZE'S PENNSYLVANIA DUTCH COUNTRY

Along the Western Highway west of Belmopan, take the turnoff for **Spanish Lookout** *and you will soon feel as if you've left Belize. There, stretching to the edge of the horizon, are folded green hills, wind-tickled fields of corn, and straw-hatted Mennonite farmers in horse-drawn buggies. Blond, freckled Mennonite children race down the dirt roads and through the corn fields, and windmills churn against a bright blue country sky.*

The Mennonites, who trace their roots to 16th-century Switzerland and Germany, began immigrating to Belize in the 1800s. Since then, they have slowly turned the unforgiving limestone ground into fruitful soil, and are now considered Belize's most prolific farmers. The remote Spanish Lookout is one of their largest greenbelts. If you drive there, take a truck. The road is very rutted and covered with rocks, and delivers a real beating to your vehicle.

West from here, off the Western Highway in the village of San José Succotz, take the hand-cranked car ferry across the gurgling Mopan River (notice the women washing their clothes). From there, a dirt road leads to **Xunantunich** (admission). One of the few Maya cities built atop a hill, Xunantunich (Shoo-NA-tu-NISH) is a stirring place looming along a limestone ridge. Presiding over the scenery is 130-foot **El Castillo**, a terraced palace with a toothy contour and a skirt of velvety green grass. In Belize, it is second only in height to a recently discovered pyramid at the Maya city of Caracol. Climb the face of El Castillo and—when you've recovered from the mesmerizing view—notice the platform topped with two temples. The temples are famous for their intricate friezes, including an astronomical frieze and a frieze portraying a headless man. The palace's exposed blue-and-white limestone, glinting in the sunlight, takes on incredible shapes.

Xunantunich flourished 1000 years ago, during the Classic Period. Covering less than a mile, its buildings encase three plazas fashioned in north-south design. Surrounding **Plaza A** are several temples, including El Castillo, decorated with intricate friezes and glyphs. Nearby, the structures around **Plaza B** are thought to be upper- and middle-class homes, hinting that Xunantunich was once occupied by a cultured, elite society. Just off Plaza A is a small **ball court**, which now resembles a grassy alley.

The ruins are an excellent place to have lunch, but you'll have to pack your own. The closest refreshments are in San José Succotz, back across the Mopan River.

One of the true joys of Western Belize is a foray into **Mountain Pine Ridge National Forest Reserve** (look for the turnoff at Mile Post 65 on the Western Highway, near the town of Georgeville), which sprawls south of the San Ignacio area. A jungle version of the Great

MAYA BUSH GUIDES

If you explore Belize's sanctuaries and preserves, chances are good that you'll have a Maya bush guide. These guides don't use programmed spiels to get you in and out. These are more like earnest pioneers whose expertise ranges from baboon and jaguar calls to wild fern species and the bizarre rituals performed by their ancient Maya ancestors. Some do not wear shoes, preferring to feel the jungle while they see and smell it. Their everyday conversations take on mystical proportions, with talk of Maya planet worship, universal energy and the healing secrets contained within the plants. When the day is done, they often retreat to the most comfortable home they know—the jungle.

Smoky Mountains, this 300-square-mile wilderness offers a delicious dose of pristine scenery. Gin-clear rivers tumble down pine-clad mountains, and streams swirl around granite boulders. Hardwood trees drip with ferns and giant bromeliads and orchids, and cool mist penetrates the air. There are valleys and ravines, and endless networks of caves. And there are spectacular waterfalls, the most famous being **Hidden Valley Falls**. Here, the water gushes down 1000 feet from a granite ledge, disappearing into the misty jungle below. You'll find it about four miles past the reserve entrance. Use the picnic tables here for lunch with a view.

A few miles farther into the reserve is the **Río On**, a river where bathtub-temperature water courses around granite rocks and creates perfect swimming holes. A little farther south, at the junction of Augustine village, you'll see signs for **Río Frio Cave**. Belize's largest and most remarkable river cave, its mouth arches more than 65 feet, beckoning visitors into its cathedral-like vault. Inside are sandy riverbeds sprinkled with boulders, and walls and ceiling with stalactites. Light filters through the entire half-mile length of the cave.

Of course, Mountain Pine Ridge harbors many more treasures, but you'll never find them without a guide. Check in San Ignacio at **Eva's** restaurant (22 Burns Avenue; 92-2267). If you plan to visit the ridge on your own, contact the **Department of Forestry** (8-22166 in Belmopan) for current road conditions.

Southwest of Mountain Pine Ridge, several hours from San Ignacio and reached only with a guided tour, is the place everyone is talking about. **Caracol**, it seems, was a supreme Maya city, surpassing even the mighty Tikal. Indeed, an altar discovered on a Caracol ball court depicts a war victory of the Lord Water of Caracol over the warlords of Tikal. The year was 562 A.D., and Caracol reigned sovereign for the next century.

Caracol slept, consumed by jungle, until 1936, when it was discovered by *chicleros*. Ever since, archaeologists and the privileged few who explored the city have marveled at its sophisticated design. Strangely, the Maya chose a location far from a good water source, then created a complex reservoir system that funnelled water to homes and crops throughout the city. Perhaps this fascination with water caused them to name their supreme warlord the Lord of Water.

No less an engineering masterpiece are the intricate causeways running out from the city center. Like spokes on a wheel, they were not only footpaths but crucial routes for transporting food and water for miles around. Caracol was both a Classic urban settlement and a ceremonial center, with its loftiest pyramid reaching 139 feet—Belize's tallest building. Archaeologists have also uncovered numerous tombs where groups of elite leaders were buried, and an Early Classic astronomical observatory.

In Belize, a flashlight is a necessity for exploring caves—and for finding your jungle cottage at night!

Excavations are still underway at Caracol, and will be for years. The sight is sometimes closed to visitors, particularly during the rainy season when the roads and footpaths are impassable. Permission to visit must be obtained from the **Archaeology Department** (8-22106 in Belmopan). It is, however, necessary to hire a tour guide, who will obtain permission for you. In San Ignacio, **Eva's** restaurant (22 Burns Avenue; 92-2267) can recommend a guide.

WESTERN BELIZE LODGING

Western Belize is a land of country cottages, ranches and jungle lodges that seem etched into the earth. Many lie more than an hour from the paved road, down winding, rocky trails that look down the sides of hills. Most have not progressed to electricity (kerosene lamps light up the night), but accommodations are usually quite comfortable. Best of all, the nature encounters and cultural experiences are unmatched. If, however, you require air-conditioning and access to restaurants, opt for a hotel room in Belmopan or San Ignacio.

Founded in the early 1800s and one of Belize's oldest cattle ranches, **Banana Bank Ranch** (off the Western Highway, near Mile Post 48; 8-23180) offers lodging in a big farmhouse as well as several cabanas. Though it is run by a couple from Montana and widely publicized, we stayed there and found the accommodations to be *less* than adequate.

However, if you're looking for a true ranch experience, we highly recommend the **Warrie Head Ranch** (Western Highway, six miles west of Belmopan; 2-77185 in Belize City). Draped across 137 pastoral acres, with grassy knolls, clear creeks and tropical fruit trees, the ranch offers nine cozy rooms decorated with Belizean tile floors, jalousie windows and whirring ceiling fans. A library exudes real warmth with its wildlife photos, board games and books on Belize. While you are here, you will be very lucky to meet Lydia, the lodge's virtuoso host and cook who rustles up giant meals of steak, chicken and fresh vegetables (for vegetarians). Moderate.

Despite its countrified name, the **Bullfrog Inn** (25 Half Moon Avenue; 8-22111) is in the capital of Belmopan. The grounds are lush and filled with singing birds, but the rooms are rather featureless. On the positive side, they are carpeted and have cool air-conditioning. The restaurant is the best in town. Moderate.

Considered the business traveler's choice, the **Belmopan Conven-tion Hotel** (corner of Bliss Parade and Constitution Drive, Belmo-pan; 8-22340) is a gracious hacienda-style hostelry with a swimming pool. But don't expect Holiday Inn-style rooms; these moderate-priced quarters are funky, featuring bright orange carpet, orange striped bed-spreads and hand-me-down furniture. Oh well, this *is* Belize!

Popular with backpackers, hikers and naturalists, **Maya Mountain Lodge** (on Cristo Rey Road, three-quarters of a mile from the West-ern Highway, near San Ignacio; 92-2164) rests on a verdant green hill-side with tropical gardens and chirping crickets. There are comfortable cottages, as well as very basic rooms with vinyl floors, plywood walls and curtained bathrooms. The real highlight is the lovely indoor-out-door dining room, with a mango tree growing through the middle. An extensive program of day trips is offered here. Moderate.

In Cayo, the **San Ignacio Hotel** (18 Buena Vista Road, San Ig-nacio; 92-2034) is as close as you get to a real hotel. Its hillside venue offers lovely vistas across Cayo and the Macal River, and there's a de-lightful swimming pool trimmed in tropical planters and wrought-iron furniture. Rooms are spacious and contemporary, adorned with Honduran mahogany furniture, and offering private balconies and ei-ther ceiling fans or air-conditioning. Moderate to deluxe.

Rubble from Maya ruins sprinkle the grounds at the remote **Claris-sa's Cottages** (off the Western Highway, about three miles from San Ignacio; 93-2462 or 92-2424). Like glorified camping, the three basic cottages have concrete floors and bamboo walls. But they reside in a breathtaking spot along a bubbling creek, where iguanas and bromeliads decorate the trees. A thatched-roof restaurant serves good food. Budget.

In a stunning hillside setting overlooking the Macal River, **Chaa Creek Cottages** (on the Macal River, about eight miles outside San Ignacio; 92-2037) gives the feeling of being pampered—in the jungle. Unsurpassed for service and deep woods surroundings, its adobe ca-banas are warm and inviting, with chestnut-colored Mexican tile floors, mahogany beds, Guatemalan blankets and thatched roofs soaring above the trees. Around dinnertime, you'll be welcomed by the owners, a gregarious couple (he's English, she's American) who are well-known around Belize. The indoor-outdoor dining room is a romantic affair offering tasty, local-grown cuisine. Before dinner, everyone gathers on the birdwatching deck, near the elegant wood bar, to trade "You wouldn't believe it. . ." stories of the day. Deluxe to ultra-deluxe.

Down river from Chaa Creek is **duPlooy's** (about nine miles outside San Ignacio; 92-2188). Though not as fancy as its neighbor, duPlooy's offers the same feeling of rural peacefulness. Accommodations range from cottages with stone floors, ceiling fans and screened porches to basic rooms (some with shared bath) in a main building. Co-owner Ken

---

When dining in Belize, order lobster and conch only in season—July though October for lobster; October through June for conch.

---

duPlooy, originally from Zimbabwe, is an avid birdwatcher who will point out the many species camouflaged in the foliage. Moderate.

Getting to **Black Rock Lodge** (on the Macal River, outside San Ignacio; for reservations, call 92-2341) takes much stamina and motivation: First you trek eight miles down a bumpy, stony road, then you hike 30 minutes through the jungle. But the scene that awaits you is more than worth it. Perched on the edge of a sheer wall of limestone, peering across the swirling river, is a cluster of fancy, thatched-roof tents engulfed in banana plants. Meals are prepared by a friendly staff, and there's a bar on site. This is camping at its best. Deluxe rates include three meals.

WESTERN BELIZE RESTAURANTS

Checkered tablecloths, arched porticoes and fresh flowers lend real charm to the **Bullfrog Inn** (25 Half Moon Avenue, Belmopan; 8-22111). The most popular eatery in town, it has an open-air terrace that faces a tropical garden. Steaks, chicken, fish and hamburgers are standard fare, and there's an attached cocktail bar. Moderate.

Across from the Belmopan bus station, the **Caladium Restaurant** (Market Square; 92-22754) features a chalkboard menu of home-cooked fare. Fried fish or chicken, pork chops, T-bone steaks and thick, frothy milkshakes are local favorites. On Tuesdays and Thursdays, go for the escabéche and curried chicken. Budget.

Some people claim you haven't been to Cayo if you haven't been to **Eva's** (22 Burns Avenue; 92-2267). The central nerve of jungle comings and goings, Eva's is where you go to book tours, meet fellow Americans, buy postcards, and hear various tales that get taller as the night (and the beer) wears on. The food is strictly a side attraction, but it's cheap and not half bad. Among the choices: chicken curry, stew chicken, rice and beans, tamales and hamburgers. Budget.

In San Ignacio, there are two possibilities for Far Eastern fare. You'll easily spot **Serendib** (27 Burns Avenue; 92-2302) by its yellow clapboard storefront. Inside are wood-paneled walls and whirring ceiling fans, and a menu of fried rice, chow meins, Sri Lankan curries and shrimp, as well as burgers and salads. Budget to moderate. More rundown, but still praised around town, is **Maxim's** (Far West Street; 92-2282). In a tiny, dark cinderblock building decorated with wildlife murals, it serves sweet and sour dishes, chop suey, curries, fresh fish and burgers. Budget.

WESTERN BELIZE SHOPPING

The **Market Square** in downtown Belmopan is comprised of stalls where vendors sell everything from copycat designer jewelry and radios to watermelons and chickens. Even if you don't buy, it's fun to watch. Open most days.

San Ignacio has a handful of interesting shops. If you're in need of inexpensive tennis shoes or leather sandals, duck into **K. K. Store** (23 Burns Avenue). Foremost among the tourist stores is **Farmer's Emporium** (24 Burns Avenue; 92-2253), which seems to carry every souvenir of Belize. Alongside these quality goods are handy items like spray paint and fresh black beans.

Toucan Gift Shop (41 Burns Avenue; 92-2211) offers beach towels with vivid Maya designs. At **Arts & Crafts of Central America** (1 Wyatt Street; 92-2823), there's a good selection of Guatemalan woven rugs and blankets and handcrafted jewelry.

WESTERN BELIZE NIGHTLIFE

In downtown San Ignacio, the **Blue Angel Club** (Hudson Street; 92-2431) is a second-floor roost with an enormous wood dancefloor outlined in chainlink fence. Crowded most every night, but most popular on weekends, when bands churn out reggae and soul music. Cover on weekends.

A giant longhouse offering fantastic views across Cayo, **Cahal Pech Disco** (Buena Vista Road, San Ignacio; 92-3380) is named for the nearby Maya ruins. Easily the most popular nightspot in Western Belize, it pulses to reggae and punta rock, compliments of top-notch local bands. Cover for men only.

WESTERN BELIZE BEACHES AND PARKS

Guanacaste National Park, fifty acres of cool, damp forest, afford a splendid walk in the woods. A guide from the visitor's center will be glad to join you, describing the abundance of life that exists along the leafy trails. Among the more interesting: armadillo houses, termite nests and logs lined with bulldog bats, who feed on fish as well as lizards and small mammals. There's also the 300-foot guanacaste tree, which the park is named for, is laden with over 35 species of air plants, many as big as normal trees. If you're lucky, the guide will pluck a pod from a cohune palm and break it open so you can taste the coconutty flavor. Bring your swimsuit for a dip in the clear, fast-flowing Belize River. Located on the Western Highway, at the intersection of the Hummingbird Highway, just outside Belmopan.

Buried deep in the rainforest, **Blue Hole and St. Herman's Caves National Park** is Belize's "other" Blue Hole—a pool of sapphire water as clear as air, with schools of fish scooting in every direction. Sunlight filters through the treetops, changing the water into greens and blues and every shade in between. Swimming is excellent here. From this cool, enchanted spot, fern-lined trails lead off into a honeycomb of caves that last for miles. The St. Herman's Caves are pitch-black and desolated, so bring a couple of flashlights, good walking shoes and a companion. Located on the Hummingbird Highway, 11 miles south of Belmopan.

Southern Belize

The least populated, least visited and most rainy region of the country, Southern Belize takes in the chunk of land from Belize City to the Guatemala border. The worn, washboard Southern Highway provides access, though its poor condition prevents many people from venturing all 202 miles. To us, the only way to visit this region is to fly. Local airlines offer service to airstrips in Dangriga, Placencia and Punta Gorda. (Notice we said *airstrips*. The closest thing to an airport is a palm tree and grass worn down by passengers waiting with their luggage.) Flying is not only much faster and extremely scenic, it costs the same as renting a car.

Heading south, about 107 miles from Belize City, is **Dangriga,** the first major town. With its downtown hubbub and harborfront vistas, it feels like a miniature Belize City. Most of the 8000 residents are Garifunas (Black Caribs), descendants of 19th-century Caribbean settlers.

From Dangriga, day trips are offered to offshore cayes and to the **Cockscomb Basin Wildlife Preserve**, about 30 miles south. The world's only jaguar preserve, Cockscomb lies in a 100,000-acre bowl of forest, ringed on three sides by ridges and mountains, including Victoria Peak, Belize's highest at 3675 feet. The Maya were probably the first human residents; ruins of ceremonial centers have been found here. Centuries later, logging camps dotted the riversides, though all that's left now are their colorful names: "Go to Hell Camp" and *Sale Si Puede* (Leave While You Can).

Today, a honeycomb of trails coils through portions of the preserve, offering hikes ranging from one hour to several days (camping is available with prior permission). You probably won't see a jaguar unless you visit at night, since jaguars are nocturnal. That doesn't mean you won't spy a boa constrictor or a red-eyed tree frog, or even a tapir (mountain cow). All live within the dense, dewy foliage, kept cool by triple canopies of trees. Along the **Curassow Trail** is a swimming hole with water so clear you can drop a coin 25 feet to the bottom and tell if it lands heads or tails. Overhead, waterfalls plunge down from the rocks.

Tours to Cockscomb can be arranged in Dangriga through **Pelican Beach Resort** (north end of town, near the airstrip; 5-22044). Or, from the southern town of Placencia, contact **Junior Burgess** (6-23139), one of the best bush guides in Belize. Cockscomb is about half-way between Dangriga and Placencia.

Most travelers find **Placencia** the most desirable place in Southern Belize. Its sands are whiter and deeper than most cayes' sand, and its seaside resorts are instantly captivating. True to its name, the area forms a peninsula where a lagoon meets the Caribbean Sea. The peninsula's northern end is a wild and windswept coast with occasional resorts. The southern end is a jumble of weathered stilt buildings perched in the sand and edged by a concrete sidewalk. There are many palm trees, but no road. Could this be the town? Remembering you are in Belize, you realize that, of course, it is!

Spend a few hours in Placencia, and you'll meet half the village (the other half comes out at night, when seaside watering holes are alive with music and rum). Young Americans and Europeans adore Placencia, and give the sleepy village a bohemian edge. Though still remote and primitive, Placencia is quickly gaining a reputation as a savvy ecotourism destination. Surrounding jungles welcome exploration and offshore reefs beckon to divers.

Perhaps no town in Belize is quite so edge-of-the-world as **Punta Gorda.** Just before the Guatemala border, it's about as south as you can get on the Southern Highway. Given the sad state of the road, it's understandable that few Belizeans ever travel to P.G. (as Punta Gorda is known in Belize), though they spend a lot time talking about it. In-

---

MASTER SLEUTH OF THE MAYA CIVILIZATION

*He has been called the "master sleuth of the Maya civilization," the Sherlock Holmes of ancient pyramids. He is **David Pendergast,** Canadian archaeologist, curator of New World archaeology at the Royal Ontario Museum, and, in Belize, a national hero.*

For nearly three decades, Pendergast has burrowed into Belize jungles to resurrect and reconstruct some of the greatest cities humankind has ever known. Living in primitive camps alongside mosquitoes and monkeys, working from dawn to dark, he and a team of Canadian archaeologists and Maya workers have uncovered everything from priceless jade to ghastly skulls. Across Belize, dinner conversations are peppered with his name, and tour guides praise his work like no other's. Perhaps in another 1000 years, he himself will be a part of Maya history.

deed, there's a certain mystique about this place where Garifuna Indians still practice sacred ceremonies, pounding on drums, shuffling their feet and calling to dead ancestors. But only rarely are outsiders permitted to witness these impassioned rituals.

What visitors to Punta Gorda will see is a quirky outpost where chickens sprint across the streets and filmy store windows advertise five-gallon buckets of pigs' tails. There are a handful of Americans here, people like Gary, who works for the local Voice of America station. Gary told us how, in the last 28 months, he survived a near-fatal attack of dengue fever and two plane crashes in the swamps. He smiles, then says even though his company will transfer him, he wants to stay another year. Life in this banana republic, he points out, is a great adventure.

There's not much to do around Punta Gorda, but the lush jungles outside town harbor several sightseeing treasures. Tours to these areas can be arranged through the **Toledo Visitors Information Center** (Front Street at the wharf; 7-22470).

Heading west from Punta Gorda, a dirt road climbs through dense rainforest, skirting Maya villages where cacao beans are drying next to thatched huts. In the village of **San Antonio**, the **San Luis Rey Church** was built in 1954 with stones from surrounding Maya ruins. No doubt some came from **Lubaantun** (five miles west of San Antonio, just past the village of San Pedro Colombia), a late Classic ceremonial center hidden in undergrowth. This isolated ruin sees few visitors, but those lucky enough to come will find Santiago Coc, the Maya caretaker who gives enthusiastic tours. Coc should know the area; in 1970, he assisted archaeologist Norman Hammond, then a doctoral student at Cambridge, with excavations.

Lubaantun means "Place of Fallen Stones," and that's just what it looks like. Within a mile of cleared jungle are mound upon mound of stones, some masked in fungi and others sprouting big trees. Eleven major buildings are set in five plazas, built atop a ridge similar to Western Belize's Xunantunich. But unlike any other Maya site, the structures here were built without any mortar. Instead, each stone was painstakingly cut to fit another—yet the only tools found were pieces of flint. Archaeologists also found grinding stones for corn and an open chamber with a human jawbone and 1000 mollusk shells, though their purpose is unknown.

But the most astonishing find was a **crystal skull**, perfectly carved from a single cube of rock crystal. Void of tool marks, its construction seems impossible. In 1926, Canadian Anna Mitchel-Hedges discovered the skull in a temple vault and took it to Canada, where it resides today. Belizeans, rightfully perturbed, believe the skull should be returned to a Belize museum.

A little farther down the dirt road, a path winds through cool jungle to **Blue Creek**. There's no sign for this marvelous swimming hole and local secret. A tangle of vines sway overhead, and schools of fish dart through the lucid water. Water gushes down from the jungle hills, creating many small falls. A quarter-mile farther on the trail are several caves and a wood shed for camping.

Back on the dirt road and heading east, a sign on an abandoned, weed-choked clunker advertises **Dem Dats Doin** (admission; for information, call 7-22470). It's owned by a Hawaiian couple who call their jungle spread a "Self-Sufficient Integrated Farm System." A guided tour introduces you to their "biogas digester," which uses pig manure to create methane gas to run their lights and refrigerator. The manure also fertilizes their gardens, which provide food (the pigs are for sale, by the way). You'll see a "solar oven," a foil-lined box that even bakes cakes, and vials where jungle plants are being converted to perfumes, rums and oils. If this weren't Belize, it would seem a very strange place!

On the Southern Highway, about 25 miles north of Punta Gorda, you'll see a sign for **Nim Li Punit**. This late Classic site lacks the scope and architectural intrigue of Lubaantun, but boasts at least 25 intricately sculpted stelae. One measures more than 30 feet, making it one of the tallest along the Maya Route. Nim Li Punit means "Big Hat," likely referring to its location along a ridge overlooking coastal plains.

SOUTHERN BELIZE LODGING

The only place we would stay in Dangriga is the **Pelican Beach Resort** (north end of town; 5-22044). A seafront oasis, it boasts spacious rooms with plank floors, ceiling fans, stuffed vinyl chairs, little refrigerators and tropical wall art—very comfortable and altogether Belizean. Plus, it has the best restaurant in town. Moderate.

In the village of Placencia, five charming cabanas rest right in the sand at **RanGuana Lodge** (6-23112). Freshly painted on the outside, the interiors feature wood walls and barrel ceilings, mounted fans, bathtubs and coffee makers. Ask for a cabana facing the sea. Moderate to deluxe.

Placencia's choicest lodging is found on the north end of the peninsula, away from the village. The **Turtle Inn** (one mile north of Placencia Village; 6-22069) looks like a place where you could wash ashore and be happy for a very long time. Hammocks are strung between palm trees and an old canoe is parked in the sand. Six cozy cabanas, built by owner Skip White, have bamboo walls, thatched ceilings and private baths. White, known as an excellent bush guide, offers excursions to surrounding jungles. Ultra-deluxe rates include three meals daily.

Twin chocolate-brown buildings along the sea signify you've reached **Kitty's Place** (1.5 miles north of Placencia Village; 62-2027). It's a comfortably worn place with warmth and character, thanks to owner Kitty Fox. Choose from apartment-style rooms with private bath and kitchen or smaller quarters with shared bath. A good restaurant and little bar are also here. Moderate.

Foremost among area resorts, and one of our very favorite Belize lodges, is **Rum Point Inn** (two miles north of Placencia Village; 6-22017 or 800-747-1381 in the United States). From the local airstrip, getting to the inn is a rewarding experience: a 20-minute boat ride through silent, shimmering mangrove canals. At the inn, you'll meet delightful owners George and Corol Bevier, former Americans who are Belize aficionados. George is a medical entomologist who has recorded the daily weather for 20 years, only to report there are no weather patterns in Belize! The inn consists of several unusual, pod-like cabanas, right on the beach, decorated with indoor gardens, Guatemalan sling chairs and comfortable beds. The ceilings are high and round and give the feeling of being in a rotunda. Meals are served family-style, with lively conversation on ecotourism. Ultra-deluxe.

Toward the north end of the peninsula, **Singing Sands Inn** (seven miles north of Placencia Village; 6-22243) is as pretty as can be. Opened in 1992, the inn is landscaped with luxuriant flowers and features a tropical restaurant. Six cabanas line the beach, each with attractive wood furniture, wood paneling and porch overlooking the sea. A quiet, relaxing place. Deluxe.

In Punta Gorda, there's just one first-rate establishment, and it opened in 1992. The **Traveller's Inn** (José Maria Nunez Street, across from the bus station; 7-22568) offers roomy rooms, adorned with thick mauve carpets, vertical blinds and shiny wood dressers and armoires. Amenities include air-conditioning and satellite television—unheard of in Punta Gorda. Deluxe.

Best of the low-end establishments, **Nature's Way Guest House** (83 Front Street, Punta Gorda; 7-22119) gives the impression it's been

---

SEEING IS BELIZING

No one is certain how Belize got its name, but theories abound. One says that it comes from the Maya word "belix," which means "muddy water." Another says it comes from "obelize," a word which British pirates used to mark dubious places.

Whatever the origin, Belizeans, having that singular sense of Belizean humor, love to use the name in puns. Everywhere you go, you'll see the signs: "Belize It Or Not," "Seeing is Belizing," "The World of Make Belize," and, our favorite, "Unbelizeable!".

Resist buying black coral in the stores. It's illegal!

---

here a very long time. Engulfed in flowering plants and vines, the funky seaside building has concrete floors of varying colors and a number of stoops and terraces. The rooms are one step up from a youth hostel, and have shared baths. The owners are an American-Belizean couple who offer local tours. Budget.

SOUTHERN BELIZE RESTAURANTS

Listen to the waves roll ashore at the **Pelican Beach Resort** (north end of town, Dangriga; 5-22044), where an entirely pleasant dining room is decorated with wavy Belizean tiles, louvered windows and pink linens. There are usually three choices for dinner, including some type of steak, chicken and grilled catch of the day. Side dishes of baked plantains and tomato pasta are just as delicious. Moderate.

In Dangriga, Chinese restaurants seem as plentiful as palm trees. Our favorite is the **Sunrise** (96 Commerce Street; 22482), where the dining room is neat as a pin. Besides chop suey and curries, you can order fried conch or fried chicken, and over ten soups, including lobster noodle and chicken and shrimp soup. Budget.

Locals and visitors gather to swap fish tales and feast on fish at **Kingfisher** (Placencia Village; 6-23175). The big, weathered clapboard building rests right on the sea, and also serves steaks and pork chops. Moderate.

Jene's (Placencia Village; 6-23112) is classic Belize. Punta rock blares from a little radio, beads dangle in the window, and a picture of a marijuana leaf proclaims: "Nature's Way of Saying Hi!" Oh, and did we mention the dust-caked fan and year-round Christmas garland? Open from early morning to late at night, Jene's serves eggs, hamburgers, fry chicken, fish sandwiches and conch steaks. Budget.

Great Placencia meals come not only from restaurants; they come from backyards. At **Brenda's Place** (near the post office, Placencia Village; 6-23137), backyard picnic tables are where terrific Belizean home cooking (compliments of Brenda, of course) is served in plates that runneth over. The menu changes daily, depending on local offerings and Brenda's mood. But count on Caribbean-style seafood, chicken and steaks. Brenda's pies are legendary. Budget.

After surveying the bare-bones restaurants around Punta Gorda, **Traveller's Inn** (José Maria Nunez Street; 7-22568) looks too good to be true. Crisp linens and fresh flowers top the tables, and an air conditioner chases away the sweltering heat. Tender grilled steaks, saucy chicken and fresh seafood are the bill of fare. Moderate.

SOUTHERN BELIZE SHOPPING

A few funky shops in Placencia are worth a stop. Local handiworks are mainstays at **Made in Belize** (Placencia Village), where shelves display crafts, jewelry and hand-painted T-shirts.

Miss Lizzies (upstairs from Jamie's Restaurant, Placencia Village) offers a mixed bag of homemade preserves, crochet, wine and used books.

The local grocery, **Wallen's Market** (near the soccer field, Placencia Village; 6-23128) stocks household items as well as postcards.

The T-shirts, cotton dresses and other last-minute items at **Rum Point Inn's** gift shop (two miles north of Placencia Village; 6-22017) are attractive and well-designed.

Other than Placencia, your only other shopping possibility is the Guatemalan market in downtown Punta Gorda. However, the clothing, radios, and beach towels sold here are better purchased across the border, on the Guatemala leg of the Maya Route.

SOUTHERN BELIZE NIGHTLIFE

In Dangriga, try the **Round House** (north end of town, across from the Pelican Beach Resort). The big, circular thatched building sits along the sea, offering rum drinks and reggae music.

It's never a bad time for a drink at the **Kingfisher** (seafront, Placencia Village; 6-23175). Boisterous and seaworn, it's always crowded.

Everyone's talking about **Cozy Corner Bar & Disco** (Placencia Village), a shuttered white house where you can dance and meet fellow travelers. Wednesday nights feature famous "chicken drops" (guess what the chickens drop).

The bar at **Tentacles** (on the water, south end of Placencia Village) is fine for a drink *before* the disco. The crustacean-shaped building looks like it's crawling out to sea.

The Sporting Life

SPORTFISHING

Many a fisherman knows the secrets of Belize waters—picturesque, unspoiled, and teeming with the kind of fish tall tales are made of. Belize's flats are world famous in fly fishing circles, and the reefs are nearly as perfect for catching prize snapper, cobia, kingfish and jack. For those who prefer inland backwater fishing, jungle rivers offer snook, snapper, jack and tarpon.

From the United States, **Angler Adventures** (P.O. Box 872, Old Lyme, CT 06371; 800-628-1447) offers a wealth of Belize fishing programs, including unique floating fishing safaris. The company has a fine reputation in angling circles, and can recommend excellent fishing lodges. Those lodges include **Paradise Resort Hotel** (north end of San Pedro, Ambergris Caye; 26-2083), **Journey's End** (northern end of Ambergris Caye; 26-2173), **Saint George's Lodge** (St. George's Caye; 2-44190); **Turneffe Island Lodge** (Turneffe Isles; 800-338-8149 in the U.S.); **Blue Marlin Lodge** (South Water Caye; 800-798-1558 in the U.S.); and **Manta Resort** (Glover's Reef atoll; 800-342-0053 in the U.S.). Many other lodges will arrange fishing trips, as well.

If you'd rather make arrangements on your own, check with one of the following Belize City tour companies: **Native Guide Systems** (1 Water Lane; 2-75819); **Belize Tours, Ltd.** (115 Albert Street; 2-75443); **Belize Land and Sea Tours** (58 King Street; 2-73897); **Mayan Tours Travel & Rental** (5536 Leslie Street; 2-31531); **Zippy Zappy Boating Services** (36 St. Thomas Street; 2-32844); or **Blackline Marine Service and Dive Shop** (Northern Highway, two-and-a-half miles north of Belize City; 2-44155).

Local fishing guides also abound throughout Belize. On Ambergris Caye, check along the waterfront in San Pedro. On Caye Caulker, **Chocolate** (22-2151 in Belize City), **Rally Badillo** (22-2190) and **Ricardo's Adventure Tours** (22-2138) offer customized fishing trips around the cayes. In Placencia, check with **Joel Westby** (6-23138), **Whiprey Caye Guiding** (6-23130), **Blue Runner Guiding** (6-23153) or **Kingfisher Sports** (6-23125).

SCUBA DIVING AND SNORKELING

Ancient Maya treasures may lie deep in the Belize jungle, but offshore, glorious underwater treasures await in the mysterious world of the sea. Here, on the world's second-longest barrier reef, dive spots come in endless varieties, from bright, shallow waters marbled with dazzling reefs to dark, deep holes dripping with underwater stalactites. The Blue Hole is, of course, the most famous dive spot, and several outfits offer excursions. From Ambergris Caye, **Out Island Divers** (26-2151) has one-day trips to the Blue Hole or the Turneffe Isles aboard its fast *Reef Roamer I.* Near the Blue Hole, **Lighthouse Reef Resort** (on Northern Caye; 800-432-3114 in the U.S.) includes a trip to the hole in its extensive daily dive program.

On Ambergris Caye, **Indigo Divers** (26-21301; San Pedro town) will take you to nearby reefs or farther out to the atolls. Also here is **The Dive Shop Ltd.** (at the San Pedro Holiday Hotel pier; 26-2437) and **Bottom Time Dive Shop** (at the SunBreeze Hotel; 26-2348). On Caye Caulker, **Belize Diving Services** (22-2143) has scuba excursions. To rent snorkeling equipment on Caye Caulker, check toward the middle of town, across from the park, in a little building that says "Snorkel Rental-Pastries."

In Placencia, stop by **Placencia Dive Shop** (at Kitty's Place, one-and-a-half miles north of Placencia Village; 6-22027). The Belizean guides here specialize in scuba and snorkeling tours to remote areas such as Laughing Bird National Park. At **Pisces Dive Service** (Placencia Village; 6-23183), Mike and Beverly McCarty offer scuba certification courses, as well as underwater photography lessons.

BICYCLING

The most enjoyable bicycling is on the hard-packed sand streets of Ambergris Caye and Caye Caulker. On Ambergris Caye, you can rent bikes at **Travel & Tour Belize Ltd.** (near the airport, San Pedro; 26-2031). On Caye Caulker, bike rentals are available at **Island Sun** (near the middle of town; 22-2215). Belize City's narrow, bustling streets don't make for great cycling, but you might try riding around the Fort George neighborhood and nearby Barracks Road. Bike rentals are available on the outskirts of the city from **E & L Bicycle Rental** (4 Eighth Street, Kings Park; 2-31157). Except for three paved roads, inland Belize is a skein of rocky, worn-out trails. Best stick to a four-wheel drive out there.

HORSEBACK RIDING

What could be more enjoyable that a scenic ride through the countryside? Out in Western Belize, **Mountain Equestrian Trails** (Mile 8, Mountain Pine Ridge Road; 8-23180 or 8-22149) is a popular, well-run facility offering rides across 60 miles of trails, including former logging trails. The ranch also features river cave float trips.

LIVING TO DIVE

The way to dive the most around Belize's fantastic reefs is to stay on a boat. Several live-aboard dive boats ply the waters around Belize's 175 cayes, dropping anchor at the Blue Hole, Half Moon Caye, the walls of Turneffe and other famous dive spots. Boats range from 16-passenger skiffs with dorm-style camping to 40-passenger yachts with staterooms. Trips typically last between one and seven nights.

*The 54-foot **Manta IV** (800-468-0123 in Florida) has one-night "camp-aboard" trips, while the 50-foot **Offshore Express** (26-2013) offers birdwatching expeditions as well as dives. The 50-foot **Reef Roamer II** (800-258-3465) anchors near Half Moon Caye and provides tents for those who want to camp on the island. The fancier, 110-foot **Aggressor** (800-348-2628) has air-conditioned cabins accommodating up to 18 people.*

HIKING

You could hike forever in the Belize jungles. Our favorite trails are, naturally, in the archaeological zones. Every major Maya site harbors a labyrinth of trails through cool, exhilarating forest with views of ancient buildings. Elsewhere, the Community Baboon Sanctuary, Mountain Pine Ridge and Cockscomb Basin Wildlife Preserve offer fantastic hiking. Unfortunately, there are few trail maps anywhere, so it's best to hike with a guide.

Among the companies that offer guides: **Native Guide Systems** (1 Water Lane, Belize City; 2-75819); **Belize Tours Ltd.** (115 Albert Street, Belize City; 2-75443); **Melmish Mayan Tours Travel and Rental** (5536 Leslie Street, Belize City; 2-45221); **Island and Inland Travel Services** (San Ignacio; 92-2421); **Chaa Creek Inland Expeditions** (near San Ignacio; 92-2037); **Maruba Resort** (Old Northern Highway, about 40 miles north of Belize City; 3-22199); **Jungle River Tours** (20 Lovers Lane, Orange Walk Town; 3-22293); **Jal's Travel and Tours** (49 Fourth Avenue, Corozal; 4-22163); **Pelican Beach Resort** (north end of Dangriga; 5-22044); and **Placencia Tours** (Placencia Village; 6-23186).

Transportation

BY CAR

There are but three paved "highways" (translation: two-lane roads) in Belize: the **Northern Highway**, which runs from Belize City north to the Mexico Border; the **Old Northern Highway**, which parallels the Northern Highway for about 40 miles; and the **Western Highway**, which starts near Belize City and heads west to the Guatemala border. Few sights are actually on these paved trails. Rather, they lie down side roads with conditions ranging from washboard to deeply rutted and layered with large stones.

The badly worn **Southern Highway** extends 202 miles from Belize City to Guatemala, which locals call "painful driving." We recommend flying to sights in Southern Belize, but driving a four-wheel-drive everywhere else. If you visit during rainy season, check local road conditions before setting off through the jungle. Many roads flood and are impassable from June through September.

BY AIR

The **Phillip S.W. Goldson International Airport**, located in Ladyville, nine miles north of Belize City, brings visitors to Belize. Several major carriers offer nonstop flights from Miami and other points in the

United States, including Sahsa, American Airlines, Continental Airlines and TACA. The Honduras-based Sahsa also offers an excellent "Maya World Fare" that allows stops in Guatemala and Honduras.

Depending on how full your flight is, you may have a lengthy wait at Belize Customs. Mondays are particularly horrendous, when Belizeans returning from weekend Miami shopping sprees have hundreds of packages that must be checked. We waited more than two hours one Monday!

On the north end of town, **Belize City Municipal Airport** serves flights within Belize and around the Maya Route. Around Belize, **Tropic Air** (2-45671 in Belize City; 800-422-3435 in the U.S.), **Maya Airways** (2-72312 in Belize City; 800-552-3419 in the U.S.) and **Island Air** (26-62435 or 26-62484 in San Pedro, Ambergris Caye) have puddle-hoppers that fly to major areas. For service to Belize's out islands, as well as to remote areas of Belize and Guatemala, call **Javier's Flying Service** (2-45332). In the late 1980s, Captain Javier Bosch flew *National Geographic* writers and photographers working on the *La Ruta Maya* issue around Central America and the Yucatán.

BY BOAT

Shuttle boats cruise from Belize City to Ambergris Caye and Caye Caulker, with usually both a morning and an afternoon departure. Launches leave from two Belize City locations: (1) across from the Bellevue Hotel, at 5 Southern Foreshore, and (2) at the Shell Station near the Swing Bridge, on the north side of Haulover Creek. The trip to Ambergris Caye takes a little over an hour and is US$10 one-way. To Caye Caulker, it's a 15-minute ride that costs US$7.50 one-way.

CUSTOMIZED BELIZE TOURS

Visitors to Belize are lucky to have several American companies that specialize in Belize travel. **Great Trips** *(1616 West 139th Street, Burnsville, MN 55337; 800-552-3419 or 612-890-4405) is the United States agent for Maya Airways and can custom design any Belizean itinerary. Manager Judy Quam visits Belize frequently, and is well-known around the country. A company called* **Sea & Explore** *(1809 Carol Sue Avenue, Suite E, Gretna, LA 70056; 800-345-9786 or 504-366-0085) employs enthusiastic and knowledgeable Belizeans who will help plan every inch of your trip.* **White Magic Unlimited** *(P.O. Box 5506, Mill Valley, CA 94942; 800-869-9874 or 415-381-8889) specializes in excursions of the most adventurous order.*

BY BUS

There's only one class of bus service in Belize, and it's closer to a school bus than a Greyhound bus. **Batty Brothers** (15 Mosul Street, Belize City; 2-72025) and **Venus** (7th Avenue, Corozal; 4-22132) offer express service from Chetumal, Mexico, to Belize City. For visitors coming from Guatemala in the west, **Novelos** (119 George Street, Benque Viejo Del Carmen; 93-22054) offers frequent daily service from Benque Viejo Del Carmen (near the Guatemala border) to Belize City.

CAR RENTALS

Renting a car gives you the freedom to explore at leisure (and avoid the hot, tinny public buses). Reputable companies recommend four-wheel-drives—a necessity for Belize's rocky roads. Be prepared to pay dearly; four-wheel-drives run about US$80 per day. Beware of companies that offer lower rates for old, gas-guzzling American cars. After paying for gas (and possibly breaking down), you will have spent more than if you had rented a new four-wheel-drive.

All the car rental companies are in Belize City. The one with the best reputation is **Budget Rent A Car** (Bella Vista Road, two-and-a-half miles north of Belize City; 2-32435), which offers four-wheel-drives in top condition. Elsewhere, try **Avis Car Rental** (at the international airport and the Radisson Fort George Hotel, Belize City; 2-31987), **Hertz Rent A Car** (Bella Vista Road, two-and-a-half miles north of Belize City; 2-32710) or **National Inter-Rent** (126 Freetown Road, Belize City; 2-31586).

If you reserve a car through a company's toll-free U.S. office, be sure to reconfirm with the office in Belize City.

PUBLIC TRANSPORTATION

Belize's public buses are not luxurious, but service is extensive and usually on time. The **Z-Line** (Venus Bus Terminal, Magazine Road, Belize City; 2-73937) runs from Belize City to Belmopan, Dangriga and Punta Gorda, and points in between. **Novelos** (West Collet Canal, Belize City; 2-77372) services Western Belize all the way to the Guatemala border. **Batty Brothers** (15 Mosul Street, Belize City; 2-72025), which offers similar routes through Western Belize, will take you to major points in Northern Belize. **Venus** (7th Avenue, Corozal; 4-22132) also offers service in Northern Belize.

Taxis are a practical, fairly inexpensive way to get around Belize City and smaller towns, but extremely expensive for trips outside town. Fares are regulated by the government, but it's always best to check the price in advance. Fares from the international airport to Belize City are US$15.

CUISINE

achiote paste—chopped tomatoes, onions and cilantro

agua—water; order it *con gas* (carbonated) or *sin gas* (without carbonation)

agua purificada—purified water

al diablo—with hot sauce

almuerzo or *la comida*—lunch, which starts at 2 p.m., traditionally the largest meal of the day

bamboo chicken—iguana

Belikin—Belize's ubiquitous national beer

boil up—a stew, usually made with fish

café con crema—coffee with cream

café con leche—coffee with milk

café de olla—brewed coffee

caldo—thick broth

camarones—shrimp

carne asada—broiled beef

cena—supper, which is usually eaten after 9 p.m.

cerveza—beer; you can order it *clara* (light) or *obscura* (dark)

ceviche—raw white fish cured in lime juice with diced onions, chilies, seasonings and tomatoes

chilaquiles—tortilla strips cooked with chilies, chicken and cheese

chile relleno—stuffed mild chili pepper

cochinita pibil or *pollo pibil*—pork or chicken with tomatoes and *achiote* paste all cooked in a banana leaf

comida corrida—daily special

congrejo moro—stone crab

cuatate—lagoon catfish

desayuno—breakfast served early and large (most hotels stop serving breakfast by 11 a.m.)

frijoles—mashed beans

gibnut—a large rodent, whose white meat is considered a delicacy in Belize

guacamole—creamed avocado

habañero—extremely hot pepper

huevos a la Mexicana—eggs scrambled with chilies and tomatoes

huevos motuleños—A traditional Yucatecan breakfast of fried eggs with re-fried beans, tomato salsa, ham, onions, shredded cheese, peas and a tortilla

huevos rancheros—fried eggs soaked in hot sauce on a tortilla

jalapeño—very hot pepper

menudo—tripe

mole poblano or *mole de pavo*—a poultry dish, usually turkey, covered in a thick sauce spiced with chilies and bitter chocolate

pan de cazón—a traditional Campeche dish that blends baby shark with layers of spicy tortillas

panucho—Yucatecan taco with shredded turkey, pickled onion and avocado

papadzules—chopped hard-boiled eggs rolled up in tortillas and served in a pumpkin seed sauce

poc-chuc—pork fillet cooked in a tangy sauce of seville orange and pickled onions

pollo—chicken

posh—a corn liquor; it is a holy sacrament among the Tzotzil, and is used in religious ceremonies

puchero—a stew make of chicken, pork, carrots, squash, cabbage, potatoes, yams, and bananas, traditionally served on Sunday in Yucatecan homes

salbutes—same as *panuchos*

salpicón de venado—cold shredded venison tossed with radish, cilantro and orange juice

salsa picante—hot sauce

sincronizada—ham and cheese in a soft tortilla

sopa de lima—chicken and lime broth

sope—soft corn shell filled with ham, beans, cheese and lettuce

tequila—a strong liquor made from the agave cactus; order it *añejo*, or aged, if you drink it straight

xtabentum—an anise-flavored liqueur made from Yucatán flowers and honey

MISCELLANEOUS DEFINITIONS

aduana—Mexican customs

alemanteca—literally means person of German descent; in highland Maya villages, it's slang for "foreigner"

alux—bewitched Maya pixie who stood around 18 inches tall

atitlán—lake; from Nahuatl, the language of Aztec slaves who came to Guatemala with the first Spanish

avenida—avenue

balneario—bathing resort

baluarte—bulwark

Belize breeze—marijuana

biotopo—biosphere reserve

brukdown—rhythmic island music, originating in the 19th-century Belizean logging camps

calesa—horse-drawn carriage, a transportation option in Mérida *calle*—street

carretera frontera—border highway

casa—house

casa de huéspedes—guest house

caseta de larga distancia—public outlet for phoning long-distance

cayuca—hand-hewn dugout canoe

cenote—sinkhole primarily found in limestone and coral terrain along the Yucatán Peninsula

Chac—Maya rain god

chicle—the gooey sap of the sapodilla tree used to make chewing gum

chiclero—worker who extracts the sap of the sapodilla tree

chultun—cistern

colectivo or *combi*—Volkswagon shuttle bus/minibus

copal—sacred incense

correos—post office

corrida de toros—bullfight

creolo—person of Spanish descent

desaparacidos—"disappeared" political prisoners

ejido—community-owned Mexican land

evangélicos—missionaries, usually from the United States

finca—plantation

garifuna—also *garinagu*; person of African and West Indian blood who immigrated from the Caribbean isles

gringo—foreigner (American)

gruta—cave

guayabera—pleated man's dress shirt

high bush—thick jungle

honorario—fee

huipil, huipiles—embroidered native blouse(s)

jimba—cane fishing pole

jumpup—festive street dance in Belize, sometimes lasting for several days

Kekchi—a distinct Belizean Maya group with its own Maya dialect

Kukulcán—Maya sun god

ladino—a person of Indian or European descent who has assimilated into the mainstream Spanish-speaking culture in Latin America

ladrón—thief

libra—pound (unit of measure)

lima—Mexican lime (larger and sweeter than U.S. lime)

limón—what is known as a lime in the United States

malecón—waterfront promenade
mercado—marketplace
mestizo—person of mixed Spanish and Indian blood
milpa—corn field; can be slash-and-burn field
Mopan—a distinct Belizean Maya group with its own Maya dialect
mordida—literally, "the bite," or a bribe
norte—north
oriente—east
palapa—thatched roof; open-walled hut with a palm thatched roof
parque—park; in Guatemala, a town plaza
parque nacional—national park
pensión—lodging similar to an English or American bed and breakfast
periférico—freeway
playa—beach
pok-ta-pok—a basketball-style Maya sport using a small rubber ball
poniente—west
posada—inn
propina—tip
punta—promontory or headland
punta rock—Caribbean-style music that is part reggae, part disco and part rock-and-roll
quetzal—a green and bright red bird with long, flowing tail feathers; a unit of currency in Guatemala
sacbé—a Maya causeway that was paved with limestone in ancient times
sleeping policeman—speed bump
sur—south
templo—temple in Maya pyramids and Spanish colonial churches
tenango—town; from Nahuatl, the language of Aztec slaves who came to Guatemala with the first Spanish
típica—native clothes
topes—speed bumps
traje—traditional village clothing
triciclo—three-wheeled, bicycle-style vehicle
turista—literally "tourist"; commonly translated as diarrhea, or Montezuma's revenge, caused by food and drink carrying unfamiliar strains of bacteria
vaquería—a Mexican cowboy fiesta with traditional dress and dancing
volcán—volcano
Yucatec—a distinct Belizean Maya group with its own Maya dialect
zócalo—main plaza or town square

Recommended Reading

A Belizean Rain Forest: The Community Baboon Sanctuary, by Robert Horwich and John Lyon. Orangutan Press, 1990. How a group of Belize farmers joined together to create one of the world's most unusual sanctuaries.

Breaking the Maya Code, by Michael D. Coe. New York: Thames and Hudson, 1992. The story of American and Soviet archaeologists' efforts to decipher Maya hieroglyphs at Palenque, Copán and elsewhere along the Maya Route.

The Codex Pérez and the Book of Chilam Balam of Maní, translated by Eugene R. Craine and Reginald Reindorp. Norman, OK: University of Oklahoma Press, 1979. The sacred book of the Itzá Maya of ancient Yucatán.

Essays in Maya Archaeology, by Gordon Randolph Willey. Albuquerque, NM: University of New Mexico Press, 1987. A leading archaeologist's theories on the rise and fall of Classic Maya civilization.

A Forest of Kings: The Untold Story of the Ancient Maya, by Linda Schele and David Freidel. William Morrow, 1990. The authors decode Maya hieroglyphs to unlock an astonishingly complex world of rulers and kingdoms. With detailed diagrams and splendid color photos.

Guatemala: A Country Guide, by Tom Barry. Albuquerque, NM: Inter-Hemispheric Education Resource Center, 1990. In-depth analysis of Guatemala politics, economy and society.

Guatemala: Eternal Spring, Eternal Tyranny, by Jean-Marie Simon. New York: W. W. Norton, 1987. Dramatic photojournalism account of political turmoil in Guatemala by a Harvard law student on behalf of Amnesty International.

Guatemala: from where the rainbow takes its colors, by Joaquín Muñoz. Guatemala: Serviprensa Centroamericana, 1975. Detailed coverage of highland Maya villages, widely available in the Spanish original and an awkward English translation.

A Guide to Ancient Maya Ruins, by C. Bruce Hunter. Norman, OK: University of Oklahoma Press, 1986. Site-by-site explanation of Maya archaeology for travelers.

I, Rigoberta by Rigoberta Menchú. London: Verso, 1984. Account of Maya village life during the Guatemalan civil war by the recipient of the 1992 Nobel Peace Prize.

Incidents of Travel in Central America, Chiapas and Yucatan, by John L. Stephens. New York: Dover Publications, 1969 (two volumes). Originally published in 1841, this book covers Stephens' explorations of Copán, Quiriguá, the Guatemala and Chiapas highlands, Palenque and Uxmal.

Incidents of Travel in Yucatán, by John L. Stephens. Dover Publications. Considered the bible of early Maya exploration, this two-volume study, first published in 1843, covers Stephens' ground-breaking discoveries along the Maya Route.

Jaguar: Struggle and Triumph in the Jungles of Belize, by Alan Rabinowitz. Arbor House, 1986. The intriguing story of a New York zoologist who survived plane crashes, drug dealers and ruthless poachers in his quest to establish the world's only jaguar preserve.

Jungle Walk: Birds and Beasts of Belize, by Katie Stephens. Angelus Press, 1989. A delightful look at Belize's wild animals.

The Last Lords of Palenque: The Lacandón Mayas of the Mexican Rain Forest, by Victor Perera and Robert D. Bruce. Boston: Little, Brown and Co., 1982. Fascinating account of life among the last un-Christianized Maya.

Lost Cities of the Maya, by Claude Baudez and Sydney Picasso. Harry Abrams, 1992. An account of recent discoveries and revelations along the Maya Route.

The Maya, by Michael D. Coe. Thames and Hudson, 1987. A thorough summary of Maya history, with fine illustrations.

Mayan Culture: Basic Facts, by Fernando Medina Ruiz. Mexico, D. F.: Panorama Editorial, S.A., 1985. Comprehensive information on Maya arts, crafts, ceremonies, geography and more, available in Spanish, English, German, French and Japanese.

The Mayan Factor: Path Beyond Technology, by José Argüelles. Santa Fe, NM: Bear & Company, 1987. This analysis of the Maya calendar, blending history, mathematics and prophesy, has become a cornerstone of New Age thought.

Mexico: A Country Guide, edited by Tom Barry. Albuquerque, NM: Inter-Hemispheric Education Resource Center, 1992. In-depth analysis of Mexico's politics, economy and society.

Mexico Mystique: The Coming Sixth World of Consciousness, by Frank Waters. Chicago: Sage Books, 1975. Erudite mix of science and mythology reaches for the heart of Maya and Toltec beliefs.

Mysteries of the Mexican Pyramids, by Peter Tompkins. New York: Harper & Row, 1976. Big, beautifully illustrated book combines the romance of early archaelogical explorations with New Age theories including pyramid power and Maya and Toltec roots in lost Atlantis.

Popol Vuh, translated by Dennis Tedlock. New York: Simon and Schuster, 1985. The mythological history of the Quiché Maya of the Guatemala highlands, based on sacred pre-Hispanic books.

The Shopper's Guide to Mexico, by Steve Rogers and Tina Rosa. Santa Fe, NM: John Muir Publications, 1989. Pratical guide to modern Mexican arts and crafts with extensive sections on Yucatán and Chiapas.

A Short History of Mexico, by J. Patrick McHenry. New York: Dolphin Books, 1970. Exactly what the title promises.

A Study of Maya Art: Its Subject Matter & Historical Development, by Herbert J. Spinden. New York: Dover Publications, 1975. Reprint of the classic 1913 work containing a detailed analysis of Maya symbolism.

Time Among the Maya, by Ronald Wright. Weidenfeld & Nicolson, 1989. Told with passion, wit and cynicism, this follows the author's eventful journey along the Maya Route.

Index

Also Available From Ulysses Press

HIDDEN GUIDES

Adventure travel or a relaxing vacation?—"Hidden" guidebooks are the only travel books in the business to provide detailed information on both. Aimed at environmentally aware travelers, our motto is "Adventure Travel Plus." These books combine details on unique hotels, restaurants and sightseeing with information on camping, sports and hiking for the outdoor enthusiast.

HIDDEN BOSTON AND CAPE COD *228 pages. $7.95*
HIDDEN COAST OF CALIFORNIA *468 pages. $14.95*
HIDDEN FLORIDA *492 pages. $14.95*
HIDDEN FLORIDA KEYS & EVERGLADES *156 pages. $7.95*
HIDDEN HAWAII *468 pages. $14.95*
HIDDEN MEXICO *444 pages. $13.95*
HIDDEN NEW ENGLAND *564 pages. $14.95*
HIDDEN PACIFIC NORTHWEST *528 pages. $14.95*
**HIDDEN SAN FRANCISCO
 AND NORTHERN CALIFORNIA** *444 pages. $14.95*
HIDDEN SOUTHERN CALIFORNIA *516 pages. $14.95*
HIDDEN SOUTHWEST *504 pages. $14.95*

ULTIMATE GUIDES

These innovative guides present the best and most unique features of a destination. Quality is the keynote. They are as likely to cover a mom 'n pop café as a gourmet restaurant, a quaint bed and breakfast as a five-star tennis resort. In addition to thoroughly covering each destination, they feature short articles and one-line "teasers" that are both fun and informative.

ULTIMATE ARIZONA *304 pages. $11.95*
ULTIMATE CALIFORNIA *516 pages. $14.95*
ULTIMATE WASHINGTON *300 pages. $11.95*
**DISNEY WORLD AND BEYOND:
 The Ultimate Family Guidebook** *300 pages. $9.95*
**DISNEY WORLD AND BEYOND:
 Family Fun Cards** *90 cards. $7.95*
**DISNEYLAND AND BEYOND:
 The Ultimate Family Guidebook** *240 pages. $9.95*
**FLORIDA'S GOLD COAST:
 The Ultimate Guidebook** *192 pages. $8.95*
LAS VEGAS: The Ultimate Guidebook *240 pages. $9.95*

VIRAGO WOMAN'S TRAVEL GUIDES

Written through a woman's eye and steeped in the grand tradition of travel literature, these guides speak directly to the special interests of solo female travelers, businesswomen and women traveling with children. Each title offers a fascinating blend of practical information and cultural insights. History, art and contemporary society are examined from a woman's point of view with fascinating results.

NEW YORK *350 pages. $13.95*
ROME *350 pages. $13.95*
PARIS *350 pages. $13.95*

OTHER ULYSSES PRESS TRAVEL TITLES

Critically acclaimed as the best resource to Costa Rica in print, *The New Key to Costa Rica* has captured the imagination of travelers everywhere. This edition is completely updated with hundreds of details on tropical rainforests, endangered species and awesome volcanoes.

THE NEW KEY TO COSTA RICA *312 pages. $13.95*

FOR A FREE CATALOG OR TO ORDER DIRECT   For each book send an additional $2 postage and handling (California residents include 8% sales tax) to Ulysses Press, 3286 Adeline Street, Suite 1, Berkeley, CA 94703. Or call **800-377-2542** or 510-601-8301 and charge your order.

About the Authors

Stacy Ritz, who penned the Quintana Roo and Belize chapters, is the author of the best-selling *Disney World and Beyond: The Ultimate Family Guidebook* and co-author of *Hidden Florida, Florida's Gold Coast* and *Hidden New England*. Formerly a staff writer for *The Tampa Tribune*, she has written for *Parents Magazine, The Washington Post, The Miami Herald, Caribbean Travel & Life, Glamour* and *Bride's*.

Richard Harris, author of the Yucatán and Campeche, Chiapas and Guatemala chapters, has written six guidebooks and co-authored *Hidden Southwest* for Ulysses Press. While working his way through college and law school as a tour guide, Harris' interest in travel writing grew. Since then he has edited more than 60 travel books and contributed to Fodor's *Mexico* guide. He lives in Santa Fe, New Mexico.

About the Illustrator

Glenn Kim is a freelance illustrator residing in San Francisco. His work appears in numerous Ulysses Press titles, including *Hidden Southwest* and *Disneyland and Beyond: The Ultimate Family Guidebook*. He has also done illustrations for the National Forest Service, a variety of magazines, book covers, greeting cards and San Francisco Bay Area advertising agencies.